GORBACHEV'S GLASNOST:
Red Star Rising

GORBACHEV'S GLASNOST:
Red Star Rising

AN EDITORIALS ON FILE BOOK

Editor: Oliver Trager

Facts On File
New York • Oxford

GORBACHEV'S GLASNOST:
Red Star Rising

Published by Facts On File Inc.
460 Park Ave. South, New York, N.Y.
© Copyright 1989 by Facts On File, Inc.

Library of Congress Cataloging-in-Publication Data

Main entry under title:

Gorbachev's glasnost.

(Editorials on file book)
Includes index.
Summary: A collection of newspaper editorials and
cartoons on the subject of the Gorbachev government
and the General Secretary's style of leadership known
as glasnost.

1. Soviet Union—Politics and government—1985-
—Juvenile literature. 2. Soviet Union—Foreign public
opinion, American—Juvenile literature. 3. Public opinion
—United States—Juvenile literature. [1. Soviet Union
—Politics and government—1985- . 2. Glasnost]
I. Trager, Oliver. II. Facts on File, Inc. III. Series.

DK288 G667 1989   947.085'4   89-11975
ISBN 0-8160-2220-8
CIP
AC

Printed in the United States of America

9 8 7 6 5 4 3 2 1

Contents

GORBACHEV'S GLASNOST:
Red Star Rising

Preface

When Mikhail Sergeyevich Gorbachev became the general secretary of the Soviet Communist Party, in March 1985, few people in the West could have predicted the sweeping changes that would take place in the ensuing four years. His policies would not only transform the U.S.S.R., but would impact throughout the world.

The problems he faced in 1985 were manifest: A creaky party bureaucracy that was resistant to change, a stagnant economic system that was unable to meet the demands of the Soviet populace, a woeful Soviet record on human rights, an expensive and unpopular war in Afghanistan, and an escalating arms race with the U.S.

Gorbachev met the challenges head on. He pushed out the party's "old guard," clearing the way for a younger, more flexible Soviet leadership. He introduced Western-style free-market economic reforms and began to open what had once been a closed society. He pulled Soviet troops out of Afghanistan. And his many diplomatic and arms- control initia-tives helped to ease tensions between the superpowers.

The Russian terms *glasnost* (openness) and *perestroika* (restructuring), the cornerstones of Gorbachev's domestic policies, have become household words in the West. Gorbachev himself has come to be known as one of the world's most charismatic and dynamic leaders.

But troubling questions arise as Gorbachev changes the course of Soviet history. Will the infusion of capitalism improve the lot of his people? How far will the U.S.S.R. go on human rights and democratic reforms? How much independence will the Kremlin tolerate among Soviet ethnic groups and among the countries of the Eastern bloc? Can Moscow be trusted to honor its arms-control commitments? Will U.S.-Soviet relations continue to advance under George Bush as they had under Ronald Reagan? *Gorbachev's Glasnost: Red Star Rising* explores these vital issues through the words and images of leading editorial writers and cartoonists.

Part I: A Nation in Change

Before Mikhail Gorbachev came to power, three Soviet leaders had died in a three-year period. Leonid I. Brezhnev, in power since 1964, passed away in 1982 at age 75. Brezhnev's successor, Yuri V. Andropov, a former KGB (state security) chief, died in 1984 at age 69, after 15 months in office. Konstantin U. Chernenko, Gorbachev's immediate predecessor, who died in 1985 at age 73, had lasted only 13 months as general secretary.

Gorbachev was 54 when he became general secretary, the youngest Soviet Communist Party leader since Joseph Stalin. Unlike the sick, dour old men who preceded him, Gorbachev was energetic, witty and charismatic. Those qualities, along with an underlying toughness and cunning, had aided his rapid rise from *apparatchik* (dutiful party functionary) to party leader.

Almost from the start, it was evident that Gorbachev had no intention of maintaining the status quo. As with any new Soviet leader, he consolidated power by replacing high-ranking holdover party officials with personnel loyal to him. But Gorbachev went further: He targeted the huge party and government bureaucracies at the national and regional levels – in some ways the very foundation of the Soviet economic system – as impediments to the modernization of the U.S.S.R. Gorbachev took careful aim at the Brezhnev regime for, in his eyes, spawning countless self-serving, incompetent and corrupt petty officials. He repeatedly asserted that the U.S.S.R.'s current economic troubles were a direct outgrowth of the period of "stagnation" under Brezhnev.

Gorbachev also cast Stalin as a villain, a man who had held the Soviet Union in a grip of terror for nearly 30 years. It was Stalin, he contended, who had set the precedent for dictatorial one-man rule, thus squelching democracy within the Communist Party. Under Gorbachev, there were shocking revelations of long-hidden Stalinist abuses, diplomatic initiatives at the Third World and nonaligned nations. The fresh approach to foreign policy, stressing pragmatism over ideology, was summed up in the phrase "new thinking."

Gorbachev's reforms also brought problems. The much-maligned bureaucracies resisted change. A conservative faction in the party – led Yegor K. Ligachev – challenged and many of the most prominent victims of Stalin's infamous 1930s purges were posthumously rehabilitated.

Gorbachev set out to change the U.S.S.R. through series of economic, political and social reforms collectively known as *perestroika* (restructuring). On the economic front, his aims were many: A shift from the traditional heavy industries (such as steel production) to high-quality, exportable consumer goods; a relaxation of central economic controls, with local managers getting more leeway in decision-making; the lifting of barriers to foreign investment, and a greater role in the economy for business and agricultural cooperatives.

Gorbachev pushed a program of "democratization," encouraging rank-and-file party members, and Soviet citizens in general, to take an active involvement in politics. The program was capped by a plan to transform the Supreme Soviet, the U.S.S.R.'s nominal parliament, into a truly representative body. In March 1989, the nation held its first multicandidate parliamentary elections since 1917.

The broad term *glasnost* (openness) summed up Gorbachev's social reforms. Soviets were for the first time allowed to openly criticize the party and the government. Some media censorship was lifted and writers and artists were granted more freedom of expression. School children learned aspects of Soviet history that had been either distorted or completely covered up. The government began to reveal problems (i.e., crime, alcoholism, pollution) that it had never before admitted existed in the U.S.S.R.

Pressured by the West, the Gorbachev regime freed prominent Soviet political dissidents held in internal exile, prisons and labor camps. Restrictions on the emigration of Soviet Jews were eased. Obstacles to religious worship were removed.

On the international front, Gorbachev tantalized the West with his many and varied disarmament proposals. He aimed new the general secretary. The Soviet people, eager to better their lives, were impatient to see the fruits of economic reform. Dissidents and liberals tested the limits of political liberalization and glasnost. Ethnic groups pressed for more independence. Soviet allies were divided over whether to emulate the new Soviet model.

"RUSSIA CAN NO LONGER TOLERATE STAGNATION AND LOW PRODUCTIVITY, SO WE'RE CONSTRUCTING A MINISTRY OF EFFICIENCY TO DOUBLE YOUR OUTPUT...."

Soviet President Chernenkno Dies; Gorbachev Chosen as Successor

Soviet President Konstantin U. Chernenko, 73, died March 10, 1985 of heart failure arising from chronic lung and liver ailments. His death came approximately 13 months after he had assumed power following the death of President Yuri V. Andropov, who had been in power before him for just 15 months. President Reagan March 11 told journalists that he would not be attending Chernenko's funeral, set for March 13. White House aides disclosed that Vice President George Bush, heading the U.S. contingent to the Moscow funeral, would carry an invitation to the new Soviet leader, Mikhail S. Gorbachev, from Reagan to come to the U.S. for a summit.

Gorbachev, the second secretary of the Communist Party, was chosen as Chernenko's successor March 11 in an emergency meeting of the Central Committee. His selection as general secretary was announced a little more than four hours after the announcement of Chernenko's death. Gorbachev, 45, was the youngest man to become the party leader since the 1924 accession of Joseph Stalin at age 45. Western analysts viewed his selection as a sign that power could be shifting away from the aged, traditionalist members of the Stalin hierarchy to a younger generation whose attitudes had not been shaped by Stalinism and service during World War II.

In his speech of acceptance to the Central Committee March 11, Gorbachev vowed to follow the "strategic line" of policies set forth by the party and his immediate predecessors. The party's most important goal, he said, was rapid economic improvement. On the international front, Gorbachev said the Soviet Union would "firmly follow the Leninist course of peace and peaceful coexistence" with the West in the spirit of the 1970s detente. Citing new bilateral disarmament talks set to begin in Geneva the following day, Gorbachev outlined the approach he said the U.S.S.R. would take. "I can only reaffirm that: we do not strive to acquire unilateral advantages over the U.S., over NATO countries, for military superiority over them; we want termination, and not continuation of the arms race."

The Times-Picayune
The States-Item

New Orleans, LA, March 12, 1985

The death of Soviet leader Konstantin Chernenko was almost anticlimactic. It had been known almost from the day he took office 13 months ago that he suffered from terminal pulmonary emphysema. He had been frail and shaky in his few public appearances. When he received flowers from a young girl during his last public appearance in Moscow less than two weeks ago, he looked like a man attending his own funeral.

The Kremlin had clearly been preparing the Soviet people and the world for the passing of the third Soviet leader in less than three years. But the swift naming of 54-year-old Mikhail S. Gorbachev as the new general secretary of the Communist Party was also somewhat anticlimactic, though it may turn out to be epochal for the Soviet Union. Mr. Gorbachev has been the obvious prospect throughout Mr. Chernenko's obviously transitional tenure, and indeed had been considered a likelier successor to Yuri Andropov than Mr. Chernenko.

Having had to deal with the deaths of three members of the old guard in rapid succession, the Politburo and the Soviet people undoubtedly saw the inevitability of a younger leader. Mr. Gorbachev is the youngest member of the Politburo, the Soviet's central ruling body, and he has behaved like a man on the way to the top for some time now. Recently in London he charmed the British with his smiles and guile.

Mr. Gorbachev's rise would mark the the beginning of the rise to power of a new generation of Soviet leaders. It most likely does not signal a new direction right away

for Soviet policies. Kremlin analysts say it usually takes about five years for a new Soviet leader to feel confident enough to offer major initiatives.

But the comparatively youthful Mr. Gorbachev appears to be in excellent health and is very ambitious. He begins his occupancy of the Kremlin's top office at about the same age Stalin was when he finally got all the Soviet reins in his exclusive hands, and it is possible that he could have as long a term as Stalin's. The new generation of Soviet leadership, though committed to the system that produced them, will certainly have some new ideas about how the system should be run, and with the old leadership fading fast, Mr. Gorbachev might beat the usual timetable for instituting changes.

Until the new Soviet leader has his feet firmly on the political ground, Moscow will undoubtedly continue the collective leadership that ran things during Mr. Chernenko's brief, shaky reign.

With the arms talks about to resume in Geneva, U.S. officials will be looking closely for the slightest nuances of change in Soviet positions. It will be surprising if they see many favorable signs of change, if any. Soviet negotiators might take an even harder line initially as a display of strength during a time of changing leadership.

Mr. Chernenko's imprint on history will surely prove to be slight. Like Mr. Andropov, his brief time at the top was transitional, and the two will probably occupy a only a footnote for having been the last of the old guard who arrived too late to power.

The Orlando Sentinel

Orlando, FL, March 12, 1985

The series of events that preceded the death of Soviet leader Konstantin Chernenko has become too familiar: countless rumors of illness, long absences, repeated denials and finally the not-so-surprising announcement that yes, yet another Soviet leader has died.

Yet for all the eulogies, Mr. Chernenko will not be remembered as a great world leader or even as a great Soviet leader. His place in history will be almost an asterisk marking a quick succession of Soviet leaders. That succession, though — from the Soviet gerontocracy to the 54-year-old Mikhail Gorbachev — is a major event, perhaps the most significant shift within the Soviet power structure since the death of Josef Stalin in 1953.

History will note that the Soviet Union did return to the arms talks during Mr. Chernenko's term. Yet it will also note that he was in power for only 13 months — the shortest for any modern Soviet leader. Also, Mr. Chernenko spent much of that time laid up in a hospital bed. Those are the kinds of facts destined for Trivial Pursuit.

Even if Mr. Chernenko had been in power longer, chances are he would not have made a firm imprint on Soviet policy. A colorless bureaucrat, he worked his way up through the hierarchy not by brilliant leadership but by riding the coattails of his mentor, Leonid Brezhnev. Once in power, his inexperience and illness made the collective nature of Soviet leadership even more collective. The decision to return to the arms talks was made less by Mr. Chernenko than by a group of leaders who saw a no-talk policy as working against Soviet interests.

His rise to power is itself telling. He got to the top because he had the support of other aging Soviet leaders who saw him as a way to protect their own power. It was a way to put off the rise of a new generation of Soviet leaders.

Mr. Gorbachev, the new Communist Party head, is clearly the leader of that new generation. In contrast to his drab predecessor, Mr. Gorbachev is an energetic, intelligent and somewhat dapper man who seems likely to bring a more dynamic style of leadership to the Kremlin. Yet as tempting as it is to think so, that change in style doesn't necessarily mean that there will be a change in policy.

Even if Mr. Gorbachev wants to take the Soviet Union in a new direction, he faces the same bureaucratic constraints as his predecessor — at least until he can strengthen his control over the Soviet bureaucracy. That could take years. And lest anyone forget, Mr. Gorbachev has risen to the top of the Soviet Union the same way as all of his predecessors: by being tough and shrewd.

Yes, the routine of Soviet succession has become too familiar. So has the business of expecting more Westernized Soviet leadership. Mr. Gorbachev is a young man by Politburo standards, signaling the rise of a new cast of characters. But a Soviet general secretary in a designer suit is still a Soviet general secretary.

THE MILWAUKEE JOURNAL

Milwaukee, WI, March 12, 1985

President Reagan offered flimsy and transparent excuses Monday when he was asked about his decision not to attend the funeral of Soviet President Konstantin Chernenko. He explained: "I had the feeling there's an awful lot on my plate right now that would have to be set aside. I didn't think that anything could be achieved by going."

Prime Minister Margaret Thatcher of Britain has a lot on her plate. So, presumably, do President Francois Mitterrand of France, Chancellor Helmut Kohl of West Germany and Prime Minister Yasuhiro Nakasone of Japan (Parliament is in session in Tokyo). But they will be in Moscow.

Equally lame is Reagan's statement that any meetings he might have with new Soviet leaders would be ceremonial and therefore pointless. Even if he were powerless to set an agenda and bring up subjects of his own choosing, Reagan should (and probably does) understand the value of symbols and ceremonies.

It appears that Reagan just didn't want to take the trouble to go. Admittedly, it could have been an exhausting trip. Yet, in a small way, it might have helped set a new tone in US relations with the Kremlin. It's a shame he shunned the opportunity.

St. Paul Pioneer Press

St. Paul, MN, March 12, 1985

In the months prior to Yuri V. Andropov's death in February 1984, when it was clear that he was ill, speculation centered as much on the age as the name of his possible successor. Would the next general secretary again come from the generation of Communist Party officials who actually lived through the 1917 Revolution, and who were adults during Nazi occupation, or would he be the first Soviet leader never to have known czarist rule and who would have been but a child during World War II? This was thought to be an important matter, particularly in terms of East-West relations.

The mostly old men of the Politburo chose on that occasion to continue their own guard, as they picked Konstantin U. Chernenko. He survived 13 months in office before succumbing Sunday at 73, the third elderly Kremlin boss to die in 28 months. His demise has led to the rise of Mikhail S. Gorbachev, 54, the youngest member of the controlling Politburo and the first of the well-pondered "younger" generation to lead his country.

Yet, while hypothesizing was keen last year about how Mr. Gorbachev and his contemporaries differed in background and presumably outlook from their older colleagues, there has been less such talk this time.

In early 1984, there was considerable discussion in the United States about whether members of Mr. Gorbachev's group were less severely molded by the Revolution and less scarred by World War II than were older Russians. If so, were they more pragmatic and less doctrinaire? Were they technocrats first, ideologues second? Were they less distrustful of the world's intentions and, therefore, less inclined to strike out?

Some of this talk will re-ignite, but there is a different cast to current commentary. The focus so far, correctly, has been on the continuity, not the change, Mr. Gorbachev likely will bring to the Soviet system.

After three episodes in which heads of state were incapable of exercising full power because of mortal illness, the collective and inelastic nature of Kremlin governance has become better understood in the West. The Soviet Union may be ceaseless in fomenting revolution elsewhere, but it is the opposite revolutionary at home. It has small patience for changing itself.

Still, one can talk legitimately about this being the beginning of a new period in the Soviet Union and in its dealings with the United States.

Unless stopped by ailment, accident or purge, Mr. Gorbachev will lead his government for an extended period; quite possibly a decade or more. As opposed to Mr. Chernenko and Mr. Andropov before him, he will have time to leave a discernible mark — as reminiscent of previous marks as it may prove.

On this side of the two great oceans, President Reagan, for all of his 74 years, is in only the second month of a second four-year term. American-Soviet relations during his first four years were divided into rough moments and less-rough moments. They were further sectioned by three Soviet regimes.

Chances are better than they have been in a number of years that the two nations can go about their contending and peace-making in a relatively straight, rather than constantly fractured, line. The decision by the two governments to start today's Geneva arms talks on schedule, despite Mr. Chernenko's death, hints at such a welcome pattern.

The Birmingham News

Birmingham, AL, March 12, 1985

As Soviet citizens re-enact the stylized drama mourning a fallen leader, the question foremost in the minds of Americans is: Will Konstantin Chernenko's death make a difference in U.S.-Soviet relations?

The answer may be a long time coming. First of all, President Konstantin Chernenko headed the Kremlin oligarchy so short a time, his influence could have been only minimal. Certainly, the colorless, even stodgy, president never had the power of a Stalin, a Khrushchev or even a Breshnev.

But neither did Andropov, the man Chernenko succeeded. Neither man was in office long enough or had consolidated his power in order to influence Soviet policy more than marginally.

Now Mikhail S. Gorbachev will lead the country as secretary of the Communist Party and probably as president, as many observers predicted. Like his prececessors, he is likely to be cautious about changing policies, were he so inclined, until his power is consolidated and is indisputable. That may be a matter of years rather than months.

The truth is the top leader is locked inescapably into historic Soviet policy. He and the Politburo in a very real sense are prisoners of a communist ideology by which all upper level politicians are judged. And the policies which they have little choice but to follow are determined by an ideology that ordains: (1) The state is supreme, the ultimate power and repository of the ultimate wisdom; (2) only one power center can exist, and only one party can represent it; (3) the communist state cannot exist alongside capitalist states; they are mutually exclusive and (4) history itself has ordained that the communist system will triumph over capitalism, so the defeat of the West and the domination of the world by communists, with Moscow as the center of gravity, is inevitable. Time is on the side of the communist system, and victory is the reward of patience and determination.

Rational observers in the West are inclined to believe that the top Soviet leaders no longer believe in these communist "truths." They deceive themselves. A search of official declarations following each party congress since Lenin's regime will reveal that the central tenets of communism are restated repeatedly and essentially without change. Furthermore, historically, no matter how the West has bent its policies, no matter how many accommodations capitalist countries have made to Soviet intransigence, the Kremlin's policies have remained essentially unchanged.

The only retreats the Soviets have made in executing those policies is in the face of overwhelming power or military strength and determination on the part of the West.

Gorbachev at 54 has been a voting member of the Politburo for only five years, although he has been a member of the Communist Party since his early 20s. How much trust the old guard places in him is questionable. He doubtless has been their spokesman for some time. He has been out front for the past six months or so, ever since Chernenko was known to be seriously ill. He recently toured Western Europe and Britain, launching a Soviet peace offensive and warning that arms control agreements depended on whether the U.S. would abandon President Reagan's Strategic Defense Initiative, the so-called Star Wars system.

As the Kremlin's No. 1 man, Gorbachev's first worldwide exposure may come during the party congress scheduled for late this year or early in 1986. In the meantime, the Soviet positions in the Geneva arms talks are not likely to change. They were established months ago and are not subject to alteration except perhaps to adopt fall-back positions in the face of U.S. determination.

No doubt, in the next few weeks, Americans will be bombarded by millions of words in the world media, some proffered by the KGB's department of misinformation, to give Gorbachev a human face. Despite warmly human images and hopeful speculation, one should remember only the very tough, only the ideologically pure and the politically clever, survive this highest level of Soviet politics.

A new leader may talk peace and accommodation, but the Soviet juggernaut is more likely to roll on, stopping only where it fears to advance.

Military, Government Changes Reported As Gorbachev Shakes Up Politburo

Marshal Nikolai V. Ogarkov had regained the post of first deputy defense minister and been named commander in chief of the Warsaw Pact's military forces, it was reported July, 17 1985. The action, according to Western analysts, continued the drive of Soviet leader Mikhail S. Gorbachev to consolidate his power, and/or spur economic changes in the leadership of the government and Communist Party.

The Warsaw Pact post was regarded as the most important position in the Soviet military hierarchy, after defense minister and chief of staff. Ogarkov, 67, had been ousted as a first deputy defense minister and chief of staff in 1984 by Soviet President Konstantin U. Chernenko.

Ivan P. Kazanets, the Soviet minister for ferrous metals, had been ousted from that post. The action was reported by the news agency Tass July 5, 1985. Tass explained that Kazanets had retired on "health grounds." However, Western analysts noted that Soviet leader Gorbachev in June had publicly criticized the minister for chronic waste in metals production. Kazanets was replaced by his deputy, Serafim V. Kolpakov.

The removal of Kazanets was one of several shakeups in the government's industrial ministries. Among the most significant, reported July 10, was the retirement of Nikolai Tarasov as minister for light industry, a post he had held 20 years. Tarasov, 74, was replaced by Vladimir Klyuev, a member of the Communist Party Central Committee.

Houston Chronicle

Houston, TX, July 3, 1985

Two major international developments: Mikhail Gorbachev is now the undisputed dictator of the Soviet Union. And Gorbachev and President Reagan will confront one another Nov. 19-21 in Geneva.

Gorbachev has made certain that he holds all the reins in the Soviet Union. His men are all in place now. They are party bosses, the kind that do what they are told.

Gorbachev's rival, Grigory V. Romanov, was ousted from the Politburo. Edward A. Shevardnadze, who has practically no foreign policy experience, has been named foreign minister, replacing veteran diplomat Andrei Gromyko. Gromyko has been put in the ceremonial post of president.

These maneuvers mean that Gorbachev will be giving the orders and Shevardnadze will be there to carry them out. Shevardnadze's reputation was made by being tough on corruption in the Georgian province. Aside from a few trips overseas, he has taken no part in forming Soviet foreign policy. But he has a proven record as a party loyalist, and that apparently is all Gorbachev wants from his foreign minister.

The task of turning the meeting between Reagan and Gorbachev into something productive will be enormous. The two men might have had a simple get-together in New York this fall when the U.N. General Assembly resumes session. Instead, they will be meeting in Geneva, and the site dictates the agenda. It is in Geneva that the United States and the Soviet Union are engaged in stalemated arms talks. The meeting in Geneva could very well make or break those talks. Either way, that would be a major turning point in history.

If one wanted to be optimistic, perhaps Gorbachev is preparing to make an arms deal to gain time to deal with his domestic problems. If one wanted to be pessimistic, perhaps Gorbachev is girding up for increased pressure on the West and more drastic crackdowns at home.

This country's job is to be prepared in either case.

SYRACUSE HERALD-JOURNAL

Syracuse, NY, July 4, 1985

After months of inertia in U.S.-Soviet relations, Tuesday saw two significant announcements — one from Moscow, one from Washington — that could signal a new round of activity.

The Soviets announced that the old curmudgeon, veteran Foreign Minister Andrei Gromyko, 75, had been "promoted" (kicked upstairs?) to the largely ceremonial post of president after 28 years as the Kremlin's chief foreign policy spokesman. Replacing him is the relatively youthful Eduard A. Shevardnadze, 57, who had been Communist Party leader of the Georgian Republic.

Meanwhile, the Reagan administration revealed that a summit meeting, a topic of speculation for months, has been arranged between President Reagan and Soviet leader Mikhail Gorbachev. (The formal announcement came a day later.) It's slated for Nov. 19 in Geneva, Switzerland.

The timing of the two announcements may have been merely coincidence, but after such a prolonged period of inactivity in U.S.-Soviet dialogue, it's not unreasonable to make a connection between them.

Most Western analysts see the Gromyko move as further evidence that Gorbachev, who assumed leadership of the Soviet Union less than four months ago, is moving quickly to consolidate his power.

Besides being a skilled diplomat and a firm Communist hard-liner, Gromyko is a survivor. He escaped Stalin's infamous purges and managed to keep the top foreign policy job through several periods of internal Kremlin turmoil. This may be Gorbachev's way of easing a venerable old public servant out of the decision-making process.

Shevardnadze reportedly has little experience in foreign policy and, unlike Gromyko, speaks no foreign languages. His chief credit is a crackdown on official corruption in Georgia. The appointment may mean that Gorbachev is going to be, in effect, his own foreign minister now that Gromyko is out of the picture.

What this means to the United States is open to speculation, and Gorbachev isn't tipping his hand. But it's reasonable to conclude that the man President Reagan will meet in Geneva will be very much in charge. For the first time in Reagan's presidency, he will be dealing face to face with the unchallenged leader of our Cold War enemy.

We can only hope that out of that meeting will come some sort of understanding that will lead to a lessening of tensions — not necessarily a thaw in relations, but a toning down of the angry rhetoric that has been exchanged recently. Whatever the outcome, such a dialogue is long overdue.

THE PLAIN DEALER
Cleveland, OH, July 3, 1985

More exciting than the recent changes in the Soviet Politburo, which are passably interesting themselves, is news that a date has been set for a summit meeting between President Reagan and Soviet leader Mikhail S. Gorbachev. The summit is scheduled for Nov. 19-21. The realignments of the Politburo can be construed as improving the meeting's chances for a positive conclusion.

Gromyko

Foreign Minister Andrei Gromyko, who plotted foreign policy for almost 30 years under five Soviet leaders, has been elevated to the mostly ceremonial post of president. Gromyko is 75 and tied to the old guard, so his transition out of the powerful Foreign Ministry was not unexpected. There even are rumors that he requested the new position.

However it came about, his departure is unlikely to make much difference. Gromyko's successor, Eduard A. Shevardnadze, is one of the Gorbachev dolls: relatively young, bright, stern toward corruption and flexibile on economic issues. He has little, if any, foreign policy experience, however, and that fact is certain to keep Gromyko in the foreign policy arena. The implication is that Gromyko has been promoted to allow him to focus more directly on the topics that interest him—arms control for example.

The other major change—the demotion of one-time contender Grigory V. Romanov—is less intriguing. Not even in this country do losing contenders for the leadership find homes in the victorious administration, especially when they come from the other party. And like the promotion of Gromyko, his replacement by another Leningrader is simply good politics. Gorbachev's efficient management of these changes refutes the generalization that Soviet politics is ruthless and without subtlety and the specific fear that he lacks political credibility and power.

□

If the Gromyko move does not herald a change in Soviet foreign policy, then obviously the nature of a summit meeting has not changed either. If anything, the timing confirms the leading topic for discussions: arms control and disarmament. November will be a month rich with arms issues. The unilateral Soviet freeze on the deployment of intermediate-range missiles will expire about then. The Netherlands will be making up its mind about the deployment of cruise missiles. The autumn session of the Geneva talks will have just concluded. And the United States will have determined its "proportionate responses" to Soviet violations of the SALT II agreement. Mid-November is taking on the shape of a deadline.

If that makes Washington and Moscow more amenable to a new arms agreement, so much the better. But the summit need not be exclusively related to arms control. Other issues deserve attention also. Among them: trade; the global economy; Warsaw Pact/NATO relations; Central America; the Middle East, and South Asia, including Afghanistan. Perhaps that list should also include some effort to produce a joint statement on terrorism.

Given the vast array of topics that deserve attention, it can be reassuring to believe that Gromyko has not been kicked up and out. Indeed, his promotion, along with the other Politburo changes, has solidified Gorbachev's position. In doing so, it provides a new consistency within the Soviet leadership on which the United States can rely, and which should help brighten the summit's prospects.

The State
Columbia, SC, July 6, 1985

WE read about approvingly of the choice of Andrei A. Gromyko as the new president of the Soviet Union, if for no other reason than he is a familiar figure and his diplomatic skills are well known by our government.

The Soviet presidency is largely ceremonial, but Mr. Gromyko, who has been foreign minister since 1958, is expected to keep his hand in while his successor, Eduard A. Shevardnadze, is learning to take his place.

Mr. Gromyko knows this country very well, having dealt with its presidents and secretaries of state since 1948 when he first went to the United Nations as an ambassador.

At age 75, he is a senior member of the ruling Politburo which is becoming more youthful as the old guard passes away. Many of the new Soviet leaders have little experience in international affairs, Soviet Premier and General Party Secretary Mikhail Gorbachev among them.

So, old Cold War warrior Gromyko, who outlasted Josef Stalin, Nikita Khrushchev, Leonid Brezhnev, Yuri Andropov and Konstantin Chernenko, will still be around to see that the United States is not mistakenly underestimated.

When he goes, who knows?

THE SUN
Baltimore, MD, July 3, 1985

When Mikhail S. Gorbachev became general secretary of the Soviet Communist Party on the death of Konstantin U. Chernenko last March, the Brezhnev era finally ended. That was the period of gerontocracy, of ossification of policy. It hardly mattered which elderly gentleman associated with the late Leonid I. Brezhnev was nominally in charge because a collective of them all was, with the generals and police chiefs exercising enormous power in that political and intellectual vacuum. It was a leadership frozen in place and mind that President Reagan had little need to know.

With the breathtaking shuffle of personnel at the top of the Politboro ratified by the Supreme Soviet this week, not four months after Mr. Gorbachev's elevation, his men are in place, his rivals are out, and the Gorbachev era has really begun. It is a milestone in Soviet history.

Because these new men are so firmly in charge and spreading their grasp, it must be assumed that all facets of Soviet policy will come under review. This is the new leadership that anyone dealing importantly with the Soviet Union must try to understand and if possible to influence. The Chinese, Indians, West Europeans, East Europeans and, yes, President Reagan, must make contact. Note yesterday's summit announcement. There is something in Moscow worth learning.

The titular elevation of Andrei Gromyko to ornamental head of state ends 42 years of his personification of Soviet policy to Americans. He was the hardline and the thaw. Josef Stalin sent him as ambassador to Washington in 1943. Nikita Khrushchev in flamboyantly taking power, named the dour technocrat foreign minister in 1957. So well did Mr. Gromyko adapt that Mr. Brezhnev, after deposing Mr. Khrushchev, not only retained but raised him in 1973 to the Politburo. And now at 75 he is the member of that generation who must as head of state approve the men who came after and legitimize what they do.

The world's ignorance of the new foreign minister, Eduard A. Shevardnadze, and his inexperience at foreign policy, suggest that the Georgian boss will be the Gorbachev device for steering foreign policy into line with general policies. Other promotions, especially the movement of Yegor K. Ligachev into control of ideology and patronage, solidify the Gorbachev takeover. The ouster from the Politburo in apparent disgrace of Grigory V. Romanov, so recently touted as a Gorbachev rival, makes the changeover vividly final.

The new men have power and the means and time to use it. What they intend to do if they are able, beyond modernize industry and agriculture, the world must try to find out.

Mike Keefe THE DENVER POST

San Francisco Chronicle

San Francisco, CA, July 5, 1985

SHIFTING ANDREI Gromyko from his long-held post of Soviet Foreign Minister to the presidency seems to betoken loss of actual authority for this enduring Russian figure.

There is gained prestige, of course, in being president of the USSR. But it is a largely ceremonial post, one that normally would have been just another titular feather in Mikhail Gorbachev's fur cap. Gorbachev, however, has pleaded press of other business, and he certainly faces a daunting task in trying to pump some vigor into his country's outmoded and sagging economy.

Gromyko, a tough, reclusive — and highly-skilled — diplomat, had made the foreign ministry (particularly its relations with the U.S.) something of a private backyard. There won't be the same focus of strength in his new position.

IT IS TRUE that Gromyko did what the Politburo and a succession of Soviet leaders from Stalin to Gorbachev decided he should do. Here was the consummate party functionary — courteous, hard-working, and totally unbending. But a functionary looked to more and more in recent years for advice on how to deal with the West.

The message from this intra-Kremlin shift seems to be that a more confident Gorbachev is anxious to call his own shots. Gromyko's replacement, Eduard Shevardnadze, is 57 and has a virtually blank slate on foreign affairs. So new foreign policy decisions are expected to emanate undiluted from Gorbachev himself.

We hope that the new Soviet leader will get some sense of what America is all about when he meets face-to-face with President Reagan in Geneva during the fall. The timing of this meeting seems propitious.

DESERET NEWS

Salt Lake City, UT, July 3/4, 1985

Though some unprecedented house-cleaning is going on in the Kremlin, there seem to be decided limits to its immediate impact on the rest of the world.

In a sharp break with the past, the chief of the Communist Party in Russia will no longer also serve as president. Instead, that largely ceremonial post will be occupied by Andrei Gromyko, Soviet foreign minister for 28 years and one of the world's toughest diplomats.

This shift, coupled with the ouster of a rival and the elevation of an obscure ally who shares his zeal for economic reform, certainly strengthens Mikhail Gorbachev's hold on the top job in Russia.

Since Gromyko's successor lacks foreign policy experience, the change might also seem to portend a shift of emphasis on Gorbachev's part — a shift from domestic affairs, his area of interest and expertise, to getting more personally involved in foreign policy. But don't count on it.

Though Gorbachev is its most dominant and visible member, the leadership of Russia is still a collective leadership whose composition changes only slightly more rapidly than the glacial pace of its policy positions. Traditionally, foreign policy is the most stable area of Kremlin affairs

While the shift involving Gromyko rewards a Gorbachev supporter and gives Gromyko a graceful exit at age 75, it's hard to believe the Kremlin will ignore the foreign policy advice and expertise of a man who has negotiated with Western leaders from Winston Churchill to Reagan administration officials. As president and as a member of the ruling Politburo, Gromyko can be expected to remain visible though less active on the international scene.

If there were any doubts about where Gorbachev's priorities are, he announced Tuesday that the Kremlin intends to concentrate on the whole complex of major tasks arising from the need to modernize the Soviet economy. This announcement is in line with Gorbachev's previously stated view that domestic reform is his most urgent task.

Succeeding to Gromyko's former post as foreign minister is Eduard A. Shevardnadze, who lacks international experience and is virtually unknown outside Russia. He is credited with stamping out much of the bribery and black marketeering that characterized the rule of his predecessor as interior minister in Soviet Georgia. He is also reputed to have instituted a blend of industrial and economic reforms similar to those expected to be undertaken by Gorbachev. But all that has little to do with the job of foreign minister

The ouster from the Politburo of Grigori Romanov, once considered a leading candidate for the Kremlin's top job, can be explained not only by his rivalry with Gorbachev or his continued insistence on hard-line policies with respect to the West. Rather, having been tainted with personal scandal, he had become an embarrassment to the Soviets.

In any government as secretive and conspiratorial as Russia's, major personnel changes are never easy to assess. But as of now, these particular shifts seem to amount more to changes in style than shifts in emphasis or direction.

THE DAILY OKLAHOMAN
Oklahoma City, OK, July 3, 1985

SOVIET leader Mikhail Gorbachev continues to consolidate his position by remaking the Politburo with men who are his contemporaries in the Communist Party structure.

Replacing Grigori Romanov eliminates a potential source of trouble for Gorbachev. Romanov, 62, was a rival for the party chairmanship after Konstantin Chernenko's death and reportedly opposed Gorbachev's selection. Now he has been retired on "health grounds."

His replacement, Eduard Shevardnadze, party leader of Georgia, puts on the Politburo a man more in the Gorbachev mode, who shares the chairman's concern for discipline and economic reform.

Not much is known of the two new party secretaries but they would not have been named if they differed with the politically aggressive Gorbachev.

The elevation of Andrei Gromyko, longtime foreign minister, to the largely ceremonial post of president, is a further demonstration of Gorbachev solidifying his power. This may be a form of semi-retirement for the dour Gromyko but it gives Gorbachev the opportunity to gather around him more of the new Soviet generation — men who were only youths when Hitler invaded Russia and who have no personal memory of the Revolution.

But don't count on them not being committed Marxists who will work to convert the world to communism.

THE TENNESSEAN
Nashville, TN, July 6, 1985

MR. Mikhail Gorbachev has further consolidated his power in the Kremlin by dismissing a rival in the Politburo, shifting Mr. Andrei Gromyko to the presidency and elevating a member to the post of chief ideologist.

Mr. Gromyko's election to the presidency was a major departure from the recent Kremlin practice of having the party leader also hold the title of chief of state. It was Mr. Gorbachev who nominated Mr. Gromyko at a session which capped two days of leadership changes, including the ouster of one-time power contender, Mr. Grigory V. Romanov from the ruling Politburo.

The official report was that Mr. Romanov was removed for "health reasons" at his own request, but it seems fairly clear he was ousted.

Mr. Gromyko is easily the Kremlin's top expert on the West. He has survived purges and six Kremlin leaderships and has negotiated with Western leaders from Winston Churchill to Reagan administration officials.

Several things might be read into Mr. Gromyko's change of status. One is that it provides a graceful end to a long diplomatic career and that Mr. Gorbachev has repaid a debt, since it was Mr. Gromyko who nominated him as Communist Party general secretary.

Georgia party chief, Mr. Eduard Shevardnadze, a new full member of the Politburo who has made a reputation for bbeing tough on corruption, was named to replace Mr. Gromyko in the foreign ministry. Since he has no notable diplomatic experience, it might be said that Mr. Gorbachev intends to take an active role in foreign policy.

That is underscored by the fact that Mr. Gorbachev was elected to the Presidium of the Supreme Sovite, which would allow him to represent the Soviet Union at international gatherings in the place of Mr. Gromyko.

Mr. Gorbachev probably forced the ouster of Mr. Romanov who was undoubtedly hurt by widely circulated stories that he borrowed priceless porcelain from Leningrad's Hermitage Museum in 1979 and smashed it during a celebration of his daughter's wedding. Reports also were that he behaved badly during his last official visit to Finland.

When Mr. Yuri Andropov died, Mr. Romanov along with Mr. Gorbachev were considered the main contenders for leadership if it passed to a younger man. Instead, the leadership post went to Mr. Konstantin Chernenko. That left the two men jockeying for position in a future leadership battle. But by the time Mr. Chernenko died, Mr. Gorbachev clearly was the contender.

Mr. Romanov was responsible for the defense industry. His speeches were hawkish and his animosity toward the West was clear. In that light, Western leaders will hardly bemoan his departure.

Mr. Gorbachev has moved with some speed in consolidating his power. And he has een moving with a sense of determination. He recently rejected a draft of the Soviet Union's five-year plan that he disagreed with, his representatives have put pressure on the Eastern bloc to cooperate more on getting Soviet industry moving. And he has made personnel changes at almost every level — putting his allies in key positions to promote his policies at the crucial party congress next February.

Mr. Gorbachev is apparently confident of his power now, and after February that power should be undisputed.

Newsday
Long Island, NY, July 9, 1985

The leadership changes in the Politburo, the seat of Soviet political power, came on the same day of the announcement that President Reagan and Soviet leader Mikhail Gorbachev would hold a summit conference in November. The two developments were more than a coincidence in that the shifts in the Kremlin would appear to have an interlocking relationship with the high-level talks between the heads of the two superpowers.

After a long diplomatic career as the key figure in Russian foreign policy, Andrei Gromyko has been moved upstairs to the presidency, a ceremonial post with far less power than the foreign ministry he headed. The appointment of Eduard Shevardnadze, the party leader of the Soviet republic of Georgia, as Mr. Gromyko's replacement marks a generational change in the Kremlin hierarchy.

The selection of Mr. Shevardnadze as foreign minister was somewhat of a surprise since he has no background in the foreign policy field. But lack of diplomatic experience was a matter of secondary importance. A more significant criterion for his appointment was that he was Mr. Gorbachev's personal choice.

Age, too, could have been a factor in the naming of Mr. Shevardnadze. At 56, he becomes an integral part of the change in the structure of Soviet leadership that began with the elevation of Mr. Gorbachev, who, in his mid-50s, is much younger than his predecessors.

By moving Mr. Gromyko out of the top diplomatic post, Mr. Gorbachev has positioned himself to take over Soviet foreign policy. And the timing of his expanded diplomatic role has been adroitly orchestrated, coming as it does only several months before the summit conference in Geneva.

It is not considered likely that any major changes in Russian foreign policy will emerge soon. But no doubt there will be changes in style that will evolve under a new and younger generation of Russian leaders, perhaps a more flexible foreign policy that could lead to improved relations between the Soviet Union and the United States.

The summit conference, the first meeting between President Reagan and Mr. Gorbachev, could be an opening phase, an exchange of viewpoints on issues with global ramifications. Geneva, as the site of both the summit and the ongoing arms talks, has a geographical symbolism, underscoring the enormous importance of the meeting between the two heads of state—and perhaps providing the stage for an agreement on control and reduction of the Soviet and U.S. nuclear arsenals.

Crisis at Chernobyl Nuclear Plant Spreads Radiation, Fear

A serious accident at a nuclear power plant in the Soviet Ukraine spewed clouds of radiation that eventually spread over other nations in Europe. The mishap, veiled in secrecy by Moscow, caused widespread fear and conjecture April 28-30, 1986.

The accident involved the No. 4 reactor in the Chernobyl nuclear plant, located in the town of Pripyat, about 60 miles north of Kiev. Western speculation and unconfirmed information led to reports of thousands of Soviet casualties, mainly due to exposure to high levels of radiation in the accident area. Western experts also speculated that the accident might actually have occurred as early as April 24.

Moscow downplayed the accident while denouncing the West for allegedly exaggerating the seriousness of the crisis. The Kremlin rebuffed most Western offers of assistance. The Soviet Union came under strong international condemnation for not initially revealing the accident and for withholding detailed information on the mishap. Western analysts noted that Moscow's secrecy conformed to a policy of not disclosing domestic mishaps. Evidence gathered outside the U.S.S.R. suggested that at least one other nuclear accident, with a high loss of life, had occurred in the country at Kyshtym in the Ural Mountains in 1957.

The lack of detailed information prompted mounting speculation in the West. As early as April 28, some nuclear experts surmised that the stricken reactor had sustained at least a partial meltdown of its core. The supposition was prompted by the presence of isotopes and iodine in radioactive fallout monitored in Sweden. A melting of the uranium fuel in a damaged reactor would cause the release of such isotopes. In turn, the speculation over a meltdown raised fears, particularly in Europe, of the possible cancers that could result from the radioactive fallout carried in the wind from Chernobyl.

Based on Soviet accounts and Western satellite surveillance, the crisis had appeared to have abated as of May 1.

However, there were new indications that the trouble persisted and might worsen. In a worst-case scenerio, a so-called "China Syndrome," the burning core – a molten slag of graphite, metal and nuclear fuel – could burn through the floor of the reactor building until it contaminated the groundwater under the building.

The plant was located next to the Pripyat River. The river fed into a reservoir that provided water for Kiev and the surrounding region. West German scientists May 8 revealed that they had been approached by Soviet diplomats seeking information on how to battle a core burn-through.

The Soviet news media May 5-8 told of the efforts "under the reactor block" to build dikes and earthworks to shield the waters from the molten core should it burn through. Meanwhile, the burning reactor continued to spread wind-borne radiation over great areas. Low levels of fallout from the accident reached the U.S. West Coast May 5.

Technical experts of the European Community (EC) May 7 recommended a temporary ban imports of on food and animals from Eastern Europe that might have been contaminated in the Chernobyl disaster. The ban, to last until May 31, covered the Soviet Union, Poland, Romania, Hungary, Bulgaria, Czechoslovakia and Yugoslavia. Banned products included milk and dairy products, fresh fruit and vegetables, fresh meat, fresh water fish, chicken, horses and mules. The EC action came as Western scientists and economists debated the impact of the accident on Soviet agriculture. Moscow, for the first time, May 5 acknowledged evidence of contamination outside the 18-mile evacuation zone around the nuclear power plant, located in the Ukranian farm belt.

Western leaders at the seven-nation economic summit in Tokyo May 5 issued a statement on the Chernobyl accident. The leaders called for a new international convention requiring information exchanges on nuclear accidents and emergencies and mildly criticized the Soviet Union for its failure to provide information about the accident at Chernobyl. Western figures on presumed deaths generally ranged from a few to thousands. West German scientists April 29 estimated that if the accident was as serious as indicated, as many as 10,000 people within a 300-mile radius of Pripyat would die of lung cancer within 10 years.

The Oregonian

Portland, OR, May 12, 1986

If the Soviet power reactor at Chernobyl didn't "melt down" in the best China Syndrome fashion, there is little occasion to rejoice, for the accident still proves that serious human and environmental damage can follow other types of nuclear reactor accidents.

An International Atomic Energy Agency official, Morris Rosen, who is leading non-Soviet investigations of the accident, has been quoted as saying that no meltdown of the reactor core occurred and that the fire in the graphite pile that moderates the reactor's has been put out.

This is by no means an end to the problem, because the reactor's fuel, believed to have been nearly exhausted at the time of the accident and hence far less lethal, is still a mass of hot decay elements that will take a long time to cool to a safe level. They are also a potential for another explosion if they contact ground or other water, releasing more lethal doses of radioactivity.

The word "meltdown," which has become a kind of scare word, means that failure of a reactor's coolant materials have permitted its uranium fuel rods to actually melt

The Argonne National Laboratory in Arco, Idaho, has reported that its April tests of a new kind of reactor encourage convictions that a reactor inherently safe from a meltdown can be built. The reactor uses metal uranium fuel instead of uranium oxide and is cooled with liquid sodium. Physical properties of the fuel will close down the reactor before it can melt, even if all coolant systems are removed, the laboratory has shown in actual "melt-down" tests run on an experimental breeder reactor.

But this solution, while good news to the industry, may be 15 years away from being translated into a commercial power-producing nuclear plant.

Scientists critical of current reactor safety, argue that fully safe reactor technology can be achieved and that current reactors would be safer if the government would only get tougher with nuclear operators.

Meltdown may eventually be removed from the lexicon of scare words, but nuclear energy safety will always be of worldwide concern — not just the responsibility of local officials in a single country.

The Burlington Free Press

Burlington, VT, May 2, 1986

In the February issue of "Soviet Life," a Russian propaganda magazine that is distributed in English-speaking countries, the Chernobyl nuclear plant was lauded as a model of efficiency; the chances of an accident were said to be so remote that they were not worth contemplating.

Yet in a gesture that undoubtedly was to be taken as a sign of the new openness of the Gorbachev era, a Soviet publication which does not appear in the West levelled criticism at the plant for its inadequacies. The author hinted that there was a genuine possibility of an accident there.

What happened Saturday at the Ukrainian nuclear facility seems to have established the author's reputation as a prophet and indeed may have much to do with the decision by the Kremlin to be stingy with information about the accident. Surely, the situation has created tensions

among the members of the Soviet's elite Politburo. It might well cause serious problems for Mikhail Gorbachev, the party leader, in his efforts to persuade others in the Communist hierarchy that he is indeed fit to hold the reins of power.

Should Americans be tempted to adopt a smug posture toward the incident, however, it should be enough to remind them of the nuclear mishaps that have occurred in this country since 1961 when an experimental reactor in Idaho Falls went out of control. The litany of accidents is long but none perhaps was more serious than the meltdown at the Three Mile Island plant outside Harrisburg, Pa., in March 1979 which led to the evacuation of hundreds from the area. There is evidence to indicate that officials of the Nuclear Regulatory Commission were less than candid with the public at that time about the dangers from the accident. The reactor, in fact, is still being

decontaminated. It is possible that it will not be used again.

Even though the commission and utilities officials claim that elaborate precautions are taken during construction of nuclear plants to prevent lethal releases of radiation, the fact is that the possibility of an accident is not as remote as the public has been led to believe. Some scientists who are critical of government and utilities policies say that several plants in the country are vulnerable to meltdowns, some of them similar to the plant at Chernobyl.

If American plants generally are required to meet higher standards, it is because knowledgeable scientists outside the government have raised questions about safety issues and because anti-nuclear activitists have called public attention to some of the potential dangers of nuclear reactors. Because scientific opinion is couched in such complex language, people are

more inclined to understand the objections of the anti-nuclear groups. It is a tribute to an open society that such groups are allowed to express their concerns about nuclear power plants.

That is not to say that nuclear plants do not have a place in the nation's power network. But it is to say that extraordinary precautions should be taken during construction and operation of the facilities to insure that they do not constitute a serious hazard to the health and welfare of the public.

However expensive and extensive such steps might be, they can be justified on the grounds that they ultimately will prevent a serious disaster which could cause death and injury to hundreds of thousands of people.

Had the Soviet Union been required to conform to higher safety standards, it is possible that the Chernobyl plant would have been properly shielded and the accident would not have been as serious as it appears to be.

Minneapolis Star and Tribune

Minneapolis, MN, May 2, 1986

The Des Moines Register

Des Moines, IA,
May 3, 1986

The fires of Chernobyl have raised disturbing questions 'for Americans mindful of some near disasters of our own, presumably safer, nuclear-power plants. Although nuclear power supplies only 13.5 percent of our electricity, the United States has more operating plants — 96 — than any other nation.

The utility companies repeatedly assure the public that the plants are safe; there hasn't been a single radiation death at a commercial nuclear plant in this country. But while the nuclear industry is long on assurance, it is woefully short on insurance.

In case of a disaster, federal law provides that liability is limited to the amount of insurance available, and that now comes to $640 million — $160 million provided by private insurers, plus retroactive assessments of $5 million per operating reactor in case of an accident. If damage claims exceed that amount, according to the law, "Congress will thoroughly review the particular incident and will take whatever action is deemed necessary and appropriate."

A 1982 study by the Sandia National Laboratory said that damages from a worst-case accident involving the Indian Point nuclear plant north of New York City could exceed $300 billion. But under the law, the victims or the taxpayers would foot almost all of the bill. The utilities would pay only a tiny fraction of the damages.

The liability limit was established under the Price-Anderson Act of 1957 because insurance actuaries had no experience upon which to estimate risks and set rates.

Today they have a better fix on the risks. But they still won't write policies to cover realistic damage potential, and the utilities won't operate nuclear plants without the protection of Price-Anderson. So the "temporary" limit, adopted in expectation that it would be needed just long enough to get the industry off the ground, remains in effect almost 30 years later.

Price-Anderson is up for its third renewal. The first two times Congress extended the act, it drew almost no public attention. But in the wake of Chernobyl, the public may indeed question whether victims and taxpayers should bear the risk of a nuclear disaster while those responsible are held only minimally liable.

Chernobyl is labeled "the worst nuclear disaster ever," but who knows what that means? Were two people killed or 2,000? Is the accident so grave that countless Soviet citizens will die in years to come from radiation illness? Or is it merely a mishap, remarkable mainly because no real nuclear disaster has ever occurred?

It could be either; it could be neither. The point is that beyond the Soviet hierarchy, the world's people don't really know and may never know. But they deserve to know. Chernobyl reinforces the truth that humans are a family and the Earth is our house. We have responsibilities to one another that transcend the rooms in that house or conflicts with brothers and sisters. Yet at Chernobyl, the Soviets behaved like the child who realized, halfway through the movie, that he'd left the bathtub filling at home, then kept silent for fear of punishment.

Mikhail Gorbachev made much of his desire for openness in Soviet society and of his campaign to prove the Soviet Union a trustworthy neighbor. But when the chips were melting down, the wall reappeared. Traditional Russian insecurity reasserted itself. Fear of internal dissent and external criticism proved more powerful than the requirement to notify other nations promptly, more powerful than the right of Soviet citizens to be informed. As Flora Lewis points out in a column on this page, it probably was no coincidence that the Soviets turned up a one-time U.S. employee Monday — after the accident but before it became a major story — to denounce Radio Liberty. Within the day, Radio Liberty would become an important source of information on Chernobyl for Soviet citizens.

Now the Soviets are lashing back at what they say are wild rumors circulating in the West of death and destruction at Chernobyl. They seem to find in those rumors confirmation of their vision of a world waiting to pounce on Soviet weakness or failure. That is the wrong lesson. The proper antidote for rumors is more information, not less. Political paranoia and secrecy cannot remove the international black eye the Soviet Union has received at Chernobyl; they only inflame it. If the Soviets learn anything from this episode, let them learn that their nuclear accident could have earned them international sympathy and understanding; that their foolish attempts to contain the news have earned them international scorn.

St. Petersburg Times

St. Petersburgh, FL, May 13, 1986

One of the seemingly obvious lessons of Chernobyl is that the four most dangerous words in any language are "it can't happen here." It's what the Russians must have said after Three Mile Island, or Chernobyl would not be the result. Nonetheless, the U.S. nuclear power industry continues to insist that what happened at Chernobyl can't happen here.

But if not, why does federal law strictly limit the industry's liability in the event of just such an accident? Why is there currently a sharp debate in Congress on how much to increase that limit, which is at present a plainly inadequate $640-million?

The reason, of course, is that utility investors and insurance underwriters measure the risk by the cold light of logic, which tells them that there is no such thing under the sun as a guarantee of perfect safety. Technology can fail. Human error can occur. There have been more than a dozen serious accidents in the United States, as recently as one in Ohio last year that threatened to replicate Three Mile Island. The Brown's Ferry reactor at Decatur, Ala., was imperiled in 1975 because a technician using a candle to check for air leaks started a fire that burned out the electrical controls for many of the safety systems. The thought of a candle nearly destroying a nuclear plant should have cured the industry of its hubris, but it did not.

By wild coincidence, the Chernobyl accident occurred two days after two congressional committees acted to increase liability limits applied under the Price-Anderson Act, first enacted in 1957. In setting the limit, originally $500-million, Congress acknowledged that nuclear power would not be feasible if the utility industry had to bear all the potential risk. Today, there is no denying that even $640-million is ridiculously low, but only two days before Chernobyl the Senate Energy and Natural Resources Committee voted 19-1 that $2.4-billion would be enough. That same day, the House Interior and Insular Affairs Committee voted 21-20 to set the limit at $8.2-billion, which outraged the nuclear power industry and prompted a walkout by Republican members to prevent final action on the bill. It is still uncertain, even after Chernobyl, whether Chairman Morris Udall, D-Ariz., has the votes to retain the higher limit. No further action is expected before May 21.

In the event of a major accident, the U.S. government would pay the damages up to the limit, less private conventional insurance coverage, and recover the money from after-the-fact assessments on all nuclear utilities. Each would be liable to only $20-million under the Senate bill, but to $80-million under the House version.

The utilities complain that the higher limits would ruin them. But $8.2-billion can hardly be called excessive, given the example of the vast tangible damage and the harm yet to be measured that Chernobyl has inflicted. In the United States, there are operating nuclear reactors within a few miles of major population centers. What would be the costs, in evacuation expenses alone, if an accident on the scale of Chernobyl occurred near Miami, New York or Detroit?

Such an accident may be unlikely here, considering that U.S. commercial nuclear power reactors use a different design and are required (unlike the government's own reactors) to have containment structures like that which served its purpose at Three Mile Island. But to say it is unlikely is to beg the question of whether it is impossible.

The United States now has 101 operating reactors, according to the International Atomic Energy Agency, slightly more than a fourth of all those in the world. Nuclear power will not be disinvented, nor should it be. It offers an abundant source of relatively cheap energy which, waste storage problems aside, is also theoretically nonpolluting. What the debate over the Price-Anderson Act points out is that nuclear energy would not be so cheap if it had to shoulder a more realistic burden of potential liability. The Price-Anderson Act is a subsidy in every respect. A higher limit means that nuclear power will cost its customers more and save them less compared to oil, coal and other sources. But it also means that it will save them less compared to energy conservation and to the potential benefits of solar and renewable energy, which have been sadly neglected of late.

Nuclear power is here to stay, but the time has come to put the true costs on the table.

THE LINCOLN STAR
Lincoln, NE, May 10, 1986

The Chernobyl nuclear plant disaster will serve as a valuable laboratory in the study of radiation effects upon human beings. That is not to diminish the tragedy of lost lives, but simply to recognize the reality of the situation.

Even if the deaths from radiation exposure are now at the low level claimed by the Soviet Union, the amount of contamination is unknown and could be far reaching.

Editorial Research Reports speculates that millions of people could suffer in the years ahead from the effects of radioactive materials deposited on the land and in the water of parts of the Soviet Union and other European countries.

The report describes the Soviet case as the most serious nuclear accident in history. It cites nuclear experts who believe radiation levels will lead to higher death rates from cancer and other diseases and probably greater problems with birth defects caused by genetic mutations.

As the human toll of Chernobyl's accident grows, perhaps the reality of all nuclear matters will sink more deeply into the world's consciousness. It is an unwanted analytical process that has been provided the world but the only thing left to do with it is to learn whatever lessons it teaches.

As is typical of people, the world has more or less resigned itself to the presence of nuclear energy. The world has come to live with something it has seemed unable to do anything about.

But before this latest Soviet nuclear accident has run its full course, the world is very likely to gain a new appreciation of the horrors of uncontrolled nuclear power. The greatest threat, of course, is that of nuclear warfare.

Should any nation ever resort to the use of nuclear weapons, the consequences would make Chernobyl look like a Sunday school picnic. Nuclear power may offer a great danger of radiation accident but nuclear weapons offer a level of human suffering of unequalled immensity.

Without a continuing awareness and appreciation of the awesome nature of such weapons, the possibility of their use is greater.

The disaster in the Soviet Union is a tragedy but it should serve as a long standing warning of the fragile hold we have on life in the nuclear environment in which we live.

SYRACUSE HERALD-JOURNAL
Syracuse, NY, May 1, 1986

While we've been distracted this week by the nuclear plant disaster in the Soviet Union, there have been a number of significant developments in our own latest case of technology gone awry — the explosion of the space shuttle Challenger.

After months of confusion since the Jan. 28 tragedy — in which seven astronauts were killed — the U.S. space program is finally starting to return to a sense of normalcy. Cape Canaveral today was to see its first launch since Challenger — an unmanned weather satellite aboard a three-stage Delta rocket. And the National Commission on Space is about to recommend to President Reagan an ambitious plan for manned space flight well into the 21st century.

Not that the Challenger episode has passed. The ugly reminders will be with us for the forseeable future. Seven flag-draped coffins were taken to Dover Air Force Base in Delaware this week, where the remains of Challenger's crew were to be prepared for burial. And new test results show that the accident was inevitable, largely due to fundamental flaws in the design of the craft that were exacerbated by cold temperatures on the morning of launch.

▽   ▽

Parallels between the two disasters, half a world away from each other, are striking. It was not really the technology that failed. Technology is neutral — bound by the laws of science and incapable of acting outside them.

The failure, instead, lies with humans who expected too much of technology, who neglected to consider all the contingencies, who smugly discounted the risks.

Before the meltdown at the plant near Kiev, Soviet engineers insisted there was no need to enclose the reactor in elaborate and costly containment facilities. The chances of an accident were so remote, they calculated, such a precaution involved unnecessary trouble and expense. Obviously, they were wrong, and that miscalculation reportedly has cost thousands of lives so far, with incalculable long-term consequences.

So it was with Challenger. We now know that the disaster was not merely bad luck, that it was bound to happen sooner or later because the techology was inadequate to perform what was asked of it. We believed those who told us it was safe. They were wrong, and we feel betrayed.

Are there other technological disasters waiting to happen? Of course. They don't have the dramatic effect of a nuclear meltdown or a spacecraft explosion, but they're everywhere. We read about them every day — asbestos, the Dalkon Shield, PCBs, Pinto gas tanks — developments touted as improvements in our quality of life that are only later unmasked as threats.

▽   ▽

This is not to say all technology is bad, but neither is it benevolent. It is a tiger that requires a sturdy cage or it will revert to nature and bite us when our back is turned. It punishes complacency. We can remain its masters only through conscientious effort.

That effort cannot be left solely to the technologists. It is incumbent upon all of us who enjoy technology's benefits to raise questions about its safety and demand real answers — not merely reassurances — before it is allowed to go forward. We can't allow ourselves to be anesthetized by vague advice to "let the experts handle it," or intimidated by patronizing claims that "it's too complicated for the layman to understand."

Laymen bear the consequences of taking too much for granted in technology. And as has been dramatically demonstrated twice this year, those consequences can be catastrophic.

Los Angeles Times
Los Angeles, CA, May 1, 1986

The automatic response of spokesmen for the U.S. nuclear industry to the Soviet nuclear disaster is to say that it couldn't happen here. They may be right—although nobody will really know until and unless the details of the Chernobyl accident are available. However, anybody who really believes that the Soviet disaster is irrelevant to the American nuclear program is mistaken.

It is true that the ill-fated Soviet reactor was of a fundamentally different design than the water-cooled and moderated reactors that are used in commercial nuclear power plants in this country. More important, it is probably true that the catastrophic release of radioactivity from the Soviet plant wouldn't have occurred if the reactor had been enclosed in a containment structure like those that the Nuclear Regulatory Commission requires of all U.S. commercial reactors. Without such a containment structure to bottle up escaping radioactivity, the Three Mile Island accident in this country seven years ago would have had far, far worse consequences.

The fact is, however, that the U.S. government operates five reactors—at Hanford, Wash., and Savannah River, S.C.—that produce nuclear weapons material, are not subject to all the regulations that apply to commercial power reactors, and do not have containment structures. Congress should insist on an immediate review to determine if these plants should be shut down.

As for commercial reactors, the disaster in the Ukraine is a useful reminder that nuclear power is not inherently safe but inherently dangerous. When nuclear power enthusiasts tell us that there isn't a chance in a million of a catastrophic accident at a given site, that is not entirely reassuring. Any system devised by human beings can fail. What makes nuclear accidents unique is that, when they do occur, the cost in lives and public health can be so enormous and long-lasting.

It is a little unsettling, with the benefit of hindsight, to read that a Soviet official once told the governor of Pennsylvania that Soviet reactors were so safe that one could be built in Red Square without danger to the populace.

A Soviet magazine recently carried an article on the Chernobyl complex itself in which an engineer boasted that working at the plant "is safer than driving a car."

At the very least the Reagan Administration should back off from proposals to make federal regulation of nuclear power plants less stringent. But a more fundamental rethinking is also in order.

In the absence of a determined, well-funded program to develop alternative energy sources as a hedge against declining reserves of oil and gas, it may not be practical to close all U.S. nuclear power plants as demanded by Ralph Nader, Helen Caldicott and other nuclear activists. However, the handwriting may already be on the wall—for both safety reasons and the diminishing economic feasibility of nuclear power.

Austrians voted in 1978 not to turn on a newly built reactor. The Danish parliament last year shelved plans to build nuclear plants. And Sweden, a world leader in nuclear technology, is planning to phase out its 12 reactors early in the next century. When you consider that no new construction of power reactors has been initiated in America for several years, it is obvious that we may be following a de facto phase-out policy ourselves.

It may not be a bad thing.

Gorbachev Spurs Major Reforms in Speech Assailing CP 'Inertia'

Soviet leader Mikhail S. Gorbachev Jan. 27, 1987 opened a plenary session of the Communist Party Central Committee with a stunning call for major political reforms, including new procedures to elect party officials. General Secretary Gorbachev's speech to the 307-member Central Committee lasted six hours. Several times he used the word "democratization" to describe the changes he envisioned in the party. Gorbachev asserted that his recommendations were a logical extension of the economic and social reforms (*perestroika* in Russian), drive for more openness (*glasnost*) and the changes in the party leadership he had initiated since 1985.

The core of his address was a strong criticism of the party's stagnation during and since the era of Soviet leader Leonid Brezhnev (in power 1964-1982). Without mentioning Brezhnev by name, Gorbachev said that the party leadership of the 1970s and early 1980s had been marked by "conservative sentiments, inertia, a tendency to brush aside everything that did not fit into conventional patterns, and an unwillingness to come to grips with outstanding socio-economic questions."

With the party in such a state, Gorbachev told the committee, the entire nation suffered. "The spread of alcohol and drug abuse and a rise in crime became the indicators of the decline in social mores." In turn, the general secretary suggested that the Brezhnev era had been a legacy of the 1930s and 1940s, when, he said, the party "misinterpreted simplistically" the ideas of V.I. Lenin, the founder of Soviet communism.

Gorbachev indicated a belief that the current social and economic problems facing his regime stemmed in large part from the bureaucratic practices and political cronyism that had become entrenched during the Brezhnev era. The general secretary maintained that the situation could be remedied only through sweeping reforms within the party.

Pittsburgh Post-Gazette
Pittsburgh, PA, January 30, 1987

When Soviet leader Mikhail S. Gorbachev first announced his policy of *glasnost* or openness, many Americans — and not just conservatives — dismissed the initiative as so much window-dressing. That reflexive reaction is increasingly harder to defend.

Yet, while heartening and refreshing to behold, Mr. Gorbachev's extraordinary efforts also inspire uneasiness. One has to wonder if Mr. Gorbachev is strong enough to prevent hard-line forces from putting an abrupt end to such flirtations with democracy, as their Chinese counterparts recently did.

This week Mr. Gorbachev called for secret balloting and a choice of candidates in Communist Party elections, while chastising the party for its inertia in dealing with social and economic problems. The proposals for electoral reform, modest as they may be by the standards of Western democracies, go far beyond any previous heresy since Mr. Gorbachev launched his *glasnost* policy.

When the Soviet leader went even further to report that he was drafting legislation giving comrades the right to file complaints in court against "illegal actions of officials, infringing the rights of citizens" he may have moved beyond the limits of official tolerance.

If Mr. Gorbachev was attempting to test his position, he could not have given his Politburo critics any stronger goading. The Soviet people, and Americans who wish them well, will soon learn if he has his troops behind him in his stated objective of "decisively changing the public mentality and remolding popular psychology, thinking and feelings."

The Washington Times
Washington, DC, January 29, 1987

The news from Moscow seems pretty dramatic. Mikhail Gorbachev is calling for "broad changes" in what passes for an electoral system, including the use of secret ballots and more than one candidate (gee!) to run for top offices. Tass waxed eloquent about the Gorbachev initiatives, referring to them as "the democratization of social life."

The reforms, if enforced, would represent a surprising swing away from Soviet tradition. "Enforced" is the operative word. Voters now cast ballots only for the Communist Party candidate, and top positions in the party and government are filled by a show of hands. The changes Mr. Gorbachev proposes already exist in law, but are ignored. If Mr. Gorbachev is serious, he need only ask the Central Committee to enforce the law.

If the changes are only an appeal for obedience to existing law, what is going on? Two things, none having much to do with democracy. Since last April when *glasnost* (or "openness") became the watchword, Mr. Gorbachev has used the term as both a superb propaganda tool and a remarkably effective lever for ejecting bureaucrats and party hacks who have resisted his agenda. It is hardly an original ploy. Lenin used the same tactic — even the term *glasnost* — in 1918 after signing decrees shackling the press and banning non-Bolshevik publications. Then as now the object was not to open up society, but to achieve greater control over the party's agenda. The party is the state, said Lenin, and it should not be thought that Mr. Gorbachev has other ideas.

Openness in the U.S.S.R. bears no resemblance to openness in the West. Moreover, *glasnost* — especially the spate of critical press articles containing revelations of official wrongdoing — is confined to specific areas in which the Kremlin has run up against party officials and others who are less than enthusiastic about Mr. Gorbachev's plans. As Lenin taught, there is more than one way to skin a bear.

The Honolulu Advertiser
Honolulu, HI, January 29, 1987

Mikhail Gorbachev's proposals for *glasnost* (openness) in the Soviet Union seem to promise movement in a good direction. But one has to wonder whether they would go far enough or fast enough, or anywhere at all.

His latest ones are for secret ballots and allowing more than one candidate to stand for office. In Russia, that's radical.

FOR NOW the talk seems mainly aimed at consolidating Gorbachev's control by sweeping the last Brezhnev remnants from power.

But Gorbachev badly wants dramatic economic improvement, and this may not be possible without giving Soviet citizens a greater stake in public affairs and at least an illusion of influence over their own lives.

Whether election reform would be for the small ruling Communist Party only or government posts too is unclear. If it touches just the party, which admits only the ideologically "pure" and advances only by patronage, it means little.

And it would be naive to look for anything like a multi-party system or true opposition candidates in the forseeable future. Nor do the changes suggest a weakening of the xenophobic nationalism that propels Soviet foreign policy.

But it would be wrong to dismiss reform because it does not instantly meet our standards. Our democracy was not born fully formed. Women had the vote, for what it's worth, in Russia before America.

SOVIET reform may be phony, aimed at luring dissidents out of the woodwork to be rubbed out. Or it may disappear as quickly as "liberalization" seems to have done in China.

But if they take hold, *glasnost*, election reform and the greater access to information that comes with computers will gradually alter Soviet society. That may not help the United States or end the Cold War, but it can't hurt.

Los Angeles Times

Los Angeles, CA, January 29, 1987

The Soviet Union is a long way from anything resembling political pluralism, much less democracy in the Western sense, but events at this week's meeting of the Communist Party's Central Committee can only be called remarkable.

Soviet leader Mikhail S. Gorbachev has been in office 22 months. During that time he has repeatedly made it clear that his first priority is the rejuvenation of the Soviet economy, which can produce first-rate nuclear missiles but can't manage to keep up with the galloping computer technology that is revolutionizing the civilian economies of Western countries.

Gorbachev has recognized that important elements of the Communist Party apparatus are part of the problem, not the solution. He wants to transform the party into an engine of change, rather than of resistance to change. And he clearly appreciates that his chances for success are far greater if he can enlist the energies of the Soviet Union's scientific and cultural elite.

The Soviet leader has gone a long way toward replacing the conservative, inflexible members of the power structure with younger men of his own choosing. Cultural controls have been relaxed. The state-run media have been encouraged to become bolder in exposing cases of corruption, inefficiency and stubborn adherence to old, neo-Stalinist ways of doing things.

So far, however, actual economic reform has been extremely modest. In recent months Gorbachev has vented his frustrations with public complaints about the roadblocks being thrown up by change-resistant party bureaucrats and industrial managers.

At this week's Central Committee plenum Gorbachev continued the process of removing holdovers from the Brezhnev era and stacking the party secretariat with his own men. Most dramatic of all, he proposed to institute secret balloting and a choice of candidates in elections to party leadership positions at local, regional and republic levels. As of now, only one hand-picked candidate for each such post stands for election; such candidates are elected unanimously by a show of hands. He also suggested worker participation in the choice of factory managers.

The extent of the change should not be exaggerated. The new, more democratic voting system will not apply to the policy-makers in the Politburo or the Central Committee. Where it does apply, the nomination process will still be closely controlled, and lower party bodies can still be overruled by officials at the next-highest level. Open debate is supposedly being encouraged, but there is as yet no evidence that criticism of the Politburo or Gorbachev himself will be tolerated. In short, the reforms are intended to enforce Kremlin authority, not dilute it.

Still, the move—if it sticks—will represent a dramatic opening up of the political process by Soviet standards. Clearly Gorbachev wants to supplement reformist pressure from the top with pressure from the bottom; the idea is that obstructionist officials will risk being voted out of their jobs.

Many Western analysts are convinced that Gorbachev is running a considerable risk himself.

In the first place, there is always the danger that the Soviet people will take Gorbachev's democratic rhetoric at face value, thus producing a revolution of rising political expectations. Of more immediate relevance, the proposed reforms strike at the heart of a system in which official position conveys privilege in the form of special stores, admission to the best universities, foreign travel and party-provided vacation resorts.

The beneficiaries of this system will not appreciate having their job security undermined. Former leader Nikita S. Khrushchev's attempts to interfere with the system are believed to have played a major role in his removal.

Gorbachev said he had Politburo approval for the reforms. But it is noteworthy that this week's Central Committee meeting was supposed to have been held late last year; the delay is believed to have been caused by resistance to Gorbachev's reform efforts within the power structure. Gorbachev seemed to be saying Tuesday that resistance has not been overcome—hence the need for "democratic" pressures on entrenched interests.

Roy Medvedev, a dissident historian who manages to keep open his pipelines to the Kremlin, commented a few days ago that "in two years Gorbachev has gone further than people thought he would. But the further he goes, the more opposition he's up against." That being the case, it remains to be seen whether the reforms approved in principle by the Central Committee this week will actually prevail.

ST. LOUIS POST-DISPATCH

St. Louis, MO
January 29, 1987

Speaking before the 300-member Central Committee of the Soviet Communist Party, Mikhail Gorbachev dropped a political bombshell: He called for the widespread use of secret ballots and a choice of candidates in the party's in-house elections. "Some comrades find it hard to understand," Mr. Gorbachev noted, "that democratism is not just a slogan but the essence of [party] reorganization."

In addition, Mr. Gorbachev made veiled attacks on the policies and programs of Stalin ("authoritarian evaluations"), Khruschev ("volunteerism") and Brezhnev ("ossified" policies). Nor did he stop there; Mr. Gorbachev denounced the party's lower-ranking leadership for widespread corruption, cronyism and abuse of power. Even for Mr. Gorbachev, who has a well-established reputation for outspokenness, the speech was surprisingly candid.

One conclusion to be drawn from the address is that Mr. Gorbachev has successfully consolidated his power base and is now strong enough to purge all of the Brezhnevian old guard and even the most powerful corrupt party functionaries.

It would be a mistake, however, to see the speech as a flowering of democracy in the Soviet Union. Mr. Gorbachev took pains to point out that Russia will remain a single-party state. Also, all candidates for party posts will still be selected by the party, and the elite will retain the ability to overturn lower-level party decisions.

The change here is more tactical than strategic: Mr. Gorbachev will use this "democratism" to weed out those opposed to his political reforms and to revitalize the Soviet dictatorship.

The Birmingham News

Birmingham, AL, January 30, 1987

The American public shouldn't become overly enthusiastic about Soviet leader Mikhail S. Gorbachev's call for revisions in his nation's election process to allow citizens "more effective and real participation." He has no intention of bringing true democracy to his communist nation.

In fact, what Gorbachev actually proposed Tuesday would change very little in the way the Soviet Union is governed, since the reforms would only take place within the Communist Party, a select group that does not include most of the Soviet people.

Gorbachev said party rules should be changed to allow its local committees to nominate more than one candidate for top leadership positions, and he called for secret ballots instead of the current practice of voting by a show of hands. Radical measures indeed, for the Soviets.

So radical that the party's 300-member Central Committee decided Wednesday not to specifically incorporate Gorbachev's suggestions, but agreed that there is a "need to broaden inner-party democracy."

Yevgeny Pozdnyakov, senior editor of the government press agency Novosti, later admitted to foreign correspondents that there had been debate over the party elections issue. He said such a change would require further discussion and then amendments to the party rules. That can't be done until the national party conference in the summer of 1988 or the next party congress in 1991. In other words, don't hold your breath waiting for it to happen.

But Gorbachev shouldn't be too disappointed. The setback is a minor one. Since he assumed power in March 1985, Gorbachev has been trying to oust entrenched Soviet bureaucrats who are holdovers from the rule of Leonid Brezhnev, the late party leader. Gorbachev's efforts at party reform now simply are aimed at that same goal.

We in the United States should not mistake Gorbachev's proposals for ideas that will actually give the Soviet people more say in how their government is run. Even if the reforms are enacted, the structure of the Communist Party will remain the same. It will only be easier for Gorbachev to replace old Brezhnev cronies with his own cronies.

BillDay Detroit Free Press Tribune Media

HEY, BIG DADDY-O, LIGHTEN UP! GIMME FIVE!!

CCCP

THE CHRISTIAN SCIENCE MONITOR
Boston, MA, January 30, 1987

THE dramatic calls for reform by Soviet leader Mikhail Gorbachev this week point to a fundamental characteristic of today's Soviet state: The economy is increasingly unable to face the intense technological and industrial competition that's occurring within the global setting.

The Soviet Union, of course, is not alone in facing profound economic sea change. It is no coincidence that even while Mr. Gorbachev was calling for modernization this week, on the other side of the Atlantic, in the United States, President Reagan was also proposing steps to boost his nation's competitiveness and productivity. And in his annual economic message, released yesterday, Reagan said he would continue to battle bureaucratic governmental efforts to "overtax, overspend, and overregulate."

The two speeches, Gorbachev's, and Mr. Reagan's State of the Union address, were delivered under different circumstances and certainly quite different time frames. One could hardly imagine the US Congress sitting through the three-hour Gorbachev address in Moscow, delivered at the opening of a two-day plenary session of the Soviet Central Committee.

Gorbachev called for a restructuring of much of his nation's leadership, within the ruling Communist Party (which he is increasingly bringing under his control), as well as in factories, universities, and shops. More party posts would be filled democratically, through open elections involving choices of candidates. Managers and administrators would not necessarily have to be party members. Competence and qualification – not just party loyalty and old-comrade connections – would be criteria for selection.

Why such a dramatic effort? Because, as the pragmatic Gorbachev realizes, the Soviet economy is far too cumbersome, bureaucratic, and, in some instances, corrupt to compete with the economies now bustling with growth and creativity – not just in the "free world," but also within East bloc and communist orbits, such as East Germany and China. Soviet growth, through most of the early 1980s, slogged in the 2 percent range, not enough to provide for major new programs. Defense spending, 14 or 15 percent of total output – twice the rate of US defense spending – continues to gobble up a huge chunk of vital resources.

Gorbachev faces a formidable task (and political risk) in persuading his fellow party members – particularly in middle-management positions within Soviet industrial and governing circles - to give up privileges garnered over the years and to meet new industrial and economic targets. Under a new five-year plan for 1986-90, the government is calling for major increases in capital spending, labor productivity, and industrial production. Indeed, some economic indicators are now believed to be on the upswing under Gorbachev.

The Soviet leader deserves credit for his modernization goals. That does mean, however, that his call for "reform" is universal: Dissidents, religious minorities, and other outsiders will presumably have to continue to wait for a later time before they are fully included in the call for more openness and democracy. And Gorbachev has not sought to imitate the bolder, and proven, market-oriented approaches toward economic reform taken by the Chinese.

Still, the Gorbachev call for modernization is remarkable – and clearly underscores the profound economic and social transformations that are taking place within the larger world economy.

Rockford Register Star
Rockford, IL, January 29, 1987

Kremlin leader Mikhail Gorbachev has a new idea to bolster Soviet leadership. Why not nominate more than one person per elective office? Why not vote for the preferred candidate with a private ballot — instead of with a show of hands?

What is he recommending, a democracy to replace the rigidity of Communism? Well, not exactly.

Unorthodox as his proposals are, Gorbachev hasn't pulled the plug on party apparatus or control. Candidates can still be screened for party "purity." So the "choice" could be controlled in that manner.

Nevertheless, Gorbachev's speech is revolutionary in terms of what now pertains in the USSR. The leader also attacked economic stagnation, corruption, moral decline. The speech will be studied by scholars with great interest.

So will the actions beyond Gorbachev's words. He's sacking a Politburo colleague, for instance, because of corruption, inefficiency and cronyism. He's raising holy Toledo because some officials forgot "real care for people, conditions of their life..."

So this guy is to be watched. His salvage plan, for a government he wants to work instead of one that drives its minions into the vodka bottle, is a massive undertaking. The result will still be communism, not democracy, although there could be some progress for the average Soviet citizen.

THE SUN

Baltimore, MD, January 29, 1987

Soviet party chief Mikhail S. Gorbachev leaves one key ideological tenet unchallenged as he tries to "democratize" the Soviet political system. There will be no attempt to curtail the leading role of the Communist Party or, indeed, to allow any other party on the ballot. Even so, Mr. Gorbachev's call for contested secret elections for party and government offices represents a momentous change in a nation plagued by stagnation, cynicism, consumerism, alcohol and drug abuse, crime, bribe-taking and toadyism. [The list is his, not ours.]

Mr. Gorbachev is seeking to loosen up the political process so he can push ahead with economic modernization programs essential to Moscow's chosen world role. Whether the Soviet leader will succeed is problematical. One has only to look at China to see the turmoil unleashed when Communist dictatorships experiment with radical reforms that are really nothing but parodies of Western democratic procedures.

Soviet party members once had faith that Draconian political means were necessary to achieve desired economic ends — a more egalitarian and productive society. But the failure of a whole series of centrally planned and directed systems has made that theory a cruel mockery, scorned even in Third World countries once mesmerized by Marxism. As a result, entrenched Communist regimes find themselves imitating their Western adversaries in ways that alarm and arouse status-quo party ideologues.

Since taking office less than two years ago, Mr. Gorbachev has been fighting the evils of the system that produced him. He has declared war on alcoholism and corruption and sloth, fired scores of unproductive officials, decreed that industrial enterprises make their own profit-and-loss decisions, released some famous political prisoners, invited defectors home and, most important, put his own people in key party and government positions. His political aim is not to undermine the party, although that is what his old guard detractors fear, but to strengthen it in his own image.

How the Gorbachev gamble turns out is of vital importance to this country. On the same day that Mr. Gorbachev was facing up to the shortcomings of the Soviet system, President Reagan went before Congress to play down shortcomings in his own government that his domestic opponents so eagerly stress. We found the contrast was not only intriguing, but on the mark.

American democracy works, mainly because its self-criticism wells up in mighty chorus from the people themselves. Soviet Communism falters because, like everything else, even its self-criticism still has to come down from the party pinnacle.

St. Petersburg Times

St. Petersburg, FL, January 30, 1987

It's time for Americans — especially those responsible for the conduct of U.S. foreign policy — to start taking seriously Mikhail Gorbachev's increasingly bold campaign to reform a stagnant Soviet society. Those reforms, if allowed to go forward, almost certainly will make the Soviet Union a stronger, more formidable adversary. However, if our government recognizes and encourages Gorbachev's efforts to make the Soviet Union more open and responsive, we may increase the possibility of breakthroughs on the basic issues now dividing the two superpowers.

Any other modern American presidency would already have shown more attentiveness to such breathtaking change in the Soviet Union. It's unfortunate that Gorbachev's campaign of reform is taking place during a period of parallel retrenchment and passivity in U.S. foreign policy.

The Soviet leader has proved that he is serious, even if the Reagan administration is not yet taking him as seriously as it should. Gorbachev knew that he could count on the support of most of the Central Committee for his efforts to modernize the Soviet economy and end decades of privilege and corruption in government and the workplace. Those reforms were put into effect at the expense of many officials who abused the authority they gained under the Brezhnev regime, but those officials' days were numbered from the moment Gorbachev came to power.

He knew that his internal *glasnost* campaign and his whirlwind foreign policy overtures would meet with more serious recalcitrance from elements of the entrenched government bureaucracy, yet he went forward. He courted Western Europe, with some success. He went to Iceland and stunned an unprepared Reagan administration with a revolutionary arms-control proposal. He has sought reconciliation with his own dissident citizens and with other communist governments, and he has introduced an unprecedented atmosphere of open criticism and debate.

And now Gorbachev is pressing his reforms at the very center of the Soviet political system. In the face of unusually overt opposition, he has demanded multiple candidates and secret balloting in the selection of party officials for local and provincial posts. Gorbachev also is expected to propose changes in the secretive selection of Politburo and Secretariat members. With all party secretary posts now in the hands of his own appointees, he is likely to get his way.

Even if all of that were to happen, the Soviet Union would not resemble anyone's idea of a Western-style democracy. Still, Gorbachev's reforms generally serve American, as well as Soviet, interests. They should be officially encouraged, not discounted.

Earlier this week, the chief American representative to the European security conference offered a rare official reaction to Gorbachev's reforms. The Soviet Union, Warren Zimmermann said, is "a different place than it was two years ago." However, he withheld judgment on whether the changes so far are "superficial or profound."

That's a fair and logical question for U.S. officials to be asking. But they could be playing a more meaningful role by actively encouraging Soviet reform, rather than passively responding to it.

The Des Moines Register

Des Moines, IA January 30, 1987

In a Soviet version of a state of the union address, Soviet leader Mikhail Gorbachev outlined a detailed plan to fight stagnation and increase democracy in his nation, and he focused for the first time on the need to reform the ruling Communist Party.

He blamed the Central Committee and the party leadership for failing to foster dynamic economic, political and artistic change during the 1970s and 1980s. "No accomplishments, even the most impressive, should obscure either contradictions in societal development or our mistakes and failings," he said.

He called for secret balloting and a choice of candidates in the party's elections of its officials, replacing the old procedure of voting yes or no on a single candidate, and proposed legislation to guarantee open debate and to protect citizens against abuses of power.

This dynamic shift in Soviet leadership, away from the stultifying resistance to change that marked the Brezhnev era, has become the characteristic of Gorbachev's rule. He has also moved to bring corrupt officials to account, allowed the press to publicize failures, such as Chernobyl and the ethnic riots in Kazakhstan, and invited cultural emigres to return to perform in their homeland.

To be sure, Soviet definitions of democratic freedom are vastly different from our own. Thousands of Soviet Jews have been forbidden to emigrate, and the plight of political prisoners has not improved under Gorbachev.

But at least Gorbachev is willing to admit the government is responsible for many of the nation's internal problems and to offer a plan to rectify mistakes. For the Soviet Union, that is a very big change from the past.

West German Pilot's Stunt Embarrasses Soviet Military

A teen-aged West German pilot landed his single-engine plane in Moscow's Red Square May 29, 1987 in a daring stunt that resulted in the dismissal of the Soviet defense minister. The pilot, Mathias Rust, was a 19-year-old resident of Hamburg. Rust piloted a Cessna 172 to Moscow from Helsinki, Finland in an unauthorized flight through over 400 miles of Soviet airspace. His plane was spotted, but apparently not challenged, by Soviet interceptors.

Rust completed his stunt by buzzing Red Square and landing within a few yards of the Kremlin Wall. Emerging from the plane in a red flight suit, Rust chatted casually with the curious crowd of onlookers before being taken into custody. The flight called into question the vulnerability of the Soviet's air defenses. According to the United States, the Soviets had been focusing increased attention on upgrading and centralizing those defenses. Ironically, the stunt took place on the U.S.S.R.'s Border Guards Day.

Rust was held at Moscow's Lefortovo Prison amid widespread speculation over his ultimate fate. Valentin Falin, the head of the official Novostoi information service, May 31 suggested that the young pilot might be released unpunished. Gennadi Gerasimov, the chief spokesman for the Soviet foreign ministry, June 1 told reporters in Moscow that a full investigation was under way and that the pilot faced possible imprisonment of up to 10 years.

Many western analysts believed that Soviet leader Mikhail S. Gorbachev used the stunt as a springboard for further consolidating his power through a shake-up of the military. Sokolov had been regarded as a traditionalist and there had been unconfirmed reports that he had lost favor with Gorbachev's ruling faction of reformists.

The Soviet Politburo, meeting in an emergency session May 30, dismissed the nation's defense minister, Marshal Sergei Sokolov, and Marshal Aleksandr Koldunov, the commander-in-chief of air defenses. Sokolov, 75, had served as defense minister since 1984.

Tass, the official Soviet news agency, May 30 said that the incident demonstrated "serious shortcomings in organizing [the] alert for the protection of the airspace of the country, a lack of due vigilance and discipline, [and] major dereliction of duty in the guidance of forces by the U.S.S.R. Defense Ministry."

Rust was sentenced Sept. 4, 1987 by a Soviet court to four years in a labor camp for his stunt. The sentence came on the third day of Rust's trial in Soviet Supreme Court in Moscow. Rust was released from a Soviet prison Aug. 3, 1988 and returned to his homeland. He had served less than one year of a four-year sentence. Rust's release was ordered by the Presidium of the Supreme Soviet, according to the official Soviet news agency, Tass.

The Honolulu Advertiser
Honolulu, HI, September 6, 1987

The lesson for Mathias Rust, the young West German who flew his small plane into the Soviet Union to land in Moscow's Red Square, is that *glasnost* or "openness" does not extend to a sense of humor about what would be called an ill-advised prank in the West.

Rust's sentence of four years in a labor camp would be considered harsh in the West, where a slap on the wrist and stern warning usually awaits those who scale the face of the World Trade Center or the like.

Americans tend to celebrate the dare-devil side of such stunts and ignore real dangers for the prankster and innocent bystanders. Certainly Rust's flight could have ended in tragedy for himself and others.

The Soviets take their borders and air security very seriously, as Korean Airlines Flight 007 gives everyone call to remember with great sadness.

World attention notwithstanding, the Soviet judge probably most wanted to discourage more such stunts. The judge did not buy Rust's story of wanting to promote world peace but saw the flight for what it probably was: "adventurism" and "self-advertisement."

The prosecutor had asked for an eight-year term. But Rust got half that in what's considered the least severe of Soviet prison camps. For the Soviets that approaches leniency.

It's hoped that this relatively insignificant though notorious case does not become an irritant in Soviet-West German relations, where important arms-control actions are imminent.

And perhaps, having made their point, the Soviets will see the virtue and the value in clemency before Rust serves his entire term.

The London Free Press
London, Ont., June 2, 1987

A Don Quixote of the air: that's Matthias Rust, the reckless 19-year-old West German flyer who managed last week to fly a small Cessna 172 more than 400 miles across heavily defended Soviet territory to a landing on a street outside the gates of the Kremlin.

Even the legendary Spanish knight would have to admire such an exploit. However, few military men — East or West — seem to be laughing.

Coincidentally, last Thursday was Border Guards Day in the Soviet Union. Did celebrating guardsmen simply toast Rust as he flew by in his Cessna?

Moscow is the only city in the world equipped with a sophisticated land-based anti-missile defence system supposedly capable of shooting down hundreds of incoming nuclear warheads. Why could it not keep track of a single, intrusive Cessna?

Soviet leader Mikhail Gorbachev is demanding answers to these and many other questions. In the meantime, he has fired the Soviet defence minister and the commander of Soviet air defence forces, while exonerating himself of all negligence or blame as head of the Soviet Defence Council.

Among top brass at the Pentagon, there is also considerable uneasiness. Few would smile at suggestions that United States military efficiency could perhaps be enhanced by trading in each of the technically troubled and cost-overridden B-1 bombers for a fleet of 10,000 Cessnas.

The biggest loser in this entire episode could well be U.S. President Ronald Reagan: Rust seems to have delivered the most telling blow yet to the long cherished, but absurd notion of a leak-proof, space-based anti-missile defence as officially envisioned at the White House. Nothing is fool-proof.

THE TENNESSEAN
Nashville, TN, June 3, 1987

SOVIET Defense Minister Sergei Sokolov has been relieved of his duties and the air defenses chief has been dismissed for negligence after a small West German civilian plane penetrated Soviet border defenses and landed in Moscow's Red Square last week.

The single-engine Cessna, piloted by 19-year-old Mathias Rust of Hamburg, flew 400 miles unhindered over Soviet territory from Helsinki to Moscow, buzzed Red Square three times and landed beside the Kremlin, the Soviet seat of power. Mr. Rust, who said he just wanted to get to know the Russians, was taken into custody and there has been no word of his fate.

But the fate of the Soviet officials deemed responsible for this embarrassment to what has been called the world's most extensive air defense system was quick in coming in a rare public firing. The Politburo held a special meeting, severely scolded the military, dismissed the air defense commander, Marshall Aleksander I. Koldunov, and announced the retirement of the defense minister.

The foreign plane incident may not have been the main cause of the action against Mr. Sokolov, 75. The incident was not mentioned in the announcement regarding him, and Mr. Sokolov is believed to have been on the way out already because of his age and because he was not a strong supporter of Soviet leader Mikhail Gorbachev's efforts to reshape Soviet society.

Thus, it seems that Mr. Gorbachev may have just seen a chance to get rid of an old-line military leader and strengthen civilian control of Soviet life. Mr. Sokolov was quickly replaced by General Dmitri T. Yazov, a deputy minister of defense, suggesting that the decision to retire the aging marshall had already been made.

But the West German's spectacular flight was the direct cause of Mr. Koldunov's firing. The Politburo said the small plane was picked up on Soviet radar and was twice circled by Soviet fighter planes as it made its way at low altitude toward Moscow. The stinging indictment said the air defense command "had shown intolerable unconcern and indecision about cutting short the flight of the violator plane without resorting to combat means."

The Politburo did not say how the airborne craft should have been stopped. But the wording of the complaint indicates that the Soviets may still be smarting from the world-wide criticism they received for their hasty act of shooting down a Korean Airlines Boeing 747 jetliner that strayed into Soviet territory on Sept. 1, 1983, resulting in the deaths of all 269 people aboard.

In the aftermath of the West German private plane incident, the Soviets are now more likely to think first of their nation's defense and not of their international image.

Commanders and fighter pilots on the borders — after weighing the different Kremlin reactions to the downing of the Korean plane and landing on Red Square — are likely to stop any foreign intruder in the quickest and surest way possible. ■

AKRON BEACON JOURNAL
Akron, OH, June 2, 1987

MATHIAS RUST probably won't receive the Order of Lenin. But as the chief of the official Novosti press syndicate in Moscow noted over the weekend, the plucky 19-year-old West German should be thanked. He gave the Soviets a relatively cost-free lesson in the flaws of their much-vaunted air-defense system.

Of course, not everyone would agree the affair was cost-free. Sergei Sokolov, the defense minister, lost his job, as did the head of the Soviet air defense forces, Alexander Koldunov. In each case, Mikhail Gorbachev moved swiftly to oust officials considered obstacles to his policies of *glasnost* or openness and reform. The new defense chief, Dmitri Yazov, is said to be an ally of the Soviet leader.

The aftermath of Mr. Rust's arrival at Red Square has reminded the world of the current volatility in Soviet politics. Mr. Gorbachev continues to struggle to solidify his power in the Kremlin. Critics, especially in the military, have complained that his approach has undermined discipline and shortchanged Soviet defenses. Indeed, they might point to the Rust flight as evidence of the troubles.

.Supporters of the Soviet leader would dutifully counter that the real problem is that his reform program has yet to grab the military. Once it does, their argument would go, the military's performance will improve, even if the military's slice of the Soviet budget is reduced.

The intensity of the infighting is great enough that it would hardly be surprising if, at some point, the theory surfaced that Mr. Rust was ignored by the air defenses in a bid to embarrass Mr. Gorbachev. Clearly, however, whatever the explanation behind the flight, Mr. Gorbachev has helped himself, effectively putting distance between his policies and the military officials who bungled.

An indication of how well the Soviet leader is doing will come later this summer when the Central Committee of the Communist Party convenes. In the meantime, the Soviets would be wise to show a sense of humor rather than grim red faces. Neither superpower has shown much amusement at anything these days. But here's a delightful story of individual spirit triumphing over massive bureaucracy and technological know-how.

The Wichita
Eagle-Beacon
Wichita, KS, June 5, 1987

THE events following the recent landing of a Cessna 172 in Red Square may reveal something about the nature of the Soviet Union under Mikhail Gorbachev.

By penetrating Soviet airspace, West German pilot Mathias Rust gave Mr. Gorbachev an excuse to overhaul the Soviet defense command. Out went several top military leaders, including Defense Minister Sergei Sokolov, the first official of that rank to be sacked since the Khrushchev era. To replace him, Mr. Gorbachev appointed Gen. Demitri Yazov, who should be a Gorbachev loyalist.

Mr. Gorbachev's actions have great significance within the history of the Soviet state. Since Lenin, there has been speculation that the Soviet Union eventually would fall victim to "bonapartism" or control by the military. Mr. Gorbachev, however, appears to have asserted the primacy of civilian leadership within the Soviet Union. The Communist Party, not the military, clearly is the dominant political force within the country.

By ousting prominent military officers and naming his own people, Mr. Gorbachev also has further consolidated his rule within the Soviet hierarchy. He never could have made such drastic changes were he not confident of his power.

Moreover, the leadership changes suggest Mr. Gorbachev is serious about downgrading the military in Soviet society. In the past, Mr. Gorbachev has spoken of the need to "rationalize" military expenditures to ensure that the civilian sector was not deprived of resources needed to improve the economy and quality of life within the Soviet Union.

The ultimate result could be less Soviet adventurism in such places as Afghanistan. Mr. Gorbachev's control over the military also could improve chances of arms control and produce a generally less aggressive Soviet foreign policy.

Like the United States, the Soviet Union has a long tradition of civilian rule. By reaffirming that heritage, Mr. Gorbachev has ensured that defense will not be the sole factor in forming future Soviet society.

"...AND YOU SAID *I'VE* GONE TOO FAR WITH GLASNOST!!"

The Clarion-Ledger
JACKSON
DAILY NEWS
Jackson, MS, June 2, 1987

Nikolai Vladimir Ilich Lenin must be rolling over in his tomb after 19-year-old Michael Rust buzzed it last Thursday in his Cessna — the culmination of a 550-mile trip from Helsinki to Moscow.

The stunning feat of this daredevil pilot in his lightweight plane should go down in aviation history. After all, it isn't every day that a teenager from West Germany defies some of the most sophisticated defense mechanisms in the most secretive nation in the world.

Rust had a little help. Officials in Moscow now claim that he slipped through 420 miles of Soviet territory unimpeded because border guards weren't paying attention. The key border operators, who were supposed to be guarding against such intrusions, were celebrating Border Guards Day which was held to honor the guards' diligence.

Rust's flight also occurred just several days before the 50th anniversary of another historic mark in aviation — that of a woman attempting to fly around the world.

Amelia Earhart and her navigator Fred Noonan left Miami Municipal Airport on June 1, 1937, in a Lockheed Electra — one of the best planes of the day. They never finished the trip, and what happened to them as they crossed the Pacific Ocean remains one of the great mysteries of that generation.

Americans have never been shy about tackling the skies — there were, among others, Charles Lindbergh, Eddie Rickenbacker and Chuck Yeager. Because some deeds of derring-do went awry, the nation has faced the ridicule and scorn of others, including the Soviet Union.

That's why Americans can take a particular pleasure in Rust's flight to Red Square, an exploit that yielded the ouster of the Soviet defense minister and head of the air defense system. Turnabout is fair play.

ALBUQUERQUE JOURNAL
Albuquerque, NM, June 3, 1987

Eluding Russian fighter pilots, baffling Soviet radar technicians, frustrating the formidable U.S.S.R. air defense establishment in its entirety . . .

It's Clint Eastwood as the daring American who steals the Soviets' most advanced prototype warplane in "Firefox." Right? Nope, it's a novice teen-age pilot from Hamburg, West Germany, in a single-engine plane built in Wichita, Kan.

American defense officials got, well, defensive. Mathias Rust's penetration of Kremlin airspace in a Cessna 172 that your brother-in-law might own was just a one-in-a-million fluke. To have even a shot at getting through the vaunted Soviet air defense requires weapon systems on the order of the B-1 bomber, Pershings cruise missiles, ICBMs.

Defense officials in the Soviet Union were red-faced. A target moving a whole lot slower than the Korean Air Lines Flight 007 managed, in the course of five hours, to cross the border, approach the only city on the planet shielded by an anti-ballistic missile system and buzz what must be one of the most heavily monitored and defended sites in the world — the Kremlin — like a fat horsefly.

If Soviet leader Mikhail Gorbachev is red-faced, it's from laughing. The incident gave him the excuse to begin a purge in the Ministry of Defense, the sector of well-entrenched Soviet bureaucracy which has been most recalcitrant about Gorbachev's reforms.

As a result, Rust, who just "wanted to talk with Russians," will get his wish and then probably get a ticket home to Hamburg despite commiting the most spectacular crime in recent Muscovite memory.

He may not have the pioneering spirit or the endurance of Charles Lindberg, but dang if Rust doesn't have Lindy's luck.

The Record

Hackensack, NJ, June 2, 1987

Sixty years almost to the day after Charles A. Lindbergh completed his thrilling solo flight across the Atlantic, another young aviator in a frail-looking single-engine plane has made the world gasp. Mathias Rust, 19, took on a challenge that could have been every bit as lethal as North Atlantic storms: He flew into the teeth of the air-defense systems of the Soviet Union. And just as they did in 1927, pluck and luck won out.

Mr. Rust's flight was not only daring but also harebrained; it could have touched off a serious international incident. But since it didn't, there's no need to hold back a smile at the way he tweaked the nose of the solemn, beribboned Soviet military establishment.

In a Pravda editorial last Thursday honoring the guardians of the country's borders, readers were assured that the Soviet frontiers were inviolable. "Every meter is under reliable surveillance," the paper said. As that happy news was being read in Moscow, Mr. Rust's Cessna 172, looking no bigger than a moth, was droning slowly by a field of Soviet antiaircraft missile implacements. His 400-mile trip through Russian air space to Moscow's Red Square took him past airfields where thousands of interceptor aircraft stayed. He even made it by two military jets that were in the air, but whose pilots apparently concluded he was just another average Russian up for a midweek spin in a private plane.

Not all the border guards were on surveillance, it later turned out. On Saturday, Pravda disclosed that 100 guards had been picked up on drunk-and-disorderly charges in Moscow's Gorky Park, where they had been celebrating Border Guard Day. Whether by chance or design, Border Guard Day was the very day Mr. Rust picked for his flight.

Smirking aside, Mr. Rust's daring jaunt shows the need for both superpowers to maintain a healthy sense of fallibility when it comes to strategic policy. Decades of military planning by the Soviet Union's best minds, 500,000 active members of the Soviet Air Defense Command, and thousands of missiles and planes failed to stop one young West German in a tiny craft rented from his local flying club.

It's unimaginable. Just as unimaginable as an Iraqi fighter penetrating the defenses of the Stark and killing 37 American crewmen. The most sophisticated weaponry in the world is no guarantee against mistakes, and even the superpowers can appear pitifully musclebound. It's a lesson both sides should keep in mind when tempted to test each other, or to design defense systems with hair triggers and no chance to recall missiles once they've been launched.

In the end, Mikhail Gorbachev has a lot to be thankful for. Humiliating as it was, the incident gave Mr. Gorbachev an excuse to clean some deadwood out of the military leadership and to reassert his own civilian control. He showed once again his shrewd understanding of public relations when he let it be known that Mr. Rust was likely to be allowed to return to West Germany without charges. It was a sharp contrast to 1968, when a young American who wandered over the Finnish border was sentenced to three years in a prison camp and was later found dead in what the Soviets then described as a suicide.

Most of all, Mr. Gorbachev can count himself lucky that he didn't have another Korean airliner disaster on his hands. Too much restraint can be embarrassing, but too little can be murderous. That's something for both superpowers to remember.

The Pittsburgh PRESS

Pittsburgh, PA, June 3, 1987

Mikhail Gorbachev has shown once again that he should not be underestimated. Moving adroitly and swiftly, he has turned what could have been a humiliation into a political victory.

The flight of Matthias Rust in a tiny Cessna — from Finland, through 420 miles of Soviet airspace, to a landing in Red Square — could have been used by Gorbachev's opponents to attack him for an inadequate defense.

Instead, Gorbachev convened the ruling Politburo and quickly sacked the defense minister, who had been resisting him, and the chief of air defense, whose men had not done their job in the flight of the 19-year-old West German pilot.

The defense minister, Marshal Sergei Sokolov, 75, had been in poor physical and political health. Gorbachev used Rust's exploit as a pretext to speed the World War II veteran's departure.

The firing and harsh criticism of Marshal Alexander Koldunov, the air defense commander, was a sign that top officials would be held accountable for the failures of their subordinates, which rarely happened before.

Gorbachev also seized the opportunity to name his own man, Gen. Dmitri Yazov, as defense minister. At 63, Yazov is relatively young and junior for the post. He is expected to cooperate with the civilian leadership's efforts to slow the growth of defense spending to modernize the overall economy.

The Kremlin leader could face a backlash by the military old guard and civilian bureaucrats who resent his changes. More likely, Gorbachev will have further consolidated his power by his decisive moves last week.

His actions brought praise from, of all people, Polish-born Zbigniew Brzezinski, President Carter's former national security adviser, who rarely has a good word for the Soviet Union. "The Soviets," he said, "have done what the American high command and political leadership have not had the guts to do — namely fire the top military men when there is a significant setback."

He's right. The deaths of 241 servicemen in the Marine barracks in Beirut in 1983, the Marine guard scandal in Moscow and the unpreparedness of the USS Stark in the Persian Gulf are examples of higher-ups escaping accountability.

If the Rust affair leads politicians here to conclude that Soviet air defenses are like Swiss cheese, they will be mistaken. The Soviets deploy 630,000 troops, 2,250 intercepter and reconnaissance aircraft, 9,000 anti-aircraft guns and 10,000 SAM missiles.

Soviet radar detected Rust's plane as it neared the frontier and fighters flew around it. The pilots thought the Cessna was a Soviet light plane, a human error that no one should expect in the future. If it had looked like, say, a cruise missile, they would have shot it down.

The Providence Journal

Providence, RI, June 2, 1987

It would be nice to draw the obvious lesson about the extraordinary 500-mile air voyage of 19-year-old Matthias Rust from Stockholm to Red Square. But what is it?

That Soviet radar and air defense systems are less effective than anyone could possibly have imagined? That the anti-ballistic missiles that surround Moscow — the only such defenses of a city in the world — are clearly unequal to the challenge of a single-engine Cessna 172?

That cunning beats strength? That the Soviet Union is to be commended for not shooting Mr. Rust out of the sky? That fortifications are more effective against elephants than mice? Take your pick; they all apply.

And they all apply because nothing applies, either. Unexpected, even bizarre, events have a way of influencing governments and history, and the fact that a West German teenager was able to fly his plane across Russia to Moscow, buzz Lenin's tomb, and land in the heart of the Soviet empire, will obviously mean more to the Kremlin leadership than any number of speeches, debates in the Politburó, five-year plans or *Tass* editorials.

Accordingly, Mikhail Gorbachev reacted swiftly: He fired his defense chief, Sergei Sokolov, and one of Mr. Sokolov's deputies, the commander of the Soviet air defenses. Mr. Sokolov had proved an impediment to the consolidation of Mr. Gorbachev's power, and this embarrassing incident gave Mr. Gorbachev a pretext to shove that impediment aside.

He knows, after all, that Matthias Rust has proved two contradictory points: That the Soviet defenses are surprisingly porous, justifying Mikhail Gorbachev's calls for system-wide reform, but that those same demands for discipline, honesty, hard work and sacrifice have not notably improved the quality of Soviet life — or, in this instance, the efficiency of the Soviet military machine.

Of course, he has proved something else, too. Before last Thursday, most people would have assumed that the final frontiers of aviation had long since been breached. Now, from the Kremlin on down, everyone knows better than that.

Gorbachev Criticizes Stalin in Major Speech

Soviet leader Mikhail S. Gorbachev criticized Joseph Stalin in a major speech Nov. 2, 1987 but fell short of a complete denunciation of the former leader. Gorbachev's nationally televised speech was the keynote address of celebrations on the eve of the 70th anniversary of the Bolshevik Revolution. Gorbachev spoke for nearly three hours at the Kremlin Palace of Congresses before 6,000 Soviet Communist Party officials and visitors from other nations. The address had been greatly anticipated both at home and abroad. It had been rumored that Gorbachev would use the occasion to sever ties with the legacy of Stalinism and to rehabilitate the memories of Stalin's foes. Stalin had become the party general secretary in 1922 and had led the U.S.S.R. until his death in 1953. According to Western estimates, millions of people had died in the 1930s from Stalin's policy of forced collectivization of the land and from his bloody purges of political and military officials.

Gorbachev told the delegates that Stalin was guilty of "enormous and unforgiveable" crimes that were a "lesson for all generations."

"To remain on a position of historical truth," he said, "we must see both Stalin's unquestionable contribution to the struggle of socialism, in defense of its gains, and his gross political mistakes, the arbitrariness permitted by those who were close to him," said Gorbachev. But Gorbachev did not go into detail on the extent of Stalin's abuses. Instead, Gorbachev merely noted that "many thousands of people inside and outside the party were subjected to wholesale repressive measures." Gorbachev balanced his criticism of Stalin with laudatory statements for the policy of collectivism ("a transformation of fundamental importance"), and with praise for Stalin's leadership during World War II.

Although Gorbachev failed to rehabilitate any of the Bolshevik leaders who had run afoul of Stalin and fallen into official disgrace, he announced that a special commission would study the possibility of rehabilitating the innocent victims of Stalinism. He made pointed references to two of the disgraced Bolsheviks, Leon Trotsky and Nikolai I. Bukharin.

Among other matters, Gorbachev defended his program of *perestroika* (restructuring) against both conservative and radical elements in the Soviet leadership. "It would be a mistake to take no notice of a certain increase in the resistance of the conservative forces that see *perestroika* simply as a threat to their selfish interests and objectives," he said.

Los Angeles Times

Los Angeles, CA, November 13, 1987

Western experts, while encouraged by Soviet leader Mikhail S. Gorbachev's announced policy of *glasnost*, have appropriately pointed out that the Kremlin's easing of restraints on dissent would be more impressive if it could not be reversed at the whim of the authorities. As long as the machinery of censorship and repression is in place, the permanence of *glasnost* will remain suspect.

Having said that, it is encouraging to note the stirrings of change in the legal framework.

Vadim Zagladin, a Kremlin official, has publicly stated that Article 190, under which dissidents have been sentenced in the past for anti-Soviet activity, might be dropped from the criminal code. He also indicated that Article 70, covering anti-Soviet agitation and propaganda, would be narrowed in scope.

This week, in an interview with the Tass news agency, Justice Minister Boris V. Kravtsov discussed the work of a review committee that is rewriting the Soviet criminal code. Among the changes that are under consideration, he said, are abolition of internal exile, shortening the list of offenses that are subject to the death penalty, reduction of maximum prison terms and expanded rights for defense lawyers.

Since the days of the czars, banishment to remote areas with harsh climates has been a standard punishment for political dissidents. In many cases the sentence to internal exile comes after a prisoner has already completed his sentence to a prison or labor camp.

Capital punishment can now be applied to a wide range of crimes, including bribery and serious economic crimes. Under the present justice system, which almost always finds defendants guilty, defense attorneys play a limited role. The change under consideration apparently would allow them to participate in pretrial investigations and give them earlier access to prosecution evidence.

It must be kept in mind that the reforms are mostly prospective; they are still in the talking stage. Cynics suspect that we are witnessing a public relations blitz aimed at advancing Moscow's interest in hosting an international human rights conference. Even if that is untrue, it remains to be seen whether Gorbachev has the will, and the authority, to move the reforms from rhetoric to reality in the face of probable opposition from conservatives. The dismissal this week of Boris N. Yeltsin, chief of the city of Moscow's Communist Party organization and an outspoken supporter of change, reinforces concerns on this score.

If the reforms that are under discussion are enacted, however, they will radically alter the Soviet criminal justice system and release creative energies that have long been stifled by censorship, intimidation and actual incarceration.

Omaha World-Herald

Omaha, NE, November 7, 1987

Philosopher Eric Hoffer once wrote that the Soviet Union was an economic failure but a military success. Some of the remarks of Mikhail Gorbachev in connection with the 70th anniversary of the Russian revolution were consistent with Hoffer's view.

The Soviet leader was blunt in his criticism of the country's economic performance. By condemning some aspects of Josef Stalin's rule, Gorbachev all but acknowledged the relationship between military success and economic failure. To make the Soviet Union a military power, Stalin demanded that the people accept a standard of living that in some cases wasn't much better than the serfdom under the czars. True, heavy industry was built up, but personal rights were non-existent and privation was widespread.

The result is the Soviet Union of today, a military giant hobbled by a Third World civilian economy.

Gorbachev's willingness to talk about the problem is a departure from past practice. So is his willingness to cut back the Soviet missile inventory. Gorbachev is in a good position to see that fewer rubles spent on missiles means more rubles to keep the economy from collapsing. One way to reduce military spending is to back away from the war-scare economy established by Stalin.

If Gorbachev is sincere, and if he is able to move the country in the direction to which he has pointed, it would be a dramatic departure. More autonomy for Eastern Europe. Further reductions in armaments and more concentration on economic growth. More *glasnost*.

Gorbachev's speech calling for mutual respect and equality between the Soviet Union and its allies came after a Soviet historian's statement that the 1968 Soviet invasion of Czechoslovakia must be reassessed. This would seem to be a break with the Brezhnev Doctrine, with which the Soviets have attempted to justify the use of force to maintain totalitarianism. It would be a break as well with the policies of Nikita Khrushchev, who invaded Hungary in 1956.

The Soviet Union may have been, as Hoffer said, a military success and an economic failure during much of its first 70 years. Now, with its tough, smart and relatively young leader, it seems to be approaching one of its best opportunities in years to achieve a more responsible balance.

THE ANN ARBOR NEWS
Ann Arbor, MI, November 6, 1987

Russia, as Churchill once said, is a riddle wrapped up in a mystery inside an enigma, but in some respects she is as predictable as tomorrow's sunrise. Take the matter of downgrading former leaders.

Dictator Joe Stalin was known to have some rather tart opinions of Lenin, but he never downgraded Lenin the way Stalin was pulled from his pedestal by Nikita Khrushchev at the 20th Party Congress in 1956. (Khrushchev in turn got his. The old shoe pounder is now an official un-person, buried in a commoner's cemetery instead of the Kremlin Wall.)

De-Stalinization continues. Last week Mikhail Gorbachev accused Stalin of "enormous and unforgivable" crimes against the state, among them the forced collectivization of agriculture and the Great Purges. Stalin, once deemed worthy to lie alongside Lenin under glass in Red Square, now seems to be the Politburo's favorite whipping boy, deservedly so.

Some time in the future if this pattern holds, another Soviet leader will rip Gorbachev up one side and down another for being soft on capitalism or some such thing. By now, the de-enshrinement of Soviet leaders is as much a tradition as the May Day lineup on Father Lenin's tomb.

The Sun
Vancouver, B.C., November 4, 1987

There are new revolutions in the Communist world that offer opportunities for better international relations and a lessening of world tension.

As it celebrates the 70th anniversary of the great revolution, the Soviet Union finds itself being dragged into a new era by a leader unlike any of the children of 1917. And China, only 38 years after its major revolution, is already on the road of its third 20th-century revolution.

The course in China is confirmed by changes in the hierarchy of government. Although Deng Xiaoping officially steps down from all positions except one, he remains the inspiration of change he began and the one job he keeps is that of head of the armed forces, which is what counts if there's trouble.

The changes reflect Deng's face anyway. His man Zhao Ziyang, the prime minister and economic reformer, is now moved up to the top post of general secretary of the central committee.

The old guard of Mao Zedong's revolution that made the Communist state in 1949 has gone. Mr. Deng also has endeavored to sweep away any vestiges of Mao's second upheaval, the cultural revolution of which he was a victim.

His own revolution is the one that is modernizing China, not only in the industrial and economic sense — that comes slowly — but in a political one.

No one ever voluntarily retired from leadership before in the new China. It certainly never happened in other Communist countries.

But having cast out the opposition and solidified his policies of reform, Mr. Deng can now sit back to watch them unfold. Further change is bound to come to China.

It is an interesting coincidence that, at the same time, the Soviet Union is undergoing great change. There Mikhail Gorbachev is modernizing the political apparatus and attempting social and badly needed economic reform.

Although he is still battling old-guard conservatives, he has begun the repudiation of Joseph Stalin, Russia's great dictator, and promised a commission to bring justice to victims of Stalin's tyranny.

Thus the two great Communist powers are going through an epoch of change. It is not confined to domestic policy. Mr. Deng began to open his country to the West and its ideas at the beginning of the decade. Mr. Gorbachev is forging a new détente and is about to reach a historic agreement with President Ronald Reagan on nuclear disarmament.

The West always watches events in the Communist world with a healthy wariness. So it should. But it can also capitalize on these changes and encourage them where they bring enlightenment and reform as well as hopes for a sounder peace.

The Idaho STATESMAN
Boise, ID, November 7, 1987

Seventy years ago today, the Bolsheviks overthrew the provisional government of Russia and ushered in Communist rule in that sprawling country of czars, hard winters and austere people.

Today, the Soviet Union is undergoing what some call the "second Russian revolution." Whether this revolution – if, indeed, it is a revolution – succeeds remains to be seen.

Regardless, today's celebration of the Bolshevik Revolution is more than of passing interest and importance to Americans.

The United States and the Soviet Union are linked in a precarious state of coexistence. The two nations – different in almost every way – walk on common ground in their competition for the sympathies and support of the rest of the world.

The Soviet Union is weather-beaten after 70 years. First came the bloody civil war between the *Reds* and *Whites*. Then came Joseph Stalin and his Great Purge. Then came World War II, which drained the blood of more than 20 million Russians. Then came 42 years of Cold War with the United States.

It's true that Soviet leaders have turned the country from a backward nation of illiterate peasants into the United States' military rival in the world. But, after the military, the clock stands still for the Soviet Union.

Even leading Soviets now admit that their country lags 20 years behind the rest of the industrialized world in standard of living and economic power.

Life expectancy in the Soviet Union has fallen since the 1960s, and the infant mortality rate is three times greater than that of the United States. The human toll has been great. The price of protecting the system has been the oppression of artists, intellectuals and dissidents – anyone who disagreed with the party line.

Leading the second Russian revolution is 56-year-old Mikhail Gorbachev who assumed power in March 1985. Mr. Gorbachev is the champion of *glasnost* (public airing) and *perestroika* (restructuring).

Mr. Gorbachev is experimenting with limited free (he calls it individual) enterprise. The Soviet press is more free to criticize government officials and report on social problems. Many dissidents have been freed from prison and allowed to leave the country.

Many, including CIA analysts, who believed that *glasnost* was a stunt for Western consumption now say Mr. Gorbachev is sincere.

Americans should welcome *glasnost* – any bit of freedom is better than what the Russian people had before Mr. Gorbachev. But they should not be lulled to complacency.

Glasnost is designed to drag the Soviet economy into the 21st Century, not to create a true democracy. Just think: The Soviet Union would be even more formidable a competitor with the United States if its economic power matched its military might.

The 70th anniversary of the Bolshevik Revolution is properly witnessed in this country not by Americans wearing rose-colored glasses, but by Americans viewing with clear eyes where the Soviet Union has been, where it is and where it might be headed.

The Register

Santa Ana, CA,
November 4, 1987

One of the great benefits of democracy is that the politicians tend to make short speeches. Another is that you don't have to listen to them. Contrast that with the plight of the poor Soviet subject. On Monday he had to listen to three hours of blather by maximum leader Mikhail Gorbachev, commemorating the 70th anniversary of the October 1917 Bolshevik *putsch*.

Western liberals like to praise the Soviet Union's moves toward reform, and there have been some improvements. In Stalin's day, Communist Party *apparatchiks* not only had to listen to his speech for hours and hours, but then they had to spend at least an hour clapping and cheering the Great Chorus-leader (as one of his titles tagged him). Picture it: hands turned pulpy red; arm muscles stiffened; knees began to buckle. But the first comrade to sit down was branded a capitalist spy and an enemy of all progressive forces throughout the world, and given a one-way ticket on a cattlecar to the Siberian Gulag.

Troubles in Stalin's time went beyond speechifying. Gorbachev himself noted on Monday that, under Stalin, "Many thousands of people inside and outside the party were subjected to wholesale repressive measures. Such, comrades, is the bitter truth. Serious damage was done to the cause of socialism and to the authority of the party."

Note that Gorbachev didn't mention the violation of the victims' rights, only that Stalin's excessive "repressive measures" had hurt "the cause of socialism." Therefore, Stalin's other actions — executing dissenters, repressing religion, destroying any vestige of independent thought or action — are implicitly applauded.

Today Gorbachev continues those policies by committing genocide in Afghanistan and Ethiopia, by enslaving an estimated 3 million people in the Gulag, and by stomping out all dissent except that of a few housebroken intellectuals. There's no real *glasnost* (openness), only a facade of minor improvements, easily reversed, to whitewash the Soviet charnel house for gullible Western observers.

Gorbachev's speech lavishly praised Vladimir Lenin, the demigod of Bolshevist ideology (though actually the prime terrorist of this century); but he had mixed praise and criticism for all Lenin's major successors: Stalin, Khrushchev, and Brezhnev. Khrushchev, who was ousted from power by Brezhnev and others in 1964, was thus partly "rehabilitated."

There's nothing surprising here. Gorbachev was just solidifying his own power base by portraying himself as Lenin's only true disciple. It was a pure power play.

Gorbachev even praised the notorious Stalin-Hitler Pact of 1939, which started World War II, and allowed the Soviets to annex Latvia, Estonia, Lithuania, and part of Poland. Gorbachev said that in 1939 the evil capitalist powers, Britain and France, were conniving to get the Soviets to fight Hitler. Maybe someday Gorbachev will "rehabilitate" Hitler and his National Socialist (Nazi) Party to the pantheon of socialist worthies.

If so, will such an infamy will be cheered as "a new realism" by liberals and other progressives in the West?

THE CHRISTIAN SCIENCE MONITOR

Boston, MA, November 4, 1987

IT is ironic that the big flap last week in the Soviet Union – Boris Yeltsin's apparent threat to resign from the Politburo – should have occurred on the pro-reform side, rather than the conservative side of Soviet leader Mikhail Gorbachev.

Mr. Yeltsin has been a Gorbachev protégé and a champion of his *glasnost* (openness, or more accurately, publicity) and *perestroika*, or restructuring. Indeed, Yeltsin has voiced reform ideas which Mr. Gorbachev himself was said to support, but to be unable to advocate himself without undercutting his own ability to function as conciliator and consensus-builder.

Yeltsin had grown impatient; change was coming too slowly for him. Hence the threat to resign.

Gorbachev might have expected opposition on his other side, from the recalcitrant bureaucrats who are presumably less than eager for change; indeed, he is presumably getting opposition, or at least resistance.

In his dramatic speech Monday to mark the 70th anniversary of the Bolshevik Revolution, he denounced Stalin's "unforgivable crimes" and promised to fill in the "blank pages" of Soviet history – which has over the years reduced important figures to mere "nonpersons." He promised the "rehabilitation" of many of those whose reputations, as well as lives, were destroyed during the Stalin era. One possible candidate for such rehabilitation eventually is Nikolai Bukharin, whose advocacy of a mixed-market economy may be seen as a prescient call for today's *perestroika*.

But Gorbachev measured his words. His speech did not go much further than Nikita Khrushchev, whom he praised, did in the mid-1950s, when "de-Stalinization" began. He referred to "victims" of the Stalin era without explicitly saying that these victims were executed, by the millions.

Gorbachev knows where he is going, but is having to do some pushing and pulling to make sure he brings people along with him. He is well into his third year in power. Whatever "honeymoon" glow a Soviet politician may be presumed to enjoy is fading. There isn't yet that much to show for *perestroika*, and indeed, things are likely to get worse for the ordinary Soviet citizen before they get much better. People are going to have to work harder, and give up some of the security and personal flexibility that slipshod industrial management has afforded them, before they see improved living standards.

On the international front, his willingness to take risks, to make concessions, to baffle the United States by actually acceding to longstanding American demands, has given him an edge in superpower relations and certainly captured the imagination of Western Europe. It can only help the Soviet Union if arms control and other means of lessening political tensions can translate into redirection of resources away from defense. But obviously he will be in trouble at home if the Kremlin thinks he has given away the store.

This is one of those turning points in Soviet history. It is not clear how long Gorbachev and *glasnost* may last. But if he moves carefully enough, Gorbachev has the opportunity to make some real changes in the Soviet Union – and the world.

Richmond Times-Dispatch

Richmond, VA, November 5, 1987

Zigging here, zagging there, Mikhail Gorbachev wended his way Monday through 70 years of Soviet history. An almost three-hour trip seems to have wound him up just about in the middle of the road. In Soviet politics, as in traffic, that can be a paralyzing place.

In Mr. Gorbachev's wish to change things, apparent since his ascendancy in the Kremlin, is the tacit admission that some things must have gone wrong. He cannot blame the party or the system it enforces, lest he erode communism's credibility with the people and lose his with the party faithful. He must hark back to individual communists to fault for errors, and rehabilitate others whose policies, sins before, are ideological blessings now. As others read tea leaves, Kremlin-watchers read tombstones. Epitaphs, not to mention events, keep getting rewritten.

Soviets and outsiders who anticipated in this anniversary speech a thorough drubbing of past policy-makers discredited by disastrous results were disappointed. So were those who anticipated a complete endorsement of reformers discredited by their rivals. Mr. Gorbachev noted, for example, the excesses of Josef Stalin, but not the grievous extent of them. Stalin contemporary Nikolai Bukharin was right to oppose forced collectivization of agriculture: "There was," Mr. Gorbachev understated, "a deficit of the Leninist considerate attitude to the interests of the working peasantry." But Nikolai Bukharin's timing was bad, fatally bad, for himself and as many as 20 million other opponents of Stalinization. Nikita Khrushchev was lauded for trying reform but made "subjectivist errors" that set back "progressive initiatives."

Leonid Brezhnev, however, was an unrelieved failure, his legacy a "growing discrepancy between the lofty principles of socialism and the everyday realities of life [that] was becoming intolerable." Mr. Gorbachev got that right. His response is *perestroika*, or the developing of a "socialist democracy" complete with grassroots participation, human rights and diversity. This "new thinking," he said, should extend to the international scene: on-site inspections for verifying arms control agreements, an "emphasis on common sense and openness," a "search for mutually acceptable solutions" while strictly safeguarding the principle of equal security."

As they might chant in the stadiums, Sounds Good, Plays Well, particularly among hopeful Westerners. If Mr. Gorbachev had not been compelled to put those goals in the context of cleaving only unto communism, and to leaven the inferred rebuke of reluctant tortoises like Anatoly Lukyanov by chiding wild hares like Boris Yeltsin, they would sound more encouraging. As it is, even Soviets themselves, unaccustomed to consultation, are unsure what course their nation will take. Writers, uncertain what will survive censors, tread carefully, as do refuseniks, workers, artists from under whom rugs have been pulled before. How then can Americans, at this point, count on change for the better, for them and for us?

"We shall never turn off that road" to communism, Mr. Gorbachev vowed at the end of his speech and, in that commitment to a system whose ideology and apparatus are stacked against democracy, may have undone all hope that went before. Same narrow road, same stalled vehicle — how much difference will a new driver make?

The Boston Globe

Boston, MA, November 4, 1987

Mikhail Gorbachev's long-awaited speech on the 70th anniversary of the October Revolution oscillated between a dynamic defense of his "new political thinking" and timorous equivocations about the history of Russia since 1917. Each of the many times he mentioned Lenin, however, the general secretary evinced a reverence that was unambiguous and utterly orthodox. As the speech itself demonstrated, nothing is more faithful to Leninism than the definition of truth as that which serves the needs of the vanguard party.

Everything Gorbachev had to say about Joseph Stalin, Leon Trotsky and Nikolai Bukharin was suffused with this Leninist principle.

Gorbachev mentioned the heretofore unmentionable Trotsky not to rehabilitate that brilliant organizer of the Red Army, who ruthlessly squashed the Kronstadt sailors' uprising, but to castigate him as a precursor of Gorbachev's contemporary opponents within the party.

Speaking as the proponent of a foreign policy founded on the need to persuade Western lenders that the Soviet Union has become a conservative big power abjuring subversion and seeking stability, Gorbachev denounced the foreign policy of the Trotskyists because "they gave priority to export of revolution."

Speaking as the champion of democratization, decentralization and limited market experiments in agriculture, Gorbachev condemned the Trotskyists because in domestic policy they gave priority "to tightening the screws on the peasants, to the city exploiting the countryside, and to administrative and military fiat in running society."

The Brezhnev holdovers and "conservatives" in the audience who heard themselves subtly compared to the "defeatist" Trotsky must have been mortified – even if they had to admire this Leninist appropriation of historical truth.

Similar political motives were discernible in Gorbachev's evaluation of Stalin's "contradictory" career. He praised Stalin because, by crushing the Trotskyists and their allies in the 1920s, he "safeguarded Leninism in an ideological struggle." Just as Gorbachev's opponents use leftist language to criticize his foreign and domestic policies, so the Trotskyists "took cover behind leftist pseudo-revolutionary rhetoric" to "make an attack on Leninism all down the line."

Stalin's forced collectivization of agriculture becomes, in Gorbachev's history lesson, a necessary stage in "socialist construction." The millions of peasants murdered by the state become victims of "excesses" that Gorbachev explains as a "departure from Lenin's policy toward the peasantry."

Seeking to put in a good word for his own drive to decentralize economic decision-making, Gorbachev attributes the peasant massacre to an administrative error: the carryover of the "administrative-command system" from heavy industry to agricultural collectivization.

Gorbachev's policies hold out the hope of a better life for people in Russia and a more stable international order. It is a shame they must still be justified as Leninist orthodoxy.

The Kansas City Times

Kansas City, MO, November 9, 1987

On the 70th anniversary of the Bolshevik revolution things undeniably are stirring in the Soviet Union. The usual massive weapons systems are trundled through Red Square in a spirit of militarism horrifying to Western pacifists. Traditional Russian nationalism and patriotic fervor that would embarrass sophisticated internationalists in Washington and London are the order of the day.

Yet there are differences in these early months of the reign of Mikhail Gorbachev. The questions are how deep those differences go, how long they will last, and what kind of society will come out at the other end. There have been false dawns in the past.

The hope of the world is that these immensely talented, energetic people will be permitted a real democratic voice in their destiny; that they will be able to exert pressure on their militarists and politicians as Westerners do as a matter of course; that dissidents and free spirits will be allowed to express themselves without fear of exile, imprisonment or economic deprivation. Not that these freedoms bring social perfection or heaven on Earth; they obviously do not. But they do let an enlightened self-interest contribute to the mix of forces that control human lives; the trial-and-error pattern of representative government permits criticism from every direction and self-correction. The rigidity of dictatorship also rules by trial and error, but only the dictators define what is erroneous.

So far Gorbachev has talked a magnificent game. He has called for democratization, which has a different meaning in the Soviet Union, and openness which also has its limits. He says he wants more internal criticism. He has said that "the arrogance of omniscience" cannot be the basis of relations with other Communist countries.

What degree of pluralism comes will be known only by results. Westerners need to remember that the Communist Party still is not a contending political party under communism, but a ruling hierarchy. In Western countries it has been an arm of Soviet foreign policy, and not really an alternative choice.

By the standards of Russian history, Gorbachev is moving with lightning speed. The West ought to give him the benefit of the doubt and every chance to put into practice what he says he wants to do. That doesn't mean cooperation must be seen in terms of concessions that undo Western alliances and military strength. It does mean patience and a cautious willingness to explore change.

The outlook for a genuine reduction of tension and hostility is better now than at any time since 1917. The West can take advantage of it and promote it without either surrender or unrealistic expectations.

THE RICHMOND NEWS LEADER

Richmond, VA
November 5, 1987

Mikhail Gorbachev is a Stalinist. From its eternal home in the unheavenly blast furnace, Stalin's ghost likely broke into a knowing smile when Gorbachev criticized the excesses committed during his regime. Uncle Joe would understand. And he would approve.

In denouncing Stalinism, Gorbachev broke no new ground. Rather, he followed textbook Communism by criticizing his long-dead predecessor. It hurts the Party not at all to dig up ancient dirt, just as long as one does not question the fundamentals undergirding the Stalinist state. The willfully naïve may consider Stalin an aberration, an extremist. But Stalin was no accident. He was inevitable.

In *Forever Flowing*, his triumphant, novel of suffering and grace. Vasily Grossman writes:

"Lenin died but Leninism did not. The power Lenin won did not pass from the hands of the Party. Lenin's comrades, aides, associates, and disciples continued the Leninist cause. ... Lenin left behind him the dictatorship of the Party he had established, the army, the militia-police force, the Cheka, the apparatus for eliminating illiteracy, the special schools for workers. ... Stalin executed Lenin's closet friends and comrades-in-arms because each in his own way hindered the realization of Lenin's innermost essence. ... [It] was Stalin who victoriously affirmed and confirmed Lenin and Leninism, who raised the Leninist banner over Russia and secured it in place there."

As Stalin obeyed Lenin, so Gorbachev obeys him, too. In *Left-Wing Communism, an Infantile Disorder* — which, by the way, casts far more light on the substance and soul of the USSR than *The Communist Manifesto*, *Das Kapital*, or the foreign desks at *The Washington Post* and CBS News and the State Department — Lenin writes:

"The strictest devotion to the ideas of Communism must be combined with the ability to effect all the necessary practical compromises, to maneuver, to make arrangements, zigzags, retreats, and so on. ..."

Uncle Mike zigs and zags, and behind every seeming retreat, every apparent maneuver, lies the desire to strengthen the Communist Party, to reinvigorate the omnipotent state. Marx and Engels said that their theory was not a dogma but a guide to action. As a dedicated child of the Revolution, Gorbachev has learned his lessons well. He would not have survived otherwise. Lenin and Stalin must be proud.

The Philadelphia Inquirer

Philadelphia, PA
November 4, 1987

"Wednesday, 7 November, I rose very late. The noon cannon boomed from Peter-Paul as I went down the Nevsky. It was a raw, chill day. In front of the State Bank some soldiers with fixed bayonets were standing at the closed gates.

"'What side do you belong to?' I asked. 'The government?'

"'No more government,' one answered with a grin. '*Slava Bogu!* Glory to God!' That was all I could get out of him ....'"

So began John Reed's classic account of the *Ten Days that Shook the World* — the Bolshevik Revolution in Russia. The situation in Petrograd (now Leningrad) back then was so anarchic that an opposition party member confidently told Reed that the Bolsheviks couldn't hold power for three days.

In fact, they have ruled for 70 years and, in so doing, have altered the course of human history. Lenin and his successors have created a state of awesome military power and built an empire that rivals anything accomplished under the czars.

And yet, Communist Russia — since 1922, the Soviet Union — is sick in body and soul. Socialism has not delivered on its promises. The workers and peasants are far worse off than their counterparts in the capitalist West. For socialism to remain a viable alternative anywhere on the planet, the world's first socialist state has to change in ways that are nearly as revolutionary as those that the Bolsheviks brought.

On Monday, Mikhail S. Gorbachev, the sixth Soviet leader since Lenin, addressed his nation on its 70th anniversary. He reviewed Soviet history and, while endorsing socialism as "the main social alternative of our epoch," found that much had gone wrong in the intervening years.

He accused Stalin, the man who built the modern Soviet state, of "enormous and unforgivable" crimes. But he was less categorical in talking of a more insidious enemy of the people, the specter that haunts the Soviet Union today — Stalinism.

He talked of how the "administrative-command system" developed during the Stalin era — the extreme centralization of political and economic power — had restricted development of the "democratic potential of socialism," a potential that he now hopes will bloom.

But he praised Stalin's murderous collectivization of agriculture — the creation of the grossly inefficient network of state and collective farms — and did not call for wholesale dismantling of a system that allows him and his cohorts to decide everything from the hours when liquor is sold in Vladivostok to the price of bread in Minsk.

Mr. Gorbachev has to tread a delicate line, pressing for reforms that he knows are essential without getting too far in front of party bureaucrats and a wary populace that fear instability more than inertia. He is fighting to reclaim a dream that was born in the streets of Petrograd 70 years ago, a dream that has all but died.

The Record

Hackensack, NJ, November 4, 1987

Based on his long awaited speech on the 70th anniversary of the Bolshevik Revolution, there is a new term to describe Mikhail Gorbachev — liberal Stalinist.

At first glance, the term seems like an oxymoron, like atheist Catholic or democratic dictatorship. After all, Stalin was, after Hitler, the greatest mass murderer in history. But believe it or not, the man who was George Orwell's model for Big Brother first emerged into the public view as something quite different — a moderate who, following Lenin's death in 1924, staked out a middle position between his rival Bolsheviks, Leon Trotsky on the left and Nikolai Bukharin on the right.

Unlike Trotsky, who was always thundering about world revolution, Stalin preached the doctrine of "socialism in one country," which held that the Soviet Union could grow and develop in a capitalist world. This struck Western businessmen such as Henry Ford as restrained and reasonable. Stalin, they concluded, was a man they could do business with. He would run his country and leave them to run theirs. He would not rock the boat.

This was the Stalin whom Mr. Gorbachev hearkened back to Monday — the good Stalin who built up industry, attempted to normalize relations with the West, and defended the Soviet homeland during World War II; not the brooding paranoid responsible for the brutal agricultural collectivization campaign of 1928-33, the show trials of the mid-to-late Thirties, and the postwar wave of anti-Semitism. The historian's task, Mr. Gorbachev declared, is to separate the positive and negative in this "extremely contradictory personality."

But coming from a new Soviet leader who has hinted at a new era of truth and frankness, this was notably half-hearted. Stalin the Contradictory is as much a myth as Stalin the All-Benificent, as he was styled during the cult of the personality. The real Stalin was not a contradictory personality but a budding monster from the start. He merely posed as a centrist to consolidate his power and prepare for the day when he could knock off his enemies on either side.

Lenin, for one, recognized Stalin for what he was and, in his last official act, wrote out a will and testament recommending that Stalin be removed from his position as general secretary of the Communist Party. Tragically, the advice was ignored, for which the Soviet people had to endure nearly 30 years of misery and mass terror.

Mr. Gorbachev's determination to find something nice to say about Uncle Joe led him to bend the truth. The new Soviet leader went out of his way in his speech to denounce Trotsky, whom Stalin, after denouncing as a Nazi, had assassinated in 1940. And while Mr. Gorbachev defended Bukharin for his conduct in the Twenties, he was pointedly silent on the phony treason charges for which he was executed in 1938.

Mr. Gorbachev also defended the Hitler-Stalin non-aggression pact of 1939 as a justified response to French and British appeasement of Nazism, ignoring the fact that Stalin allowed himself to be lulled into complacency and was totally unprepared when Hitler turned on his erstwhile ally and invaded in June 1941. Millions died because of Stalin's miscalculation, an error that the Kremlin still cannot bring itself to admit.

Clearly, Mr. Gorbachev is under intense political pressure and fears that too thorough a debunking of the Stalin myth might trigger an ideological chain reaction impossible to control. So he has opted for something halfway, a partial debunking that goes not much further than Khrushchev's famous address before the 20th Party Congress in 1956. Despite his call for "an honest understanding of our enormous achievements as well as of past misfortunes," it is clear that what Mr. Gorbachev wants is something less — honesty to a point.

Charleston, SC, November 4, 1987

In his address marking the 70th anniversary of the Russian revolution, General Secretary Mikhail Gorbachev provided evidence to bolster the arguments of those who are skeptical about the "democratization" of the Soviet Union.

Perhaps the most telling tip-off for skeptics was Mr. Gorbachev's lukewarm denunciation of Joseph Stalin. The great reformer announced that he has set up two committees to look at the Stalin era and report back. It is a sad state of affairs when Mr. Gorbachev, in the age of *glasnost,* manages to come out with only a weak echo of Nikita Khrushchev's fiery indictment of Stalinism 30 years ago.

The speech failed to establish if Mr. Gorbachev is pursuing a restrained policy of reform because he fears a backlash from communist hard-liners or whether his aims are more prosaic and, perhaps, decidedly pragmatic. The picture that emerges from his address is of a leader who wants to make the Soviet Union an economic powerhouse in order to realize Lenin's vision of world revolution. In Mr. Gorbachev's own words, "The main thrust of our foreign policy has remained unchanged. We have every right to describe it as a Leninist policy of peace, mutually beneficial international cooperation and friendship among nations."

In short, Mr. Gorbachev's address was disappointing. He is not telling the Soviet citizens the same story that his slick public relations machine is telling the rest of the world. That may be because Mr. Gorbachev fears that he will be ousted, like Mr. Khrushchev, if he tries to break the totalitarian mold imposed by Leninism. It may also be because Mr. Gorbachev seeks only economic reform and will only allow liberalization to the extent that it promises to produce a more efficient and willing work force.

Despite the depressing prospect that Mr. Gorbachev hopes to use *perestroika* to bring changes to Soviet society, while changing nothing of importance in the totalitarian system, the historical outlook is encouraging. It is now quite clear that the future that Lenin envisioned does not work. Marxist-Leninism has failed throughout the communist world and the forces of history will decide what replaces an ideology that is following fascism to the scrap heap. Despite Mr. Gorbachev's desire to contain change, and harness it to provide the power that will revive Marxist-Leninism, he cannot even imagine let alone control, the forces that he has unleashed.

The Oregonian

Portland, OR, November 6, 1987

Dwight Eisenhower was president, and Richard Nixon a young and ignored vice president. There was no wall in Berlin, and U.S. nuclear dominance was overwhelming. The American automobile industry was internationally dominant, and Ronald Reagan was a Democrat.

That was the state of the world when a Soviet leader first said the things about Josef Stalin that Mikhail Gorbachev said in his much-heralded speech on the anniversary of the Bolshevik Revolution this week. Gorbachev's speech is considered a breakthrough, and in some ways it is, but its main achievement is to bring Soviet openness all the way to where it was in 1956.

At that time, Soviet leader Nikita Khrushchev, in a speech to the 20th Party Congress, first attacked the barbarities of Stalin's 30-year regime. But Gorbachev's speech is still considered a sign of advancing *glasnost* because since the fall of Khrushchev, Stalin has been steadily regaining position, and now any attack on him is again considered bold and courageous.

How far Gorbachev felt he could go in the speech shows powerfully how far *glasnost* still has to go.

"Some expected it to be a radical review of history," said dissident Soviet historian Roy Medvedev. "Others expected he would just scratch the surface. I expected somewhere in between, and that's about where it came out."

American leaders speak on history mostly at building dedications, and what they say is ignored even by the architects. But a Soviet leader's version of past events is closely watched as a clue to present events, and a friendly mention of a Bolshevik dead half a century is read as encouragement for a writer thinking of publishing a novel today.

Gorbachev's speech shows again that in the Soviet Union the past will continue as the obedient servant of the present. "Historical truth isn't the issue," pointed out Soviet expert Stephen Cohen of Princeton University. "The issue is the great political struggle under way in the Soviet Union."

Gorbachev's willingness to criticize harshly certain aspects of the Soviet past is encouraging. But it is also worth remembering that we have been here before, and that from this point the Soviet trail can lead backward as well as forward.

LOS ANGELES HERALD

Los Angeles, CA, November 4, 1987

Winston Smith, the protagonist of George Orwell's chilling novel "1984," spent his days rewriting and re-rewriting history to match the latest requirements of Big Brother. Over the decades, many Soviet historians have been devoted to a similar task, with truth the victim. In his Monday speech commemorating the 70th anniversary of the Bolshevik revolution, Mikhail Gorbachev gave his nation's scholars some cause for concern that the latest rewriting of Soviet history already underway may still fall far short of reality.

Gorbachev

Despite the predictions of most Kremlinologists a year or two ago, Gorbachev has made clear that his reforms aren't window-dressing to deceive the West into letting down its guard. He is determined to remold the Soviet Union economically and politically, though it is uncertain — even to him — just how far his proposed changes can go.

In that light, his speech was disappointing. Not because it included the usual adoration of the coup of October 1917, of the Bolshevik's patron saint, Lenin, and of the "great achievements" of the Soviet Union. To sharply criticize those would be to challenge the source of his own power. Rather, it was Gorbachev's relatively soft handling of Josef Stalin, arguably the bloodiest ruler of the 20th century.

Perhaps to appease his conservative critics, Gorbachev toned down his remarks by hedging on the number of Stalin's victims and praising him for modernizing the nation. In fact, the Stalinist legacy — and the Leninist as well — must be fully explored and publicized if the Kremlin's reformers expect to have any chance of success.

That look at the past may be greatly aided by Gorbachev's reviving of a commission started by Nikita Khrushchev to examine Stalin's actions and "rehabilitate" those who suffered at his hands. That means filling the blank pages or, in Russian terms, the "white spots" that now disguise and distort Soviet history.

It should not mean just another Winston Smith-style official revision. What is needed is open scholarly debate fueled by access to the Kremlin's prodigious archives.

Gorbachev would have to muster considerable courage to take this route. Filling in all those white spots would present great risks for him and his colleagues. Fully exposing their nation's past might well elicit citizen demands for a comprehensive restructuring of its present that goes well beyond anything the Kremlin's most radical pace-setters have in mind: real democracy.

THE CHRISTIAN SCIENCE MONITOR

Boston, MA, November 2, 1987

THE on-again, off-again superpower summit between Mikhail Gorbachev and Ronald Reagan is apparently on again – for early December in the United States.

This is a positive development for both nations and for world peace. For reasons similar to those we will shortly list, a visit by Ronald Reagan next year to the Soviet Union would likewise advance world understanding.

Not to meet your "enemy" is to forgo the opportunity to stand in his shoes, to understand his point of view, and possibly to make him your friend.

Many supporters of Mr. Reagan, and Mr. Gorbachev, are opposed to such meetings. They fear that unwise concessions might be made on subjects like arms control. Indeed, this was the case with the summit in Iceland a year ago, when Reagan and Gorbachev suddenly engaged in a game of one-upmanship on reducing nuclear arsenals.

For this latest summit, Mr. Reagan was right to declare that the proposed signing of a midrange missile accord need not be linked to a meeting. This called Moscow's bluff in a last-minute attempt to bring Reagan's Strategic Defense Initiative into the negotiations. The subject can still be discussed at the forthcoming summit, but it should not be made a condition for such a meeting. Reagan was right not to give in.

Gorbachev has been having his own domestic political troubles, which may have led him to attempt to avoid a US visit now. His having renewed his interest in coming may be a sign that he has put his own house in better order.

Whatever.

A visit to the United States would be the relatively young Soviet leader's first such venture.

If he expects to find a leadership or a nation supine or confused by the stock market slide, bedeviled by budget and Supreme Court conflict, preoccupied with television entertainment and materialism, he should be in for a surprise.

There is something rock-solid about the democratic West.

Gorbachev's visit will only make Americans want to show him their best, the values on which they have built a free society – not a perfect society, but one that is nonetheless advancing individual rights and opportunities for all.

Such visits are usually held to fairly tight schedules.

But we invite our readers to suggest – in letters to this page – what they would show Mr. Gorbachev on his US visit if they had the chance.

For our part, we would like the opportunity to be host to him in Boston, where the Revolution began, as a place to begin showing him what America is all about.

Detroit Free Press

Detroit, MI, November 4, 1987

THE MOST INTERESTING and, in many ways, most important part of Soviet Leader Mikhail Gorbachev's address opening the week-long celebration of the 70th anniversary of the Bolshevik coup was about the country's formative years, the era of Lenin and Stalin.

Mr. Gorbachev offered his interpretation of those dramatic decades and set new boundaries for revisionist analysis. From now on, this line will be toed by official Soviet historians and invoked by countless officials. Revised history books will be published and libraries stocked with them.

The whole procedure may smack of Orwell, but that's the only way for Mr. Gorbachev to assure legitimacy for the fundamental reform he is trying to implement in the Soviet Union. In a political system that purports to adhere to "objective" and "logical" laws of history, no major change in political direction can be plausibly justified without rewriting history. In the Soviet Union, it always boils down to facing the Stalinist legacy.

The treatment of this legacy by the creator of *glasnost* falls considerably short of the expectations of his supporters who had hoped that he would simply set the record straight, pay respects to Stalin's millions of victims, and give Soviet historians the license to seek the objective truth. This didn't happen. Mr. Gorbachev, while he became the first Soviet leader to publicly denounce Stalin's atrocities, was less direct and less specific in his condemnation of the genocidal policies than Nikita Khrushchev in his unpublished address 21 years ago. Technically speaking,

Mr. Gorbachev made the contents of Mr. Khrushchev's speech public.

An analysis of the components of Mr. Gorbachev's presentation, however, offers insight into the Soviet leader's priorities and plans. He seemed determined to sound reassuring and positive. He highlighted all the successes he could think of and searched for redeeming features in former leaders, Stalin included. The elevation from official obscurity of reformers such as Mr. Khrushchev and Nicolai Bukharin, the architect of Lenin's New Economic Policy, and the obvious refusal to return Leon Trotsky, the key proponent of exporting the revolution, to the Soviet pantheon are telling hints.

In sum, Mr. Gorbachev used the occasion to lay out and defend his agenda. While his reforms clearly have their limits — *glasnost* or not, for example, the right to interpret the Soviet past remains the domain of the state — the changes that the Soviet leader is advocating are substantial and may have far-reaching consequences for his country and the rest of the world.

THE SACRAMENTO BEE

Sacramento, CA, November 8, 1987

Two major events last week provided a measure of how rapidly the two major Communist powers have moved to change themselves in recent years: In Moscow, Soviet leader Mikhail Gorbachev made a speech in which he sharply attacked past Soviet failings and pledged to continue his reform program, a speech critics said was too timid; in Beijing, an unprecedented transfer of power to a new generation of Chinese leaders went off without a hitch only months after a crackdown on liberal reformers seemed to presage a counterrevolution by aging conservatives.

In tracing Soviet history since the Bolshevik revolution 70 years ago, Gorbachev trod a cautious path — more cautious than many in the West had hoped or expected — between laying bare all the sins of the past and offering up the traditional Communist self-congratulation that characterized the stagnant years of the Brezhnev era. Thus his denunciation of Stalin was, at most, no more critical than that offered 31 years ago by Nikita Khrushchev. Somehow the enormity of Stalin's crimes was shrunk so that the millions of Soviet citizens who were murdered or starved in the forced collectivization of agriculture during the early 1930s became "thousands," and their deadly fate was euphemized as "wholesale repressive measures."

Westerners, and Soviet dissidents, may justly fault this and other shadings of the brutal historical record. But no institution ever makes the worst case against itself. And Gorbachev, however much in command he may be, still must contend with deeply entrenched forces — in the Kremlin and in the far-flung Soviet Communist Party apparatus — that would stop his reforms in their tracks if they could.

In fact, a close reading of Gorbachev's nearly three-hour speech leads to the conclusion that his vaunted campaigns for *glasnost* (openness) and *perestroika* (restructuring) are still very much on track. Moreover, on arms control he seemed more eager than ever to move beyond agreement with the West on medium-range nuclear weapons to a treaty reducing the number of strategic missiles. Even more impressive was his signal to Moscow's East European satellites that the Kremlin's hold on their policies may be relaxed.

On domestic themes, Gorbachev pulled no punches in exhorting his colleagues to promote democratic participation and to "expose and neutralize the maneuvers of ... those who act to ... trip us up, who gloat over our difficulties ... (and) who try to drag us back into the past." To balance that, he also chided "the overly zealous and impatient ... who voice their disappointment with what they regard as a slow rate of change, who claim that this change does not yield the necessary results fast enough."

Doubtless Gorbachev was mindful, in walking that tightrope, of the fate of Khrushchev, whose freewheeling style led to his abrupt ouster in 1964. Such caution 23 years later may disappoint Westerners, but Gorbachev is still pressing reforms far more sweeping than anything Khrushchev contemplated. His tempered speech is no reason to write off this remarkable man's revolution within a revolution.

What is still remarkable in Moscow is coming to seem almost routine in China, though it is not. Men who were once paraded around in dunce caps or sent to labor camps by Red Guards wore conservative business suits to a Communist Party Congress at which Deng Xiaoping ushered in a new generation of leaders and retired a number of elderly conservatives from key posts.

After nearly a year of inner-party turmoil brought on by student demonstrations demanding greater freedom, Deng's reformist program has survived and even been strengthened. By resigning his own most powerful party post, he was able to induce other octogenarians to stand down and to place four of his "youthful" followers (average age: 62) on the five-member Politburo Standing Committee. The 83-year-old Deng is expected to wield great power even from the sidelines so long as his health permits.

The changeover and the ascent of Zhao Ziyang, Deng's hand-picked successor, to the post of Communist Party general secretary mean that the anti-reformist conservative counterattack has been blunted. Yet Deng's biggest coup may have been winning approval of the separation of party and state functions. In principle at least, that will allow China's modernization to proceed free of the dead hand of party ideologues. Whether it works out that way depends on many factors, including how well the system can assimilate Western management and technical know-how and purge retrograde party functionaries from low-ranking positions, especially at the factory level.

Neither Gorbachev's *glasnost/perestroika* campaign nor Deng's quasi-capitalism implies a conversion to Western-style democracy. Both countries are still run by totalitarian Communist elites with awesome military and police powers at their disposal. What the world is witnessing are belated attempts by two badly run dictatorships to streamline themselves in order to improve the lot of their own people and to make themselves more competitive in an essentially capitalist world that they still reject.

That poses a potential challenge to the West, but the response need not be a negative one based on the zero-sum calculation that improvements in Communist societies must, by definition, weaken the security of the free world. Such thinking is at the root of so much that divides East and West. Gorbachev and Deng, whatever their motives, have dared to challenge deep-rooted assumptions at home and in the global arena. Surely the leaders of less-rigid Western societies can match that boldness.

Wisconsin ⚖ State Journal
Madison, WI, November 4, 1987

Mikhail Gorbachev has simultaneously acknowledged internal opposition to his campaigns of *glasnost* and *perestroika* and repudiated Josef Stalin, the ruthless dictator who is still revered by the same Soviet hard-liners who oppose him.

In the People's Republic of China, reformist Deng Xiaoping has retired but a new generation of leaders dedicated to his goal of market-oriented economic reforms and an opening of doors to the West appears firmly in command.

Has the clank gone out of the "Iron Curtain?" Has the millenium of East-West relations dawned?

While there is always reason for optimism, we must bear in mind that Gorbachev's reforms at home — even if they prove successful — may not mean reform of Soviet policy abroad. All good communists still want victory without war. This week's celebration of the 70th anniversary of the Bolshevik Revolution has given Gorbachev a chance to revise selected chapters of Soviet history, but when he speaks of reviving "socialist democracy," the accent remains heavily on the socialist.

Stalin was the object of strong criticism in Gorbachev's Kremlin speech on Monday — but so was Leon Trotsky, Stalin's arch-foe and a man assassinated in 1940 for advocating a more democratic style of Soviet leadership.

In China, neither Deng nor his successors show signs of extending their reformist zeal much beyond the marketplace (although it is hard to understand how they will keep China's masses down on the farm once they have tasted their brand of capitalism).

Let's welcome the changes behind the Iron Curtain, but let's not forget that in almost all ways it is still very much made of iron.

BUFFALO EVENING NEWS
Buffalo, NY, November 6, 1987

AS THE Soviet Union observes the 70th anniversary of the Bolshevik revolution this week, both the Russian people and Soviet observers around the world are digesting a remarkable speech marking the anniversary by Soviet leader Mikhail Gorbachev.

The speech, a historical review of the 70 years of Marxist rule, was a mixture of fact and fiction that offers clues as to what the Soviet party line will be and what changes may be expected at home and abroad. The address, which included a denunciation of Stalin, suggested that Gorbachev's policy of controlled change amid an atmosphere of openness will continue.

In words reminiscent of Nikita Khrushchev's 1956 speech assailing Stalin's reign of terror, Gorbachev said that Stalin had been guilty of "enormous and unforgivable" crimes and that "many thousands of people inside and outside the party were subject to wholesale repressive measures."

Gorbachev sought to counteract the trend toward rehabilitating Stalin that developed in the two decades after Khrushchev's fall from power. He specifically rejected two tenets of neo-Stalinism — that Stalin didn't know about the crimes done in his name and that much of the repression was necessary in the early years of the Soviet state. While supporting the collectivization of agriculture, Gorbachev denounced the excesses in implementing the policy.

The speech was a major step toward revealing the lies that have been perpetuated in the past, but it also demonstrated Gorbachev's caution in steering a middle course between radical change and the ideological rigidity of much of the Communist Party's bureaucracy. While denouncing Stalin, he did not go into details of the enormity of his crimes and the millions who died under his tyranny.

There is hope for further revelations of the truth, however, in a new investigation of the Stalin years, which, Gorbachev said, "was not seen through to the end." A commission will continue to explore the evils of the period.

Gorbachev also made a vigorous appeal for his new domestic policies, which he called "a renewal of socialism" but actually include the limited use of profit motives and market forces to reinvigorate the stagnant Soviet economy. He faces opposition from some elements of the Soviet bureaucracy that are marked by ideological orthodoxy and abhorrence of change.

In his asserted view of the world, Gorbachev rejected the orthodox Marxist view of the inevitability of conflict between Marxist and capitalist systems. He said such clashes are giving way to a new era of cooperation in an "interrelated, interdependent" world. The free world must remain on guard, but his profession of this less doctrinaire approach lends hope for more progress in negotiations on arms control and other international problems.

Overlooked in the Soviet celebrations was the bitter truth that the Bolshevik revolution did not replace a tyrannical czar but the liberal Kerensky government that had won power in a revolution the preceding February. The Kerensky government might have developed into a modern democracy, but the tiny band of Bolsheviks, exploiting the chaos and misery of war and revolution, staged their own revolution.

This year is also the sad 70th anniversary of the Kerensky government, which fell to mobs incited by Bolshevik promises of "land, peace and bread" and was followed by an evil tyranny more ruthless than that of Ivan the Terrible or any of the czars.

Today, however, the door to new freedoms has been opened slightly, and Gorbachev's new leadership may bring turbulent change to the Soviet Communist Party and new directions at home and abroad.

THE ATLANTA CONSTITUTION
Atlanta, GA, November 5, 1987

So Monday's three-hour opus was the speech to which Mikhail Gorbachev was said to have devoted most of his vacation time during a mysterious 56-day departure from public view during August and September.

He could have put that time to better use helping Raisa around the house.

For the supposedly candid Soviet party boss to castigate Josef Stalin for his personality cult and high crimes was no eye-opener. In fact, Gorbachev overlooked millions of Stalin's victims, justified Stalin's ruthless collectivization of the Soviet economy and hardly dared speak the names of Bolshevik comrades murdered on Stalin's orders.

For all his talk of glasnost (openness) and perestroika (restructuring), the single solid proposal that Gorbachev made in the direction of democratization was to expand powers for local governments, presumably at Moscow's expense. But even this small gift was wrapped tightly in party ribbons.

The foreign policy portions of Gorbachev's address were especially disturbing — not that it's surprising he would cast Mother Russia on the side of the angels. But when it came to admitting error, he wasn't the least bit contrite about the ravaging of Afghanistan or the subjugation of Eastern Europe. No, what seemed to trouble Gorbachev in retrospect was his predecessors' inability to confront the forces of Western imperialism (read that Washington) more vigorously.

Mikhail Gorbachev

But far and away the most significant portion of his speech was contained in one line: "We must not give in to pressure to those overly headstrong and impatient people who do not want to take into account the objective logic of the restructuring."

That underscored note of caution may be a tipoff that Gorbachev will cast aside his reformist signal-caller, Moscow party chief Boris Yeltsin. It surely means Gorbachev must pay deference to elements high in the party who cling to an orthodox ideology and to the privileges of their rank.

Indeed, it is a setback for Gorbachev and for his precious perestroika. Kremlinology being one of the more inexact sciences, it had been presumed he was firmly in charge. Obviously, he's not. So patience, comrade. Marx's millennium will take a little longer.

Communist Party Conference Backs Gorbachev Program

The 19th All-Union Conference of the Soviet Communist Party (CP) ended July 1, 1988 at the Palace of Congresses in Moscow. Tass, the official Soviet news agency, July 4 published six resolutions approved at the gathering. The conference, which had opened June 28, featured debate that was often blunt and unrestrained. The openness of the gathering stunned many Soviet citizens, millions of whom were mesmerized by television and newspaper coverage of the event.

The first day of the conference, and a closing speech by General Secretary Mikhail S. Gorbachev, were televised live in the U.S.S.R. From the second day on, up to and including the voting on resolutions, the meeting was held behind closed doors, with newspapers and edited TV accounts provided later in the evening and the following day. The conference was the central topic of conversations among ordinary people in towns and cities throughout the nation. Never before had the Soviet public been allowed to view candid disagreements at a high-level party meeting. Yulia Karasyoda, a student, told a U.S. reporter in Red Square July 1: "You might not understand this in America, but for the first time in our country we know our leaders."

Gorbachev alluded to the history-making meeting in his closing address July 1. "Nothing of this kind has occurred in this country for nearly six decades...One can say that *glasnost* (openness) was one of the protagonists of the conference," he told the 5,000 delegates. In his speech, the Soviet leader pointed to the "apprehensions" among many that *perestroika* (restructuring), his program of reforms, would weaken the role of the party. "To my opinion, the conference has given a sufficiently clear and convincing answer to this question: No," he said. "While remaining the ruling party, the party has all the necessary levers to play its guiding role, and the main of them are the 20 million Communists through whom the party pursues its political course in all spheres of society's life."

Delegates addressed the CP June 29 through July 1 in an atmosphere that was sometimes charged with emotion. One of the first speakers June 29 was Leonid I. Abalkin, a senior economic adviser to General Secretary Gorbachev. Abalkin surprised many onlookers by questioning whether the country could, "while retaining the Soviet organization and the one-party system, ensure a democratic organization of social life."

The comment drew a sharp rebuke from Gorbachev, who was seated with the party leadership behind the speakers' podium. The general secretary chided Abalkin for having too little faith in his (Gorbachev's) political reforms.

Another June 29 speaker, Vladimir P. Kabaidze, the manager of a machine-tools factory, pronounced a litany of complaints about bureaucratic interference with his work. Kabaidze was strongly applauded when he said: "It's useless to fight the forms. You've got to kill the people producing them."

One of the many startling moments during the conference came June 30, during an address by Vladimir I. Melnikov, a party official from the Komi region of Siberia. Melnikov called for a purge of the so-called "old guard" of the party, saying, "Those who were active in the past pursuing the policy of stagnation cannot remain and work in the central party and the Soviet organs. Each one should answer for everything, and do so personally."

Gorbachev then interrupted, asking Melnikov to be specific about whom he was speaking. Melnikov turned around to face the general secretary and answered: "I would refer, in the first place, to Comrade Solomentsev, to Comrades Gromyko, Afanasyev [and] Arbatov." Mikhail S. Solomentsev was the chairman of the watchdog CP Control Committee and a Politburo member. Andrei A. Gromyko, also a Politburo member, was the president of the Soviet Union. Viktor G. Afanasyev was the chief editor of *Pravda*, the Communist Party newspaper. Georgi A. Arbatov was the head of the U.S.A. and Canada Institute, a Moscow think-tank, and a trusted adviser to Gorbachev. The reference to such influential figures by name brought gasps from the delegates. Gromyko, seated in the front row of the leadership contingent, gave no indication of being upset.

The Boston Globe

Boston, MA, July 1, 1988

Mikhail Gorbachev's opening address to an extraordinary Communist Party conference will not make the queues of shoppers vanish overnight. His vision of a revitalized society will not bestow capacious living space on citizens, nor repair the rusty machinery peasants and workers must operate in collective farms and factories. But the address does mark the end of one era and the beginning of another in the political history of the Soviet Union.

All Gorbachev's exhortations for change were deduced from a single axiom – that the centralized, repressive system bequeathed by Stalin has been a failure. This uncharacteristic communist capacity for self-criticism is the necessary point of departure for the general secretary's radical program to restructure the governance, the economy, the legal system and the culture of his country.

Gorbachev's proposals to dissolve the monolithic party-state by removing the party from everyday management of the economy and administration imply a momentous rejection of the power system created by his predecessors.

Despite his repeated salutes to Lenin and the party's Leninist principles – the rhetorical price reformist virtue must still pay to Bolshevik vice – the world's most powerful communist was indicting his forebears for having perverted the prerevolutionary promise of Marxism. Instead of creating the classless society evoked in Marxist scripture, Gorbachev intimated, they had allowed Stalin to institute the absolutist rule of a party oligarchy. All Gorbachev's reforms begin from the premise that the Soviet Union cannot solve its many daunting problems without dismantling the dictatorship of the party.

When he calls for a socialist state founded upon law, he implicitly concedes that for the past 70 years Soviet society has been subject to the arbitrary power of the party bosses. When he demands that elected legislatures acquire genuine lawmaking powers, he admits that the original revolutionary slogan, "All power to the Soviets," has been transmuted into a cynical farce. His plan to reduce the tenure of top officials to two five-year terms and to hold competitive elections decided by secret ballot amounts to an acknowledgment that the present system of lifetime sinecures has produced a ruling class of indolent, inefficient and corrupt officeholders who are no more accountable than Mafia dons.

Gorbachev's break with the past cannot, by itself, make the stagnant Soviet economy suddenly productive, nor overcome the resistance of party "conservatives" who fear losing their privileged positions. His purpose in calling the first party conference since 1941 is to have this august body ratify the grand design of the reforms set out in his speech. Hereafter, his legalistic dismantling of the old system will become the party line, and those who oppose it openly will risk being accused of factionalism.

The Seattle Times

Seattle, WA, June 30, 1988

MIKHAIL Gorbachev is a natural political mechanic, but he clearly belongs in marketing. The retooled government he unveiled before a Communist Party conference this week was packaged for sales in both domestic and export markets.

The Soviet Union's economy is a shambles, and Gorbachev forthrightly blames a lethargic, complacent party bureaucracy for stifling all incentive for recovery.

Gorbachev wants to infuse the dynamics of competition and the rewards of capitalism into a moribund economic system that is controlled from the top down by party edict.

To slacken the party's leash, Gorbachev gently proposes to transfer power from the party to elected officials in legislative bodies at national through local levels. Even the leadership of the country would pass to a president selected by a new national legislature.

At first blush the changes are dramatic, but many of the recommendations mirror the existing structure. The new president — pick a name, say Gorbachev — would continue to lead the Communist Party and be head of state.

In the same 3-1/2 hour speech, Gorbachev called for stronger guarantees of civil liberties, but warned that democratic rights cannot be used to promote anything as undemocratic as opposition parties. Some things will never change.

Beyond stroking a domestic audience, Gorbachev is also making a pitch to foreign observers, particularly Europeans eagerly looking for a signs of a new, benign Russian bear.

One important stake is the North Atlantic Treaty Organization. The United States has been pressuring its European allies to pick up more of the cost of their own defense. Bringing U.S. military forces home from Europe has political and budgetary appeal for a financially strapped Congress.

Our allies, such as prosperous West Germany, are looking hard the other way as the bill is shoved in their direction. Instead of spending more on NATO, the West Germans, and other Europeans, strain to see less risk.

They behave as if Soviet reductions in intermediate-range missiles aimed at Europe, combined with Gorbachev's latest talk of democratizing his national government, might make NATO seem downright unneighborly.

Political entrepreneur Gorbachev understands that the potential market for his new, improved Soviet Union is much greater than the consumers he already controls.

THE TORONTO SUN

Toronto, Ont., June 27, 1988

The Communist party conference starting tomorrow couldn't come at a more interesting time, smack in the middle of the rat-a-tat-tat of the Tit-for-Tat war.

We expel Soviet spies. And the Soviets, miffed that we're actually showing gumption and not playing patsy, throw out Canadians in retaliation.

This brouhaha has chilled Soviet-Canadian relations and given our loony left the colliwobbles.

They think we should have just ignored that the Soviets were continuing to spy on us, the proof that when you peeked under the Iron Curtain, nothing really had changed in the shabby Kremlin spy world.

Ironically, tomorrow's conference in Moscow is supposed to be Mikhail Gorbachev's monument to the "sweeping changes" he's fathered.

Heaven knows, just about all the reforms under discussion for the rest of this week — curbs on the party power and limits to terms in office — are badly needed in that totalitarian twilight zone.

We're all for them and any other reforms under glasnost and perestroika. But unless they herald genuine *democratic* change, they're just more PR glitz.

Indeed, live TV coverage will be limited to the opening and closing of the conference. Some glasnost!

No wonder expectations for the conference have withered since Gorbachev first proposed it early last year.

There are even signs Gorby himself may be in trouble. Even he, who should know better, underestimated the power of inertia in the USSR.

As a result many of his supporters have been excluded from the conference by entrenched local party officials.

That's not all. Gorbachev's search for help in the capitalist world has come unglued lately. Low oil prices have cut into his ability to buy western technology. And now even Canada is turfing his spies.

We will watch with interest, but also with the same wariness British PM Margaret Thatcher demonstrated in her speech to our Commons: "Old ways die hard and there is still little evidence that the Soviet Union's long-term foreign policy objectives have changed."

The world waits for that to be proved wrong.

The Atlanta Journal
AND
THE ATLANTA CONSTITUTION

Atlanta, GA, July 4, 1988

After three years of fits and starts, the Gorbachev revolution got under way in earnest with last week's festival of glasnost, otherwise known as a Communist Party conference. In it, General Secretary Mikhail Gorbachev shook to their very core the guardians of the old orthodoxy in the party and the country's massive bureaucracy.

The goings-on during the special conclave in Moscow may have been astonishing to outsiders, but they were positively breathtaking for ordinary Soviet citizens.

Never before had they been privy to open infighting amid the upper councils of the party. Or able to witness in their living rooms, via remarkably candid televised highlights, accusations of obstructionism, incompetence, abuse of authority and corruption being leveled, even face to face, against party bosses. Soviets whose spirits haven't been crushed into utter submission by the weight of centuries of czarist and Communist tyranny are being given reason to hope.

To hope for what?

Surely not just for a wider range of consumer goods of better quality or a little break from the soul-numbing routine and regimentation of everyday Soviet life.

No, what Gorbachev, himself a creature of Leninist ideology, offers goes far beyond cosmetic fixes in a rusted, creaking system. It is nothing less than a fundamental overhaul, but one that is well within the framework of his collectivist background.

Let us in the West not mistake Gorbachev's vision for the social democracies of Scandinavia. His communism with a human face is nonetheless communist. Still, his program can hold promise both domestically and for the world.

Predictably, he keeps the Communist Party as the lone compass by which the Soviet Union fixes its direction. Yet he dares to decentralize decision-making, erect barriers between a too-long-dominant party and the state, demand accountability and substitute for the arbitrary exercise of power a rule of law with at least some civil liberties.

Are outsiders overidealistic and perhaps misguided to cheer Gorbachev's efforts when, after all, he hopes perestroika will reverse the Soviets' accelerating slide toward the level of third-rate powers?

By no means. The world can learn to live with a stronger Soviet Union if it is more governed than ruled, more stable, more predictable and more honest with itself. Granted, none of these happy developments is assured under Gorbachev's restructuring, not even after the hearty approval his reforms received at the close of the party conference. High hurdles remain in the form of entrenched and selfish underlings, fractious nationalities, an inert body politic.

One thing is certain. If the Soviet Union stays on its old, well-worn path, it can't help but become less stable and less predictable and probably more rather than less dangerous. There's nothing sappy about wishing to avoid that outcome.

The Philadelphia Inquirer

Philadelphia, PA, July 3, 1988

The Soviet Communist Party may never be the same. For the first time, during its special conference last week, the party power structure was exposed to the glare of television. Its stormy debates — shown up close and personal — pitted liberal reformers against conservatives and were the most animated since Joseph Stalin crushed all debate within the party in the 1920s. Soviet viewers, accustomed to viewing snippets from dull, lifeless party meetings, were enthralled. The fractious conference marked a crucial new stage in Soviet leader Mikhail S. Gorbachev's fledgling efforts to introduce some form of democracy into Soviet politics.

The Soviet leader was less successful in translating revolutionary words into changes in the political system. The conference had been intended to galvanize his lagging program of economic reforms by firing a goodly number of party hacks and transferring some power from the party to elected institutions. Mr Gorbachev was unable to get rid of the hacks — this time. As for political changes, he had trouble even getting the delegates to discuss giving up some of their political power; it remains to be seen how much power a new parliament will have.

But the conference — the first of its kind since 1941 — was an extraordinary event just the same. By encouraging delegates to behave differently, by creating an atmosphere in which the most powerful political figures could be criticized by unknowns, in front of television cameras, with the critics apparently emerging unscathed, Mr. Gorbachev has changed the rules of political behavior and ushered in a new level of public debate. Unless Vladimir Melnikov, a party leader from the Komi region of Siberia, loses his job for saying that two members of the ruling Politburo should be canned, other citizens presumably will feel safer airing their views.

That is not to say that warning indicators were not flashed to show that the new debate has limits. The conservative delegates who denounced the new press freedoms were a reminder that the fight for openness in Soviet society is far from won. Mr. Gorbachev refused to support reformer Boris N. Yeltsin whose criticism of the slow pace of reform cost him his job as Moscow party chief last fall. Yet Mr. Yeltsin was able to engage in an astonishing debate at the conference with conservative Politburo member Yegor K. Ligachev, even if his moving plea for reinstatement fell on deaf ears.

With the veil of secrecy pierced by the glare of television, and with their foibles revealed by words and expressions — Soviet leaders lost the air of untouchability that shielded them from public accountability. The Soviet public may want to know more, like the delegate who complained that Soviets know more about President Reagan's income than they do that of their own leaders. Perhaps the public will want to have more control over these men, who are only human after all. Such changes are part of a process of democratization that at best will take decades. This conference was a promising beginning.

LOS ANGELES
Herald Examiner

Los Angeles, CA, July 7, 1988

Westerners haven't felt so warm and fuzzy about the Soviet Union since they helped us win the war. The "evil empire" is showing signs of a political thaw, with the televising of the recent contentious debates at the historic Communist Party Congress. Even Ivan on the street is speaking up as never before. And General Secretary Mikhail Gorbachev is sweeping in a new program of political and economic restructuring. But does this mean Gorbachev and the Soviets can be trusted?

At this point, the Gorbachev reforms remain more a wish list than a reality. But they do signal how far things have progressed in the three years since Gorbachev assumed power.

Clearly, the party apparatchiks, bureaucrats, secret police and military establishment aren't the only ones he needs to persuade. During seven decades of Communist Party rule, something like a public consensus has emerged in the Soviet Union — by default or design — that seems willing to trade away basic Western freedoms for stability and security.

The result has produced great economic deprivation and horrific abuses of human rights, along with scientific, economic and cultural stagnation. What Gorbachev seeks now probably has far less to do with idealism than a gut instinct for survival: The Soviet economy can't produce enough guns to satisfy its security demands or enough butter to feed its population.

Assuming the Gorbachev program succeeds, would a reconstituted Soviet Union necessarily look more like a friend — or an even more threatening foe? Until now, the West has assumed that the U.S.S.R.'s adopting more of our values would ease superpower tensions; we're not so sure. Historically, more wars have been fought over territory and resources than conflicting ideologies.

The true test of Gorbachev's democratic tendencies may occur outside of the Soviet Union, when Eastern Bloc countries began implementing their own political and economic restructuring. Will Gorbachev welcome those warming trends?

THE ⬛ SUN
Baltimore, MD, July 6, 1988

The Communist Party extraordinary conference portends extraordinary change in the public life of the Soviet Union. General Secretary Mikhail Gorbachev's drive for perestroika or restructuring of political and economic life had strong opposition within the Communist Party before the conference, and still does after it. The adopted resolutions as published, while embracing such reforms as limited terms of office, omitted such other Gorbachev ideas as a strong presidency. Perhaps this will come, perhaps not.

What was breathtaking in Soviet experience was the holding of the conference itself, the candor of the speeches and the openness of media coverage. Not everything was televised for the public. But even some of the more controversial speeches that were kept off the screen were later published in newspapers. What delegates could debate, ordinary citizens can debate as well. Once public policies have been made the public's business, the public will go on treating them that way.

Ordinary Soviet citizens have heard policies debated, leaders denounced and inside conclaves revealed. That means they now are empowered to discuss these affairs, hold opinions and make those opinions felt. A powerful genie is out of the bottle. It could be put back in, as only a totalitarian police state can stuff a genie back in a bottle, but at a fearful cost.

Mr. Gorbachev and his allies on the Central Committee meant to turn on this force. They hope to use public opinion against the obstructions in reform in the regional party apparatus and the Central Committee. They have summoned public opinion into being.

The risk is high. Delegate after delegate talked of shoddy goods, machinery that fails, bureaucratic suffocation. Having been told that changes at the top of the party structure and openness for the intelligentsia will bring practical results, these delegates await the results. Yet nothing runs better in Russia this week than last.

The aim was to make the machinery more responsive to genuine public opinion, to create diversity within the one political party, and to make officialdom more responsive. Each of those reform ideas stops short of what Americans would call a democracy. But the program runs the risk that ordinary citizens of the Soviet Union will begin to want democracy. Mr. Gorbachev and his colleagues must find great fault with the status quo if they are willing to court this risk.

DESERET NEWS
Salt Lake City, UT, July 3, 1988

No one can say for sure where the Soviet Union is headed after the nation's Communist Party ended a rare conference this past week. The 5,000 delegates heard unprecedented arguments over such formerly taboo issues as a freer press, the "mistake" of Afghanistan, religious rights, the economy, more elections and elections by secret ballot, limits on terms of office, and many others.

The debate was often sharp, and whether Soviet leader Mikhail Gorbachev can carry out his program is still an open question. The conference closed with no clear indication as to the fate of many of his reforms.

Perhaps the best clue will come from what happens in coming months to two individuals — Soviet President Andrei Gromyko, who was foreign minister for 28 years, and Vladimir I. Melnikov, a local party boss in the region of Komi.

During the conference, Melnikov addressed the delegates and said the Soviets want high officials who served under Brezhnev — the target of much criticism — removed from office. When asked for specific names, Melnikov mentioned two people, one of them, Gromyko. "Comrade Gromyko has fallen behind the times," he declared.

In years past, such open criticism of a major figure by a minor official would have been greeted with stunned silence. This time, the delegates actually applauded.

However, next day, the 78-year-old Gromyko was honored with the chairmanship of one of the closing sessions. He was shown on public television standing at the lectern, conducting the meeting.

If Gromyko remains in public positions and Melnikov vanishes into Siberia, it will be a demonstration of the lack of substance behind "glasnost." But if Melnikov stays and Gromyko goes — well, almost anything might become possible in Russia.

Los Angeles Times
Los Angeles, CA, July 8, 1988

It will take months and perhaps years for tangible results of last week's remarkable Communist Party conference in Moscow to manifest themselves. But General Secretary Mikhail S. Gorbachev almost certainly had it right when he said that changes in Soviet life that the conference was designed to validate were irreversible. The same is true not only of East-West relations but also of the way the West will shape policies in the future.

For most Westerners the conference was a flimsy copy of democracy, but it was real enough to move some of the present generation of Soviets to tears. It moved others to fire off telegrams to the Kremlin to say what they thought about the sharp exchanges among Communist leaders for whom wooden was the preferred style for decades.

The telegrams were what Gorbachev wanted as he piloted the congress into its berth in history. In fact, a flimsy copy of democracy is his best hope of getting grass-roots support for keeping the Communist Party bureaucracy away from the working parts of government and the economy until he can get both performing more smoothly. It will be easier for Gorbachev to weed out the party's dead weight if, for example, Soviet citizens learn to holler at the agriculture minister about a shortage of meat instead of grumbling at the butcher. The party conference was a stunning lesson in hollering, watched in wonder by millions of Soviets who had simply never seen anything like it in their lives.

The general secretary's *perestroika* campaign, his effort to reshape the way the Soviet Union's government and economy work, is as fascinating to the West as it is to the Soviets, millions of whom had despaired of knowing anything better than numb acceptance of the bare minimums in life.

Changes in Moscow will provoke similar changes in the Western world. How much of the tension can be wrung out of the superpower relationship between the United States and the Soviet Union is no more than a good guess. But relations had already changed enough last week for the Pentagon to stage a series of flashy war games for an important visitor, Marshal Sergei F. Akhromeyev, chief of the Soviet armed forces general staff. And after a U.S. Navy ship shot down a civilian Iranian Airbus over the Persian Gulf, killing the 290 passengers and crew members, a Soviet response that only months ago would have had the word *brutality* somewhere in it went more like this: "We warned you that something terrible would happen one day with that concentration of force. Now it has."

In the context of past superpower relations, that remark borders on disengagement. Akhromeyev will not just watch troops maneuver and climb into a B-1 cockpit; he will discuss with top Pentagon officials how forces in both countries can be rebuilt to reduce their capability for sudden offensive thrusts anywhere in the world.

The Moscow party conference should also mean a change in White House perspective on foreign policy. For nearly 40 years American relations with other countries have had less to do with the countries themselves than with whether they had a role to play in the military standoff between East and West. The need for taking that into account never will go away entirely, but for now it is not the most burning question. By fastening the attention of both superpowers on their own problems, the conference may start a trend toward looking at the world the way it is rather than the way it should be. That would be refreshing.

THE CHRISTIAN SCIENCE MONITOR

Boston, MA, July 1, 1988

ST. LOUIS POST-DISPATCH

St. Louis, MO, July 4, 1988

The juxtaposition of the Communist Party Conference in Moscow and the Fourth of July offers an unusual opportunity for Americans to reflect on how valuable their freedoms are — and on how other countries are beginning to realize that such freedoms are necessary to nourish the best that people everywhere have to offer.

Just a glance at the list of reforms proposed by General Secretary Mikhail Gorbachev to the party conference presents a vivid picture of how far apart the two countries are. The improvements that Mr. Gorbachev would like to bring to his country — more local governmental control in the hands of elected councils, personal rights of privacy, a more individualized agriculture policy — are not only commonplace in the United States, they are an accepted part of our heritage.

The document that Americans celebrate today, the Declaration of Independence, did not grant that heritage automatically, of course. American patriots fought fiercely to win their political freedom from the British; even after that aim was accomplished, it took one false start, the Articles of Confederation, before the basic form of government and its inherent individual liberties were enshrined in the Constitution.

But it is not so much the specific freedoms that should come to mind on Independence Day as the spirit behind them. The American spirit of questioning authority, of individualism and iconoclasm, has long been the engine that drove the United States to be a leader among the world's nations. It is no accident that the symbol of the Fourth of July is fireworks; their brilliance and noise and explosive power exemplify what this country is all about.

That kind of freewheeling spirit needs to be nurtured, and it thrives best in an atmosphere that is quintessentially American but often bewilders citizens of other countries. The Japanese tendency toward conformity and respect for authority runs counter to our tendency to declare independence, almost at every opportunity; similarly, the traditional Soviet rule by fear and suspicion would hardly tolerate the open exchange of ideas and dissent that characterize American democracy.

Now, Mr. Gorbachev seems to be acknowledging that such openness is the key to success in the late 20th century. Not surprisingly, his calls for glasnost and perestroika are viewed with suspicion by a bureaucracy and a citizenry long used to the exact opposite. Freedom is not always easy to deal with; the more choices you have, the harder it is to choose, and learning how to choose wisely comes only with practice and with the assurance that the penalty for wrong choices will not be too harsh. Countries like the Soviet Union are only now talking about giving their citizens such assurance. Americans have had it for generations, and that freedom is what we celebrate on the glorious Fourth.

MIKHAIL GORBACHEV, for all his political keenness, could have appeared a lot like a speaker who had walked into the wrong hall. There he was, the man whose face has been splashed on every cover page available, expounding reform to a gathering of dour men who applauded only when he threw a sop to conservatism.

As has been known all along, reform in the Soviet Union is a delicate task. Reform challenges decades of communist orthodoxy and centuries of authoritarian rule. Mr. Gorbachev's lengthy opening speech to delegates assembled in Moscow for an extraordinary Communist Party conference was a tortuous exercise in seeking common ground without sacrificing principle.

Still, the forthright calls for change were there. The General Secretary proposed a new form of presidential leadership that would transfer power away from the party bureaucrats – thousands of whom sat in his audience. He outlined the revitalization of local soviets, or elected administrative bodies, which would allow the same transfer of power at a grass-roots level. These proposals included some items to soothe the conservatives, such as giving the chairmanship of each soviet to the local party boss. In the Soviet context, they are revolutionary nonetheless.

The economy was Gorbachev's major target – and for good reason. Gains in the production of food and consumer products must be engineered; if things slog along at the current bare-necessity pace the average citizen could view his program as little more than an abstraction. Gorbachev laid into the bureaucratic intransigence that · has thwarted his efforts to put decisionmaking authority in the hands of the front line producers who, he affirmed, have to be free to respond to market demands. "We must make the farmer sovereign master," he proclaimed.

Personal freedoms were accorded equal eloquence. Gorbachev asserted "the rights of citizens to the inviolability of their private life" – a none too subtle jab at the intrusive arm of the KGB. He reaffirmed the Communist view that religious belief is "unscientific," but added "this is no reason for a disrespectful attitude to the spiritual-mindedness of the believer, still less for applying any administrative pressure to assert materialistic views."

Reform-minded Soviets, along with many in the Western world looking on, hope the silence that greeted such ringing statements won't speak louder than the statements themselves.

Gorbachev has sketched out his vision of a new Soviet future in detail. His notion of a democratic society may never fit perfectly with Western concepts, but he is clearly drawing on the democratic experiences of other nations in piecing together a new structure for Soviet government. He is a Communist, but a Communist determined to see his system evolve away from the ice age of Stalin.

What will that evolution bring? A more prosperous Soviet Union, a friendlier and freer one, or one marginally different but still adversarial towards the West? When the party conference is over, the work of implementing reform will go on.

To make *perestroika* and *glasnost* matters of law, not just vision, Gorbachev will need the support of the 5,000 somber delegates he addressed in Moscow, and the consent of a vast and calcified bureaucracy. This support is not yet guaranteed.

The Washington Post
Washington, DC, July 3, 1988

THE QUESTION of the century has been whether a full-blown totalitarian system, such as the one imposed by the Communist Party in the Soviet Union, could be transformed or at least substantially changed from within. No answer has yet been given, but the party conference held last week in Moscow demonstrates that the question is still open. This is a lot more than you could say up until fairly recently when General Secretary Gorbachev starting breaking the crockery.

At the conference, unimaginably spontaneous things went on in a setting where the stage directions ("all rise," "stormy applause") used to be given by party command. The icons of the historical Soviet past were assailed. Sitting Politburo members were told they had outstayed their time. A dismissed Politburo member was allowed to argue his case for returning to favor. The top man himself was challenged to make his program work. Delegates were accused of criminality. Angry protests were made against the workings of the system. Many of these astonishments, moreover, were televised live: Soviets were let in directly on what their rulers do to an extent unheard of before.

Though much of what happened is still unknown, it is clear enough that Mr. Gorbachev created a format (the party conference) and used a technique (unprecedented openness, or glasnost) he hoped would undermine the resistance to his reform. Some part of the resultant convulsion could have been planned or predicted. But much of what he was doing had to be a sheer gamble. He was risking, moreover, much more than an unusual and, by Soviet convention, unseemly display of public disorder in high places.

He was taking the chance that the turmoil of accusations, quarrels, counterattacks and reappraisals that were the stuff of the meeting would show up the party for all to see as an organization unfit to hold power, or at the least unfit to hold power in the old unwatched, unchallenged and unaccountable ways. On the other side was risk too. For when the party's ways are changed—and that is what the week's struggle was about—the political system becomes something very different in its nature, in its operation and in the expectations people have for it, at home and abroad.

There are two kinds of "success" possible in this sort of exercise. One is reaching the leadership's final goals. Mr. Gorbachev has not done this, and he may not even know where he is going; certainly he is hard put to manage the process he has set loose. The other is unhooking the system from its old moorings. This Mr. Gorbachev has done to a considerable extent. He has accomplished the feat of forcing the political system to take up his agenda of all-consuming change. The Soviet system is now in something resembling a float.

Not, of course, a completely free float. If there was an unmistakable giddiness on view in Moscow last week, there also remains in place, available for use in a cynical restoration, the machinery of a controlled system: an apparatus of compulsion and persuasion, habits of communist rule (and the Russian past). As much as Westerners would like to believe that democratic impulses, even when they appear in utterly improbable circumstances, are irreversible, no one can be sure of that. The turmoil, the promise (and the power of Mr. Gorbachev) could yet come to an abrupt end. Certainly he has risked all of this. But it is also apparent from what has gone on so far, especially in the turbulence of the televised party conference, that movement within totalitarian systems *is* possible, that history, even under the most thorough of repressive systems, does not come to a halt, that pressures for reform cannot be stamped out forever. And the implication of that is that even if this movement comes to grief or stops far short of what people in the West hope for it, the process will recur in the future—the instincts it has activated in the Soviet Union will always be there.

The TENNESSEAN
Nashville, TN, July 1, 1988

IN his opening speech to the Communist Party conference, Mr. Mikhail Gorbachev extended his reach for reform, but what he may grasp may be far less than he wants.

The general secretary called for sweeping change in the Soviet Union, including creation of a full-time legislature with real power and election of a president with duties akin to those of some heads of Western countries.

He also proposed that farmers be made masters of the land in a program that would allow them to lease the soil they till to quickly increase production and end chronic food shortages. Although he stopped short of suggesting the dismantling of the collective farm system, he seemed to be urging a more capitalistic system in agriculture.

Although he promised freer expression and more attention to the country's more than 100 nationalities, Mr. Gorbachev had some warnings about his policy of "glasnost" or more openness. He said that does not mean he will tolerate formation of new political parties. Nor, he said, should the policy be abused by those trying to redraw political boundaries.

In the political sphere, Mr. Gorbachev said strict demarcation of functions between the party and government organizations is needed to ensure the success of his social and economic reforms.

The idea of directing some power away from the party is likely to be regarded as heresy by the old-line Communists. Many of those in party ranks consider that the party's control of all aspects of Soviet life is the essence of socialism.

Nor do the older heads — even those from the hinterlands — relish the idea of restructuring the governing mechanisms so as to create a full-time legislature and a president with power instead, presumably, of a general secretary at the top.

Mr. Gorbachev had already set off debate throughout the country about the Communist Party and its future. The general secretary had hoped that local party organizations would elect delegates to the conference who were committed to change. But many of the delegates are not reformers; they are traditionalists who have grown up in the system and find it difficult to conceive of a somewhat different arrangement.

Mr. Gorbachev's greatest challenge then will be to convince the conference, and beyond that the people, that change is necessary — not only economic change, but political change as well. He will have to depend on his own charisma and intellect to persuade both groups, and hope that he has enough loyal supporters to help pull it off. ■

News-Tribune & Herald
Duluth, MN, July 4, 1988

Is Mikhail Gorbachev serious about structural change in the Soviet Union? If so, will he be able to accomplish such change?

The Communist Party conference called in Moscow last week by Gorbachev, the first such national Soviet convention in nearly half a century, has captured headlines across our nation for the candor and the vigor of Gorbachev and some of the nearly 5,000 party delegates. They advocate basic political and economic change in the Soviet Union's totalitarian socialist system, change unprecedented since Josef Stalin's reign of terror.

Soviet watchers, including many here in our region who have been expanding their Soviet understanding through the Duluth-Petrozavodsk sister city program, are trying to fathom both the sincerity and the possibility of Gorbachev's proposed changes. They foresee increased prospects for increased bilateral exchanges, a greater traffic in culture as well as in commerce. Indeed, increased commerce, increased access to Western technology and Western money, is perhaps the root cause of Gorbachev's sweeping changes. Both we and they could conceivably benefit, culturally and economically, from that.

Yet even with Gorbachev's seemingly radical changes, the differences between our two government systems would still be vast; our social and governmental systems would still be in basic conflict. But understanding could increase and international tension decrease.

All this, of course, can come to pass if, and only if, Gorbachev's bold words are translated into bold domestic action. We are not optimistic that such will happen; we are, however, hopeful that it may.

Gorbachev Assumes Soviet Presidency

The Supreme Soviet, the U.S.S.R.'s nominal parliament, Oct. 1, 1988 confirmed Communist Party General Secretary Mikhail S. Gorbachev as the president of the Supreme Soviet Union. He succeeded the retired Andrei A. Gromyko. The Supreme Soviet Sept. 30 session continued the sweeping shake-up in the party leadership begun by the CP Central Committee, at Gorbachev's behest.

Lev N. Zaikov, the boss of the Moscow city CP and a full (voting) member of the Politburo, nominated Gorbachev for the presidency in a brief speech. Gorbachev was confirmed, without debate, by a unanimous show of hands by the 1,500 Supreme Soviet members.

By assuming the presidency, Gorbachev became the head of state in addition to being the head of the party. The head of the government, Premier Nikolai I. Ryzhkov, was one of his proteges. Gorbachev in June had initiated a process under which the presidency – actually the chairmanship of the Presidium (executive council) of the Supreme Soviet – would have meaningful powers.

Gorbachev, in an acceptance speech, told the legislators that *"perestroika* (restructuring) and the renewal of our society" had "entered a new age...Stormy discussions and meetings and analysis of the mistakes of the past are no longer enough. We need practical headway and real improvements...especially where people's living standards are concerned." Gorbachev continued: "The working people are not satisfied with the way our government and economic bodies, public organizations and many party committees work."

In another action at the Supreme Soviet gathering, Marshal Viktor M. Chebrikov was replaced as the head of the KGB (state-security apparatus). Chebrikov, who had been named the party secretary in charge of legal affairs Sept. 30, remained a full Politburo member. The removal of Chebrikov's base of power came as no surprise to observers. He had been the only known high-ranking member of the leadership to align himself with Yegor K. Ligachev, Gorbachev's main rival in the Politburo.

THE ☀ SUN
Baltimore, MD, October 10, 1988

By solidifying his grasp on the Kremlin apparatus and conferring on himself the trappings as well as substance of power, Mikhail S. Gorbachev comes to resemble more closely the Soviet dictators whose mistakes he vows to undo. To combat the terrifying legacy of Josef Stalin, become the next Stalin. To stamp out the stultifying cult of Leonid Brezhnev's personality, raise Mikhail S. Gorbachev onto the pedestal.

It is not really so surprising. Mr. Gorbachev is a Russian and a Communist. If he sends journalistic lances to prick the balloons of Stalin's reputation, there is no debunking Vladimir I. Lenin. The sources and legitimacy of power as Mr. Gorbachev exercises them are those that Lenin erected. It was Lenin who made the Soviet system synonymous with police state, who used the czarist secret police and army to impose his vision of communism on a divided and largely unwilling people.

There is no doubting Mr. Gorbachev's desire to liberate the creativity of Soviet peoples by freeing them from red tape and shackles of inherited practice. His criticisms of Soviet economics resemble those made by ideological critics of communism. In the interest of economic productivity, at the base of state and political power, he clearly intends reforms and liberations that have a greater-than-economic dimension, extending into the intellectual and even spiritual spheres, however distasteful some of that may be to Mr. Gorbachev himself.

But to impose this on fourth generation bureaucrats, the party functionaries raised by Mr. Brezhnev for their limited vision and unlimited loyalty, Mr. Gorbachev requires unhindered cooperation at the top, unbrooked by opposition. The criticism he allows to flow will not be of himself. Diversity, pluralism, separation and balance of powers, whatever their virtue lower in the hierarchies, still have no place at the summit of Soviet power. The general secretary proceeds as his predecessors have. He knows no other way.

The old cold warrior Andrei A. Gromyko was removed from the presidency so that Mr. Gorbachev could take the position for himself as Mr. Brezhnev had. This does not enhance Mr. Gorbachev so much as the presidency. Mr. Gorbachev's power flows from his position as general secretary of the Communist Party controlling patronage in party, government, state, military and security establishments. He is taking the role of president to enlarge the importance of government structure.

The Gorbachev revolution is to be less confrontational in foreign policy, to encourage initiative and problem-solving by Soviet people, to decentralize decisions and liberate do-ers from dictation. To achieve this, he dictates it. He is not asking Soviet peoples if they want it. To allow differences of opinion, he pushes aside those who object. No one is quite sure how far Mr. Gorbachev means to go, though clearly not all the way.

The Philadelphia Inquirer
Philadelphia, PA, October 9, 1988

One of the top jobs in the Soviet political hierarchy has no counterpart in the United States. On the ruling Politburo, there is always one man — traditionally, the number two man — in charge of ideology. He is considered the principal arbiter of which policies — both at home and abroad — can be safely called Leninist. The ideologist's pronouncements are important because they inevitably affect policy in areas ranging from the limits of dissent to the possibilities for rapprochement with the West.

Thus it is no small matter that there is a new chief ideologist in the Kremlin this month. Vadim A. Medvedev, an economist who was promoted to the Politburo just 10 days ago, has taken over the responsibilities previously held by Michael S. Gorbachev's conservative rival, Yegor Ligachev. That Mr. Medvedev is the leadership's most junior member suggests that ideology itself is declining in importance. And where Mr. Ligachev had tried to hold the line for orthodoxy against the forces of reform, Mr. Medvedev's philosophy could loosely be described as "anything goes (so long as we call it socialist)."

This is important not just for the Soviets, but for the entire world — particularly the United States. The latest shake-up in the Kremlin has reinforced the notion of a more flexible, pragmatic Soviet foreign policy — unclouded by the need to pursue an epic class struggle against imperialism.

Mr. Gorbachev has been moving in that direction since 1985, but Mr. Ligachev was sending very different signals. In a highly publicized speech last August, he re-emphasized the "class" character of Soviet foreign policy and the importance of the worldwide struggle for "social and national liberation." Any other approach, he said, "only confuses the minds of the Soviet people and our friends abroad."

Now Mr. Ligachev is overseeing agriculture, and Mr. Medvedev, in his first major speech, has reaffirmed the Gorbachev line. He rejected Marxist-Leninist orthodoxy in both domestic and foreign affairs: attacking state ownership of productive property at home and class warfare abroad. "Universal values," such as avoiding war and preventing ideological catastrophe, are now more important than the struggle between the classes, he said.

Clearly, action is what counts in these matters. But the transfer of the ideology portfolio to Mr. Medvedev means that, for now at least, there are virtually no philosophical boundaries to a more accommodating Soviet approach to the outside world.

Richmond Times-Dispatch

Richmond, VA, October 8, 1988

A one-party state has its disadvantages: The inertia of plump bureaucrats is one. A one-party state has advantages, too, one of which Mikhail Gorbachev availed himself of last week: naming oneself president and replacing opponents in high bureaucracies with supporters. Mr. Gorbachev, in the parlance of American presidential campaigns, would be described as having "a vision" of Soviet society and the "fire in the belly" to achieve it. He also has the concentrated power to revamp the party line in a parliament accustomed to toeing it.

Never mind that the world calls the, say, Chilean version of that concentration of power simply, and derisively, dictatorship. The Soviet version, the world calls progress. And (as in Chile), progress it may prove. If *perestroika*, or restructuring, is to happen, it must come from the top down.

During his recent visit to Siberia, President Gorbachev heard both the people's calls for adequate food, shelter and medical care and their complaints that his reforms have not provided them. He returned to Moscow apparently determined to prove that the fault lies not in his policy of reform but in the lack of dedicated reformers.

It is no accident that Mr. Gorbachev's new chief ideologist is an economist, or that his maiden speech endorsed butter over guns, reform over rhetoric, internal change over external meddling on the Soviet agenda. The new head of the KGB, the secret police whose primary targets have been dissident Soviets, is a Gorbachev ally unlikely to bridle at the combination of *glasnost* and commerce evident in Moscow's recent deal with a U.S. firm to supply that formerly forbidden tool of anti-Soviet propagandists, the copy machine. The Old Guard in Soviet foreign policy gives way to New Thinkers whose latest suggestion is a freeze on superpower force levels in Asia and Europe.

For the Soviets, these changes may mean a better life. For the rest of us, they could mean a quieter world. But neither is a sure bet.

Not even as newly (self-)proclaimed head of state can Mikhail Gorbachev move the Soviet ship of state quickly, smoothly through a top-to-bottom overhaul. He cannot move too slowly on reform or his program will lose public support. He cannot move so fast that he galvanizes the anti-reform movements in the party and the bureaucracy.

The political unrest evident among Armenians and Estonians, among Poles and Romanians is as much an invitation to reinstitute repression as an argument for further freedoms. If Mr. Gorbachev has begun to ease back the lid only to have the top fly off, the we-told-you-so's now hunkering down in the Kremlin will uncross their arms and nail it down tight.

The necessary economic progress requires fundamental changes in the Soviet system, not just advantageous deals with foreign capitalists whom Moscow insists pay $1.80 for a ruble the world values at 12 cents. If the Soviets are to share the rewards of the market economies, they will also have to share the risks.

Likewise for conventional and nuclear arms control: Reductions in both tensions and defense expenditures could benefit both superpowers. But the freeze on forces in Asia, for example, would freeze a Soviet advantage in weaponry and proxy armies which a genuinely new and peace-loving Moscow would not need.

The answer to the inevitable question — What should Washington do to help Mr. Gorbachev achieve his Moscow millennium? — is this: Be at least as wary as the Soviet people of Mr. Gorbachev's ultimate success, and be as flexible as U. S. national interests permit. The American president who bases his policies of trade, aid and arms control on the certainty that Moscow's motives are utterly benign and Mr. Gorbachev will ultimately prevail not only endangers U. S. security. He also lessens the chances for genuine, lasting change in the Soviet Union.

Lincoln Journal

Lincoln, NE, October 10, 1988

What news agencies are able to report in and from the Soviet Union these days continues to be nothing short of amazing — considering the tightness of Communist authorities for decades.

One wonders how the Soviets reacted to a story in the weekly *Moscow News* a few days ago. It dealt with mass killings under Josef Stalin; in bloody particular, executions at a city near Minsk in the 1930s. At least 102,000 Soviets were slain there.

So-called "enemies of the people" were bound and gagged near freshly-dug ditches and then gunned down, in some cases one bullet doing the work of two. Moscow News found witnesses who said "gunshots resounded night and day, winter and summer." Pulling the triggers were agents of Stalin's secret police, then called the NKVD. The successor of that terrorist outfit is today's KGB.

It is impossble to imagine any internal publication providing that murderous story as recently as three years ago.

Likewise, back then, we would not have known that local authorities in the town of Chernobyl — population 10,000 at one time — currently are demolishing the ghost community. This was widely reported over the weekend. The explanation given in *Pravda* was that Chernobyl's structures are considered impossibly contaminated by the world's worst nuclear power plant accident 2½ years ago.

Sad to say, the United States government does not have a spotless record in making public information which citizens should have access to.

Last week, the Department of Energy finally revealed there had been many serious accidents up to 1985 at the five-reactor South Carolina plant making nuclear weapons. Information about extensive radioactive contamination and fuel-melting episodes was deliberately kept from the American people.

How authorities thought they could block outside knowledge of a 1970 incident when it took 900 people three months to clean up a radioactive water spill is difficult to imagine. Still, when an activist group two years ago made a report about a near catastrophe at the plant in 1960, members were once more dismissed as kooks.

This kind of patronizing attitude is an understandable reason why there is such scepticism about nuclear power, why public confidence flags. Those in charge — in the government and in industry — do not have a track record of fully leveling with the American people. "Trust us" no longer has the selling power it once did. And in a properly functioning democracy, such dubiousness is cause for great concern.

The Washington Post

Washington, DC, October 2, 1988

BORIS YELTSIN is the Soviet politician who was fired for being too ardent a supporter of Mikhail Gorbachev. Speaking last spring of Yegor Ligachev, then the No. 2 man in the Soviet Communist Party Politburo and leader of the conservative opposition, Mr. Yeltsin said: "Of course it would be possible to carry out the process of change more energetically if there was another man in his place." This is what now seems to have happened in Moscow. Mr. Ligachev was, if not neutralized, then taken down a big peg in the restructuring that Mr. Gorbachev engineered in the Soviet Communist Party and in the government—engineered in a not-so-open power play worked out apparently while Mr. Ligachev was on vacation. The task of consolidating the political support needed to permit Mr. Gorbachev to proceed with his reform program is an immense and continuing one. The sweep of the latest personnel changes, however, shows he is dead serious about making progress.

Mr. Ligachev, 67, who formerly had the party's ideology portfolio, is not gone from the Politburo but has been reassigned to a major but more workaday portfolio, agriculture. It is a field in which Mr. Gorbachev, himself a former agriculture chief, is in a position to second-guess him. The 79-year-old veteran of the Kremlin big time, Andrei Gromyko, most recently a chair-warming president, lost that post.

Mr. Gorbachev has the presidency now and obviously means to use it. The longtime Soviet ambassador in Washington, Anatoly Dobrynin, who had shown Mr. Gorbachev the foreign policy ropes, also retires, to be replaced by a Gorbachev protégé. And so on. Meanwhile, Mr. Gorbachev slashes away at the structures and habits of the bureaucracy.

In and out of the Soviet Union, great doubt remains whether perestroika can accomplish what its author envisions, which seems to be a society that runs better but still has a communist party at its helm. This is a difficult and perhaps inconsistent proposition, and so far Mr. Gorbachev, facing the drag of a system little given to change, has not had a full chance to make a test of it. One part of his response has been to scale back some of the reforms—to the point of dismaying some of the people he had counted on to help him drive ahead. Another part of his response has been to move old people out of the way and to replace them, at the working level as at the policy level, with, what one of his new Politburo choices calls "people who support perestroika." By his latest stunning moves, Mr. Gorbachev does not so much solidify his power position as commit the Soviet Union more deeply to a tremendous experiment in modernization that many officials and individuals in the country continue to question. More action and more tension: that is the prospect.

ARGUS-LEADER
Sioux Falls, SD, October 10, 1988

U.S. experts are still analyzing the recent leadership changes in the Soviet Union. It's clear even to casual observers, however, that the biggest beneficiary has been Soviet leader Mikhail Gorbachev, general secretary of the Communist Party.

Gorbachev emerged from two days of wheeling, dealing and meetings with the additional title of president, a largely ceremonial position formerly held by veteran Soviet hand Andrei Gromyko, who retired.

Gorbachev's double role gives him more power to force through his reforms.

But there is also at least preliminary justification for the United States to view the changes as an encouraging sign.

The Soviet Union is by no means turning democratic, in the U.S. sense of the word. And although Gorbachev has shown he can be a power player, he also appears to be increasingly willing to deal with internal problems with some accommodation and negotiation.

That same flexibility may hold true in foreign policy dealings with the United States.

The recent shake-up included the biggest personnel changes in Soviet leadership since Gorbachev became party leader 3½ years ago.

Gorbachev retired two full and two candidate Politburo members and promoted four others. He also promised that government councils would take on a greater responsibilities in the everyday management and that the Communist Party would limit itself to policy matters.

"The soviets (governing councils) will take on their shoulders the major burden of state work," Gorbachev said in a speech. "As the situation changes, we must change accordingly."

Analysts say the changes will help Gorbachev in his drive to restructure the Soviet economy and government. The changes are viewed as an attempt to further prod the slow-moving Soviet bureaucracy. Gorbachev has complained publicly that his reforms are taking hold too slowly. He says he wants to provide more and better food, housing, clothing, education and medical help to Soviet people.

Some analysts say Gorbachev needed to wield power in both the Communist Party and in the Soviet government in order to separate them, as he promised to do when he first rose to power. He appears to be decentralizing power at the bottom of the power structure and centralizing it at the top.

Naturally, Gorbachev's personnel changes advance his loyalists at the expense of the old guard.

If nothing else, the Soviets are focusing energy on their own problems and inefficiencies rather than on international adventurism.

THE SACRAMENTO BEE
Sacramento, CA, October 5, 1988

There's a paradox in Mikhail Gorbachev's newest shake-up of the Kremlin hierarchy: To persuade his fellow citizens, and officialdom, to embrace his policy of restructuring the Soviet system through decentralization and democratization of decision-making, he has had to centralize power more than ever in his own hands. Now that he has done so, it's still an open question whether he can succeed in making his reforms work.

By having himself elected to a strengthened presidency, Gorbachev acquires power over government as well as party functions, a fusion signaled months ago at a special party conference but one not expected to happen so soon. And by removing or reassigning remnants of the party's old guard and replacing them with men of his own stripe, Gorbachev strengthens his chances of implementing his reform program at the top. The difficult part, even supposing his power in Moscow is now supreme, will be in translating policy into practice throughout all the layers of overlapping party and government bureaucracies.

A measure of Gorbachev's sense of urgency was the suddenness of last week's Communist Party Central Committee meeting, followed immediately by a session of the Supreme Soviet (parliament) at which the Politburo shake-up was rubber-stamped. Whether the urgency resulted from widespread complaints about the failure of Gorbachev's policies to improve the Soviet standard of living, or from a threat to his leadership from within the hierarchy, can only be guessed at. What seems certain is that Gorbachev is determined to turn over more of the day-to-day responsibility for running the country to the government bureaucracy and to confine the Party's main function to setting policy. There's strong evidence of that in the decision to slash the Central Committee staff's size by 50 percent and to reduce the number of Central Committee departments from 22 to 6.

Gorbachev's principal opponents have not been entirely routed. Yegor Ligachev lost his post as chief ideologist and foreign policy adviser, but will head the party's agriculture department, a post in which he can distinguish himself or, if productivity continues to languish, take the blame for failure. Another hard-liner left over from the Brezhnev era, Viktor Chebrikov, lost his job as head of the KGB, the Soviet secret police, and his KGB successor will not be a Politburo member. Chebrikov, however, remains in the Politburo, and as head of the legal affairs department could be instrumental in bringing about — or slowing down — the judicial reforms that so many Soviet citizens would welcome.

Once again Gorbachev has surprised both his friends and enemies by moving to consolidate his own power in the name of creating more power for others down the chain of command. If he succeeds, he would create new freedoms while removing much of the state-guaranteed security that Soviet citizens have learned to count on, and lately to defend, even as they grumble about the system's inadequacies. Persuading them that giving up some security and accepting more responsibility is the surest way to improve their lives may be the most formidable task Gorbachev has ever faced.

DAILY NEWS

New York, NY, October 4, 1988

AT THE MOST OBVIOUS LEVEL, it's a high irony: Bear No. 1 chases all the other big and medium bears out of the woods, locking up absolute control for himself. Why? To usher in democracy. Mikhail Gorbachev's moves suggest Peter the Great or Joe Stalin a whole lot more than Tom Jefferson.

For himself, there is the title "president" added to his chairmanship of the all-dominant Communist Party. Out, or shunted aside to impotent positions, is a large handful of the once-powerful, including President Andrei Gromyko and senior foreign-policy adviser Anatoly Dobrynin.

Into power come younger, leaner men, Gorbachev loyalists. Iron Mike's main remaining visible rival, Yegor Ligachev, gets the agriculture administration portfolio. That honor may turn out to rank with helmsman of the Titanic. And there's a restructuring of the monolithic, all-pervasive Soviet bureaucracy that may ultimately squeeze thousands of petty despots out of power.

And all of that was done without a single public debate. Without one dissenting vote.

Long live *democratizatsia!*

So what does it mean?

It means that a very powerful, very crafty man has solidified his rule of the Soviet Union. And it is reasonable to believe, with reservations for safety, that he is a man who for practical reasons sees a vital need to reduce the hostility between his nation and the free world and to curtail the size and cost of armaments, including nuclear weapons.

It also means that Gorbachev clearly recognized that a dramatic purge was vital to his reign. It clearly is costly to him to have to practice raw dictatorship after three years of preaching democracy and openness.

And what should it mean to Americans?

Well, it's a mixed message. If, say, Gorbachev disappeared tomorrow, U.S.-Soviet relations would be less stable than before—with familiar if unloved foreign-policy leaders and functionaries out, with an atmosphere of despotism hanging over the succeeding rulers. For all his talk of democracy, there is less institutional democracy in the Soviet Union today than there was a week ago. But it is also likely that the people in line to succeed Gorbachev in case of any demise but a coup are more tolerant of democracy and of the U.S. than their old-line predecessors.

Never get between a bear and its young. Especially a very big bear.

TULSA WORLD

Tulsa, OK, October 4, 1988

WHEN the Soviet government called home its ambassador to the United States and other high-ranking officials in foreign countries last week, Kremlin-watchers around the world asked, "What's up?"

The answer came over the weekend: A major shakeup in the Soviet leadership, with more power falling into the hands of Party Chairman Mikhail S. Gorbachev.

On Friday, it was announced that Gorbachev would succeed retiring Old Guardsman Andrei Gromyko as president. There were other important changes in the leadership, including the KGB. All were calculated to advance Gorbachev loyalists.

Perhaps more important, Gorbachev announced that the Supreme Soviet, the nation's nominal parliament, would assume a greater role in everyday management of the country. The Soviets (government councils) also were promised more power, obviously at the expense of the central Communist party apparatus.

These are more than cosmetic changes. They fit in with Gorbachev's promise to restructure the Soviet economy and to bring more voices into the decision-making.

The West must continue to watch the changes in the Soviet Union with caution. But there is no longer any doubt that Gorbachev is serious about liberalizing the Soviet Union's internal politics and economics.

None of this means that the Soviet Union is turning democratic in the Western definition of that word. But it does mean that Gorbachev plans to deal with the Soviet Union's severe internal divisions with some accommodation and negotiation.

The same is almost certainly true of the Soviet Union's foreign policy.

That's good news.

The Idaho STATESMAN

Boise, ID, October 4, 1988

It is hard not to admire and stand in wonder at what Mikhail Gorbachev is doing in the Soviet Union.

If Mr. Gorbachev survives, he could go down as one of the most influential political leaders of this century. If he is toppled, he may be remembered as a river boat gambler who lost.

Last week Mr. Gorbachev moved swiftly to consolidate his power and to send a strong message to the entrenched Soviet bureaucracy that he will not let his reforms die.

First, Mr. Gorbachev arranged the ouster of the Soviet Union's president, Andrei Gromyko, who had served at the highest echelons of the Soviet government since the days of Joseph Stalin.

Mr. Gorbachev also stacked the Communist Party's ruling Politburo with his own people, ousting most of the members who stood in the way of his reforms.

The shakeup was the biggest one since former Soviet leader Nikita Khrushchev ousted the "anti-party clique" in 1957.

Mr. Gorbachev's reforms are welcome from the standpoint of human rights. The Soviet Union is far from a democracy, but there is more toleration for opposite points of view and less censorship.

A number of dissidents, including Nobel Peace prize winner Andrei Sakharov, have been released from captivity because of Mr. Gorbachev. The Soviet Union has loosened its emigration policies.

Mr. Gorbachev has improved relations with the United States and other western countries.

Even Mr. Gorbachev's economic reforms are welcome in the sense that they could improve the living standards of Soviet citizens.

But Mr. Gorbachev's reforms should not be of just academic interest to Americans. If Mr. Gorbachev succeeds, the United States will have to deal with the Soviet Union as an economic power as well as a military one.

For now, though, it is fascinating to watch this charismatic leader work his stuff like a quarterback moving his squad down the field toward the goal line. Part of the fun is watching and waiting to see whether he scores a goal or runs out of downs.

THE BLADE
Toledo, OH, October 4, 1988

THE Russians have had their big meeting, and there has been a shake-up. Andrei Gromyko, who seemed to take the same vitamins that General Franco took, has been forced out. He lived through and adapted to every regime since Joseph Stalin's time. Gone, too, is Anatoly Dobrynin, long-time ambassador to the United States and an established fixer among the good old boys of the politburo. It is a new day, but what kind? Perhaps not even Comrade Gorbachev knows.

Experts will continue to debate the question of whether the new Soviet leaders can actually achieve change. It is not at all clear that they can.

And the same experts will continue to talk about just what the new Soviet society entails. Is the goal to be a more efficient communist nation with more rational priorities or a less centralized and controlled socialist nation where private economies and personal initiatives are possible? Will such privacy and economic experimentation lead to a yearning for political democracy?

And no one knows what the ethnic diversity of the socialist republics portends. Or whether the Russians can retain in the long run some hold on all of the satellite countries.

Yet one thing is very clear. Mr. Gorbachev is not kidding. He is not just pushing some new line of propaganda; he wants change. His boldness is perhaps the greatest power the Soviet Union now possesses. In a nation that is really an awful mess, this man has created the possibility and the hope of change.

Consider that Alexander Solzhenitsyn has been invited to come to the USSR; that Ronald Reagan has lectured on capitalism at the University of Moscow; that the Russians meet with U.S. diplomats and release political prisoners that they previously would not admit existed.

Last week the Voice of America was allowed into the Soviet Union. The USIA will send a correspondent to Moscow straightaway. Think of it, the Voice of America existed precisely *because* the USSR was closed to Western thought and propaganda. Essentially Mr. Gorbachev is taking down the Iron Curtain — a piece of it anyway.

Some of these acts are window dressing, but they are something more, too. They show a cynical realization that real communism does not work, so why not try something else and keep the myth for ·packaging? On a deeper level Mr. Gorbachev and his reforms represent the triumph of reason. How does Ivan Sixpack profit from the cold war? Mr. Gorbachev, by being both cynical and rational, is not a Marxist but a Machiavellian.

The Sun Reporter
San Francisco, CA, October 5, 1988

Mikhail Gorbachev's elevation to the presidency of the USSR represents an incredibly fast change in the direction in which the Soviet people must go. All the media are criticizing the fact that a meeting of the Communist Party heirarchy was precipitously called last weekend which resulted in the elevation of Gorbachev and his close associates who believe in his program of *glasnost* and *perestroika*.

The seriousness of the impending crisis in the USSR over the economy and standard of living has been given primacy of action. While most people criticize the hurried calling of such a meeting, which will probably change the whole character of the USSR, we, for one, admire the decisiveness of Gorbachev's actions in re-emphasizing his determination to press ahead and develope a new and improved life for all of the Soviet citizens.

Gorbachev has laid his credibility on the line. We hope that he will be victorious in changing the mode of action of those party and government officials who are reluctant to give up their positions of power.

The leadership of the USSR and the People's Republic of China have both undertaken an almost impossible task — so much so, that it is mind-boggling.

We are at an important crossroads in history, when strong men with strong ideas are prepared to move ahead without fear or timidity, to change the direction of the national struggle so as to more adequately serve the will of the people for a better way of life, with greater individual freedom and more participation of the people in the great call for the transformation of the communist states into real instruments which serve the needs of the people.

Such behavior is truly impressive, and we are hopeful that success will be achieved. The efforts of 1.25 billion citizens in China and the USSR are on the move. The outcome is not yet known, but the people believe in their leaders, and the leaders apparently feel a call to a great crusade.

THE ARIZONA REPUBLIC
Phoenix, AZ, October 1, 1988

IN his espionage thriller *Moscow Rules*, novelist Robert Moss observes that in the Soviet Union if you hope to win at the game of power politics, you had better play by Moscow rules. Mikhail Gorbachev, the general secretary of the Communist Party, knows the rules.

In less than four years, Mr. Gorbachev has risen from obscurity as a junior member of the ruling Politburo, a man responsible for agricultural affairs, to undisputed leader of the Soviet Union.

Mr. Gorbachev's final power play came dramatically and unexpectedly this week when he took both his opponents and supporters by surprise, convening a special plenary meeting of the party's Central Committee. So hastily was the Central Committee plenum called that key Gorbachev allies — Foreign Minister Eduard Shevardnadze, Defense Minister Dmitri Yazov and Army Chief of Staff Sergei Akhromeyev — were caught abroad and had to rush back to Moscow.

What Mr. Gorbachev accomplished was a bloodless purge of the remaining old guard, Politburo opponents widely viewed as blocking progress on the *perestroika* and *glasnost* campaigns to restructure and invigorate the moribund Soviet economy.

Mr. Gorbachev's chief rival, ideology watchdog and No. 2 man on the Politburo, Yegor Ligachev, was demoted to the general secretary's old job of agriculture minister, and the venerable Andrei Gromyko was retired from the Politburo altogether. This clears the way for his removal as president, which could happen as early as today during a special meeting of the Supreme Soviet. This in turn makes possible the election of Mr. Gorbachev to that office.

If that happens, Mr. Gorbachev would head both the party and the state, a consolidation of personal power not seen since the death of Josef Stalin. In addition to the removal of Mr. Gromyko, three other members of the Politburo were retired and replaced with Gorbachev allies, leaving only two pre-Gorbachev members of the ruling body.

That something was in the wind had been obvious ever since Mr. Gorbachev returned from his traditional summer vacation. In a series of speeches and press interviews in recent weeks, Mr. Gorbachev has blasted the snail's pace of economic reform. Stung by the growing public disillusionment with *perestroika* — a program that greatly raised expectations, but has failed to deliver — Mr. Gorbachev moved decisively against revanchist elements in the party believed to be blocking his reforms.

Mr. Gorbachev's coup d'etat is an effort to rid the bureaucracy-bound economy of red tape by transferring economic powers from party hacks to elected government officials. Should the West stand on the sidelines cheering Mr. Gorbachev on to success? Experts disagree.

Is an economically more successful, more competitive Soviet Union in the West's interests? Some believe that it would be better for the West if Mr. Gorbachev were to fail and the Soviet economy were to continue to stagnate. By forcing the Soviet leadership to spend less on defense, this would enhance Western security.

Among others, Margaret Thatcher, however, believes that a hungry bear is a more dangerous adversary. This view presumes that a more economically efficient Soviet Union can be corrupted by consumerism and that rising economic expectations will fuel demands for political liberalization. The dispute, however, is academic, since the West can do little or nothing to influence the internal economic situation in Russia.

Mr. Gorbachev is now solidly in control, and the last obstacles to *perestroika* are falling. If his economic reform campaign fails to deliver the better standard of living advertised, no one is left to blame. It is now Mr. Gorbachev's ball game, and he made the rules.

The Record

Hackensack, NJ, October 7, 1988

Mikhail S. Gorbachev has bought more time for Russia's "second revolution," but that may not be much of a victory. In an artful power play, Mr. Gorbachev has taken on the post of president, bounced four Politburo members, sent conservative rival Yegor Ligachev packing, and reshuffled the Communist Party apparatus. Mr. Gorbachev is in charge. No question about it. But now comes the hard part. He has to do something with his power.

Mr. Gorbachev has confounded experts who said he was headed for a fall. That was an easy conclusion to draw. Three and a half years into one of the most ambitious reform programs since the time of Lenin, Mr. Gorbachev doesn't have much to show for himself. There's a new mood of openness, a lot of outraged conservatives, but not a great deal more. Shoppers still waste hours hunting for meat and vegetables and return home to overcrowded, shoddy housing. The country's economy is still a mess, and demonstrations are shaking Armenia and Azerbaijan. Thanks to Mr. Gorbachev's political skill and his iron will, however, he came out of last weekend's emergency meeting of the Central Committee with more power than he ever had before.

But that power may not get him very far. He's got to enliven the Soviet Union's stagnant bureaucracy and apathetic work force. Even harder will be reconciling some seemingly impossible contradictions. His country's economy must become more efficient at everything from getting potatoes to grocery shelves to catching up with the latest computer technology. But that would require concessions to free-market pricing and decentralized decision making. Mr.

Gorbachev says that's what he wants, and a top aide called this week for more experiments with capitalist-style economics.

Sounds great. But such changes, after years of rigid controls, carry a cost. Food and housing become more expensive, and workers in over-staffed industries get fired; the ones who stay work harder. Inflation rises. All this is especially painful to people used to a protective government. Such problems recently led Chinese leaders, also officially committed to injecting a dose of capitalism into their economy, to announce they're slowing the pace of change.

Change will also be hard to achieve without an open clash of competing ideas and philosophies. Yet Mr. Gorbachev left the impression with this most recent meeting that openness in the future may be permissible only as long as it's useful to him and his policies. By removing many of his critics from their positions of influence, Mr. Gorbachev indicated that he no longer will accept criticism of his ideas of restructuring. He also seemed to be saying that he doesn't want other Kremlin leaders competing on an equal basis.

Mr. Gorbachev realizes that the Soviet Union today is interesting chiefly as an example of advanced arteriosclerosis. He also realizes that everday Russians have had it with a Third World standard of living imposed upon them in the interests of idelological purity and of maintaining a first-class military. But despite Mr. Gorbachev's new ideas, his agenda still rests on an autocratic system and a highly centralized bureaucracy. And that sounds very much like a recipe for more stagnation, not for revolutionary change.

The Oregonian

Portland, OR, October 2, 1988

Andrei A. Gromyko once said that Mikhail S. Gorbachev had a nice smile but iron teeth. President Gromyko just found out how hard those iron teeth bite. Friday came the news that Gromyko, adviser to Soviet leaders back to Josef Stalin, would retire from the Politburo. This clears the way for the general secretary to become president.

Gromyko's ouster was one of a dizzying number of other unexpected changes. Another holdover from earlier regimes, Mikhail S. Solomentsev, also left posts in the Politburo and Party Control Commission. And Gorbachev's chief rival and the Kremlin's No. 2 man, Yegor K. Ligachev, was demoted. The most puzzling departure was that of Anatoly F. Dobrynin, one-time ambassador to Washington and until Friday the party foreign affairs secretary. Dobrynin was an architect of Gorbachev's new political thought and behind the general secretary's wooing of Western public opinion.

According to Soviet experts contacted by The Oregonian, the Kremlin shakeup looks at first crack like a strengthening of Gorbachev's position from what it was at last June's party conference when such changes were expected. According to Leon Aaron of the Heritage Foundation, Friday's move even enhanced the general secretary's position over what it was as recently as two weeks ago. Then he was under fire for the failure of perestroika to put food on Soviet shelves or cut waiting lines, as well as for his inability to control Russia's ethnic disruptions.

There's no doubt that Gorbachev has solidified his support. As Richard Staar, director of the Hoover Institution's International Studies Program, remarked, perestroika can succeed only if Gorbachev establishes control over and cuts back the Soviet bureaucacy. The departure or demotion of perestroika's enemies may allow him to do that.

Still, Gorbachev may have consolidated his position only for now. In what the American Enterprise Institute's Thomas Robinson says could have been a preventive strike against an impending assault by Kremlin hardliners, Gorbachev apparently could not vanquish his opposition. Ligachev remains in the government as minister of agriculture — a key to perestroika's success if the post has real power. Dobrynin's departure may have been the price Gorbachev had to pay to Kremlin hardliners.

In other words, Gorbachev's enemies live, and true consolidation may only come if the general secretary can translate the theories of perestroika into full meat cases and grocery shelves, and soon. For the United States, that means continued uncertainty about the leadership of the world's other superpower.

'All those in favor of giving comrade Gorbachev considerably more power . . .'

Soviet Parliament Backs Constitutional Changes

The Supreme Soviet, the U.S.S.R.'s nominal parliament, Dec. 1, 1988 approved changes in the Soviet constitution that would reorganize the nation's political structure in 1989. The vote came at the end of a three-day session. The approval came amid a backdrop of a nationalist political challenge from the Baltic region and worsening ethnic violence in the Transcaucasus region. The unrest was a major topic of debate among the legislators.

The constitutional changes had been proposed by General Secretary Mikhail S. Gorbachev at the opening of the Communist Party conference in June. (See pp. 42-47.) In a speech to the legislators Nov. 29, Gorbachev had asserted that the constitutional revision was necessary to "exclude the possibility of any part of the state machinery getting beyond the control of the people and their representatives."

Addressing the nationalism issue, Gorbachev promised that the changes would give the republics more "independence...The strength of the union must rely on the strength of its constituent republics as sovereign socialist states."

The key proposal was the transformation of the current 1,500-member Supreme Soviet – an essentially passive body that translated party dictates into law – into a more representative bicameral legislature with genuine powers. The upper house of the new legislature, to be known as the Congress of People's Deputies, would have 2,250 members, 1,500 would be elected at the local and regional levels. The remaining 750 would be chosen by party organizations, youth groups, unions and popular fronts. The 400-450 members of the lower house, which would take the name Supreme Soviet, were to be picked by the Congress.

Since Gorbachev had assumed the presidency in October, the reorganization would mean a further consolidation of his control over the Soviet ruling structure. Soviet critics argued that, contrary to enhancing "democratization," the reorganization would serve to concentrate power in the hands of a single figure.

The New York Times

New York, NY, December 2, 1988

A real national legislature with clearly stipulated powers ... unfettered debate ... a 10-year limit on holding office ... contested elections ... an independent judiciary. These are among the departures in what Mikhail Gorbachev calls "a rule-of-law state" made possible by "the direct involvement of the Soviet people in politics."

Moscow ratifies these changes even as reports come from the Caucasus of 100,000 Armenians and Azerbaijanis fleeing their homes in fear of further violent ethnic clashes.

The Soviet leader pushes ahead with glasnost and "democratization" despite the risks and challenges to Moscow's central authority and to Communist Party control. The moves seem to reflect the conviction that perestroika, economic reform, cannot succeed without a much greater measure of freedom. Mr. Gorbachev and his colleagues are taking big chances in an experiment Americans can only applaud.

Loosening the reins has led to the turmoil in the Caucasus, and assertions of autonomy in the Baltic republics. Mr. Gorbachev has handled these situations gingerly, on the eve of his first visit to New York. And he has dramatically underlined his intention to plow ahead with yet another glasnost landmark — ending decades of jamming Radio Liberty, the Russian-language service of the Munich-based, U.S.-financed Radio Free Europe.

Thus millions of Soviet citizens will now have freer access to the uncensored news coverage of their own internal affairs given by Radio Free Europe, as distinguished from the Voice of America, whose broadcasts have not been jammed for two years.

While rejecting demands that republics get a veto over laws passed by a parliament yet to be established, Mr. Gorbachev has not cut off the debate. His remarks have been conciliatory. In his speech this week he called for more, not less discussion: "Indeed, can there be anything more revealing than public debates in which the candidates parry questions, put forth their views and, if you like, show their worth?"

Still, in weighing the claims for the new Soviet charter, the wary will recall the famous Stalin Constitution of 1936, which also seemed to promise freedom but under Communist tutelage. The reality was sardonically described then by a Soviet cynic: "No elections could be fairer. They put up the candidates, and we elect them."

The "they" are still there, tens of thousands of party officials at all levels of government, in every plant, office, regiment and collective farm. But what is dramatically different is Mr. Gorbachev's attitude. He is reaching outside the party, to the people. In a totalitarian state, that's not only a bold idea; it's revolutionary.

In his first years in power, Mr. Gorbachev tried to bring about needed economic reforms principally by removing the old clique from the upper party echelons. When that proved insufficient, he moved against the party bureaucracy. Now he pushes deeper still, against ingrained popular resistance to change and toward an unprecedented and perhaps unachievable mixed dictatorial-democratic system.

The Honolulu Advertiser

Honolulu, HI, December 1, 1988

Just 50 years ago, the Soviet Union's three Baltic republics — Estonia, Latvia and Lithuania — were free. So it's no surprise that their people are among the Soviet citizens most outspoken in demanding more local autonomy and less centralized control from Moscow.

Last week the top-level Presidium of the Supreme Soviet, chaired by Soviet President Mikhail Gorbachev, rejected Estonia's "declaration" of limited sovereignty, which included the right to review all new Soviet laws.

While that predictable response was a setback, it was not the end of a festering problem. This week, in a compromise, Gorbachev told the Supreme Soviet, or parliament, that he would try to accommodate the Soviet republics' desire for autonomy.

For example, Gorbachev is now proposing to give all 15 republics stronger representation in one house of parliament, the Soviet of Nationalities. And he proposed creating a special commission to settle the division of powers between the central government and the republics.

But Gorbachev is also stressing the economic unity of the Soviet Union and emphasizing that the country would move toward greater cooperation among the republics, not less, in the name of economic reform.

No Moscow leader would last long who permitted a satellite nation to leave the Soviet orbit, much less so if an integral republic won real independence.

So this is the United States' dilemma. We favor greater freedom for Soviet citizens who desire it. But we also believe success for Gorbachev's *glasnost* (openness) and *perestroika* (reorganization) reforms are to our long-term advantage.

If hard-line Soviet leaders believe the empire is unraveling, a backlash against Gorbachev will certainly result.

If we encourage the Baltic peoples to push too hard for independence, the Soviet reaction could be the heavy-handed repression visited upon Hungary, Czechoslovakia and Poland. That is something we would be unable to prevent — or stop.

The Atlanta Journal
THE ATLANTA CONSTITUTION
Atlanta, GA, December 6, 1988

Back in 1936, Josef Stalin produced the illusion of a constitution that, in fact, gave all power to the party rather than to the people. At long last, that gross distortion, that landmark in Soviet newspeak, has been altered, perhaps dramatically so, after three days of spirited, high-level give-and-take — and even dissenting votes — in Moscow.

Last week's constitutional conclave was no mere attorney's exercise, though Mikhail Gorbachev as the Soviet's only party boss ever to be trained for the law has an understandable hankering common to those so trained to tidy up the legal structure.

Mr. Gorbachev's intent clearly is to cut through the overgrowth of the Communist bureaucracy, which has taken to day-to-day Soviet decision-making and long-term policy formulation the way a wisteria winds itself, ultimately fatally, around its host tree.

So, with the changes, the Soviets have the makings of a genuine legislative body that genuinely debates issues before it, an independent judiciary, contested elections, even checks and balances like a two-term limit for public officeholders. All of these are worthy institutions in and of themselves, but merely grafting them to an innately dictatorial system hardly means the beginning of a democratic transformation.

Much depends on how the new tools are used. The changes do allow Mr. Gorbachev, having already reshaped the leadership at the Politburo level, to penetrate down deeply into the resistant, multi-layered bureaucracy and to force its cooperation in his essential economic restructuring program. Trickle-down perestroika, as some cynical analysts are calling it in Moscow.

Unhappily for Mr. Gorbachev, he must contend with fundamental contradictions. He wants to strip defenders of party privilege of their ability to obstruct him; yet in investing his office with the legal muscle to do so, he opens himself or his successors to all-too-alluring and corrupting influences. He wants to diffuse power to the level of the local soviets for more efficient, informed decision-making; yet his promises of restructuring are seen by some frustrated minorities as an invitation to secede, which, as Estonia knows, it clearly is not.

Mr. Gobachev works without a net, with little leeway for missteps or time to produce results — a sobering thought for his American hosts on the eve of his visit to New York. For those who question the wisdom of our cooperation with a man who yearns for a confident, better-managed and more productive Soviet Union, let them compare that with the current alternative: an enemy that feels inferior, is struggling to sustain itself and claims world attention only because of its nuclear arsenal.

One way lies a competition Americans should have no reason to fear. The other way lies the potential for confrontation that could give us nightmares.

The San Diego Union
San Diego, CA, December 2, 1988

Many Americans have come to equate Mikhail Gorbachev's campaign of *glasnost*, or openness, with freedom of expression in the Western sense. That concept, which was defined most clearly by the 18th Century Age of Enlightenment, enshrines free speech as a virtual absolute in democratic societies.

But the emerging Soviet policy of *glasnost* bears scant resemblance to the First Amendment, as the Kremlin's announcement this week regarding Alexander Solzhenitsyn illustrates.

Mr. Solzhenitsyn's harsh critique of modern life has offended not only the Russian authorities but also many Westerners. Yet the novelist's strident condemnation of American ways has not prevented his works from becoming best-sellers in this country as well as elsewhere around the globe.

The same would be true in the Soviet Union if publication of Mr. Solzhenitsyn's works were not prohibited by the government. Earlier this week, the Kremlin's top ideologist shattered any hope that *glasnost* would tolerate the iconoclastic views of Mr. Solzhenitsyn, who lives in forced exile in Vermont. Politburo member Vadim A. Medvedev held a press conference to declare that circulation of the writer's books will remain permanently banned in his homeland.

The decision surprised some observers in the Soviet Union because Mr. Solzhenitsyn is best known for his scathing attacks on the Stalin era. Under General Secretary Gorbachev, Moscow has encouraged an open reappraisal of monumental crimes committed during the reign of terror of Joseph Stalin. One of the most compelling indictments of Stalin's rule is *The Gulag Archipelago*, Mr. Solzhenitsyn's most famous work.

As explained by Mr. Medvedev, however, the writer's criticism of Vladimir Lenin, the founder of the Communist upheaval in Russia, is "in fundamental contradiction to our social and political order, to our ideology, to our attitudes toward our history, our revolution and Lenin." To permit Soviet citizens to read Mr. Solzhenitsyn "is to undermine the foundations on which our present life rests."

Such are the rather narrow limits of freedom of thought, *glasnost*-style. Lenin and his teachings remain above reproach. Any Soviet citizen who violates this standard still risks a trip to the gulag himself. Meantime, Mr. Solzhenitsyn is about to celebrate his 70th birthday in exile, grateful perhaps for the American-style openness he enjoys in the West.

Lincoln Journal
Lincoln, NE, December 6, 1988

Whether the Soviet Union in its 15-republic constituent parts is more of a "democratic" system now with adoption of major governmental reforms — including "socialist checks and balances" within the context of a one-party system — is pure guesswork. It depends upon one's definition of democracy. From the North American perspective, there is next to nothing in the history of the Russian empire which fairly can be described as a strong, grassroots democratic tradition.

Always at the center of the Russian and subsequently the Soviet experience is an autocratic and hopefully benign central power, unilaterally imposing its will throughout the social organization. One does not find past decades of local Russian or Soviet self-government, or essential regional independence or self-sufficiency during which democratic values and habits as we know them were bred into the popular bone.

This does not apply, of course, to the luckless Baltic states (and now republics), incorporated into the Soviet Union against their will nearly 50 years ago by aggression and treachery. We speak here mainly of old Russia and the Asian regions.

President and General Secretary of the Communist Party Mikhail S. Gorbachev successfully stuffed reform from above down the Soviet Union's throat last week. He called the changes a major step toward "a new, democratic Soviet Union . . . In this revolutionary period, we are blowing up the old structure."

Let us hope. The old structure lodged a weight of oppression on the common people in social contract exchange for basic physical protection and economic existence. We have already seen how quickly long-constrained personal self-expression broke to the surface all across the Soviet Union once Gorbachev's daring policy of glasnost was implemented.

The Soviet people are now letting off steam; endlessly, according to recent visitors.

Gorbachev shrewdly knows that the dynamism he wants to inject into the turgid, failing Soviet system is impossible without easing up on human rights, without taking economic risks, without confronting the entrenched power of the Communist party heirarchy. The constitutional reforms rammed home last week therefore represent an historic initiative, within the Russian and Soviet dimensions.

But painting them as democratic in the Western tradition is pure Madisonski Avenue stuff.

The
Des Moines Register

*Des Moines, IA,
December 2, 1988*

Mikhail Gorbachev has discovered the danger of mixing freedom and autocracy.

Violent clashes in the southern Soviet republics of Azerbaijan and Armenia have left at least 20 people dead in recent days.

Estonia, the tiny Baltic state that came under Soviet rule during World War II, meantime has challenged Moscow's authority by declaring that its laws and constitution would prevail over those of the Soviet Union.

Both conflicts go to the heart of Gorbachev's fundamental dilemma: opening the Soviet economy without losing political control.

Estonia and the other Baltic states are among the most economically advanced of the 15 Soviet republics.

If allowed to prosper, they would serve as models for the rest of the country. That may be why Gorbachev didn't order tanks into Estonia.

Instead, he went on national television to rebut Estonia's claim, saying it was unconstitutional to override Soviet laws and the constitution. He then praised the republic for voicing its concerns, saying that "in Estonia, just like everywhere else in the country, the process of perestroika (restructuring) is under way."

Gorbachev then noted that the key to resolving problems of interethnic relations lies in "harmonizing relations between the center (Moscow) and the republics."

The battle between Moscow and the republics is reminiscent of the fight in the United States over states' rights vs. federal rights. This country, eventually, allowed autonomy to the states insofar as they do nothing to undermine the unity of the nation.

In the Soviet Union, likewise, officials seem to be pressing for limited autonomy for the republics in such areas as language, culture and decentralized control of economic planning. But these measures fall short of the right to secede from the union.

That may not satisfy Estonia. During a meeting of the Supreme Soviet, the nation's parliament, the president of Estonia criticized Gorbachev's plan for political reform. There is no political system that suits each republic, said Arnold Ruutel, "so we have developed our own."

That the Estonian leader dared to voice such criticisms, in itself, indicates a dramatic departure from the Soviet Union of the past. How far Gorbachev will let that dissent translate into structural political changes remains to be seen.

©1988 HERBLOCK
Washington Post

'When I learn tricks, I expect yum-yums.'

Portland Press Herald

Portland, ME, December 1, 1988

Dramatic evidence of Soviet leader Mikhail Gorbachev's effort to open his society has been mounting all year. Among the most dramatic have been Gorbachev's proposals to establish a rule of law and restructure the power of Soviet leadership, tolerate some ethnic dissent, give new emphasis to individual effort and show a willingness to allow a measure of public criticism. So far, so good.

Criticism that goes to the heart of Soviet social and economic repression, however, remains off limits. For evidence of that we need only look to the Kremlin's continuing ban on works by Alexander Solzhenitsyn, widely regarded as the greatest living Soviet writer.

To allow Solzhenitsyn's searing works on punishment and the intrusive control of human life in the Soviet Union to be published there "is to undermine the foundations on which our present life rests," Vadim A. Medvedev reaffirmed this week. Medvedev, described in reports from Moscow as "the top Kremlin ideologist," is the official keeper of the Communist Party line.

It is a post without parallel in this country. So, too, is the fear that an artist's view of truth, openly expressed, can topple the government. Were the fear shared here, we would have no such books as "The Grapes of Wrath," "The Red Badge of Courage," "Soul on Ice" or even "Uncle Tom's Cabin."

But we do. And that, as Robert Frost once said, has made all the difference.

THE ARIZONA REPUBLIC
Phoenix, AZ, December 1, 1988

THE more skeptical of Western Kremlin observers suggest that, while the furor over "political reform" in the Soviet Union is of passing interest, the day the government publishes a Moscow telephone book — well, that will be the time to take the reformist hoopla seriously.

The Supreme Soviet, what passes for a parliament, has been meeting this week to implement the political reforms the Communist Party adopted under Mikhail Gorbachev's tutelage last June. Coming on the heels of ethnic uprisings in Armenia and Azerbaijan and a declaration of autonomy in upstart Estonia, the meetings have been unusually rowdy, at least by the staid standards of that docile legislature.

What do these "reforms" mean? Some in the West have been aflutter over the anticipated establishment of a "Western-style parliament" when the Supreme Soviet votes today to dissolve itself. But as actress Tallulah Bankhead once remarked about an especially dull Broadway play, "There is less in this than meets the eye."

The Gorbachevization of the Soviet government amounts to superficial procedural changes that leave unchallenged the fundamental power of the Communist Party. Tinkering with the relationship of the party to the government might appear revolutionary in the context of Soviet history since 1917, but until the party's monopoly power is diluted by the legalization of competing political structures, the benefits of *perestroika* will be temporary.

Mr. Gorbachev has sought to replace the 1,500-member Supreme Soviet with a full-time elected legislature that will draft laws, engage in debate and hold meaningful votes. As now structured, the Supreme Soviet exists merely to rubber-stamp party decrees. This new legislature would be chosen by a 2,000-member Congress of Peoples' Deputies, which would be popularly elected by multiple-candidate ballots.

The trouble is that all candidates must be from the Communist Party, so it is difficult to see how this loosens significantly the party's grip on the government. Even more amusing, the new legislature, consisting entirely of party members, is being touted as a "Western-style parliament," though what one-party Western parliament these reports have in mind is not indicated.

Mr. Gorbachev was forced at the last moment to back away from some of his more controversial proposals — proposals that would have centralized yet more power in the presidency, which he assumed in October, and in the national parliament. Nonetheless, it probably is only a matter of time before the party finds new means to assert its control of the restructured government.

THE SACRAMENTO BEE
Sacramento, CA, December 3, 1988

"Reform is ripe and must be carried out without delay," Mikhail Gorbachev said. And so, even as blood flowed in ethnic strife in the streets of Armenia and Azerbaijan, the Supreme Soviet this week approved the first phase of Gorbachev's sweeping experiment in new forms of Soviet governance, a voyage with no clear destination and untold risks along the way.

For Americans accustomed to an image of the Soviet Union as an unchanging monolith, every day brings fresh astonishment: Gorbachev's efforts to pull the Communist Party bureaucracy back from day-to-day oversight of society, economy and government; the attempt to empower popularly elected legislatures; the open challenge to Moscow's authority from the Baltic republics, with Estonia bidding for "sovereignty" within the Soviet Union; the vigorous, open debate over Gorbachev's constitutional proposals and the dissenting voices on the final vote; the end to the jamming of foreign radio broadcasts.

No one can now doubt the determination behind Gorbachev's drive to use democratic devices to loosen the dead hand of bureaucracy on Soviet life. He has faced squarely the Soviet Union's central contradiction — modern, growing economies and dynamic technological innovation are impossible in centrally planned economies and Communist states that insist on a monopoly of information — and he has chosen to infuse a degree of freedom into Soviet society as a catalyst for change and growth.

But already Gorbachev's drive to resolve one contradiction has highlighted another: the inherent tension between the center and periphery in a multinational empire long held together by military force and terror. In Estonia, Latvia, Lithuania, Armenia, Azerbaijan, Georgia and the Ukraine, *glasnost* has been interpreted not just as permission to criticize Communist corruption and managerial incompetence, but as a license to air long-suppressed ethnic grievances against neighbors or to surface national aspirations of autonomy from Moscow's imperial rule.

Gorbachev has not created those contradictions; he has simply been bold enough to confront them. But in doing so, he has unleashed forces and aspirations that will not be easily controlled under the basic ground rules of continued Communist and Russian hegemony. Like the new governmental institutions he has created, Mikhail Gorbachev's present course is an improvisation.

"All of us are now learning our lessons," Gorbachev says. "All of us are in a school of democracy." If history is a guide, Russia's aptitude for reform is limited; Russian rulers have periodically planted hot-house blooms of modernity and liberalism only to have them shrivel up in the society's authoritarian permafrost. Because the alternative is international crisis and a return to the brutal darkness from which the Soviet Union is just emerging, the rest of the world must hope that Gorbachev and his supporters are more diligent and successful pupils than their forbearers.

Omaha World-Herald
Omaha, NE, December 5, 1988

The Supreme Soviet — the two-house parliament of the Soviet Union — has passed President Mikhail Gorbachev's constitutional reforms, 1,344 to 5. The result is a newly-fashioned presidency and a sort of national congress that will be elected March 26. This is part of Gorbachev's attempt to restructure the government, revitalize the economy and establish the rule of law in the nation's political life.

Creating a constitution that works is not easy. The Soviet Union has never had a real legally guaranteed constitution such as those in the Western democracies. The 1936 Soviet constitution of Josef Stalin, with its liberal guarantees of political and civil rights, bore little resemblance to actual conditions under the country's leaders from Stalin to Chernenko.

The oldest functioning constitution in the world is that of the United States. That the oldest constitution is only a little more than two centuries old gives some idea of the difficulty of preserving a functioning legal blueprint over time.

The new Soviet constitution could be the first true, legal, binding blueprint for government in the Soviet Union. It could lead to some of the same kinds of problems that America's Founding Fathers wrestled with. The relationship between the central government and regional governments. The separation and balance of powers. Federalism, suffrage and the role of the courts.

Like constitution-makers in other nations, Gorbachev and his supporters must do their best to see that the document on paper can survive the challenges of real people and real issues. The military, the Communist Party bureaucrats and the KGB are still powerful elements in Soviet society. They have seen how raw power can be used to neutralize legal guarantees in the past and may be tempted to use similar tactics in the future.

Gorbachev and his political allies face a formidable task under conditions much less favorable than those in 18th and 19th century America.

Rockford Register Star

Rockford, IL, December 6, 1988

Eleven dead. More than a hundred injured. Some 1,200 under arrest for curfew violations. What does all this spell? It spells G-L-A-S-N-O-S-T. And it spells trouble for Mikhail Gorbachev, the Soviet Union's top boss.

The statistics derive from the Soviets' southern Caucasus republics where ethnic bad blood has reigned for years between Armenians and the Azerbaijanis.

Once Gorbachev loosed glasnost upon the Soviet Union, his policy of openness was taken literally by various constituencies. They include Estonia which tried to declare its independence totally from the Soviets, only to hear a big "nyet" from Gorbachev. They include restive Lithuania.

But the "troubles" brewing between Armenia and Azerbaijan started last February with 34 Armenians dead. Since then, the fighting has become more sanguine. The latest rupture is told in the statistics above.

What Armenia wanted to do, only to be denied permission from Moscow, was to annex the Armenian enclave of Nagonor-Karabakh from Azerbaijan. The Azerbaijanis also said "nyet."

Ethnic traditions are not the only cause of rivalry between Armenians and Azerbaijanis. Armenians nurture a Christian religion. The Azerbaijanis are Moslems.

So there is this testy, murderous difference between the two. And there is the larger problem of a Soviet that gobbled up these little states long ago, including their strife.

Now it surfaces and the military go in with rifles loaded. If World War I could start with the assassination of an archduke in Sarajevo, Yugoslavia — which it did, then do not underestimate what the Armenians could trigger in the Soviet Union. The tremors could reach as high as Gorbachev's job. They could spread unrest to satellite states such as Poland and Czechoslovakia. That's why the world stands watch — and waits.

BUFFALO EVENING NEWS

Buffalo, NY, December 7, 1988

THE SUPREME SOVIET, a rubber-stamp parliamentary body, has traditionally met for only a few days a year, when it approves — without debate or dissent — the decisions that have been made by the Communist Party hierarchy.

That is likely to change under President Mikhail Gorbachev's reform program, which the Supreme Soviet now has formally approved.

The reforms were shaped by an unusually open and spontaneous party conference in Moscow last summer, and the debate and dissent evident at last week's meeting of the Supreme Soviet indicated that the new spirit had begun to alter that body. Whether the reforms will result in real freedom for the Soviet people remains an open question.

On the surface, the reforms look promising. There will be elections with more than one candidate for each position, and a parliament that will elect the president and take a more active role. Some power is supposed to be shifted from the Communist Party to elected legislative bodies, both nationally and in the various Soviet republics.

Possibly significant in terms of shaking up the entrenched bureaucracy of the party is a provision mandating a limit of two five-year terms for all senior officials, including Gorbachev. Throughout the 71-year history of the Soviet Union, all leaders have ruled, like the czars, until they died or were deposed.

How well the new political system works cannot be known until the national election scheduled for next March. Meanwhile, Gorbachev's entire program of political and economic reform faces threats that he may not have foreseen.

The freer discussion allowed under Gorbachev's policy of "glasnost," or openness, has unleashed protests and demands for more independence from the Baltic states of Estonia, Latvia and Lithuania, which were independent countries until they were seized by Stalin in 1940.

The other Soviet satellites in Eastern Europe may also protest against Soviet domination.

There is also a new restiveness among the various non-Russian nationalities that make up the Soviet population. Ethnic problems have brought mass rioting and deaths in Azerbaijan and Armenia.

In addition, Gorbachev faces problems in the economic sector, where he is depending on his new use of individual initiatives to invigorate the failing Soviet economy. There have been no dramatic gains so far.

Some old-line communists in the hierarchy no doubt yearn for the simplicity of the old ways, under which all decisions were made in the Kremlin and any sign of dissent was brutally crushed.

Gorbachev is visiting the United States and the United Nations this week with his position strengthened as a result of the ratification of his reforms. His skillful handling of the reform program and his political opponents make him supreme at home for the moment. But if his reforms do not produce results, opposition to him can be expected to grow.

THE CHRISTIAN SCIENCE MONITOR
Boston, MA, December 2, 1988

MIKHAIL GORBACHEV wanted the Baltics to be a showcase for *perestroika*, a place where restructuring is working. And by Soviet standards the three small republics have done well.

But a loosened grip by the Kremlin freed up more than productivity; it also unleashed nationalistic feelings that have simmered in Estonia, Latvia, and Lithuania ever since they were absorbed into the Soviet Union a half-century ago.

Political rumblings for autonomy have reverberations in Armenia, Soviet Georgia, the Ukraine, Central Asia, and other parts of Mr. Gorbachev's sprawling domain. The violent conflict between the Armenian and Azerbaijani republics has flared again in the last few days, resulting in 18 deaths, by the latest reports.

The Soviet leader feels these tremors as he rushes to complete a rebuilding of his country's political structure – a structure designed to consolidate executive authority and give real power to the legislature. The Communist Party's Central Committee has given its OK to the plan, and the Supreme Soviet – the country's current rubber-stamp national legislature – followed its lead yesterday. In a remarkable break with the past, however, five delegates voted against parts of the Gorbachev package; and 27 abstained. All the dissenters were from the Baltics.

Gorbachev sees his efforts as crucial, giving him the ability to cut through bureaucratic sludge and carry out reform, and giving the Soviet people a taste of democracy through elective bodies with genuine policy-making authority. Others, such as Andrei Sakharov, have warned that the ultimate result could be the opposite of democracy – a dictatorial executive who accumulates power instead of sharing it. The country's ingrained, repressive political culture gives that dark vision credence.

The Estonians, joined by the Armenians and the Georgians, are worried about centralization, too. They see Gorbachev's plan as an encroachment on the rights of their republics.

Under the Soviet Constitution, those rights have been extensive – on paper. They include the right to secede. Of course no republic has ever been allowed to exercise these rights, though Estonia seemed to be putting them to the test with its recent declaration of sovereignty.

Gorbachev declared that declaration "totally unacceptable." He took particular exception to the Estonians' effort to revive private property, making clear that such an idea is still heresy in the cradle of communism. Gorbachev's speech to the Supreme Soviet, however, took a conciliatory approach, offering the republics greater representation in the new lawmaking apparatus and putting some legislative restraints on his new presidential powers.

The Baltic nationalists were undeterred. Lithuanian President Vitautas Astrauskas proclaimed, "We are tired of living under orders from above." The Estonian party leader, Vaino Valjas, asserted, "We will not retreat."

Under present circumstances, it's hard to know which direction is a retreat. The constitutional changes being pushed by Gorbachev may do away with the hollow powers now accorded republics, but they may end up giving republics more actual autonomy over their economic destinies. Politics is another matter. It's doubtful anything like the kind of quasi-independence desired by the Estonians will be allowed.

Reformers in the Baltics have pursued their path of separate development under the banner of *perestroika*. Gorbachev puts forth his plan for a revamped government under the same banner – yet his goals and the Estonians' are colliding.

The Estonians, unfortunately, may be about to learn that what *perestroika* giveth, it can also take away.

The Charlotte Observer
Charlotte, NC, Decmember 4, 1988

There has been astonishing liberalization in the Soviet Union under Mikhail Gorbachev. Soviet citizens now have freedoms scarcely imaginable a few years ago, and the reforms continue. Their country last week even stopped jamming Radio Liberty (as it stopped jamming Voice of America broadcasts in 1987).

Glasnost is real; let us hope it endures. But it also has limits, as the Kremlin also demonstrated a few days go in dashing hopes that the works of Soviet exile Alexander Solzhenitsyn might be published there soon. "To publish Solzhenitsyn's work is to undermine the foundations on which our present life rests," said top party ideologist Vadim Medvedev.

Freedom of speech and press remain a gift, not a right, in the Soviet Union, and only as broad as the regime allows. The debate in the Soviet Union is about reforming and perfecting communism, not about abolishing it. The challenge from Alexander Solzhenitsyn is more fundamental.

The regime's objection to him is not merely political, but almost theological. For people who treat Lenin as an icon, Mr. Solzhenitsyn's harsh portrait of him and his system is blasphemy. Whether the leadership's attachment to Leninism is a matter of faith or expedience, what is at stake for them is the legitimacy of the Soviet system.

Though the Soviet Union appears to be becoming dramatically less threatening in many ways, it is still a very alien political culture. That does not make the substantive reforms less real, less welcome or less hopeful. But Mr. Medvedev's blunt remarks from very high in the Soviet leadership are a reminder that Soviet democraticization is not yet democracy. The stark difference between Western and Soviet systems, and the flood of conflicting signals from within that still-mysterious country, combine to make rea understanding both more difficult and more important.

THE ▰ SUN
Baltimore, MD, December 5, 1988

Whatever the Soviet constitution said was the system of government, this past half-century, did not matter. The party ruled, with its own massive bureaucracy. Government was a hollow shell of formalism And the party's leader intimidated or tyraﹰﹰ it with the secret police. That was the system Josef Stalin devised. It is what his successor Mikhail S. Gorbachev has formally overthrown and replaced, with his new blueprint rubber-stamped by the Supreme Soviet, in the Stalinist manner.

Inside the Soviet Union and out, analysts and observers and ordinary citizens need time to decide whether they think the system has changed, or only the formalism. Now there will be a powerful government chief under law. It will be Mr. Gorbachev, who will remain general secretary of the Communist Party. People will call him by his governmental title, which will translate as president. But there will be confusion whether Mr. Gorbachev's word goes because he will be president, or because he is general secretary, which is what Stalin was.

The new system will call for contested and presumably honest elections of 2,250 people to a Congress of People's Deputies, which will meet annually as an electoral college. Where the current 1,500 Supreme Soviet meets annually or infrequently to approve decisions and hear speeches, the new Supreme Soviet will have only 542 members, chosen by the Congress of People's Deputies from its own ranks, who will meet often as a working legislature.

The government will be a real government, Mr. Gorbachev says. It could be a safety valve to make the regime more responsive to public opinion behind the backs of the Communist Party bureaucracy. Or it could be no more than a new formalism disguising the massive power at Mr. Gorbachev's fingertips. Mr. Gorbachev calls it a return to the system that Vladimir I. Lenin constructed before Stalin perverted it. The official creed is that Stalinism is dead, Leninism lives.

Mr. Gorbachev comes to dine with President Reagan and President-elect Bush Wednesday fortified by the enactment of his constitutional changes as well as the usual promises of more open debate and liberalized emigration, while troubled by ethnic unrest and the latest hijacking. A little democracy is called a dangerous thing. Mr. Gorbachev is trying to save communism by introducing a little democracy.

Soviets to Rewrite History Textbooks

Long-held concepts of ideology were reshaped as previously veiled chapters of history were uncovered. It was reported in the West June 1, 1988 that Soviet elementary and secondary schools had canceled final exams so that textbooks could be rewritten to conform to the new versions of history and new concepts of economics.

Izvestia, the government newspaper, June 10 said in a front-page editorial that the old Soviet textbooks were filled with "lies...The guilt of those who fooled with generations [of students] is gigantic and without measure." It was reported in the West Oct. 19 that students for the first time were being encouraged to openly discuss shortcomings in the Soviet system, past and present.

The Wichita Eagle-Beacon

Wichita, KS, June 15, 1988

THE Soviet Union has decided to restore the deleted periods in its history. Since the 1917 revolution, Soviet history has been subjected to cuts and edits. It has now become a question for Soviets as to what is true and what is false.

Soviet history books have been thrown out. Soviet schools' customary year-end written history exam has been canceled. This has affected millions of school-age children who will take a revised oral exam. This is an evident upheaval. This is the type of progress about which the Soviets usually never openly speak.

But General Secretary Mikhail Gorbachev has promised a policy of glasnost (openness) and perestroika (restructuring). He has been open about the problem in Soviet history, and he is attempting a reconstruction of that history.

The problem isn't resolved yet, though, by any means. The Politburo in the past either has ignored or re-written history. There had been some optimism in the 1950s as well. At that time, Soviet leader Nikita Khrushchev was making history with his revelations about the Stalin era and he was widely acclaimed. He had a prominent place in Soviet history books. Later in 1964, when Mr. Khruschchev was replaced by Leonid Brezhnev as the Soviet leader, Mr. Khruschchev disappeared from the written page of Soviet textbooks. Then, later in 1987, Mr. Khrushchev again was acclaimed as the "brave leader" who had condemned the crimes of Stalin.

It is possible that Mr. Gorbachev's perestroika could meet the same fate as Mr. Khrushchev's historical review. Mr. Gorbachev's reform program has resistance from mid-level party and government officals.

Mr. Khruschchev, while the Soviet leader in 1956, canceled Soviet history exams. In 1988, Soviet schools once again are unsettled. There has been too much alternating between fact and fiction in history textbooks for some Soviet people to know what to think. Some Soviet children aren't troubled by the change in their history books. They are adjusting. It is a part of their life. But other children are confused.

Study at school is seen as the primary duty of Soviet children. This generation of children depended on their schools to help fulfill that duty. The constant reshaping of history has become a question for some of these children. They ask what is pretense and what is truth. Mr. Gorbachev has asked for mutual trust between the Soviet Union and the United States. The next generation of Soviet citizens may have a difficult time in respecting and understanding the objective of mutual trust.

Omaha World-Herald

Omaha, NE, July 28, 1988

Newspeak is not dead. George Orwell's description of the tortured thought processes of totalitarianism still has validity.

A case in point: A Soviet delegation to a conference on Eastern Europe conceded recently that Josef Stalin broke the Yalta agreements and precipitated the Cold War by seizing Eastern Europe after World War II. But the delegation would not admit that communism existed in Eastern Europe because of Stalin's actions.

The delegation was able to take the first steps toward admitting Stalin's role but refused to call into question the legitimacy of the Communist regimes in Eastern Europe. Glasnost has its limits, apparently. Yet if Stalin did not impose communism by force on Poland, Czechoslovakia, Hungary, East Germany and other Iron Curtain countries, who did?

Both the Hungarians and the Czechs — in 1956 and 1968, respectively — broke with the Stalinist system, more or less with ease — until Soviet tanks rolled in to reassert control. These facts are widely known, even to members of the Soviet delegation.

The truth is that communism has operated much like a fundamentalist religion in the Soviet Union. It has its theories of historical inevitability; its sainted founder; its dogmas, martyrs, pogroms, holy wars. To admit that it has no legitimacy in Eastern Europe is to deny sacred dogma — that communism is an inevitable historic force, the last phase of human history and the highest form of human society.

With these dogmas shattered, the system built by Stalin and preserved by his successors would be exposed for what it is: a shabby form of social fascism imposed by a murderous dictator on nations and peoples who wanted no part of it.

The final irony is that the Soviet delegates argued that any change in the status of Eastern European countries would be a violation of the Helsinki Accord of 1975, which calls for non-interference in the affairs of sovereign European countries. The delegates admitted that Stalin broke the Yalta agreement, which was supposed to mean exactly the same thing — non-interference. Newspeak was never more blatant.

The Hartford Courant

Hartford, CT, June 17, 1988

The ideological fermentation in the Soviet Union has produced another stunning development: The government decided that the version of history taught to schoolchildren is so inaccurate that they wouldn't be given final examinations in the subject this year. The once supposedly infallible Soviet regime now seems eager to proclaim its fallibility.

Canceling the tests was explained as a way to stop the transmission of historical untruths. "The guilt of those who deluded one generation after another, poisoning their minds and souls with lies, is immeasurable," said the newspaper Izvestia. It praised the cancellation as evidence of a "triumph of new thinking" and a "readiness to discard the traditional approaches."

These are heady days in Moscow, and ideas appear, disappear and dart through the air so bewilderingly that it's hard to know exactly what to make of the government's decision. It might be little more than window-dressing for glasnost, the policy of openness championed by General Secretary Mikhail S. Gorbachev. Calling attention to the country's repressive past could build support for glasnost and Mr. Gorbachev at the important party conference this month.

Yet there's reason to think that calling off the exams signifies more than shrewd politics. By denouncing and discarding the old history curriculum, Soviet officials have promised a fresh and presumably much more honest examination of their country's painful and often tragic past. If they break their word, their credibility will suffer, as will the image of glasnost, a movement upon which Mr. Gorbachev's future is likely to depend.

What's most startling about this event isn't the regime's public confession that what generations of Soviet schoolchildren were taught wasn't entirely true. It's the implication, obvious to all Soviet citizens, that their government systematically misled them for decades, that it subordinated the truth to its political interests.

How thoroughly the authors of Soviet history books will overhaul their descriptions of their country's past remains to be seen. But it's already clear that in allowing, if not instigating, this revolutionary approach to writing and teaching about history, Mr. Gorbachev has taken another step of breathtaking boldness.

Los Angeles Times

Los Angeles, CA, June 15, 1988

It helps to have some questions when you are groping for answers. In the Soviet Union, which is struggling to distinguish facts from the party folklore of its 70 years under communism, that is not an easy combination to put together. So 53 million Soviet students got no final history examination this year because the shortage of questions is almost as severe as the shortage of answers about Soviet life and leadership since the revolution of 1917.

It may help to think of the difficulties that Soviet history teachers are laboring under in the following way: Imagine how teachers in this country would react to revelations that Woodrow Wilson was addicted to arriving secretly at secret covenants and Winston Churchill was a German spy. Imagine how the teachers would react if they knew that there was more—much more.

The root of the Soviet school dilemma is that what is in the newspapers and what Soviet General Secretary Mikhail S. Gorbachev is saying on television bear no important relation to what is in the history books. And skipping one year's history test is in many ways the least important manifestation of the way that kind of intellectual and literary turmoil is affecting all of Soviet society.

The most fundamental accommodation for the history books so far is the re-creation of hero Josef V. Stalin as a tyrant who turned the revolution that he inherited from V. I. Lenin into a bloodbath. The West had known about Stalin for decades. Many Soviets did, too, but they could neither write nor talk about it openly until now. At another level, the books must accommodate the party's lifting of men like Nicolai I. Bukharin, once regarded by Lenin as his possible successor, out of the shadows of history. Stalin ordered him shot as a traitor.

The rehabilitation of Stalin's victims continues apace, with four more cleared this week of the accusations that Stalin made against them. Among them were Lev B. Kamenev and Grigory E. Zino-

viev, who shared power with Stalin after Lenin's death until he nudged both men down the leadership ladder, finally ordering them shot in the 1930s.

It was even suggested in print in Moscow recently that Lenin himself made possible the use of terror as a tool of leadership in the Soviet Union because he did not stop it at the outset.

That in turn has led Soviet analysts, again in print, to question whether there is some congenital flaw in Marxism as practiced by Lenin and his successors that invites terror and dictatorship.

None of this could have happened without the policy of *glasnost*—sometimes translatable as *plain talk*—that Gorbachev has promoted as a means of getting ordinary Soviets involved in his efforts to restore momentum to the nation's sagging economy.

Gorbachev wants to hack away much of the nation's bureaucratic superstructure, give away much of the Communist Party's power over day-to-day operations of government and industry, and open up the system to more citizen participation. A combination of caution among ordinary people drummed into them during decades of tyranny and fear among bureaucrats of losing power has made his campaign a cliff-hanger for months.

In two weeks the Gorbachev campaign will come to the highest cliff of all, a national party congress—the first of its kind in nearly 50 years—that will give him, or withhold from him, the changes in law and custom that he needs to continue the reforms.

The congress is a test of the lessons of history that cannot be postponed until the new textbooks are written. It is a test that we hope Gorbachev passes, partly because a nation busy with its own domestic problems is less likely to be thinking in terms of conquest and partly because the Soviet people deserve whatever freedoms they can get—perhaps as a first step toward what the West would recognize as freedoms.

WORCESTER TELEGRAM

Worcester, MA, August 30, 1988

A letter printed in the Soviet newspaper Izvestia recently has been boiling up a tempest in the glasnost/perestroika teapot.

It was one of those little tidbits that has lent new fascination to the pastime of Kremlin-watching in these days of Soviet openness and restructuring. A librarian from the Crimea reported that library officials in major cities of the Ukraine had been ordered to purge their shelves of the writings of a number of pre-Gorbachev Soviet leaders along with writings by several ideologists whose ideas no longer conform to the party line.

The purge apparently is part of the official campaign to discredit the reputations and thinking of the past — particularly of the Brezhnev era, now described as "the period of stagnation."

Such a letter stirs conflicting reactions in the West. The apparent attempt to rewrite the history of the Brezhnev era evokes disturbing echoes of the intellectual purges of the past. Soviet history has been rewritten regularly to denounce former leaders and serve new ideological directives.

However, it would be naive to believe that the Soviet Union, or any totalitarian society, could shed all its bad habits in a few months or years. And to the extent that the proscribed writings are blatant propaganda, the order that they be removed could be seen as a hopeful sign of Moscow's broad commitment to the openness and restructuring Gorbachev is promoting.

There is also the question of the provenance of the letter: It might have been an unsolicited offering from a feisty librarian, but it also might have been published by Soviet authorities to drive home the message that the bad old days of Brezhnev have decisively given way to a new order.

But the most telling fact is that the letter was printed at all. Whether it was an official plant or a legitimate correspondence, we hope the dialogue it has provoked serves as a clear expression of new openness. If not, this episode is apt to be purged from the record when the history of the Gorbachev era is rewritten.

The Providence Journal

Providence, RI, September 3, 1988

Close observers of the Soviet scene continue to wonder whether Mikhail Gorbachev's professed desire for *glasnost* ("openness") will lead to a fundamental change in policy — a willingness to accept the truth about historical developments and to allow honest debate about current events.

Or is it primarily a new and more sophisticated means to accomplish a customary Kremlin practice — helping to erect a "cult of personality" around the current leader by denigrating the character and policies of his immediate predecessors?

A recent flap in the Moscow press raises this issue anew, but does little to help clarify the matter. According to a letter purportedly written by a librarian in the Crimea, which was published in the government's official newspaper *Izvestia*, public libraries have been directed to rid their collections of political and economic works written in the years leading up to Mr. Gorbachev's takeover of the Communist Party leadership in March 1985. The ostensible goal, according to the letter, is to remove the heaps of fraudulent and self-aggrandizing materials that had been published to inflate the ego and the reputation of the late Leonid Brezhnev.

Such a *ukase* from the Kremlin would surely be a dramatic stroke. But ridding Soviet libraries of materials that contain systematic propaganda, intentional distortions and outright falsifications would be a prophylactic task comparable to Hercules' effort to clean out the Augean stables. It would require junking virtually all works of history and social science published in the Soviet Union since the Bolsheviks seized power in 1917 — an unlikely prospect.

Indeed, the Soviet Culture Ministry immediately denied the veracity of the letter published by *Izvestia*. According to a spokeswoman, the instructions were not to remove all the Brezhnev-era materials, but to discard duplicate copies so as to free up shelf space for newer or previously restricted works.

That would be a more plausible command and a more commendable goal. As part of Mr. Gorbachev's ongoing campaign to impugn the Brezhnev era, those two decades now officially referred to as "the period of stagnation," towns, streets, buildings and the like all over the Soviet Union are being renamed. It would be farcical if library bookshelves were now to be restocked on the same principle of historical effacement and revenge. It would be no improvement to replace propaganda from the Brezhnev reign with propaganda, more fashionable but equally one-sided, from the Gorbachev era.

As a reader of *Sovietskaya Kultura* recently complained: "Blame everything on Brezhnev — is this really fair? For some reason, today's leadership is always good and the past leadership is always bad." Soviet citizens are all too familiar with this pattern; they are now demanding something different and better — the plain, unvarnished truth about the past and the present.

The Hartford Courant

Hartford, CT, April 12, 1988

Word has trickled out in the Soviet press and via Western visitors that the Soviet Union has suffered a cultural calamity that may rank with the floods that devastated Florence in the 1960s.

But perhaps a better analogy would be the destruction of the ancient Alexandrian libraries.

Soviet scholars have revealed that sometime in February, a fire at the Academy of Sciences library in Leningrad destroyed at least 400,000 books and periodicals, many of them irreplaceable publications dating to the 17th century.

Among other treasures that are now reportedly threatened by water damage and mold because of the fire are manuscripts by Pushkin, Dostoyevsky, Lermontov and other writers whose works were housed in the library's Institute of Russian literature.

Soviet scholars are criticizing library officials for suppressing news of the calamity at first, and downplaying the loss. But perhaps the officials' timidity isn't surprising — it's a courageous Soviet bureaucrat who admits wrongdoing or error, even in the age of glasnost.

What may be more significant is the fact that Western experts have offered help with repair, restoration and salvage that apparently is being accepted by Soviet authorities. Would the Russians, a proud people, have accepted such help even a few years ago — or would their instinct have been to keep their embarrassment entirely to themselves?

The Soviets revere literature, especially that of their own authors. Most, if not all, Americans sympathize with their loss, and might well hope that from this disaster may come new understanding — perhaps even new cultural bridges.

The Arizona Republic

Phoenix, AZ, August 22, 1988

A couple of hundred years from now, scholars may find it passing strange that Russian history books contain a paucity of data about politics and economics in the Union of Soviet Socialist Republics for the quarter of a century prior to 1985. What in the world happened? they may ask.

What will have happened is what is happening now. Public libraries in the Soviet Union are being purged of political and economic books written before the enlightened Mikhail Gorbachev, the popularizer of *glasnost* and *perestroika*, came to power.

According to a letter from a librarian published in the government newspaper *Izvestia*, village libraries have been ordered to clear their shelves of pre-'85 volumes dealing with these two sensitive subjects.

The librarian, who identified herself as being from the Crimea, a region on the Black Sea, also said that writings being removed included those of two former Soviet leaders, Leonid Brezhnev and Konstantin Chernenko, as well as those of Mikhail Suslov, a longtime Kremlin ideologist, and others now in disgrace.

The letter said the purge order covered "outdated" material from 1961 through March 1985, when Mr. Gorbachev was named general secretary of the Communist Party. That would take in the Khrushchev-Brezhnev-Chernenko era.

With typical Soviet clarity, the director of the state culture agency in the Crimea said the directive from the central Ministry of Culture in Moscow was only a recommendation and was not politically motivated. Merely a "cleaning out of the book fund," he said. Besides, he added, no one was employed in the Crimea's libraries with the name signed to the letter — suggesting that, even in the era of *glasnost*, one has to be careful.

Equally forthright, a Foreign Ministry spokesman said the action sounded like a "local initiative" by officials who were "doing more than necessary" to set the nation on the right course. He didn't explain precisely what he meant.

The irony of the order — or recommendation or whatever it was — is that it would do the very thing Brezhnev was blamed for doing: covering up the country's problems and repressing independent political and cultural thinkers.

The Gorbachev policy of *glasnost*, or openness, encourages a more accurate and honest examination of Soviet history. Mr. Gorbachev has called for the elimination of "blank spots," taboo subjects such as the repressions under Soviet dictator Josef Stalin. Similarly, Mr. Gorbachev champions economic reform under a policy of *perestroika*.

It makes no sense that a man who calls for taking the wraps off materials that were closed to the public for so many years would now sanction banning books because, as the letter in *Izvestia* said, they are "no longer topical."

Unless, of course, Mr. Gorbachev speaks out of both sides of his mouth.

The Hutchinson News

Hutchinson, KS, June 15, 1988

The Soviet government, caught up in its frenzy of reform, has officially acknowledged what many people have known for a long time — Soviet history, as it is taught to its citizens, is a patchwork of distortions, untruths and blank spots.

The admission was recently published in a commentary on the front page of Izvestia, a government-sanctioned journal as much to blame for historical distortions as the texts circulated in Soviet schools.

Now the government has canceled final exams for 53 million Soviet children because the history they have learned is clearly wrong.

Educators are in the process of correcting "the bitter fruit of our own moral laxity" as Izvestia termed the historical misstatements.

The Soviets should be applauded for this novel and noble Soviet change of pace. But a caution ought to be emphasized.

Now that the government has acknowledged past misstatements, what assurance do the Soviet people have that this "new history" will hold any more truth than the "old" history.

It is not unusual for new communist regimes to denounce the outrageous actions of their predecessors. It provides a new blackboard on which to chalk new directions.

For now the words sound too good to be true. After all, there are several more moves the Soviets have yet to make.

When, for instance, will the Soviet press be freed from government shackles? When will Soviet writers, those who have remained in their country and those who have expatriated, be allowed to publish and circulate their works freely and without fear of retribution? Once the Soviets have rewritten their history, will the Soviet citizen have access to other histories, those that are written without government sanction?

The statements made in Izvestia, if they are to be believed, denote a positive change of direction, one that bodes well for a society in which truth is so alien.

St. Paul Pioneer Press & Dispatch

St. Paul, MN, June 16, 1988

"Hey, Teach, didja see the story in the paper? The Russians canceled the history final for 53 million kids. How come you can't do it for this class?"

Do you remember reading why the Soviet government canceled the exam?

"The story said they'd been teaching the kids the wrong stuff."

Right. Before Gorbachev's time, Russian students studying their own history got a prettied-up version. Teachers and textbooks left out whole pieces and lied about other pieces.

"You mean they just slid right by the embarrassing stuff?"

You've got it.

"You mean if it had been us we wouldn't have studied about Watergate and the   tnam protesters and like that?"

Maybe not at all. Certainly not the way we did. What other topics might have looked different to you if American presidents decided what we ought to know?

"Well . . . *most* topics. Slavery. The Civil War. Treaties with the American Indians. Prohibition. The My Lai massacre. It's creepy to think what it would have been like to have some Big Brother telling us what to believe about those."

That's exactly what the Russians had been doing with their history. What do you think about the flip-flop they're making now?

"You're always saying, 'Let history speak.' So they've switched to that, from thought control? Awesome."

Good word for it. Now, do you think I'm still going to make you take that test?

(Groan) "Yeah, Teach, don't tell us again, 'So you can show me that you're ready for your future because you understand your past.' "

Friends, you are ready for that exam. Class dismissed.

Portland Press Herald

Portland, ME, August 19, 1988

Glasnost, Mikhail Gorbachev's open window on Soviet life, became isinglass-nost this week. And once again the issue is Soviet history.

According to a letter from a librarian in the Crimea, published in the official newspaper Izvestia, Soviet public libraries have been ordered to remove from their shelves all political and economics books written before Gorbachev assumed power three years ago.

Taken literally, the purge order would leave Soviet libraries all but empty. And that, the Soviet Culture Ministry quickly countered, would be absurd.

Instead, the ministry claimed, the order was meant to clean out endless copies of documents accumulated during Leonid Brezhnev's 18 years in power. And accumulate they did. During the Brezhnev era, Soviet libraries were routinely forced to stock 100 copies of Brezhnev's memoirs, speeches and documents.

Now they're gathering dust. No surprise there. Still, rather than a centralized order directing librarians which books to clear from their shelves, why not let each library decide for itself, based on what its readers want to read?

Granted, for a country which is busy rewriting its history, that's a radical idea. Already this year, thousands of Soviet students were excused from history exams while books were rewritten to match Gorbachev's new policies of glasnost and perestroika. Now, Soviet history will apparently underscore Josef Stalin's rule of terror and Brezhnev's corruption.

That's all the more reason to leave earlier versions available so Soviet citizens can see how they were manipulated. Otherwise, robbed of an opportunity to know history, they could be condemned to repeat it.

Buffalo Evening News

Buffalo, NY, June 15, 1988

IN WHAT surely must be a historic act in itself, the Soviet Union has canceled the entire country's June history exams. The reason: An explosion of long-suppressed facts, freed by the openness of "glasnost," has left students and teachers too confused to proceed.

The importance of this move, which affects 53 million Soviet young people, goes a long way beyond giving students a reprieve from tests. It is an unusual admission of past wrong by the Soviet state.

Soviet students hadn't been able to help noticing something. As Mikhail Gorbachev's glasnost policy opened the way for a closer look at the past, articles contradicting the history texts proliferated, with the discrepancy particularly noticeable where Stalinism and its crimes were concerned. What was a history teacher — stuck with a textbook and a syllabus that looked more and more like a work of fiction — to do?

For the rest of the world, the fact that Soviet students had been getting a misleading picture of events was hardly news. But imagine the effect on a Russian history class. A nation that has been taught for decades to be unquestioning of the official Communist viewpoint — with draconian penalties for dissenters — suddenly couldn't avoid asking questions, and even saw some questioning officially encouraged.

The cancellation of the exams was announced in Izvestia, the government newspaper. The paper said the decision is intended to end the passing of lies from generation to generation, partly to keep from further perpetuating vestiges of the Stalinist system that the new leaders see as strangling the nation's economy and creativity.

The Soviet Union still has a long way to go to becoming a democratic society. Until it has multiparty elections that offer choices, a representative government and basic rights such as the West enjoys, it will not be free.

But Gorbachev's moves toward some free-market principles, limitations on officials' terms and greater openness bespeak at least a welcome trend. Letting truth burgeon to the point where kids can't take their history tests is evidence of a further turn in the course of Soviet government.

Soviets Admit Map Fraud

Viktor R. Yashcenko, the Soviet Union's chief cartographer, Sept. 2, 1989 admitted that maps of the U.S.S.R. had been routinely falsified for the past 50 years as a security measure. An interview with Yashcenko was carried in *Izvestia*, the government newspaper. "People did not recognize their motherland on the map," Yashcenko said. "Tourists tried in vain to figure out where they were." He announced that accurate maps of the country would henceforth be released.

ST. LOUIS POST-DISPATCH
St. Louis, MO, September 8, 1988

For Viktor Yashchenko, the Soviet Union's chief cartographer, it must have been the most professionally embarrassing interview in his career. In the pages of *Izvestia*, Mr. Yashchenko admitted that for the past 50 years, nearly every public map issued in the Soviet Union has been inaccurate. Even imprecise maps, such as those with scales of 40 miles to the inch, were doctored. Whole cities were "moved" from their real locations — or disappeared altogether. Major rivers were rerouted by miles and whole mountain ranges shifted. Coastlines and railroad lines were regularly redrawn.

The reason for all of this falsification, according to Mr. Yashchenko, were orders from Soviet dictator Josef Stalin, who feared that foreign nations would use the maps in their war plans against the Soviet Union. The process began in the late 1930s, when the Soviet secret police took over all map-making duties. The only accurate maps were classified top secret; everything else was false.

Apparently Hitler's armies brought their own maps. They found Leningrad and Stalingrad without once getting lost. The only people confused by the bogus maps were in all likelihood tourists and Soviet citizens. What has made the Soviet map falsification policy particularly ludicrous was the development of photo spy satellites over 25 years ago, which has allowed the West to map all of the Soviet Union fully and accurately.

Western cartographers have long known about Soviet map falsification and they have responded favorably to Mr. Yashchenko's promise that all new Soviet maps will be accurate. Maybe Moscow will next declassify the telephone books.

THE SACRAMENTO BEE
Sacramento, CA, December 8, 1988

One of the most vexing questions about Russia has always been centered on why things — the airline reservation system, the telephones, the food distribution system — don't work. Is it because the technology is bad and the workmanship shoddy and unmotivated, or because they've intentionally sabotaged things so that they don't work? The standard Marxism-is-inefficient argument has always favored the former, but there are good reasons to hold with the latter.

Now comes an official Soviet acknowledgment that, in the case of maps — maps of Russia, street maps of Russian cities, indeed the whole Soviet Atlas of the World — things were purposely faked, and have been for the past 50 years. Towns were put in the wrong place, or moved from place to place; rivers run to places where they don't run; streets are left off; major landmarks (among them KGB headquarters in Moscow's Dzerzhinski Square, known to every Muscovite) intentionally omitted. All this on the orders of the KGB and its predecessor, the NKVD, which controlled Soviet cartography and regarded accurate maps of Mother Russia as a state secret. It seems to have dawned only belatedly on the KGB that any nation with the resources to put a satellite in orbit can map every Soviet alley and tree with accuracy. The CIA's map of Moscow, available to all U.S. diplomats and to many others, is the most accurate map of the Soviet capital in existence.

The Russians have promised to start rectifying all this. The government chief cartographer says: "We received numerous complaints. People did not recognize their motherland on maps. Tourists tried to orient themselves in vain on the terrain." No wonder when three different versions of the Soviet Atlas have the East Siberian town of Logashkino in three different places, while a fourth doesn't have it at all.

The question now, of course, is how long the rectification will take: The estimate is that it will be years. Once purposeful distortion ends, normal inertia and incompetence may take over. But then paranoia is probably also a form of incompetence, as the Russians, in this case at least, have now learned.

PORTLAND EVENING EXPRESS
Portland, ME, September 7, 1988

In the United States, we're wondering why so many of our students are ignorant of the basic facts of geography.

In the Soviet Union, ignorance of geography has been official government policy for the last five decades.

In a statement making public something that's been known to Westerners for years, the Soviets' chief mapmaker admitted last week that for the past 50 years, the secret police had been deliberately falsifying all sorts of Soviet terrain features on everything from road maps to tourist brochures.

Indeed, the best street map of Moscow, depended on by diplomats and correspondents sent to that city, is produced in Washington, D.C., by the CIA.

So why did the Russians find it necessary to do all this?

Put it down to Stalinist paranoia if you will, but spies use maps, you know, and if you just move a river here or a mountain range there, you can send those capitalist running dogs around in circles.

The revelation that Soviet revisionism has extended to street names and buildings was apparently prompted by two things: first, under Mikhail Gorbachev's policy of openness, citizens began complaining that the maps of their country weren't exactly useful for anything but wallpaper.

And second, Russian rulers seem to have realized that satellite photography has made it difficult to hide the Urals anymore.

This is what happens when the secret police double as the National Geographic Society. If you can make people disappear for years, what's a city block?

This whole story sounds like a Yakov Smirnoff joke — you remember, he's the Russian refugee comedian who says, "In the U.S. you can always find a party — but in Russia the Party can always find *you*."

Maybe not. Especially if they've been using their own maps.

Pittsburgh Post-Gazette

Pittsburgh, PA, September 7, 1988

Mikhail Gorbachev's policy of glasnost is now one for the books — the geography books, that is.

In the latest example of the new Soviet policy of openness, the chief mapmaker of the U.S.S.R. has admitted that for the past 50 years his nation deliberately has published inaccurate maps of the country, changing boundary lines and omitting important buildings — including the headquarters of the KGB.

Viktor R. Yashchenko, the chief of the Soviet Geodesy and Cartography Administration of the Council of Ministers, said the policy of falsifying maps dated back to the 1930s. It reflected a paranoia and penchant for secrecy that continued long after the development of satellite photography allowed other nations to make accurate maps of Soviet locations.

Now, Mr. Yashchenko said, only accurate maps will be published.

Americans tempted to feel superior about the re-mapping of the Soviet Union should remember that, even with accurate maps at their disposal, American teen-agers are notoriously poor at identifying many American states, let alone foreign countries.

Now that Soviet students will have access to accurate geographical information, a map gap may be on the horizon.

THE SUN

Baltimore, MD, September 17, 1988

If the U.S. wants to bomb an obscure village in Siberia or photograph a back street on the wrong side of Moscow, it can do so with total accuracy. Satellite sensors work. CIA maps of the Soviet Union are accurate. Moscow keeps no geographic secrets from our eyes in the sky. It keeps them only from the Soviet people and tourists lacking access to CIA maps. This has made no sense for decades, but the practice is only now being ended.

Viktor R. Yashchenko, chief of the Soviet mapping agency, came clean in an interview with *Izvestia*. For a half-century, his agency has taken directions from the security police to omit or falsify locations of land features and facilities, to unlist streets, to mis-locate bridges. Features would be deliberately misplaced by 5 to 25 miles, enough to throw off any 1940s bombardier.

The mapmakers did this under the order of Josef Stalin a half-century ago, lest Soviet maps lead an invading army or fifth column. Stalin died. Satellite mapping came in. Tourists went crazy using old, falsified or no maps. Russians knew their maps lied to them about the streets where they lived. But the practice went on, because no one stopped or reversed it. Government bureaucracy is like that, and paranoid Communist secret police bureaucracy is more so than others.

Till this year. *Glasnost*, it's wonderful. Soon the Russians will have maps almost as good as the CIA's. American maps show the location of such sensitive facilities as the Central Intelligence Agency and National Security Agency. Well, why not? The Russians spies know, why can't we? Only now, under Mikhail Gorbachev, is the Soviet Union coming around to similar common sense. It's a small step, but progress all the same.

The News and Courier

Charleston, SC, September 20, 1988

Russia, in the memorable words of Winston Churchill, is a riddle inside an enigma. It isn't, of course. It only seemed that way to Sir Winston because all he had at his disposal was a Soviet map.

The Soviet Union has at last officially acknowledged that maps available to everyone but the very highest officials — maps of the USSR, street maps of Soviet cities, indeed, the entire "Soviet Atlas of the World" — have been purposely faked for the past 50 years.

Towns were intentionally put in the wrong locations, or moved from place to place; rivers run to places where they don't run; streets were left out; and major landmarks (among them the KGB's looming headquarters in Moscow's Dzerzhinski Square, known to every Muscovite and every student of Soviet history the world over) were purposefully omitted.

All this on the orders of the KGB and its predecessors — the NKVD, OGPU, MOE, LARRY and CURLY — which controlled Soviet cartography and regarded accurate maps of the Motherland as a state secret.

It doesn't seem to have dawned on the pinheads of state security that a nation such as the United States with the resources to put satellites into orbit could effortlessly map every back alley and tree in the USSR with pinpoint accuracy.

It must be a source of enormous embarrassment to the Kremlin that the most accurate map of the Soviet capital available is the CIA's map of Moscow, which is available to diplomats, journalists and others traveling to the Soviet Union.

THE CHRISTIAN SCIENCE MONITOR

Boston, MA, September 12, 1988

THE folks at the US Central Intelligence Agency must be sighing: They're likely to lose their 15-year claim to drawing the most reliable street maps of Moscow.

The wave of *glasnost*, or openness, sweeping the Soviet Union has finally crested over the agency that maps Mother Russia. That nation's chief cartographer recently admitted that for 50 years the government, under state security police guidance, has deliberately fudged all of its public maps. The motive was to render maps unreliable for spies, invading armies, or untrustworthy members of the proletariat at home who would aid and abet them. The disclosure comes as no news to Western mapmakers, who have based their renderings on satellite photos. Nor does it come as news to Soviet citizens: Tourist maps routinely omit the names of major streets, distance scales, and significant landmarks, such as the KGB building in Moscow – though many a Muscovite will point you in the right direction, thank you.

The cartographer claims the Kremlin will set things right: No more now-you-see-them-now-you-don't cities. No more rail lines doing the rhumba from one map edition to the next. Why the change? Economic restructuring and planning gets tough if your project has to cross a river when the map you've read correctly says you're still miles away from it.

One hopes that the Kremlin finally sees some value in trusting the people it leads with tidbits as damaging to state security as the shape of the highway that rings Moscow (a *perfect* circle or a square with rounded corners, take your pick). Soon after the head mapmaker's disclosure, a KGB department head published an article lamenting the Kremlin's obsession with secrecy. In a remarkable statement, considering the source, he wrote: "People's trust and support can be obtained only in exchange for trust to the people."

True enough. But the proof is in the mapmaking. We'll know *glasnost* is for real when Raisa and Mikhail (Gorbachev) start buying vacation maps from the local newsstand, use them to drive from Minsk to Pinsk, and actually get there.

Gorbachev Urges Co-op Farm Revival

Soviet leader Mikhail S. Gorbachev March 23, 1988 called for a revival of the nation's cooperative farms. The general secretary's comments were made in Moscow to a national congress of collective farmers. It was the first such congress since 1969. Gorbachev had been raised in a farm region of Russia, and he had risen within the Communist Party as an agricultural expert.

Cooperative farms had been created under the regime of V.I. Lenin, the founder of Soviet communism. Subsequent leaders had deemphasized cooperatives in favor of state-run farms. Cooperative farms (*kolkhozes* in Russian) were largely self-sufficient and specialized in such produce as eggs and fruit. Under the system, farmers banded together to share the ownership of agricultural equipment and buildings. They were free to determine which crops to plant. They could keep some of their produce for personal consumption and share the profits from sales to the state. In contrast, the giant state farms (*sovkoves* in Russian) were subsidized by the government, run by managers employing salaried workers, and were under rigid production quotas. The state owned all equipment and buildings, determined which crops would be planted, and allocated the produce to the state market.

Gorbachev told the farmers' congress: "We should revive cooperatives not in their old, often too-primitve forms, but in the form of a modern, high-standard cooperative movement extensively integrated both within its own framework and with government-run enterprises."

Gorbachev criticized the favoritism toward state farms shown by past Soviet leaders. He said that the attitude had made farm cooperatives no more than "junior partners" in the economy, and had "delayed solution of the food problem."

The general secretary introduced to the congress draft legislation on cooperative farms. Among other things, the measure would give cooperatives new legal rights, encourage them to form joint ventures with state farms, and would allow them to contract with foreign buyers. The legislation also had a provision on so-called "team contracts," under which cooperatives could rent land to resident workers, usually whole families. The workers would sell an agreed amount of their produce back to the cooperatives. The workers could make whatever use they chose of the produce not sold to the cooperative, including selling it directly to consumers. Under Gorbachev, the U.S.S.R. had experimented with the team-contracts concept in Estonia and Siberia.

The Washington Post

Washington, DC, October 17, 1988

MIKHAIL GORBACHEV'S education in socialist agriculture presumably began when his peasant father was swept into one of the dictator Stalin's collective farms. Later, as Leonid Brezhnev's farm chief, he had six years to learn the limitations of simply throwing money—greater investments—at the grossly inefficient structure Stalin had designed to tame a resisting peasantry. In his characteristic style, Mr. Gorbachev has already turned the glare of glasnost on the manifest failings of the current system. But only in recent weeks has he made the political breakthrough—circumscribing the power of his chief Politburo rival, Yegor Ligachev—that now allows him to undertake the "leap forward" in agriculture that he has been contemplating for some time.

The problem is simple: farmers working for wages in huge factory-like collectives have little incentive to produce—Soviet farm productivity is about one-tenth the American level. Mr. Gorbachev intends to tackle the problem at the producing end by allowing—by stirring: many will hang back—individual farmers or groups of farmers to lease land and work it themselves. Their success will depend in good part on the terms set for the services they will necessarily have to acquire from state organizations. Even more important will be the terms set for the marketing of their products. How much of the crop will they have to sell at farmer-subsidized state prices, how much in the widening free market that Mikhail Gorbachev envisions? And how will city dwellers react to the higher food prices that freeing up the market will surely bring?

Overall, Mr. Gorbachev's perestroika is under heavy attack precisely for failing to make a difference in the lives of ordinary people. Diet is a central item in the standard of living, and the Soviet diet, though long on calories, is still painfully short of fresh fruit and vegetables and decent meat. Many experts inside and outside the Soviet Union had thought Mr. Gorbachev would do better to follow the example of China and Hungary and start his restructuring on the farms, where the first results are only one growing season away—in industry, results take many years. This approach would seem to hold promise for city dwellers and farmers alike. It is big political news that Mr. Gorbachev is extending reform to this vital sector now.

The Hutchinson News

Hutchinson, KS, November 4, 1988

Here it is 1988, and they're still flailing Jimmy Carter and arguing about the grain embargo of 1979.

Going into the final week of the campaign, George Bush was scaring voters with the charge that Michael Dukakis was another Carter who'd embargo grain to the Soviets at the drop of a hat.

He wouldn't either, Dukakis retorts. And besides, Dan Quayle favored the embargo.

It's all so silly. Critics blame every farm ill since the blizzards of the 1880s on the grain embargo, imposed by Carter in response to the Soviet invasion of Afghanistan. Actually, a couple of inches less rain, a couple of degrees more temperature can affect a farmer's income more.

The embargo wasn't a big campaign issue in 1980. Reagan didn't campaign against it, wasn't in favor of lifting it in 1981 — the State Department was adamantly opposed — which is why Sen. Quayle voted against lifting it.

But by 1984, the grain embargo had become the Willie Horton of the campaign. By 1988, it's a pretty tattered issue.

You can't ask Bush because he isn't taking questions, but ask yourself: If the Soviets were to invade Poland next year, do you think a President Bush (or Dukakis) would keep on selling them grain?

The Des Moines Register

Des Moines, IA, September 6, 1988

The story is being told in Moscow about five farmers in the village of Saltykovka who organized a cooperative to raise pigs. They planned to produce 300 tons of pork a year to sell for profit.

But people in the area called the farmers "money grubbers" and "new bourgeoisie." Three times their barn was set on fire, finally driving them from business.

In the Soviet Union, people often can't buy meat at any price. When it is available, the price is low in state-owned stores, but the quality is miserable.

Yet there is hostility to the point of arson to an enterprise that might produce good pork, because the organizers might make money.

Ingrained attitudes die hard. For decades, Soviet ideology has instilled hatred of "bourgeois" thinking. Now Mikhail Gorbachev is counting on it to overcome the national embarrassment of a superpower that is unable to feed its people properly.

In the most striking move yet in its economic restructuring, the Soviet government will allow individual farmers to lease land from the state for up to 50 years and allow them to hire farm workers. Individuals also will be allowed to own tractors and other farm equipment that previously were considered "means of production" which under communist orthodoxy could only be owned by the state.

Even in the surprising place the Soviet Union has become, the farm reforms are astonishing. This is the same country that under Josef Stalin killed perhaps 20 million people during the forced collectivization of agriculture.

Now Gorbachev is trying to recreate that which Stalin destroyed.

China pioneered the way in the late 1970s, dismantling collectives and turning plots of land over to individual families. China now eats better than in generations, and the income earned by farm families stimulates the rest of the economy.

But it will be difficult in the Soviet Union, not only because of hostile attitudes to overcome but because it takes more than breaking up the collectives. There must be reforms up and down the line in the farm-supply sector, in marketing, in processing, in distribution and retailing.

Agriculture may be the biggest test yet of Gorbachev's perestroika, and the key to its success.

THE KANSAS CITY STAR

Kansas City, MO, August 26, 1988

It is in this country's economic interest to sign another long-term grain sales agreement with the Soviet Union.

It also is of political interest to the current Republican administration. The current one expires in September. American agriculture is watching as U.S. officials with the agriculture and state departments are negotiating with the Russians. Officials hope to extend the current five-year pact and to get the Soviet Union to agree to buy even more grain than the minimum 9 million metric tons now called for.

Sales to the Soviet Union have been iffy in the past. Soviets looked upon the United States as an unreliable supplier following grain embargoes and the use of food as a weapon against political enemies. The Russians also like to go where the price is right. The signed agreement with the Russians to buy so much wheat and corn, with the option of also buying soybeans, helps to put stability into U.S. sales and keeps a big customer.

Nowhere can the signing of this pact be more important than in the wheat country of Kansas and throughout the Midwest. The Soviet Union was the top buyer of U.S. wheat in the last marketing year, and 404 million bushels of the 447 million sold were of hard red winter wheat, which is grown in Kansas.

In two of the current pact's years, the Russians did not meet the minimum goals of wheat purchases, although they exceeded them in the previous two. But under the U.S. government's export enhancement program, with its subsidies for purchases of American grain, the Soviets became better buyers once again.

The fact that this country is locking the Soviets into huge purchases is comforting to farmers here. The Soviet Union needs grain because of its domestic shortages. Unlike Third World countries which also need grain, the Soviet Union has money to pay for its purchases. But it is extremely erratic in buying habits unless pinned down. A new grain trade agreement would do that.

The Hartford Courant

Hartford, CT, September 3, 1988

Mikhail S. Gorbachev's campaign to restructure the Soviet economy is vulnerable to this bit of sarcasm: "Where's the beef?"

The beef is literally and figuratively on the Soviet farm. True reform has been dormant in the bedrock of Soviet socialism — in state-owned collective farms, state-controlled markets and one-party politics.

It is one thing to release a few hundred political prisoners, allow Soviet citizens to read Western newspapers, rehabilitate discredited comrades, shake up the Communist Party and permit small, one-employee businesses. These liberties and measures could be easily wiped out.

It's another thing to allow Soviet citizens to form their own companies, operate private farms and sell crops in a market, permit political parties and offer meaningful autonomy in the republics. There would be no turning back from such reforms, not without bloodshed.

Mr. Gorbachev, whose campaign for liberalizing institutions and restructuring the economy is still in its infancy, has taken one of his boldest steps yet. Soviet farmers will be allowed to rent land from the state, buy their own tractors and trucks and hire farmhands. Although land would still be owned by the state, the renters would be given half-century leases.

The changes promise a return to family farming and the end of a six-decades-old tragedy. No sector of the Soviet population was more brutally forced into communism by Stalin than were the farmers. Peasants and landowners were stripped of their lands and forced into giant farms where they toiled for the state. Hundreds of thousands were murdered or died of famine.

Collectivization has been an abysmal failure marked by food shortages.

Soviet farmers will at last have the chance to show that a modified form of private enterprise can work in a socialist state. Ironically, while the Soviet Union resurrects the family farm, the family farm in America is in jeopardy. We are in the age of agribusiness here, and the bigger the farm, the more likely its survival.

Could this be what some political scientists call convergence — they will move a bit closer to capitalism and we will move a bit closer to centralized agriculture?

Rockford Register Star

Rockford, IL, October 29, 1988

From his seemingly bottomless bag of amazing tricks, Soviet leader Mikhail Gorbachev pulled out a whopper — a proposal to abandon collective farming, a basic symbol of the communist system. Figuring that food fills bellies better than does failed theory, Gorbachev wants to free all of Soviet agriculture.

Over Soviet television, that new medium of *glasnost,* Gorbachev criticized the system of collective farming, praised experiments in the private leasing of farms, suggested that "the entire agrarian sector ... follow this path," and vowed to "stop the process of depeasantization and to return the man back to the land as its real master."

Wow!

This reversal of Stalinism ranks among Gorbachev's boldest. Once again he is releasing genies that likely can never be put back in their bottles.

Doubtless there will be resistance to this reform of agriculture, especially among state farm bosses, but any great improvements on the consistently sorry performance of the collective system surely will win over the public. Fuller stomachs are happier stomachs.

As Gorbachev himself puts it: "I would support any approach that proves itself."

What wonder will come next in the Gorbachev revolution? Nothing seems out of the question anymore.

The Providence Journal

Providence, RI, October 17, 1988

Soviet President Mikhail Gorbachev announced a major break from Marxist practice last week. The reform proposal would largely abandon collective farm policies that have left Soviet citizens hungry for over half a century.

Under the plan, Soviet farmers who now toil for wages on state farms will be able to lease plots of land and sell what they produce on their own.

While much to be applauded, the reforms coming from Mr. Gorbachev may strike many Soviet citizens as painfully ironic. In a speech commemorating the 70th anniversary of the Russian Revolution last year, the Soviet leader defended the policy he now plans to abandon, characterizing as historical necessities the "excesses" of Josef Stalin's policy of forced collectivization.

As a direct and premeditated result of that policy, millions of peasants and *kulaks* (small landowners) who refused to join collectives starved to death in the early 1930s. Soon, their descendants will be allowed, and even encouraged, to leave the state farms.

However, says Mr. Gorbachev, they will not be *forced* to leave the collectives their ancestors were *forced* to join

or starve. That irony would apparently be too cruel even for Mr. Gorbachev.

Nevertheless, he does seem to recognize that half-way measures to reform the collectives are flawed: "No fool is going to go to work on a lease contract as long as he can have a salary without earning it" at a collective, Mr. Gorbachev said in answering a question after his announcement last week.

Still, that unfortunate class of hungry people known as the Soviet citizens has every reason to applaud even half-way moves in the right direction. It is about time Soviet leaders expanded a longrunning agricultural experiment under which 5 percent of arable land has been leased. On that land grows an estimated *40 percent* of all Soviet food.

Another painful irony will be felt by the man supposedly put in charge of Soviet agriculture: Yegor K. Ligachev. As a hardline Marxist and critic of Mr. Gorbachev's policies, carrying out these reforms may well stick in his craw. Still, we expect he will accept the task with a smile. A job in Moscow beats one in Siberia. Anyhow, the boss was himself the farm czar before becoming the Soviet leader in 1985, so who knows?

BUFFALO EVENING NEWS
Buffalo, NY, August 29, 1988

EXTENSION OF the longstanding program of U.S. grain sales to the Soviet Union will help the American farmer, the U.S. economy and the nation generally. A five-year grain agreement will end next month, and the two countries plan a one-year extension while negotiating a new long-term pact.

Plagued by crop failures, the Soviets have recently been buying more than the minimum of 9 million tons prescribed in the agreement. In the first nine months of this fiscal year, they have paid $1.6 billion to American farmers for over 15 million tons of grain.

Current negotiations center on the volume of guaranteed sales. The United States seeks a higher minimum, so that the sales will be predictable and not disruptive of the grain markets. Moscow wants flexibility, seeking to reduce the minimum but to have the right to buy more if it wants to.

President Reagan has opposed some forms of East-West trade, but he has always favored grain sales to the Soviet Union, even when President Jimmy Carter imposed a grain embargo to protest the Soviet invasion of Afghanistan. While the pending agreement merely continues the past pattern of grain sales, it comes as welcome news to farmers and has positive implications for the administration in this election year.

While the grain sales are simply good business, without the strategic aspects of some East-West trade, they have been involved in controversy over the years.

In 1972, when Russia first entered the U.S. grain market in a big way with a purchase of 12 million tons, the size of the purchases pushed up prices in the United States and created controversy for the Nixon administration.

Today, however, the grain markets have adjusted to annual sales of this scope, and the new agreement is not expected to disrupt U.S. markets. American farmers, indeed, depend on the exports to the Soviet Union, which is the biggest buyer of American wheat.

While this year's drought has pared stockpiles somewhat, the surpluses are still believed adequate to handle the Soviet purchases.

These American grain surpluses are striking demonstrations of the productivity of the American farmer, and the continued Soviet shortages show that, despite the reforms sought by Soviet leader Mikhail Gorbachev, Soviet agriculture remains stagnant.

Gorbachev has encouraged Soviet peasants to set up their own farms so that "a person becomes the genuine master of the land," but few have done so. Marshall Goldman of the Russian Research Center at Harvard University calls the current state of Soviet agriculture "abysmal."

Goldman estimated that 20 to 30 percent of Soviet crops rot in the fields because of inefficiency and the lack of storage and distribution facilities. There are not enough barns or elevators to store the grain, and many rural roads are so poor that the grain cannot be transported efficiently.

It is ironic that the Soviet Union is a superpower as far as military might is concerned, but after 71 years of farming under Marxist principles, it still cannot feed itself.

The Boston Globe
Boston, MA, September 10, 1988

A once-promising scheme for fertilizing crops in arid regions of the southern Soviet Union has become an ecological disaster that threatens to become counterproductive. With hard work and luck, the losses may be contained and even reversed; whatever its outcome, the project stands as a warning to the rest of the world to be highly chary of major modifications to regional patterns of water flow and plant life.

The Aral Sea, one of the world's largest inland waters, was a relatively stable, mildly saline lake fed by several major rivers. In 1960, earlier irrigation projects drawing on those rivers were sharply expanded, cutting off the natural flow of fresh water into the Aral.

The consequences, detailed in the magazine Science, included a rapid drop in the Aral's water level, which had been expected. The unpredicted consequences were extensive blowing of a variety of salts from the Aral's exposed bottom, which contaminated farming areas being fed by the irrigation projects, and a sharp drop of foliage in river delta areas because of a falling water table. Weather patterns gradually shifted, making summers hotter and winters colder, compounding the existing problems of aridity in the region.

Attempts to reverse the problem even included plans to divert river water from streams flowing into the Arctic Ocean. Mikhail Gorbachev canceled the plans when he came to office, because of the cost and the possibility that the diversions would create ecological problems in Siberia.

A variety of less dramatic measures, such as more efficient use of irrigation water, drilling for large untapped reservoirs and improved return of irrigation runoff water, may help stabilize the Aral in the next decade, leaving it a smaller but less dangerous body of water than its present salty self. In the interim, ecologists and others should sift its history for lessons about massive alterations, such as the stripping of tropical rain forests. Mankind is being very hard on its planet.

THE DAILY OKLAHOMAN
Oklahoma City, OK, May 21, 1988

JUST because some farmers in southwestern Oklahoma are driving Soviet-made tractors doesn't necessarily mean the Russians are plowing new ground in international trade.

That assurance comes from John Lien, a farm machinery expert with the International Trade Administration. He says Soviet tractor sales in the United States are insignificant and cites figures to prove it.

Last year, U.S. tractor imports from the Soviet Union totaled only 1,447 with a value of around $1.5 million. More than half of the machines were in the 30-to-40 horsepower class.

More than 108,000 tractors were sold in this country in 1987, and only about 16 percent — those over 100 hp — were American-made.

The United States doesn't sell any tractors to the Russians, Lien explained, because there's no market. The primary export markets for U.S. tractors are Canada and Australia.

"The Soviets, with their government-controlled economy, built 150,000 to 200,000 tractors last year, and they build all sizes," Lien said. All carry the same name: Belarus.

Commerce Secretary William Verity is on a crusade to expand U.S.-Soviet trade, which now amounts to about $2.75 billion annually.

The administration is far from united behind Verity's goal. Defense Secretary Frank Carlucci says the trade initiative makes it difficult for the United States to complain about a $2.1 billion line of credit granted to the Soviet Union by a group of West German banks, which he believes will just give the a Soviets more money to use on military activities.

Even harsher criticism comes from Transportation Secretary James Burnley. He said a Commerce Department decision to allow a U.S. company to lease space on the Soviets' orbiting space station for experiments was a dangerous mistake. By helping subsidize the Kremlin's space program, he warned, America could be helping an enemy build a greater capacity for wartime use and also doom our own space commercialization initiatives.

Curb on Independent Publishers Set

The Soviet government Feb. 1, 1988 announced a ban on the creation of independent publishing and printing operations. Private publishing houses and printing plants had sprung up around the nation in the wake of Soviet leader Mikhail S. Gorbachev's economic reforms and policy of *glasnost* (openness).

The chief spokesman of the Soviet foreign ministry, Gennadi I. Gerasimov, confirmed that the ban had been ordered by the state committee for publishing, known as *Goskomizdat*. "One reason [for the ban] is a lack of newsprint," Gerasimov explained. "Another reason is a lack of machinery. And the third reason is that they [*Goskomizdat*] don't want the competition."

Gerasimov said that *Goskomizdat*, rather than allow independent publishing, would instead create a program under which authors of fiction could have their works published at their own expense.

The editors of 30 independent Soviet publications met in Moscow May 8, 1988 to strengthen mutual cooperation. The journalists included Sergei I. Grigoryants of the independent journal *Glasnost*, Lev M. Timofeyev of *Referendum* and Aleksandr Podrabinek of *Express Khronika*.

"The aim is to set up a club of independent editors for the exchange of information, so that we all know who is printing what and where," Grigoryants explained.

THE CHRISTIAN SCIENCE MONITOR
Boston, MA, April 12, 1988

WE had grown so used to a monolithic Soviet press that it's still a little jarring to see Pravda and another state-published newspaper lock horns. But maybe we'd better get used to it.

Last week Pravda aimed a full-page editorial at an article in Sovietskaya Rossiya, official paper of the Russian Republic, written by an obscure university lecturer from Leningrad. She had raised broad concerns about the reforms begun by Mikhail Gorbachev, lamenting unbridled public debate, modernization in the arts, loss of party discipline, and the denigration of Stalin, to name a few complaints.

Pravda saw her article as an anti-*perestroika* manifesto. Its stern rebuke of those who would revert to the "old thinking" was said to have been penned or authorized by a top Politburo ally of Mr. Gorbachev. The editorial called it "improper" for a publication to give space to views like those held by the Leningrad academic. Such views work against reform and progress, Pravda intoned – indicating again that *glasnost*, or openness, may have its government-defined limits.

Still, this kind of journalistic contentiousness is something not seen since the Soviet Union's earliest days. As the editor of Moscow News, one of the country's more liberal papers, put it, "*Glasnost* and debate are something so new to us that sometimes it gives us a headache."

Beneath the printed skirmishes rumbles a massive struggle to shape the Soviet economy into something it's never been: a productive, efficient operation. Gorbachev has been promoting *perestroika*, or economic restructuring, for a number of years now. Results so far are slim. Last year the USSR had its slowest economic growth of any year since World War II, save one. The stage was set by this, as well as discontent in some quarters over the planned pullout from Afghanistan, for a potshot at Gorbachev.

Quickened action on Afghanistan and other diplomatic fronts probably reflect the Soviet leader's desire to clear his decks and concentrate on the domestic economy. Gorbachev's surest way of fending off critics, certainly, is to show real gains in output and efficiency. That would indicate his "new socialism" indeed has a future.

Meanwhile, he can rebuff the "go slow" crowd with assertions that the old ways compiled an indisputably miserable record. Evidence of the need for reform – from stories of bureaucratic ineptitude to choking air pollution in some industrial centers – may pop up in the Soviet press with added frequency. Gorbachev needs to build all the pro-*perestroika* momentum he can muster.

The Boston Globe
Boston, MA, November 8, 1988

Even as they applaud Mikhail Gorbachev's innovations, Soviet dissidents and Western democrats find themselves debating a crucial question: Will Gorbachev's reforms usher in a new political order, or have they been fashioned in accordance with the shrewd conservative dictum that for things to remain the same they must change a little?

Does Gorbachev want to preserve the Bolshevik power system by modernizing it, or is he willing to permit a new system to evolve in order to achieve modernization?

A proposed new press law for the Soviet Union suggests a preliminary answer to that question. The answer, alas, seems to be that Gorbachev's rationale for changing the system is to preserve its essential traits.

If adopted, the new press law would prohibit the regular publication of papers, magazines or bulletins by any "social organization" not legally registered. Anyone violating this statute would be liable to legal penalties.

An immediate consequence of such a law would be to proscribe the myriad of unauthorized publications that have sprung up in all parts of the Soviet Union during the past three years. This blooming of a hundred flowers was made possible not merely by Gorbachev's positive policy of glasnost, but also by a negative anomaly in the old system. Until now, there simply was no law making some publications legal and others illegal. There seemed no need for such a law. Stalin's terror made it unthinkable for a private citizen to publish anything. In Brezhnev's time, when a dissident had to be punished for mimeographing a subversive publication, he or she was charged with "anti-Soviet agitation" or with spreading "false information slandering the Soviet state."

The inconvenience of these statutes, for the ruling class, is that they are blatantly political. Adoption of the new press law would provide an administrative rationale for shutting down all the independent papers and magazines that have come into being since Gorbachev inaugurated glasnost.

In the name of his vaunted plan to make the Soviet Union a socialist society based on law, Gorbachev would restore the party's monopoly on the means of information. Under the guise of rectifying the Stalinist penchant for arbitrary rule, the new statute on the press would deprive citizens of a right no Soviet ruler had ever bothered to take away from them, legally.

Even in the editorial offices of official publications, there is overt opposition to the new press law, since its provisions against libel would have a chilling effect on any journalist contemplating an expose of some local party baron.

Gorbachev is no Thomas Jefferson. He seeks not freedom of the press, but an official press to lead the cheers for his policies, rousing an alienated populace from its torpor and exposing the evils of his dead predecessors.

THE INDIANAPOLIS NEWS
Indianapolis, IN, November 3, 1988

TV screens in the Soviet Union are being filled with a whole assortment of new images — screaming rock bands, America's Mr. Rogers, Britain's Margaret Thatcher, and Soviet politicians actually disagreeing with one another in public.

It's all part of Mikhail Gorbachev's effort to open up Soviet society and bring his country into the second half of the 20th century.

The most widely noted turning point was during the Chernobyl nuclear accident in April 1986, which official Soviet media ignored for days, following longstanding party policy that disasters only happen in the United States.

Chernobyl focused international scrutiny on the woeful shortcomings of the Soviet news media, much to the embarrassment of Gorbachev. So now domestic disasters — fires, floods, plane hijackings, train wrecks — are reported on the national media. In typical Soviet style, however, disaster coverage is delayed a full day before airing — to minimalize sensationalism, perhaps, but also to secure clearance from party officials.

Yet despite the past's strong hold, Soviet television is making relatively rapid strides toward today. Much of the change occurred under the regime of Leonid Brezhnev, who got televisions out to the people. In 1960, according to Jonathan Sanders of World Monitor magazine, only 5 percent of the Soviet population could watch TV. Now more than 93 percent can.

What all those TV screens are showing is a marked change from the numbing propaganda that for years has ruled Soviet airwaves.

The 9 p.m. daily news show, Vremya — the most official of official broadcasts — has been a leading outlet for shaking up the old order.

During the June conference of the Communist Party, Vremya stunned Soviet viewers by showing a party delegate attacking prominent Politburo members by name. The next night, Vremya covered a bitter exchange between former Moscow party boss Boris Yeltsin and his Politburo enemy Yegor Ligachev. This kind of public squabbling, so common in the West, is unprecedented in the Soviet Union.

Glasnost has also brought contentious westerners into Soviet TV rooms. "British Prime minister Margaret Thatcher became an overnight hero to many Soviets last spring," Sanders writes, "when she took on and trashed several Soviet journalists in a 50-minute television interview."

ABC News anchor Peter Jennings, talk-show host Phil Donahue and even a game-show team of Russian-speaking Columbia University students have all made their way across the Iron Curtain onto popular Soviet TV shows.

This freer flow of information and culture on Soviet airwaves is promising and welcome. But as long as the party still owns every significant media outlet, all these new freedoms can be revoked just as quickly as they emerged.

The Hartford Courant
Hartford, CT, April 6, 1988

Who, five years ago, supposed that the Soviet Union would give its citizens routine access to Western newspapers and magazines? Probably no one. Yet such a dramatic policy change appears to be in the offing.

An aide to Soviet leader Mikhail S. Gorbachev recently said he expected the government to soon let ordinary citizens read Western periodicals. Finding the publications there is extremely difficult, and reading them requires official permission.

The significance of such a move would be much greater if no news or opinion from Western sources reached the Soviet people. The government, however, seems to have stopped jamming Western radio broadcasts. Printed material from the West is circulated secretly among intellectuals.

Still, allowing periodicals and newspapers form London, Paris, New York and Rome to be freely read would be a big step toward an open Soviet society. Printed news stories and commentary can carry much more information than can radio programs, so the potential for thoroughly and objectively informing Soviet readers about world events, including events in their own country, is enormous.

Such a policy change would benefit Mr. Gorbachev, who wants to be seen, at home and abroad, as embodying a new, enlightened style of Soviet leadership. It might also reflect an effort by the Soviets to shed their longstanding inferiority complex. The leaders wouldn't encourage cultural, economic and political comparisons if they feared the results.

But what would be best about letting the Western periodicals circulate is that it could at last bring the Soviet masses into full-fledged world citizenship. They probably would begin to feel involved as never before with peoples and problems outside the sphere of their government's influence.

No one can tell where such an awakening would lead. But it's clear that the Soviet Union, and the rest of the world, would be better for it. In countries as in individuals, ignorance spawns and nourishes fear and belligerence. Knowledge promotes confidence and cooperation.

The Wichita Eagle-Beacon
Wichita, KS, August 19, 1988

SOVIET television has changed over the past year in keeping with Soviet leader Mikhail S. Gorbachev's reform. Soviet television has made a leap in programming that has fascinated and even startled Soviet viewers.

Until this year, tractor exhibitions, folk festivals, morning exercises and language lessons were the usual television offerings in the USSR. There had been ideas for less traditional programs but they were forbidden during the Leonid Brezhnev era.

In 1985, Mr. Gorbachev sought to change the television industry and a few discussion shows were created. Last year a new show was aired. Mr. Gorbachev chose to use the television medium as a proving ground for his controversial ideas, and three young hosts of the new talk show saw themselves as "lieutenants of reform." They talked openly about the reforms in the USSR that once had been restricted topics.

In order to increase Soviet optimism for reform, the Soviet people have witnessed footage from the disaster scenes in Afghanistan, showing blood and bodies on a gravel road. A young man is seen in a veterans hospital as well. He says he is a Soviet soldier and did what he was told to do, but he doesn't know what the Soviet forces were doing there or if they should have been there at all.

Television has been capturing more attention than even Pravda, the official Communist Party newspaper. With the withdrawal on schedule of Soviet forces from Afghanistan being shown on television, the event is being regarded as proof by Soviet officials of Mr. Gorbachev's triumph in foreign policy.

Officials don't ignore television programming, as it's a barometer of public opinion shaped by Mr. Gorbachev. Television is helping the Soviet leader stand his ground. With a few shows transforming television in the Soviet Union, it's no wonder Mr. Gorbachev is being called the great communicator by those in the East and in the West.

Or is that the great manipulator?

Brezhnev's Son-in-Law Convicted in Corruption Scandal

The Soviet foreign ministry Feb. 3, 1987 confirmed the arrest of Yuri Churbanov, the son-in-law of the late Soviet President Leonid I. Brezhnev. Churbanov, 50, was married to Brezhnev's daughter, Galina. He had served as a first deputy minister of internal affairs until his demotion to a lesser post within the ministry in 1984.

Gennadi I. Gerasimov, the chief spokesman of the foreign ministry, disclosed that Churbanov had been arrested for "corruption and bribe-taking." He said that an investigation of the case was under way but declined to give further details.

A military tribunal Dec. 30, 1988 sentenced Churbanov to 12 years of hard labor for corruption. The trial had opened Sept. 5. Churbanov had pleaded guilty to abuse of power but innocent to accusations of bribe-taking. Churbanov was convicted of receiving the equivalent of US$1 million in bribes related to fraud in the cotten industry of the central Asian republic of Uzbekistan.

Six other defendants, tried along with Churbanov, were convicted of bribery and sentenced to prison terms ranging from eight to 10 years.

Separately, the name of the late Soviet leader Brezhnev would be removed from one city, a city district and two local squares, it was reported by Tass, the official Soviet news agency, Jan. 6, 1988. Most of the places had been named in Brezhnev's honor in November 1982, following his death. Brezhnev's memory had fallen into disfavor under Soviet leader Mikhail S. Gorbachev. Tass explained that the residents of the Brezhnev sites had petitioned the Communist Party and Soviet government to be rid of his name.

The Courier-Journal & Times

Louisville, KY,
September 7, 1988

CORRUPTION in the bureaucracy isn't new to Russia. Nikolai Gogol so savagely satirized official misdoings in *The Inspector General* that he was forced to flee to Rome to escape the hostile public reaction. Nor is official deceit new. Gogol covered that in *Dead Souls*.

What is rare is official acknowledgement that they exist — and in the highest places. So when *Pravda* carries a headline, "The Son-in-law and His Godfathers," over its account of the trial of Yuri Churbanov, and uses phrases like "organized crime" and "mafia" to describe protection rackets and extortion rings in Uzbekistan and other republics, Soviet citizens know things have changed.

And when the government's chief map maker acknowledges in *Izvestia* what the West has known — that public maps were deliberately falsified on orders of the secret police — another doorway has opened. Glasnost is prevailing.

The distortions fooled no one. They didn't even fool Soviet citizens, who wondered why KGB headquarters was omitted from the map of Moscow, and who knew the highway ringing Moscow is elliptical, not square. If the deception served any purpose, it was to make it harder for Soviet citizens to find their way about — and out. The broad-gauge Soviet railroads fill that same function.

In Mr. Churbanov's corruption trial, the charges involve a network of conspirators at the top of both state and party organizations who allegedly skimmed off millions of rubles. But it goes deeper. Mr. Churbanov, a mechanic who rose to the post of deputy interior minister and thus one of the nation's top law-enforcement officers, was married to the daughter of Leonid Brezhnev, whose failings as premier are intertwined with the charges against Mr. Churbanov.

In the Stalin era, Mr. Churbanov probably would have had a secret trial before being shot. Now the whole world is going to be privileged to hear his whole ugly story. Gogol would have loved it.

Winnipeg Free Press

Winnipeg, Man., September 11, 1988

Unprecedented is becoming an overworked adjective to describe the multiplying rivulets of information pouring out of cracks in the granite facade of the Soviet state bureaucracy as Mikhail Gorbachev's *glasnost* policy spreads its wings.

It seems better to think of these information leaks as rivulets rather than a flood for two reasons. One is that large areas of Soviet official life remain off limits, including aspects of sensitive historical events. The other is that all the information coming out so patently serves the political goals of the Soviet leader himself.

That said, there is much to enjoy in the irregular revelations because the Soviet Union remains today for most outsiders what Winston Churchill called it in a broadcast talk 49 years ago: "A riddle wrapped in a mystery inside an enigma."

This week alone there has been the amazing spectacle of high Soviet officials placed on trial for gargantuan corruption during the rule of the late Leonid Brezhnev, a claim by one Soviet historian that Brezhnev was a virtual vegetable for the last six years of his reign and detailed coverage of a Soviet space crisis that could have ended in disaster.

All three revelations can fit comfortably into the description of serving Mr. Gorbachev's goals. These goals include galvanizing the inefficient Soviet economy and discrediting the bureaucratic deadwood left over from the time before March, 1985 when Mr. Gorbachev and his new broom arrived in the musty corridors of the Kremlin.

Changing the air inside the Kremlin is hard work, as is shown by the case of the czarist falcons. It took a two-year Herculean effort by *Moskovskaya Pravda*, a Moscow morning newspaper, to establish the fact that Kremlin museum employees have been fighting a plague of big, aggressive crows by launching at them even more aggressive falcons of the kind that Ivan the Terrible and other counter-revolutionary despots used for hunting in past centuries.

The modest success of the experiment may have had some bearing on official denials that either problem or solution exists. The noisy crows damage the gold leaf on Kremlin onion domes, kill spruce trees by stripping them of bark, eat the tulips and dine on neighborhood sparrows. Since the falcons began dining on them, the crows have developed their own version of the Krasnoyarsk radar. When the falcons soar, the crows stay away. When the falcons sleep, the crows return.

The corruption trial, with its 1,500-page indictment, its televised display of a king's ransom in gold coins, cash and jewels, is ostensibly about dirty dealings in the Soviet Central Asian republic of Uzbekistan. It is really an indictment of Brezhnev and all his greedy cronies, the point being driven home by the fact that the key defendant is Brezhnev's son-in-law, Yuri Churbanov. Mr. Churbanov had the wit to marry Galina, Brezhnev's daughter, after which it was suddenly realized that he was overdue for promotion from junior policeman to general. Instead of fighting crime, he committed it, taking payoffs, bribes and kickbacks.

The record of Brezhnev and his cronies is further clouded by the claim of Soviet historian Roy Medvedev that Brezhnev died in January, 1976, was brought back to life, then spent the time until his November, 1982 final death as a virtual automaton. The claim is that he was kept going by cronies fearing loss of opportunity to dip their snouts and trotters in the hog trough.

Open coverage of the Soyuz spacecraft's problems was useful for persuading cynical Soviet citizens that change is really happening, as well as for persuading foreigners of the same thing. Public criticism, after its safe return, of the capsule commander's competence, showed that even the revered cosmonauts can be hauled on the carpet if they display the kind of inefficiency that damages expensive machinery and incurs costs.

The message from all three events is that no one, no matter how high, whether alive or dead, is immune to criticism if it can be shown that their actions shamed the country or posed a threat to *perestroika*, Mr. Gorbachev's term for overhauling the Soviet economic structure. The other message is that, in Moscow or on vacation in the Caucasus, he is calling the shots.

The Des Moines Register

Des Moines, IA, September 8, 1988

Soviet leaders have a way of legitimizing their rule by putting the alternative on trial. The "period of stagnation" is on trial now in the person of Yuri Churbanov, son-in-law of the late Leonid Brezhnev.

The Brezhnev era lasted nearly two decades. It was a time during which life was rather comfortable for the Soviet elite, with access to special stores and other privileges not available to the masses.

There was rigid adherence to the ideology of central planning. After all, the system worked fine — for the privileged elite. It also supported a military buildup that assured the Soviet Union never again would be humiliated, as happened in the Cuban missile crisis.

But the Soviet people endured living standards unworthy of a nation with pretense to greatness. The economy was at a standstill as the Soviet Union slipped farther and farther behind the West in everything but megatonnage.

Churbanov could hardly be a better symbol of the era. After becoming the third husband of Galina Brezhnev (the first two were circus performers, as was a purported lover after the marriage), Churbanov rose quickly to near the pinnacle of Soviet power and enjoyed a life of opulence.

There were private planes and limousines, a country dacha and seaside villa, imported wines and the finest foods. This in a nation where people must stand in line to buy lumps of greasy sausage — when it's available.

Churbanov stands accused of accepting more than $1 million in bribes from the "cotton mafia" in Uzbekistan, who were regularly allowed to falsify the size of the cotton crop in the region. Satellite photos allegedly show vast areas purportedly growing cotton to be nothing but desert.

The trial is a sensation in Moscow. It has it all — corruption, nepotism, the absurdities of central economic planning, and even Galina Brezhnev's eye for muscular circus performers.

The Brezhnev era now is in official disgrace as a time of moral decay. Mikhail Gorbachev likes the contrast with his own era of openness, economic restructuring and a higher moral tone — on the surface, at least.

What's unclear is how much — deep down — the system has really changed, and indeed whether it is capable of changing. That won't be known until long after the trial of Yuri Churbanov.

The TENNESSEAN

Nashville, TN, September 11, 1988

IN a show trial in Moscow there is an apparent attack on the late Leonid Brezhnev, the Soviet leader from 1964 to 1982, that may leave him little reputation.

The trial, which is liberally covered by the Soviet media, concerns Mr. Yuri Churbanov and eight co-defendants. Mr. Churbanov is married to the only daughter of the late Mr. Brezhnev. At the height of his power Mr. Churbanov was a candidate member of the Central Committee, the No. 2 man in the ministry of the interior, and a three-star police general.

The indictment against Mr. Churbanov was read at the beginning, and it was so lengthy that at one point, the prosecutor and one judge dozed off. It contained details of charges that the Brezhnev son-in-law accepted bribes totaling 656,883 rubles — $1.04 million.

Mr. Churbanov lived high on the hog. In addition to money, so the indictment says, he accepted gifts of household items, fine wines and cognac and had expensive fruit flown to him on a regular basis.

Investigators are said to have assembled 110 volumes of documents in the case which will likely reveal widespread corruption not only by Mr. Churbanov, but also of other Brezhnev confidants and relatives. It may even include the late Soviet leader himself.

The Soviet media have already begun to hammer at the memory of Mr. Brezhnev. One account says he was incapable of ruling during the latter period of his life. So there seems to be a concerted attack on the Brezhnev era.

There is political significance. Obviously, Mr. Mikhail Gorbachev is trying to distance himself from the Brezhnev period, and at the same time trying to send the message that corruption will not be tolerated.

It might be a blow to Mr. Yegor Ligachev, the second-ranking member of the Politburo. On several occasions Mr. Ligachev has criticized the blanket condemnation of Mr. Brezhnev and last year described the period as a time when people's lives "became materially and spiritually richer." Those words will haunt him now since the trial will underscore who became materially richer during the Brezhnev years.

The trial will be even more lurid as it goes along, and by the end Mr. Brezhnev will be totally repudiated and his ruling years a black mark on history. ■

The News and Courier

Charleston, SC, September 19, 1988

The Communist Party newspaper Pravda has published an unprecedented article saying "there are grounds to believe" that the late Bolshevik leader Leon Trotsky "was not an enemy of the revolution and socialism" during his years in the Soviet hierarchy between 1917 and 1924. The article is the clearest sign yet that Mikhail Gorbachev intends to honor his promise to fill in the "blank spots" of Soviet history.

Few names trigger Vesuvian scorn in the Soviet Union as surely as Trotsky's. Since Stalin exiled him from the USSR in 1929, Trotsky has been officially declared a "foreign agent" and the word "Trotskyism" is a term used to describe profound anti-Sovietism. To be called a "Trotskyite" in earlier days was to be handed a death sentence. Many of the hapless Bolshevik leaders whom Stalin sent to the cellars of Lubyanka and Lefortovo prisons or the Artic death camps during the great purges of the 1930s were first labeled "Trotskyites."

Leon Trotsky was the Bolshevik pseudonym of Lev Davidovich Bronstein, one of Lenin's earliest collaborators. During the 1905 Revolution, Bronstein was chairman of the St. Petersburg Soviet. Arrested by the czar's police and briefly imprisoned, he was expelled from Russia and eventually landed in New York, where he taught high school in the Bronx. (When he returned to Russia in 1917 after the March Revolution and helped the Bolsheviks seize power the following October, The Bronx Home News carried the wonderfully provincial banner headline: LOCAL MAN LEADS REVOLUTION.)

The newspaper may have overplayed Trotsky's role in the Bolshevik coup, but the Soviets have ignored it for 60 years. Trotsky was, among other things, the founder of the Red Army and he is credited by historians with formulating the Bolsheviks' victorious campaign in the Russian civil war. A gifted speaker and author of voluminous historical and theoretical works, Trotsky quickly earned the enmity of Stalin, who saw in him a powerful adversary. Stalin engineered Trotsky's ouster from the party and his eventual exile from the USSR. Obsessed with Trotsky and infuriated by his caustic comments published abroad, Stalin had him murdered in Mexico in 1940. The revolution does indeed eat its own.

Some of the other old Bolsheviks who battled Stalin for power after Lenin's death in 1924 — such as Lev Kamenev and Nickolai Bukharin — have already been rehabilitated by a special commission set up by Mr. Gorbachev. And even though the Soviet leader personally criticized Trotsky during the Revolution Day speech in Moscow last November, Soviet historians have been given greater freedom to openly discuss various figures from the past.

The great irony of Stalin's life, wrote a disaffected communist in 1937, is that one day he would come to be charged with "Trotskyism." The remark was prescient. It's author was Trotsky.

Soviets Disclose Budget Deficits

Finance Minister Boris I. Gostev Oct. 27, 1988 disclosed that the Soviet Union would have a budget deficit of 36.3 billion rubles (US$58 billion at the official exchange rate) in 1988. He admitted that the government had kept deficits hidden for several years.

"This is not a problem that has cropped up all of a sudden," he said. "It is the result of an unbalanced economy, of excessive subsidies, of huge losses caused by extensive management methods, parasitic attitudes and passive financial policy." The finance minister's statement was the first detailed public discussion by a high-ranking Soviet official of the nation's fiscal troubles. In the past, the Kremlin had either pronounced budgets balanced or boasted of budget supluses.

The announced deficit would amount to about 4% of the Soviet Union's gross domestic production, including the unofficial economy, according to the *New York Times*. The comparable figure for the U.S. for the latest fiscal year was 3.1%.

Later, in an interview with foreign reporters, Gostev announced that the Soviet Union was planning to create a stock market. He also said that the nation would totally revise its tax system, using Western models, in the 1990s.

Yuri D. Maslyukov, the chairman of the State Planning Committee (Gosplan), Oct. 27 reported to the Supreme Soviet that the economy was undergoing a "social reorientation" toward satisfying consumer demands. The planning chief told the legislators that 1988 had seen the "beginning of a growing dynamism of the economy." However, he cautioned against a "smug complacency in light of the improving general economic indicators."

In a related development, a coalition of seven U.S. companies April 13, 1988 had signed an agreement with the Soviet Foreign Economic Consortium to pursue joint business ventures. The pact was signed in Moscow. U.S. Commerce Secretary C. William Verity Jr. and 500 American business executives, including the representatives of the seven companies in the coalition, visited the Soviet capital April 11-13 to attend the 11th annual convention of the U.S.-U.S.S.R. Trade and Economic Council. The coalition called itself the American Trade Consortium. It consisted of Archer Daniels Midland Co., Chevron Corp., Eastman Kodak Co., Ford Motor Co., Johnson and Johnson, Mercator Corp., and RJR Nabisco Inc.

The Dallas Morning News
Dallas, TX, October 27, 1988

This week's meeting between West German Chancellor Helmut Kohl and Soviet President Mikhail Gorbachev may be the first phase in Moscow's grand scheme to cement a European loan commitment of $8 billion in hard currency. Why would Mr. Kohl and other European leaders go along with it? They are, to begin with, anxious to increase trade with the Soviet Union and apparently believe that strengthening Mr. Gorbachev's political base through the granting of loans will assist in that process.

The West Germans have their own agenda, beginning with their vaguely defined yearning for German reunification. While Moscow has no intention per se of granting that wish, Bonn appreciates the fact that the Soviets did give East German leader Erich Honecker approval to visit West Germany last year and have begun allowing some of the 2 million ethnic Germans in the Soviet Union to emigrate.

The results of Soviet efforts at political reform (*glasnost*) and economic reform (*perestroika*) will not be known for some time. And it could be true, as some European leaders now believe, that East-West tensions can be reduced. But Washington is justified in its caution, reflected in a recent Senate resolution calling for talks between the U.S.

and its allies on the implications of extending credits to Moscow.

An obvious question arises from Europe's new generosity toward the Soviet Union, which none of its leaders seem quite prepared to answer: What sense does it make for Western Europe to extend billions of dollars in loans and credits to the Soviet Union and then milk both U.S. taxpayers and its own to pay the offsetting billions in maintaining NATO readiness against the conventionally superior Warsaw Pact?

Since West Germany, Italy, France, Britain and Japan already may have their minds made up about proffering these loans to Moscow, they should at least place some conditions on the Soviets. Western nations should insist in no uncertain terms that the Soviet Union begin making drastic reductions in Warsaw Pact conventional forces to eliminate its overwhelming advantage, as opposed to simply sparring over this critical question of Western defense.

Should Chancellor Kohl return home from Moscow $8 billion poorer and with a stack of scientific, human rights and economic agreements and no new understanding regarding conventional force parity, his diplomatic trip may just have to be reclassified a mugging.

The Honolulu Advertiser
Honolulu, HI, November 4, 1988

The Soviet Union's first admission that its national budget has been in the red for the past decade shows some interesting parallels with the U.S. deficit predicament. But this is one race we are still winning.

Soviet problems are reflected in various ways. For example, U.S. military sources say the reduced number of Soviet warships and sailing time in the Indian and Pacific Oceans seems to more reflect a budget squeeze than Moscow's new policy of less confrontation and more diplomatic activity.

The Soviet finance minister put their deficit at about $55 billion in U.S. dollars. Some Western analysts suggest it could actually be twice that, and much more of a problem for Soviet President Gorbachev than is being suggested in this first revelation there is a problem.

But, while the higher figure would still be well behind last year's U.S. deficit of $155 billion, the Soviets also seem more optimistic about their problem. "We'll try to get rid of it in one year," said the finance minister in Moscow with what may prove overstated optimism.

In any event, no presidential candidate here this year is talking in terms of getting rid of our deficit fast, even if it is an enormous drain on the economy. In fact, failure to adequately address the issue, and face up to the possible need for a tax hike, is one of the major failures on both sides of this campaign.

The Dallas Morning News

Dallas, TX, October 3, 1988

Parker Bros. is developing a Russian-language version of the cutthroat board game Monopoly. Considering that the game gave millions of Americans their first taste of buying, selling and cheating the capitalist way, the idea of making the game compatible with Soviet communism is intriguing.

Instead of Park Place, Russians might deal for real estate on Arbat Place. Instead of the B&O Railroad, they might buy the Siberian Railroad. At the worst, instead of "Go To Jail" they might land on "Go To The Gulag."

Of course, the Soviets cornered the market on monopolies long ago, since their system doesn't allow competition. Maybe we better wish they don't get too good at it.

The San Diego Union

San Diego, CA, October 27, 1988

The haste with which Western Europe is falling over itself to lend money to the Soviet Union should be a source of deep concern to Congress, the Reagan administration, the American people, and everybody else in the Free World.

Decades of Marxist controls, isolation and stagnation behind its self-imposed Iron Curtain have left the Soviet economy weak, disorganized, and uncompetitive. To resuscitate this wasted society, Mikhail Gorbachev's *perestroika* needs nothing so much as massive injections of Western capital.

According to the British journal, *The Economist*, The Soviet Union's budget deficit is now about 14 percent of its gross domestic product. By comparison, America's deficit is 3 percent of its GNP. Much of the Soviet debt has been incurred on armaments and training. "Soviet statistics have been doctored to hide the true size of military spending, much of which is concealed under other headings, and with understated prices for military equipment," asserts *The Economist*.

The Soviet people are beginning to demand butter to match the Kremlin's guns. Mr. Gorbachev well knows that to meet rising demands he must underpin his economic reforms with political reforms. Hence his impressive consolidation of personal power.

European bankers have been quick to spot the trading opportunities in a renascent Russia. Within the space of 10 days, banks in West Germany, France, Great Britain, and Italy have offered the Soviets more than $7 billion for projects ranging from a $540 million nuclear reactor to vehicle plants and food-processing factories.

Many of the loans will be spent on modernizing the Soviet Union's light industry, most of which is archaic by Western standards. Moscow is earmarking the money for factories producing consumer goods.

On the other hand, Soviet loan appeals to Japan have met a far different reception. Tokyo analysts describe the granting of credit to the Soviet Union as "unlikely," largely because of cool relations resulting from the Soviet refusal to return to Japan the Kuril Islands off Hokkaido seized by the Soviets at the end of World War II.

American reaction to the new Soviet loans by the European democracies has been cool. Sen. Bill Bradley of New Jersey spoke for a lot of Americans: "It would be a tragic mistake if Western capital enables the U.S.S.R. to put off the hard choice between guns and butter."

In the 1970s, free-world banks advanced billions of dollars to the Soviets, who then undertook the greatest military buildup in peacetime history. Moscow pushed into Africa, Afghanistan, Central America, and Southeast Asia. Their trucks and weapons came from factories paid for by the West.

The question Congress must face is: Should the United States continue to defend Western Europe through its NATO commitments at the cost of $150 billion annually and stand idly by while our principal allies, who are doing too little in their own defense, are financing the adversary?

Pentagon officials believe Western credit will enable the Soviet Union to continue financing global commitments and adventures inimical to U.S. interests. Indeed, the Republican Party platform calls for an end to such loans because they "provide the Soviet Union with desperately needed hard currency to bolster its weak economy and facilitate Soviet purchase of U.S. technology."

Furthermore, the $7 billion credit already approved is only the thin edge of the wedge. West German finance expert Peter Pietsch, of the Commerzbank, the third-largest private bank in the country, forecasts: "Credit not only from West Germany but from all of Western Europe will be increasing and expanding in coming years."

The incoming administration must give this problem its urgent attention. If necessary, it must consult with America's European allies through the 24-nation Organization for Economic Cooperation and Development and formulate ground rules for regulating future loans and lines of credit to the U.S.S.R.

Of course, this action carries the risk of offending America's European allies by imposing controls on the free flow of capital, but the risks attaching to unrestricted credit for the Soviet Union are infinitely greater.

Omaha World-Herald

Omaha, NE, October 29, 1988

The Soviet Union is showing the world a different face, a demeanor that at times is almost humble.

For decades, the Soviets have presented a facade of arrogant, brutish power — admitting no faults and blaming everything wrong in the world on the Western democracies. Now, suddenly, they are admitting that they have food shortages, corruption, budget deficits, incompetent bureaucrats and general economic and political difficulties.

Official newspapers and magazines are acknowledging for the first time that airplane crashes, prostitution, drug addiction and youth gangs exist within the nation's borders.

The Soviet Union, in this new posture, somewhat resembles the Wizard of Oz. The curtain has been pulled, showing not a mighty wizard but a fragile little man. The pompous, thundering voice and the special effects that created an aura of power around him were all the result of a sound and light show.

The Soviets still have a formidable military machine, of course, but the economy that underpins that machinery is weak. Following the directives of Stalin, the Soviet Union and most of its satellite states in Eastern Europe invested heavily in big industries such as steel, cement and coal. They did not develop consumer goods to be sold on the world market. Several Third World nations such as Brazil and South Korea can now supply steel and heavy machinery and basic industrial goods cheaper than the Soviets, and the quality is better.

The Soviets simply have little to sell on the world market and have not been able to provide their people the basic consumer goods that citizens in industrialized Western countries take for granted.

As a result, the government of Mikhail Gorbachev has come to the West with hat in hand. Prime Minister Helmut Kohl of West Germany is one of a number of West European leaders who have been invited to the Kremlin recently, apparently to set up some kind of European Marshall Plan to shore up the reform-minded regime of Gorbachev. Prime Minister Margaret Thatcher of Britain will have none of it, and the Reagan administration has expressed skepticism.

If the Soviets are serious, they will continue with disarmament talks and make more gestures like the plan to convert the treaty-breaking radar installation at Krasnoyarsk into a civilian-controlled space research station.

The Philadelphia Inquirer

Philadelphia, PA,
August 2, 1988

Soviet emigres returning to their homeland as tourists virtually all come back with the same report: The intellectual climate has changed incredibly over the last couple of years; the standard of living, if anything, has gotten worse.

That the mountains of liberalizing decrees have done little or nothing to reduce the lines in the shops or to put more meat on the table casts doubt on the viability of Mikhail S. Gorbachev's programs. No one realizes that more than the Soviet leader himself, who at a major Communist Party meeting last week railed against his fellow officials' "callous attitude" toward the ubiquitious lines for food and services that rob people of their energy and optimism.

Mr. Gorbachev said that the Politburo is on the case and is preparing "urgent and cardinal measures" to improve food supplies. Consumers might find that language heartening if Soviet leaders, including Mr. Gorbachev, had not been making similar promises for decades. And when Mr. Gorbachev exclaims, as he did Friday, "How can we tolerate this!" all but the most blindly loyal citizens know the answer: The party bosses live in a world of perks and privileges that exempts them from the travails of lines and shortages.

The only way for Mr. Gorbachev to move beyond hollow promises is to chip away at the main obstacle to consumer satisfaction in the Soviet system — state ownership and control of virtually all the nation's land and means of production. Each new wave of reforms takes him a little farther in that direction. He is now talking about leasing unlimited amounts of land to private farmers and even of turning over failing factories to entrepreneurs.

While he insists "there is nothing non-socialist about this," he is in fact retreating from the Marxist-Leninist precepts that are at the heart of the Soviet state. His goal is to create an ideal hybrid that combines the best aspects of socialism and capitalism, but there is no working model. All the success stories in the world — whether in the West or in Asia — are relatively unimpeded free market economies. The more Mr. Gorbachev moves in that direction, the better off Soviet consumers are likely to be.

Arkansas Gazette

Little Rock, AR, October 31, 1988

Kipling (or somebody) once advanced the theory that Russians took on a new set of problems when they tried to emulate the West. During one important interlude in its history, the Soviet Union claimed to have invented just about everything, but that strategy seems to have been abandoned.

Finance Minister Boris I. Gostev made no claim the USSR had discovered a painless way to finance government operations when he confessed his country was running large budget deficits. Neither, for that matter, did he credit the United States with having demonstated the magic of debt financing.

For the first time since the revolution, the Soviet government acknowledged that revenues were failing to match spending. The deficit for 1989 is expected to be 36.3 billion rubles, or about $58 billion. The budget was reported at 494 billion rubles ($790 billion), which meant the deficit was about 7 percent of expected spending.

The United States can do better than that. President Reagan offered (and Congress adopted) a 1989 budget that exceeds $1 trillion and the deficit is likely to be about $150 billion. That works out to a debt growth equal to about 15 percent of spending. America *should* do better in deficit spending than most countries. It has had more experience.

In acknowledging the deficit, Gostev confirmed the ferment in the Soviet Union. The view from the historic perspective has always been that changes in the giant country would come, regardless of who happened to be running the show. In the absence of an undercurrent, Mikhail S. Gorbachev could never have come to power. Now there is unmistakable evidence that he is speeding the innovations.

It is safe to assume this is not the first Soviet deficit. Others have been covered by fiscal legerdemain and, in the closed economy of Joe Stalin, there was no reason to reveal that revenues did not match spending. Gorbachev has realized that the entrenched communist economic system could not keep Russia in step with the remainder of the developed world, process the vast resources, and raise living standards. Soviet ideology had to bend if the economy was to be salvaged.

The hazard now is that Gorbachev and his successors, having discovered the joys of deficit spending, will pursue the course toward the brink of self-destruction. Any politician knows that borrowing money is less painful than collecting taxes to cover the bills. Debt expansion is an open invitation to initiate spending programs that make the citizens feel safe and happy but that saddle succeeding generations with massive burdens. "Star Wars" purchased on credit is more appealing than a pay-as-you-go Strategic Defense Initiative.

Indications are that Gorbachev, having come late to the game of deficit financing, plans to make a serious effort to balance his budget. Apparently there are ample opportunities to cut waste and fraud by closing inefficient operations, trimming the bureaucracies, and rewarding efficient producers. On the revenue side, the contorted communist ideology is expected to allow more private initiative and to collect taxes on the profits.

So far as can be determined, no one in authority has promised to *increase* tax collections by *reducing* the rate. Clearly Gorbachev still has not achieved the level of sophistication that is practiced in other parts of the developed world. There is also a possibility that the demonstrations he has seen have not convinced him the approach works.

The Boston Globe

Boston, MA, October 14, 1988

If there is one axiom shared by capitalists and Marxists, it is that economic forces cause political effects. Hence ideologues for both sides should agree that West Germany's offering of a $1.6 billion line of credit to the Soviet Union may be a momentous event – a premonitory sign that the Cold War of the last half-century could be petering out.

Arranged by a banking consortium that the Deutsche Bank leads, this is the biggest credit line the West has ever provided to Moscow. Though it is a purely commercial arrangement not guaranteed by the Bonn government, the signing of the agreement will serve as a highlight of Chancellor Helmut Kohl's visit to the Soviet Union later this month. The political implications of the event are recognized by all parties.

The link between perestroika and Western credits has long been obvious. Gorbachev cannot restructure the stagnant economy bequeathed to him by his predecessors without substantial loans from the Europeans, the Japanese and, eventually, the United States.

In the three-and-a-half years since Gorbachev ascended to power, it has been evident that his drastic alterations of the party line had as a principal purpose the need to alter perceptions of the Soviet Union in the capitalist democracies. The changes he wrought in Soviet foreign policy, tolerance for dissent, emigration, political structures and economic practice – all served to prepare for the day when Soviet borrowers would knock on the doors of foreign bankers, asking for loans.

Nor were Gorbachev and his teammates timid about saying they hoped to instill trust abroad, to make Moscow a respectable member of the community of nations. When Foreign Ministry spokesman Gennady Gerassimov had to explain the goal of dramatic changes taking place in his country, that slick packager of the new Soviet image dropped his customary sardonic tone, saying simply: "We want to be a civilized nation."

For many right-wingers in the United States, nothing has seemed more frightening than the prospect of lending shrewd Marxist-Leninists in Moscow the funds to prop up their evil empire. Should bankers and businessmen in the West suddenly cast off all reservations about commerce with the Soviet Union, the knee-jerk anticommunists would lose a large part of the political capital they had invested in the cold war.

Although the question of whether to finance perestroika has been one of the issues ignored in the presidential campaign, the next president will not be able to evade it. A wise defender of American interests will want to give Gorbachev a lift along the capitalist road.

The Des Moines Register

Des Moines, IA, June 28, 1988

Mikhail Gorbachev has the classic problem of dismounting the tiger. How does he do it without being devoured?

The Soviet leader knows he must introduce elements of a market economy and other freedoms to get his creaking empire moving. Yet things are likely to get worse before they get better.

The negative effects of market forces — such as layoffs, tougher workplace discipline and higher prices — will be felt before any of the offsetting benefits of a more vigorous, productive economy.

The communist government has an implicit social contract with the Soviet people. Sure, consumer goods are scarce and shoddy in the workers' paradise. But in exchange for their stoic acceptance of a standard of living unbecoming to a superpower, the people have things such as guaranteed employment, low bread prices, cheap rent and other security blankets.

How does Gorbachev convince the Soviet people to surrender their security blankets before he can yet deliver the consumer goodies that will make the sacrifice worthwhile?

A suggestion: Open the Soviet market to unlimited amounts of Western consumer goods.

The desire for Western goods in the Soviet Union is legend, typified by tourists being propositioned for their Levis. Moreover, Soviets are noted for having plenty of spending money. There's not much to buy, but a wad of cash is kept handy just in case something does turn up on the market.

Opening the market to Western goods could allow Soviet consumers to see an immediate improvement in their lot, while at the same time providing a tangible demonstration of Gorbachev's resolve to bring the Soviet Union fully into the world community.

It's unlikely to happen. Opening itself fully to Western goods would require a big change in national psychology. The Soviet Union has a virtually self-contained economy. The price for economic self-sufficiency is high: stagnation and the inability to keep up with the West. But it is part of the security blanket.

Then there are the risks of competition. Who'd buy Russian shoes if they could buy Italian? Who'd buy a Soviet washing machine if they could buy American? Perestroika is supposed to expose Soviet factory managers to competition, but that would probably be more than they could handle.

Opening the Soviet Union to Western consumer goods — glasnost in the marketplace — would be a bold stroke indeed, but it might put Gorbachev right back astride another tiger.

The Boston Globe

Boston, MA, November 7, 1988

One measure of the Soviet economy is its ability to compete with international goods in difficult markets. The Soviet Union has had considerable success with such staple items as oil and natural gas, which are freely exchangeable with oil and gas from other sources, but it has had limited success with manufactured goods, particularly consumer goods. There are signs, however, that it has made gains, which has given it more confidence about that competition. That should be healthy for all parties.

Next month, the Soviet government will hold its first comprehensive trade fair in the United States. The fair, to be held at the Javits convention center in New York, will exhibit 4.500 products, ranging from toys to machine tools, that Soviet Union enterprises are ready to export to the United States.

Whether Americans are prepared to buy such goods is another matter – one that will depend on their evaluation of the goods' quality and price and the reliability of service.

That Soviet industry is prepared to take the chance in open markets is an indicator of improvements in at least some sectors of its economy.

Americans may misunderstand or underestimate aspects of the Soviet economy because of its bad reputation for turning out consumer goods and its notorious record of providing poor service and inadequate spare parts for keeping things working, and for its weak showing in the computer field. In fact, Soviet successes have been notable in some highly complex undertakings, as its space program illustrates clearly.

The improvements are certainly spotty, and Soviet President Gorbachev's insistence on major revamping of the economy points to significant shortfalls. But the trade fair indicates that an interesting start has been made, with perhaps more to come, and the commerce it may engender can only improve East-West relations and stimulate both economies.

Anti-Alcoholism
Measures Set

The Soviet government instituted a series of measures aimed at combating rampant alcoholism in the Soviet Union. The measures were announced by Tass, the official news agency, May 16, 1985.

Alcoholism was a major problem in the U.S.S.R. It was the third most prevalent ailment in the nation, after heart disease and cancer. Alcohol poisoning accounted for more than 50,000 deaths a year in the Soviet Union, according to Western statistics. Alcoholism was also considered a key factor in declining Soviet worker output, and contributed to crime and divorce. According to Western statistics, up to 80% of robberies and assaults in the Soviet Union were alcohol-related, as were 75% of murders and rapes. Western analysts believed alcohol figured in up to 45% of the divorces in the U.S.S.R.

The annual Soviet consumption of liquor was believed to be about 4.5 gallons a year per person 15 years or older, the highest average in the world.

The anti-alcoholism measures included:

■ Raising the legal drinking age to 21 from 18.
■ A gradual decline in the production of vodka and other liquors, beginning in 1986.
■ A ban on the sale of fruit-based high-alcohol beverages.
■ Prohibiting the sale of liquor before 2 p.m. on workdays.
■ Stricter penalties for public drunkeness and drunk driving.
■ Improved treatment for alcoholics.
■ Soviet leader Mikhail S. Gorbachev May 15 visited the Kirov machinery plant in Leningrad, the nation's second-largest city. It was his first trip to a Soviet city, other than Moscow, since assuming power in March. Gorbachev toured the plant and spoke to its workers, urging them to raise productivity and avoid the ills of alcohol.

A factor in the Soviet Unions's 1988 budget deficit was revenues lost to the state by the cutback in the sales of alcoholic beverages during the Kremlin's three-year campaign against alcoholism, according to Finance Minister Boris I. Gostev Oct. 27, 1988. Alcoholic beverages were subject to high sales taxes in the U.S.S.R. The Council of Ministers, or cabinet, had approved a plan to ease the anti-alcoholism campaign, it was reported in the West Sept. 27. Under the plan, restrictions on the production and sale of vodka would remain in place, but Soviets would have greater access to beer, cognac and wines. The U.S.S.R. had instituted sugar rationing, it was reported in the West April 25, because of a nationwide shortage caused by the clandestine making of home-distilled vodka.

Roanoke Times & World-News

Roanoke, VA, August 11, 1985

EVERY ARMY has its Beetle Baileys, soldiers in name only who would rather goof off and have a good time than do their duty. Maybe that's the way to explain the story about four Soviet soldiers who traded their tank for two cases of vodka. Or maybe it says something about the overall quality of Soviet fighting forces.

This story was written by Ota Filip, a Czechoslovak emigre who contributes occasionally to a newspaper in Frankfurt, West Germany. Filip says reliable sources gave him this account:

During Warsaw Pact maneuvers in Czechoslovakia last fall, a four-man Soviet tank crew got lost as darkness fell. The weather was cold, rainy and foggy, and the crew felt a need for some personal antifreeze. Their vodka ration had been cut because of a government campaign against alcoholism; so they drove into a village, found a tavern that was still open, and bargained with the owner.

After a couple hours of merrymaking, the four left the tavern with two cases of vodka (24 bottles) and several pounds of herring and pickles. The tavern-keeper retained a wedding ring left by one of the soldiers. He also kept the tank, which he dismantled and sold for scrap. The tankers were found sleeping off their binge in a forest two days later.

Maybe it's just an amusing anecdote. But it echoes the message of a book published a couple of years ago, "The Threat: Inside the Soviet Military Machine." To learn what the typical Soviet soldier is like, author Andrew Cockburn interviewed many of the thousands of Soviet Jews who served a hitch in the Red Army and then were allowed to emigrate to the West.

From this, Cockburn drew up a composite of Pvt. Ivan Ivanovich, the average Soviet draftee. Ivan, like Beetle Bailey, comes off as lazy and poorly disciplined. He is also discontented, ignorant, and a heavy drinker. Not exactly your model fighting man.

His commanders don't look much better. They would be much more concerned about covering up the story of the great tank caper in Czechoslovakia than making an example of the errant crew. Anyway, to judge from Cockburn's book the soldiers may have gotten the better part of the bargain with the tavern-keeper. Soviet tanks are badly designed and underpowered, and they break down about every 100 miles. The undependability of these machines is one reason the Russians make tens of thousands of them.

This incident suggests that NATO officers might need to write another tactical scenario into their battle plans. Along with rockets, cannons and other anti-tank weapons, near the front stockpile thousands of cases of vodka and munchies. Then airdrop leaflets inviting Soviet tank crews to a big party. Free parking, comrades — right next to the recycling center.

The London Free Press
London, Ont.,
August 8, 1985

The story of four thirsty Soviet soldiers who traded their tank for 24 bottles of vodka offers a little comic relief to otherwise gloom-and-doom military news.

The wayward foursome, according to a West German newspaper, became lost on recent Warsaw pact manoeuvres in Czechoslovakia and found refuge at a village pub where, after running out of money, they persuaded the publican to accept their parked tank in exchange for more booze. The innkeeper was so pleased with the deal that he threw in some herring and pickles as "a gesture of comradeship."

The yarn, attributed to a Czech emigre author who in turn says he heard it from "reliable sources," claims the tank crew was found two days later snoozing in a forest, and their escapade was uncovered when pieces of the dismantled tank were sold to a metal recycling centre.

Though apocryphal, the account has a certain universal appeal to those familiar with the sentiments of rank-and-file servicemen who become fed up with discipline and bored with military routine. They're reflected in the widespread tendency to petty larceny when troops are presented with an opportunity for bartering government property for personal benefit.

It even makes the Soviets seem more human, somehow, to think that such capitalistic corruption may exist in citizens of such a totalitarian state.

While it does not exactly follow the Biblical admonition of beating swords into plowshares, trading one tank for a case of vodka opens up intriguing possibilities should this sort of defalcation catch on.

Makes one wonder what a Sam missile might fetch.

The Dispatch

Columbus, OH, August 12, 1985

Military lore of nations throughout history is loaded with stories of hard-drinking soldiers, but a story coming out of Czechoslovakia is sure to go down as a classic. It proves, too, that the recently announced Kremlin crackdown on alcoholism in the Soviet Union is coming none too soon.

Reports have it that the crew of a Soviet tank that was taking part in last fall's Warsaw Pact military maneuvers managed to get lost on a particularly dank and dreary day. The tank wound up in a remote village and, since the crew's vodka supply was getting low, they pulled the tank up to a tavern. They didn't have much to bargain with, but managed to get one bottle of vodka when the tank commander traded in his gold wedding ring.

That wasn't nearly enough, however, so the crew cut a deal with the tavern owner: two cases of vodka in exchange for the tank. The barmaster was so happy with the deal that he threw in seven pounds of herring and pickles for free.

When discovered asleep a few days later in a nearby forest, the crew told officials they didn't know what had become of the tank. Their story started to unravel, however, when a local junk dealer reported that he had just received large amounts of high-quality steel from a local businessman. The tavern owner, it turned out, was cutting the tank up and selling it for scraps.

It isn't known what has become of the crew and the tavern owner, but it can be surmised that the incident will spur Soviet officials to greater effort in trying to stem the consumption of alcohol by soldiers and civilians alike. Kremlin officials announced in June that they had had enough of alcohol-inspired crime and absenteeism and were taking action to reduce public dependence on spirits.

They'll need all the luck they can get. Alcoholism has long been a major problem in the Soviet Union, but rarely before has such meaning been given to the word "tanked."

The Philadelphia Inquirer

Philadelphia, PA, May 25, 1985

Soviet leader Mikhail Gorbachov is trying to crack down on an old Russian problem — alcoholism — for new reasons. It is the Soviet Union's third most prevalent ailment after heart disease and cancer and the main reason life expectancy for men is declining.

The reason for the new campaign is the damage that drinking does to labor productivity. Pravda wrote recently about how productivity plummets after paydays and weekends because of drunkenness, and factory managers have written to newspapers complaining of drinking on the job.

Mr. Gorbachov has made labor discipline the heart of his campaign to revive the flagging Soviet economy. How well his anti-drinking measures are accepted will be one of his first major tests before the Soviet public.

Drinking certainly is not a problem novel to the Soviet Union. But Russians, to whom shots of vodka are an essential element of any celebration, are the world's biggest consumers of hard liquor. Sociologists, Western and Soviet, offer varied explanations: the role of drinking in the culture, rapid urbanization, loss of some of the nation's values or boredom at lack of after-work entertainment, a problem hinted at in the government's promise of more recreational facilities along with its package of stiff measures against alcohol abuse.

The campaign against the "green serpent," Russian slang for vodka, won't be easy. The last czar and the early Bolsheviks tried to ban alcohol without success during World War I, and previous campaigns against drinking have led to production booms in homemade moonshine. Raising the drinking age from 18 to 21, imposing heavy fines on public drunks and moonshine makers, decreasing production of alcoholic beverages — all may have no more success than America's experiment with Prohibition.

But Mr. Gorbachov's success or failure in rallying public support for his teetotaling measures will reveal much about his ability to rally Soviets jaded by the past few years of geriatric leaders. He has been flashing his style on Leningrad streets, buttonholing workers in front of television cameras to warn them that drunkenness is a critical problem for the country. Even if the anti-alcohol campaign falls short of its goals it should give some signs of whether Soviets are willing to sacrifice, and to work harder, at the behest of more dynamic leadership at the top.

THE PLAIN DEALER

Cleveland, OH, May 19, 1985

You may be certain that when Soviet authorities drop all reticence about drunkenness, alcoholism must be doing serious damage to the social fabric of the socialist paradise. It hasn't helped the work ethic either. A Soviet newspaper estimates that restricting the sale and consumption of vodka could increase productivity 10%.

Hard drinking in the Soviet Union is akin to the drug problem in the United States, although Soviet statistics indicate an even broader range of citizens is affected. The ability of the proletariat to live exemplary lives and build a sturdy socialist economy is deeply impaired.

Television and newspaper campaigns in recent weeks have prepared the Soviet people for tough new measures that include raising the drinking age from 18 to 21, phasing out sweet, fruit-based alcoholic drinks and delaying the opening of liquor stores on work days. Production of vodka will be cut back, but prohibition, in effect earlier in the century, evidently was considered unworkable, even in a police state.

To compensate for shrinking supplies of booze, the government has promised to increase the availability of soft drinks, juices, jams and fresh fruit to replace the banned sweet liqueurs. It seems naive to imagine hardened drinkers cheerfully turning to such substitutes, but the Kremlin does appear to realize that a stick without a carrot won't work.

The Russian reputation for serious drinking predates communism by many centuries. Indeed, prohibition that was introduced at the start of World War I was repealed by the Bolsheviks in 1924. You have to believe, however, that those early communists expected to build such an enriching, fulfilling society that nobody would turn to liquor for refuge.

The fact is that both teen-agers and women have joined menfolk in a monumental binge that is cutting life expectancy, causing physical and mental damage, increasing the divorce rate and contributing to crime, including most murders, rapes and robberies. Why so many Soviet citizens are drinking their lives away is a fascinating question for outsiders and a compelling one for the Kremlin.

The most likely reason apppears to be boredom; a lack of variety in Soviet life, an absence of challenge. Religion is discouraged, political dissent is crushed. In the absence of spiritual outlets, consumerism is the prevailing creed, but the Soviet system is unable to deliver the goods. The new laws against drinking, which Soviet leader Mikhail Gorbachev appears to be counting on to revive productivity, no doubt will deter some. The laws will not get to the heart of what ails one of the world's most repressive social and economic systems.

the Charleston Gazette

Charlotte, WVA, March 23, 1988

UNTIL a few years ago, the Soviet Union used to boast a great deal about its system of free medical care. But under Mikhail Gorbachev's policy of *glasnost*, the gulf between the claims made for Russian health care and the reality is wide indeed.

Start at the beginning, with birth. The U.S.S.R. ranks a sorry 50th among the world's nations in infant mortality — after Barbados and ahead of the United Arab Emirates. Officially, the Soviet infant-mortality rate is 25.4 deaths per 1,000 live births, but Western experts estimate the number is closer to the 35-40 range.

(The United States, while much higher up on the ladder, still has nothing to boast of. In America, the infant mortality rate currently stands at 11 per 1,000 live births, making it a backward 17th among all nations. What a miserable commentary this is on the world's two "great" superpowers.)

Provided Ivan lives beyond his first year, he can expect a greater likelihood of lung cancer, up from 26 deaths per 100,000 in 1961 to 74 in 1982. But the greatest danger to a Soviet's health is heart disease, a problem not helped by the country's indulgence in heavy smoking, as well as heavy drinking.

Should he become ill, Ivan can't look forward to staying in a comfortable, sanitary hospital. Over one-third of the U.S.S.R.'s district hospitals operate without hot water, while 27 percent have no sewage facilities. There are chronic shortages of basic health care supplies such as bandages and disposable hypodermic syringes — no small consideration in the era of AIDS.

Incredibly, 40 percent of Russian medical school graduates can't read simple X-rays or cardiograms. And, while Americans can sue for malpractice, there is no law in the Soviet Union that will get rid of incompetent physicians.

Altogether, the picture of Soviet health care is bleak. Far from being a nation capable of conquering the world, it seems to be one that can't even handle a common cold.

WORCESTER TELEGRAM

Worcester, MA, September 28, 1988

Could Mikhail Gorbachev's political future depend on a shot of vodka served at room temperature without vermouth, tonic or orange juice? Would the Soviet leader founder because he tried to cut the alcohol intake of his country's citizens?

Perhaps not. But drinking in the Soviet Union is no small matter, and Gorbachev has learned that the hard way. He was forced to lift his despised restrictions on alcohol sales.

The drinking controls that he imposed in 1985 have reduced public drunkenness and crimes in the Soviet Union. But the same controls also hurt the economy and created a sugar shortage as citizens turned to illicit moonshine. Just as important, they have built a tremendous resentment among the public.

Now the government has given orders to increase production of wine, beer and vodka in state-controlled distilleries. Liquor stores will be allowed to have longer business hours. Wine, beer and champagne will once again be sold in grocery stores. Those popular little wine and beer bars, where Ivan and Natasha can drown their sorrow leaning against the counter, will reopen again.

The new policy should do away with the long lines of thirsty customers outside the stores, creating angry scenes. But it does represent a minor setback for the Kremlin's No.1 reformer.

The anti-drinking campaign was an important part of Gorbachev's grand design, and with good reason. Alcoholism is a major problem in the Soviet Union, causing serious social, law enforcement and production problems. But putting Soviet citizens on the wagon has proved risky at a time when Gorbachev needs popular support.

Gorbachev may be getting good reviews for glasnost and perestroika in the West, but in his own country he has been losing the battle of the bottle. His willingness to compromise indicates that the Soviet leader hasn't forgotten the old Leninist principle: two steps forward, one step backwards.

The Courier-Journal & TIMES

Louisville, KY, April 29, 1988

POOR Mikhail Gorbachev. He tries to wean his hard-drinking countrymen from alcohol by making vodka scarcer and more expensive and what happens? A Soviet sugar shortage, that's what happens.

Sugar is being rationed because too much of it has been going to make moonshine liquor. The Russians love sweets, but many of them love booze even more.

In the United States, some experts advocate taking the profit out of illegal drugs by making them legal. Similarly, at least one Soviet economist believes the government should quit trying to curb liquor production and should concentrate, instead, on public education to combat alcoholism.

That may be good advice. In any event, the present approach doesn't seem to be working. The crusade for sobriety was supposed to boost workers' productivity, as well as improve their health. But according to a report by U. S. intelligence agencies, the Soviet economy basically remained stuck in neutral last year. Industrial production edged forward a bit, but agricultural production fell three percent.

The intelligence report warns that, unless Mr. Gorbachev "can achieve better results this year, ...tensions within the (Soviet) leadership are certain to mount."

In other words, if Mr. Gorbachev and his crew of self-proclaimed reformers want to keep their jobs, the Soviet economy had better start delivering the goods. For many disgruntled consumers, the proper consumer goods mix includes sugar and vodka.

Pittsburgh Post-Gazette

Pittsburgh, PA, September 21, 1988

After three years of relative sobriety, Ivan apparently has fallen off the wagon.

The devastating economic losses the Soviet Union has suffered since Mikhail S. Gorbachev imposed sharp restrictions on alcohol production and sales have forced the government to loosen up and make vodka and other spirits more readily available.

Curiously, the effort to reduce absenteeism due to drinking and improve the productivity of workers appears to have produced much the same reaction in that country as the "noble experiment" of Prohibition did here in the 1920s and 1930s.

Moonshiners quickly emerged in great numbers in the Soviet Union and were consuming so much sugar in their stills that a severe shortage was created. Comrades were not only concocting bathtub vodka but, more dangerously, processing cleaning fluids and other toxic liquids containing an alcohol base to drink.

Though booze was never totally banned under Mr. Gorbachev's edict, its availability was curtailed and it was usually necessary to wait outdoors in lines for so long that the bottle obtained became almost medicinal in purpose.

According to the spiritually uplifting report in Pravda, operating hours of liquor stores are now to be expanded and, what's more, wine and beer will once again be sold in grocery stores. The latter, the Soviet consumer might be heartened to know, is a service not extended in even such progressive corners of the capitalist Western world as Pennsylvania in the Northeastern United States.

'Please, Poppa Gorbachev. I'm too young to go out on my own. You know I don't have any initiative. You've said so yourself. Who'll look after me? I'll starve, Poppa!'

THE RICHMOND NEWS LEADER
Richmond, VA, September 26, 1988

The Soviet Union's hierarchy apparently is learning a lesson the U.S. learned the hard way almost 60 years ago: Prohibition doesn't work. Big Mike Gorbachev perhaps thought a crackdown on booze would be easier to impose in his nation of conscript-citizens, but he was wrong.

For almost three years, Soviet citizens have been dissuaded from drinking by scarcity, high prices, and limited outlets where they can buy booze. As a result, to be sure, the Soviets are drinking less, but they also are getting testier and much less tolerant of official shortcomings. The state has lost jillions of rubles in much-needed revenues, and the ranks of militia have had to be beefed up to control unruly lines outside state liquor stores.

Soviets also have turned to dangerous liquor substitutes, such as cleaning fluid, that have caused widespread injuries and even deaths. Enterprising moonshiners have depleted sugar supplies to produce vast quantities of booze outside the state's control. When sugar ran low, they turned to candy as a substitute, and Soviet sweet tooths went begging. Sound familiar?

Now Gorby and the state — in the face of overwhelming discontent among the masses — are relenting. Some controls will be relaxed to permit greater production of vodka and other liquor, and the number of shops selling booze will be increased. In effect, the Gorbachev regime is admitting failure in its joyless campaign to wean its subjects off liquor. In view of growing protests and street demonstrations by angry citizens, perhaps Gorby and his crew might heed the wisdom of an ancient Russian czar who said, 'The joy of Russia is drinking. She cannot do without it."

Could it be that the commissars are learning — contrary to Marxist theory — that booze, not religion, is the opiate of the masses?

The Pittsburgh
PRESS
Pittsburgh, PA, April 29, 1988

As any student of America's "noble experiment" — Prohibition — could have told Mikhail Gorbachev, it's easier to declare war on alcohol, as he did three years ago, than to get people to stop drinking.

Nevertheless, Gorbachev had no choice but to try to cut vodka consumption soon after he came to power. Drunkenness was endemic.

Russia was the only developed country with declining male life expectancy. Industrial accidents and alcohol-related crime were twin plagues.

Despite all that, the general secretary's first major domestic reform was unpopular. He cut liquor production, boosted prices and ordered many state-owned breweries and distilleries to convert to non-alcoholic beverages.

The results were hardly what Gorbachev expected. He touched off a vast upsurge in moonshining — in fact it is Russia's only growth industry — and sugar, much of it imported, disappeared from store shelves.

As Prohibiton-era Americans made bathtub gin, thirsty Soviets have set up small stills in homes and apartments. They distill an illegal alcohol called "samogon" from grain, fruit or potatoes, and use sugar to raise the alcohol content.

Russians, who have a national sweet tooth, are angry over the lack of sugar, which they use heavily in tea, jam and cakes. And to separate the moonshiners from a key raw material, the authorities have started to ration sugar.

The system is failing in the Black Sea city of Odessa, where the bootleggers are especially canny. For a bottle of harsh, home-made vodka, they demand money — and a sugar-ration coupon, so they can make more alcohol.

Experts estimate that bootleg liquor has almost made up for the cutbacks in state production. An economist points out that the government is losing revenue and should increase its output before moonshining grows into organized crime.

The soundest way to curb Russian-style drunkenness, sparked by boredom and deprivation, would be to raise the standard of living and offer products to compete with vodka for workers' rubles.

Unfortunately, Soviet leaders, including Gorbachev, are better at talking about quality consumer goods than at delivering them.

Soviet Dissidents Form an Independent Party

A group of Soviet dissidents met in Moscow May 7-9, 1988 to form an independent political party, the Democratic Union. Under the Soviet constitution, the Communist Party (CP) was the U.S.S.R.'s only legal political entity. The organizers of the Democratic Union viewed its formation as a logical extension of the "democratization" reforms initiated by Soviet leader Mikhail S. Gorbachev. But Gorbachev in 1987 had said he saw "no need for any other party" in the U.S.S.R.

It was believed to be the first time since 1979 that dissidents had attempted to organize opposition to the CP's political monopoly. Estonian nationalists in January 1988 had called for the creation of an independent party but apparently had not tried to form one themselves.

The Democratic Union's organizational meetings involved over 100 people from about 20 Soviet cities. They included liberals, social democrats, human-rights activists and members of informal political clubs. The nation's older, well-known dissidents were not involved in the Democratic Union. Instead, the participants appeared to be mainly in their 30s. Some members described themselves as the "children of Prague Spring," explaining that they had become disillusioned as teenagers in 1968, when the Soviet Union led an invasion of Czechoslovakia to overthrow a reformist regime. (See pp. 158-161.)

One of the organizers, Aleksandr Rukashov, May 8 told a Western reporter that the new party would seek to run candidates in elections. "The union's position is to put political opposition to the totalitarian dictatorship of the Communists."

The group scattered its meetings among several apartments in Moscow. The police May 8 detained and questioned 14 activists, all nonresidents, and then ordered them to leave Moscow. Five members of the Democratic Union, along with journalist Sergei I. Grigoryants, were arrested May 9 in an early morning raid on Grigoryants's residence. Grigoryants was the editor of the independent journal *Glasnost*. He was not a member of the new party and was skeptical about the group's ability to accomplish significant change. Nevertheless, Grigoryants allowed the activists to hold a meeting at his residence, which was also the journal's office. (See pp. 58-59.)

According to dissident sources, the editor was immediately charged with "resisting authorities" and was sentenced to one week in jail. Three of the arrested activists were said to receive five-day jail terms.

The Democratic Union was able to complete its organizational meetings and draft a founding charter May 9. The document stated that the party was dedicated to "economic pluralism, a multi-party system, a legal opposition press and independent trade unions."

Richmond Times-Dispatch

Richmond, VA, May 22, 1988

The Muscovite who, among his lesser sins, recently called Moscow University "a stagnant swamp" was jailed earlier this month. Freed on Monday, Sergei Grigoryants, editor of the dissident periodical *Glasnost*, returned home to find the meager equipment with which he and his Press Club Glasnost produced the bimonthly magazine confiscated, the ownership of his home imperiled, and a charge of defaming the Soviet state (the penalty: up to three years in prison or internal exile) looming.

Mr. Grigoryants knows the drill: His more than eight years in Soviet prisons and labor camps are the lot of an "anti-Soviet agitator," otherwise known as troublemaker, which Mr. Grigoryants is. Former underground publisher of underground publications, he took Mikhail Gorbachev at his word — *glasnost* — and moved above ground. No. 5 of *Glasnost*, for instance, carried articles on economic reform entitled "Mute Glasnost," "Great Promises and Two Pennies Worth of Hope," "Notes of a Skeptic," "Flaws and Prescriptions."

His current problems with officialdom, Mr. Grigoryants suspects, stem less from his writings than his approval of a hardy band of Soviets who are trying to form a political party, the Democratic Union, in opposition to the Communists. He sees in his arrest and harassment three warnings. The first is to get Soviet dissidents to lie low during Mr. Gorbachev's coming summit meeting with President Reagan. The second is to get the Americans to lay off human rights in the Soviet Union. The third is to remind Mr. Gorbachev that the greater threat to his liberalization comes not from fledgling democrats but from the police and the KGB.

"Stalinism," wrote one A. Voyeikov in "Flaws and Prescriptions," "is more than a senseless economic policy that runs contrary to the interests of the people. True regeneration cannot be accomplished without a deep restructuring of the entire sociopolitical mechanism, without all-encompassing democratization, which, incidentally, is consistent with the approach of Mikhail Gorbachev."

Is it? When Soviet police shut down the magazine named for one of the twin pillars of Mr. Gorbachev's regime, the world has to wonder how serious he is about *glasnost* and how much control over its opponents he can — or chooses to — exert.

Lincoln Journal

Lincoln, NE, May 20, 1988

There's a case to be made that if there is a single Russian to blame for a massive chunk of the U.S. federal deficit increase during the Reagan raj, it would be Sergei Georgievich Gorshkov, who died the other day at age 78. Sad to say, his iron influence will be felt for a very long time.

Gorshkov was the driving commander-in-chief of the Soviet navy for 29 years and a full member of the Soviet Communist Party Central Committee for a quarter-century. He relentlessly exploited those two positions. He revolutionized the Soviet fleet from a small, domestically defensive force, to a navy capable of sustained worldwide combat and power projection.

Top officers of the U.S. Naval War College habitually quoted Adm. Gorshkov — he wrote much — with great respect and, not infrequently, with a kind of awe. Some drew parallels with Adm. Alfred Mahan, famed theoretician of U.S. Navy global doctrine in the 19th and 20th centuries.

Not since Peter the Great has anyone accomplished more in building a modern navy for Mother Russia. Adm. Elmo Zumwalt, former chief of naval operations, called Gorshkov the most effective naval leader of modern times.

By now, the link between Adm. Gorshkov and doubling of the federal debt — by more than an unprecedented $1 trillion — during the tenure of the Reagan administration should be obvious.

Saying it needed to counter Gorshkov's accomplishments, the Reagan administration undertook a crash program to build a 2½-ocean, 600-warship, 15-carrier task force Navy. Neither the Air Force nor the Army were as favored as the Navy in the Reagan military-spending explosion.

Gorshkov, therefore, inevitably reshaped U.S. military relationships, war thinking and diplomatic options. For contributions to his nation, Hero of the Soviet Union was a modest decoration.

⚎ The Cincinnati Post

Cincinnati, OH, May 21, 1988

Soviet police and KGB authorities have sent a chilling message just before the Reagan-Gorbachev summit: Despite the slogans of "glasnost" (openness), they retain full power to suppress unwelcome ideas. They can still exercise that power ruthlessly against Russians who step out of line.

The authorities have evidently decided not just to harass Moscow's most important new independent periodical, but to put it out of business. They recently raided the office of the journal "Glasnost," the name of which was deliberately chosen by editor Sergei Grigoryants as a test of the official slogan. They arrested Grigoryants, held him for a week — and seized or destroyed all the facilities that he needs to resume publishing.

When Grigoryants returned to his office after being released, he found it sealed off by a police squad. He was told that he would have to produce documents proving that the office and printing press belong to him — a bureaucratic process that could keep him tied up for months. He also learned that the journal's files and manuscripts had vanished.

Grigoryants founded "Glasnost" only about 10 months ago, but it quickly acquired a readership and influence far beyond its small circulation. From the beginning he published it completely in the open: He even sent complimentary subscriptions to Gorbachev and the other members of the Communist Party Central Committee. Its articles were often reprinted in other independent journals or published abroad in translation.

The authorities responded by denouncing the editor in the state-controlled media but did not stop him from publishing — until now. Since his jail stay, he has heard that he may face criminal charges for defaming the state; his punishment could be as much as three years in the Gulag. The authorities obviously want to intimidate Grigoryants and the dozens of other dissident journalists who have been inspired by his example.

Gorbachev, a master at manipulating U.S. opinion, has won far more credit here than he deserves for his limited reforms. The crackdown on "Glasnost" shows that the limits are a lot narrower than we would like to think.

The Philadelphia Inquirer

Philadelphia, PA, May 17, 1988

The bold, if quixotic, attempt last week to start a genuine opposition party in the Soviet Union was one of those events that allow Westerners to measure the progress of political tolerance in Mikhail S. Gorbachev's Soviet Union. How would the *glasnost* gang handle this latest challenge to its authority? Would the 100-odd conspirators be packed off to Siberia? Would they merely be harassed? Or would they actually be allowed to go about their business in peace?

As it turned out, the KGB came down hard, but not too hard, on the founding fathers of the Democratic Union. More than 20 people were temporarily detained after the group's first meeting May 8. When that failed to dissuade them, their leader, Sergei Grigoryants, was formally arrested the following day. A few years ago, Mr. Grigoryants could have looked forward to seven years of hard labor for anti-Soviet activity. For now, he has been jailed a mere seven days.

From the authorities' point of view, a liberal assault on the premise of Communist rule is more an annoyance than a threat. If the Russians ever summoned up the energy to oust the Communists, they'd be more likely to opt for a right-wing dictatorship than a Western-style democracy. *Democracy,*

as defined by the Gorbachev-era reformers, means a more open way of choosing leaders within the confines of Communist rule. That Mr. Grigoryants paid such a small price for his impudence is a reflection both of his inability to cause real harm at home and of his genuine potential to become a human rights martyr in the West.

If Mr. Gorbachev were to make a list of his main political concerns, the activities of rambunctious dissidents like Mr. Grigoryants would probably be placed near the bottom. Far more worrisome are the *non*-activities of the placid majority — the untold millions of workers, farmers, managers and party apparatchiks who pay only lip service to Mr. Gorbachev's reforms. Last Tuesday, the day after Mr. Grigoryants' arrest, the Soviet leader was complaining to a gathering of newspaper and magazine editors that conservatism and confusion continued to cripple his efforts to make the nation's faltering economic system more rational and productive.

So there is indeed a political drama being played out in the Soviet Union, a struggle over whether the Soviet system can be made to respond to reforms. Seen in that full context, appeals for multi-party democracy are an interesting, but inconsequential, sideshow.

THE INDIANAPOLIS STAR

Indianapolis, IN, May 19, 1988

Discussing the process of selecting delegates, a political party leader said, "There's not going to be any of the quota system we had in the past — so many workers and peasants, so many women, and so on."

No, the leader is not Paul Kirk, national chairman of the Democratic Party, which has an "equal representation rule" mandating that 50 percent of participants in party deliberations, such as conventions, be women.

The quoted leader is Mikhail Gorbachev, Soviet Communist Party general secretary and in effect head of the government.

Addressing leading Russian newspapermen in Moscow, he said the main goal is to choose "the most active supporters of *perestroika*" for next month's scheduled conference of some 5,000 party delegates.

Perestroika, his ambitious program to reform Soviet society, is vital, not the delegates sex or occupation. It's not clear if Democrats are embarrassed that the world's No. 1 communist appears more issue oriented than are they with their gender quotas.

Gorbachev admitted that his reform plan has created "real turmoil in the minds of many people — workers, intelligentsia and leading cadres, not only below, but at the top."

He added, "The panic has reached such a level — and this is very serious — as to question whether *perestroika* is something destructive which is denying the value of socialism . . . and leading to destabilization."

He was referring to recent public debates between backers and opponents of reform.

But it is more a matter of people being confused rather than outrightly opposed to his plan, and once it is fully comprehended it will gain wide acceptance, he said. He urged the media to contribute to that understanding.

That reform does not include tolerating an opposition political party was proven the very next day when the USSR accused a group of making a "blatantly anti-constitutional" call for a multi-party system. One organizer, Sergei Grigoryants, was jailed for a week after KGB secret police raided a country home where the dissidents had met to form a new party.

The state-run Tass news agency assailed journalists who covered the dissidents' three-day meeting as those "whose contacts with self-styled political figures go far beyond the bounds of professional duties."

It seems Tass doesn't know that when people try to form an opposition party in a dictatorship, that *is* news and hence a professional newsperson has a duty to cover it.

Perestroika is a plan to boost the stagnant Soviet economy by easing some state restrictions on domestic enterprises and on foreign investments. It also allows more debate on issues. It is not a plan to give people the right to choose their own leaders — the very essence of democracy.

Lenin's body lies amouldering in the grave but his one-party state goes marching on!

Edmonton Journal

Edmonton, Alta., May 12, 1988

Last weekend about 100 people gathered near Moscow to form a new political party — the Democratic Union. Police arrested and held 19 of them — a predictable response in an authoritarian state.

Yet the Soviet Union needs a reflective rather than reflexive approach to this major test of the open society promised by Mikhail Gorbachev. The general secretary of the Communist party of the Soviet Union has spoken only of democratic reforms within the party, which is constitutionally the supreme arbiter of Soviet life.

Yet as the weekend dissidents reasonably asked, what is true democracy without political pluralism, independent trade unions and the right to elect a popular government?

Their efforts put Gorbachev in a difficult position. The Democratic Union says it supports the Soviet leader's reforms and merely wants to take them further.

If Gorbachev allows them to organize, his conservative rivals may see it as caving in to the dissidents' demands. If he cracks down on the fledgling party, he will undermine his promises of openness and democratic reform.

There may well be a day when political pluralism becomes a reality — it has been attempted unsuccessfully several times in the past. But if Gorbachev appears to endorse that goal, his days of power may quickly end. Conservative resistance to his reforms is as strong as ever — the power struggle within the Soviet leadership is far from over.

Recent media attacks on the cult of bureaucracy, the efforts to come to grips with Stalin's reign of terror — these are enough to send the conservatives to the barricades to defend the privileges and status they enjoy in an authoritarian society. To them democracy is the ultimate threat.

The Democratic Union's demand that the Soviets withdraw soldiers from territories brought into the Soviet sphere after the Second World War is another interesting challenge. It is akin to the desire of postwar Britons, withdrawing from the empire, who were more intent on building a better life at home than propping up imperial glory abroad.

The changes Gorbachev has set in place may take on a life of their own: once the doors of freedom are pried ajar, they cannot be easily shut. Even if the Democratic Union is silenced for now, more demands for pluralism will follow.

Toronto, Ont., May 11, 1988

Mikhail Gorbachev exploited glasnost and perestroika — openness and reconstruction — as twin banners to proclaim his new, improved brand of communism.

He proved himself a skilled marketer, a master of PR. The two Russian words quickly became part of the everyday international vocabulary.

And hope was revived in the USSR. For example, human rights activist Sergei Grigoryants started a magazine called *Glasnost* to record political progress.

This week, Grigoryants was arrested and given a week in jail. His crime? Trying to found a new political party, a long-overdue alternative to the communist monolith.

Grigoryants wasn't alone, of course. The KGB rounded up dozens of members of the Democratic Union.

And Gorbachev has failed the first real test of glasnost.

"The whole idea of the Democratic Union is to challenge the stranglehold of the Communist party on Soviet society," said one of the new party's members.

This was more than the Kremlin could stomach.

While Gorbachev loudly proclaimed he wouldn't let hardliners stand in the way of his reforms, the KGB was out arresting the dissidents.

Of course, Gorby wants it both ways. With the Reagan-Gorbachev summit only three weeks away, he doesn't want anything to reflect badly on human rights in the Soviet Union. But he's not prepared to allow freedoms to flourish either.

Ironically just last week Ronald Reagan acknowledged there'd been some improvement in the Soviet human rights record. The current crackdown on dissidents should wipe out that impression.

Gorbachev has said he is seeking greater democracy as part of his reform package aimed at halting the country's economic woes but he has emphasized that the Communist party will remain in control.

No wonder the U.S. Congress is leery of entering into a missile reduction treaty with the USSR without guarantees there'll be full inspections on both sides.

Soviet openness applies only to publishing more consumer complaints about shoddy goods or bureaucratic corruption. The system itself remains sacred.

Birmingham Post-Herald

Birmingham, AL, May 18, 1988

Under the spell of Mikhail Gorbachev, many Western leaders — including President Reagan — have started giving the Soviet Union the benefit of the doubt on human-rights issues. Reagan recently said that Moscow has been showing "a willingness to respect some human rights."

Five days after the president's conciliatory speech, Soviet police arrested 14 members of the Democratic Union, a new group that has called for the legalization of political parties other than the Communist Party. They also seized papers and copying equipment from the offices of the independent journal "Glasnost."

The Soviets have relaxed a few of their repressive policies, but they are still a long way from putting into practice the human-rights agreements that they have already signed — such as the Helsinki pact. Until they do so, the White House should insist on raising these issues at every summit, including the one scheduled for May 29.

The Kansas City Times

Kansas City, KS, May 25, 1988

Yes, the state certainly has a right to defend itself from armed terrorism, from conspiratorial activities leading to violence and threatening the unity or security of the state, and from direct calls for violence—but not from speech! There is only one measure of the true value of speech: an openly expressed public opinion. History has repeatedly shown us that persecuted speech eventually reveals itself as the truth.—Lev Timofeev in Glasnost

As of now, Lev Timofeev's essay on freedom of speech as exercised in the magazine ironically called *Glasnost* stands as a remnant of Soviet totalitarian whim. The magazine has been closed down. Its editor, Sergei I. Grigoryants, told *The New York Times* that authorities had destroyed his files and manuscripts and taken over his printing equipment.

Grigoryants had been in jail for a week. He was arrested at his home at a meeting of members of the Democratic Union—people who had hoped to organize an opposition party. Grigoryants merely was listening to them. He is said not to be very sympathetic to their cause, but was willing to help.

What was so diabolical about the magazine that caused this upheaval? Police ransacking Grigoryants' house and cordoning it off? *Glasnost* carried reports of demonstrations. It had open letters to the likes of George Shultz and Mikhail Gorbachev asking for exit visas. It carried all kinds of opinion: attacks on prejudice, diatribes against "Zionism," pleas for religious tolerance, discussions of vandalism. In short, the kind of perennial issues, large and small, that confront humankind in all societies.

But in the Soviet Union this is not permitted outside carefully directed channels. Criticism must be prescribed from the top down. It must remain within careful norms.

That is not freedom. It is the same rigid statism beamed from a different direction. If the marching orders come from a relatively enlightened source at this moment, they can come from a different source at another time. It has happened before. Freedom cannot be turned off and on like water from a faucet. It is either there for all or it is not there at all.

The Providence Journal

Providence, RI, May 23, 1988

When last summer Sergei I. Grigoryants of Moscow gave his new publication the name Glasnost, it did two things: It aligned the magazine with Soviet General Secretary Mikhail Gorbachev's liberalization movement and introduced a built-in irony for that time, surely never out of Mr. Grigoryants's mind, when the authorities would act to close it down

That moment arrived early this month, 10 months after the publication was founded, and it was more emphatic than a simple forced closure of operation. Publisher Grigoryants was arrested and taken to jail. Although released after a week, he is still rumored to face possible charges of defaming the Soviet state, the punishment for which could earn him three years in prison or internal exile. In addition, his printing equipment was confiscated and his files and manuscripts destroyed — just to be sure he got the message. Things do not bode well for the future of Mr. Grigoryants or of Glasnost.

From a business point of view, Glasnost was not much of a magazine. Nevertheless, it had a following among Muscovites yearning for literary as well as political freedom. It appeared twice a month, rarely exceeding 200 copies. As with underground (samizdat) publications, its articles would be retyped and passed on by faithful readers. We have never seen a copy, but can well imagine its crude appearance. The editorial offices where Mr. Grigoryants was arrested were in a house on the outskirts of Moscow, certainly not to be mistaken for any kind of publishing row.

Despite its humble circumstances, the publication had become a widely sought source of information for many Soviets. In fact, issues would occasionally be taken out of the country and translated in the West. The West, in turn, viewed it as a concrete indication of the reality of Mr. Gorbachev's reforms. If its shutdown doesn't challenge the Soviet leader's sincerity, that's only because it may signify a challenge to his control.

The questions about its discontinuation are still unanswered. Mr. Grigoryants asserts that it was the work of the police and KGB anxious to show Gorbachev supporters they are still in charge when it comes to citizens' rights in the Soviet state. Tass called it a warning to dissidents considering demonstrations during the coming summit.

Whatever the reason for the actions, the result seems clear and a bit Orwellian: Glasnost without Glasnost. Openness without openness.

The Houston Post

Houston, TX, May 11, 1988

Glasnost, Soviet leader Mikhail Gorbachev's vaunted policy of openness, has its limits. More than 100 young dissidents and the editor of a magazine named Glasnost have been rudely reminded where the line is drawn.

The dissidents formed a political party last weekend to challenge the Soviet Communist Party, the only party allowed in that land of the proletariat. The aims of the new Democratic Union would seem reasonable enough to Americans — political, economic and spiritual pluralism, a legal opposition press and independent trade unions. But all that is anathema to the Kremlin Communists.

Police swooped down on the meeting, detaining a score of those present. The editor, Sergei Grigoryants, who let dissidents use his office, was also arrested and sentenced to a week in jail. It might be argued that they would have been treated more harshly in the pre-Gorbachev era. But that isn't the point. Glasnost means glasnost, or it doesn't. A policy permitting a half-open society is a sham.

Soviet Party Regulars Humbled in Parliament Elections

The Soviet Union March 26, 1989 held its first nationwide multicandidate parliamentary elections since 1917. The step toward Western-style democracy had unexpectedly embarrassing results for the Communist Party (CP) leadership.

Voters across the country chose among candidates to fill 1,500 seats in the new 2,250-seat Congress of People's Deputies. The remaining 750 seats of the restructured parliament had been reserved for deputies picked by the party and by labor, social and youth organizations.

The voter turnout was reported to have been heavy, even in some districts where there was only one candidate on the ballot. Candidates ran with no opposition in about 25% of the districts. In other distrcits, there were as many as 12 candidates on the ballot. An election was not valid unless a minimum of 30% of the eligible voters in a district cast ballots.

The preliminary results disclosed by government and party officials gave a broad picture of the outcome. It was evident from the official reaction that the voting did not go as the leadership had anticipated. Where Soviet leader Mikhail S. Gorbachev had intended the elction to result in a vote of confidence for his reformist policies, the result instead appeared to show deep dissatisfaction with the status quo and a desire for even more sweeping change.

Populists, liberals, radicals reformists and ethnic nationalities defeated party regulars in many districts. In other districts, some party loyalists won seats with a bare minimum of the necessary votes.

Party bosses were not exempt from the humiliation. In the most noteworthy defeat, Yuri F. Solovyev, the CP first secretary of the Leningrad region, and a nonvoting member of the Central Committee Politburo, failed to win a seat even though he was the only candidate on the ballot in his district. Under the rules of the election, an unopposed candidate had to receive at least 50% of votes cast in his or her district. Voters in Solovyev's district were reported to have crossed his name off their ballots en masse.

Pravda, the Communist Party newspaper, March 28 omitted mention of Solovnev's defeat in a summary of election results. The official news agency Tass mentioned it in passing. Local media coverage in Lenningrad of the results simply named those who had won seats.

Leningrad city CP boss Anatoly Gerasimov was soundly defeated by ship-builder Yuri Boldyrev. Leningrad Mayor Vladimir Khodyrev, running unopposed, was a victim of a "crossout" campaign.

Five Ukranian regional party leaders ran unopposed in their districts and each failed to reach the 50% mark. Kiev party leader Kostantin I. Masik and the city's mayor, Valentin A. Zgursky, were defeated.

Nationalist candidates in the Baltic region trampled nonnationalist party regulars. It was reported that in Lithuania, some 31 of the 42 seats went to nationalists.

In another hotbed of nationalist tensions, the Transcaucus region, Armenian activists charged that the elections had been rigged in favor of antinationalist candidates.

The second secretary of the Moscow region, Yuri Prokofyev, failed in his bid. Moscow Mayor Valery Saikin also failed, in spite of a vigorous campaign that had included Gorbachev-style "walkabouts." Some Western observers viewed the defeats of Prokofyev and Saikin as a spillover from the triumph of Boris N. Yeltsin, the populist former party boss of Moscow. Yeltsin won Moscow's at-large seat in the new parliament with 89% of the vote over Yevgeny A. Brakov, the managing director of the Zil automobile works. *Pravda* March 28 announced Yeltsin's victory but did not say it was a landslide. The item was buried on page two.

Gennadi I. Gerasimov, the chief spokesman of the Soviet foreign ministry, March 28 told reporters that the party would carefully study the meaning of the results. He suggested, but did not say outright, that the defeated party officials might be removed from power.

"Party leaders must have not only the confidence of the party, but the confidence of the people," Gerasimov said. "We'll have to look at it."

President Gorbachev met with a group of senior Soviet editors March 29 in the chambers of the Central Committee. The gathering was private, but one editor later said that Gorbachev expressed the opinion that the elections were no cause for alarm.

Chicago Tribune

Chicago, IL, March 28, 1989

Ronald Reagan once told a favorite old joke to Mikhail Gorbachev, about an American who informed a Russian that he was free to stand in front of the White House and say, "Down with Ronald Reagan!" The Russian replied that the communist system is just as tolerant: He also was free to stand in front of the White House and say, "Down with Ronald Reagan!"

The joke is looking more dated all the time. Even before Reagan was out of office, the day had come when a Soviet citizen could publicly denounce his own leaders. Sunday, the day came when a Soviet citizen could walk into a voting booth and cast a ballot against the official candidate of the Communist Party. For the first time in nearly 72 years, an exercise in real democracy has occurred in the nation that invented totalitarianism.

From all appearances, the election for the new Congress of People's Deputies was honest. Views that once would have earned a sentence in the Gulag will be represented in a government policymaking body.

Early returns showed 89 percent of the vote going to deposed Moscow party chief Boris Yeltsin, a maverick critic of the old regime and an advocate of political pluralism. Muscovites elected two other reformers; a third made a runoff. The Leningrad party chief got trounced, and the regional party chief, a Politburo member, apparently also lost.

Meanwhile, an opposition group in Lithuania said each of its 39 candidates either finished first or forced the leader into a runoff. Candidates of the Estonian People's Front rolled up lopsided victories over communist opponents. A small victory for liberty lay in the choice of many citizens not to vote at all—which in past elections was a crime.

This is hardly Western-style democracy. A third of the places in the new congress were reserved for the Communist Party and other officially recognized institutions. More than a quarter of the rest were uncontested. With rare exceptions, the fundamental legitimacy of the current system was not questioned.

Equally important, no one knows yet how much power the congress will have. Clearly, it will be inferior to the Supreme Soviet, whose members will be chosen from this body. How they will be selected is another important but unanswered question.

Still, the fragrance of freedom was unmistakable in the electoral campaign. Old-line party hacks, once immune to public sentiment, were forced to plead for votes from ordinary people. Reformers took relish in the chance to decry the suffocating rigidity of the old system. Long-stifled popular resentments bubbled up like lava out of a volcano.

Presiding over all this was the architect of reform, Mikhail Gorbachev, whose chief purpose in office seems to be to continually surprise the rest of the world. The new parliamentary body is a way to harness the Soviet peoples' frustrations with communism and to dilute the power of Gorbachev's party enemies. The country's intractable economic stagnation has made such dramatic steps unavoidable.

Clearly the new legislature will help his efforts at reform. It will provide a forum for the wide-ranging debate he has opened up in his country, focusing a constant scrutiny on the government's conduct. It will also stand in the way of those who would like to retreat from Gorbachev's path. Changes like this one are designed to make reform irreversible—regardless of what happens to its author.

Gorbachev declared after the election, "The master of the country has spoken." No one in the Soviet Union has serious doubt that the real master is still the Kremlin. That isn't going to change anytime soon. But now it is just possible to imagine a day when the Soviet people will be the rulers and not the ruled.

The News and Observer

Raleigh, NC, March 30, 1989

For a country with a 72-year history of repressive totalitarian rule, the elections in the Soviet Union were of historic importance. It was only the second contested national election in Soviet history, and the results of the first, held soon after the 1917 revolution, were canceled by Lenin. But as fervently as Americans would like to see it, democracy is nowhere near full flower in the land of the czars and commissars.

Undeniably, Sunday's vote reflected widespread discontent with the Soviet status quo and the pace of change. There were embarrassing — even humiliating — defeats for the Communist Party.

In Moscow, Boris Yeltsin, who had been tossed out as a party leader, got 90 percent of the vote running against an official party candidate. In Leningrad, six leading Communist officials were defeated. In the Baltic republics, candidates favoring self-rule and independence from Moscow scored striking victories. There were even upsets of a Politburo member and several other senior Communist officials who had no opposition. Enough voters crossed the candidates' names off the ballot to force a new election.

But in some ways the anti-establishment victory was more apparent than real. Before the election, the Communist Party had handpicked a third of the members of the new Congress of People's Deputies, including President Mikhail Gorbachev. And while Mr. Gorbachev won an endorsement of his change-oriented policies, he also was left with the ticklish job of delivering on the reforms he has promised and keeping peace in an obviously divided and volatile party.

How well Mr. Gorbachev can deliver on his pledge of a better life for ordinary Soviets will be the real test of the election's significance. If he fails, it could lead to a resurgence by hard-liners and a return to a far more repressive form of government.

The Providence Journal

Providence, RI, March 28, 1989

Like Carl Sandburg's fog, Soviet democracy is coming on little cat feet, one very furtive and tentative step at a time. Indeed, it is stretching the term a little to call this weekend's election of a national legislature "democracy," but in contrast to the past, and in hopes for the future, we'll call it that anyway.

Nobody is quite certain what the powers of this Congress of People's Deputies will be. Just about all of the candidates for open seats were members of the Communist Party — Mikhail Gorbachev himself has spoken with contempt about multi-party democracy — and nearly half the places will be filled by appointments from official organizations. So the only innovation was the choice for voters between two aspirants running for the same seat.

In the long history of the Soviet Union, that is some innovation. Commentators have tended to say that this is the first time Soviet citizens have enjoyed such a choice in 60-plus years. Well, that's one way of putting it. It is dangerously wrong, however, to suggest that democracy ever flourished in the early days of the Bolshevik revolution, or was a feature of Czarist Russia. Of course, it was not — and therein lies the danger. For this is a society that is not only unacquainted with democracy, but historically devoid of any experience whatsoever in popular rule.

What we have seen during these past few weeks of electioneering, and in the months and years of *glasnost* and *perestroika*, is the natural thirst of the Soviet population for change. Nearly everybody agrees that the Marxist-Leninist experiment has failed — Mr. Gorbachev admitted as much in his United Nations speech — and failed to the tune of millions of lives, decades of terror, and generations of misery. And it is encouraging to observe that the process of reform seems to lean in the direction of social, political and economic freedom.

But a single, one-party ballot does not make a democracy, and while the engine of state now features such passengers as Boris Yeltsin, the Party-based populist, and various representatives from the Baltic republics, it is wise to remember where the real power lies. The Soviet Union has embarked on a fascinating trip, but it is miles from resembling a democratic state. The character of the government, the fundamental creed of the regime, the national aspirations of Soviet foreign policy — these have yet to be modified at all.

Mr. Gorbachev knows that a taste of democracy merely whets the public appetite, and is mindful of resistance to change and reform. But can anyone manage a slow-motion revolution? Nobody yet knows. So while we are interested and gratified by these extraordinary events, we are watchful and cautious and skeptical as well.

Newsday

Long Island, NY, March 28, 1989

Flowers, appropriately, brightened at least one Moscow voting booth Sunday. They accompanied the budding of a new democracy in an old dictatorship. Soviet citizens cast their ballots in the Soviet Union's first multi-candidate election since shortly after the Communist Party took power more than 70 years ago.

But a bud is not a blossom. The voting may indeed herald a new era of freedom; the victory of an anti-establishment candidate may indeed portend a loosening of totalitarian ties. At present, however, that is conjecture. What is certain is that the Soviet Union still is far from democratic: The Communist Party remains the only legal party there.

The contested elections result from Soviet leader Mikhail Gorbachev's new policy of glasnost, or openness. The law that permitted them, he said, "advanced the political thought and social activity of the people, and this is what we wanted to achieve."

It may have achieved a bit more than he expected. In the election campaign, the man he fired in 1987 as Moscow Communist Party boss, Boris Yeltsin, denounced the economic failures under Gorbachev that have kept store shelves empty. But when ballots were counted Monday, Yeltsin had been rewarded with 89.4 percent of the vote. He resoundingly defeated a traditional party loyalist.

Yeltsin will represent the capital in a new Congress of People's Deputies. Voters chose 1,500 of its 2,250 seats Sunday, about 1,100 in contested elections; candidates for the other seats were either unopposed or are being chosen separately by officially sanctioned organizations. By law, the Communist Party is guaranteed 100 seats. Gorbachev himself was made one of the deputies last month.

The congress will meet once each year to decide important issues, elect a president and choose by secret ballot a 542-member Supreme Soviet, which will be the nation's actual working legislature.

In all of this, there will be no turning back. Those who have sipped the nectar of freedom cannot return to their former austere diet. Sunday's vote is a real step forward. But it is a small one. The Soviet Union has a long way to go before democracy flowers there.

DAILY ✠ NEWS

New York, NY, March 28, 1989

THEY'VE GONE AND DONE IT. For the first time since 1917, people in the Soviet Union have cast ballots that allow a choice between candidates. That's 180 degrees from Soviet "democracy" of the past: the sovereign right to vote for each and every boss the masters of the empire told you to.

The practical effect of Sunday's elections? Nil. No change. The new 2,250-seat Congress of People's Deputies will not be a democratic legislature, any more than there was one before. In the entire election, 82% of the candidates were Communist Party members, so there'll be no straying from the party line on big policy matters.

But forget substance. The symbolism is more important. And it is of profound significance. Tens of millions of Soviet citizens now have had, for the first time in their lives or imaginations, the experience of casting ballots on real choices. And, amazingly, many of the winners were candidates who challenged nominees of the party hierarchy.

For most of the last 80 years, simply to talk of such an idea in public could have led to a labor camp or a firing squad.

President Mikhail S. Gorbachev took a big risk. But if he is not toppled by hard-liners, or brought down in some more obscure and ironic way by his own "reforms," he will gain much. Domestically, his very personal reform politics has gained great strength and credibility. Externally, it gives him a legitimacy that comes only from popular mandate, the absence of which weakens all despots.

But ultimately this is what will be remembered, come what may: Thousands of Soviets gave speeches, and millions heard them, free of the stark and immediate terror of offending police or bureaucrats. However bored Americans may feel by their politicians, when you've never heard of such a thing, and never dared to dream of it aloud — well, when it happens, you can never, ever forget.

TULSA WORLD

Tulsa, OK, March 28, 1989

SOVIET citizens tried something new Sunday: an election in which there was more than one choice for some offices.

The voting was preceded by a campaign in which candidates and citizens actually debated issues and expressed opinions.

No, the Soviet Union hasn't suddenly achieved representative democracy. More than 80 percent of the candidates for the new 2,250-member Congress of Peoples' Deputies were Communist Party members; 25 percent of the seats were uncontested and the new "congress" won't have much power.

But in allowing a free choice for even a few not-very-powerful offices, President Mikhail Gorbachev has let a powerful genie out of the bottle. With this small taste of freedom and the notion of having some voice in their own government, the Soviet people will almost certainly demand more power.

Oddly, the most publicized winner in Sunday's voting was one of Gorbachev's most famous critics, Boris N. Yeltsin, who had been fired from a powerful Moscow municipal office in a quarrel with the Gorbachev government. He won his seat in the new congress with a huge margin.

The election symbolized great hope in the Soviet Union. There is also a risk. If things move too fast, stubborn conservatives could be frightened into abandoning the Gorbachev reforms.

One thing is certain. A mighty force has been released in the Soviet Union. Things will never be the same in that country again.

THE CHRISTIAN SCIENCE MONITOR
Boston, MA, March 29, 1989

SOMEWHERE, Vladimir Ilyich Lenin must be rubbing his eyes in wonder.

Soviet citizens by the millions have voted in a free and open election in which the very structure and purpose of the state have been questioned. Thousands of candidates were selected in a town meeting atmosphere where many Communist Party hacks learned the true meaning of *glasnost* and *perestroika.*

Yes, it's easy to be cynical about this historic exercise in democracy, Soviet-style. No serious talk of a real multi-party system yet. An army of 18 million bureaucrats is still in place. And doubts remain about how much power the new 2,250-member Congress of People's Deputies will have. But last summer's party conference – the first in nearly 50 years – whetted appetites for something new, and now that it's been tasted, political palates are forever changed.

With the election afterglow fading, the bulk of Mikhail Gorbachev's challenge becomes more obvious and more imperative. The problems: How to control the democratic cat now that it's out of the bag? Liberals and conservatives will both be testing the political limits. How to deal with Baltic and other nationalistic groups? They're already pushing for economic independence.

And the toughest problem of all: how to build a healthy economy? The Soviet Union imports 36 million tons of grain a year because 20 percent of domestic crops are lost to bureaucratic mismanagement. Agricultural subsidies amount to 18 percent of the Soviet budget, contributing to a deficit three times the US's.

The Soviet leader is betting all this political openness (*glasnost*) will impel economic restructuring (*perestroika*). But how much time does he have? Very few Soviet citizens feel their standard of living has improved during the four years Gorbachev has been in power. The overwhelming election victory of gadfly Boris Yeltsin in Moscow – who's been calling for an end to official privilege and the dismantling of the power of the party bureaucracy – is a clear indication of discontent.

But Comrade Yeltsin has also been urging even more radical reform and an acceleration of *perestroika,* so there is certainly more desire for change. "We are passing through the most difficult years now," Gorbachev told a crowd in Kiev recently. But he reminded them that the Soviet Union has seen far worse in its short history, and he urged them not to "lose heart." That's our wish for the Soviet people too as we welcome their important step toward democracy.

The Houston Post
Houston, TX, March 30, 1989

HISTORIANS MAY SOMEDAY DESCRIBE the Soviet Union's parliamentary elections this week as an aberration in that totalitarian Communist state, or the beginning of democratization. Either way, they will be remembered.

Soviet voters took advantage of their first contested national elections in 70 years to send a message: They are tired of Communist Party officials who support the stagnant status quo. Those party candidates who failed to win seats in the new Congress of People's Deputies won't lose their current posts, at least not immediately. But their humiliating defeats could shorten their bureaucratic careers.

By giving the combative populist, Boris Yeltsin, 89 percent of the vote in his race against an establishment candidate, Moscow voters registered their disdain for the arrogant, pampered party elite, with its limousines, weekend *dachas* and other perquisites.

Nationalism reared its head in such places as the Ukraine and the Baltic republics of Latvia, Estonia and Lithuania. Powerful Communist Party officials, even some running uncontested, were rejected. High-ranking military officers also fared badly in the voting.

This was a stunning rebuff to the hardliners in the party who oppose change and a boost for President Mikhail Gorbachev's *perestroika,* his program of sweeping economic and political reforms. Yet even Gorbachev may be discomfited by the landslide victory of Yeltsin, his former protege. The outspoken maverick was ousted as Moscow party boss and Politburo member in 1987 for criticizing party privilege and the slow pace of *perestroika,* or restructuring.

The next step in Gorbachev's carefully engineered reform plan is as critical to his success as this week's vote. The new 2,250-member congress — 1,500 deputies chosen by popular election and 750 named by the Communist Party and other organizations — will pick from its ranks a full-time parliament of more than 500 members and a new president. The Soviet leader seems certain to succeed himself in that job. But he must also control the parliament if he is to loosen the Communist Party's tight grip on the levers of government.

Though Gorbachev appears to have been the big winner in this week's elections, the results revealed deep and widespread discontent with the system. If *perestroika* , as instituted, fails to deliver a better life for Soviet citizens, he can't pass the buck.

St. Paul Pioneer Press & Dispatch
St. Paul, MN, March 28, 1989

BY the standards of Western democracy, the Soviet election Sunday wasn't much. The 1,500 winners in the national election will join members chosen by the Communist Party and other organizations to form a 2,250-member Congress of People's Deputies. It is certain to be dominated by the establishment.

But by Soviet standards, the voting and its outcome were remarkable. Anti-establishment candidates not only were allowed to run, but made strong showings. The most notable is Boris Yeltsin, who took more than 90 percent of the vote in his district. Mr. Yeltsin, an ousted Moscow party boss, hit political pay dirt campaigning against abuses by the elite while most of the country is suffering increased deprivation from a new order that often seems more like chaos.

The new congress won't be a power center, but it will reverberate with the distinct voices of loyal opposition for the first time in Soviet history. The politically canny Mikhail Gorbachev is bound to be listening, and so is the West.

The News Journal
Wilmington, DE, March 30, 1989

THE PEOPLE of the Soviet Union have spoken. They are dissatisfied with their government representatives and they want change.

Soviet citizens turned out in large numbers in Sunday's parliamentary election — first free election since 1917 — and ousted numerous high-ranking Communist Party officials. In their stead, they voted in new delegates to the 2,250-member Congress of People's Deputies. In several instances, when there was no choice because only an incumbent's name was on the ballot, voters expressed discontent by crossing out the name. Important Communist Party functionaries in Leningrad, Kiev and elsewhere found their names crossed out on more than half of the ballots and were denied seats in the next congress.

Then there was the amazing victory of Boris N. Yeltsin in Moscow with 89.4 percent of the vote. Mr. Yeltsin, who was ousted from the Politbureau a couple of years ago because he wanted more rapid change than the entrenched bureaucrats could tolerate, had run a populist campaign, often addressing large crowds in the Soviet capital. He is a former ally of Soviet leader Mikhail Gorbachev and may be able to strengthen the latter's hand in moving forward with reforms.

Mr. Gorbachev took a gamble when he called for free elections. He was looking for popular support for reforms, and he seems to have obtained it.

But now comes the challenge of implementing those reforms — getting farmers to produce more, putting more consumer goods on the market, providing more housing, permitting more local control, reducing central planning and allowing more freedom of expression.

It's easy enough for citizens to vote *nyet* on those in parliament. But it is difficult for the new officials to formulate effective programs. And the Soviet people have to both work hard to make the new programs work and understand that success is not achieved overnight.

Holding free elections only begins change. It's like a long novel's first chapter. Now come development of plot, delineation of character and progress to a climax. The true meaning of the elections won't be known until that climax is reached.

Part II: U.S.-Soviet Relations

Relations between the U.S. and U.S.S.R. have long been characterized by distrust and mutual suspicion. From the "Cold War" period (the late 1940s through the 1960s) to the uncertain rapprochement of the "detente" era of the 1970s, the two countries remained implacable adversaries. The threat of nuclear war not only overshadowed the superpowers, but the world as a whole.

There was no reason to believe relations would improve when Ronald Reagan assumed the U.S. presidency in 1981. A hardline anticommunist, the president in 1983 used the memorable phrase "evil empire" to characterize the U.S.S.R. Reagan championed a massive build-up of the U.S. military to counter what he viewed as the Soviet menace. He convinced America's Western European allies to base U.S. intermediate-range nuclear missiles on their soil. And he began what was to be his most controversial military program – the Strategic Defense Initiative (popularly known as "Star Wars") – which he envisioned as a space-based shield of high-technology weapons that would protect the U.S. against Soviet intercontinental ballistic missiles.

Reagan met his match in General Secretary Gorbachev. Like the president, the Soviet leader was amiable, but firm in his beliefs. Gorbachev equaled Reagan in the ability to use the media to sway public opinion.

Over the course of three years, the two leaders held five meetings and eventually reached a point of mutual respect. They first met in Geneva in November 1985. Their discussions in Reykjavik, Iceland, in October 1986, were abrasive. The Soviet leader received a warm reception in Washington in June 1987, as did the president when he went to Moscow in May 1988 (during which Reagan backed away from his "evil empire" statement). Their last meeting during the Reagan presidency was in New York City in December 1988.

A high point of U.S.-Soviet relations came at the Moscow summit, when the two leaders exchanged formal documents of ratification of a treaty to eliminate intermediate-range nuclear forces (INF). The treaty, signed at the Washington summit, was the first ever agreement to rid the world of an entire class of nuclear arms. But the INF treaty was not the only sign of improved relations. In the years 1985-89, the superpowers agreed to bilateral measures on cultural, scientific and educational exchanges, enhanced trade and joint business ventures. The superpowers cooperated on finding ways to cool regional conflicts around the world. And, under steady Western pressure, the Kremlin began to raise restrictions on the emigration of Soviet citizens while at the same time adopting a more permissive attitude on human rights.

As George Bush assumed Reagan's mantle, the U.S. and Soviet Union were negotiating a treaty to reduce strategic (long-range) nuclear weapons, and superpower tensions appeared to be at an all-time low. Both the Gorbachev regime and the Bush administration indicated that they wished the two nations to continue drawing closer.

S. Korean Passenger Plane Shot Down After Violating Soviet Airspace

A South Korean commercial airliner en route from New York to Seoul was shot down Sept. 1, 1983 after overflying strategically sensitive Soviet territory. All 240 passengers and 29 crew members were believed killed when the plane, a Boeing 747, disappeared in the Sea of Japan after being struck down by a heat-seeking missile launched by a Soviet jet fighter. According to Korean Air Lines, the dead passengers included 81 South Koreans, 61 Americans, 28 Japanese, 16 Filipinos, 10 Canadians, six Thais, four Australians and single passengers from India, Malaysia, Sweden and Vietnam. The 29 crew members were all South Korean. Among the U.S. passengers was Rep. Larry McDonald (D, Ga.), chairman of the extreme right-wing John Birch Society.

Accounts of the downing of the plane that began to emerge were sketchy and marked by rhetoric that intensified steadily over the next few days. The Soviet Union Sept. 1 claimed that a plane flying without navigational lights had violated Soviet airspace and resisted efforts by Soviet planes to guide it. A statement carried by the official press agency, Tass, said "the intruder plane did not react to the signals and warnings from the Soviet fighters and continued its flight in the direction of the Sea of Japan."

U.S. Secretary of State George Shultz the same day charged that the U.S.S.R. had downed the South Korean plane, knowing that it was an unarmed civilian airliner. Shultz offered an unusual glimpse into U.S. intelligence-gathering operations when he disclosed that the U.S. routinely monitored Soviet military transmissions. A replay of electronically-recorded communications by a Soviet fighter pilot had indicated that he had sighted the South Korean plane, fired on it and reported it destroyed, Shultz revealed. Shultz acknowledged that Flight 007 had been flying over Soviet territory, but did not explain why the jetliner had strayed so far off course. President Reagan Sept. 1 condemned the jet's destruction as a "horrifying act of violence" and demanded an explanation from the U.S.S.R.

The United States Sept. 4 disclosed that a U.S. reconnaissance plane had been in the vicinity of the Korean Air Lines jet when it passed over the Kamchatka Penninsula. The admission followed the suggestion by a Soviet general that the South Korean plane had been mistaken for a U.S. RC-135 reconnaissance plane. An RC-135 had, in fact, been flying a route that intersected that of the Korean Air Lines plane, the U.S. revealed, but a White House statement maintained that the closest the two planes ever came was about 75 nautical miles from each other. U.S. officials noted that the shapes of the planes were considerably different, and that although they could not be distinguished on radar screens, the Soviet pilot, according to the transcripts, had made visual contact with the passenger plane.

President Reagan, in a nationally televised speech Sept. 5, denounced the Soviet Union for what he described as the "Korean Air Line massacre." He avoided taking any major retaliatory initiatives, however, announcing only minor punitive measures that were widely viewed as symbolic and unlikely to have any appreciable effect on U.S.-Soviet relations. A majority of the countries in the North Atlantic Treaty Organization reportedly agreed at a meeting in Brussels Sept. 9 to impose a two-week ban on civilian flights to and from the Soviet Union. President Reagan Sept. 8 directed that the two U.S. offices of the Soviet airline Aeroflot be closed, and that three Aeroflot officials be expelled from the U.S.

The Soviet Union used its veto power Sept. 12 to block a resolution stating that the United Nations Security Council "deeply deplores the destruction of the Korean airliner and the tragic loss of civilian life therein." The vote was nine to two, with four abstentions. Poland joined the U.S.S.R. in voting against the resolution. The four countries that abstained were China, Nicaragua, Zimbabwe and Guyana.

THE INDIANAPOLIS STAR

Indianapolis, IN, September 2, 1983

If the world needed proof of the brutal nature of the Soviet regime, it has it now in the senseless, barbaric gunning down of a commercial Korean jetliner. The aircraft accidentally and innocently strayed into Soviet air space and the price paid was the lives of 265 human beings.

The tragedy was not precipitated by some trigger-happy military crew acting in haste and without consultation with superiors. The Korean aircraft was tracked on Soviet radar for more than two hours and the MiG fighters which intercepted it — as many as eight, according to reports — were in constant contact with their ground control.

Communications monitored by the Japanese report that there was visual contact with the Korean jet and that a MiG pilot confirmed the firing of a missile and the destruction of his "target."

There are no mitigating circumstances and no basis for plausible explanations. Diplomatic apologies and negotiated settlements are not appropriate. Among civilized people the incident is, pure and simple, the murder of 265 helpless people.

One of the terrible ironies is the death of Rep. Lawrence P. McDonald, D-Ga., national chairman of the John Birch Society, an organization frequently denounced as paranoiac about communism. McDonald, then, has become a victim of paranoia come true.

The real delusion, however, is that the Soviet Union is just another member of the family of nations. Rather, this incident confirms the contempt the Soviets have not only for international law but for the humaneness that marks a civilized society.

Rockford Register Star

Rockford, IL, September 2, 1983

Inconceivable ... appalling ... outrageous ... revolting ... barbaric ... completely inexcusable.

There simply are no words to adequately describe the shooting down of a peaceful passenger plane and the 269 persons aboard.

Soviet actions as spelled out in detailed reports from Washington and from Japan fully deserve the condemnation of the entire world.

Was there provocation? Probably in that the Boeing 747 apparently had wandered into Soviet air space. But how provocative can a jumbo airliner be? And under what twisted logic would such a "provocation" justify firing a deadly missile at an airliner?

Is there a possibility that this was the act of some irresponsible fighter pilot with an itchy trigger finger? Of course that possibility exists. But radio transmissions monitored in Japan clearly indicate Soviet fighter pilots in close communications with their ground command during the entire 2½ hours they trailed the jumbo jet.

And even if this tragedy was triggered, literally, by one irresponsible individual, what does that say about the nation which gives such a person a trigger to pull?

Washington and Tokyo are fully justified in the anger they've expressed officially to the Soviets and in their demands for explanation.

But we can't imagine an acceptable explanation for such a grave violation of international laws and such an humanitarian act.

No, the Soviets stand accused today before all mankind for a terribly violation against humanity.

Rocky Mountain News

A Scripps-Howard Newspaper Reg. U.S. Pat. Off. Colorado's First Newspaper—Founded in 1859

Denver, CO, September 3, 1983

AMERICANS have justifiably reacted with fury over the Soviet Union's shooting down of a Korean airliner and many would like to see the United States take the strongest of retaliatory measures.

Obviously, the murderous act requires a strong official response from this country. But it would not be in the interest of the United States or of the world to overreact.

It is elemental that the attack be condemned in the sharpest terms and that a demand be made of the Soviet Union for a full explanation of the details of the episode and of what prompted it to kill 269 innocent passengers and crew of an unarmed commercial aircraft.

The United States also should take the lead in marshalling world opinion against the savagery of the Soviet regime.

Past that, though, officials face a delicate task in deciding how far to go.

In earlier times such an aggression would have been considered an act of war. But it goes without saying that a response that could escalate events into a shooting war is out of the question.

There have been demands in some quarters that the grain treaty just signed with the Soviet Union be revoked and that all trade with the Soviet Union be stopped. U.S. officials would have to weigh where the consequences of such actions would fall heaviest — on us or them. In any event, responses of this nature would fail unless they were supported by other nations of the free world. So if the U.S. does decide to act, it ought to round up support first.

If the Soviet leadership has any sense, it will acknowledge that it made a terrible mistake and apologize. So far it has done nothing but lie and try to put the blame on others.

If there is any good that can come out of such a tragedy it is the opening of the eyes of everyone in the world as to exactly what kind of leaders they are dealing with in the Soviet Union.

The Idaho STATESMAN

Boise, ID, September 2, 1983

The question preying upon millions of minds today is how a Soviet fighter plane came to shoot down an unarmed Korean jetliner.

The Soviets' few statements — that the airliner failed to identify itself and that Soviet fighters attempted to escort it to an airfield — are not likely to assuage anyone's outrage. The attack, which apparently took the lives of all 269 people aboard the plane, defies rationality. There can be no justification.

Still, the Soviets must explain.

All that is known points to a deliberate decision by someone in the Soviet military to destroy a plane that, under the circumstances, could hardly have been taken for anything other than what it was.

The Soviets had tracked the Korean Air Lines Boeing 747 for 2½ hours. According to Secretary of State George Shultz, at least eight Soviet planes reacted to the KAL flight at one time or another. The Soviet pilot who fired the missile apparently had the 747 in sight when he fired. He was continually in contact with superiors on the ground and told them it was a 747.

Did the Soviets believe the plane, which they say violated Soviet airspace, presented some threat? If so, why? One would think that the innocent nature of such a plane would be evident even at night.

Did the Soviets try to persuade the Korean Air Lines pilot to alter his route, either by radio or through signals? Was there a warning shot fired?

What happened?

Such questions, which have been directed to the Soviets by our own State Department, are not raised out of mere curiosity. They lie at the heart of a matter of vital concern to everyone on Earth.

Peace today is maintained through an armed truce between the Soviets and the West, each side fearing and respecting the power of the other, each side depending upon the other's willingness and ability to act rationally.

On Thursday, the Soviets broke that truce with an act that, by all available accounts, makes no sense. None of us can rest easy until that act is explained and assurances are made that such a thing can never happen again. Much more explanation — plus an apology from President Yuri Andropov — must be forthcoming from the Soviets.

The Providence Journal

Providence, RI, September 2, 1983

The loss of 265 lives aboard a South Korean jetliner has left the world shaken — more shaken, indeed, than most air tragedies do. Neither bad weather nor mechanical trouble seems to have been involved. Instead, according to U.S. accounts (derived from sensitive intelligence-gathering devices), the Boeing 747 jumbo jet — unarmed, on a routine civilian flight — was blasted out of the sky by a missile fired from a Soviet fighter near Soviet-owned Sakhalin Island north of Japan.

Such an attack is a barbaric outrage, as an incensed Washington was insisting yesterday. Shooting down an unarmed civilian aircraft can never be justified, regardless of whether the plane is offending a government by violating its air space. There are many ways to bring an intruding plane under control short of shooting it down. Did the Soviets try any such steps? The record is unclear. Regardless, shooting the plane down cannot be seen as anything other than a wanton, criminal act. Those aboard the downed Korean plane appear to have been murdered, as surely as if they had been lined up against a wall and shot.

It seems agreed that the Korean plane, Flight 007 en route from New York to Seoul by way of an Anchorage refueling stop, went off course and strayed into Soviet airspace — not once but twice. It first flew over the Kamchatka Peninsula and over the Sea of Okhotsk, and then over Sakhalin Island. Both U.S. and Soviet officials say the flight was tracked for two and a half hours. Tass, the Soviet press agency, said yesterday that the plane carried no navigation lights and failed to respond to radioed queries. Soviet air-defense fighters, added Tass, "tried to give it assistance in in directing it to the nearest airfield." The Soviet account made no mention of the plane's having been shot down.

Full details of this grim and mysterious event may never be learned. So far as is known, the plane's crew sent no radio message to indicate that Soviet aircraft were nearby. All the crew and passengers are presumed lost, and the Soviets are unlikely to level with the rest of the world if one of their pilots did indeed shoot down the Korean jet. But the detailed U.S. account, unless it can be effectively refuted, depicts an example of callous behavior that even by Soviet standards has to be considered cold-blooded and brutal.

Technical and navigational questions abound. Was the pilot off course? If so, did he know it? And, if so, why is there no evidence of radio contact with some ground station, somewhere? If the Soviets indeed tried to establish radio contact, as they claim, what kept the Korean pilot from replying?

None of these questions, however, can alter the fact of an appalling international tragedy, one heavy with political overtones. The loss of the Korean plane underscores, in all-too-vivid fashion, the shaky state of East-West relations and the constant perils of a world dominated by heavily armed superpowers. If the Soviets shot down the jetliner, it was an act utterly impossible of justification or explanation, one providing all too grim a reminder of the Soviets' habit of behaving in world affairs according to their own rules. One hopes Soviet officials make decisions about their nuclear missiles with more care and thought than was evident in the episode of the Korean jetliner.

Soviet Union and Allies Withdraw from L.A. Olympic Games

The Soviet Union May 7, 1989 announced that it would not participate in the 1984 Summer Olympic Games in Los Angeles. The announcement by the Soviet National Olympic Committee said that the participation of its athletes in the L.A. games was "impossible" in light of the "cavalier attitude of the U.S. authorities to the Olympic Charter."

The announcement pointedly avoided any use of the term "boycott" to describe the Soviet withdrawal. (The term had been widely used in the West to describe the U.S.-led movement in 1980 to keep nations out of the Summer Olympics in Moscow, to protest Soviet military involvement in Afghanistan.) Bulgaria and East Germany soon followed suit in announcing their own withdrawals from the L.A. games. They were joined May 11-13 by Vietnam, Mongolia, Czechoslovakia, Laos and Afghanistan. Most of the non-participants cited concern over security at the games as the justification for their withdrawal.

The finality of the Soviet withdrawal was made clear May 14 when Marat V. Gramov, the chairman of the Soviet National Olympic Committee, called his nation's decision "irrevocable." Speaking at a Moscow news conference, Gramov blamed the pullout on an "anti-Soviet crusade" in the U.S., asserting that the Reagan administration had been plotting to induce the defections of Soviet athletes through kidnappings and the use of "psychotropic chemicals to affect the nervous system." He contended that an adviser to President Reagan, Michael Deaver, had endorsed the activities of the Ban the Soviets Coalition, an umbrella organization of anti-Soviet groups in Los Angeles. President Reagan said that the reasons stated by the Soviets were "absolutely false," and asserted that "no one in the history of the Olympics has ever done so much as we're doing to insure" the safety of the athletes.

The Salt Lake Tribune
Salt Lake City, UT, May 10, 1984

There could be any number of reasons the Soviet Union decided not to send its athletes to the Summer Olympics in Los Angeles in July. But one way or another they are all tied directly to the unusually bad relations now existing between the U.S. and the USSR.

Given this bleak state of affairs, it was only natural that the Soviets would seize the timely opportunity to repay the U.S. in kind for boycotting the 1980 games in Moscow. Such a Soviet response was anticipated in these columns four years ago when The Tribune questioned the wisdom of President Carter's attempt to wreck the Moscow Olympics in protest to the Soviet invasion of Afghanistan.

Despite this understandable urge to settle old scores, the Soviets would hardly have pulled out of the 1984 games if they felt that the present state of relations with their major adversary were conducive to attainment of hoped-for policy concessions.

Conditions, of course, are anything but conducive to concessions and there are ample signs that the Kremlin has given up on being able to do business with the Reagan administration. With no prospect that swallowing their immense pride and going to Los Angeles would have a worthwhile payoff, the decision not to compete was all but inevitable.

There is an element of plausibility in the official Soviet excuse that the United States refused to provide adequate "security" for the 1,000 or so athletes and coaches the USSR would have sent. Although they have

their in-house experts on the United States, those who run the tightly controlled Soviet empire find it impossible to understand why the mighty U.S. government cannot prevent demonstrations and other types of anti-Soviet protest from taking place.

Fear of mass defection by Soviet athletes tempted by the many charms of Southern California has been suggested as a factor in the boycott. That notion can be dismissed out of hand. Indeed, a few might have tried it, but Americans are fooling themselves if they think many Soviets, least of all star athletes who get preferred treatment at home, are burning with desire to live in this country or anywhere else outside the USSR.

It has been suggested that the Soviets think sitting out the summer games will embarrass Mr. Reagan and contribute to his defeat in November. If so, they have again confirmed their lack of understanding of things American. Many in this country blame Mr. Reagan for the sad state of U.S.-Soviet affairs. But they can be counted upon to resent such ham-handed intervention in domestic politics.

Even so, Soviet refusal to compete at Los Angeles should be taken as a distressing indicator of how things stand after almost four years of Reagan stewardship. His vaunted resolve to negotiate from a position of superior strength or not negotiate at all has produced a frightening stalemate so dense that even the once-noble Olympic spirit cannot penetrate.

THE PLAIN DEALER
Cleveland, OH, May 9, 1984

The Soviets have until June 2 to change their minds about pulling out of the 1984 Summer Olympic Games. We hope they do. As a test of athletic prowess, the games are virtually meaningless without the participation of the Soviet Union, just as the 1980 Moscow games were diluted by the absence of the United States.

The threat of Soviet revenge for the U.S. boycott in 1980 is nothing new. It has hung over the Los Angeles Olympics for four years. The Soviets do not take embarrassment lightly, which may be why they exploited some recent developments to justify their decision not to compete.

From the Soviet standpoint, there is room for concern. A key Soviet official has been denied a visa on the grounds that he is a KGB agent. An anti-Soviet group is believed ready to tempt Soviet athletes to defect.

Of course, the Soviets are being hypocritical. They would be the first to ban from their country an alleged CIA agent fronting as a sports official. There is no doubt that they would suppress dissident groups; they banished possible troublemakers from Moscow in 1980.

Because this is a free country, Washington can do nothing about anti-Soviet groups in Los Angeles so long as they stay within the law. Moscow's charges that the U.S. government is conniving to whip up hysteria against Soviet athletes seem exaggerated if not downright paranoiac. Most Americans with any interest in the 1984 Olympics want the games to go on and the Russians to be there. They want to see the world's best in action.

The Soviets have been whining for some time about the whole idea of going to Los Angeles. Evidently they despise the city. Some of their complaints are echoed by many Americans. LA has smog and other typical urban American amenities: crime and a high cost of living. Those considerations by themselves would not have kept the Soviets away. They exist in perpetuity; the Soviets could have exploited them any time in the past four years but waited instead for more political excuses.

Now that Moscow has made its decision, Olympic officials are waiting for the other shoe to drop in the form of reaction from the East European satellites and other Soviet allies. Some of them have been quoting Soviet allegations in their press, but a general boycott would indicate the raw political necessity of maintaining subservience to Moscow rather than a true allegiance to the Soviet point of view.

Perhaps Moscow simply wants Washington to sweat. In fact, the withdrawal will hurt the Soviet Union's own athletes and, indeed, other competitors more than anyone else. It might also damage the games commercially and would be an undeserved blow to those in Los Angeles who have worked hard to stage the event at the lowest cost to the U.S. taxpayer.

The decision is not likely to hurt the Reagan administration. If anything, the action will fuel the anti-Soviet mood that the president has attempted to exploit. It would be better for the Soviets, having made their point about a clumsy decision of the United States four years ago, to reverse their decison and send a team to Los Angeles this summer.

The Boston Herald

Boston, MA, May 9, 1984

THE SOVIETS, behaving like a pack of petulant children, have chosen to keep their athletes at home to demonstrate their displeasure with the United States. On the flimsiest of pretexts they opted to boycott the Summer Olympics to be held in Los Angeles, thus setting a new standard for global spoilsports.

The Soviets maintain that the U.S. has failed to be able to guarantee the security of its athletes, an accusation that flies in the face of reports that the security preparations for the Games are second to none. It makes sense — at least to most of us not tuned in full time to propaganda — that the U.S. would do all within its power to make sure athletes of all countries feel both welcome and safe.

Accomplishing that goal during these troubled times won't be easy. International terrorism — some of it even fostered by the now fearful Soviets — has been a source of constant worry for Olympic organizers.

With the haunting memory of Munich all too fresh, no one in this country surely wanted L.A. to forever be linked in the minds of the world community to such human tragedy. Is that such a difficult idea for the Soviets to comprehend? Is there not a certain logic to that?

True, it was a mere four years ago that the United States protested the Soviet invasion of Afghanistan and the slaughter of thousands of innocent people by boycotting the Moscow Olympics. But what great international incident prompted the current display of Soviet petulance? What great cause, what loss of life, what violation of ideals has brought this response?

Now, as it was for our own athletes four years ago, the big losers are those who have trained for years and years for a chance to bring home the gold, to compete against the finest athletes each nation can produce. How sad for those fine Soviet athletes to become the latest pawns in their nation's political game.

And how sad for us, as well, not to be able to watch them compete and join in the kind of sportsmanship that is the essence and spirit of the Olympics.

The Oregonian

Portland, OR, May 9, 1984

Let's skip the propaganda from the Soviet news agency Tass. The Soviet Union's decision to boycott the 1984 Summer Olympic Games in Los Angeles was a predictable, eye-for-an-eye retaliation for the U.S. boycott of the 1980 Moscow Olympics.

The political issues that prompted these boycotts will be debated ad nauseam. But the fact remains that the Olympic Games over the last two decades have been permeated with national and international politics, their idealistic purpose exploited and abused.

If the Olympic Games are to survive as a forum for apolitical sports competition between individual athletes, they should be moved to a neutral, permanent site, preferably to the place of their origin in Greece.

President Carter would not have called for a boycott of the 1980 Games had they not been in Moscow, nor would the Soviet Union have announced it would not participate in the 1984 Olympics had they been held in a nation outside the United States.

In other words, it is not the Olympic Games that are being boycotted in these matters of state, it is the host nations that are being targeted. But it is the Games that are penalized.

The U.S. boycott of the 22nd Olympiad in Moscow was justified as a proper foreign policy response to Russia's outrageous invasion of Afghanistan. The Soviet Union's retaliatory boycott is founded on little more than the myths that the United States would provide less-than-acceptable security for Soviet participants and spectators in Los Angeles and that the United States somehow had undermined — no specifics were given — the Olympic charter.

While it is doubtful that the Soviets can be persuaded to change their minds, Olympic officials should take steps to convince other socialist countries that this is not their propaganda war. It is a limited foreign policy exchange between successive host nations.

The Soviet intention to boycott the Los Angeles Olympics will hurt America's effort to showcase capitalism and free enterprise, just as the American withdrawal from the Moscow Games undercut Russia's elaborate 1980 plans to showcase its system of government and way of life.

Athletic competition, ironically, will survive without the Russians — better with them, but not lost without them.

Members of the International Olympic Committee should recognize soon that the Olympic Games themselves have become a hostage of nations willing to play the Olympic card as part of their foreign policy deck. As a first act of depoliticizing the Games, they should be moved away from playgrounds where political propaganda scores more points than athletic prowess.

The Morning News

Wilmington, DE, May 10, 1984

SO THE RUSSIANS aren't coming. The official reasons given by the Soviet Union for withdrawal from the XXIII Olympiad are without merit. The real reason the Soviet athletes won't participate is revenge.

The Soviet Union was deeply offended by the boycott of the 1980 Olympics in Moscow. The Soviets mobilized the country to prepare for the sports spectacle: Magnificent new stadiums were built; modern electronic and telephone equipment was installed; whole neighborhoods were rebuilt; a new air terminal was constructed. The Moscow Olympics were to be a showcase, a demonstration of the wonderful things a Communist state could achieve.

And the party was spoiled by the United States. President Carter called for a boycott of the Moscow Olympics to protest the Soviet invasion of Afghanistan. Nearly 60 other nations followed America's lead.

It was clear during 1980 and 1981 that Soviet citizens bitterly resented the boycott. Even those who oppose the government on many issues were dismayed at not being able to show the positive aspects of life in the Soviet Union. There was talk among ordinary people, as distinct from the expected government claptrap, that mixing sports and politics was bad business.

This is the same talk we hear now in this country. The games will be held in Los Angeles, with or without the Soviets and their political allies. But, like the 1980 games in Moscow, they won't be of the same high quality. How could they be with many of the world's best athletes absent?

International politics has been an aspect of the Olympic games for years. What else would one call the feverish struggle for medals between the Western nations and those of the Soviet bloc? The games are as much ideological proxy battles as tests of physical strength, skill and endurance among world class athletes.

By withdrawing from this year's games, the Soviet Union will get its revenge. Our nation's pride will not be damaged much and the economic losses will not begin to compare with the financial devastation the Soviets suffered in 1980. But it will be done.

The boycott should not have surprised anyone. The Russians have long memories, thin skins and a deep sense of retribution. The United States did not present them with a reason to boycott the Olympics; they manufactured one.

Reagan Speeches Hint at Softened Stance on Soviet Negotiations

President Reagan visited Ireland at the beginning of a 10-day European tour that featured Reagan's attendance at the World War II D-Day commemoration in Normandy June 6, 1984 and culminated with his participation in the economic summit in London. In Ireland, Reagan's speeches focused on the prospects for resuming nuclear arms reduction talks with the Soviet Union.

Addressing a joint session of the Irish Parliament in Dublin June 4, Reagan expressed willingness to consider the Soviet proposal for a new treaty on the "non-use of force," set forth by the Soviets and their Warsaw Pact allies in January 1983. Reagan said: "If discussion on reaffirming the principle not to use force, a principle in which we believe so deeply, will bring the Soviet Union to negotiate agreements which will give concrete new meaning to that principle, we will gladly enter such discussions."

The U.S. previously had rejected the Soviet proposal to agree to "non-use" of conventional force, on the grounds that all nations had already agreed to such a principle in the United Nations charter and in other documents.

In a nationally televised White House news conference June 14, President Reagan also prepared to relax his conditions for holding a summit meeting with Soviet President Konstantin U. Chernenko. Reagan had previously maintained that direct talks with Chernenko would have to be carefully prepared and deal with concrete issues, a stance that he had been urged to change by Republican Senate leaders Howard Baker and Charles Percy. Reagan told reporters June 14 he was "willing to meet and talk any time" with Soviet leaders. The President said he would not insist on "a preconstructed meeting in which you've got a list of points," but that he opposed the kind of get-acquainted session that he had charged had "led to great expectations...and great disappointment" under previous administrations.

The Honolulu Advertiser
Honolulu, HI, June 9, 1984

Whatever the reason behind it, President Reagan's new peace offensive is a welcome switch from the image of a world leader dangerously prone to military solutions.

The "new" Reagan should be enouraged to keep it up — and not just because the election is coming in November.

THERE IS room to question how deeply felt Reagan's more moderate posture toward the Soviets and some other communists really is, given his views and record in the past.

Certainly part of it is political. He is popular at home, but surveys among Americans show a rising "fear of war" as a key issue and the perception that Reagan at the least has been deliberately inconsistent in pursuing peace. Europeans are much more critical and nervous about him.

So it is no coincidence that Reagan brought out the olive branch in time with his European trip.

First there was Secretary of State George Shultz's trip last weekend to Managua to discuss the potential for better relations with the Marxist-backed government of Nicaragua the U.S. has been seeking to destabilize, if not overthrow.

Then there was Reagan's well-received Monday speech to the Irish parliament where he proclaimed he is willing to enter negotiations on a non-aggression pact with the Soviet Union, a top Kremlin priority.

As commentators have noted it was a clear and skilled effort by Reagan to change his image with Americans as well as others from a leader, as he puts it, with a reputation for an itchy finger to a pilgrim for peace.

SINCE THEN there have been occasions for following up in the same vein at the D-Day anniversary in France and at the summit meeting in London.

Will it work?

Indications are Reagan, a man who again recently tried to sell the MX missile as "the peacemaker," can with his considerable communication skills establish an image with at least American voters of actively pursuing arms talks, reduced tensions and maybe even negotiations on Central America.

Others, in Europe and elsewhere, may be more skeptical, especially if the reality of our efforts does not match the Reagan image-making. The Democratic Party will also be keeping a more critical score in months ahead.

Still, that is best judged later. For now, after three and a half years, Reagan is at least paying more positive attention to the premier issue of our times.

The Chattanooga Times
Chattanooga, TN, June 14, 1984

In the wake of his meeting with leaders of the industrialized nations of the free world last week, President Reagan told reporters Soviet intransigence on arms control negotiations may be due to uncertainty in Russia: "[I]t's beginning to occur to some of us that maybe the silence is because they don't know what to say right now." The statement dramatizes the potentially dangerous lack of understanding between Washington and Moscow. We guess at their motivations; they guess at ours. Meanwhile, a nervous world awaits progress by the superpowers toward controlling the nuclear menace.

Mr. Reagan may be right in attributing Soviet stonewalling at least in part to shifting power bases and a quick succession of leaders in the Kremlin. But the president cannot escape responsibility for the deterioration of U.S.-Soviet relations during his presidency, as even Senate Majority Leader Howard Baker tacitly acknowledged in a speech Sunday.

Speaking at commencement exercises at Dartmouth College, Sen. Baker observed that "acrid rhetoric...has polluted the dialogue between superpowers..." The senator didn't blame Mr. Reagan, of course, but the fact is the president began his campaign of denunciation against the Soviets within days of taking office and continued it with gusto until the dawning of this election year softened his tone.

As the election draws near, Mr. Reagan is coming under increased pressure from fellow Republicans to do something to assuage national concern over the breakdown in relations with the Soviet Union. In his Dartmouth speech, Sen. Baker bucked the Reagan position and called for regular summit meetings between the superpowers. He underscored the strength of his position by saying the should begin "now,...whenever we can bring these two heads of state together." Sen. Baker, joined by Republican Sen. Charles Percy of Illinois, followed up with a personal meeting with the president Tuesday to urge an early meeting with Soviet leader Konstantin Chernenko.

Mr. Reagan's response was to restate his position that a summit should be held only when the stage has been set for announcement of some breakthrough or major agreement between the nations. Through a spokesman he asserted that regular summits would not, in and of themselves, solve the problems between the two countries; but that is not the point.

The point is that the nuclear stockpiles of the two superpowers threaten the earth and that the two men who control that immense power should know one another and talk face to face about issues which divide them. There is no risk in talking but considerable risk in the uncertainty bred of silence between the superpowers. Personal understanding and rapport which could be developed through regular consultations would serve the world well in time of crisis.

That understanding is crucial to developing a constructive relationship with the Soviets and underlies the commitment of Democratic presidential contender Walter Mondale to regularly scheduled summit meetings. The prospects that the sage advice of Sens. Baker and Percy will be acted upon would be much improved if the White House changed hands come November.

The Wichita
Eagle-Beacon

Wichita, KS, June 5, 1984

The most important things President Reagan told the Irish Parliament on Monday really were aimed at Moscow, not the Irish. His declaration of American friendship, his attempts to explain his Central American policy, which many of the Irish don't like, and his deploring of sectarian violence were important, to be sure. But the success of the Reagan trip will be measured more by the response of the Soviets to the president's plea for "greater dialogue" with the Kremlin "to guard against miscalculation or misunderstanding in troubled or strategically sensitive areas of the world."

In the interest of such improved communi-

cation, Mr. Reagan said, the United States would be willing to discuss the Soviet call for a treaty renouncing the use of force in Europe if Moscow will consider U.S. proposals at the Stockholm Conference on European Disarmament for reducing war risks. This country even would be willing to stop, and perhaps reverse, its deployment of intermediate-range nuclear missiles in Europe — as part of an arms control agreement with the Soviet Union. But "for such an outcome to become possible," the president said, "it will be necessary for the U.S.S.R. to return to the bargaining table in earnest."

American-Soviet relationships at the Stockholm conference have been amicable enough on the person-to-person negotiator level. But the Soviet Union has refused to allow any policy level compromises, even on such U.S. proposals as East-West agreements to limit the size of military maneuvers in Europe and to exchange some kinds of military data.

American missiles in Europe worry the Irish, too, and that is one of the reasons for the anti-Reagan demonstrations in Ireland during the president's visit. The Irish view of Mr. Reagan's policies and performance — not only in Europe but in Central America and elsewhere — may not be critical to the implementation of those policies, except in the context of America's reliance on its allies for geographic as well as moral support. But the Soviet leadership should give serious thought to Mr. Reagan's appeal for a revival of U.S.-Soviet discussions about tension-creating issues and arms control. It's to be hoped the initial Soviet rejection of the president's plea will be reconsidered.

The Washington Times

Washington, DC, June 11, 1984

If Moscow were consistent in its statements about arms control, President Reagan's speech last week to Ireland's parliament should have had them dancing with joy in the Great Palace of the Kremlin. Instead, Tass issued one of those characteristically banal statements rejecting Mr. Reagan's overture as a political gimmick to soften his "trigger-happy" image in Western Europe. So much for good intentions.

There was a measure of irony, though, in Moscow's response. When the president said that the United States was prepared to consider a mutual renunciation of force in Europe, provided the Soviet Union considered other ideas to reduce tension, he was repeating almost verbatim Moscow's proposal last winter to the 45-nation Stockholm meeting on European security.

What happened to sour Moscow on its own idea? For one thing, the author of the original proposal died. Two major turnovers within 18 months in the top echelons of the Kremlin hierarchy have caused almost

insurmountable inertia in a regime that, even in good times, is not noted for the alacrity with which it formulates policy.

A more important reason for Soviet intransigence has to do with domestic problems. With a U.S. presidential election in the offing, the Kremlin hopes it can gain a little breathing room to deal with the frustrations generated by the inability of Marxism-Leninism to achieve the blessings of a prosperous society.

In a sense, though, Tass did flirt with the truth. Mr. Reagan's words were indeed aimed at the West Europeans. In expressing his willingness to embrace a previously tendered Soviet proposal, the president demonstrated the sort of judicious flexibility that gives the lie to Moscow's heavy-handed portrayals of American intransigence. That ought to pay handsome dividends in uniting the allies for the important rounds of arms negotiations certain to materialize after the November election.

The Burlington Free Press

Burlington, VT, June 5, 1984

After months of reciting the cold war rhetoric that was reminiscent of the 1950s, President Reagan in his Monday address to the Irish Parliament took a more conciliatory tone toward the Soviet Union by offering to stop — even reverse — the deployment of medium-range nuclear missiles in Europe in exchange for arms control agreements with Moscow.

His offer indicated that Washington is willing to meet the Soviets halfway in working out treaties to slow the pace of the arms race. It represented a shift in the anti-Soviet rhetoric that has been emanating from the White House in recent months. The escalation of unpleasantries between the two governments has created the impression that their differences are irreconcilable. Stung by foreign policy reverses in several areas, the new Russian leadership apparently has gone into hibernation, insulating itself from the rest of the world until it can get its bearings. At the same time, it appears that the Soviets are continuing the buildup of their strategic and tactical forces in anticipation of a confrontation with the West. An isolated and sullen Russia could be a dangerous adversary because of the difficulty of ascertaining its intentions.

Washington and Moscow have been equally guilty of indulging in militant rhetoric since Konstantin Chernenko took over as Soviet leader. Chernenko has scant knowledge of the world outside the Soviet Union and is ill-equipped to deal with the subtleties of foreign policy. His advisers in the Kremlin apparently have convinced him that it is futile to negotiate with the United States on any issue until after the November election. They apparently hope that Reagan will lose the election and want to do what they can to assure that result.

Soviet conduct has frightened people in several Western countries because they believe they will be caught in the crunch of a Russian-American nuclear war. Deployment of medium-range missiles in North Atlantic Treaty Organization countries has persuaded Europeans that they are a step closer to such a conflict. They expect the Soviets to respond by adding more medium-range missiles, aimed at the heart of Western Europe, to their arsenal.

In his speech, Reagan said the United States wants "greater dialogue" with the Kremlin to prevent "miscalculation or misunderstanding" in troubled areas of the world. As evidence that this country is "prepared for peace," Reagan held out

the possibility of stopping or reversing the deployment of the medium-range missiles if the Soviets accept proposals that are being considered at the Stockholm Conference on Disarmament in Europe. They call for limitations on the size of Warsaw Pact military maneuvers in Europe, mandatory advance notification of military exercises and an exchange of data to "produce greater transparency" between the forces in the East and the West. The Soviets have merely called on the West to agree to a pact renouncing the use of force.

"If discussions on reaffirming the principle not to use force ... will bring the Soviet Union to negotiate agreements which will give new meaning to that principle, we will gladly enter into such discussions," Reagan said.

The United States "will remain ready" to work with the Soviets toward a "more peaceful world," he said.

In taking such a conciliatory stance toward the Soviet Union, Reagan has sent a signal to Moscow of a willingness on the part of the administration to adopt a flexible approach in dealing with the issue of arms control.

Now the men in the Kremlin must emerge from their shell and demonstrate similar flexibility.

Reagan's U.N. Address Avoids Criticism of Moscow

President Reagan adopted his most conciliatory stance yet toward the Soviet Union in an address to the 39th session of the United Nations General Assembly Sept. 24, 1984. The two superpowers, he said, had "a particular responsibility to contribute political solutions" to regional conflicts, which could "set off the sparks leading to worldwide conflagration."

Reagan said he was "disappointed" that the talks proposed by the Soviet Union to prevent the militarization of outer space had not materialized in September and expressed hope that such talks could begin by the end of the year. Washington and Moscow needed "to extend the arms control process to build a bigger umbrella under which it can operate – a road map, if you will, showing where during the next 20 years or so these individual efforts can lead," the President said. Toward this end, he proposed that the U.S. and U.S.S.R. seek by the spring of 1985 to "institutionalize regular ministerial or cabinet-level meetings between our two countries on the whole agenda of issues before us, including the problem of needless obstacles to understanding."

More specifically, Reagan said, such talks could "consider the exchange of outlines or five-year military plans for weapons development and our schedules of intended procurement." The President said the U.S. would "welcome the exchange of observers at military exercises and locations" and renewed earlier U.S. offers of on-site verification of nuclear weapons tests.

The optimistic speech, devoid of formerly standard references to the Soviet military presence in Afghanistan and alleged human rights violations, appeared to be the culmination of an election-year softening in Reagan's approach to U.S.-Soviet relations. The President had begun his speech by suggesting that the U.S. had attained the position of military strength needed to negotiate with Moscow. "America has repaired its strength," he said. "We are ready for constructive negotiations with the Soviet Union."

Soviet Foreign Minister Andrei Gromyko, in a 75-minute speech to the General Assembly Sept. 27, however, delivered a harsh attack on U.S. foreign policy since World War II. In a reference to the President's speech, he charged that the Reagan administration's policy was that "Strength, strength, strength and, above all, strength is the guarantee of international peace. In other words, weapons, weapons and ever more weapons."

TULSA WORLD

Tulsa, OK, September 26, 1984

PRESIDENT Ronald Reagan in a talk before the United Nations has called for negotiations on arms control and other moves to ease tensions between the U. S. and Soviet Russia.

The president's offer won't satisfy those who think the only block to arms control is "Reagan's refusal to sit down and talk" with the Soviets. These critics have a way of blaming the U.S. for most of the evils of East-West confrontation.

But their pessimism, while based on the wrong reasons, is well-founded.

For one thing, the superpowers' tragic, wasteful preoccupation with nuclear arms is not a cause so much as it is an effect. It is the result of vast differences between the American and Soviet views of the world.

These differences are not going to be quickly settled by talks between the leaders of the two countries.

To be sure, a start must be made. Agreements that benefit both can be reached.

But the Soviets must be convinced that they cannot achieve their goals without agreements. If they can achieve the disarmament of the U. S., for example, through disruption of NATO members, through agitation by citizens of the western alliance for unilateral disarmament, they will not negotiate.

Why bargain when the other side is doing what you want without concessions on your part?

The president's announcement that "America has repaired its strength . . . we are ready for constructive negotiations with the Soviet Union," is perhaps the best hope for worthwhile negotiations with the Soviets.

THE CHRISTIAN SCIENCE MONITOR

Boston, MA, September 27, 1984

IN his speeches to the United Nations and World Bank, in his White House turnstile greetings of a half-dozen foreign ministers or heads of state, including those from the Soviet Union, Canada, and Israel, in his private chat with former President Richard Nixon and his sidekick Henry A. Kissinger, both veterans of Washington-Moscow negotiations, President Reagan has clearly earmarked this as "foreign-policy week" of the 1984 campaign.

It would be unfortunate, however, to dismiss the burst of White House interest in the fundamentals of diplomacy as so much electoral posturing. And it would be as sorry to miss the opportunity this presidential campaign affords to lift Western thinking to the discipline and vision needed to win world peace.

Giving the timing, public skepticism about Mr. Reagan's new conciliatory tone should come as no surprise. Add to that the recollection that just a year ago, this week's Soviet guest at the White House would not travel to the UN opening conference because the White House would not intercede to guarantee the safety of his landing in the New York area. Just a month ago in Dallas, the President and his administration's spokesmen were still at their rhetorical drubbing of the Soviet leadership. And on the campaign trail last week in Iowa, Mr. Reagan repeated his conviction that rebuilding US military might must precede effective negotiation: "As I will tell Soviet Foreign Minister Gromyko when I meet with him in a few days, we seek no territorial expansion and are making no effort to impose our will on anyone," he said. "But we will never again allow the United States of America to let down its guard."

Add, too, that for the public, apart from what a leader says and does, there is the inherent difficulty of assessing a leader's intention.

Yet what Mr. Reagan said about building a structure for negotiating with the Soviets — institutionalizing regular ministerial or Cabinet-level meetings on the full range of US-Soviet difficulties, erecting an umbrella negotiating approach for the several separate missile and space weapon forums, and drawing up "a road map . . . showing where during the next 20 years or so these individual efforts can lead" — surely sounds like the right way to go.

In part Mr. Reagan was extending an olive branch to the Kremlin; but it was a branch without leaves — that is, there were no specific proposals for arms talks themselves. The conciliatory tone reflected the ascendancy on this occasion of the President's diplomatic chieftains, who have continually had to compete with the President's confrontational military advisers for his attention. How that internal competition would be resolved in a second Reagan administration would be up to Mr. Reagan himself to decide. The public favors a militarily strong America. Yet the President cannot mistake the equally high priority that Americans and their allies put on improved relations with the Soviet Union.

___

It is time for Mr. Reagan to place US diplomatic rearmament on the same plane as military rearmament.

It is hard work to make peace: Note that the figure for peace is a sword turned into a plowshare. Diplomacy, institutions for negotiation, regularized summits deserve the same lead time — running to a generation and more — as is now given to sophisticated weaponry. There can be no illusions about improved relationships; they emerge from recognizing shared interests, not from happy talk. Yet instruments for peacemaking require investment, too.

This newspaper is now inviting its readers to propound strategies for peace — looking back from the year 2010 and describing how world peace was achieved in the intervening 25 years. You may have noted the "Peace 2010" contest outlined on a preceding page. Such a time frame suggests to us the scope of the task.

A "foreign-policy week" is far from enough.

In the current election campaign, both candidates should outline their road maps for peace — a bipartisan journey leading through presidencies beyond their own.

WORCESTER TELEGRAM.

*Worcester, MA,
September 26, 1984*

President Ronald Reagan can't please some people, no matter what he does or says.

For three years, critics have been climbing all over him because of his tough stance toward the Soviet Union. Now that he is proposing talks on arms and other things, they are jeering him as a political opportunist.

Walter Mondale says he should have been saying these things three years ago instead of wasting all that time in pointless confrontation. The Boston Globe says that Reagan "is now adopting the coloration of a peacemaker." The New York Times says that Americans should judge his speech "skeptically."

Well, maybe so. Maybe Reagan is motivated by nothing more than pure political cynicism. But it may be a mistake to jump too readily to that conclusion. The president is not a cynical person. He may be ready to give the Soviets a hearing. He may be ready to make compromises on arms control that he would not make three years ago when he believed our defenses were in poor repair.

Our feeling is that neither the Soviet government nor the American people should sell Reagan short. His speech at the United Nations General Assembly was an initiative that deserves careful consideration and a measured response. The next move is up to the Soviet Union.

Arkansas Gazette.

Little Rock, AR, September 26, 1984

President Reagan's speech before the United Nations General Assembly was correct in form and tone even if its substance brought few changes to the posture of East-West relations only six weeks before Mr. Reagan faces the political judgment day of a presidential election. While the words of reconciliation are welcome and seem to be in vogue in recent days, they should be judged ultimately by Mr. Reagan's willingness to act in a way that gives them appropriate substance.

What is happening in East-West relations this week begs for perspective. It is customary for an American president to address the UN General Assembly in the fall, just as Mr. Reagan spoke to the body a year ago in a form and a tone that were similar to those he used this year. One does not employ unseemly language on the world stage, which is the speaker's platform at the UN, and expect to emerge with a peaceful image intact. Assuming a statesmanlike pose is the only acceptable conduct in that forum. Indeed, Mr. Reagan sounded much the same even when addressing the General Assembly in the wake of the Korean Air Lines massacre.

That so much is being made of Mr. Reagan's meeting with Soviet Foreign Minister Andrei Gromyko tells a great deal about the low estate of United States-Soviet relations since 1981, when Mr. Reagan first took office and began calling the Soviet Union an "evil empire" run by liars and cheats. Until Mr. Reagan's days in the White House it had been customary for the Soviet foreign minister to pay a call after a regular appearance before the UN. That is what Gromyko is doing this time and the visit gains in attention because it means that Reagan, at last, is having a face-to-face meeting with a high Soviet official — one of those liars and cheats, if you will.

What, if anything, will come of this tableau staged in New York and Washington may be known in time, but let it be said and resaid that Mr. Reagan's rhetoric sounds a great deal better when he is speaking to a broader international audience than when he is speaking principally for domestic political consumption.

What he said at the UN is a far cry from what he said at the Republican National Convention just a few weeks ago. Neither the substance nor tone is the same when Mr. Reagan speaks of an "evil empire," or demands that Congress provide ever more funding to "rearm America" and correct what he has perceived (erroneously) to be a weakness in relation to the Soviets in nuclear arms.

Engineering perceptions and then selling them is an integral part of politics at any level. The world, in the UN speech, is asked to believe that because the United States has now "repaired its strength" it suddenly is in a position to conduct "constructive negotiations" with the Soviet Union. The implication in this remark is that Mr. Reagan has not been interested until now in having "constructive negotiations" with the Soviet Union, which explains why all rhetoric over the last few years about being constantly ready to talk if the Russians would only come to the table has had such a hollow ring to it. The Soviets are hardly innocents on this score either, but uncovering a few layers of the Reagan record is important to an understanding of what has been happening in high exposure over the last week.

Whether Mr. Reagan has shucked his bellicose ideology and actually is "born again," just six weeks ahead of a presidential election, on the issue of arms control is the question now placed upon the American public agenda. The answer, like the question, will turn largely on perceptions not only among the American people but also among the Kremlin leadership.

Crisis 'Hot Line' Between U.S., U.S.S.R. to be Modernized

United States and Soviet officials July 17, 1984 initialed an agreement to modernize the 21-year-old "hot line" between Washington and Moscow. The exchange of diplomatic notes at a closed ceremony at the State Department in Washington, D.C. amended the original 1963 hotline agreement. The documents, which did not require congressional approval, were the culmination of a year of bilateral negotiations.

The new accord provided for the addition of a high- speed facsimile transmission system to the 64-words-per-minute teleprinters currently in use. The facsimile equipment, which was to be installed with 18 to 24 months would triple the speed of word transmissions and would be capable of transmitting graphic material such as maps and charts.

President Reagan, in a statement following the initialing, called the agreement "a modest but positive step toward enhancing international stability and reducing the risk that accident, miscalculation or misinterpretation could lead to confrontation or conflict" between the U.S. and the Soviet Union. Moscow had portrayed the hot line negotiations as discussions on technical improvements rather than arms control talks and had insisted on a closed ceremony for the initialing, according to Reagan administration officials.

The State

Columbia, SC, July 28, 1984

THE agreement of Washington and Moscow to improve substantially the so-called "hotline" between the two capitals is an encouraging development at a time when their relationships are the worst in many years.

Upgrading the communications link is not a signal that the superpowers are ready to take up talks on disarmament which the Soviets walked out on in December. Some quiet diplomacy is going on to begin new talks on banning space weapons, but there's no sign of renewing the strategic arms negotiations.

The hotline agreement, however, does show that American and Russian officials can work together with beneficial results for both sides. That may not be enough of an accomplishment to encourage other discussions. The Kremlin appears to have put its relationship with the White House on hold until after the November Presidential election.

When the new hotline arrangements were signed, the event was quietly toasted by a few representatives of the two governments with only one State Department photographer present. The Soviets did not want to publicize their cooperation.

If we cannot read much more into the results, the improvement of the direct communication link with Moscow still must be regarded as important. This is the means of communication between the heads of the two states when and if there is a crisis, and the intentions of each must be understood by the other.

The first hotline was agreed to in 1963. It was a teletype circuit through Washington-London-Copenhagen-Stockholm-Helsinki-Moscow. In 1971, the hotline became a satellite system, using both U.S.A. and USSR satellites. The telegraph circuit was kept as a backup.

According to the Arms Control Association, the new agreement adds a high-speed facsimile capability. It will speed up word transmission to triple the present rate, and will provide for transmission of graphics, maps and charts. No video or voice system has been negotiated.

While the information is classified, the system is known to have been used on four occasions by the United States. It was used during the 1967 Arab-Israeli War to clarify American fleet movements in the Mediterranean so the Soviets would not misunderstand them.

That the system exists is reassuring. Miscalculations and misunderstandings can be quickly dealt with. But that is no guarantee a crisis will not get out of control and touch off a confrontation of the superpowers.

Far better, of course, will be a strategic arms control agreement on the nuclear missiles now aimed at targets and awaiting an order to fire.

The Virginian-Pilot

Norfolk, VA, July 24, 1984

The hot line is a misnomer. The crisis-communications link between the White House and the Kremlin lately has been as cold as the deep freeze in relations between the two nuclear megapowers.

The ice has been so thick — encrusting every issue from arms to athletics — that for months the United States and the Soviet Union could not even agree to modernize the 20-year-old hot line. It needs modernizing. It plods along at the speed of a teletype — which it is. But 60 words a minute can be excruciatingly slow when nuclear missiles can leap continents in minutes.

Last week, after a year of Cold War delay, the two countries finally agreed to hot-line improvements to provide fast, fast relief in crisis situations. Soon high-speed printers will be installed for near-instantaneous transmission of texts, maps, charts and pictures.

Besides the technological advantages, the agreement is beneficial because it signifies that both sides are talking to each other again. Give some credit to the Soviets for risking election-year exploitation by the Reagan administration. And give some credit to the administration for not bringing out brass bands to accompany a claim of a diplomatic coup. The administration instead quietly described the hot-line agreement as "modest."

But the administration also characterized it as an overture to more harmony. Let's hope so. Both sides have plenty to talk about after a year of cold shoulders.

ALBUQUERQUE JOURNAL

Albuquerque, NM, July 23, 1984

Modern communications technology is about to catch up with the nuclear warhead missile age. The Washington-Moscow crisis "hotline" is being updated after serving both governments well for 20 years.

The Direct Communications Link, which has seen limited, but important use, will be expanded and improved, which should reduce the risk of a happenstance triggering a confontration between the United States and the Soviet Union.

The existing "hotline" relies upon an all-too-slow 67-word-a-minute teletype, particularly if a finger were hovering over that red button.

The new system will utilize a satellite relay and be capable of transmitting maps, diagrams and words.

President Reagan suggested upgrading the "hotline" in 1983 as one of a series of "confidence-building" measures with the Soviets. An agreement to improve the system was initialed recently by representatives from both sides.

The agreement and the improved system could lead to other confidence building accords to lower the risk of a nuclear confrontation between the superpowers. While a modest step, an improved "hotline" has long been needed.

Newsday
Long Island, NY, July 19, 1984

The agreement to upgrade the hot line between the United States and the Soviet Union is a small but welcome step toward putting relations between the superpowers on a safer and more rational footing.

The hot line, which was originally installed shortly after the 1962 Cuban missile crisis, ensures rapid communication between the White House and the Soviet leadership. Although the Reagan administration refuses to disclose whether it has ever used the system, it is known to have been activated at least five times: during the 1967 and 1973 Middle East wars, the 1971 India-Pakistan war, the Turkish invasion of Cyprus in 1974 and the Soviet invasion of Afghanistan in 1979.

Under the new agreement announced Tuesday after a year of negotiation, the communication link will be technically improved to allow for speedier teleprinting and the almost instantaneous transmission of maps and graphics. Swift communication of that type could, as President Ronald Reagan noted in announcing the accord, "play a crucial role in helping to resolve certain types of crises or misunderstandings."

The agreement certainly doesn't indicate any important breakthrough in U.S.-Soviet relations. Reagan described it correctly as "a modest but positive" move to reduce the risk of nuclear war by accident or miscalculation. Nor will it automatically clear the way for resumption of negotiations on the far tougher issue of arms control.

But it does signal some small progress. And in doing so, it could help create the right circumstances and the appropriate atmosphere for the resumption of nuclear arms talks.

The Des Moines Register
Des Moines, IA, July 21, 1984

The new U.S.-Soviet hot line agreement took 14 months to negotiate, and it will take another 18 to 24 months to install the new equipment — time for no end of crises and wars. But it was a good idea after the Cuban missile crisis of 1962, and it is a good idea now.

Diplomacy can act fast, but normally it moves at glacial speeds. Months can go by before there is a straight answer to a question. It is highly desirable to have an emergency channel for quick top-level communication.

The 1963 hot line, still in place, is simply a telegraph wire with a teleprinter at each end, and translators and technicians on call. It never was what it is popularly imagined to be — the "red phone" that Ronald Reagan can pick up and use for talking to Konstantin Chernenko.

In 1971, Soviet and U.S. satellite links were added, but the terminal speed remained a mere 66 words per minute. Now two new high-speed facsimile terminals are to be added, three times as fast, and with capability of transmitting high-resolution maps, charts and photographs.

Since 1963, the hot line has been used at least five times, including during the 1967 and 1973 Arab-Israeli wars, when the United States and the Soviet Union favored opposing sides. The equipment is tested daily.

Arms talks between the two superpowers were stalled, but they have agreed to talk about the Bering Sea boundary, cultural exchanges and fishing quotas. And now they have agreed to modernize their emergency communications link. Good.

St. Paul Pioneer Press
St. Paul, MN, July 20, 1984

The understandable anxiety created in some quarters by President Reagan's continued tough anti-Soviet Union talk was reduced somewhat this week when negotiators in both countries reached agreement on a proposal that should help temper the threat of an accidental nuclear war.

The agreement, signed in Washington Tuesday, calls for upgrading the famous Hot Line linking the leaders of the two superpowers.

Opened on Aug. 30, 1963, following the Cuban missile crisis, the Hot Line transmits messages between the two leaders via phone lines and ponderously slow teleprinters. When nuclear missiles can reach their targets in 20 minutes or less, 66-word-a-minute teleconferences are an international danger.

The new system will modernize the Hot Line by using ground lines, satellites and high-speed printers to enable the two leaders to quickly exchange messages, maps, photographs and charts. These new capabilities should help both sides quickly extinguish perceived threats ignited either by misunderstanding or computer error.

As praiseworthy as the agreement is, it is only one step on the long road to a more secure future. Some weapons-control experts in the U.S. are calling for the establishment of "nuclear risk reduction centers" in both Washington and Moscow. They would be staffed by Soviet and American military experts and linked to top military and political officials in both nations. Last month, the Senate endorsed the concept.

The Soviets, in turn, have expressed an interest in improving communications during international terrorist incidents. Some justifiably fear that such an incident could trigger a nuclear confrontation between the two superpowers. Both ideas should be pursued.

AKRON BEACON JOURNAL
Akron, OH, July 19, 1984

THE AGREEMENT between the Soviet Union and the United States to upgrade the hot line between the two countries is, as President Reagan described, "a modest but positive step" toward reducing the chance of nuclear war by miscalculation.

It is also — Mr. Reagan did not say — a sign of the severe strains between the superpowers. A part of Soviet-American relations for 21 years, improvements in the hot line should be a matter of routine, not of hope.

As relations have cooled over the past 3½ years, many have been eager to grasp at any sign of improvement — for instance, a longer than usual meeting or another scientific agreement.

This week plans were made to install a new version of the hot line, an important part of crisis management that has been used no less than five times in two decades. The new hot line will speed up transmissions and allow each side to send maps and other graphic materials.

The superpowers have also agreed to talk about establishing a boundary in the Bering Sea, fishing quotas, cultural and scientific exchanges.

As encouraging as these steps are, it is unfortunate that Mr. Reagan has reached a point in his term where he must, in effect, start over again with the Soviet Union, talking first about noncontroversial matters and slowly approaching arms talks. But clearly, that is the case and, not surprisingly, both sides share the blame.

After the hot-line agreement was signed this week, officials from both sides toasted, and then resumed their rhetorical battle.

Moscow petulantly accused Mr. Reagan of engaging in a "game of words" about the Soviet-proposed space weapons talks. For his part, Mr. Reagan blamed the Soviets for the lack of arms talks, reminding his audience that Moscow left the bargaining table last winter.

Short of an arms treaty as the election nears, Mr. Reagan is likely to continue to blame the Soviets for his gunslinger image. But what he really means is that superpower relations are at their lowest point since the hot line was installed.

Beyond modest steps, much difficult work lies ahead to ease tensions and improve relations.

Wisconsin State Journal
Madison, WI, July 20, 1984

In the all-to-thin annals of arms-control achievements, the hotline agreement just reached by the United States and the Soviet Union is not a big chapter.

But should the hotline be needed again, the agreement may prove important indeed.

Negotiators have been meeting in virtual secrecy for more than a year to talk about upgrading the 21-year-old hotline between Moscow and Washington.

Created by President Kennedy after the Cuban missile crisis in 1962, the hotline has long conjured the image of a bright red telephone on the president's desk, allowing instant communication with the Kremlin.

Actually, it is a teletype machine in the Pentagon that transmits messages at the agonizingly slow speed of 66 words a minute. It takes six minutes to send the typical two-page message.

Under the new agreement, equipment will be installed allowing messages to be sent at triple the old speed. Other equipment will allow maps, photos and charts to be transmitted for the first time.

It's remarkable in this age of instant communications and virtually instant missiles that the world's most important hookup is so slow.

The agreement is a result of President Reagan's initiative; he deserves credit for this modest but potentially critical upgrading of the hotline.

Moscow Condemns U.S. Plans for Antisatellite Missile Test

The White House Aug. 20, 1985 announced that the United States was preparing for its first test of an antisatellite missile (ASAT) against a target in space. The test would not, the announcement said, violate the United Nations Charter or any existing treaties with the U.S.S.R., including the 1972 ABM (antiballistic missile) treaty.

Congress in 1984 had released $19.4 million for three ASAT tests, upon these conditions: that it be given 15 days' advance notice of the tests, that it receive presidential assurances that the tests were necessary for national security, and that the tests not violate existing treaties or interfere with ongoing efforts to negotiate limits on space weaponry.

Both the U.S. and the Soviet Union had begun developing ground-launched ASAT missiles in the 1960s. The systems were designed to destroy reconnaissance satellites, which flew in relatively low orbits. The current U.S. ASAT program aimed at developing air-launched missiles that could destroy early-warning and communications satellites, which orbited high above the Earth.

The Air Force in 1984 had conducted its first, and only, test of an air-launched ASAT missile. The 1985 U.S. test was to involve an ASAT missile carried by an F-15 jet fighter. The target was to be an obsolete U.S. satellite that was still in orbit. The plan called for the plane, guided by radar, to release the missile in high altitude. The missile, guided by on-board infrared sensors, was to destroy the target satellite by high-speed collision rather than by explosion.

Tass, the Soviet news agency, Aug. 21 warned that the U.S. decision could force the U.S.S.R., which had announced a unilateral moratorium in 1983, to resume its own ASAT tests. The U.S. move, Tass asserted, was in effect a negative response to a Kremlin proposal that the United Nations sponsor an international conference on curbing space weapons. Tass restated that the Kremlin's view that the U.S. ASAT development was tied to the U.S. Strategic Defense Initiative ("Star Wars"). The Reagan administration maintained that its antisatellite and antimissile programs were separate entities.

The Miami Herald
Miami, FL, August 28, 1985

SOMETIME in September, an Air Force F-15 pilot will launch a small, complex, nonexplosive rocket at an older, low-orbiting U.S. satellite and attempt to disable it. One hopes that the pilot's timing is better than that of the Reagan Administration, which scheduled this test only two months before President Reagan and Soviet Premier Mikhail Gorbachev are to hold their November summit meeting.

The Administration's rationale for testing the anti-satellite (ASAT) system now is that the Soviets already have an operational ASAT system and the United States doesn't. That's true — as far as it goes. The Soviets' ASAT system is old, ground-based, and is believed incapable of striking at U.S. satellites in orbits higher than about 22,000 miles above the Earth. The Soviets unilaterally halted their own ASAT testing in 1983.)

The U.S. test, by contrast, involves a system that — if it works — would be immensely more flexible because its smaller rocket could be launched from aircraft. The Air Force has had lingering problems with the ASAT device. It packs 235 parts into a container about the size of a gallon of milk, and neither its design nor its cost has been fixed.

In Washington, armaments experts on both sides of the issue concur on one factor: The ASAT system's technology is inseparable from that involved in research on the Administration's Strategic Defense Initiative (SDI), popularly called "Star Wars." The 1972 anti-ballistic-missile (ABM) treaty between the United

ASAT Weapons

States and the Soviet Union permits research on SDI-type systems but bans their actual deployment. The treaty doesn't cover ASAT systems.

Clearly, however, lessons learned in research on anti-satellite weapons would be applicable to systems designed to down ABMs. Given the level of U.S.-Soviet mutual intransigence and each nation's determination to match the other's excursions into new weaponry, the Administration's planned ASAT test is both a provocation and an invitation to escalate the arms race.

Such a provocation might be defensible if it involved merely the sequential next step in an existing program of testing or if its timing required unchangeable conditions, such as the "window" for launching space missions. Neither condition obtains here, however. This ASAT test's timing seems based on little more than a spurious "we gotta match the Soviets" argument and the President's stated belief that ASAT treaties are unverifiable.

Even while saying that, however, the President has told Congress that his Administration will make every good-faith effort to negotiate a treaty curbing ASAT devices. Then why time this test so near the summit meeting? Why not, instead, wait until after the summit and, if those talks produce no progress on an ASAT agreement, determine whether to proceed with this test?

The Grand Rapids Press
*Grand Rapids, MI,
August 23, 1985*

President Reagan's plan to launch a satellite-destroying missile into space this fall could knock down more than just its target.

The proposal is likely to cripple prospects for advancement in the November summit between Mr. Reagan and Soviet leader Mikhail Gorbachev. It could also set back Geneva progrss toward an arms control treaty.

National security adviser Robert McFarlane justifies the launch on grounds that this country needs to "play catch-up ball" with the U.S.S.R., which has a monopoly on space weaponry. Mr. Reagan told Congress the testing is crucial to the nation's security. Neither, however, makes a strong enough case to justify the military and diplomatic risks.

Although the Soviets have an anti-satellite (ASAT) system which they have repeatedly tested in space since the late 1960s, their missiles amount to something of a blunderbuss when contrasted with American weaponry. The U.S.S.R.'s ground-based satellite slayers require at least 24 hours between their firing and the time they find their target.

Additionally, the Soviet missiles are capable of hitting only relatively low-flying targets. They can strike American spy satellites which fly in low orbits but can't touch communications satellites, upon which the nation is so dependent. The Soviet space tests of their weaponry, which concluded three years ago, were successful only half of the time.

By contrast, this country's ASAT missile is one-eighth the size of the Soviet weapon and 24 times faster in finding its target. The American ASAT, whose components have all been successfully tested on the ground, is believed to be faster, more flexible, more reliable, and considerably more effective than the Soviet counterpart. Once launched from the fighter jet, the American weapon can travel at 500 miles a minute, while the Soviet arm's pace is 13 miles a minute from ground to target. Even the Central Intelligence Agency agrees that the Soviet system is no threat to U.S. satellites.

Little if anything is to be gained by testing this nation's ASAT system. If there is hope of negotiating a ban on such weapons, it will be hurt by the fall launching.

The White House is engaging in bureaucratic doublespeak on this subject. Mr. Reagan says the launch is necessary because of the "growing threat" of the Soviet system to American satellites — despite the contrary findings by the CIA.

White House spokesman Larry Speakes lauds the launch plan as a potential incentive for the Soviets to begin serious bargaining with the United States. In his next breath, he says the test would have no bearing upon the Geneva talks.

Rather than propel the Soviets to the negotiating table, the American anti-satellite missile test is likely to drive them back to the missile drawing boards. That is the way arms races go and that is how the United States and the Soviets have accumulated enough firepower between them to blow up the world several times over.

President Reagan through most of this year has made a point of his desire for a mutual U.S.-Soviet reduction in weapons. The ASAT missile can be helpful in advancing that hope. All he needs to do is return it to the shelf. In the absence of a real Soviet threat, the risk of such a hold is insignificant. The chance of avoiding another round of expensive and dangerous arms development, on the other hand, is great.

The Hartford Courant

Hartford, CT, August 25, 1985

It's very difficult, if not impossible, to stop the president from doing something that he is determined to do — even when Congress lays down the law.

Look at U.S. aid to contra guerrillas in Nicaragua. When Congress banned such aid, President Reagan vowed to find a way to continue helping in the attempt to overthrow the Sandinista regime. He did help, by having his staff at the National Security Council assist the contras clandestinely.

The latest Congress-be-damned attitude comes in the area of anti-satellite weapons that travel as fast as 500 miles a minute in space toward their targets — yet another form of Star Wars. The president has authorized the first U.S. test of this weapon in space.

A little background:

In 1983, Congress stipulated conditions when it allowed the Air Force to conduct three tests. The president must certify a test at least two weeks before an experiment. He cannot issue certification unless his administration is endeavoring to negotiate with the Soviets an arms agreement to limit anti-satellite weapons. He must show that such testing will not impair prospects for arms control negotiations. He must also make certain that the testing is in accordance with the anti-ballistic missile (ABM) treaty of 1972.

It takes great imagination to believe that these criteria are being met.

Negotiations to limit anti-satellite weapons haven't even begun.

How can the president show, with credibility, that the testing of such a new weapon will not impair prospects for arms control negotiations? He can't.

The testing will jeopardize the ABM treaty. This agreement prohibits the United States and the Soviet Union from building defensive systems against ballistic missiles. It permits laboratory testing of ABM systems, but not field testing.

President Reagan's Scowcroft Commission described the ABM treaty as "one of the most successful arms control" agreements, because it virtually halted the anti-missile arms race.

The beginning of anti-satellite field testing will signify the beginning of the end of this treaty. Weapons developed to destroy satellites in space can also be used to shoot down ground-based intercontinental ballistic missiles. The technology for both weapons systems is similar.

What Mr. Reagan has done is simply state his opinion that "such testing would not constitute an irreversible step that would gravely impair prospects for negotiations on anti-satellite weapons." Note the qualifying words "would not constitute an irreversible

step." We would be taking a step backward, but it would not be irreversible, he is saying.

White House spokesmen pointed out that the Soviet Union began the competition in anti-satellite weapons by conducting tests a few years ago. In fact, the first tests were conducted by the United States in the 1950s.

Soviet President Yuri V. Andropov announced in August 1983 a unilateral moratorium on the deployment of anti-satellite weapons. In June, the Soviets proposed a moratorium on the development of such defensive weapons systems. U.S. officials agreed to discuss the subject in Geneva, but no such discussions have been scheduled.

The White House announcement on the testing of anti-satellite weapons came on the same day that Robert C. McFarlane, the president's national security adviser, gave a speech on the prospects for improved U.S.-Soviet relations. He said "even incremental improvements" would be hard to achieve without changes in Moscow's approach and its thinking on major issues.

What about changes also in Washington's approach and its thinking on major issues? Has there been a strong hint of change? The president's authorization of testing this version of Star Wars weaponry shows change in the wrong direction.

Newsday

Long Island, NY, August 22, 1985

Imagine two vast armed camps, each with an extensive array of outposts, sentries and patrols to warn against a surprise attack by the other. Now imagine that one camp has the ability to overrun some — but not many — of the other's outposts, leaving the second camp marginally more vulnerable than it was. Finally, imagine the second camp pursuing measures that might enable it to wipe out most, if not all, of the warning systems employed by the first.

This last, in essence, is what the United

States is doing by proceeding with tests of a much more sophisticated antisatellite weapon (ASAT) than the cumbersome and unreliable Soviet model. And by doing so, Washington is challenging the Soviets to play catch-up, as they've done successfully with new weapons from the hydrogen bomb to the multi-warhead missile.

Today's intelligence satellites are like patrols or sentries, transmitting information to each of the superpowers about the other's satellite launchings, missile tests,

troop and ship movements. The earliest warning of an attack by an enemy's strategic missiles would probably come from satellite sensors. The power to destroy satellites at will is the power to deny vital information about external threats. Both the United States and the Soviet Union would be better off if neither had this destructive capability.

For precisely that reason, Congress has prohibited American ASAT tests against real targets unless the president certifies that several conditions have been met. One is that the United States is making a good-faith attempt to negotiate mutual and verifiable limitations on ASAT testing with the Soviet Union. Another is that a U.S. test won't seriously impede those negotiations.

This week the Santa Barbara White House offered the required certification and let it be known that a new ASAT test could be expected sometime after 15 days had elapsed. That's bad timing — barely two months before a scheduled U.S.-Soviet summit meeting in Geneva.

Tuesday's White House statement gave a notably pessimistic assessment of the prospects for an ASAT agreement. A comprehensive ban, it said, "is not verifiable or in our national security interests." This amounts to a self-fulfilling prophecy: If the American ASAT proves successful against orbiting targets, the chances for any meaningful ASAT limits will be seriously diminished. The weapon is so compact and easy to conceal that a ban on deployment will be all but impossible for either side to verify. In short, this is one more case where a technological advance is a retreat for U.S. security.

The Union Leader

Manchester, NH, August 22, 1985

President Reagan's notification to Congress that he intends to proceed with the first anti-satellite weapons test in space has drawn cries of anguish from all the expected quarters —the Kremlin, Congress and the liberal news media. (The similarly politicized clergy will soon be heard from, once they shift gears from their current cause celebre —exploiting South Africa's internal problems to their full violent revolutionary potential.)

Reagan's critics adapt themselves easily to Moscow's credo: *What's mine is mine. What's yours is negotiable.* Unconcerned that the Soviet Union already has a functioning anti-satellite system, they claim U.S. possession of same will undermine prospects for success at the

November summit meeting between President Reagan and Soviet leader Gorbachev. And, anyway, they contend, the Soviets haven't conducted any ASAT tests recently and, in fact, have announced a moratorium and urged the United States to follow suit.

In this Year of Our Lord 1985, it is astounding that even Moscow's "useful idiots" are unaware (a perhaps too charitable assumption) that declaring a temporary moratorium after they've achieved some technological success they'd deny America is an old Soviet trick.

And that the *only* viable way to negotiate with Moscow's masters of deceit is from a position of *demonstrable* strength.

Time Interviews Gorbachev; Reagan Asks Soviet TV Time

Soviet leader Mikhail S. Gorbachev Aug. 26, 1985 accused the United States of waging a "campaign of hatred" against the U.S.S.R. The remarks were made in Gorbachev's first formal interview with Western journalists, which appeared in the Sept. 9 issue of *Time* magazine. The major topic of the interview was U.S.- Soviet relations, with an emphasis on arms control and the scheduled November meeting in Geneva between Gorbachev and President Reagan.

Gorbachev expressed "regret" that relations between the two countries were not improving. He cited Washington's repeated charge that recent Soviet arms-control offers were propaganda ploys, saying: "It is hard to understand why our proposals have provoked such outspoken displeasure on the part of responsible U.S. statesmen," he said. "Anyone even slightly familiar with the matter would easily see that behind our proposals there are most serious intentions and not just an attempt to influence public opinion."

The White House had dismissed a unilateral moratorium on nuclear tests announced by the Soviet Union in July, claiming that the U.S.S.R. had completed its 1985 testing program before the announcement.

The Soviet leader challenged the U.S. to a propaganda "competition" by matching Moscow's arms control initiatives, and chided Washington for playing down the coming Geneva summit as a mere "get-acquainted" meeting between the two leaders.

President Reagan, in a speech of welcome Sept. 10 to visiting Danish Premier Poul Schluter, responded to Gorbachev's remarks. Describing the summit as a possible "beginning point for better relations," the President warned against "wishful thinking and public relations campaigns" in advance of the parley. Reagan told the audience he intended to remind Gorbachev of "why we believe they represent a threat to us and to the Western world."

A week earlier, the White House disclosed that the U.S. had requested Soviet TV airtime for President Reagan in January, and that the request had gone "not only unanswered but unacknowledged." White House spokesman Larry Speakes said that U.S. officials were "pleased that Mr. Gorbachev was able to present his views to the American public," and that Reagan would like equal access to Soviet media in order to present Washington's position on bilateral relations. The statement contrasted with U.S. press reports that Reagan administration aides were annoyed that *Time* had given the Soviet leader a popular forum for what they regarded as propaganda.

St. Petersburg Times

St. Petersburg, FL, September 6, 1985

Assuming President Reagan is capable of stifling his penchant for Rambo references and nuclear-attack jokes, a brief presidential appearance on Soviet television could serve a limited but useful purpose. If nothing else, it might mollify an administration increasingly irritated by Soviet leader Mikhail Gorbachev's largely successful pre-summit public relations campaign in the West.

Using *Time* magazine and a U.S. congressional delegation as intermediaries, Gorbachev has done a masterful job in the past week of continuing to create a benign, reasonable, capable image for himself. President Reagan, the acknowledged master communicator, must be frustrated that he has no similar access to the Soviet public.

BUT THE SOVIET Union is not a democracy, and a direct presidential appeal to the Soviet people cannot possibly be as meaningful as Gorbachev's overtures to us. Furthermore, this back-and-forth public posturing prior to the November summit may detract from the real business of preparation for an encounter that may determine the immediate future of U.S.-Soviet relations in general, and arms control in particular.

Presidential spokesman Larry Speakes admitted as much — even as he pressed the Soviets to allow the President to appear on Soviet television. "We do not intend to enter into a debate in the media," Speakes said. "Preparations for the meeting in Geneva are best conducted in confidential diplomatic channels."

ONE PUBLIC miscalculation by either leader could destroy the pre-summit work that has been performed away from the glare of the television cameras. Rather than spending his time rehearsing a speech for the Soviet man in the street, Mr. Reagan — hardly the most knowledgeable President in terms of the details of arms control and the other vital issues sure to be raised at the summit — should be doing his homework in private.

The Reagan-Gorbachev summit is not a debate or a declamation contest to be won or lost. Its results will be judged on substance, not style or personality. Many Americans who have met the new Soviet leader find him to be a charming man. If Soviets were given a chance to watch Mr. Reagan give a televised speech, they probably would be similarly impressed with him. But will charm end the arms race?

WORCESTER TELEGRAM

Worcester, MA, September 10, 1985

The first impression the reader gets from the Time magazine interview with Mikhail Gorbachev is that the Soviet Union has found its most formidable leader since Josef Stalin.

The second impression is that Gorbachev seems to want to improve relations with the United States so that he can devote more resources to revitalizing the ailing Soviet economy.

There is no question but that President Reagan and his advisers face an unexpected challenge at the summit talks in Geneva in November. They will not be dealing with the doddering Andropov or Chernenko mouthing the boiler-plate rhetoric of Andrei Gromyko. Gorbachev has masterfully solidified his control in the Kremlin and, according to Jerry F. Hough's article in Foreign Affairs, he has a somewhat different agenda.

If Hough is correct, Gorbachev considers the Soviet economy his main problem. Although he is a Marxist to the bone, he feels that Soviet foreign policy must rest on a strong economy at home. The implication is that he wants to spend money on improving agriculture, industry and management rather than on new weapons systems. For that reason, Reagan's Strategic Defense Initiative must be stopped, because it would require Moscow to spend billions of rubles in new space weapons.

It is easy to be cynical about Soviet public statements. They are always laced with propaganda, and Gorbachev's are no exception. His offer to suspend nuclear tests came when he knew that the United States had scheduled tests designed to develop the nuclear element for lasers in space. The recent leak from Moscow that he is prepared to reduce nuclear missiles substantially resembles similar airy proposals that the Soviets have made for years.

In short, Gorbachev poses a formidable challenge. Whether he is prepared to make real concessions and arrive at real agreements will be tested in Geneva.

STAR WARS

SYRACUSE
HERALD·JOURNAL
Syracuse, NY, September 5, 1985

The new Soviet leader, Mikhail Gorbachev, turns up frequently on American television and has granted several interviews to Western reporters. Experts on Soviet strategy say his availability is part of a pre-summit media blitz to create a favorable impression of Soviet positions.

The U.S. television networks are happy to provide Gorbachev and other Russian leaders with all the attention they desire. That's natural after decades of icy Soviet dealings with the Western media.

Beginning even before he assumed power, Gorbachev showed his media savvy by mesmerizing the British press — and Prime Minister Margaret Thatcher — during a visit to England last December. He has since stepped up the frequency of contacts.

All the attention Gorbachev is getting throws a wild card into November summit expectations. In any previous encounters with Soviet leaders, U.S. presidents had no worry about winning the propaganda battle at home. American reporters *had* to concentrate on them because access to Soviet leaders was impossible.

▽   ▽

Gorbachev has served notice that will no longer be true. In the long run, the increased access will benefit U.S. citizens because it will give them a broader perspective of U.S.-Soviet issues.

Larry Speakes, President Reagan's press spokesman, raises a valid point, however. When, he wonders, will the president get the same kind of attention on Soviet television? He has urged the Soviet Union to allow Reagan "direct access" to the Russian people through a televised speech?

It's not as though the administration is asking for something it would be unwilling to offer to Gorbachev. Months ago, Charles Wick, director of the U.S. Information Agency, wrote to the Soviet government asking for television time for President Reagan or some other American leader. Wick said any such offer would be reciprocated on American television.

There is precedent for such an exchange: In 1972, Richard Nixon spoke directly to the Soviet people at the end of his visit to Moscow. Later that year, then-Soviet President Leonid Brezhnev concluded his visit to the United States with a televised address.

▽   ▽

Chances are no such exchange will take place as long as Gorbachev finds relatively smooth sailing for himself in the American media. Why give up any part of a newfound advantage?

Actually, the Soviet government has little to fear from a single Reagan speech. In this country he may be the "Great Communicator" but in the Soviet Union his speech would be little more than a momentary diversion. It could hardly undo years of calculated anti-American rhetoric in the Soviet media.

Even so, we'd be very surprised if the Soviets even bother to acknowledge the American requests. What *might* get Reagan on Russian television are some hardball questions from American reporters the next time they interview Gorbachev. Let's see them make him squirm a little as they ask him what he fears from a Reagan appearance. It shouldn't be hard; they've had plenty of practice on American politicians.

The Hartford Courant
Hartford, CT,
September 7, 1985

White House spokesman Larry Speakes has a point: Soviet officials appear on American television frequently, but almost never do the Soviet people see and hear a U.S. official say anything that hasn't gone through their government's information filters.

Although the U.S. ambassador to Moscow traditionally speaks on Soviet television on the Fourth of July, the only U.S. president given TV access was Richard M. Nixon. His 1972 appearance was followed the next year by an address on American television by President Leonid I. Brezhnev.

Anticipating his November meeting with Mikhail S. Gorbachev, and probably prompted in part by a Time magazine interview with the Soviet leader, President Reagan is asking to be allowed to speak on Soviet television. A similar request, made in January by Charles Z. Wick, director of the U.S. Information Agency, has drawn no response.

The Soviets may be concerned by what Mr. Reagan would say, given some of the harsh rhetoric he has directed at them in the past. But surely they can see that fuller communications between the two peoples can lead to better superpower relations, which would be mutually beneficial.

Mr. Gorbachev evidently likes to project an image of modernity, progressiveness, even novelty. Let him strengthen that image first by supporting Mr. Reagan's request, then by speaking to Americans on U.S. television.

Summit, Conducted Under Press Blackout, Brings No Breakthroughs

U.S. President Reagan and Soviet leader Mikhail S. Gorbachev Nov. 21, 1985 concluded a hectic three-day summit meeting in Geneva. The two leaders spent about five hours in private discussion, far more time than had been anticipated in pre-summit preparations. The talks were described by them and their aides in such terms as "frank," "cordial," "lively" and "businesslike." There were no breakthroughs on such divisive regional conflicts as Afghanistan and Central America, but the summit ended with the signing of six bilateral agreements, and with the likelihood that Gorbachev would visit the United States in 1986.

The bilateral pacts pledged U.S.-Soviet cooperation on cultural and scientific exchanges, a resumption of civil aviation ties, improvement in air safety in the northern Pacific region, consular exchanges (New York City and Kiev), magnetic fusion research, and environmental protection. At the signing ceremony, the two leaders spoke of pursuing peace through further face-to-face discussions, beginning with a summit in the U.S. sometime in 1986. They issued a joint statement on accelerated negotiations to "prevent an arms race in space and to terminate it on Earth, to limit and reduce nuclear arms and enhance strategic stability." The joint statement said that both sides supported the "principle" of "50% reductions in nuclear arms," as well as "the idea of an interim INF [intermediate-range nuclear forces] agreement."

Reagan told reporters at the ceremony that he viewed the Geneva summit as a "fresh start" in U.S.-Soviet relations. "We've packed a lot into the last two days and we are headed in the right direction." He said that he left Geneva "determined to make peace in the world."

Gorbachev held a press conference at the Soviet mission after the signing ceremony. He denounced the U.S. Strategic Defense Initiative ("Star Wars") and indicated irritation with Reagan for the President's refusal to budge on the issue during their private talks. Gorbachev warned that the U.S.S.R. would invoke an "effective" response to a U.S. space-based antimissile system.

The U.S. contingent in Geneva included First Lady Nancy Reagan; George P. Shultz, the secretary of state; Robert C. McFarlane, the White House national security adviser; Richard N. Perle, an assistant secretary of defense; and Donald T. Regan, the White House chief of staff. The Soviet contingent included Raisa Gorbachev, the wife of the general secretary; Foreign Minister Eduard A. Shevardnadze; Anatoly F. Dobrynin, Moscow's ambassador to the U.S.; Marshal Sergei F. Akhromeyev, the military chief of staff; and Georgi A. Arbatov, an adviser to Gorbachev on U.S. affairs.

The first day of the summit began with separate announcements by both sides that the discussions would be held under a press blackout.

Detroit Free Press
Detroit, MI, November 22, 1985

TWO STATE dinners, two formal teas, and five hours of private talks later, Summit 1985 is over. President Reagan and Secretary Gorbachev have returned to the nations they lead with not a great deal more than a feeling for one another and a better understanding of where each stands on some major global issues. But that is enough. We did not and could not fairly have expected more. Our two nations have been at loggerheads for decades. More than geography and ideology separate us. We view the world in radically different ways and through the prisms of disparate experiences.

We are encouraged by the initial remarks of both leaders as they prepared to leave Geneva. Both spoke of having made "a fresh start" in improving relations between their two nations. Most encouraging of all, the Soviet leader said that he and the president "discovered that we do seek to share a certain initial premise . . . the understanding that a nuclear war cannot occur, that there can be no winners in a nuclear war."

That understanding is no guarantee that at sometime, somewhere in the world nations may not take up nuclear arms against one another. But it means that the leaders of the world's two most powerful nations have looked into each other's eyes knowing each has the means at hand to destroy the planet and recoiled from such a decision.

The summit had its more predictable moments. There was some prickly talk about U.S. plans for the Strategic Defense Initiative, and Secretary Gorbachev made it abundantly clear that he will seek to link his nation's plans for arms reduction to an as yet unmade promise by the United States to back off Star Wars. But it remains a bargaining point, and the leaders have agreed to host one another for further talks in 1986 and 1987.

The struggle to secure and maintain peace is a long and difficult process, and one summit does not change that reality. But the meetings in Geneva this week have apparently been a positive contribution to the process.

The Washington Post
Washington, DC, November 22, 1985

IT WAS at the least a civil summit. Whatever differences were expressed in their long sessions alone, in public President Reagan and General Secretary Gorbachev were at pains to display restraint and amiability. A hint of frustration seemed to touch Mr. Gorbachev's remarks at his press conference yesterday. The president acknowledged last night to Congress that he had paid Mr. Gorbachev "the tribute of candor." Yet on the surface, cordiality and forbearance reigned.

There is always the risk, in these summit extravaganzas, that the chemistry will go sour or that differences will widen into misunderstanding or worse. By this standard it would have been enough for the president to come home cloaked in an aura of relief that relations had gotten no worse. In fact, both leaders said that something more positive was achieved in the way of mutual understanding and that a political impulse was given to arms control. That two more summits are in the offing is reassuring. Much can be said for a subdued and steady approach to Soviet-American relations, especially when the gap in formal positions and in leaders' perspectives is so broad.

Still, the relative thinness of tangible results is notable. The exchanges and humanitarian relief and other items were something, but the summit did not produce agreement even on the full list of lesser bilateral accords that had earlier been described as fit for Geneva sanction. Nor was there public sign of any decision on the large arms control issues or on the regional disputes that lie at the heart of Soviet-American rivalry.

For Mr. Gorbachev, one can guess that his failure to stop the American Strategic Defense Initiative, which the Kremlin had characterized as his chief summit mission, had something to do with his readiness to paint as successes the less tangible atmospheric modifications. At his press conference he insisted that slamming the door on SDI was the continuing Soviet condition for "radical" cutbacks in offensive arms. Nonetheless, the final joint statement recorded his agreement to seek "early progress" in "areas where there is common ground." The "areas" named exclude the Soviet priority of space arms but include the American priorities of deep cuts in offensive strategic arms and an interim accord on missiles in Europe.

The secretary of defense and some others had urged Mr. Reagan not to trade away SDI or to extend the controls of SALT II. Mr. Reagan evidently didn't. Nonetheless it seems premature to conclude that "Weinberger won" on the Washington arms control battlefield or, for that matter, that the perfunctory language in the joint statement on regional issues means there are no chances for restraint there either. The deepening of consultation could turn out to be important.

It would have been useful if the two men had worked out the framework for arms control that was being talked about in the administration before the president left Washington. But for them to come out of their first summit talking, and talking civilly, makes Geneva an accomplishment. For Ronald Reagan, who neither wobbled nor froze (as the various anxious feared), it was a personal accomplishment too.

The News American
Baltimore, MD, November 24, 1985

President Reagan, in his Thursday night speech to Congress and the American people: "There were over 3,000 reporters in Geneva, so it's possible there will be 3,000 opinions on what happened."

Boy, you can count on *that*. The postmortems have begun and will continue and then continue some more, most guaranteed to bewilder and bore us all. Thus we'll keep ours very short, leaving the detailed and scholarly analysis to the deep thinkers.

Because President Reagan and General Secretary Gorbachev met, we are convinced that the human race is safer from incineration than it was a week ago.

"I would be so bold as to say that the world has become a more secure place," said Mr. Gorbachev, and we think he believes it. And said the president: "There's always more room for movement, action and progress, when people are talking to each instead of about each other."

We have no illusions that all will be sweetness and light from now on. The president made that plain in his speech before Congress. But if you think (as we do) that the fingers are farther from the nuclear buttons this Sunday than they were last, it's hard not to count the Geneva get-together a success.

ALBUQUERQUE JOURNAL
Albuquerque, NM, November 22, 1985

In Geneva this week, the leaders of the two most powerful nations in the world went face to face and decided they will meet to talk again next year and again in 1987, no small matter considering the fact it had been six years since the last meeting for such leaders.

Both President Reagan and Soviet leader Mikhail Gorbachev are calling their summit meeting a success, even though there was no breakthrough on an arms control agreement, no human rights understanding, no evidence that regional conflicts will be resolved the sooner as a result of this conference.

A world hopeful for a lowering of the nuclear Demosthenes sword hanging over civilization was to be disappointed by the failure to produce an arms control agreement, or a plan to prevent extension of the arms race into space. Even in the planning stages for the Reagan-Gorbachev summit, however, there was no great expectation for such a superpower breakthrough.

In addition to a slight thawing of relations between the two leaders and their nations, the summit did generate agreements for cultural and sports exchanges and for air traffic safety arrangements.

The six hours of one-on-one talks hold the promise for much more than the on-camera charm and personal diplomacy that marked the publicity wars of the first summit for the president and the Soviet leader. Gorbachev now should have a better understanding of the thoughts underlying the president's public statements about the Soviet Union.

Reagan, by the same token, should have a better and more detailed understanding of the hopes and phobias of his strongest international adversary. From out of that meeting should come the realization that both sides want peace and that both sides recognize that there can be no winner of a nuclear war.

Perhaps in their next meeting, the president and Gorbachev can seed the common ground they plowed in Geneva. The anxiety level, if not the survival, of Americans, Russians — all of mankind — hangs in the balance.

CHARLESTON EVENING POST
Charleston, SC, November 22, 1985

No sooner had the summit meeting at Geneva concluded than some commentators began totting up winners and losers. Perhaps their efforts were inspired by the popular desire television seems to have induced for instant resolution of problems, for instant gratification. There were no winners or losers at Geneva — at least no immediate winners or losers. The ultimate goal of the conference, regardless of how the agenda was phrased, was the promotion of peace through the limitation and reduction of American and Soviet nuclear arms. That goal cannot be reached in two days, two weeks or two months. Maybe not in two years.

That's not to say it cannot be reached. Nor is it to imply that no movement toward the goal was made at Geneva. On the contrary, signs of movement were the most encouraging consequence of the meeting between President Reagan and Secretary General Gorbachev.

During their private discussions (private in the sense they included translators but no other aides), the two leaders obviously disagreed strongly on what are widely regarded as key points in arms control. For example, Secretary Gorbachev offered to cut back on nuclear bombs if the United States would abandon its proposed "Star Wars" program. Mr. Reagan would have none of that. Other "serious differences" remained after the more formal sessions as well, yet the two principals agreed to quicken the pace of arms talks.

They announced they will hold a second summit meeting next year — probably in Washington — and a third in 1987. Inasmuch as the last such meeting between top leaders of these two nations was held six years ago, the announcment seems to signal changes that could enhance prospects for peace.

One change is an apparent thaw in relations between the United States and the Soviet Union, as manifested in the "personal" diplomacy in which President Reagan and Secretary Gorbachev engaged. Another change is that the scheduling of summit meetings in 1986 and 1987 affords an opportunity to move away from occasional encounters that carry with them high risks and into an era in which meetings of national leaders might become regular elements of dialogue between West and East.

It was much too much to expect an arms pact to result from the Geneva meeting. It is not too much to hope that, in President Reagan's words, the two days of talks will "inject a certain amount of momentum into our work on the issues between us, a momentum we can continue at the meeting we've agreed on next year."

There is no reason to pretend that the ideological differences between the United States and the USSR can be lessened in future summits — or even that they should be. There is the best of reasons to hope that periodic exchanges of high-level views at subsequent summit meetings might lead initially to recognition of the need for restraint, and ultimately to agreements on verifiable reductions in nuclear arsenals.

The Idaho STATESMAN

Boise, ID, November 22, 1985

There were no bombshells and no break-throughs at the Geneva summit. Still, it was a success.

It was a success even though President Reagan and Soviet General Secretary Mikhail Gorbachev achieved no agreements on arms control. It was a success even though Mr. Reagan stood firm in refusing to negotiate on his Strategic Defense Initiative – called "Star Wars" – a weapons system the Soviets insist will escalate the arms race.

Mr. Gorbachev has proposed cutting back on nuclear weapons in exchange for limits on Mr. Reagan's SDI. He didn't change Mr. Reagan's mind on this issue and Mr. Reagan didn't change Mr. Gorbachev's.

But look at what was accomplished at the summit. Mr. Reagan and Mr. Gorbachev – frequently meeting in private with only their interpreters present – learned where the other stood, and why. They defined and aired their reasons for disagreement. And they agreed to meet again in two more summits – one in 1986 and one in 1987.

As Mr. Gorbachev said, "The meetings contained the possibility to move forward." Most significantly, he said that "In the course of that meeting we uncovered that we (and the Americans) do seek to share a certain initial premise ... the understanding that a nuclear war cannot occur. That there can be no winners in a nuclear war."

Of course, preventing nuclear war takes more than nice-sounding words. And hopefully, the two future summits will lay the groundwork for the arms control and cooperation that will give these words some substance.

But for now, the important achievements are these: The two men came away determined to meet again; they listened to each other; and they managed to air their disagreements without name-calling or hostilities. That's not a bad beginning.

The Philadelphia Inquirer

Philadelphia, PA, November 22, 1985

After all the hullabaloo, how does the Reagan-Gorbachev summit meeting stack up against expectations, or lack thereof?

It was encouraging to see the two leaders side by side, talking civilly and acting as if both recognized the need to confront each other's realities. It was "a good start," President Reagan reported with apparent confidence to Congress last night.

Even if neither convinced the other of a thing, four hours of face-to-face conversation (after expectations they would spend only 15 minutes alone) must leave each with some better comprehension of the other's mind.

Granted, neither man changed his thinking. Both made that clear. There was no agreement on the key issues; sharp exchanges took place, and neither man seemed to have shifted course on their arms control differences. No progress was announced on U.S. concerns about human rights or regional disputes. Opportunities were missed to reach substantive guidelines on arms talks or to extend SALT II. But as the President's address last night illustrated, the two leaders seem finally to have found a better way of dealing with each other than hurling insults. Two future summits have been scheduled, providing some needed routinization of contact between the American president and the Soviet leader after a six-year hiatus. That's especially useful because it puts the role of summit meetings more clearly in place.

What, after all, can be expected from a summit? In the past, when successful, they almost always crowned months or years of lengthy negotiations that ironed out disputes before the leaders met. Or they served as excuses for Soviet and U.S. leaders to size the other side up, sometimes for good, sometimes for ill.

No summit meeting can solve deep-rooted problems. What it can do — as in Geneva — is focus world attention on knotty issues and spur American and Soviet leaders to clarify their thinking. This in turn leads to deadlines that prod their respective bureaucracies to churn out new ideas.

Had this summit not been scheduled, probably neither side would have produced the recent arms reduction proposals that come closer — despite remaining differences — to a negotiating framework than anything seen in years.

Had no follow-up summits been scheduled, this progress might have quickly dissipated, but the target dates of the two future meetings will provide stimulus to Moscow and Washington to narrow their differences.

So regularizing summits is all to the good for keeping both countries on track and giving each leader a regular chance to feel the other out. But summit dates alone can't guarantee that progress will be made.

Decisions that loomed large before Geneva — such as whether President Reagan will swap limits on missile defense in space for deep Soviet cuts in offensive weapons, and whether Mikhail S. Gorbachev will offer a realistic formula for doing that — still wait to be made. Summit or no summit, the responsibility for peace remains squarely in their hands.

The Courier-Journal

Louisville, KY, November 23, 1985

JUDGING FROM their own post-summit assessments, the face-to-face meetings between Ronald Reagan and Mikhail Gorbachev in Geneva did, indeed, mark the "fresh start" that U. S.-Soviet relations have so badly needed. Now comes the hard part.

Anticipated follow-up summits in the United States next year and in Russia in 1987 almost surely will depend on how much progress is made by U. S. and Soviet arms negotiators in the months ahead. This week's summit didn't settle the outstanding differences between the two leaders on "Star Wars" and other major nuclear weapons issues. At best, the Geneva meetings only provided some momentum that may carry over in the soon-to-be-resumed arms talks.

Luck will be a factor, too. A crisis neither side wants could blow up suddenly in the Middle East or in some other region where both the U. S. and Soviet Union have major interests. Nor can one rule out a major miscalculation or blunder by one or both of the superpowers. The Eisenhower-Khrushchev meeting in 1960 came to an abrupt halt when the Soviet leader angrily announced that an American U-2 spy plane had been shot down over Soviet territory. And President Kennedy's 1961 Vienna summit with the same Mr. Khrushchev was followed, only two months later, by East Germany's construction of the Berlin Wall.

But the stakes are even bigger these days, with the superpowers aiming thousands of nuclear missiles at each other. The threat of mutual annihilation is a powerful incentive both for nuclear arms cutbacks, the top Soviet priority, and for cooling global hot spots, a major objective of Mr. Reagan. And there's the growing need, on both sides, to reduce military spending that is contributing to severe dislocations in the U. S. and Russian economies.

"Enduring competition" will surely continue to test U. S.-Soviet relations, as President Reagan warned in his report to Congress Thursday night. And Americans who are true to their country's democratic principles will never cease to regard the Soviet system as inimical to freedom and other values we hold dear. But these values would not survive nuclear war — and neither, perhaps, would the human race. That's why it's so important that this week's "fresh start" in Geneva yield more tangible results before Mr. Reagan and Mr. Gorbachev meet again. •

Sunday News Journal

Wilmington, DE, November 24, 1985

THERE WAS NO talk of "evil empires" and "capitalist bullies" at Geneva last week. The handbooks of caustic characterizations were left behind in the United States and in the Soviet Union.

There was no major breakthrough on arms control at the meeting between President Ronald Reagan and Chairman Mikhail Gorbachev. There are those who contend that the meeting was a failure because the two men left Switzerland without reducing the world's nuclear arsenal. They are wrong, very wrong.

It has been seven years since the leaders of the world's two most powerful nations have talked face-to-face. These have been years of bitterness and name calling. Tensions have steadily mounted, not only in the United States and the Soviet Union, but throughout the world.

The two nations have not directly confronted each other militarily. But they have, through proxy nations, tried to infuriate each other. Both have had some success here.

There had to be an end to this bickering and, it seems now, that the meeting in Geneva was the end — and the beginning of a new era of toleration.

The two nations have fundamental differences on several levels. They will remain. Still, it is possible to cooperate in areas where national security is not threatened. The agreement reached to resume U.S.-Soviet cultural exchanges is an example. The establishment of new consulates in Kiev and New York City, is another.

The two leaders also agreed to establish new communications links to improve air safety in the North Pacific and to exchange information on solar energy research.

For a world in the shadow of nuclear terror, these are small glimpses of light. Yet, they are light.

Messrs. Reagan and Gorbachev had sharp exchanges when they talked of arms control. The president held fast on his Strategic Defense Initiative proposals. The chairman was in no mood to yield on land-based missiles. Still, the two men agreed to accelerate the arms control negotiations scheduled to resume in January.

Most encouraging of all, the president and the chairman apparently were able to talk bluntly with each other without resort to acrimony. Both described the meetings as useful and positive. They agreed to meet again.

President Reagan described his meetings with Mr. Gorbachev to the joint session of Congress this way: "*We met, as we had to meet. I had called for a fresh start — and we made that start. I can't claim we had a meeting of the minds on such fundamentals as ideology or national purpose — but we understand each other better. That's the key to peace. I gained a better perspective, I feel he did, too.*"

That is no failure.

The Toronto Star

Toronto, Ont., November 22, 1985

Summit meetings, Prime Minister Brian Mulroney said in an Ottawa speech less than a month ago, are instruments in the pursuit of peace; they are not peace itself. And so it proved in Geneva this week as the leaders of the world's two superpowers met for the first time in six years. U.S. President Ronald Reagan and Soviet leader Mikhail Gorbachev achieved a welcome degree of warmth and cordiality.

Who could have imagined, for instance, that the man who scarcely a year ago spoke of the Soviet Union as "an evil empire" would be seated cosily before an open fire beaming at that empire's leader? And that the man who has often accused the Americans of war-mongering should beam back at the U.S. president?

By breaking the ice in Geneva, and by agreeing to meet twice more in the next two years, Reagan and Gorbachev have given the world hope that peace may be attainable. But more is needed than apparently friendly conversations between two powerful men and their signatures on a high-minded, carefully worded document that says all the right things but commits neither side to anything of substance.

The hard work of disarmament — the only sure pathway to peace — has still to be accomplished. Soviet and American officials have been talking sporadically about arms control for years; progress has been made at a snail's pace and often not at all. Talks are to resume in Geneva in mid-January and may start sooner in the wake of the summit meeting. Reagan and Gorbachev set some goals for the talks. Their agreement mentions a 50 per cent reduction in nuclear arms by both countries, a total ban on chemical weapons and the destruction of any existing ones in either country, and the establishment of methods to verify that control measures are carried out.

These are certainly disarmament goals with which Canada agrees. In his Ottawa speech, Mulroney mentioned some others. They include a comprehensive test ban treaty that would apply to all countries, not just the U.S. and the U.S.S.R.; the prevention of an arms race in outer space; and the building of enough confidence in the permanence of arms control so that military forces in Europe and elsewhere can be reduced. They are worthy objectives for the Prime Minister to continue to push.

Reagan and Gorbachev have sent a clear signal to the arms negotiators that they expect some progress toward disarmament goals. The agreement they signed said forthrightly, "A nuclear war cannot be won and must never be fought." That is a statement to which the whole world can put its signature.

Daniloff, Zakharov Set Free; Reagan Denies Direct Swap

Nicholas Daniloff, the Moscow correspondent for *U.S. News & World Report* magazine was arrested by the KGB (the Soviet internal-security and intelligence agency) Aug. 30, 1986 in the Lenin Hills, a wooded section of Moscow. The dispute surrounding his continued detention and subsequent release cast a pall over U.S.- Soviet relations.

According to Ruth Daniloff, the reporter's wife, he had gone to the area at the telephone request of a Soviet acquaintance, identified only as "Misha," for an exchange of farewell gifts. Daniloff was preparing to leave the Soviet Union in September, at the end of a five-year tour as the magazine's Moscow correspondent. Daniloff met Misha at the appointed spot and gave the Soviet two American novels. Misha handed the reporter a sealed package that was supposed to contain newspaper clippings from Frunze, Misha's native city in south-central Soviet Asia. Misha quickly left the scene. Moments later, Daniloff was surrounded by KGB agents and was arrested. He was taken to Lefortovo detention center in Moscow.

There, according to Ruth Daniloff, the agents opened the package and found two maps marked "top secret" and photos of Soviet military installations and equipment. Tass, the official Soviet news agency, Aug. 31 announced that Daniloff had been apprehended while "engaging in an act of espionage" and would be held pending an investigation and the filing of formal charges.

Western analysts viewed the Daniloff arrest Aug. 30 as a retaliation by Moscow for the arrest in the U.S. of Gennadi Zakharov, a Soviet physicist attached to the United Nations. Zakharov had been taken into custody in New York City Aug. 23 after allegedly paying an employee of a U.S. defense contractor to turn over classified documents. He was accused of espionage and faced life in prison if convicted. Moscow denied a link between the Daniloff and Zakharov cases.

Daniloff and Zakharov were set free Sept. 29 and Sept. 30, 1986, respectively, under an arrangement worked out by the foreign ministers of their two countries. Both men swiftly returned home. Daniloff had been confined to the Soviet capital, in the custody of the U.S. embassy, pending a trial for espionage. Zakharov had been confined to the New York City area, in the custody of the Soviet mission, pending a trial on espionage charges. The spy cases had disrupted U.S.-Soviet relations for a month. The breakthrough had come Sept. 28, in a three-hour meeting between U.S. Secretary of State George Shultz and Soviet Foreign Minister Eduard Shevardnadze in New York City. The meeting had been the fourth between the two men regarding the issue, beginning Sept. 19 in Washington, D.C.

With no prior announcement by either superpower, the Soviets allowed the reporter and his wife to fly from Moscow to Frankfurt, West Germany Sept. 29. It was unclear if the charges against Daniloff were officially dropped by the Soviets. He did not have to appear in court. In effect he was simply expelled from the U.S.S.R. on short notice.

Before boarding the plane to Frankfurt, Daniloff spoke to reporters in Moscow. He repeated the assertion that he had been framed by the KGB. "I must say I leave more in sorrow than in anger," he said.

Zakharov Sept. 30 appeared in U.S. District Court in the New York City borough of Brooklyn. In a four-minute arraignment before U.S. District Judge Joseph McLaughlin, Zakharov pleaded no contest to the spy charges. McLaughlin waived sentencing on two of the three counts in the espionage indictment – conspiracy and attempting to transmit classified information to a foreign power. The judge sentenced Zakharov to five years' probation on the remaining count of illegally obtaining classified information and barred Zakharov from serving his probation on American soil. The judge then ordered him to leave the U.S. within 24 hours. Zakharov and an entourage of Soviet officials drove from New York to Washington, where Zakharov boarded an Aeroflot flight to Moscow. Before leaving, he told reporters that he had been "set up" by U.S. intelligence. "I am not a spy...I am grateful to the Soviet Union for getting me out," he said.

In announcing the freeing of Daniloff and Zakharov, President Reagan Sept. 30 fervently denied that a swap had taken place. "There was no connection between these two releases," he maintained.

NEW HAMPSHIRE

SUNDAY NEWS

Manchester, NH
September 7, 1986

Even as the Soviets were winning the praise of their Western apologists for a new "openness" last week — they actually admitted a cruise ship had sunk — they were calmly and cold-bloodedly showing their true colors in the kidnapping of a U.S. reporter.

In the final analysis, and this is a point some in the West will never grasp, the Communists will do exactly what they darned well please in their unflagging, never-changing goal of world domination.

It's not that the Reds don't care about world opinion. They do, and when they wish it, they can be masters at its manipulation. But when push comes to shove, the Soviets will always dispense with the niceties and the concern for public relations.

The Soviets know that world opinion is an especially forgetful thing when it comes to their misdeeds, that they can — and do — get away with anything. (Shooting down passenger planes, invading foreign countries, torturing their own citizens.) This is in part due to the understandable tendency of many people to simply not believe that the Soviets are as bad as they really are.

It's much nicer to go through life not having to think that there is a power over the hill that would enslave you.

But also contributing to this amnesia in world opinion re the Soviets is a Western diplomatic mentality — in our own State Department as well as in Europe — that holds that we simply misunderstand poor Mother Russia (and sweet, innocent Red China, too).

This is the kind of gross stupidity that leads to suggestions of "swapping" an alleged Soviet spy for a U.S. reporter held hostage in Moscow; that putting the Red spy in his ambassador's custody won't mean much (other than a chance for the two to trade secrets).

There are, no doubt, some Americans who will even insist there is no difference between Moscow seizing and charging the U.S. reporter and the U.S. arresting yet another Soviet agent.

The differences, of course, are many. The simple one being that the Russian would get a fair trial in America.

The Hartford Courant

Hartford, CT, September 3, 1986

The Kremlin denies it, but let us hope that the detention of American magazine correspondent Nicholas S. Daniloff is only a petulant retaliatory gesture on the Soviets' part: You arrest one of ours, we'll take one of yours. If such is the case, the Soviets might be more readily embarrassed into letting Mr. Daniloff go.

Sinister symmetry does mark the two recent episodes of alleged espionage that have strained pre-summit relations between the superpowers. The FBI, which last month arrested Gennadi Zakarov, a Soviet national employed by the United Nations, claims their suspect paid an FBI informant for classified material.

Gennady Gerasimov, the chief Soviet foreign ministry spokesman, says in turn that Mr. Daniloff, who works for U.S. News & World Report, was caught in an act of espionage Saturday when a Soviet acquaintance gave him a package later found to contain top-secret maps.

There, however, similarity between the two cases ends: The arrest of a member of the Soviet diplomatic corps and the arrest of a U.S. journalist are quite different things. A certain percentage of diplomats of all nationalities almost certainly function as intelligence agents for their governments.

That Mr. Daniloff — a respected newsman with considerable experience covering the Soviet Union — was spying is nearly unthinkable. His wife reports Mr. Daniloff thought he was being given scarce out-of-town newspapers — something every journalist covets.

Most likely, the reporter's arrest was a blundering miscalculation by a Soviet bureaucrat insufficiently aware of the importance Mikhail S. Gorbachev has attached to reforming the Soviet system and improving communication with the rest of the world. The Soviets have hinted Mr. Daniloff may be released within several days, and that hint lends credence to the theory.

On the other hand, the order for Mr. Daniloff's arrest — or setup — may have come from the Kremlin's top levels. That would be a powerful signal that the putative winds of change blowing from Moscow since Mr. Gorbachev's ascension to power aren't as warm as they seem.

Either way, the detention by the Soviets of a U.S. journalist — without charges, and pending a KGB investigation — is extremely unusual and cannot be condoned. If securing Mr. Daniloff's immediate release requires a full-court press on Moscow from the Reagan administration, let it come.

The Boston Herald

Boston, MA, September 3, 1986

DESPITE the best efforts of the American intellectual elite to make the Gorbachev regime look like a vodka drinking version of the New Frontier, the Soviets — in arresting U.S. News and World Report correspondent Nicholas Daniloff — persist in acting like, well, like the Soviets.

At first, the world was told that Daniloff was arrested for spying, and that's no white collar crime in the Soviet Union. Now we are told that he won't be charged until at least the middle of next week.

The game being played here should be obvious: the Soviets will release Daniloff if the U.S. drops espionage charges against Gennady Zakharov, the Soviet national employed by the United Nations and arrested by the FBI in New York last week.

Nowhere could the contrast between free and democratic societies and totalitarian ones be more clear. If the Reagan administration refuses this craven deal, then the Soviets can jail Daniloff on the manufactured evidence against him.

If we give in to it, then the message will be that whenever we arrest a Russian for spying in this country, all Gorbachev has to do is scoop up some innocent American and demand a trade.

The Daniloff arrest is also further evidence of a tougher Soviet attitude when its people get caught spying. The rules of the "game" are being changed.

The efforts to absolve Gorbachev are going to ridiculous lengths. There are even reports appearing in the U.S. press now that this was a "rogue" KGB operation, unauthorized from above. First, no KGB officer who values his career (his life, even) would create an international incident on his own authority. Second, Gorbachev would not be lying on the beach if there were the slightest hint that his secret police agency was out of control.

This is a carefully calculated act of state terrorism. The Reagan administration must hold fast to the rule of law and work for Daniloff's freedom, or risk more Daniloffs in the future.

The Washington Post

Washington, DC, September 9, 1986

THE SOVIETS who took the American journalist Nicholas Daniloff hostage last week have now compounded the original outrage by charging Mr. Daniloff with espionage and announcing that he will be tried as a spy. Mr. Daniloff, the Moscow correspondent of U.S. News & World Report, was kidnapped by the Soviet government, the one that spends so much of its time complaining that its benign and peaceful purposes in this world go woefully unacknowledged by the United States.

The talk coming out of Moscow has been uncommonly cynical, even by Kremlin standards. Its spokesmen have taken to parody in describing the various legal "protections" Mr. Daniloff will get and in putting forward the preposterous view that this trial, if it occurs, will have the purpose of discovering the truth. This imitation due process is a farce. So are the Kremlin's unconvincing lamentations that the United States has let a little matter get in the way of resolving the great life-and-death issues that confront and divide the superpowers. If Mr. Gorbachev & Co. wanted to get on with the business currently being negotiated between this country and the U.S.S.R. they would not be holding Nick Daniloff hostage.

Mr. Daniloff has been imprisoned for 10 days now. In that time the U.S. government, which began by speaking in a number of voices and not very coherently, has finally managed to get more coherence—and indignation—into its message. The president publicly warned the Soviets yesterday about the consequences of their hostage-taking. But even as the government toughens up, one can expect considerable numbers of people to go the other way. It is already being hinted at that Mr. Daniloff may have violated some Soviet laws unconnected to the seizure of the package the authorities planted on him. As the Soviet system—its rules, habits and statutes—is fundamentally inimical to the practice of journalism as we understand that term in the West, it would be surprising if the Soviet authorities could not find some law to incriminate any journalist in Moscow who has been doing a good job.

What is important is that we in this country—for once—not sink into the sea of doubt that often marks these hostage episodes. We do not need to go around looking for clues as to how some misguided action on the part of the United States impelled the Russians to do this. We don't need to buy the line that Nick Daniloff must have been doing something shady. We don't need to accept the idea that there is some rough equivalence between Mr. Daniloff and the apprehended Gennadi Zakarov.

Above all, we do not need to settle into that bemused state of mind whereby we subtly transform an outrage into a way of life, a kind of business-as-usual condition, letting the unjust imprisonment of this man become a kind of intermittent but semipermanent "issue," one that loses all its urgency and its impact. The Soviets must be made to understand a) that there is a real price for this and b) that it will get higher, not lower, with the passage of each day.

The San Diego Union

San Diego, CA, September 4, 1986

Not since the dark days of Stalin had the Kremlin seized an American citizen from the streets of Moscow and imprisoned him on a trumped-up spy charge. Yet the arrest last week of Nicholas Daniloff, a correspondent for *U.S. News & World Report*, is a reminder that Mikhail Gorbachev's celebrated "westernizing" of the Soviet regime is a figment of credulous minds.

Mr. Daniloff was abruptly surrounded by KGB agents at a park in Moscow's Lenin Hills, near his apartment, after he met briefly with a teacher from the Soviet republic of Kirghiz. An acquaintance of Mr. Daniloff, the teacher had telephoned him earlier and proposed the meeting in order to give the journalist a parcel of newspaper clippings. Such private encounters with Russian dissidents are standard procedure for American correspondents, inasmuch as Soviet citizens who meet openly with foreigners risk harsh government reprisals.

Before Mr. Daniloff had the opportunity to open the packet he had been handed, the KGB men shoved him into a car and whisked him away. He was told the material he had received included maps and photographs stamped "top secret."

This obvious setup, crude even by the KGB's standards, befits a bad spy thriller. But other correspondents have been similarly ensnared by the KGB's operatives in various ploys over the years to embarrass the United States.

What makes the Daniloff case so grave is that, instead of being detained briefly as were earlier journalists, he is being held indefinitely while the Soviet authorities weigh whether to prosecute him in a show trial reminiscent of the Stalin era.

The best explanation for the Kremlin's seizure of Mr. Daniloff lies in the FBI's recent arrest in New York of Gennadi Zakharov, a Soviet official at the United Nations, who is charged with espionage after paying an informant for U.S. secrets. The Kremlin wants back its spy and appears to view Mr. Daniloff as the perfect hostage to swap in return.

Surprisingly, the State Department is playing right into Soviet hands by hinting it wants the federal magistrate in New York to release Mr. Zakharov into the custody of the Soviet ambassador in Washington. That move presumably would pave the way for Mr. Daniloff to be freed in exchange.

Maybe so. But by rewarding Moscow for its outrageous conduct, the State Department would make tempting targets of any American journalist, businessman, or tourist in the Soviet Union who could be used as pawns by the Kremlin in future endeavors.

The White House has at its disposal more sensible means by which to redress this grievance. One is to call an immediate halt to preparations for a Reagan-Gorbachev summit until the Daniloff case is resolved. It is unthinkable to us that Ronald Reagan should play host in this country to Mr. Gorbachev while he is holding an American hostage in a Moscow jail.

At the same time, the arms talks in Geneva and other avenues of Soviet-American cooperation should be closed until Mr. Daniloff is freed. The American Society of Newspaper Editors already has canceled a scheduled U.S. tour by a delegation of Soviet journalists. Other private groups in contact with Soviet citizens should voice their concern for Mr. Daniloff by similar actions.

In these ways Mr. Gorbachev will come to understand that he has seriously misjudged Americans' willingness to tolerate the intolerable.

The Boston Herald

Boston, MA, October 9, 1986

OUR elation over the release of Nicholas Daniloff and Yuri Orlov should not be allowed to obscure the fact that there are other Kremlin prisoners, most in a far more precarious position than the American journalist during his imprisonment.

A doctor's group, the International Physicians Commission for the Protection of Prisoners, seeks to publicize the plight of gulag inmates, specifically their medical problems.

The organization, composed of doctors from the U.S., Canada, Britain, France and Israel, has accumulated substantial evidence on the mistreatment of Jewish dissidents in Soviet prisons.

According to Dr. Martin Motew, commission co-chairman, refuseniks are regularly mistreated in ways designed to impair their health. One prisoner was confined with active tuberculosis patients. Others were forced to stand for hours in cold water.

Prisoners also are abused by being compelled to do hard labor, without proper food or clothing. Some have sustained internal injuries in the course of interrogations.

The commission hopes to publicize the plight of Soviet prisoners, at international forums and, by a concerted letter-writing campaign, to pressure Moscow to provide adequate medical care for its victims.

By increasing public awareness, perhaps they will succeed in making the issue a topic for discussion at the upcoming Reagan/Gorbachev meeting in Iceland.

The Dispatch

Columbus, OH, October 1, 1986

It's almost too good to be true: The Daniloff crisis is over, accused Soviet spy Gennadiy Zakharov was subjected to American justice and released, a prominent Soviet dissident is being freed, arms limitation talks continue, the superpower summit is still on and President Reagan and General Secretary Gorbachev will meet early next month to talk things over.

This is creative diplomacy at its best, an example of what can be achieved when diplomats want results. Everybody wins and the whirlwind of events make observers willing — indeed, eager — to forget that the context of the crisis was changed to allow for success.

In breathtaking succession this week, Moscow and Washington announced the details of an agreement that had been reached to end the crisis that developed during the last few weeks. It started when U.S. officials arrested Zakharov on spy charges. The Soviets then arrested Nicholas Daniloff, a Moscow correspondent for *U.S. News and World Report*, and charged him with espionage. Charges and countercharges were exchanged and the situation reached the point where it appeared that a hoped-for summit between Reagan and Gorbachev would be canceled, sending damaging shockwaves through U.S.-Soviet relations.

But then U.S. Secretary of State George Shultz and Soviet Foreign Minister Eduard Shevardnadze got to work. In a series of closed-door meetings, the pair evolved a resolution acceptable to both sides. Included in this accord was the release of Yuri Orlov and his wife. Shultz said Orlov, reported to be in poor health, was the "driving force" behind the Helsinki Monitoring Group of civil rights activists.

Of greatest importance is the fact that Reagan and Gorbachev will meet in Iceland Oct. 11 and 12 in a session billed as a meeting to allow the pair to prepare for a formal summit in the United States later this year.

The impetus to this agreement was, however, the obviously deep commitment to improved relations felt in both capitals, and the determination by each nation not to allow the present opportunity for progress to slip away.

This bodes very well for the future. Washington and Moscow have demonstrated that they can work and cooperate together. They have demonstrated that they can trust each other to keep promises and that mutual benefits can be achieved when lines of communication are left open. This type of experience is essential — and has been missing — when attention is turned to the high-stakes and extremely complicated area of nuclear arms limitation negotiations.

The consequences of the developments of the last few days will likely be felt for years and, because of the determination of the leaders of both countries, the consequences are likely to be all good.

Rockford Register Star

Rockford, IL, October 2, 1986

A swap by any other name is still a swap.

The administration riles at the suggestion that it traded Nicholas Daniloff for Soviet agent Gennadiy Zakharov, but that clearly is what happened.

And it is regretable that a swap was required to get Daniloff away from his Soviet captors because the Soviets now have been told they can seize any American as a hostage to force us to trade for their spies.

But none of that is the important factor in this unfortunate case. More important is that there were no alternatives to this trade. Instead of criticism, the president deserves praise for negotiating the trade successfully.

At this late stage of the game, it was the only thing President Reagan, or for that matter Soviet leader Mikhail Gorbachev, could do — short of declaring war on each other. The situation, which was badly handled at the beginning by all concerned, was serious but certainly not serious enough to risk endangering world peace or arms reduction hopes.

The Daniloff-Zakharov affair was a dark cloud over summit preparations. In fact, a summit could not have taken place in the atmosphere of abiding tension that ensued after the arrests of these men in hostile countries.

Thus, although it appears President Reagan backed down from his original posture that there would be "no trade" for Daniloff, he actually had no option. He did the only thing possible in working out the agreement that won the release of both Daniloff and Zakharov a day apart.

There are those in this country who object to any negotiations with the Soviets. They will criticize the Daniloff-Zakharov deal as "surrendering" to the Soviets. They will object even to discussing arms control because "you can't trust the Russians."

But we must wonder what options they would prefer. Either we exist in peace with the Soviets, or we go to war with them. Either we attempt to find mutually-beneficial agreements, or we attempt to impose our will upon them by force of arms.

Some of these people probably would have had the United State wage war on the Soviet Union to free Daniloff. But that, we suggest is a suicidal approach to solving world problems.

Actually, it is encouraging that top Soviet and U.S. leaders finally decided to dispense with the whole messy situation and focus instead on the need for critical talks on arms controls.

The positive outcome of this entire incident is a recommitment by both sides to a summit meeting. Reagan and Gorbachev will meet Oct. 11-12 in Iceland.

In this instance, also, the Reagan administration is careful about labels. U.S. officials are calling it a "pre-summit meeting," at which the leaders will prepare to meet later this year in the United States for the real thing.

Perhaps they do not want to raise false hopes about what may be accomplished at the two-day meeting. Perhaps there has not been enough progress in the lower level arms talks for the two leaders to hope to conclude meaningful arms agreements.

But the important factor is that Reagan and Gorbachev are meeting — face to face. Their goal is to lay the groundwork for a formal summit meeting, perhaps before Christmas.

That being the purpose of the meeting, they can call it anything they want. We call it progress.

U.S., Soviets Quarrel Over Reykjavik Arms Stance

The U.S. and Soviet Union gave differing interpretations of an understanding on nuclear weapons reached by the two sides during a preparatory summit in Reykjavik, Iceland. The interpretations left confusion over exactly what U.S. President Ronald Reagan and Soviet leader Mikhail S. Gorbachev had agreed upon. The Reykjavik talks had collapsed over the U.S. Strategic Defense Initiative ("Star Wars"), but news emerged from the meetings that the superpowers had reached broad understandings on arms control prior to the breakdown.

The talks were conducted under a news blackout, so the disclosure of the understandings to the Western press came through unidentified sources close to the Reykjavik negotiations. That process appeared to have added to the controversy. Reports out of Reykjavik said that the two sides had endorsed a goal of eliminating strategic missiles within 10 years.

The confusion began when Reagan briefed U.S. congressional leaders Oct. 14, 1986. U.S. Sen. Sam Nunn (D, Ga.) later quoted the President as telling the legislators:"We put on the table a proposal to eliminate within 10 years all nuclear ballistic missiles and everything else, including bombs.'"

U.S. Secretary of State George Shultz disputed Nunn at a press conference called to clarify the U.S. position at Reykjavik. Shultz said that the U.S. had proposed a 10-year delay in deploying a Star Wars system. During the period through 1991, both sides would cut their nuclear arsenals (ballistic missiles, warheads, bombs, long-range bombers and cruise missiles) by 50%. From 1991-96, Shultz told reporters, both sides would proceed to eliminate only their remaining ballistic missiles.

General Secretary Gorbachev added to the debate Oct. 22, when he appeared on Soviet television to explain Moscow's position at Reykjavik for the second time since the talks. Gorbachev ridiculed the notion that Reagan's purported statement had been misinterpreted. "I state: the President did, albeit without special enthusiasm, consent to the elimination of all, I emphasize all...individual nuclear arms." Gorbachev stressed that it was he, not Reagan, who had pushed the proposal.

Some knowledgeable observers dismissed the growing furor as post-Reykjavik manueverings by the superpowers. Others asserted that the matter raised questions about Reagan's competence as an arms negotiator. If the President had agreed to eliminate all nuclear weapons, the analysts asked, had he considered all the strategic or political implications?

The Reagan administration Oct. 29 issued to the press a document aimed at answering the growing questions on the matter. In essence, the paper restated the account given by Shultz Oct. 17. White House spokesman Larry Speakes Oct. 23 stepped in to clarify the matter. He admitted that the two leaders had talked about eliminating all nuclear weapons, but said they did not set a time limit or reach any firm agreement on the issue.

The Washington Times

Washington, DC, October 21, 1986

As U.S. negotiators map their strategy for the next round of arms-control talks with the Soviets, they should bear in mind what the Reykjavik summit has revealed. Moscow thinks SDI can work, perhaps because its own 17-year-old Star Wars program already has borne fruit. And the American public, which Michail Gorbachev had hoped would turn against President Reagan, thus far has given the president and SDI overwhelming support.

These realities color every aspect of future arms-control discussions, particularly those involving the deal struck tentatively at Reykjavik and "unstruck" when the Soviets introduced a killer proviso limiting SDI to the laboratory. Prior to that, both sides had agreed to cut their ballistic missile forces by 50 percent. With SDI, this might have been a reasonable reduction. But without it, 50 percent reductions would have no effect whatever on either side's ability to launch a devastating first strike.

Soviet ICBMs carrying roughly 6,000 war-heads still could deliver a knockout blow against America's halved missile force. Moreover, reducing submarine-based missiles by 50 percent would leave the remainder doubly vulnerable to anti-sub forces, unaffected by the agreement.

As for eliminating ballistic missiles, Henry Kissinger has explained the problem:

"No conceivable verification scheme could account for the tens of thousands of warheads in the arsenal of both sides. A reserve force would therefore have to be left to protect against possible violations. Provision would have to be made against possible threats from third countries. Before they knew it, the negotiators would be back at the starting point: to analyze the lowest level of nuclear weapons consistent with mutual security."

Perhaps technological developments eventually will resolve this difficulty, but for the forseeable future nuclear disarmament is impossible and SDI remains America's only reliable defense.

THE DAILY OKLAHOMAN
Oklahoma City, OK
October 16, 1986

CONTINUING Soviet assaults on President Reagan's Strategic Defense Initiative raise questions about the real motive for opposing an approach designed to make nuclear weapons obsolete.

All along Soviet propaganda has depicted the SDI as an offensive-weapons system. Americans, with their penchant for popular slogans, have unwittingly aided the distortion by sticking SDI with the nickname, Star Wars. Unfortunately, it carries a connotation of nuclear warheads bent on destruction.

In reality, the SDI is a wide-ranging research effort to develop the most feasible concept of anti-ballistic missile defense. Emerging technologies offer the possibility of non-nuclear options for destroying missiles and their nuclear warheads in all phases of their flight.

These include sensors for identifying and tracking missiles, ground and space-borne interceptors and directed-energy weapons to destroy missiles and warheads and a command, control and communications capability to operate a layered defense.

Such elements could not be used as offensive tools. Yet Soviet leader Mikhail Gorbachev has persisted — both at the Reykjavik meeting with Reagan and since in talking to his own people — in condemning SDI as a great offensive threat to Russia.

It is clear Gorbachev's whole idea in inviting Reagan to a "pre-summit" meeting was to try to defeat the SDI. Analysts say the Kremlin fears the SDI as a threat to its existence as a superpower. The Soviets achieved nuclear parity with the United States in the 1970s at great cost. They have to rely on their offensive nuclear capability to keep that identity. Eliminating offensive weapons would reduce their superpower status.

Thus, Gorbachev, for domestic consumption as well as impressing skeptics in the United States, emphasizes SDI as a "new class of weapons of mass destruction." He questions the logic of building a defensive system if nuclear weapons are to be eliminated. But the SDI's purpose is to keep the Soviets honest until this happens. If this suggests the United States doesn't trust them, they have only themselves to blame.

The Kansas City Times

Kansas City, MO, October 29, 1986

Within the next few days the U.S. is expected to formally propose strategic nuclear weapons reductions of 50 percent within five years and the removal of intermediate missiles in Europe. All ballistic missiles would be eliminated in 10 years. The Soviets already have rejected even greater arms reduction plans because they did not accompany strictures on the Strategic Defense Initiative which Washington says it cannot accept. That is the way it ended in Iceland.

It is difficult to know what to make of this latest Reagan package. It may very well be a consolidation of what the president thinks he said to Mr. Gorbachev. But one unavoidable conclusion must be that it is a further White House attempt to contain damages of a summit that spun wildly out of control.

Someday whole cycles of memoirs and confessions will be written about what really happened at Reykjavik. Publishing houses will devote themselves to the autobiographies of those who were there. Until then one can only look at the unfolding evidence and conclude that the president cannot be allowed to wing it at these affairs; that the United States cannot afford to let him go into a room with a man like Mikhail Gorbachev and improvise.

The emerging picture is one of chaos in the immediate aftermath of Reykjavik, with aides running around in panic asking, "What did he say?" Within the past few days the number of "misspokes" has reached record levels. We do know now that Mr. Reagan told Mr. Gorbachev that, "If we agree . . . we can refer this to our delegation in Geneva to prepare an agreement that you could sign during your visit to the United States." Perhaps this needs to be seen in the context of many other words. By itself, it shows a rather wistful priority on a dazzling showbiz finish to the arms race.

The proposals that now are supposed to go to Geneva are impressive, even if they fall short of the elimination in 10 years of all nuclear weapons. Already they have startled Europe with visions of having to depend on conventional forces instead of the American nuclear deterrent.

Ten days ago Sen. Sam Nunn begged the president to "pull our zero ballistic missile proposal off the table before the Russians accept it." The ballistic missile formula remains a puzzle, although Mr. Reagan seems to be taking cruise missiles and bombers out of the equation.

But can anyone be sure?

The Oregonian

Portland, OR
October 25, 1986

Earlier this month, the most common themes in the 1986 election campaign were reducing the deficit, military spending reform and not raising taxes. Last week, as part of viewing the Iceland summit as a triumph, the administration sought to add another: unquestioning support of the Strategic Defense Initiative.

If entertaining two contradictory ideas at once is a challenge, what should we call fielding four?

At a time when the future consists of red ink as far as the eye can see, the largest, most incalculable cost of all, the budget for "Star Wars," is now supposed to be ruled out of discussion.

The base figure for the weapons system is $770 billion, or half of the entire U.S. defense budget for the last five years. Few, however, take the figure literally, given the traditional cost overruns in defense procurement and the difficulties of pricing technology, equipment and software that have not yet been devised.

Other estimates range into the trillions. Former Secretary of Defense Robert McNamara warned last week that even after the initial costs, maintaining the system and updating it to face new offensive technologies might cost $100 billion to $200 billion annually.

Warnings that neither military nor economic security would be enhanced by expanding the arms race into space have been met by an implied suggestion that the Soviet economy, smaller and less advanced than the American, would break under the strain before ours did.

It might be a close race. The Soviet economy is indeed weaker, but also more disciplined, and certainly our match in determination to spend whatever seems militarily necessary. Meanwhile, the U.S. government has a $2 trillion deficit, $200 billion annual deficits and an economy that seems to be getting worse instead of better. Already, interest on the deficit — the immovable, uncuttable budget item — mounts toward $200 billion a year.

Explaining his unshakable commitment to Star Wars, the president last week told a group of junior high school students, "I couldn't give up your future."

But the future does not have to be lost militarily. It can also be mortgaged — and foreclosed.

Los Angeles Times

Los Angeles, CA, October 31, 1986

For a few more days, the struggle for control of the U.S. Senate will upstage the struggle for control of nuclear arms. Then Washington can get back to the lessons of the Reykjavik summit.

Perhaps the intrusion of politics was useful. The Reagan team's frowns of failure at the summit's end, the painted smiles of success that replaced them, the fudging in Washington over just how far President Reagan and General Secretary Mikhail S. Gorbachev moved toward disarmament are history. What counts, now, as it did then, is the future and, details aside, Reykjavik is a foundation on which to build.

The central meaning of the conversations in Iceland is that the two leaders understand that the arms race has gone far enough and that they should be cutting their nuclear arsenals, not adding to them. An outline for achieving that—born at Reykjavik—is on the table in Geneva.

Reykjavik also showed that there can be no deal on offensive nuclear weapons without a negotiated deal on defensive weapons.

Gorbachev's price for cuts in missiles was a slowdown in Star Wars, a price the President was not then prepared to pay. Gorbachev's price should have come as no surprise to Reagan. His own defense secretary, Caspar W. Weinberger, told him a year ago that an expanded Soviet defense network would require the United States to build more American offensive missiles.

Soviet officials are not likely to cut offensive weapons without knowing where the U.S. defense project is going. Americans cannot design a sensible defense system without knowing how many offensive missiles the Soviets have. Unless ground rules are negotiated for defense systems in both countries, there is little hope that either would, in the end, agree to cuts in offensive weapons. Any attempt to negotiate on other grounds would just leave the teams at Geneva talking in offensive-defensive circles.

The President does not have to give up much to bargain on defenses. The wheels have pretty much come off of his grandiose version of Star Wars anyway. A growing majority of scientists reject his claims that a shield can be built to protect all America from nuclear weapons; they still support research, as do we, although at a slower and more disciplined pace. And the major Star Wars debate in Washington in 1987 will not be over the President's vision but over using technology at hand to defend American missile silos.

Congress is losing its taste for billions of dollars it will take under the President's crash research program just to find out what Star Wars might and might not do. As Sen. William R. Cohen (R-Maine) told National Journal recently, the country doesn't have the resources to commit to a program for which there still is "no architecture."

Not long after the President proposed Star Wars in 1983, a defense analyst said that the system would never work but it would serve a purpose anyway by shaking up decades-old beliefs about arms control and the value of deterring war with the threat of devastating retaliation for any first strike. Shaking up those beliefs has led both countries back to the basics. Arms control started out as something that would come in stages, with each successive treaty moving the world away from the dangers of nuclear war.

The goal was set at Reykjavik. The experts at Geneva now can get closer to the goal by filling in the details—how to balance offense and defense, what to do with conventional weapons—and produce something that both the President and the General Secretary can comfortably sign.

SYRACUSE
HERALD-JOURNAL
Syracuse, NY, October 16, 1986

Soviet chief Mikhail Gorbachev is getting plenty of public relations mileage out of the collapse of the Iceland summit. It's pretty much a matter of politalking, the ability of politicians to cash in on public sentiment simply by batting their gums while actually doing nothing at all.

Make no mistake, President Reagan, too, is using politalk to his advantage and, we think, will continue to win this war of words against the Soviets. Actions, after all, speak louder than all the politalk in the world.

Let's face it: Despite all the post-Reykjavik rhetoric about historic opportunities and the sighs over the missed chance at "a drastic solution of problems of war and peace," the world was no safer or more dangerous on Monday morning than it was on Saturday night.

No matter what the chief politalkers and the assistant politalkers say or how much they try to assess blame, all that was accomplished in Iceland was billions of empty words, the politalkers' favorite fare. What we may be observing now is nothing short of politalker heaven.

But President Reagan has a major advantage in the politalk-credibility battle with Gorbachev, however. It is this: While Gorbachev piously politalks about peace prospects in Iceland, the Soviets have an estimated 115,000 troops in Afghanistan fighting a rag-tag army of guerrillas.

The Soviets are trying to politalk that, too, of course. While Afghanistan is usually off-limits to Western reporters, the Soviets have brought in foreign journalists to watch the Soviets withdrawal of 8,000 troops from the war-torn (thanks to the Soviets) nation.

That move apparently is just as substantial as what happened — or should we say didn't happen — in Iceland last weekend.

▽   ▽

Defense Secretary Caspar Weinberger said the Soviets recently increased their troop force, making the much-politalked-about withdrawal meaningless.

A Soviet general called Weinberger's claim an "open lie," but even Weinberger was understating his case: The withdrawal of 8,000 troops is insignificant when we consider that more than 100,000 Soviet troops remain.

Just as it's impossible to be a little bit pregnant, Afghanistan can't be a little bit free until it completely free — when all Soviet troops are withdrawn and the Afghans are able to choose their own government.

If there is an "open lie" here, it is clearly on the tongues of the Soviets, who have been knee-deep in Afghan blood for seven years now. All the Soviet politalkers' words in Moscow and Kabul cannot and will not change that.

The Philadelphia Inquirer
Philadelphia, PA, October 28, 1986

The Soviet leadership seems convinced that it has President Reagan over a barrel on the administration's obvious confusion over what was agreed to verbally at the Reykjavik summit. At issue is whether Mr. Reagan agreed to eliminate *all* strategic nuclear weapons over 10 years or whether he drew the line with the already-momentous proposal that both sides eliminate intercontinental ballistic missiles, but hold on to bombers and long-range cruise missiles.

Secretary of State George P. Shultz, admittedly exhausted at the time, said the night the summit ended that Mr. Reagan had signed on to the broader proposal, a dramatic reversal of four decades of strategic doctrine. But in addressing the nation the following night Mr. Reagan said that he only had proposed eliminating ballistic missiles.

The official version seemingly clear, Mr. Reagan and Mr. Shultz briefed congressional leaders the following day and, to the amazement of arms experts, like Sen. Sam Nunn, (D., Ga.), they said that the President had agreed to scrap the entire strategic nuclear arsenal. Sen. Nunn could conclude only that there was "a genuine question" over what the administration had agreed to.

Now the Soviets, smelling blood and generally miffed about Mr. Reagan's enthusiastic stumping for the "Star Wars" missile defense program, have gotten into the act. Soviet leader Mikhail S. Gorbachev last week publicly contended that the President — "albeit without special enthusiasm" — agreed to do away with all strategic nuclear weapons. Then, in a move that the administration has denounced as dirty pool, one of Mr. Gorbachev's top foreign policy aides held a special press conference to quote directly from Soviet notes of the meeting.

This dispute, further evidence of how quickly relations have soured after the first burst of post-Reykjavik optimism, underlines the political risk of trying to resolve momentous and complex issues in a single weekend of negotiations, particularly when the chief negotiators — the President and Mr. Shultz in this case — do not have that firm a grasp of the issues.

Mr. Reagan erred in getting in over his head. The Soviets, apparently more interested in embarrassing the President than in keeping negotiations on track, have compounded the error.

The fact remains that, thankfully, no agreement was signed at Iceland. Whatever the President said to Mr. Gorbachev, it is clear today that the United States does not favor eliminating strategic nuclear weapons within a decade. The two sides should quit bickering and turn their attention to shaping a genuine arms accord that they both could embrace unequivocally.

The Miami Herald
Miami, FL, October 23, 1986

SO NEAR and yet so far: That was the universal summation, from participants and observers alike, of the recent "nonsummit summit" at Reykjavik, Iceland. Since that dolorous description was issued, both Washington and Moscow have discovered some rays of hope in the post-Reykjavik gloom.

In one sense of course, neither superpower had a choice. It's simply unthinkable that they could allow the disagreements that torpedoed that meeting to be accepted as unalterable and permanent. Both sides recognize the peril, and the cost to their economies, of resuming an unrestrained arms race. Both know that whether they like one another or not, the United States and the Soviet Union must continue to negotiate.

Since Reykjavik, statements from both sides have displayed a welcome affirmation of this fact of superpower *Realpolitik*. Secretary of State George Shultz said last week that the reason he looked tired and disappointed in his news briefing just after the summit collapsed was that he was ... tired and disappointed. Now, from Moscow, come hints to the Reagan Administration and its European allies that the Soviets might accept some out-of-laboratory research on President Reagan's beloved Strategic Defense Initiative.

The Soviets portray this as less a change of heart than that their position at Reykjavik had been misunderstood. Whatever its origin, it offers a glimmer of optimism that there is fruit to be found in the continuing U.S.-Soviet arms talks in Geneva — if only both sides are willing to climb high enough up the tree.

In retrospect, one can view Reykjavik as less a failure than a clarifier of boundaries. The Soviets displayed a willingness to make unprecedented cuts in both intermediate-range and long-range nuclear missiles — but theirs was an all-or-nothing offer. If President Reagan wouldn't agree to stop all except laboratory research on SDI, then no deal.

Mr. Reagan told them nothing doing. The rest might well have been history, but instead it is developing into what it should be, must be: prologue. The door that seemed to slam shut with such force at Reykjavik appears now to have bounced open a crack. Let's hope that this Soviet feeler on Star Wars research is enough of a wedge to open the door enough for resumed arms-control negotiations to slip through.

THE RICHMOND NEWS LEADER
Richmond, VA, October 16, 1986

Before Mikhail Gorbachev went to Reykjavik, the USSR announced a withdrawal of some Red Army troops from Afghanistan. Easily excited Westerners interpreted the announcement as another sign of Gorbachev's Liberalism. Mondale voters and reporters for "All Things Considered" probably called home to tell Mom the good news.

After Gorbachev returned to Moscow, news reports confirmed that the USSR had launched what observers call "one of the most brutal campaigns" yet in its war to subjugate Afghanistan. The administration revealed that the so-called withdrawal actually refers to the regular rotation of units. Replacements already are on their way.

"Brutal" aptly describes the Soviet offensive. Soviet jets strafe villages. Soviet artillery fires indiscriminately into cities. The Soviets are attacking one of the few areas where freedom-fighters operate effectively. Afghan civilians are dying.

Those criticizing President Reagan for not trading Star Wars for vague promises to reduce arms in the future should train their eyes on Afghanistan. While Gorbachev smiled for the press and while his wife dispensed chocolates to Icelandic children, Soviet troops killed and maimed countless Afghans whose only crime is their desire to be free.

The Providence Journal
Providence, RI, October 18, 1986

The Kremlin was confused, but the American people stood decisively behind the President in the aftermath of the weekend summit in Iceland. The Reagan administration has positioned itself smartly to take advantage of this rare scenario at the Geneva arms control talks. U.S. negotiators have placed before the Soviets the same choice that President Reagan placed before them in Reykjavik.

The choice is whether to accept the agreements forged in Iceland, on medium-range missiles in particular, without linking them to the strategic defense question. The Kremlin, after some shuffling, has said *nyet*, but perhaps the Soviets can be persuaded to change their minds. If not, then the onus for derailing the arms cuts will in any event be off Mr. Reagan and back where it should be — on Mikhail Gorbachev. It was the Russian, after all, who blocked progress in Iceland, startling everyone by linking the Euromissile pact with the Strategic Defense Initiative. These had been decoupled at the 1985 summit.

All three network news polls show the American people in overwhelming agreement with Mr. Reagan's handling of the summit and his refusal to barter extensive research and testing on SDI for arms cuts. The polls showed more support for the SDI program than ever before. And they showed that Americans by a large margin blame Mr. Gorbachev, not Mr. Reagan, for what happened at the so-called "collapsed" summit.

This might reflect the public's apparent desire to rally 'round the President at a critical pass in the superpower relationship. As such, it might wither a bit over time. For this reason, U.S. negotiators were on the ball in calling swiftly for a special session in Geneva devoted expressly to the matters discussed in Iceland.

The more so because, in a departure from form that seems to bespeak confusion at the Kremlin, top Soviet officials earlier this week had been saying different things about the same topic — that topic being whether arms agreements are still linked to an agreement on strategic defense.

On Wednesday, Mr. Gorbachev reportedly told Argentine President Raul Alfonsin that the two realms of arms control could only be considered as a "package." The same day, chief Soviet arms negotiator Viktor Karpov said, "We are ready to discuss and solve the questions separately. . . ." On Thursday Soviet Foreign Ministry spokesman Gennady Gerasimov said that Mr. Gorbachev "cannot divide this package," though it remained unclear just what position the Soviet leader himself was taking.

By Friday, the Soviets seemed to have got their act together. They're going with linkage.

In revealing an apparent confusion on linkage, the Soviets have granted the United States an opportunity to focus public attention on the issue. If there is linkage, there may well be no agreement. With Mr. Gorbachev having announced his intention to mobilize world opinion to pressure the U.S. public to put the squeeze on the Reagan administration to kill the Strategic Defense Initiative, it was important that Soviet intransigence be made clear without delay.

That, it seems, has been done.

The Kansas City Times
Kansas City, MO, October 21, 1986

Maneuvering continues over exactly what happened at Reykjavik and what might happen at Geneva now. Much, if not most, certainly is propaganda. What remains of substance is impossible to tell. Yet hope prevails.

The Soviets are hinting, says an American spokesman, that there might be further compromise on testing for the Strategic Defense Initiative. How nice. But then Georgi Arbatov, the Soviet propagandist and expert in all things American, explains with his usual charm that the Russians are perfectly willing to furnish President Reagan with "some face-saving devices," if that is what he needs. Some offer.

In Europe, North Atlantic Treaty Organization officers are pondering a Europe without the intermediate Soviet SS-20 and U.S. Pershing II rockets. It was Europe that wanted the Pershing IIs in the first place, out of the fear that the U.S. would not respond with intercontinental missiles should Europe come under attack or intimidation from the SS-20s. Also, the elimination of the intermediates could leave much of Europe vulnerable to short-range Soviet missiles assuming the NATO equivalent could not reach the Soviet Union. Moreover, the Soviets have the swift intermediate range Backfire bomber while the U.S. F-111s are growing older.

The real problem for Europe is that in a return to dependence on conventional (nonnuclear) forces, Europe would have to provide much more money and manpower to defend itself. But as Secretary of State George Shultz observes, Europe has more than enough manpower, and with U.S. industrial productivity, far outdistances the productivity of the Soviet Union and its satellites. The gross national product of Western Europe is about equal to the American. What Europe may not have is the will to kick the habit of dependence on American nuclear protection.

What reductions, if any, can come from the present standoff should become apparent in the weeks ahead. The Soviets may believe that Mr. Reagan is bluffing and they may call what they think is his bluff. They might be surprised. Mr. Reagan's man, George Shultz, has been asked what security would remain for the West with complete nuclear disarmament in the face of Soviet superiority in conventional forces. Mr. Shultz, in answering, asks another question: What security is there in continually living 30 minutes away from obliteration?

The Washington Post

Washington, DC, October 26, 1986

PHASE 1 of the post-summit process was dejection; Phase 2 was a recovery of hope; Phase 3 was the effort to establish exactly what happened in Reykjavik—and Phase 4 is now developing. It's the effort to work out an alliance policy that satisfies American strategic considerations and the European allies' requirements too. This doesn't mean Phase 3 is finished. On the contrary, the White House and Mr. Gorbachev have been engaged in an extraordinary public debate over what was actually offered and agreed on in the hurly-burly of Iceland. Nonetheless, the emphasis now, at least on the American side, is to ensure that henceforth policy takes into full account the implications of trying to move rapidly to a Europe and a world without the different sorts of nuclear arms that the two leaders discussed cutting or eliminating at Reykjavik.

There are two considerations here. The first bears on Europe and the Strategic Defense Initiative. The Europeans are dubious about SDI but, out of deference to the leader of the alliance, they hesitate to get into the middle of the Soviet-American argument over it. Still, they do not want SDI to become an obstacle to Soviet-American arms control, which remains their political priority. To keep Moscow from using SDI as a wedge, Mr. Reagan will have to consult very closely with the Europeans as he goes along.

Then, like many strategic thinkers (including Pentagon officials) in the United States, the allies fear Europe might fare poorly if it is deprived of the nuclear forces that generations of Westerners have seen as compensating for Moscow's superior conventional forces. These alarms seem to have induced the administration, as it returns to Geneva, to edge back from some of the grander strategic proposals discussed in Iceland. The summit also made it urgent to reconsider the conventional arms balance in Europe. At Vienna on Nov. 4, the latest Helsinki meeting begins. There Washington must blunt the expected Soviet attempt to remove all-European issues of human rights from this all-European forum. Further, it must devise the framework in which all the allies (including France) can enter talks on conventional forces and make them work. With nuclear cuts, either Western conventional forces must go up to match Moscow's advantages in forces-in-being and proximity, or Soviet forces must go down.

Mr. Gorbachev declares that the United States is "twisting" the results of Iceland. In the same breath he complains that while he came to Reykjavik with fresh proposals, Mr. Reagan arrived "empty-handed." But this is not the whole of it. Mr. Gorbachev went to Iceland announcing a modest purpose. Once there, he unveiled a strategy of surprise and tried to rush Mr. Reagan. Things moved fast—too fast, as is demonstrated by the continuing argument over whether the two agreed to destroy ballistic missiles or also other strategic offensive arms.

It may be thought an embarrassment now for Mr. Reagan to consolidate his policy at the more modest end of a scale marked, at its other end, by the extravagance of Reykjavik. But this would be a small and passing embarrassment and one far preferable to accepting a Soviet reading that is not in the American interest. Mr. Gorbachev will have no difficulty understanding this, as he settles down.

The Hartford Courant

Hartford, CT, October 18, 1986

The three major American television networks flooded viewers with information about the Iceland summit before President Reagan and Soviet leader Mikhail S. Gorbachev had even shaken hands. Then two news blackouts cut the coverage to a trickle.

One blackout was planned — the news moratorium agreed upon by both sides to relieve pressure on their leaders. The other blackout wasn't expected, although perhaps it should have been. There were football and baseball games on Sunday, the day the summit ended, and they dominated the airwaves.

The official blackout was supposed to prohibit statements by officials of either government, in public or private, about the substance of the negotiations until they were over. The intent may have been admirable, but it was a bad idea nonetheless.

For one thing, blackouts aren't reliable. Summit stakes are so high that both sides are sorely tempted to use the news media to try to advance their positions or undercut the opposition. The temptation proved irresistible in Reykjavik.

One Soviet official last Saturday morning criticized the U.S. position on nuclear weapons testing. Another later told a reporter of his optimism that arms agreements would be reached. Publicly, White House spokesman Larry Speakes angrily accused the Soviets of violating the blackout understanding; privately, he did so himself, by discussing summit prospects with several reporters last Saturday night.

The other drawback to summit blackouts is that they needlessly deprive the public of information about the status of the negotiations. It's possible to describe summit talks, at least in general terms, without interfering with progress. But officials naturally prefer the easier route of silence.

If the U.S. and Soviet delegations can be forgiven, if not excused, for agreeing to say nothing about the summit while it was going on, the major American TV networks deserve no such tolerance. Their performance Sunday on the world's biggest story was disappointing.

When Secretary of State George P. Shultz called a news conference to discuss the lack of tangible results at the summit, only NBC and CBS provided live coverage. And only CBS covered (in part) President Reagan's post-summit speech to U.S. military personnel in Iceland.

The networks had ample time Sunday for baseball and football, however, and that suggests an explanation for their scanty coverage of the summit's results: With millions of dollars' worth of advertising time sold for the games, was it asking too much to expect a lot of attention to a contest like the one in Reykjavik?

THE ARIZONA REPUBLIC
Phoenix, AZ, October 24, 1986

AT last, a Soviet offer the Reagan administration can't refuse.

In his 90-minute television speech to the Soviet people the other day, General Secretary Mikhail Gorbachev revealed a proposal he laid on the negotiating table at Reyjkavik. He offered to end the Russian jamming of the Voice of America if President Reagan would permit the Soviet Union to set up its own broadcasting station in or near the United States. According to Gorbachev, Reagan promised to think about the proposal. The president should do more than that. He should publicly accept it. Let's see if Gorbachev is serious.

Thomas Jefferson believed passionately that in a free marketplace of ideas the truth will inevitably emerge victorious. "Enlighten the people," he wrote, "and tyranny and oppressions of the body and mind will vanish like evil spirits at the dawn of day."

The American people and their democratic system of government have less to fear from an unembargoed exchange of ideas with the Soviets than do the dictators in the Kremlin.

Radio Liberty and Voice of America broadcast via powerful transmitters in Europe into the Soviet Union in several of the 15 different languages spoken inside the Russian empire. The Soviets have no comparable facilities in North America. The Reagan administration should strike an agreement allowing the Russians to compete with rock 'n' roll, easy-listening, talk shows, country Western disc jockeys and classical stations. It is unlikely the Voice of the Politburo will find much of an audience here.

The people of the Soviet Union and Eastern Europe, however, rely upon the objective and uncontrolled information offered in Western radio broadcasts from VOA and the BBC because they know their own media offer nothing more than government-controlled propaganda.

Reagan should accept Gorbachev's offer. The United States can hold its own in a Cold War of the airwaves.

BUFFALO EVENING NEWS
Buffalo, NY
October 18, 1986

DESPITE THEIR FAILURE to conclude a final agreement on arms control at Reykjavik, President Reagan and Soviet leader Mikhail Gorbachev made remarkable, and some would even say spectacular, progress in that direction.

Thus, it is encouraging that during the few days since the end of that so-close-and-yet-so-far summit in Iceland, both sides — rather than slipping back into separate pockets of diplomatic isolation — indicate that the search for arms control accords will continue, as it surely must.

Reagan, negotiating highly complicated matters at a brief summit meeting, was right to reject the Soviet demand that he drastically curb research, testing and development on the Strategic Defense Initiative in order to win Soviet consent to dramatic mutual reductions of offensive nuclear weapons.

Though Reagan did offer some significant concessions, he concluded that what Gorbachev demanded went too far in curtailing the SDI program.

SDI, popularly known as Star Wars, is a defensive, not an offensive, system. As the Reagan administration has stressed, the successful development of SDI could serve as an insurance policy against Soviet cheating on cutbacks of offensive weapons. It might also help guard against future attack by some third nuclear power not a party to an arms-reduction treaty.

In recent days, the Soviets have flashed conflicting diplomatic signals about the relationship of SDI to other kinds of arms control. Before the summit, they indicated that an agreement on reductions in medium-range missiles in Europe and the Far East need not depend on resolving differences over SDI. At Reykjavik, on the other hand, Gorbachev linked everything to SDI.

Since the summit, Kremlin officials have spoken ambiguously on this point, some saying the issues were coupled and others saying they were not. The Soviet negotiating positions on this question will presumably be clarified as the Geneva talks proceed.

There is no reason why reductions in medium-range missiles need to be tied to SDI. Also, it might still be possible to adjust differences over SDI research, testing and development as well as move toward additional, verifiable limits on nuclear testing.

The overriding point is that the areas of agreement that surfaced at Reykjavik should not be neglected. After Reykjavik, the leaders of both superpowers agree on two things: Those talks produced unexpected progress, and the search for new arms accords should not stop.

Reykjavik suggested a lessening of superpower differences over nuclear arms control, not the reverse. The Reagan-Gorbachev summit should be seen as neither an end nor a beginning, but simply a step in a continuing series of steps that can yet lead to major arms reductions and a less forbidding nuclear world.

St. Petersburg Times
St. Petersburg, FL, October 16, 1986

"A government that will break faith with its own people cannot be trusted to keep faith with foreign powers."
— President Reagan, in his Monday night televised address.

"The whole question comes down to: 'Is deception going to be a tool that the government can use in combating a very significant national security problem,' and I think that the answer . . . has to be yes."
— White House national security adviser John M. Poindexter, speaking to a group of reporters in Washington Tuesday.

The President is right, and Poindexter is wrong: Governments have an obligation to "keep faith" with their people by, among other things, telling them the truth. If a government can't be trusted to keep its commitments to its own people, the President argued, how can it be trusted to keep its commitments to other governments?

Of course, the President was talking Monday night about the Soviet Union, not the United States. He made the valid point that the Soviets' domestic human-rights abuses naturally have a negative effect on our readiness to trust the Soviets in the context of arms control and other U.S.-Soviet negotiations. In particular, the Soviet leadership routinely uses its government-controlled press to mislead the Soviet people, or to withhold vital information from them. That trait is not lost on American negotiators seeking ways of verifying Soviet compliance with proposed or existing agreements.

"Disinformation," or *dezinformatsiya,* is a Soviet invention — one that many Reagan administration officials, including Poindexter, apparently envy. In the particular case defended by Poindexter Tuesday, the administration planted false news stories last August purporting to describe increased Libyan terrorist activity and possible American retaliation. The idea, he says, was to confuse Libya's Moammar Gadhafi and destabilize his regime.

But information, whether true or false, cannot be so easily controlled. The disinformation may have reached Gadhafi, but it also reached Congress, it reached the leaders of other governments, it reached ordinary American citizens who pay attention to the news.

The Poindexter policy isn't just wrong, it's stupid. By sacrificing its credibility in support of today's cause, the administration endangers its credibility for tomorrow's.

For example, the White House has had a hard enough time winning allied support for legitimate anti-terrorist action. With this summer's disinformation campaign now revealed, how quick will other governments be to trust future American claims of Libyan terrorist activity? How quick will they be to join in coordinated retaliation? For that matter (to put the government-citizen relationship in the context used by the President), if the White House reserves the right to tell the truth only when it feels like it, how can it ask the American people to trust implicitly its version of events at last week's U.S.-Soviet sessions in Iceland?

Finally, the disinformation campaign reveals the cynicism of the administration's attempts to crack down on official "leaks" of information. While one half of the White House is busy threatening prosecution of officials or journalists involved in the disclosure of supposedly "secret" information, the other half is busy leaking its own classified intelligence (true and false) that happens to serve the administration's purposes.

At least some White House officials see nothing wrong with manipulating the press and the public through disinformation and intimidation. As the President pointed out Monday night, that's the way the Soviet Union, not the United States, is supposed to do business.

U.S., Soviets Trade Diplomatic Expulsions

The United States and the Soviet Union traded diplomatic expulsions Oct. 19-20, 1986 in a dispute that cost the U.S. the services of 260 Soviet nationals employed at its Moscow embassy and Leningrad consulate. The dispute was rooted in the Daniloff affair of September 1986. (See pp. 98-101.)

Washington Sept. 17 had ordered out of the U.S. 25 members of the Soviet mission to the United Nations who had been identified by the Reagan administration as intelligence agents. The move was in apparent retaliation for the spy charges lodged by the Soviets against *U.S. News & World Report* reporter Nicholas Daniloff. Moscow had repeatedly warned that it would retaliate unless the expulsion order was lifted.

The Kremlin Oct. 19 ordered five American diplomats to leave the U.S.S.R., four from the U.S. embassy in Moscow and one from the U.S. consulate in Leningrad. Moscow claimed that the diplomats had engaged in "impermissable activities," a euphemism for espionage. The announcement of the expulsion made no reference to the ouster from the U.S. of the Soviet U.N. staffers, but Western analysts saw a direct link. The highest ranking of the five was William Norville, a first secretary at the embassy.

In Washington, U.S. Secretary of State George Shultz Oct. 19 protested the expulsions and hinted at a retaliation. The retaliation came Oct. 21 when the Reagan administration ordered 55 Soviet diplomats to leave the U.S. by Nov. 1. It was the largest number of Soviets ever included in a single U.S. expulsion order. The Reagan administration had long maintained that the Soviet diplomatic missions in the U.S. were a haven for spies and should be reduced in staff size. One U.S. official Oct. 22 said that the expulsion of the 55, coupled with the ouster of the 25 U.S. staffers, amounted to a "decapitation of the Soviet intelligence network in the U.S."

Los Angeles, CA
October 23, 1986

At the Reykjavik summit, President Reagan and Soviet leader Mikhail Gorbachev were scheduled to discuss the recent U.S. banning of 25 Soviet U.N. envoys, the incident that began the current diplomatic-expulsions war. This messy little game of tit-for-tat might have been avoided if they hadn't instead focused exclusively on arms control.

The controversy arose with the Reagan administration's justifiable concern over the number and conduct of Soviet diplomatic personnel assigned to the U.S. Until the mass expulsion of Soviet envoys this week evened things out, Moscow had some 300 diplomats here: 50 more than the U.S. had in the Soviet Union. In addition, about 800 Soviets work for the United Nations in New York.

Many of those people keep busy with diplomatic duties, but undoubtedly a large percentage are here to spy. And, certainly, U.S. intelligence agents are well-represented at the American embassy in Moscow. But the more than 1,000 Soviets on "government" business in the U.S., compared to the 251 Americans working for the U.S. in the Soviet Union, gives the Russians a huge edge.

U.S. Sen. Daniel Moynihan also charges that in addition to engaging in the normal espionage activities, the Soviets are utilizing microwave technology at their facilities in New York City and Long Island to eavesdrop on American telephone conversations. And Moscow's new embassy, located on one of the highest points in Washington, reportedly enhances the Soviets' ability to listen in.

There's no easy solution to this troublesome situation. But at Reykjavik, Reagan and Gorbachev didn't even try to come to terms with it. High-level U.S. and Soviet officials should make up for that oversight and begin negotiating this issue. If they don't, tit-for-tat will further deteriorate superpower relations.

THE BLADE

Toledo, OH, October 16, 1986

THE AMERICAN embassy under construction in Moscow has become yet another obstacle to the seldom smooth path of relations between the two superpowers. Work has been halted on the structure because "sophisticated listening devices have been implanted in everything," according to a news report from the Soviet capital.

U.S. investigators searching the structure, which is five years behind schedule and $80 million over its budget, have concluded that eavesdropping equipment has been installed in precast floors, prefabricated concrete columns, and steel beams. It is becoming a security nightmare, and some officials have concluded that the $167 million building may have to be demolished and rebuilt from the ground up. In its present state it is worthless.

Moreover the building has construction flaws, including mortar on the brick facade that could crumble in Moscow's winter weather. This is probably the result of incompetence rather than malevolence.

Meanwhile, Russian families have moved into a new embassy compound on a hill well above most of Washington, D. C. They cannot occupy the offices until the U.S. embassy in Moscow is finished, but it is feared that Soviet intelligence agents will be able to monitor private, commercial, and government messages with equipment that did not exist 16 years ago when the site of a former Veterans Administration hospital was sold to the Soviet Union.

It is obvious that the United States is getting the worst of the bargain. But aside from complaints by some members of Congress, there is no evidence that the State Department or any other government agency is taking steps to halt what could be one of the most strategic Soviet espionage centers in the western world.

The reciprocal arrangement between the two countries to build new embassies has been carried out in bad faith by the Russian side.

Washington has been played for a sucker by the Soviet Union. The Government should admit its costly mistake, drop the embassy-construction agreement, and prevent the Russians from establishing new and effective electronic eavesdropping posts in both Moscow and Washington.

Richmond Times-Dispatch

Richmond, VA, October 24, 1986

Paring down to "parity" is how the State Department explains the latest expulsions of Soviet diplomats from the United States. The Soviets, who preach superpower parity but practice superiority, don't want it seen that way. But they have somehow got to be disabused of the notion that they are *entitled* (a) to maintain a larger contingent of diplomats here than they allow the United States to maintain there and (b) to spy with impunity under diplomatic cover.

It is a question not only of basic fairness but of national security, as even Congress agrees: Convinced by numerous studies of heavy U.S. losses to Soviet military and civilian espionage, Congress decreed last year that the Soviet diplomatic complement in Washington and San Francisco equal the American diplomatic complement in Moscow and Leningrad.

Never mind that, counting the Soviet delegation to the United Nations and Soviets assigned to the U.N. Secretariat, the Soviet Union actually has several hundred more "diplomats" here than we have there. Never mind that U.S. diplomats in the Soviet Union enjoy nothing near the access to the public given Soviet "diplomats" via the U.S. media. For years the Soviets have resisted parity even in the size of the two superpowers' respective embassies and consulates. They have consistently rejected proposals that parity be reached by increasing the American delegation to the U.S.S.R. to the size of the Soviet delegation to America.

Shaving their delegation has become the only alternative. If the Soviets threaten to decimate the American diplomatic presence by continuing to expel Americans in retaliation — 10 have been ousted so far — they ought to find their own contingent decimated likewise.

As to which capital will be more hurt by the withdrawal of Soviet janitors, typists, etc., employed in U.S. offices in the Soviet Union, make it Moscow: It will be easier for Washington to send over a janitor who janitors than for Moscow to recoup the loss of a janitor who spies. U.S. diplomats will be inconvenienced, purposely: In the Soviet system, which works, as much as it works, on the basis of whom you know and what favors you can exchange, American diplomats just lost their knowledgeable folk. Still, if the lights go out in Spaso House, the U.S. ambassador's Moscow residence, they can be made to flicker in Washington, too.

"Petty," charges Mikhail Gorbachev, but petty it isn't. Washington has bent over backwards to ignore even overt Soviet espionage and to combat it by example. The Soviet response has been egregious. Holding journalist Nicholas Daniloff hostage to a Soviet spy, literally studding the new U.S. embassy building in Moscow with electronic bugs — this and more the Soviets have done, all under the assumption that Soviet espionage must go unremarked, not to mention unchallenged, lest the "dialogue" on more important issues collapse.

Acquiescence in this blackmail has gone on far too long. If the Soviets truly want an arms control accord, they won't be deterred by the United States' exercise of its prerogative to protect itself from espionage. And if the United States wants true arms control, it is past time that Washington established the principle that the Soviets should expect to get only as good as they give, whether in diplomatic niceties or in arms control negotiations.

The Philadelphia Inquirer

Philadelphia, PA
October 23, 1986

One might think that, after going eyeball-to-eyeball over the Daniloff case and eyeball-to-eyeball over "Star Wars," the American and Soviet leaders would want to give their eyes a rest. Not a chance. The two feisty warriors are at it again this week, testing each other's patience and mettle with the heaviest series of diplomatic expulsions in the history of the relationship.

The Soviets struck the first blow Sunday by expelling five American diplomats in retaliation for the U.S. expulsion of 25 employees at the Soviet U.N. mission during the height of the Daniloff affair last month. The State Department responded Tuesday by booting out 55 Soviets, arguing that when the dust cleared each country would have identical numbers of nationals on the other's soil (the United Nations is necessarily excluded from those totals).

Not surprisingly, the Soviets fired back yesterday, expelling five more Americans and withdrawing the services of 260 Soviet citizens who occupy a host of supporting jobs at the U.S. Embassy in Moscow and the consulate in Leningrad. The Americans' preference for using cheap Soviet labor for nonsensitive secretarial and blue-collar work was the main reason for the imbalance in the two missions.

It would be comforting to blame both sides equally for this unnecessary squabble, but the evidence suggests otherwise. Sunday's Soviet expulsion order, justified or not, represented a scaled-down response to the U.N. expulsions. The Reagan administration could have retaliated in the same spirit — a spirit justified by the advances made at Reykjavik — but chose instead to turn the matter into a major confrontation.

If the State Department was so convinced that the Soviet representation should be reduced, it should have dealt with the matter at an earlier date and in a less confrontational manner. Like it or not, the Soviet ceilings were consciously set higher to allow them to import all of their own workers, a choice that was open to the Americans as well. If the rules were to be changed, the Soviets should have been given time to adjust.

Never one to pass up an opportunity, Mikhail S. Gorbachev went on television last night to denounce the American expulsion order and link it to U.S. militarists' desire to prevent a post-Reykjavik arms accord. American officials, he charged, "have taken action in recent days that to the normal human mind appear simply wild after such an important meeting."

Would that he were wrong.

THE SUN

Baltimore, MD, October 23, 1986

All hail to Mikhail S. Gorbachev. The Soviet party chief has ordered the withdrawal of Russian nationals working (and spying) at the U.S. embassy in Moscow and the U.S. consulate in Leningrad. And through his spokesman he has proclaimed the "principle of reciprocity and equality" in the staffing of American and Soviet diplomatic posts.

Most Americans not employed by the State Department have favored such actions for years. But it took a spate of espionage cases, a burst of congressional ire and some tit-for-tat expulsions of diplomats before and after the Reykjavik summit to gain Soviet indirect acceptance of the "substantial equivalence" required by U.S. law.

For years the United States has permitted the Russians to maintain diplomatic staffs in this country that vastly exceed the size of U.S. staffs in the Soviet Union. The presence of hundreds of Soviet citizens in the secretariat of the United Nations and in the Soviet mission itself was bound to give the Kremlin a numbers edge. But unfortunately, the Russians secured additional advantages in their regular diplomatic missions simply because we allowed them to. Consider:

□ The Soviet Embassy in Washington and the Soviet consulate in San Francisco employ only a handful of Americans that the Soviets themselves recruit. In contrast, U.S. missions in the Soviet Union have had on their payroll 260 Russians selected by the KGB-connected Diplomatic Service Bureau. No doubt, Mr. Gorbachev's dismissal order will cause temporary inconvenience for the Foreign Service. But the wonder of it all is that the order came from Moscow, not Washington.

□ The Kremlin says it has 300 people working in its Washington and San Francisco missions compared with 460 persons employed at U.S. diplomatic posts in Moscow and Leningrad. If we subtract those 260 KGB-selected employees mentioned above, Moscow enjoys a 100-person edge — even using Soviet figures.

We suspect that both superpowers, without losing face, would like to end the present tit-for-tat game in expelling diplomats so they can explore arms control proposals offered at the Reykjavik summit. If so, Mr. Gorbachev's attempt to declare a defeat a victory is well-timed. Americans should generously allow him to co-sponsor the principle of equivalency in the staffing of American and Soviet diplomatic posts.

Moscow Hosts Peace Forum

The Soviet Union hosted an international forum on peace Feb. 14-16, 1987. The forum's formal theme was a "Non-Nuclear World for the Survival of Mankind." It was attended by over 700 artists, scientists, business executives and some public officials from 80 nations. Although sponsored by the Soviet government, the forum was organized as a private conference and participation was by invitation only.

Prominent Western participants included: former Canadian Prime Minister Pierre Elliott Trudeau; writers Graham Greene of Great Britain and Norman Mailer of the United States; American industrialist Armand Hammer; actors Gregory Peck and Kris Kristofferson of the United States and Peter Ustinov of Great Britain; musician/performance artist Yoko Ono; physician/peace activist Dr. Bernard Lown; and Social Democratic politician Egon Bahr of West Germany.

Perhaps the most unexpected participant was Andrei Sakharov, the Soviet dissident physicist who had been released in 1986 after 17 years of internal exile. (See pp. 202-205.) Sakharov addressed the forum Feb. 14, in his first appearance at a major official function since his return from exile. Foreign journalists were barred from hearing his 10-minute speech, but forum participants later told the press that the physicist had appealed for a more democratic Soviet Union.

The highlight of the forum was an address by Soviet leader Mikhail S. Gorbachev on Feb. 16, the closing day. The one-hour speech was nationally televised in the U.S.S.R. Gorbachev expressly linked his drive for economic and political reforms in the Soviet Union to his arms control intiatives. "You have arrived in the Soviet Union when essential revolutionary changes are under way," he told the participants. He told them that the changes were "irreversible." The general secretary surprised some onlookers by failing to offer new initiatives on arms control. Instead, he devoted part of his speech to criticizing the U.S. for considering a broad interpretation of the 1972 ABM (antiballistic missile) treaty in order to facilitate development of the Strategic Defense Initiative.

Los Angeles Times
Los Angeles, CA, February 18, 1987

Mikhail S. Gorbachev disappointed those who expected him to use the extraordinary party that he hosted in Moscow over the weekend—a peace forum attended by movie stars, novelists, scientists and assorted other famous folk from all over the world—to announce some new, dramatic arms-control proposal. It didn't happen. Instead, the Soviet leader used the publicity-generating presence of his glamorous guests to press the theme that the Soviet Union wants and needs peaceful and stable relations with the West so that it can concentrate on domestic concerns.

Soviet foreign policy, Gorbachev said, "is more than ever determined by domestic policy, by our interest in concentrating on constructive endeavor to improve our country. This is why we need lasting peace, predictability and constructiveness in international relations."

Gorbachev's conciliatory plea deserves to be treated seriously. There is ample evidence that the rejuvenation of the Soviet economy really is his top-priority goal; it makes sense that his reform program could be pursued more vigorously if East-West frictions could be eased. Western governments obviously must give him a chance to demonstrate his sincerity.

So far, though, the plain truth is that the Soviet leader has not done all that he could do to overcome suspicions that his rhetoric of peace and accommodation is mostly for propaganda effect.

Gorbachev, for example, talks a good game about removing Soviet troops from Afghanistan. But, when you examine the fine print, Moscow is still demanding peace on its own terms, paying no more than lip service to the Afghan people's right to self-determination.

The Soviet leader lambastes President Reagan's apparent intention of bulling ahead with the testing of "Star Wars" components. The Times has repeatedly expressed its own concern about the President's refusal to accept meaningful restraints on Star Wars development. But if Gorbachev himself is willing to work out an agreement drawing the line between acceptable and unacceptable forms of research and testing of missile defense systems, he and his negotiators should plainly say so. If he really is interested in reducing the chance of nuclear war, he should stop using the impasse on Star Wars as an excuse to block agreement on the reduction of offensive missiles of medium and intercontinental range—an area in which the two sides are within negotiating distance.

The return of dissident Andrei D. Sakharov to Moscow from enforced exile in Gorky, together with the release of 150-odd political prisoners, is certainly welcome. But Gorbachev's avowal of a new, more relaxed policy on human rights would be more credible if human-rights pronouncements were being publicized inside the Soviet Union; instead, they are being made by Foreign Ministry spokesmen basically for foreign consumption.

Finally, it is hard to square Gorbachev's soft words with the Soviet propaganda campaigns alleging that the disease AIDS was concocted by U.S. biological-warfare experts, and suggesting that the American CIA was somehow responsible for the assassination of Swedish Prime Minister Olaf Palme.

It was with such thoughts in mind that a bipartisan majority of the U.S. Senate voted overwhelmingly on Tuesday for a resolution cautioning the Soviets against efforts to "exploit American domestic politics or divide the United States from its allies."

The overall positive tone of Gorbachev's speech on Monday was encouraging. There is a reasonable prospect that he meant what he said. But, as a State Department spokesman noted, it can't be accepted as gospel until the Soviet Union does more to close the gap between words and deeds.

THE DAILY OKLAHOMAN
*Oklahoma City, OK
February 18, 1987*

EVER since he took over as head of the Soviet government, Mikhail Gorbachev has fascinated some people in the West who want to believe he's different from his predecessors.

He has impressed them with his intelligence, suave demeanor and candor. They believe his drive for more openness in government presages deep changes in Soviet society, especially in its attitude toward human rights.

Thus, many of them gathered in the Kremlin the other day for a world forum on "peace and disarmament." Delegates included Soviet and foreign (including U.S.) scientists, film stars, doctors, businessmen and other public figures.

No doubt they took Gorbachev at his word when he told them the Soviet Union is changing its approach to human rights and also that his arms control proposals show it is prepared to give up its status as a nuclear power and reduce all other weapons to minimum needs.

We'd all like to believe the leopard has changed its spots and that the Soviets are not still committed to global communist expansion. Yet people not blind to Russian history under Marxism know that Gorbachev is a product of the Soviet system and cannot change it without junking that ideology.

As George Urban, director of Radio Free Europe, wrote a year ago, Gorbachev cannot challenge his legacy without undermining his claim to leadership and the legitimacy of the Soviet system.

The Providence Journal

Providence, RI, February 18, 1987

Harold Macmillan, the wise old British prime minister who died last December at the age of 92, used to say that action is important in politics, but the appearance of action is essential. Mikhail Gorbachev, the wise young (55) General Secretary of the Soviet Communist Party, clearly understands Macmillan's thesis. Better yet, he is putting it into practice.

In the superpower game of chess, Mr. Gorbachev is proving that action for its own sake, movement, rhetoric, balm and spectacle may sometimes be their own reward, and that the superficial trappings of reform can generate the same volume of applause as the real thing.

Indeed, he may believe that it is not "pressure ... from the West" but "socialist choice" that has impelled him to reorganize his bureaucracy, free some political prisoners, and conduct nuclear diplomacy in public. He may believe that, but it's not necessarily so: It is Western pressure that helps to guide his hand, and it takes the form of public relations.

Mr. Gorbachev has learned what his predecessors did not fully appreciate: That in the Age of the Bomb, the West is so anxious for friendly signals it will sometimes overestimate the importance of nearly any Soviet gesture or pronouncement.

This is not to say that Mr. Gorbachev's reforms are insignificant; they are not. It *is* to say, however, that propaganda is designed to distort perceptions rather than clarify vision, and that the best weapon in any diplomat's briefcase remains perspec-

tive. Mr. Gorbachev is a master showman, and his brilliance may sometimes be blinding.

Consider the Moscow Forum for a Nuclear-Free World and the Survival of Mankind, currently convening in the Soviet capital. The name nearly stands by itself; a final communique would be redundant. The Kremlin has assembled an extraordinary cast of characters from all corners of the globe: The credulous, the ingenuous, the fearful and the faithful, believers in arms control, believers in profit, seekers of friendship and cultivators of publicity.

Andrei Sakharov, who until recently languished in internal exile, is now rubbing shoulders with actors, disarmers, bankers, and novelists. Scholars like Yoko Ono are in earnest conversation with entertainers like John Kenneth Galbraith. All have been treated to Mr. Gorbachev's energetic oratory, and each has been invigorated by the daily release of this activist or that dissident.

Let a hundred Forums flourish, we say. The Soviet Union seldom conducts its affairs in public, and even a breath of sunshine, or a glimpse of Norman Mailer, might ease the burden of monotony and repression. Let each delegate work his way to Dr. Sakharov, however, and ask him about the nature of his country's system, the condition of human rights, and the relative importance of celebrity gatherings to the principle of liberty, the deliverance from fear, or the kindling of the spirit of democratic rule.

The Star-Ledger

Newark, NJ, February 28, 1987

The new "openness" of the Soviet Union that Russian leader Mikhail Gorbachev is vigorously promoting as a hallmark of his modernization movement was given a new wrinkle at an international "peace forum" in Moscow. It wasn't so much what Mr. Gorbachev had to say, but what was more impressive was the illustrious list of honor guests the Kremlin had gathered for the occasion.

In his address, the Soviet leader reiterated a litany of familiar charges against the Reagan Administration. He accused the President of trying to undermine a Russian proposal—a bargaining chip put on the table at the Geneva summit meeting in 1985—to prevent an arms race in space (Star Wars Initiative) and to enhance strategic arms stability.

Among the several hundred carefully selected prominent guests who heard the hour-long Gorbachev speech was the Soviet dissident, physicist Andrei Sakharov. Asked about his reaction to the address, Mr. Sahkarov, with his customary candor, replied: "Good ideas, but not new."

That was precisely the point. The Gorbachev speech was of secondary importance. What was more important was the international "window dressing" provided by the select audience—the religious leaders colorfully arrayed in black, white and saffron robes, the mix of capitalists with resident Communists, scientists and the celebrity presence of film stars and well-known authors.

Perhaps the most dramatic note was the unexpected presence of Dr. Sakharov. Not that the Nobel Prize-winning scientist did not belong with the elitist gathering, but that it was less than two months since he had been released from a lonely internal exile in the closed city of Gorky.

The peace forum was a cleverly devised backdrop to focus international attention on the Gorbachev regime, its purportedly more enlightened stance on human rights, and its commitment to a more open stance with the West. Mr. Gorbachev has shown that he can be an articulate, well-informed "point man" in promoting the latest version of Soviet revisionism.

Give the man his due. He has a charming quality that sharply contrasts with the dour, intimidating demeanor and the ponderous rhetoric of his predecessors in the Kremlin. But the full measure of Gorbachev policies and reforms will be in deeds, and not in words, nor carefully orchestrated peace forums with elitist international audiences.

" GLAD YOU COULD MAKE IT. "

Amerika Miniseries Aired Drawing Broad Criticism

The controversial television miniseries *Amerika* aired Feb. 15-20, 1987 in the United States. *Amerika* portrayed the U.S. 10 years after a Soviet takeover. It starred Robert Urich and Kris Kristofferson. Ironically, Kristofferson, who played an anti-Soviet patriot in the program, was attending the Moscow peace conference when the program debuted. (See pp. 110-111.) The 15-hour miniseries, produced by Capital Cities/ABC Inc., cost a record $40 million. Based on preliminary ratings, about 70 million Americans watched the opening episode Feb. 15. But the ratings plummetted during the remainder of the week due, according to commentary, to the presentation's turgid pace and complex plot.

The Soviet Union and U.S. peace groups denounced the miniseries as anti-Soviet propaganda. On the other side, some American conservatives argued that the program did not accurately reflect the horror of Soviet occupation. ABC Television offices in several U.S. cities were picketed by peace activists Feb. 15.

In related developments:
■ Chrysler Corp. Jan. 27 withdrew the commercial advertising, valued at about $5 million, it had planned to run during *Amerika*. In a statement, Chrysler explained that its "upbeat product commercials" would be "inappropriate" for the program.
■ Kristofferson Feb. 12 taped a 30-second public service announcement praising the United Nations. The action was taken partly to offset the U.N.'s strong objections to *Amerika*. In the program, the Soviets used soldiers, identified as U.N. peacekeeping troops, to subjugate the American populace. The U.N. symbol was incorporated into the flag of the occupying forces.

Pittsburgh Post-Gazette
Pittsburgh, PA, March 12, 1987

One of the most dramatic examples of media hype — and anti-media hype — was the controversy earlier this year about the television mini-series "Amerika."

The ABC drama, which depicted life in a future Soviet-occupied America, was savaged by critics on the left who seemed to believe that it would foment hatred against the Soviet Union, with God knows what consequences for world peace. At least during its production, some right-wingers seemed to attribute similarly miraculous powers to a mere piece of entertainment. Now Americans would finally wise up about the Evil Empire!

Well, we can all breathe a sigh of relief. According to a survey by a professor at George Washington University, "Amerika" came, was seen but did not conquer any attitudes. The poll conducted by Prof. William Adams showed that the series had no measurable effect on attitudes toward the Soviet Union, the United Nations or U.S.-Soviet relations.

Concluded Prof. Adams: "It takes more than a television mini-series to shift longstanding opinions on fundamental issues." No kidding.

Chicago Tribune
Chicago, IL, February 18, 1987

Political theater is to theater as military music is to music. Just this week Americans have been treated to two marvelous examples.

ABC-TV is running an interminable miniseries called "Amerika" about a Soviet takeover of this country. It has stirred up so much controversy that you have to wonder who is more confused about what is reality and what is showbiz, the network or its liberal antagonists.

Made-for-TV movies, whether of the teary-eyed disease of the week variety or the so-called "docudramas," are not exactly models of political subtlety, or any other kind of subtlety, for that matter. Good guys and bad guys are the stuff of melodrama and miniseries, in the grand tradition of the old horse operas with the guys in the white hats prevailing over the guys in the black. But TV is nothing if not dedicated to equality of opportunity. Sometimes it makes the patriots the bad guys, sometimes it makes them the good guys. Business people fare similarly, as do U.S. intelligence agents, cops, journalists and so on.

What TV does not do is make the same person both good and evil, as mixed as human nature is mixed, nor does it make history as complex and morally ambiguous as it always turns out to be. Instead, we get alternating simple-minded TV visions of the future.

First it was "The Day After," which demonstrated the proposition that nuclear war is hazardous to health. Now it is "Amerika," which asserts that it is better not to be Red. The only wonder is that anyone takes any of it seriously.

Another kind of political theater is taking place in Moscow, in between "Donahue" shows. The Soviet Union invited a lot of American celebrities to go over for what is billed as an international peace conference. Some of the usual suspects showed up: Norman Mailer, Gore Vidal, Yoko Ono, John Kenneth Galbraith and Kris Kristofferson, who has the dubious distinction of starring in both shows simultaneously, because he has a leading role in "Amerika."

They got a chance to hear Mikhail Gorbachev describe his vision of the new Soviet state. Only days after secret police thugs violently broke up a street rally in Moscow, Mr. Gorbachev said, with unintended irony, that the new approach to human rights "is there for all to see."

The purpose of the celebrity delegation was, as always, to be there to be seen. It became part of the stage setting, which is the whole purpose of being a celebrity in the first place. And it does not really matter what the purpose the play really serves, or who is doing the directing.

The Augusta Chronicle
Augusta, GA
February 18, 1987

It ended.

The long years of resistance to Communist takeover of a free people simply folded like a collapsed deck of cards.

That's the haunting basis of the week-long ABC-TV miniseries, "Amerika," and it's no wonder the Soviet Union and its domestic apologists are screaming foul.

This drama about life in the United States under Soviet occupation is striking a responsive chord among many Americans because a stark lesson is there for all to learn.

The fall of America in "Amerika" reminds us of those dark days in April 1975, when South Vietnam fell to Communist slavery — one of the most shameful pages in U.S. history.

We do not belabor the matter of recriminations, since what is past is past. We note, only because the record speaks so clearly, that Vietnam was lost because of astoundingly naive and stupid policies, and because of unabashed failure to realize that Communist "peace" agreements aren't worth the paper they are printed on.

And these things were compounded then due to a U.S. Congress which lost its determination to resist the spread of a communistic New Dark Ages over Southeast Asia.

"Amerika" focuses on this same U.S. collapse of will which resulted in slavery for the Vietnamese people.

The series subtly asks how a free people can allow their freedom to be taken away without a fight.

That's excellent food for thought, especially for young people often subjected to leftist propaganda in our high schools and colleges.

We must ask again: Will a free America fall in the real world, as "Amerika" suggests, because complacent men and women have grown tired of defending anything?

We hope not but we wonder.

THE SAGINAW NEWS

Saginaw, MI, February 25, 1987

Poor "Amerika." Nobody loved it and a lot of people left it.

This was the television series with a minimum guaranteed audience — everyone who just "knew" what it ought to say, or was going to say.

As this fictional world turned out, not often did those preconceived notions coincide with the vision of Donald Wrye, who did the actual writing and directing. What he had in mind, said Wrye, was an exploration of how Americans might react to losing their freedoms under foreign domination. Russia? Well, as it was pointed out on the "Viewpoint" post-mortem, would anyone have believed Bermuda?

It is also a little hard to believe Wrye and the ABC network could not have predicted that the show would be viewed through glasses colored in tones of individual political beliefs. For different reasons, that audience would have been satisfied only if "Amerika" had indulged in 14½ hours of Russian-bashing.

Then the left, which seems to forgive any Soviet transgression, including the original alliance with Hitler, on the grounds of "peace," could say, see, we told you so. The other side could, conversely, cheer a portrayal of Soviet monstrosity.

Well, Wrye had other literary ambitions. "Amerika" began in lethargy and concluded in ambiguity, with a whimper, not a bang-up victory for liberty or, alternatively, brutal crushing of it. The show people were looking for, said network chief Brandon Stoddard, is "another show."

Maybe America needs a sequel. "Amerika" got lost in rhetoric — sometimes its own, but mostly that of people who refuse to respect an artist's intentions.

The Hutchinson News

Hutchinson, KS, February 17, 1987

Not to worry, komrades. "Amerika" won't get them aroused.

Those Amerikanskes could be more of a threat to international kommunism if they really got serious about demokracy. They've been getting lazy about demokracy lately.

As kommunists know, demokracy works only when the people make it work, and will fail when the people don't bother to get informed, get involved and get with it.

So relax, komrades. The Amerikanskes won't get any revolutionary message from "Amerika." It's so boring the only message those Amerikanskes are going to get watching "Amerika" is from their bladders.

THE CHRISTIAN SCIENCE MONITOR

Boston, MA, February 18, 1987

WHAT is real? In the United States we are asked to look at a television series, "Amerika," and imagine that Americans have handed over to fictitious Russians the democratic freedoms that Americans fought a revolution, a civil war, numerous civil rights wars, and continuous other legal and personal battles to ensure. As if to mock the fiction, the Miss America pageant goes on amid a controversy over whether contestants should parade in real furs or fake.

Meanwhile, in Moscow with a "c," Mikhail Gorbachev stages a "peace pageant" of his own, to which Gregory Peck and Kris Kristofferson were invited. We are finding it hard to discern whether dissident Iosif Begun has been released or is still detained – much as outsiders are straining to perceive whether the release of 140 other detainees, the publishing of long-banned books, and other signs of "freedom" within the Soviet Union are real or imagined.

In Washington, again, the latest reports in the Iran scandal are of a dark side to Project Democracy, the undertaking President Reagan announced in London during his first European tour in 1982. Project Democracy was advertised as a kind of free-enterprise foreign policy effort, with older democracies supposedly leading the way in by fostering free institutions like the press, political parties, and universities. Billionaires were invited to support it. Unfortunately, the undertaking apparently soon acquired a secret side – a covert network of communications, emissaries, arms suppliers, and transportation facilities, under the direction of the National Security Council's former employee Oliver North. Such an operation, designed to circumvent the established foreign policy apparatus with its legislative and judicial review, mocks the true meaning of democracy. What fantasy land must officials and their colleagues inhabit when they determine that a democracy's tasks are too urgent to be decided openly and left to the elected representatives of the people?

Another irony: Today marks the 40th anniversary of the first Voice of America broadcast to the Soviet Union. The Voice seems like an almost quaint institution, now that television satellites bring Moscow and Washington spokesmen together for instant discussion or confrontation. Yet the Voice has played a long and useful role in reporting on world affairs. The daily Voice dispatches, heard by millions of Soviet citizens, help build a foundation for democratic freedom there by broadcasting an independent view of world affairs.

Times change. Mr. Gorbachev can see that the Soviet Union needs to release some of the creativity of the Soviet intelligentsia, its scientists and managers, if his state is ever to meet its economic and cultural goals. With every inch of freedom comes the risk of greater expectations, which if not realized can lead to bitterness and dissent. Given the strains within the Soviet system and the history of repeated repressions, the West should be cautious in expecting either too much or too little of Gorbachev's *glasnost*. When he contends that peace with the West is requisite for his freedom experiment to succeed, he is probably right. He may be about to give up on the Reagan administration, which wants to reinterpret the ABM Treaty to permit "star wars" deployment.

In Washington, the Reagan administration's credibility comes under daily review. Does it mean what it says about democratic idealism, or is it secretly and willfully pursuing a separate agenda?

Freedom is a process that West and East cannot afford to trivialize.

Richmond Times-Dispatch

Richmond, VA, March 5, 1987

Liberal critics of ABC's "Amerika" have indignantly denounced the miniseries, charging, among other things, that it would poison relations between the two superpowers and give viewers a bad impression of the Soviet Union. It turns that out they had nothing to worry about. Americans, it seems, already had a bad impression of the Soviet Union, and "Amerika" did little to change it.

According to a George Washington University poll of 1,110 adults before and after last month's showing of "Amerika:"

• An "overwhelming majority" of those surveyed believed there would be mass executions, concentration camps and less freedom of speech if the Soviets took over.

• Sixty-three percent said they believed the Soviets would like to take over the United States.

• Before "Amerika" aired, 69 percent said they would rather be dead than red. After it aired, the figure was 72 percent.

• Forty-five percent of those surveyed believe that the grim portrayal of life in "Amerika" is an accurate depiction of what life would be like under Soviet occupation. Another 25 percent said it would be even worse.

Maybe the real problem here is not a TV program. Maybe, just maybe, it's the Soviets themselves.

U.S., Soviets Agree on Treaty to End INF Missiles

U.S. President Reagan Sept. 18, 1987 announced that the U.S. and Soviet Union had tentatively agreed on a treaty for the global elimination of medium-range nuclear missiles. The two sides had begun work in Geneva on reconciling separate draft treaties on intermediate nuclear forces (INF). The provisions of the announced accord would be incorporated into a final treaty. The INF breakthrough had been negotiated by U.S. Secretary of State George Shultz and Soviet Foreign Minister Eduard Shevardnadze, and their staffs, Sept. 15-17 in Washington, D.C.

Reagan made the formal announcement of the agreement at a brief White House news conference that was attended by Shultz. "I am pleased to note that an agreement in principle was reached to conclude an INF treaty," the President told reporters. "I want to congratulate Secretary Shultz and Foreign Minister Shevardnadze and their delegations for their outstanding efforts over the past three days."

In addition, Reagan said, the two sides had agreed to mount an "intensive treaty on bilateral 50% reduction of strategic (long-range) nuclear weapons. Reagan also announced that Shultz and Shevardnadze would meet in Moscow in October to finalize arrangements for a summit meeting in the U.S. between the President and Soviet General Secretary Mikhail S. Gorbachev. The summit was expected to take place before the end of 1987, probably in the late autumn. The two leaders could use the meeting to sign an INF treaty.

When the President invited questions from the floor, one reporter asked him if he still believed the Soviet to be an "evil empire." Reagan replied: "I still don't think its lilly-white."

Shultz took the podium after the President left the briefing room. The secretary expressed optimism on slowing down the arms race. However, he cautioned: "There are still a lot of very important problems to be worked out." At a press conference at the Soviet embassy in Washington Sept. 18, Foreign Minister Shevardnadze told reporters that the INF accord "marked a common success for all mankind."

Neither the U.S. nor the Soviet Union gave specific details of the tentative accord announced Sept. 18. The U.S. press gleaned some details from statements, both on and off the record, by U.S. officials close to the Shultz-Shevardnadze talks. The two sides were reported to have traded concessions with regard to arms control. The compromises were not limited to INF weapons.

The key concession by the Soviets had come Sept. 17, when Shevardnadze agreed that West Germany's 72 Pershing 1A missiles would not be included in the text of a U.S.-Soviet INF treaty. An important concession by the U.S. had been reported Sept. 15. In answer to a major Soviet objection, the U.S. agreed that it should begin removing INF missiles from Western Europe as soon as the treaty too effect. Washington had previously insisted that the Soviet arsenal, superior in number, be cut to the level of the U.S. weapons, at which time the two sides would make simultaneous reductions.

Initial reaction to the tentative accord was laudatory, but some U.S. politicians tempered their praise Sept. 18. U.S. Senate Majority Leader Robert Byrd (D, W. Va.) said, "I am optimistic that there is progress, but we will have to review the treaty language and the fine print. The Senate may add reservations or understandings of its own." U.S. Rep. Les Aspin (D, Wis.), the chairman of the Armed Services Committee of the House of Representatives, told reporters: "I think that it's essentially a political agreement. Its political implications are far more important than the military agreement.

The Grand Rapids Press

Grand Rapids, MI, September 20, 1987

Since last Friday, there's been a patch of sunlight lying across the deep and dark shadow of the nuclear arms race. Though much more waits to be done, the meeting last week between Secretary of State George Shultz and Soviet Foreign Minister Eduard Shevardnadze was an unusually positive step toward a safer world.

The two leaders met to iron out an agreement on short and medium-range missiles. Under the accord, which is still a few steps from completion, the U.S. and Soviets would begin to eliminate their stockpiles of the shorter range missiles, most of which are in Europe. Two stumbling blocks to a treaty apparently were cleared: The two sides agreed to a compromise on the 72 West German missiles that carry U.S. warheads, and a consensus is near on verification procedures. Barring unforeseen problems, President Reagan and General Secretary Mikhail Gorbachev will meet this year to sign an intermediate nuclear forces (INF) treaty.

Those were accomplishments enough for a meeting between American and Soviet diplomats. But Mr. Shultz and Mr. Shevardnadze went further. They agreed to begin negotiations in December on a test-ban treaty and gave hints that similar talks on reductions in strategic nuclear weapons might also be arranged. Moreover, the Soviets have shown in recent months a new willingness to discuss reductions in conventional forces in Europe.

It's difficult to be overly optimistic where superpowers and war machines are concerned. For 40 years, while the nuclear stockpiles multiplied, the two countries have reacted to each other with the utmost suspicion and fear. The arms race has slowed on occasion, only to speed up again or take another dangerous turn.

The difference now seems to be a Soviet leader acutely aware of the economic wear-and-tear caused by an unending defense buildup and an American president smart enough to see an opportunity for peace and seize it. Mr. Gorbachev knows his nation will not thrive if it does not diversify its economy and cease building fences of nuclear weapons separating his people from the rest of the world. He is not about to disarm his nation, but he and Mr. Reagan apparently are willing to think the hitherto unthinkable: that the nuclear arms race can be ended without endangering world peace.

There are skeptics in Congress and in the Soviet Politburo; the extent of their influence will be discovered in the coming months. Some senators are rightly concerned that an INF agreement will leave the Soviets with a clear superiority of conventional forces in Europe. But Mr. Gorbachev's apparent openness about talks regarding non-nuclear forces should defuse some of that criticism. Besides, how can one argue against a reduction of nuclear arms because of other inequities in the defense picture? If we wait for parity on all levels before completing an arms deal, a treaty likely will never be signed.

It's not hard to set up insurmountable obstacles to an arms accord, or any kind of agreement for that matter. What's hard is to inch forward, to take the political heat, to move patiently and deliberately to reduce the threat of nuclear annihilation. That's what the U.S. and Soviets are doing these days, and their success, in this opening act at least, is worth applauding.

Herald News

Fall River, MA, September 21, 1987

President Reagan has announced that he and Mikhail Gorbachev will meet in Washington before the end of the year to sign a treaty eliminating medium and short range nuclear missiles from the armaments of both the United States and Soviet Russia.

The President's announcement followed several days of negotiation between Secretary of State Shultz and Foreign Minister Shevardnadze. Those negotiations took place in an atmosphere of increasing optimism, and their successful conclusion came as no surprise.

The announcement that a treaty eliminating medium and short range missiles has been generally received with enthusiasm abroad, although Lord Carrington, speaking for NATO, pointed out it will leave western Europe vulnerable.

This is certainly true, and is one of the principal reasons why the negotiations have taken so long. Western Europe has depended for its own safety since the end of World War II on the nuclear shield provided for the most part by this country.

If both superpowers lower their nuclear shields, the defense of western Europe will depend on conventional forces and weapons.

But it is no secret that the conventional forces and weapons in the Soviet Union and its satellites far outmatch those in the west.

NATO with that in mind must set about rebuilding its defenses, and while the United States will participate in that process, its European partners will have to assume a larger role than they have been accustomed to play.

This is the price the west must pay for the elimination of medium and shorter range nuclear missiles. It is a mistake to assume that their elimination can be carried out without exacting a price in return.

The relief that will be felt at the removal of some aspects of the nuclear threat will soon be replaced by concern over the new effort and expense NATO must assume in order to strengthen western defenses.

But at present the dominant emotion here as well as abroad is enthusiasm for the new treaty, and if Gorbachev comes here to sign it before January, the President will be able to end 1987, which has been far from smooth sailing for him, on a positive note.

With all the reservations that many Americans justly feel about the new treaty, it does represent a lessening of the nuclear threat at least for the time being, and that is good news for us all.

What it portends for the future is another question, one that will not be answered for some time to come.

The Record

Hackensack, NJ, September 21, 1987

How did it happen?

With Secretary of State George Shultz and Soviet Foreign Minister Eduard Shevardnadze reaching tentative agreement Friday on a treaty banning short- and medium-range land-based missiles, this is the question of the hour. How could an administration once opposed to the very notion of détente now be on the verge of the most important arms agreement since the early Seventies?

The answers can be found on both sides of the superpower gulf. In Washington, the Reagan administration has undergone a sea change. The president, who once denounced the Soviet Union as "the focus of evil in the modern world," is now politically weaker, badly wounded by the Iran-contra scandal. Partly for that reason, the ideological composition of his administration has changed. Hawks like Assistant Defense Secretary Richard N. Perle, United Nations Ambassador Jeane Kirkpatrick, Communications Director Patrick Buchanan, and Navy Secretary John Lehman are gone; moderates like Secretary of State George Shultz and Chief of Staff Howard Baker are in command.

The president has gotten the message that his "evil empire" talk and his administration's huge arms buildup alarmed a large segment of the public. The American people know that nuclear war is unthinkable and unwinnable.

They are leery of another Vietnam and have no stomach for another anti-Communist crusade. Détente, despite years of abuse by hard-liners, is not so unpopular with the average voter. Americans want their presidents to sit down with the Soviets and negotiate. They favor arms control, along with joint U.S.-Soviet measures to reduce international tension.

•

The changes in Moscow have been, if anything, even more dramatic. When Mr. Reagan took office, his Soviet counterpart was Leonid Brezhnev, an aging, infirm bureaucrat who was as feeble politically as he was physically. Mikhail Gorbachev, by contrast, is showing extraordinary creativity and flair in the game of international diplomacy. In the Reagan administration's early days, it was an article of faith that Soviet totalitarianism left absolutely no room for dissent, debate, or internal change. The sweeping reforms that go under the name glasnost have shown that Soviet society is not as frozen and immutable as was once believed.

Thanks to these political and societal shifts on both sides, a good bit of common sense has managed to sneak through the battle lines. It has produced, at last, the first significant arms-control advance in this decade.

The Des Moines Register

*Des Moines, IA
September 22, 1987*

The public and the White House are understandably thrilled at the prospect of a U.S.-Soviet summit in which President Reagan and General Secretary Mikhail Gorbachev will sign their first arms-control agreement.

The treaty, which would ban medium-range nuclear missiles in Europe, comes after more than six years of tedious negotiating and political maneuvering. Its military impact will be minor; it eliminates only 2,000 of the 25,000 nuclear warheads in U.S. and Soviet arsenals. But the political ramifications are enormous.

The agreement marks a dramatic departure by President Reagan from the "evil empire" rhetoric that once characterized his approach to U.S.-Soviet relations. The summit will also be seen by members of the Soviet Politburo as a test of Gorbachev's ability to deal both with the United States and his own military bureaucracy.

But euphoria over the emergence of what some analysts have labeled Detente II should not mask the serious challenge still ahead for U.S.-Soviet relations. Star Wars, long-range nuclear missiles and the defense of NATO Europe are not dealt with in this plan.

Gorbachev has offered to begin talks on cutting strategic nuclear arsenals next year. But the Soviets have always predicated such talks on cuts in the Star Wars program, and it is unlikely that President Reagan will abandon what has become his pet project in his final year in office.

Additional progress on arms control is also contingent upon a new military strategy for NATO. The ban on medium-range nuclear weapons returns Western Europe to a defense based on conventional military forces and the threat of a U.S. submarine-launched nuclear strike. Any additional cuts in nuclear arsenals, therefore, will have to include a rethinking of NATO defense strategy.

"This doesn't solve all the problems by a long shot," warned Secretary of State George Shultz.

But even if the agreement is not a solution, it is a start. As such, the summit should mark not the end of U.S.-Soviet arms-control negotiations, but the beginning.

The Register-Guard
Eugene, OR, September 22, 1987

Soviet leader Mikhail Gorbachev will come this fall to the United States, where he and President Reagan will sign the first treaty between their two nations that actually reduces, not just limits, nuclear weaponry. This is an enormously encouraging development, but any parades would be premature. A variety of obstacles could frustrate a successful summit. Even if the treaty is signed, it will be only a beginning.

On Friday the two nations announced an agreement in principle on a treaty that would eliminate two classes of nuclear missiles: those with a range of between 300 and 600 miles, and those with a range of between 600 and 3,000 miles. The accord would ease the risk of nuclear war in Europe, thereby achieving a long-standing aim of American and NATO policy.

Various ideas for limiting, freezing or eliminating Soviet and American nuclear weapons in Europe have been seriously proposed by both sides during the past five years. Indeed, the deployment of American Pershing and cruise missiles in Europe was intended to counter Soviet short-range SS-4 and mid-range SS-20 missiles and eventually force their withdrawal. If the arms treaty is signed and observed, this difficult and expensive strategy will have proven successful.

But the treaty is not yet ready for signature. Important questions of timing and verification must still be negotiated. Even if those issues are settled, ratification by the Senate is far from certain. Some senators don't trust the Soviets to abide by any arms agreement. Others have come to believe that American nuclear weapons in Europe are a necessary counterweight to the Soviets' superior conventional forces. And still others will attempt to use an arms treaty as a vehicle for broader arms control, foreign policy and even domestic issues.

Despite these obstacles, there's good reason to hope that a final treaty will be negotiated and ratified. Both Gorbachev and Reagan could use the political boost they would receive from a success in the arms control arena. Reagan is ideologically well positioned to achieve an agreement; few could accuse him of placing too much trust in the Soviets or of weakening American defenses. Gorbachev, for his part, reportedly needs to consolidate his position with a foreign policy achievement.

Elimination of short- and medium-range missiles, however, should be regarded as only the first step. The treaty would scrap a total of about 2,000 missiles — more than three-quarters of them Soviet. But both the Soviet Union and the United States would retain more than 20,000 nuclear weapons. While the agreement would represent a reduction in weaponry, nuclear arsenals would still be dangerously and expensively overstocked.

A treaty that scraps a few missiles should be taken as proof that greater efforts could lead to further agreements to dismantle some more. There are, of course, many barriers to further progress — including disagreements over the course of Reagan's Strategic Defense Initiative and arguments over compliance with past treaties. But even a relatively small step would demonstrate that progress is possible.

The agreement-in-principle announced Friday is significant in itself. If a final accord is signed and ratified, the threat of a hair-trigger nuclear war in Europe will recede. But such an agreement would acquire truly historical significance if it was the first — not the only — arms-reduction treaty. The first flower of spring is welcome, but better yet is the promise of more blossoms to come.

Wisconsin ⚖ State Journal
Madison, WI
September 21, 1987

For the first time since the dawn of the nuclear age, an arms-control treaty that would actually *eliminate* atomic weapons instead of simply limiting how many new missiles or bombs can be built is within the grasp of the United States and the Soviet Union.

Many details remain unsettled, but the "agreement in principle" announced by Secretary of State George Shultz and Soviet Foreign Minister Eduard Shevardnadze is unalloyed good news.

Those who would angrily denounce it as a "giveaway" or deride it as meaningless either don't want an arms-control treaty at all or don't want to admit that President Reagan's "hang tough" approach to checking the arms race is beginning to pay dividends.

No one should interpret this agreement to ban all intermediate-range missiles as meaning the nuclear sword of Damocles is no longer hanging over our heads. It is still there, and as sharp as ever. But to eliminate an entire class of nuclear weapons in one stroke is certainly a step toward more dramatic cuts in atomic arsenals.

Once details about verification and staging are worked out in Geneva, the United States and the Soviet Union will begin junking a combined 1,000 missiles in Europe and Asia. About two-thirds of those weapons are Soviet SS-4, SS-12, SS-20 and SS-23 missiles aimed at Western Europe, Japan and the People's Republic of China. The United States will scrap more than 330 Pershing II and "cruise" missiles; a dispute over U.S. warheads on 72 West German Pershing 1-A missiles is also close to settlement.

Another result of last week's meetings is that Reagan and Soviet leader Mikhail Gorbachev will hold a Washington summit, probably this fall. And while not directly linked to the intermediate missile treaty, Shultz and Shevardnadze said talks will begin by Dec. 1 on a possible nuclear test-ban treaty. That's a promising development because it signals a mutual desire not to replace scrapped missiles with newer models.

Finally, this agreement will knock the dust off U.S. and Soviet proposals to make deep cuts in each nation's long-range arsenals. Remember Reykjavik? That October 1986 "mini-summit" ended with Reagan and Gorbachev storming off empty-handed, but they left behind on the table a U.S. blueprint for deep cuts in long-range missiles, bombers, sea-launched missiles — the works. Gorbachev has since proposed his own version.

Let's hope that last week's "agreement in principle" quickly becomes an agreement in black and white for Senate consideration. Then, both sides should figure out how to blunt the nuclear sword, once and for all.

The Boston Globe
Boston, MA, September 19, 1987

If the US-Soviet agreement in principle to ban medium-range and shorter-range nuclear missiles becomes a turning point in the arms race, historians will count it as a triumph not only for US and Soviet leaders, but also for the millions around the globe who have pushed them in the right direction.

The reductions are less important than the precedent that will be set. The agreement will cover missiles with ranges from 315 to 3125 miles. These make up about 4 percent of the nuclear arsenals, and not one of the missiles has been targeted on the United States. Yet by agreeing for the first time to destroy weapons, the superpowers have set the stage for hacking away at redundancies elsewhere in the thicket of nuclear deterrence, especially in long-range missiles, which pose a far greater threat.

The administration will argue, with some justification, that the agreement has vindicated President Reagan's policy of pressing a huge military buildup so as to be able to "negotiate from strength." Obviously, the buildup helped concentrate the Kremlin's attention on the absurdity of continuing the relentless buildup of decades past.

The new leadership of Mikhail Gorbachev was also crucial. Gorbachev's recognition of the pointlessness of competition in overkill, and his willingness to seek compromise and exhibit flexibility where his predecessors would have held fast, helped break the superpower lock-step.

If progress follows in more important areas of arms control, the president and his advisers will share the credit with the members of Congress – prominently represented by Sen. Sam Nunn (D-Ga.) – who saved the Anti-Ballistic Missile Treaty and protected the administration from its instinct for military excess.

Behind Congress stands a second group, the freeze movement and its successors – citizens who have educated themselves about arms control, organized politically, and placed ending the arms race high on the national agenda.

This week's agreement will mean nothing if the buildup in long-range missiles is not stopped. It is ironic that President Reagan has repudiated the SALT treaties, which would do that. Until they are replaced with something better, the door to a continued arms race is wide open.

It is fine to be firm at a bargaining table. It is no less important, however, to have a sound negotiating position. In arms control, to hang tough with a poor negotiating position – for example, scrapping SALT and the 1972 ABM treaty and placing all bets on "star wars" – is the path to impasse and greater peril.

The overriding question now is whether there will be an agreement to improve upon SALT by achieving deep cuts in strategic missiles. This is what Reagan says he wants. Yet the Soviets, even as they accepted the agreement on intermediate-range nuclear missiles, made it clear that strategic cuts will depend on the United States' willingness to live within the ABM treaty and postpone the development of "star wars" space defenses for 10 years.

TULSA WORLD

Tulsa, OK, September 19, 1987

THE arms agreement between the United States and Soviet Union calls for praise, but the step must be taken carefully.

It's President Reagan's first arms accord with the Soviets and would ban medium- and shorter-range nuclear missiles. It would be the first agreement that would ban an entire class of nuclear weapons.

The pact also calls for a summit before the end of the year between Reagan and Soviet leader Mikhail Gorbachev.

The treaty would require dismantling 332 U.S. missiles in West Germany, Britain, Italy and Belgium aimed at the Soviet Union. In return, the Soviets would destroy 462 missiles targeted on Western Europe and another 221 pointed at China and Japan.

The two sides disagreed on a timetable but the difference was "essentially technical."

It all sounds like good news and is drawing kudos from both sides. And, of course, any step to protect the world against nuclear destruction is welcome.

But the U.S. must not become complacent in its defense measures. Although both superpowers will retain ample supplies of long-range nuclear weapons, the Russians retain a definite edge in conventional forces.

The U.S. has relied on its nuclear arsenal for the protection of Europe and has to some extent let its conventional force slide. Russia, on the other hand, has continued to make defense its top priority. The Soviet economy revolves around its military machine.

Banning short- and medium-range missiles — those with a range of 315 to 3,125 miles — leaves serious questions about the safety of Western Europe. Russia would have the upper hand in a conventional war in Europe.

And the Soviets have not shied away from confrontation. That's easy enough to document in countries such as Afghanistan and Ethiopia.

The U.S. while making a good-faith effort to reduce its nuclear arsenal must beef up its conventional forces. That may mean better training, pay and incentives for those serving in the military.

As both Secretary of State George Shultz and Soviet Foreign Minister Eduard Shevardnadze said: "It's a beginning."

And it's a good one, but the U.S. must proceed with caution.

The Union Leader

Manchester, NH, September 22, 1987

The arms pact being promoted with the Soviet Union is a most dangerous step backward for this nation, which is the ultimate target of communism.

The Communists are chess players. They let us concentrate on the move to give up one pawn while they plot toward boxing us into future moves that will put us at their mercy. If you don't believe it, note what their own Foreign Minister said of the new pact:

"We consider this particular treaty just step number one. We don't think that it is a big achievement in itself. The second step, which is a more important step (is an agreement) on strategic offensive arms."

And when the Soviets talk about strategic offensive arms, they are really talking about our only defense against their weapons — the SDI or Star Wars, if you will.

It is correct that step number one is not a big achievement. It concerns only 6 percent of the total nuclear missiles. We Americans are cheered by the fact that they give up 2,000 warheads to our 350, which is the pawn they offer in order to gain the more important goal. We ignore the fact that they retreat a few hundred miles into the security of their homeland and we retreat halfway around the world, leaving Europe to face the massive Soviet conventional forces.

The Communists are no fools. They know the only way they can survive is to destroy free enterprise. Lulling us into euphoria by signing useless agreements is part of their plan. Otherwise, why should they be hailing this treaty as progress?

There is no logic to signing deals with a regime that is publicly breaking the last one we made, a regime that is pursuing its bloody takeover of the free world while talking peace.

THE DENVER POST

September 21, 1987
Denver, CO

THE U.S.-Soviet "double-zero" agreement — in which both sides will ban intermediate-range nuclear missiles — is one small step for mankind away from the precipice of nuclear war.

Banning just one class of weapons, of course, cannot banish the specter of atomic annihilation. But the double-zero treaty still does double duty for the cause of human survival.

First, the agreement removes a particularly nettlesome factor from the nuclear equation. The U.S. and the Soviet Union can still hurl intercontinental missiles at each others homelands — or devastate each other with submarine-launched missiles.

But ICBMs take perhaps 30 minutes to complete their voyage to destruction. In contrast, a Pershing II missile fired from West Germany could strike Moscow with lethal precision in only eight minutes, while Soviet counterparts could wipe out key NATO command posts in Europe with equal speed. Such short flight times aroused fears of "decapitation" in both the NATO and Warsaw Pact camps — the possibility of a nuclear surprise attack wiping out key command and control facilities before the targeted country could respond. Eliminating such missiles thus reduces the potential for a first strike and ensures more time to think and evaluate in a crisis.

Similarly, submarine-launched missiles can reach many military targets swiftly — but generally lack the accuracy for "decapitation" strikes. Thus, the elimination of these short-leashed weapons gives the world a little more breathing room in a crisis.

The second — and greater — benefit is political. The first arms control agreement in the Reagan-Gorbachev era is a sign that the second cold war may be winding down — eight years after the Soviet invasion of Afghanistan sent superpower relations back into the deep freeze. As Colorado Sen. Tim Wirth noted Friday, the agreement raises hopes for a joint U.S.-Soviet ban on nuclear testing as well as subsequent trims of the existing nuclear arsenals.

We trust the treaty will be ratified as soon as the details are finished and it is formally presented to the Senate. It may be only one small step toward a true and lasting peace. But it is a step. And as the Chinese proverb so aptly puts it, a journey of a thousand miles begins with a single step.

The Washington Post

Washington, DC, September 17, 1987

PRESIDENT REAGAN on Tuesday oversaw the signing of an agreement with the Soviet Union to set up "nuclear risk reduction centers" in the two capitals. The event reflected and warms the atmosphere in which the two superpowers are currently working toward more conspicuous agreements. But the new agreement, which results from unusual lobbying in Moscow as well as Washington by Sens. Sam Nunn and John Warner, has its own importance in raising the profile of an area of overwhelming common concern.

The agreement commits each country to open a nuclear risk reduction center in its capital to keep 24-hour watch on "events with the potential to lead to nuclear incidents." It's more complicated than it may seem. Nuclear risks come in two categories. Those that are commonly though far from universally accepted are the risks that a government creates and tolerates, even as it tries to minimize them, in the course of building and deploying nuclear weapons. A government relying on a strategy of nuclear deterrence will not want risk reduction to inhibit the organization or conduct of its defense, and the agreement does not invade this sphere. The other kind of risks arises from "accident, miscalculation or misunderstanding," in the language of the new agreement, whose operating premise is that an adequately sharp line can be drawn between the two kinds.

Identifying risk reduction as a separate government function, one to be performed by its own office or bureaucracy, is new and raises considerations of turf, management and efficiency. Ideally, after all, the whole executive branch ought to be a nuclear risk reduction center, and there should be no need for any responsible official to be urged to tend to this supreme task. The practical difficulties—of sharing information and intelligence, for instance, or of communicating in a crisis—have induced the two governments to go slow. They are holding off on joint manning of the centers. They have given no specific mandate to the centers, but evidently are prepared to test certain possibilities of cooperation on nuclear terrorism or on nuclear threats by third parties. The initial emphasis is to be on rerouting certain routine, already existing exchanges of nuclear information through the new facilities. The shared intent seems to be to explore what usefully can be done. At least it's a start.

St. Petersburg Times

St. Petersburg, FL, September 22, 1987

The agreement between the United States and the Soviet Union to eliminate all their short and medium-range nuclear missiles comes as good news to a world that had begun to despair of halting the arms race. So why is the Senate Foreign Relations Committee threatening to delay ratification of the promised treaty?

The simple answer is that the new agreement, for all of its undeniable value, is less important than the 1972 Anti-Ballistic Missile (ABM) Treaty, which the committee is trying to protect.

Ideally, a decision to scrap the missiles in Europe ought to lead to a treaty reducing the much larger and powerful strategic nuclear forces that the superpowers aim at each other's heartlands. But that can't happen if the United States insists on sacrificing the ABM treaty to the testing or deployment of the Strategic Defense Initiative, commonly known as Star Wars. The Soviet Union would be forced to counter Star Wars in the cheapest available way, which would be to deploy enough new heavy missiles to overwhelm any U.S. defense.

The ABM treaty was intended to forestall just such a no-win situation. It limited each side to just one ground-based defensive installation and prohibited either the testing or deployment of space-based missile interceptors. At least that's how most people have read it, including the senators who ratified it and the members of the Foreign Relations Committee today. The Reagan administration contends, however, that the treaty would permit it to test critical Star Wars components in space.

To reach that conclusion, the administration has been forced to argue that the Senate was misled in 1972 by the Nixon administration officials who testified in support of the treaty. What they said was one thing, says the Reagan White House; what the U.S. and Soviet negotiators had agreed to in secret session was another.

Sen. Sam Nunn, the foreign relations chairman, insisted on reading the negotiating record for himself and assured the Senate that it supported no such cynical conclusion. Both the public and private record contravene any claim to the testing of space-based systems. But the administration still clings to its untenable position that what U.S. negotiators told the U.S. Senate in 1972 was not to be trusted.

If not then, why now? That's the reasoning behind Nunn's warning, as reinforced by a committee report issued Sunday, that the committee might have to delay the forthcoming Euromissiles treaty while it reads for itself the record of the negotiations that led to it. Of course, Nunn adds, that wouldn't be necessary if the administration agreed — as it should — to abide by the strict original interpretation of the 1972 treaty.

It's regrettable — indeed, tragic — that the Senate should even have to consider holding one worthwhile agreement hostage for another. But the Senate's caution is understandable given the strength of the administration's obsession with the untried, untested, unnecessary and very likely unaffordable Star Wars scheme. On the same day that Secretary of State George P. Shultz and Soviet Foreign Minister Eduard Shevadnadze reached their historic agreement in principle on the Euromissiles, Defense Secretary Caspar Weinberger approved a new testing phase intended to hurry Star Wars along. On Sunday, Frank C. Carlucci, the national security adviser, abandoned any pretense that Star Wars is simply a research program. "We intend to develop it as rapidly as we can and deploy it when it is ready," he said on *Meet the Press*.

Fortunately, however, the Senate should not have to delay the Euromissile treaty in order to make its point about protecting the ABM treaty. It needs simply to stand firm on the restrictive language in its defense authorization bill, affirmed by a floor vote last week, which prohibits the administration from conducting Star Wars tests in space without subsequent specific congressional approval. (A similar provision is in the House defense bill.) Mr. Reagan may veto that, but time is on Congress' side. The administration will have to have a defense spending bill at some point, and the same restriction can be added there.

The forthcoming agreement on Euromissiles is worthwhile for its own sake. It represents the first-ever decision to dismantle an entire nuclear weapons system. It proves that arms reductions are possible despite past rhetoric.

Mr. Reagan is entitled to this triumph. More to the point, so is all humanity.

The 🌳 State

Columbia, SC, September 20, 1987

FOURTEEN years ago, President Nixon and Soviet Premier Brezhnev signed SALT I — an agreement to limit defensive anti-ballistic missiles and to freeze levels of some offensive weapons. Friday, the fading spirit of detente between the two nuclear superpowers was cautiously revived with the announcement that the United States and the Soviet Union had reached an "agreement in principle" to ban medium- and shorter-range nuclear missiles. President Reagan himself added the icing with word that he and Soviet leader Mikhail Gorbachev will hold a summit — their third — before the end of the year.

In a brief announcement from the White House, the President was understandably upbeat — exuberant, almost — and why not? Things have not gone well for the Administration during the past year. The Iran-Contra debacle cast grave doubts as to his capacity to conduct foreign policy and the nomination of Robert H. Bork to a vacancy on the U.S. Supreme Court is under heavy siege by liberals and many Democrats on Capitol Hill.

A summit to sign a major arms agreement will most certainly — and rightly so — boost Mr. Reagan's stock in the United States and among our allies who have had their reasons to be skittish at recent pronouncements and policies of this Administration.

Cautious enthusiasm from abroad was immediate. In a terse, two-sentence statement, the North Atlantic Treaty Organization said, "we hope that an agreement will be the beginning of a process in which we can live at a much lower level of armaments for the same security."

The proposed treaty outlined Friday would be the first ever to ban an entire class of nuclear weapons. The agreement would do away with missiles with a range of 315 miles to 3,125 miles and would require the dismantling of 332 U.S. missiles in West Germany, Britain, Italy and Belgium that are aimed at the Soviet Union. In return, the Soviets would destroy 462 missiles targeted on Western Europe and another 221 pointed at China and Japan.

The American warheads on Pershing 1-A missiles installed in West Germany would not be a part of the treaty despite earlier Soviet insistence that they be included. Those warheads are, instead, part of a cooperative agreement with the West German government and would be removed under a plan already announced by Chancellor Helmut Kohl.

Indeed, Mr. Kohl's bold announcement last month that his country would dismantle the Pershing missiles was a crucial breakthrough and paved the way for the U.S. and Soviets to snap a deadlock which came to a head earlier in the summer. In July, Mr. Gorbachev had said the Soviets would accept the so-called "double zero" option, eliminating INF (intermediate-range nuclear forces) missiles, provided West Germany's Pershing missiles were included. At that time, U.S. negotiators refused to discuss the German missiles.

Arms control efforts have progressed at a decidedly measured pace since the Nixon-Brezhnev agreement of 1973. Before Mr. Nixon left office a year later, the two sides had agreed to limit underground nuclear weapons tests. In 1979, President Carter and Mr. Brezhnev agreed to the SALT II treaty that limited some strategic offensive weapons. At about the same time, NATO agreed to deploy Pershing II and cruise missiles to Western Europe to counter a Soviet buildup of SS-20 rockets.

The U.S. and the Soviets remained alarmingly aloof from each other during Mr. Reagan's first term in office. It was not until November, 1985, one year after his re-election landslide, that Mr. Reagan and Mr. Gorbachev held their first summit — a get-acquainted ice-breaker in Geneva at which the two leaders did little more than feel each other out and come to an exchange agreement on scientists and artists. Last year's followup summit at Reykjavik accomplished even less, largely because of Mr. Gorbachev's insistence that one of Mr. Reagan's pet programs — the Strategic Defense Initiative (Star Wars) — be abandoned.

The INF treaty now on the table needs fine-tuning, including details on verification and a timetable for dismantlement. It will also require ratification by two-thirds of the U.S. Senate. While the proposed pact does not address the issue of longer-range missile warheads, it reflects genuine progress towards the ultimate goal of total nuclear disarmament.

THE BILLINGS GAZETTE

Billings, MT, September 21, 1987

A tentative nuclear arms agreement between the Soviets and the United States will be poked and prodded over the next few months and for good reason.

Basically, the "agreement in principle" would impose a worldwide ban on U.S. and Soviet missiles with ranges from 315 miles to 3,125 miles.

Soviet Foreign Minister Eduard Shevardnadze called the tentative agreement "a common success for all mankind, for all civilization."

Secretary of State George Schultz said it was "an important beginning" in arms control.

Senate Majority Leader Robert C. Byrd pointed out that a treaty is not a treaty until the Senate says it is — by a two-thirds vote.

There are two technical points that must be clarified over the next few months. First, there must be a means of verification that will ensure that neither side cheats, and second there must be a timetable for the withdrawal of the arms.

But the real debate goes much deeper than that.

The Soviets have an overwhelming superiority in conventional weapons poised on Europe's eastern border. And U.S. cruise missiles were deployed, in part, to offset that threat.

Pulling the mid-range missiles out of Europe would leave the nations of NATO more susceptible to Soviet attack.

Some Europeans believe that if the Soviets were to attack using only conventional weapons, the United States would be very hesitant to counter-attack with the only means possible — strategic nuclear weapons.

The possibility that the U.S. would sacrifice Europe if confronted by the thought of nuclear war lies heavily on some European minds.

And that raises the very real question: Will the pact push our allies closer to the Soviet camp?

East and West Germany, for example, have recently concluded talks aimed at improving relations between those two countries.

There are other points that need consideration, too.

The United States and the Soviet Union are deadlocked on strategic weapons negotiations because of the U.S. Star Wars development and the Soviet conventional arms superiority.

The negotiators say there has been some movement on the question of human rights in the Soviet Union and talk of the pullout of 115,000 Soviet troops from Afghanistan, but those points are miles away from settlement.

And while these negotiations go on, the rest of us sit on pins and needles, hoping these people who hold our lives in their hands will negotiate with the intent of finding peace and not advantage.

There is movement here, and it seems that we must be thankful for that. The pact indicates, at least, an benign interest in finding a solution to the madness of Mutually Assured Destruction.

In the next few months, we will likely see whether that indication has real promise.

Reagan, Gorbachev Hold Summit; Sign INF Treaty, Discuss Arms

U.S. President Ronald Reagan and Soviet leader Mikhail S. Gorbachev held a summit in Washington, D.C., Dec. 8-10, 1987. It was the first visit to the U.S. capital by a Soviet leader since Leonid Brezhnev in 1973.

More than 5,000 journalists from around the world were accredited to cover the parley. Gorbachev's manner, mainly relaxed and amicable, made him a popular figure with the press and the U.S. public alike. An ABC News/*Washington Post* poll in the U.S., made public Dec. 6, had given the Soviet leader a 59% "favorable" rating, only four points below that of Reagan.

Reagan and Gorbachev were reported to have made some progress on an agreement to reduce strategic (long-range) nuclear weapons by 50%. But neither man gave ground on the contentious dispute over the U.S. Strategic Defense Initiative ("Star Wars"). Other prominent issues included human rights, regional conflicts and bilateral trade. Both sides hailed the summit as a major event in U.S.-Soviet relations.

The Soviet leader arrived on an Ilyushin-62M jetliner at Andrews Air Force Base in Maryland on the afternoon of June 7. He flew in from Great Britain, where he had met with Prime Minister Margaret Thatcher. Gorbachev was greeted in the U.S. by a delegation led by Secretary of State George Shultz. At the close of his initial remarks upon disembarking from his plane, the general secretary said to Shultz: "The visit has begun...So let's hope. God help us."

President Reagan and General Secretary Gorbachev signed the Intermediate Nuclear Forces Treaty (INF) in the White House's East Room on the afternoon of Dec. 8. Vice President George Bush, members of the Reagan cabinet, U.S. congressional leaders and Soviet officials attended the ceremony. The treaty was a culmination of six years of bilateral negotiations on medium-range missiles. In a brief statement before the signing, Reagan cited "the wisdom of an old Russian proverb...*doveryai no proverai.* Trust but verify."

"You repeat that at every meeting," Gorbachev retorted with a smile.

After the ceremony, President Reagan told the onlookers, "Today, I for the United States and the General Secretary for the Soviet Union, have signed the first agreement ever to eliminate an entire class of U.S. and Soviet nuclear weapons. We have made history."

Gorbachev said that the treaty would become "a milestone in the chronicle of man's eternal quest for a world without wars."

The pact called for the destruction, rather than the dismantling, of all U.S. and Soviet missiles with approximate ranges of 300-3,400 miles.

The two nations had a variety of options for destroying the weapons, including launching them into the ocean. Longer-range INF weapons included the U.S. Pershing IIs and ground-launched cruise missiles and the Soviet SS-4s and SS-20s. The Soviet's SS-12s and SS-23s made up the shorter-range weapons. West Germany's 72 shorter-range Pershing 1A missiles, with their U.S.-controlled nuclear warheads, were not part of the treaty. The agreement included a 13-year verification program that called for both resident and short-notice on-site inspections. The verification measures were the first of their kind in any U.S.-Soviet arms treaty. About 140 INF-related facilities came under the treaty, but not all were subject to inspections.

Gorbachev met with members of Congress at the Soviet embassy Dec. 9. The General Secretary had declined an invitation to meet the congressional contingent on Capitol Hill. The rejection was an apparent reaction to his not being allowed to address Congress. During the gathering, Gorbachev lobbied to overcome congressional opposition to the INF treaty. The pact could not be implemented until ratified by the U.S. Senate. After the parley, Rep. Robert Michel (R, Ill.) characterized the Soviet leader as "a very smart individual, very attuned to our system..."

Later that morning, Reagan and Gorbachev held their third meeting at the White House. The discussions revolved around the thorny issues of strategic arms and the Soviet intervention in Afghanistan.

Gorbachev and his entourage Dec. 10 departed from the U.S. The two countries issued a joint statement saying that Reagan had accepted an invitation from Gorbachev to visit the Soviet Union sometime in the first half of 1988.

The Grand Rapids Press
Grand Rapids, MI, December, 8, 1987

The glitter and ceremony of the Washington summit have left the centerpiece in the affair, the missile-reduction treaty, as little more than an ornament.

That's unfortunate, and dangerous.

Left unattended, the Reagan-Gorbachev agreement abolishing intermediate-range nuclear missiles will almost surely fall victim to the forces of prejudice and fear on Capitol Hill, and to masters of distortion outside of it. That is one reason why a considered, mature airing of the agreement in the Senate next month is so necessary.

But, for now, one needn't be a nuclear strategist or a political scientist to see good in the general lines of the accord. This is, most importantly, the first arms treaty which actually *reduces* the total stockpile of nuclear weapons. More than 1,000 U.S. and Soviet intermediate-range missiles will be destroyed, eliminating that class of weapon from each nation's nuclear arsenal. In contrast, 10 previous nuclear-weapons agreements sought only to freeze or restrain growth of forces — with a notable lack of success.

Almost as significant are the treaty's tight verification provisions. For the first time, the Soviets have agreed to on-site inspection of their armaments factories and missile sites to prevent cheating. Inspectors, on each side, will monitor destruction of missiles and will have authority to make unannounced checks of missile sites to insure the destroyed weapons are not replaced. Previous agreements, at Soviet insistence, left verification to spy satellites.

The Soviets in talks leading to this treaty also provided unprecedented detail about their missile capabilities, and they have agreed — again, for the first time — to an unbalanced retreat, resulting in the destruction of more Soviet than U.S. missiles.

The most lasting feature of the accord is the groundwork it lays for further reductions, both in chemical weapons and in long-range nuclear arms. Indeed, with a verification procedure already in place, chances for a major pullback on the intercontinental missiles seems likely in 1988.

Senate hearings and debate next month ought to examine all of those points and the many more features of the 200-page accord. Senators should hold their fire until that review is completed.

One other aspect is worth noting. President Reagan early in his administration took a fearful political beating — here and in Europe — for insisting on placement of U.S. cruise and Pershing intermediate-range missiles in Western Europe to counter the Soviet nuclear force in Eastern Europe. The affair produced a Soviet walkout from the Geneva arms reduction talks and massive anti-U.S. demonstrations in West Germany and England.

The president is due credit for his tenacity and firmness in sticking with that unpopular position. His resolve was a major factor in bringing the Soviets around. The agreement signed today, in fact, is essentially the same one Mr. Reagan proposed in 1981 — and rejected then by the Soviets.

There seems no reason to think this accord heralds a new era of detente. Neither, however, is there reason for regret in that; the nuclear buildup in the detente era was considerable. This treaty is a lesson in arms *reduction* progress through courage, patience and foresight. The Senate, in reviewing the agreement, should show some of those qualities on its own.

The Record

Hackensack, NJ, December 10, 1987

The leaders of the United States and the Soviet Union agree to call each other "Ron" and "Mikhail." They swap banter with what looks like genuine warmth. The Soviet national anthem is played at a festive ceremony on the South Lawn of the White House. President Reagan and General Secretary Gorbachev sign the most important arms-reduction agreement in more than a decade. They talk easily about an arms cut to come that would have seemed unthinkable a few months ago. These gray days of early December have turned into a time of unexpected hope.

To build on this new spirit of accord, it's important that Mr. Reagan and Senate Democrats join forces to defeat the handful of hardline legislators who will try to kill the treaty that does away with both sides' medium- and short-range missiles. A new web of verification procedures, which allow each side to inspect each other's missile installations and factories, will be added to the existing network of spy satellites. That should be enough to prevent cheating. The treaty itself, which eliminates whole classes of missiles and marks the first actual reduction in Soviet and American nuclear arsenals, is enough to justify the mood of excitement in Washington and Moscow.

The treaty is, however, only a beginning. It affects only 4 percent of both sides' nuclear missiles. It leaves untouched some 28,000 nuclear warheads and launchers that can devastate the earth. It's to these weapons that Mr. Reagan and Mr. Gorbachev have agreed to turn. Both leaders say they hope to agree on a 50 percent reduction before Mr. Reagan leaves office. The political and strategic problems in working out such an accord shouldn't be lost in the wave of good feeling. But it's a welcome change to see Mr. Reagan pursuing this goal instead of brandishing his rhetoric about the "evil empire."

There's a lot more to be gained from the new mood of cooperation than the narrow advantages it offers the two leaders. Granted, Mr. Reagan badly wants a significant arms accord to go into the history books with the Iran-contra fiasco and the budget deficit. Mr. Gorbachev needs a breathing spell from the arms race to pursue his own goal of domestic restructuring. But the reality is that both countries would benefit if they could devote more energy and resources to competing in world marketplaces with such nations as Japan and West Germany.

A year from now, Mr. Gorbachev may be out of power, a victim of the countless bureaucrats alarmed by his proposals for change. Election-year politics in America may have made impossible the consensus needed to move forward on arms reduction. But for now, we can bask in the unexpected warmth of the drama being played out in Washington.

St. Petersburg Times

St. Petersburg, FL, December 13, 1987

If summits are for history as well as for current consumption, it's too soon for President Reagan or General Secretary Gorbachev to claim success for their meeting last week.

When historians decide, they'll ask not only whether the treaty on medium- and short-range missiles was ratified (and kept), but whether it led to reducing conventional forces in Europe and, above all, to cutbacks in strategic nuclear weapons.

Bowlers might see it this way: A strike in the first frame is wasted if the next two balls go in the gutter. But to pursue the analogy for a moment, that strike is the best way to begin the game.

The Euromissiles treaty, as noted earlier, is a genuine achievement. For the first time since Hiroshima, it calls for the elimination of an entire class of nuclear missiles. It also sets the precedent of having American and Soviet inspectors on each other's soil to verify compliance, which can only improve the outlook for the strategic arms talks at Geneva.

The treaty had been agreed on beforehand, of course, so the summit played only a ceremonial part. As to the overall agenda, which Mr. Reagan pronounced a "clear success," it certainly did no harm and appears to have helped. It failed in resolving the dispute over interpretation of the 1972 Anti-Ballistic Missile (ABM) Treaty or in evoking any sign of Soviet conscience as to emigration and other human rights. It succeeded, however, in settling some secondary strategic arms issues, such as the maximum lifting power of Soviet launchers and sub-limits on nuclear warheads for ballistic missiles.

The most conspicuous achievement — which Mr. Reagan and Mr. Gorbachev see in very different ways — was their agreement not to let the ABM dispute obstruct the strategic arms talks. Whether that's good or bad depends on what results. If Mr. Reagan takes it as license to break the ABM treaty by field-testing components of the Strategic Defense Initiative (SDI), it might become impossible to reach a strategic arms agreement.

The Soviets still insist that one of the terms for such a new treaty would be guaranteed compliance with the old ABM treaty for a certain number of years.

When Gorbachev was asked whether the summit had "made it any less likely that the arms race will be extended into space," he replied, "I don't think so." What he has done is to let Mr. Reagan save face. The president won't have to confess, at least for now, that he has been wrong to claim the treaty would allow Star Wars testing in space. Gorbachev can only hope Mr. Reagan will leave it at that.

Gorbachev also knows that Congress has effectively barred such provocative testing of Star Wars components for most of the 13 months left in Mr. Reagan's term. Having shouldered the burden of keeping Mr. Reagan from making a rash mistake, the Congress can't let it down now.

In his speech to the nation Thursday night, the president once again spoke of Star Wars as a certainty: "When we have a defense ready to deploy, we will do so." That decision will not be his, or even his successor's. SDI managers don't know at this point whether the technology would work. They can't even say how much it would cost — by some estimates, $1-trillion — or whether the nation could afford it. Those choices will fall to Congress, in five years or more. If the United States and the Soviet Union have agreed by then to steep reductions in offensive weapons, the need for defensive weapons would be not only arguable but moot.

There can be no strategic arms reduction agreement, however, if the two sides do not take the first step their leaders agreed to at the Washington summit. The U.S. Senate has no business more important than ratifying the Euromissiles treaty without any unfriendly amendments or reservations. Those who oppose it may not all expect war, as Mr. Reagan asserted, but they are working to make war more likely.

News-Tribune & Herald

Duluth, MN December 9, 1987

It's signed, but it's not sealed and it's certainly not delivered. "It" is the arms-control agreement signed Tuesday by President Reagan and Mikhail Gorbachev in the White House.

Designed to eliminate intermediate-range nuclear missiles within three years, the treaty bearing signatures of the leaders of the two most powerful nations on Earth does not mean it is in effect — or ever will be.

The jubilation felt by many that the two nations have just made the world a little safer — and little is the word; this is just a start — from nuclear annihilation must be tempered by concern that the U.S. Senate might not ratify it.

While the Soviet Union's totalitarian system enables it to decide beforehand if it will accept the terms, our democratic system calls for the consent of the Senate. And the Senate has balked before on arms control, just as it balked almost 70 years ago when President Woodrow Wilson tried to bring America into the League of Nations.

There were indications from within the Senate Tuesday that the treaty might have fairly smooth sailing, although there are powerful members of that body who openly are opposing it. Much of the reason for the opposition is reflected in a column on this page by Constance Hilliard.

We have previously expressed our support for this treaty in hopes that it might be a start toward broader nuclear disarmament. We still believe that, and we believe the Senate should approve it.

If any progress is to be made in arms control, a certain amount of trust that the partners will act in good faith must be present, even if everyone involved has not been completely trustworthy in the past.

While it is a chance that many are unwilling to take, it is a chance that must be taken.

THE LINCOLN STAR

Lincoln, NE, December 11, 1987

The U.S. and Soviet signing of an intermediate nuclear forces (INF) agreement is a very major international development, from whatever point of view you take. One can make all sorts of comparisons of military strengths and weaknesses and can postulate the convictions of Western Europe and conclude the treaty threatens the free world.

We reply to that, nonsense. To rid the world of thousands of nuclear warheads when there are many more thousands remaining in land, sea and air arsenals of the major powers could hardly be considered dangerous.

The INF treaty, even if finally adopted by Congress and the Communist Politburo, is not that decisive in terms of nuclear war. The world could have just as big and dreadful war without such intermediate range weapons as it could with them.

And if you think the Soviet Union, absent the threat of those intermediate weapons, will be tempted to march conventional forces across the face of Europe, you have little appreciation for reality. Reality is that such a move would trigger World War III so fast it could make your heart stop. And millions of hearts would be stopped if that ever happened.

Even if the Soviets saw a military advantage, why would they want to press it? Why would they want to seek such a hallow victory, leaving millions of their own people dead, millions more suffering untold hardship and their country left in devastation?

None of that makes any sense and the Soviet Union really is not demonstrating such a level of stupidity.

Mikhail Gorbachev is striving to turn his country around; to reshape communism into a form that offers greater hope of achieving the quality of life that remains the unfulfilled promise of the bloody Bolshevik revolution. If he succeeds, Soviet society would undergo tremendous change and national aspirations would be altered; all toward greater harmony with Western values.

These are distant matters, to be sure, but the INF treaty is one seed planted in the vastness of Soviet soil. The seed could wither and die or could sprout and be trampled out but why would we not want it given a chance?

If all the optimism of the INF treaty is ultimately trashed, the world will have lost little more than a bit of temporary euphoria. If the treaty should realize its full potential, an unprecedented state of world peace could be achieved.

THE SACRAMENTO BEE

Sacramento, CA, December 12, 1987

According to plan, Mikhail Gorbachev and Ronald Reagan signed a treaty this week to eliminate land-based intermediate-range nuclear missiles from Europe. And, as expected, they failed to make real headway on human rights and regional issues like Afghanistan, Cambodia, Central America and the Persian Gulf. Judged by those results, the third summit meeting between the two leaders achieved what it was expected to — no more, no less.

Yet in one important respect the stage was set for substantial further progress toward a major arms control objective: a treaty, perhaps as early as mid-1988, that would drastically reduce the number of strategic missiles on both sides. By finessing their differing interpretations of the 1972 anti-ballistic missile treaty, thus avoiding a clash over how far the United States may go in developing the Strategic Defense Initiative, Reagan and Gorbachev were able to agree on numerical limits on long-range missile warheads that the Soviets previously had tied to curbs on SDI.

Roadblocks remain. Even the INF treaty will not slide through the Senate without a fight; nor can a lame-duck president be sure that a strategic arms pact will win the required two-thirds Senate majority in the thick of a presidential election campaign. And it's possible that the Kremlin will have second thoughts about delinking strategic arms negotiations from SDI. Nonetheless, it's remarkable that an implacably anti-Communist American president and the leader of one of the most secretive, xenophobic societies in the world have now endorsed a detailed plan that will, among other things, place American and Soviet inspectors in each others' missile factories and bases for years to come.

Progress on arms control came despite deep differences in other areas, and illustrates the degree to which the superpowers have moved away from the Carter doctrine that linked strategic questions to human rights and regional issues. Those questions remain on the agenda, certainly for this country. Gorbachev may bristle at questions about the treatment of Jews and dissidents in the Soviet Union. Even so, he seems to understand now that Americans, however ready they are to deal with him on military and political questions, will never lower their voices about Moscow's appalling human rights record. Nor can he assume that the United States will not, if circumstances warrant, relink these issues.

Gorbachev repeatedly talked to his American hosts about the need for "new thinking" in the Soviet-American relationship. There is such a need, yet the gap between his interpretation and ours of what that means is still wide. If this week's summit narrowed that gap just a bit, there's every reason to hope that the process so well begun by Reagan and Gorbachev can continue.

THE SUN

Baltimore, MD, December 13, 1987

The Reagan-Gorbachev summit and what it produced changes the political dialogue for 1988. In their 1984 platform, the Democrats charged that the Reagan administration "has no answer other than to escalate the arms race." Such rhetoric has become inoperative. Republicans described nuclear deterrent forces as "the ultimate guarantor of America's security," a sentiment the GOP can hardly trumpet in light of President Reagan's espousal of a nuclear-free world.

With public opinion clearly in favor of the president's accomplishments, the Republicans would seem to have secured a definite political boost. Yet Republicans being Republicans, they are quite capable of blowing this advantage. Sen. Jesse Helms is heading a band of Senate conservatives passionately opposed to the Reagan-Gorbachev INF treaty to eliminate intermediate-range nuclear forces.

All of which puts the Democrats in a peculiar position. The dynamics of the ratification debate beginning Jan. 19 will make such stalwart anti-Reagan Democrats as Robert Byrd and Alan Cranston informal floor whips for that man in the White House. This could make things awkward for their campaign against the president's Strategic Defense Initiative, especially since SDI no longer seems an insuperable impediment to a treaty drastically reducing long-range offensive weaponry.

Among the six Democratic contenders for the presidency, arms control is not an issue. They all favor Ronald Reagan's treaty. So instead of attacking their old Nemesis, the Democrats have to attack the GOP conservatives who are attacking *their* old hero. Massachusetts Gov. Michael Dukakis frames the issue by asking: "Do we need any further proof that the radical right has a stranglehold on the Republican Party?" It is a line that will have to be dropped once the Gipper proves that Helmsmen cannot block his treaty.

Among the six Republican contenders, arms control is very much an issue. Since Pete du Pont, Al Haig, Jack Kemp and Pat Robertson (all longshots) are against the INF treaty, logic suggests they would be apoplectic if a strategic arms cut comes out of a Springtime Moscow summit.

So far, George Bush has been able to bask in the reflected light of the summit, the only GOP contender fully in support of the INF and its possible follow-on. It has been a definite plus. But Senate GOP leader Bob Dole has assured Mikhail Gorbachev that the treaty will be ratified, and he will play a very visible role in crafting the Senate resolution that will make this possible.

So here we go: Democrats favor a treaty a concession-minded president of their own choosing could not have gotten. And conservative Republicans oppose a treaty only tough, conservative arms control policies could have secured. However, it's only foreign policy. The economy controls elections, right?

SUMMIT SOUVENIR PHOTO OPPORTUNITY

The Hutchinson News

Hutchinson, KS, December 10, 1987

The numbers aren't etched in granite.

But the latest indication is that the United States will junk 850 missiles, and the Russians 1,900.

That will remove all the missiles designed to explode 300 to 3,000 miles away from the launching pads. By some scientific accounts, the 2,750 missiles would easily be capable of destroying the planet forever, no matter where they landed.

Even after the elimination of these missiles, however, the world's stockpiles will be hardly dented. The current guess is that there will be well over 21,000 nuclear missiles left in place now, with the assembly lines still churning out new and improved versions.

The treaty is a decent and reasonable start to something big. Indeed, it already is something big, since it clearly reflects the nations' determination to put less faith in arms and more faith in people as a source of defense in coming years.

The Toronto Star

Toronto, Ont., December 10, 1987

First the euphoria. Then the hangover?

"We made history," cried a jubilant Ronald Reagan. And they did, of course. What's equally important is the reaction of the world since the signing of the historic treaty that destroys all those missiles.

The world's delighted, ready to embrace an era of peace and good will that will last year 'round.

We've been cheering too. So why be a party pooper and mention hangovers?

Unfortunately, the headaches hover over anyone who examines the reality that only one class of weapons has been wiped out. That leaves more than 90% of the nuclear arsenals of the two giants, enough to maintain the threat of holocaust many times over.

Even assuming the Soviets will play absolutely straight with verification, a reluctant assumption for us, the threat remains that's implicit in their goal of imposing the dictatorship of the proletariat, a threat backed by both all their other missiles and superior conventional forces.

Mikhail Gorbachev got a taste of democratic reality yesterday when he met U.S. congressional leaders. He left many of them with legitimate worries, even though passage of the treaty through Congress seems certain.

The worriers find it impossible to ignore the Soviet threat to a Western Europe stripped of missiles. They note that the treaty doesn't address human rights or the Soviets' persistent malicious meddling.

Gorbachev may have told Reagan he's willing to get out of Afghanistan, but talk is no substitute for action. We've already seen one withdrawal that wasn't.

This is one of the media events of the century, a triumph of hype and symbolism. We welcome the achievement while remaining as skeptical as some congressmen.

That's not to say it isn't important. If the world thinks it is, it is, because we live in a curious time where perception's as important as reality.

Nevertheless, we must not forget that real peace involves much more than eliminating a class of weapons already made redundant by technology.

So we cheer these baby steps in the right direction as we demand proof this is a true dawn of Soviet freedom.

The London Free Press

London, Ont., December 12, 1987

In comparison with the Reykjavik fiasco last year, this week's more carefully prepared summit between Soviet leader Mikhail Gorbachev and President Ronald Reagan was an historic success, though it may have fallen short of the exaggerated expectations entertained by some observers.

To be sure, little more was accomplished than the formal signing of a previously concluded (INF) treaty banning intermediate-range missiles, but that was a significant achievement in itself. It's the first agreement to require reductions, not just limits, in the number of nuclear missiles available to each side.

The treaty now goes to the United States Senate, where it is expected to be ratified by the necessary two-thirds vote.

Meanwhile, negotiations are proceeding on a related Strategic Arms Reduction Treaty (START), but little progress seems to have been made on this issue during the summit. The two sides still cannot agree on whether the 1972 Anti-Ballistic Missile (ABM) Treaty should have a strict (Soviet) or broad (U.S.) interpretation, but Gorbachev seems less concerned about this problem inasmuch as budget restraints imposed by the U.S. Congress have slowed development of Reagan's cherished strategic defence initiative.

According to the British-based International Institute for Strategic Studies, the U.S. now has 7,900 nuclear warheads on ballistic missiles; the Soviet Union, 10,056. At the Washington summit, both sides agreed that these totals should be reduced to 4,900 each, but

disagreement persists on crucial questions having to do with limits on different types of missile launchers.

Still, there is some hope that agreement on a substantial strategic arms treaty might be reached in time for a return visit to Moscow by Reagan next summer, but it's far from certain. The issues are much more complicated and far more important than those involved in the INF treaty.

There was some frank talk at the summit about irreconcilable differences over other matters, such as Soviet human rights abuses and the continuing occupation of Afghanistan. Perhaps the best aspect, though, is that Gorbachev and Reagan maintained a cordiality that bodes well for the continuing relations between their two countries.

St. Louis Review

St. Louis, MO, December 11, 1987

For most of the 42 years since the dawn of the nuclear age, the two superpowers have been developing and stockpiling huge arsenals of powerful atomic and hydrogen weapons. On both sides the basic strategy has been M.A.D. (Mutually Assured Destruction). Both the United States and the Soviet Union have had the potential to destroy each other — and the rest of the world as well — many times over. This balance of terror has been, and still is, the major deterrent to direct conflict between the two nations.

The threat to the world's environment from nuclear weapons' testing led to the treaty banning such tests in the atmosphere and limiting the signatories to underground tests. The ABM (anti-ballistic missile) treaty, never ratified by the U.S. Senate, but observed in principle, has limited the rate of growth of the superpowers' nuclear arsenals.

Now for the first time our two nations have agreed to the elimination of an entire category of weapons — the intermediate range missiles. Again, for the first time, the Soviet Union has agreed to on-site inspections as a back-up to the sophisticated methods of monitoring which have been in place on both sides for years. The United States has consistently maintained that a treaty without adequate methods of verification would be worthless. The change in the Soviet position on verification made the new agreement possible.

The most hopeful aspect of the new treaty is the expressed willingness of both sides to take up the challenge to reduce their stockpiles of long-range strategic weapons. If this treaty is successful and nuclear weapons are gradually eliminated, the focus of national and world security will shift to conventional weapons in which the Soviet Union enjoys an overwhelming superiority. The maintenance and development of conventional weapons and forces will likely be far more costly than nuclear weaponry.

The need to work for limitation of the size and equipping of non-nuclear forces will become paramount. The relationships among the United States and its allies could well be altered as the U.S. nuclear umbrella over Western Europe is reduced. The economies of Western Europe will be affected as reliance on the United States for defense and the era of the "bigger bang for a buck" fades. The new treaty will bring problems as well as the euphoria of the moment, but we are cautiously optimistic. For a welcome change the problems for the defense and the economy will come from a reduction in armaments.

RAPID CITY JOURNAL

Rapid City, SD, December 9, 1987

If you think the Intermediate Nuclear Force treaty will change the way people think, think again.

Long before Mikhail Gorbachev's trip to Washington was certain, three major schools of thought within our European NATO allies began working toward new goals — all of which are old goals in new garb.

The first school believes in continued deterrence. Grieved at losing its beloved medium-range nuclear missiles, this group is clamoring for "modernization" and "restructuring" of NATO military forces. Those terms are blinds obscuring the lurking actual motive — continuing escalation of the arms race. If they can't have ground-launched cruise and Pershing 2 missiles, they'll build other delivery systems. They'll use combat aircraft and submarines to replace the ground-based missiles that would be scrapped by the INF treaty.

Unsurprisingly, this view is popular among military bureaucracies and defense contractors.

The second group believes that peace actually can be kept with fewer weapons. This group believes the number of arms in existence can be reduced. Believers view INF as a first step toward ending the arms race. They want to reduce the numbers of all types of weapons, maintaining parity as weaponry dwindles. Ultimately, the only systems remaining would be defensive, with offensive weapons so reduced that invasion by either side is impossible.

This is the concept of making war obsolete that President Reagan pushes when trying to sell his Strategic Defense Initiative to Americans. Gorbachev claims to belong to this school, as well. So do many other European leaders.

Then, there are the so-called pragmatists. This group's main purpose is to make certain the U.S. remains tied to Europe. They view the missile withdrawal as a mistake, but accept it as accomplished fact. They are scrambling to find other ways to keep the U.S. presence in Europe. They benefit by having to spend less on their own defense, and also from the massive expenditures made by the United States in maintaining a strong presence in Europe.

The pragmatists include many political and business leaders.

Which school of thought will win out? Time will tell. But the jockeying for post-INF influence demonstrates that the treaty hasn't done anything to change the way people think. And that's the most important change of all if arms control is ever to become a reality.

St. Petersburg Times

St, Petersburg, FL, December 9, 1987

The true significance of the Intermediate-range Nuclear Forces (INF) agreement signed Tuesday by President Reagan and General Secretary Gorbachev is not easy to characterize.

It is the first arms control agreement signed by the leaders of the two nuclear superpowers since the signing of the second Strategic Arms Limitation Treaty in 1979, which with Mr. Reagan's opposition never was ratified by the U.S. Senate.

The INF agreement also is the first arms control pact under which an entire classification of missiles actually will be destroyed. The United States and the Soviet Union, after Senate ratification of Tuesday's agreement, will destroy within three years about 2,800 medium- and short-range missiles with the capacity to carry about 3,800 nuclear warheads. The warheads will not be destroyed. They will be recycled into other weapons.

The agreement helps to create complex political and military problems for the Western Alliance. Western Europe is perceived to be more vulnerable to the threat of Soviet conventional military power, a concern that now begs for attention. The United States will need to strengthen its political ties to European nations. That task is more challenging since Gorbachev has become so popular there.

The agreement's breakthrough is the plan for its verification: first-in-history, on-site inspection of missile production plants. American observers will be stationed in the Soviet Union and Soviet inspectors in this country. That is a level of exchanging information for the purposes of arms control never before achieved.

As both Messrs. Reagan and Gorbachev noted in their remarks, the agreement can be a first step toward another treaty dealing with the centerpiece nuclear weapons, strategic missiles. Yet the reality is that further steps down that path collide with President Reagan's dream of a Star Wars shield protecting America from hostile missiles, a dream he says he will never give up.

It was interesting that Mr. Reagan and Gorbachev spoke similar words about a strategic agreement. "It is my hope," the president said, "that progress will be made toward achieving another agreement that will lead to a cutting in half of our strategic nuclear arsenals." Gorbachev said he came to the United States "with the intention of advancing the next and more important goal of reaching agreement to reduce by half the strategic offensive arms in the context of a firm guarantee of strategic stability." That last phrase is a reference to Star Wars. Neither nation would agree to reduce strategic weapons while there is a chance the other might deploy a defensive system which would be more effective defending against a smaller number of targets. It's as simple as that. Until that conflict is resolved or side-stepped, there will be no agreement cutting strategic arsenals in half.

One way of measuring Tuesday's agreement is in the transformation of Ronald Reagan. Until about two years ago, he had never seen an arms control treaty he liked. He vigorously opposed every step toward reducing nuclear weapons, whether by Republican or Democratic presidents. As president, he filled his administration with hard-line opponents of arms control as well as some supporters, and refused to resolve their policy differences until about a year ago. Now, approaching the end of his term, Mr. Reagan's thoughts of his place in history apparently have caused him to mellow. He deserves praise for these changes.

Mr. Reagan's transformation also suggests the great power and durability of the political idea that governments can control nuclear weapons if their leaders have the wisdom and the will to do it, which may be the most hopeful thought in the history of the INF treaty.

THE DENVER POST

Denver, CO
December 9, 1987

PRESIDENT Reagan and Soviet General Secretary Mikhail Gorbachev made history yesterday, signing a treaty to eliminate intermediate range nuclear forces — the first pact abolishing an entire class of nuclear weapons.

But whether their achievement endures and signals a further diminution of mankind's nuclear nightmare depends upon whether the U.S. Senate ratifies the treaty.

As of now, America's participation in the treaty is no more than a personal promise by Reagan. It will not bind future U.S. administrations unless the Senate ratifies it. And it has been 15 years since any arms-control agreement mustered the two-thirds majority required by the Constitution for Senate approval.

The INF pact is at least the 23rd arms-control agreement signed by both the U.S. and the Soviet Union. The first — the Geneva protocol outlawing poison gas and bacteriological warfare, was signed by the U.S. in 1925 and the Soviets in 1928. But the Senate dawdled for nearly half a century before ratifying the treaty in 1974.

President Richard Nixon inaugurated the modern era of restrictions of strategic nuclear weapons in May 26, 1972, at Moscow when he signed the first Strategic Arms Limitation Treaty. SALT I was ratified by the Senate Aug. 3, 1972 — the last time the Senate has ratified an arms-control treaty.

Leonid Brezhnev and Jimmy Carter signed the follow-up SALT II treaty in Vienna in 1979, but it has not been ratified. To this day, the most important arms-control agreement in the postwar world has no legal force in the U.S. Its sole force is a personal promise by Carter, later affirmed and then modified by Reagan, to abide by SALT II's terms.

The Soviet Union cannot be forever expected to sign treaties with this country unless we formally promise to abide by them. Furthermore, the senatorial dithering on arms control makes the U.S. look vacillating and warlike in the eyes of our allies and the world. Our European allies unanimously favor the INF treaty. It is not only the first treaty ever to scrap an entire class of nuclear weapons; it also sets a precedent with on-site verification procedures that will send hundreds of Soviet inspectors to the United States and Western Europe, and a corresponding American contingent to the Soviet Union.

The INF treaty should be ratified by the Senate and given the full force of law. Any senator who votes against it is contributing to the reckless endangerment of the human race.

MARGULIES
©1987 HOUSTON POST

Coolness Between First Ladies as Husbands Meet in Washington

Nancy Reagan and Raisa Gorbachev met for coffee at the White House Dec. 9, 1987. A swarm of reporters trailed along as the U.S. First Lady took her visitor on a tour of the official residence. Although each repeatedly denied it, a coolness was evident between the two. Mrs. Gorbachev several times stopped to speak with the journalists, only to be hurried along by Mrs. Reagan. At one point, a reporter asked the Soviet First Lady if she would like to live in the White House. She replied through an interpreter: "I would say that, humanly speaking, a human being would like to live in a regular house. This is a museum."

In concert with the summit, the Soviet Novosti news agency Dec. 9 issued biographical information on Mrs. Gorbachev that had not been generally known in the West. Among the information reported by Novosti was that "Raisa Maximova Gorbachevna, was born in the Siberian City of Rubtsovsk, in a family of a railway engineer."

THE SAGINAW NEWS
Saginaw, MI, December 11, 1987

Those suspicious of Gorbachev's visit to the United States were right. The Soviets' secret plan is now apparent, even transparent.

Look at the clues. Mikhail and Raisa holding hands in public; no Gary Hart syndrome there. The admission that they engage in pillow talk — just like Nancy and Ron. The engaging smiles. The wisecracks. Meetings with media moguls, moneyed industrialists, interest groups. Calculated demonstrations that behind the cheerful exterior is a smart, tough guy.

It all builds on strongly favorable opinion polls. So he doesn't speak English, but so what? A lot of things Reagan says require interpretation and clarification, too.

The clincher came Thursday morning. Gorbachev was late to his meeting with the president because he climbed out of his limousine and spent five minutes pressing the flesh and working the crowd. The only thing missing was a baby to smooch.

Yes, it's obvious. The missile treaty was only a cover for the real Kremlin design. The Democrats have a problem, and Smiling Mike's the solution. The scary thing is that, at the moment, it is not at all certain that he would fare poorly as someone's nominee for president of the United States.

THE BLADE
Toledo, OH, December 12, 1987

NO QUESTION about it, Mr. and Mrs. Mikhail Gorbachev were the toast of Washington, D. C., this week, showing that the nation's capital really is a fairly small town after all — if gawking at celebrities is a sign of a small town.

Summit media watchers, however, focused on a little side drama of the event, the supposedly chilly relations between Raisa Gorbachev and Nancy Reagan. Mrs. Gorbachev did not mind upstaging her hostess and even resisted being swept along by Nancy Reagan on a tour of the White House, symbol and home of the imperial presidency.

As one report had it, White House aides, exasperated by Mrs. Gorbachev's independent turn of mind, were reduced to sniping about her wardrobe. And, of course, the dresses worn by both women were reported in breathless detail.

Both the President's wife and the Soviet general secretary's wife are getting something of a bum deal. They were, as usual in such cases, pushed into the subordinate roles of host and sightseer while their husbands were dealing with the affairs of the world. Yet both are well educated, no doubt have their own, independently formed views on world issues, and have shown considerable spunk in resisting the usual stereotypes of the dutiful wives of world leaders.

Mrs. Reagan has been portrayed unfairly for years as a woman whose principal public role was to look adoringly at her husband while he spoke. More recent accounts indicate that she has opinions on issues, including the nuclear arms race, and she may have had some influence on her husband's thinking.

She certainly had influence in other ways, including the ouster of Donald Regan, the pugnacious former White House chief of staff, who angered the First Lady.

Raisa Gorbachev has a somewhat different problem. She is lively and intelligent, too, but lives under a governmental system in which wives of political leaders are seen rarely and heard from almost never. Some observers speculated that she had tried to play an understated role so as not to provoke the heavies in the Kremlin who dislike Mr. Gorbachev's policies and probably him as well.

It boils down to the fact that the summit-covering army of journalists in Washington were forced to look for stories where they could find them. Some have concentrated on the reported points of friction between two intelligent and high-spirited women. The tendency among some reporters is to view the top women in the summit spotlight as a pair of fluffballs.

That they are not; they have both public and private lives and, on the whole, deserve respect for their success in balancing those roles rather than the cheap shots about their activities in the White House and elsewhere in Summitsville.

Omaha World-Herald
Omaha, NE, December 4, 1987

Vanity of vanities, all is vanity, wrote the author of Ecclesiastes. Some Soviet citizens are saying much the same thing these days about the stylish Raisa Gorbachev. A reference to her was the only item Soviet censors cut from an American television interview with her husband, General Secretary Mikhail Gorbachev.

The Soviet leader discussed a number of sensitive military and political topics during the interview. That the censors' only cut in the Soviet broadcast of the interview was Gorbachev's statement that he discusses "everything" with his wife may say something about the sensitivity of the Gorbachevs to criticism of Mrs. Gorbachev.

She reportedly once used an American Express gold card to charge items at an exclusive Paris shop. Her trim figure, stylish clothing and international travel with her husband have not won her universal admiration in the Soviet Union.

Part of the problem may be that she is a walking reminder that quality consumer goods are not widely available to the general public in the Soviet Union. Party members and their families have the privilege of shopping at exclusive stores where Western goods are available — but most go about it quietly. Because Mrs. Gorbachev is in the limelight, it is difficult to hide the fact that top officials have a much higher standard of living than ordinary citizens, which conflicts with the party line.

The Gorbachevs have impressed Westerners with their charm, style and intelligence. But tastes vary. The criticism of Mrs. Gorbachev suggests that some of the qualities that make the Gorbachevs interesting to Americans may very well be the things that turn some Russians off.

The Providence Journal

Providence, RI
December 12, 1987

Vladimir Nabokov, the Russian-born writer who emigrated to the United States, once noted how Soviet diplomats were always affronted by the crude manners of American statesmen who invariably spoke to them, when standing, with their hands in their pockets.

His observation points out the delicacy of etiquette in foreign relations: the Americans had no idea that they were violating a long-time Slavic social convention. In the same way, the first-time Westerner to Japan often fails to slurp his soup with the expected, complimentary decibels.

Yet watching Raisa Gorbachev's diplomatic dance with Nancy Reagan this week, one got the impression that her rumbling out of step was not the product of happy ignorance, but rather of calculated design.

Admittedly, meaningful dialogue is difficult through an interpreter, and all the more uncomfortable when every word is being scribbled down by reporters for, if not posterity, the next day's papers. But Mrs. Gorbachev seemed to be intentionally trying to rile Mrs. Reagan with condescension and trivia.

She spoke critically of the First Family's living quarters, calling them more like a museum than a home, and quizzed Mrs. Reagan on the dates and periods of her furnishings. More grievously, she held up the tour, heedless of her hostess's attempts to keep it on schedule, to linger before her beloved cameramen and news reporters. When Mrs. Reagan urged an exit, she persisted — disregarding accepted rules regarding hosts and guests that are universal.

Of course, how the First Lady and the wife of the general secretary of the Soviet Communist Party get along is of little international consequence, even when they each have — as we are told they do in this case — the welcome ear of their husbands. Mrs. Gorbachev's behavior is far from jeopardizing the INF treaty or threatening world peace.

What it does do however is remind us of character. Though dressed with her customary stylishness (are the people who admire her love of clothes the same ones who years ago criticized Mrs. Reagan for hers?) Raisa Gorbachev has nevertheless risked resurrecting an image of a people of boorish stubbornness — the very image that her husband, we had thought, was succeeding in dispelling.

Lexington Herald-Leader

Lexington, KY, December 15, 1987

When she toured the White House with Nancy Reagan, Raisa Gorbachev did everything but spit on the furniture to demonstrate her disdain for things American, and, in particular, things Reagan. How Mrs. Reagan will get even in Moscow next year is anybody's guess; but pity the fool who rains on the first lady's media parade.

Mrs. Gorbachev called a Nixon portrait "a typical picture of the 20th century." Later, she grumbled about the bad light in another room. She also called the White House a "museum," and opined to reporters about how unpleasant it must be to live in such a place.

Indeed, while Ron and Mikhail were chumming it famously, Nancy and Raisa were getting about as friendly as a pair of mud wrestlers. Mrs. Reagan's aides made fun of Mrs. Gorbachev's baggy hose and rhinestone belt buckle. Mrs. Gorbachev didn't invite Mrs. Reagan to visit her at home in Moscow.

Stylish she may be, but Mrs. Gorbachev obviously lacks her spouse's gift for public relations. But then, there's only room for one first lady in Washington, and Nancy Reagan made it clear long ago that she has no intention of relinquishing that role to anyone.

Pittsburgh Post-Gazette

Pittsburgh, PA, December 11, 1987

The distractingly cool behavior of Raisa Gorbachev and Nancy Reagan toward one another raises the question of the appropriate role of an unelected spouse at historic events like summit conferences.

Are the wives of the summiteers inviting undue attention with their less than cordial conduct? Or are journalists, with their thirst for the trivial, letting their heads be turned from the more important business at hand? (Some might cite this editorial as support for the latter possibility.)

Whatever the explanation, the apparent coolness between Mrs. Gorbachev and Mrs. Reagan has competed for public attention with the more substantial activities of their husbands. Perhaps the scrutiny is related to the "First Lady" syndrome in this country that seems to require of the president's spouse an active involvement in public affairs not common in other countries. Does Madame Mitterrand or, to switch sexes, Denis Thatcher garner such attention?

It's a perilous discussion to be drawn into because of the danger of being tarred as sexist. Criticize the public roles being played by the two wives and some feminists might inquire whether you would rather see Raisa and Nancy in the kitchen rustling up a state dinner together.

Hardly, but both women should realize that when they shift the focus from arms control to the sort of looks and gestures they are exchanging, they are intruding themselves more than a leader's spouse (of either sex) should. This is not their show.

Americans Tour
Soviet Radar Site

Three members of the U.S. Congress returned from a surprise visit to a controversial Soviet radar facility Sept. 8, 1987 to question the Reagan administration's repeated assertion that the facility was part of an elaborate system to guard against nuclear missile attacks.

Reps. Thomas J. Downey (N.Y.), Jim Moody (Wis.) and Bob Carr (Ill.), all Democrats, were taken to the radar site at the end of week-long trip to the Soviet Union sponsored by the National Resources Defense Council (NRDC), a private group that monitored Soviet military activities. The Soviet government had never before allowed U.S. politicians to visit secret military sites.

In arguing for his own "Star Wars" missile defense plan, President Reagan and his aides had repeatedly charged that the Soviets were already building a system to defend against incoming missiles, in violation of the 1972 ABM (antiballistic missile) treaty, which banned most defenses. As evidence, Reagan cited the large, so-called phased array radar being built near Krasnoyarsk, Siberia several hundred miles north of Mongolia. The treaty banned all early-warning systems, except ones located near a national border and directed outwards. The Krasnoyarsk radar was apparently directed towards the eastern half of the Soviet Union. The Soviets claimed that the radar was intended for tracking satellites, but military analysts said that its orientations made it better for tracking incoming missiles than satellites.

The legislators concluded in a report that if the radar was intended for early warning of an attacks, it would violate the letter of the ABM treaty, but "not its purpose." Anthony R. Battista, a respected staff member and expert on military electronics for the House Armed Services Committee who accompanied the group, said that Soviet officials had said to him that the radar was tuned to a frequency that was too low for tracking satellites, but not ideal for detecting missiles. On the other hand, Battista said that the unit would not be very useful as part of an antimissile defense system, since it was not built solidly enough to withstand the buffeting winds and electromagnetic pulses that would be generated in nuclear warfare. "We judge the probability of Krasnoyarsk functioning as a battle-management radar to be extremely low," the lawmakers wrote.

Downey told a press conference that if a radar unit of such "shoddy" construction were built in the U.S., "we would have a scandal of major proportions." The lawmakers were allowed to shoot more than 1,000 photographs and several hours of videotape in and around the facility. They acknowledged that the film would be invaluable to U.S. intelligence experts, who had relied on satellite photographs of the site.

The NRDC had been urging the Soviet Union to allow visitors to the radar site for more than a year. Final approval came after 14 members of the Soviet ruling Politburo were polled by phone, the legislators said they had been told. The visit was seen as part of an effort by the Soviets to show that they were willing to allow the public verification procedures necessary for an arms control agreement.

General Secretary Mikhail S. Gorbachev Sept. 16, 1988 made an offer on the disputed Krasnoyarsk radar facility. Gorbachev offered to place the radar complex under international supervision for undefined nonmilitary space research. In response to the offer, the White House Sept. 16 restated its demand that the radar complex be dismantled.

The U.S. State Department Dec. 14, 1988 announced that it had been informed by the Soviet Union that two disputed radars would be destroyed in compliance with Washington's wishes. The radars with the Western codenames "Pawn Shop" and "Flat Twin," were located near the Soviet city of Gomel. The Reagan administration had charged that they violated the 1972 ABM treaty. State Department spokesman Charles E. Redman Dec. 13 welcomed the dismantling of the Gomel radars, but said that the "crucial issue of the Soviet [radar] violation at Krasnoyarsk remains unresolved."

U.S. and Soviet representatives met Oct. 31 to Nov. 2 in Geneva on the matter of the Krasnoyarsk radar, but had failed to reach agreement. Moscow restated its offer to turn the Siberian facility into a space-research center. Washington continued to insist on the facility's destruction.

The Atlanta Journal
THE ATLANTA CONSTITUTION
Atlanta, GA,
September 14, 1987

"We consider it a violation (of the ABM treaty), period," says White House spokesman Marlin Fitzwater. "They didn't build it to show drive-in movies."

"It" is the Krasnoyarsk radar complex deep in Siberia, which the Reagan administration insists is a prohibited system designed to track incoming U.S. missiles and which the Soviets maintain is a perfectly permissible device to monitor satellites.

Fitzwater's cutesy remark is the White House's idea of a fitting put-down of the conclusions of three U.S. congressmen just back from an intriguing trip to the Soviet Union. The Kremlin gave them, four staff members and two independent U.S. scientists the extraordinary privilege of wandering all over the suspect radar complex, taking photographs, even scooping up samples of concrete. It was glasnost, squared.

OK, so the three congressmen are all Democrats disposed to disbelieve Reagan gospel. But they weren't born yesterday, either. Their leader, Thomas Downey of New York, is exceptionally bright and just as suspicious of the Soviets as the next American.

The congressmen's findings flatly contradict previous administration alarms:

• The complex is not now in violation of the ABM treaty; it won't be operational for several years (and it's behind schedule).

• If it was supposed to house an antimissile warning system, it would be hardened against nuclear attack. It isn't.

• For such a supposedly crucial element of our adversary's defense network, the workmanship is incredibly slipshod.

Granted, the congressmen's on-the-scene report is not definitive, but it is disturbing. If we are in fact overstating the radar complex's importance, then we're creating a bargaining chip for the Soviets, one that they can offer to dismantle if we will only dispose of a genuine asset of ours.

At the very least, the Downey group's on-the-spot findings should spur the administration to re-examine its long-distance evaluation. Or does it consider itself infallible?

The Houston Post

Houston, TX, September 14, 1987

Soviet leader Mikhail Gorbachev has scored a slick propaganda coup by allowing a delegation of U.S. congressmen to visit the controversial Krasnoyarsk radar installation deep inside Siberia.

The Reagan administration has cited the giant phased-array radar as a major violation of the superpowers' 1972 anti-ballistic missile treaty. It is 500 miles inside Soviet territory instead of on the perimeter of the country, as required by the pact. And it could direct the interception of hostile missiles in a nuclear war.

After touring the site last week, however, some of the lawmakers questioned the administration charge. Instead of a bunker hardened to resist a nuclear blast, they found shoddy concrete buildings still under construction. In a remarkable display of *glasnost,* or openness, they were permitted to take photographs and talk with Soviet officials about the radar, which is not yet in operation.

Perhaps the visit was intended to warm U.S.-Soviet relations as the superpowers near agreement on a pact to scrap all medium-range nuclear missiles. But it also enhances the Soviet leader's peacemaker image abroad. And it bolsters congressional opponents of President Reagan's Star Wars anti-missile defense program.

In trying to divine Gorbachev's motives for opening the Krasnoyarsk radar, let's not forget that its location is a clear ABM violation. It also faces north, making it a better missile detector than the satellite tracker the Russians say it will be. What about that, Mikhail?

The Dispatch

Columbus, OH, September 1, 1987

A treaty once callously dismissed by Soviet Foreign Minister Andrei Gromyko as "an excuse to peek through the neighbor's fence" was put into effect last week when American military officials for the first time inspected a Soviet troop movement.

While Americans might — and probably should — view the exercise with some skepticism, it would be unwise and premature to discount it entirely.

The State Department said four military officers traveled to the Soviet Union to view a planned maneuver involving 16,000 Soviet troops at Minsk. The treaty signed last year in Stockholm by 35 nations gives all parties the right to on-site inspection of conventional troop movements.

While the United States has good reason to trust the Soviets least where the military is involved, it is nonetheless important to pursue ways to reduce tensions and suspicions that are unfounded.

Although other Americans have gone to the Soviet Union to "observe" military activities under other agreements, this was the first time U.S. officials went as "inspectors" pursuant to a treaty under which they could not be refused entry.

The treaty only covers conventional military maneuvers from the Atlantic Ocean to the Ural Mountains in the Soviet Union. The Russians could not, therefore, inspect troop movements on American soil, only in Europe.

If U.S. officers come away from this experience with a better understanding of their Soviet counterparts, the treaty will have served a useful purpose beyond its intent to build trust between the superpowers.

The more that U.S. military officers can know about their Soviet counterparts — how they think, their methods of operation, their chain of command, and the personalities of those who hold important positions within the chain of command — the easier it will be to predict Soviet responses to events.

This knowledge could be crucial should a crisis emerge. Any opportunity to gain insight into the Soviet mentality should be welcomed, and pursued in its own right.

Coming as a prelude to a hoped-for superpower agreement involving the first-ever agreed destruction of a whole class of nuclear weapons, this troop movement inspection is at least a foothold in the continuing quest for improved relations with the Soviet Union. There are many levels at which cooperation between the two nations can be pursued. While neither side will ever fully trust the other, the pursuit of understanding at every level can help create a broad relationship that will endure setback.

The treaty allowing participating nations to inspect European troop movements is a small step in the right direction.

Newsday

Long Island, NY, September 14, 1987

That was an extraordinary and important event last week when a group of American officials were allowed to visit a large Soviet radar at Krasnoyarsk. And *potentially* it was an event with major implications for the future of Soviet-American relations.

Extraordinary because allowing a group of American congressmen not only to visit but to photograph a Soviet defense facility is without precedent. This is the most vivid illustration so far of the Soviets' new attempt at openness. Of course, there are public relations benefits for them, and clearly they aren't revealing any highly valuable state secrets; what the American delegation photographed could also be seen in great detail by spy satellites. But until recently the Soviets considered it a shooting offense to photograph an army cafeteria.

The event is important because it undercuts the view that the radar proves the Soviets can't be trusted to carry out the provisions of any arms control agreement. The reality seems far more ambiguous. Krasnoyarsk appears to be the result of a bureaucratic fiasco in which the Soviet army started building a radar without understanding that it would violate the Anti-Ballistic Missile Treaty. The radar, according to American experts, is definitely not designed as a battle management station (as opponents of arms control have charged); it's too vulnerable to attack. Now the Soviets are indicating that they do not want Krasnoyarsk to be an obstacle to an future arms control agreements.

The potential long-range implication is a major change in Soviet military doctrine: If the new leadership accepts the fact that in a nuclear world it's more important to emphasize crisis stability than nuclear war-fighting capability, this would open the way for major advances in arms control.

There is probably a battle going on between the older Soviet military establishment — which must look at the Krasnoyarsk visit with horror — and the newer progressive elements aligned with General Secretary Mikhail Gorbachev. He is certainly in control now, but who will ultimately prevail is uncertain. It's obviously premature to make any fundamental changes in American military planning.

But it's also important for this administration and the next to recognize that something extraordinary is happening in the Soviet Union. There may be opportunities for easing tensions and creating a more stable relationship with an adversary. The possibility of a major change must not be dismissed.

Soviets Cease Jamming Voice of America

Officials of U.S.-financed Radio Liberty and its sister station, Radio Free Europe, Nov. 30, 1988 said that the Soviet Union had stopped electronic jamming of its broadcasts into the nation after 35 years. Jamming of Voice of America broadcasts had ended in May 1987 and jamming of British Broadcasting Corp. programming had ceased in January 1987.

According to the *New York Times*, the Soviet action left only Czechoslovakia and Bulgaria still jamming the broadcasts. Czechoslovakia Dec. 17 announced that it had ended the jamming.

In a related development, the Voice of America, run by the U.S. Information Agency, Sept. 28 was granted permission to open a permanent bureau in Moscow.

Los Angeles, CA, May 31, 1987

The Soviet Union's decision to cease jamming Voice of America broadcasts into that country is good news for Soviet listeners — and the West. But the U.S.S.R. still has a way to go before glasnost, or openness, becomes a part of Soviet airwaves.

For decades, the Soviets periodically have used powerful transmitters to block Western broadcasts translated for and aimed at East bloc listeners. The practice was explicitly prohibited in the 1975 Helsinki accords, but in recent years that provision was more or less ignored. Jamming intensified, for instance, after the Soviets' 1968 Czechoslovakian invasion, their 1979 Afghanistan invasion and the rise of Poland's Solidarity union in 1980.

Since its inception in the late 1940s, the Voice of America has attempted to present truthful, non-ideological reportage about international affairs, especially about life in the West. Like the much older BBC World Service, the VOA — as part of the U.S. Information Agency — depends for its credibility on freedom from government interference. Most of the USIA's directors, which have included in their ranks the famed CBS correspondent Edward R. Murrow, have fought hard to preserve its journalistic integrity.

Last January, the Soviet Union suspended its jamming of Russian-language BBC broadcasts just before a Moscow visit from British Prime Minister Margaret Thatcher. The current USIA director Charles Wick suggested a similar motive behind the unjamming of VOA on the eve of his visit to Moscow last Friday.

But the Soviets apparently have increased their interference of two other USIA broadcast services, the more ideological Radio Free Europe and Radio Liberty, and they continue to interfere with West Germany's Deutsche Welle service as well as Israel's Kol Israel programs.

Western broadcasters still have a problem, but also an opportunity. While the Soviets are busy jamming Radio Free Europe and Radio Liberty, the U.S. should strengthen its commitment to the Voice of America.

In so doing, we're in a better position to insist on Soviet compliance with the Helsinki accords for all international broadcasting.

The Charlotte Observer
Charlotte, NC, May 27, 1987

In today's world it is futile to try to stop people from listening to what they want to hear, says a top Soviet official by way of explaining his country's decision to stop jamming Voice of America broadcasts. Fine, but . . . .

But what? Well, say American officials, the VOA jamming may have stopped, but jamming of other Western services has increased. Indeed, engineers say that at least two of the Soviet jammers previously aimed at the VOA have simply redirected their interference to target Radio Free Europe and Radio Liberty. It also appears that there is increased jamming of German and Israeli broadcasts. The pattern is familiar: When jamming of British broadcasts was ended in January, shortly before the Moscow visit of British Prime Minister Margaret Thatcher, U.S. officials said the jamming was simply refocused on other targets.

While welcoming the end to the jamming of VOA, U.S. officials noted that a "more convincing demonstration of glasnost (openness) would be a Soviet decision to end all jamming."

Even that would be only a tiny step toward internal freedom in the Soviet Union, where the rush of reforms has not dismantled the legal tools of repression. While it is fine to applaud progressive steps, however small they may be, the West should not forget how long and little traveled the road is to real openness and freedom in the Soviet state.

THE PLAIN DEALER
Cleveland, OH, May 31, 1987

As director of the United States Information Agency, Charles Z. Wick's ego hasn't gotten any smaller. Preparing to leave for Moscow last week to negotiate some cultural exchanges, Wick suggested that the Soviet Union had suddenly ceased jamming Voice of America broadcasts in order to "make the trip even more pleasant." Even if that's true, it's nothing to be proud of. Conservative essayist William Safire, for example, remains critical of Wick's performance in Reykjavik last year. While there, Wick supposedly agreed to permit Soviet propaganda broadcasts into the United States from Cuba in exchange for VOA's freedom. He specifically did not include the two more powerful Western broadcast tools: Radio Liberty and Radio Free Europe.

As it turns out, when the Soviets ceased jamming the relatively innocuous VOA, they turned their jamming transmitters against Radio Liberty and Radio Free Europe. It should not escape your attention that although both the latter broadcasts are American funded, only VOA is a federal program, directed by the USIA. Is Wick's ego so large that he would deliberately sacrifice Western European broadcast projects for his own pet project? It's not outside the realm of credible speculation.

□

Regardless of its genesis, VOA's new freedom sends mixed signals about Soviet Premier Mikhail Gorbachev's ideas of liberalism. A decision to allow Soviet citizens to hear VOA seems to reinforce the success of his glasnost (openness) campaign. Yet, at the same time, opposition from older Soviet ideologues is growing stronger. Several publications have been warned to mute their reporting of sensitive social issues such as drug abuse, prostitution and police brutality. Some literary magazines that blossomed with the glasnost thaw likewise have been dampered. Those retreats suggest that the old-guard Soviet Bolsheviks have begun a coordinated effort to combat liberalization.

Meanwhile, Soviet Bloc nations are hedging their bets. Gorbachev visited Romania last week in part to encourage acceptance of his new brand of liberalism. The Soviet leader was warmly received, but in his official toast, Romanian President Nicolae Ceausescu pointedly refused to endorse Gorbachev's campaign. Romania always has a reputation as the Warsaw Pact's most independent nation, but other Soviet Bloc nations, with far closer ties to Moscow, also are ambivalent.

The surges of liberalization and retrenchment form a familiar pattern in most maturing socialist nations. As the ranks of the original revolutionary cadres wither, second-generation leaders begin pressing for economic progress at the expense of ideological purity. Thus, in Vietnam and China, liberal encroachments on central planning and other traditional restraints ebb and flow. It's no different in the Soviet Union. VOA's new broadcast ability might indeed be a symbol of glasnost. More probably, though, the decision is merely a temporary diversion from the the old guard's new restraint on the ideas and information in more influential sources—Moscow's literary magazines and the European radio stations that Wick sold out.

Los Angeles Times
Louisville, KY, May 24, 1987

ADD THIS to life's little ironies: The Soviet Union, that land that isn't known for freedom's ring, has quit jamming the broadcasts of news and views from the Voice of America. But the United States, now celebrating the 200th birthday of the Constitution, will not tell most of its own citizens what it is beaming to those Russians — or to anyone else.

"We hope the Soviet decision on V. O. A. signals a sincere initiative to open up their closed society. It's a positive step," Charles Wick, head of the Voice's parent, the U. S. Information Agency, said. We hope so, too, and now we hope Mr. Wick and his colleagues will work to open up their own society.

For it is against the law in this land of the free for this newspaper to print the text of messages that the Voice of America beams abroad. It is against the law in this land of the free for the people who work at the Voice office in Washington to send you copies of the news reports and editorials that are aired in nearly every nook and cranny of the world. It is against the law in this land of the free for you to copy down the material if you visit the Voice office and — after proving you're a historian or a scholar or a newspaper person —

ask to see the reports.

The law in question is the Smith-Mundt Act of 1948, one of several laws governing the Voice of America. The statute declares that any information prepared for or broadcast by the Voice "shall not be disseminated within the United States." It was passed because the legislators didn't want the government to set up a propaganda network to brainwash the folks at home. But instead of keeping us from being propagandized, it is keeping us from being informed about what our own government is doing and saying abroad.

Voice of America broadcasts contain a mix of news, entertainment and educational material. And each week since 1982, the Voice has been broadcasting 10 to 12 editorials in as many as 42 languages to listeners abroad. The editorials are written by members of an eight-person policy office, and presumably they reflect the views of the Reagan Administration on current issues.

We say "presumably" because the Voice won't send us copies of those editorials. So we can't say for sure. If you're really interested, you could buy a short-wave radio, or, these days, give a call to your Aunt Natasha in Leningrad. She can tell you what's going on here in the land of the free.

The Dispatch
Columbus, OH, May 28, 1987

The Soviet Union has stopped jamming Voice of America broadcasts and, in as sporting a gesture as the Kremlin may be capable of, challenged the U.S.-financed station to keep listeners interested.

The Soviets may have to do likewise. The jamming cessation may be a signal that the superpowers are willing to take the next step toward increasing understanding between their people.

That step is an exchange of radio programming that would give each nation the opportunity to reach millions of listeners in the other nation.

Such an exchange was discussed last fall during the summit between President Reagan and Soviet leader Mikhail Gorbachev. While no formal accord has been announced, American officials are known to be interested in the possibility.

Charles Z. Wick, director of the U.S. Information Agency, the organization that supervises VOA operations, has said in the past that the amount of programming and methods of keeping track of it would have to be negotiated.

On the surface, Soviet officials

described the decision to stop jamming VOA broadcasts as an effort to dispel the mystique that developed around VOA since the early 1980s when the radio broadcasts were jammed.

This came at a time when relations between the Soviet Union and the United States were deteriorating in the aftermath of the Soviet occupation of Afghanistan.

"If something is forbidden it tastes sweeter than what it is," a Soviet official said this week. "After the sweetness of the forbidden fruit, I hope they (Soviet listeners) do not get a bitter aftertaste now."

American officials can be expected to work even harder to continue the quality of news and information programming beamed into the Soviet Union.

There now exists an opportunity to reach many people who might otherwise have been unable to receive the VOA because of the jamming.

This opportunity to ease tension and increase understanding is certainly a welcome one.

FORT WORTH STAR-TELEGRAM
Fort Worth, TX, May 29, 1987

It may be too much to hope that the Soviet Union's cessation of jamming Voice of America broadcasts into that country will be permanent. Nevertheless, it is impossible to suppress that hope.

While it is possible that the jamming has been stopped for the first time in eight years because of the impending visit of the director of the U.S. Information Agency to the Soviet Union to discuss cultural exchanges, there is a good chance that the unjamming of VOA is another facet of Soviet leader Mikhail Gorbachev's *glasnost* (openess) campaign.

The downside of the unjamming of VOA, of course, is that the jamming transmitters that were focused on those broadcasts now appear to be used to intensify interference with Radio Free Europe and Radio Liberty broadcasts. True *glasnost* would allow broadcasts also to reach Soviet listeners without official interference.

Of course, expectations concerning the Soviet Union — where certain freedoms taken for granted in this country are unheard of — must be tempered with realism. Gorbachev may be the closest thing to a benevolent dictator to head the Soviet government in years, but the Soviet Union is still a totalitarian state.

The Radio Free Europe and Radio Liberty broadcasts are sharply critical of Soviet policies and misadventures and fit cozily in the official Soviet definition of propaganda. The VOA broadcasts are mixtures of straight news, features and entertainment. They are more effective communications for the West because they do not proselytize.

If the Soviets insist on jamming some American broadcasts, it is in the best interests of all involved that the VOA's broadcasts be the ones to go unjammed.

The Seattle Times
Seattle, WA, May 27, 1987

WHEN the Soviets signed the Helsinki Pact 12 years ago, they agreed to stop jamming foreign radio broadcasts to announce, at long last, that Voice of America broadcasts in Russian and other Soviet languages are free of interference.

An end to the jamming of VOA programs apparently is a part of Mikhail Gorbachev's reform program. But like so many other Gorbachev reforms, the clearing of the air waves is incomplete. Radio Free Europe and Radio Liberty broadcasts aimed at the Soviet empire are still being drowned out. In fact, some of the Soviet jammers previously beamed at VOA transmissions have been redirected against the other two U.S. stations.

Radio Free Europe and Radio Liberty have a particular bite. Many of their programs are prepared by refugees from Warsaw Pact nations.

It will be up to the VOA to keep Soviet listeners informed about the continuing difficulties experienced by its "competition."

Reagan, Gorbachev Hold Moscow Summit

U.S. President Ronald Reagan and Soviet General Secretary Mikhail S. Gorbachev met in Moscow May 29 to June 2, 1988 for the fourth summit. It was the president's first visit to the Soviet Union. During the summit, Reagan, known for his hard-line anti-Soviet stance, noticeably softened his views. There were no breakthroughs on arms control, but two relatively minor accords were signed. Among other issues, human rights caused the most disagreement. At the end, Reagan spoke of his U.S.S.R. visit in glowing terms, but Gorbachev complained of "missed opportunities," dampening the overall optimism that emerged from the summit.

Air Force One, the presidential jet, landed at Vnukovo Airport, east of Moscow, at 2 p.m. May 29. The large U.S. contingent included First Lady Nancy Reagan; George P. Shultz, the secretary of state; Frank C. Carlucci, the secretary of defense; Howard Baker, the White House chief of staff; Lt. Gen. Colin L. Powell, the White House national security adviser; and Max M. Kampelman, the chief arms-control negotiator. The Americans were driven to the Kremlin's Grand Palace, where Gorbachev and Reagan spoke at a welcoming ceremony in the ornate St. George's Hall.

Speaking in Russian, Gorbachev said that his three previous summits with Reagan had weakened "long-held dislikes" and broken "habitual stereotypes stemming from enemy images." He added, "Mr. President, you and Mrs. Reagan are here on your first visit to the Soviet Union, a country that you have so often mentioned in your statements. Aware of your interest in Soviet proverbs, let me add another one to your collection: 'It's better to see once than to hear a hundred times.'"

The President said that he had come to Moscow to continue the "step by step" progress in superpower relations. Reagan used a Russian proverb – *Rodilsya, Toropilsya* ("It was born, it was not rushed") – to illustrate his point. "We both know there are tremendous hurdles to be overcome," he added.

Following the welcoming ceremony, the two leaders adjourned to the palace's St. Catherine's Hall for their first discussion of the summit, which lasted 70 minutes. The meeting was private, but reports surfaced that Gorbachev bristled when Reagan pushed the human rights issue. The President presented the Soviet leader with 14 cases involving Soviet political prisoners and would-be emigrees. Gorbachev was reported to have suggested that Soviet legislators and U.S. members of Congress meet regularly on the human rights issue.

President Reagan hammered at the human rights issue in afternoon speeches May 30 at the Danilov Monastery in Moscow and at Spaso House, the U.S. ambassador's residence, where the Reagans stayed during the summit. At the monastery, a 13th-century Russian Orthodox complex, the President called for the Soviet government to permit closed churches to be reopened. Americans, he said, "feel it keenly when religious freedom is denied to anyone anywhere."

An hour later, Reagan met with 98 Soviet dissidents and "refusniks" (persons, mainly Jews, who had been denied permission to emigrate). "You have the prayers and support of the American people, indeed, of people throughout the world," the President told them.

The superpower talks May 30 focused on arms control. Reagan, Gorbachev and key aides met for nearly two hours in the morning. Defense Secretary Carlucci held a three-hour discussion with Marshal Sergei F. Akhromeyev and Dimitri T. Yakov, the Soviet defense minister. Gorbachev made a surprise proposal to gradually reduce the active-duty troops of the North Atlantic Treaty Organization and the Warsaw Pact by 500,000.

The U.S. and Soviet Union signed nine separate agreements May 31. Two of the nine pacts pertained to arms control. They were signed by Secretary of State George Shultz and Soviet Foreign Minister Eduard Shevardnadze. Reagan and Gorbachev witnessed the signings but did not take part in the ceremony because the agreements were considered minor. One of the arms agreements required either superpower to notify the other 24 hours before the test launching of a land- or sea-based ballistic missile. The notice was to include launch site and planned impact site. The other arms pact codified a 1987 agreement in principle on an exchange of monitoring the yields of underground nuclear tests.

Minneapolis Star and Tribune

Minneapolis, MN, June 2, 1988

Ronald Reagan is not a great administrator, a fact reinforced recently by former White House officials turned authors. But Reagan deserves credit for being a brilliant head of state. He performed especially well in that role during the Moscow summit which ends today. Despite regrettable lapses — notably his remark about "humoring" American Indians, discussed in an editorial below — the president was an eloquent spokesman for the American perspective on U.S.-Soviet relations.

Tone was an important ingredient of that eloquence, and Reagan's was just right. From his landing in Moscow, the president persistently pressed the Soviet Union to improve its record on human rights. And he often made his point by referring to poignant passages from that nation's own literature. In private discussions, his provocative emphasis on the human-rights theme elicited prickly responses from General Secretary Mikhail Gorbachev. But in public, especially during a Tuesday exchange with university students and Wednesday's press conference, Reagan coupled his criticism with enthusiastic endorsement of Gorbachev's efforts to improve Soviet conduct.

At times Reagan seemed to be interpreting Gorbachev to the Soviet people and encouraging them to support the general secretary's far-ranging political and economic reforms. Reagan may have gone too far in attributing most human-rights abuses to bureaucrats run amok, but his point is valid: The Soviet Union has many foot-dragging apparatchiks who see safety in the status quo and danger in a more liberal human-rights policy.

On arms control and the evolution in U.S.-Soviet relations, both leaders, but especially Reagan, wisely downplayed their personal relationship and emphasized instead the need for steady work at narrowing differences between the two nations. The INF treaty, ratified by the Senate just in time for the summit, is the first impressive fruit of that narrowing. With continued hard work, the two sides eventually should resolve disagreements over strategic defense and agree to major reductions in strategic nuclear arsenals.

That agreement most likely will not come during Reagan's remaining months in office, which causes Gorbachev some frustration. But the end of an American administration is an artificial deadline. Pushing too hard to beat it risks miscalculations that might retard or even derail the difference-narrowing process Reagan and Gorbachev have started. Stable U.S.-Soviet relations — and arms treaties that endure — require a base of understanding capable of surviving changes in the leadership of either nation.

In a toast delivered Tuesday night, Reagan told Gorbachev that "on matters of great importance, we will continue to differ profoundly." But, the president continued, "On specific matters of policy we have made progress, often historic progress. And perhaps most important, we have committed our nations to continuing to work together." Reagan captured the summit spirit precisely. It wasn't a diplomatic spectacular; it was one conversation in a dialogue that needs to continue long after Reagan and Gorbachev have passed from power.

Roanoke Times & World-News

Roanoke, VA, JUne 1, 1988

GRANTED, it may have been a bit presumptuous for Ronald Reagan to use part of his state visit to Moscow to meet with some well-known dissidents and whip up sentiment for civil rights in the Soviet Union. Were the shoe on the other foot, Americans might not cotton to Mikhail Gorbachev's touring black ghettos or Indian reservations in this country, listening to grievances of the downtrodden and then lecturing the United States on how it should treat its minorities.

That, however, is a quibble. The president has a gift for the stirring symbolic gesture, and this surely qualified. His meeting with those protesters and refuseniks, who were rounded up and bused by American officials to the U.S. ambassador's residence, was a public-relations triumph. It showcased Ronald Reagan at his best, and it made a point about human rights that Soviet authorities could not ignore. (Indeed, they tried on their evening news TV program to defuse its impact.) And if the event irritated the Kremlin — well, nobody promised that detente, let alone *glasnost*, would be a rose garden.

Speaking Monday to several dozen Soviet citizens who have felt the back of the Soviet system's hand, Reagan said that although there have been "hopeful signs" of improvement in that country, "there can be no relenting for us now. We must work for more, always more." He added: "I came here to give you strength, but it is you who have strengthened me."

A number of dissidents interviewed afterward by The Washington Post said the event moved them deeply. Lev Timofeyev, a former political prisoner in the U.S.S.R., now editor of the Independent Journal, commented: "We've had many substantive working meetings with American officials. But today was a great precedent. To hear such things from an American president in the middle of Moscow is a great symbol for us."

On an evening TV news program, a Soviet official, Genrikh Borovik, grumbled that the event was propagandistic and "a waste of time" for Reagan in a visit that held more important things in store. Things such as arms-control discussions.

Arms control is important. But if the superpowers' leaders are to talk about what divides them and their political systems, there can be nothing more basic than human rights. Of course, in practice the United States falls short of its own ideals. But the Soviet Union has consistently and flagrantly ignored or violated the rights its people supposedly are guaranteed in its own constitution. Things are better for many dissidents under Gorbachev. But this is not because he is a democrat at heart, but because he sees the need for flexibility and openness to revive the Soviet Union, especially its moribund economy.

This is not simply a matter of a visiting American president's trying to impose Western values on an alien culture. At Helsinki in 1975, the U.S.S.R. was one of several signatories to a treaty that — among other things — pledged participants to allow their citizens to emigrate freely and to "respect human rights and fundamental freedoms, including the freedom of thought, conscience, religion or belief . . ." For more than a decade, the Kremlin treated those commitments as virtually a dead letter, and it still is a long way from fulfilling them all. Consider Reagan's words in Moscow as a little reminder.

Lincoln Journal

Lincoln, NE, June 3, 1988

Now that the distraction of that noisy, know-it-all Amerikanski crowd has passed, it's time in Moscow to get down to the truly important items on the calendar for June 1988.

That could only mean the first Soviet Communist Party conference since 1941. American presidents and summits come and go. Not so crossroads events which may determine the authoritarian state's direction for the next decade or so, plus who effectively will be at the head of the Marxist-Leninist parade in the immediate future.

The most unusual party conference is scheduled to begin June 27. Even more extraordinary is the agenda. The proposals for party restructuring — limits on length of leadership for any one individual, secret balloting — and national economic change are unlike anything of Russian experience since the immediate post-Revolutionary period.

Dynamic Mikhail S. Gorbachev is the most visible point man for Soviet reform. But Westerners err if they judge that all proposed systemic changes in the Soviet Union breathlessly hang upon Gorbachev's personal fate, and his success at the 19th All Union Party Conference.

The Russia of Josef Stalin is gone. Years of urbanization and education have transformed the Soviet Union while we paid no attention and clung to strereotypes. Before World War II, peasants constituted more than half of the country's population. Today, they are less than 13 percent of the total. The urban working class now amounts to 61 percent of the population, with white-collar workers representing about 25 percent. There are sophisticated, unfulfilled elites independent of the ruling Communist Party apparatus.

These, in fact, are the people for whom Gorbachev may have the greatest appeal. The lively views of some of them entered American homes last week, via television. President Reagan surely was on the mark telling students at Moscow University they were living in an exciting dawn of national change, with increasing possibilities of personal freedom and a better life.

Which is simply to suggest that even if Gorbachev sustains a setback in the party conference by forces saying he is moving too fast, the rigid Soviet societal and political ice already has fracture lines.

Wisconsin State Journal

Madison, WI, June 1, 1988

Soviet leader Mikhail Gorbachev has been gritting his iron teeth the past few days over this pesky American president's naggings about human rights. ". . . It is my impression that probably both sides do not have a very good idea of what the real situation on human rights is in the Soviet (Union) and the United States," Gorbachev said, suggesting that Ronald Reagan is somehow guilty of throwing rocks from inside a glass house.

Gorbachev says he welcomes expanded U.S.-Soviet exchanges, but sets as a condition that "this should be done without interfering in domestic affairs, without sermonizing or imposing one's views and ways . . ."

There is no need for a translator to understand what Gorbachev is really saying: He's being upstaged at home by the "Great Communicator," who is busily meeting with Soviet dissidents, touring monasteries and generally being a dacha-to-dacha salesman for freedom of speech, economic activity and religion. Comrade Gorbachev is not amused that Reagan is being Reagan in Moscow.

Well, that's just too bad. Gorbachev has known from the start that his policy of glasnost would be a two-way street, and he could have guessed that the first American president to set foot on Soviet soil in 14 years would put his claims of openness to an old-fashioned American test.

For Gorbachev's policy of glasnost to become firmly rooted in the change-resistant Soviet society, he must lead by example, showing tolerance for diverse opinions and, yes, buttinski American presidents.

Gorbachev may think Reagan the ungracious guest, but the Soviet leader has everything to gain in the eyes of his own people by keeping his grumblings to a minimum. If the Kremlin can't grin and bear criticism of its internal policies from an American president, it certainly won't tolerate debate from within.

●

Reagan may have grasped the problem of human rights in the Soviet Union, but he could use a lesson in American history. In response to a question at Moscow University on Tuesday, the president said it might have been a mistake for the U.S. government to "humor" Native Americans by allowing them to continue their "primitive lifestyle" on reservations. He said he can't understand why American Indians have complaints about their lot in life, because some of their lands "were overlaying great pools of oil. And you can get very rich by pumping oil."

That kind of insensitivity toward civil-rights issues at home will not help Reagan in his efforts to promote human rights abroad.

The Union Leader

Manchester, NH, June 1, 1988

When Ronald Reagan arrived in Russia, 20 Russian Bibles went on sale in Moscow. What would be normal here was unprecedented there. One Russian said that it was the first time in his life that he had ever seen Bibles on sale in the city.

This propaganda ploy — "of course the Soviets allow religious freedom" — sums up this summit meeting, where the Soviets will sell us the line that they are just ordinary, peace-loving folks like us. And Americans will swallow the bait.

Gorbachev smiles, the people wave, 20 Bibles are sold and, unfortunately, many of our leaders and many of our people will applaud this latest treaty as a sign of peace. The constant fear talk of nuclear war has made us well prepared to accept any sign of peace. Add to that the reassurance of cultural exchanges and student visits and we're suckers for the pitch.

The Soviets do not have to destroy us. We will destroy ourselves with our wishful thinking and our belief that 20 Bibles prove there is a change in the Communist goal of ultimate world domination.

The Augusta Chronicle

Augusta, GA, June 1, 1988

The first trip to Moscow by an American president in 13 years pitted the Reagan Revolution against the Russian Revolution.

Ronald Reagan made some frank, startling pronouncements in the citadel of Marxism-Leninism. And Soviet Communist Party boss Mikhail Gorbachev let him get away with it.

The man once denounced by the Kremlin as the spokesman of "Wall Street capitalism," standing by a bust of Lenin, told Moscow University students yesterday that economic democracy is the wave of the future. He specifically cited the free market success of South Korea, Singapore and Taiwan. Those countries, of course, have been damned for years as "reactionary" by hard-line ideologues at that very university.

The most anti-Communist U.S. president of this century also praised mainland China and Soviet ally India for limited free market experimentation.

India, incidentally, is now following more of the supply side Reagan economic gospel rather than the socialism its economists learned at Moscow U. The prime minister has slashed government regulations, import barriers and taxes and demanded that Indian industry modernize and learn to compete for the march into the 21st century.

President Reagan's summit exposure to the Soviet people — through the Soviet media, no less! — and his particular emphasis on a free economy and human rights may be doing more to inform younger Soviets than all of the broadcasts aired by Radio Free Europe and the Voice of America.

Significant, too, is that Kremlin propaganda doesn't talk any more about the traditional Marxist view of a fatal crisis in the capitalist system.

As Soviet agriculture expert (and Gorbachev friend) Alexandr N. Yakovlev, now says: "The forecasts of the development of the capitalist system, of the boundaries of its viability and of the reserves of its survival were found to be largely oversimplified. It (the propaganda) all has to be abandoned."

Theoretician Karl Marx, in effect, was all wet.

The Dallas Morning News

Dallas, TX, June 1, 1988

President Reagan's speech delivered Tuesday to students at Moscow State University will be remembered as one of the high points of this United States-Soviet summit.

A man of lesser political sensibility than Ronald Reagan easily could have used this platform for one more Russian-bashing speech on human rights. But the president rose to the moment to talk in terms that painted pictures of what freedom of information, of thought, of communication and of the market really are. He spoke to a Soviet audience clearly groping for social and political definitions in the midst of change as Soviet leader Mikhail Gorbachev leads the nation on a rocky path presumably toward greater openness.

For President Reagan to speak directly to the Soviet people in this way was especially meaningful. This is because the Soviet Union is only partially buttressed by the strength and ruthlessness of the KGB and Soviet Red Army. An even more powerful force in maintaining the repressive status quo is Soviet society, the values of the people themselves. These values have been throughout the history of the Soviet state been represented by an acquiescence to political repression in exchange for minimal guarantees of economic security. President Reagan, in addressing the younger generation of Soviets, was talking to those who will in time define the values of their society as they assume positions of leadership.

While the central theme of this summit is arms control, the human rights dimension is what the dream of world peace inevitably springs from. The chasm created by differences in values between the two superpowers is an even wider gulf than the elements of contention within the treaty negotiating process. A free society espouses public accountability for the decisions of its government. In a totalitarian one, its citizens close their shutters and lock their doors to escape responsibility for governmental actions.

President Reagan penetrated to the nub of the issue when he said: "Freedom is the right to question and change the established way of doing things." When Soviet society, beginning perhaps with the students in that audience, decides to embrace those ideals, not only will human rights in the Soviet Union be guaranteed, but the reasons for the arms race effectively will have vanished.

The Hartford Courant

Hartford, CT, June 2, 1988

"**Y**ou are talking about another time, another era," President Reagan said in Moscow where he disavowed the assertion he had made in his first term that the Soviet Union is an evil empire.

It is indeed another era — for the Soviet Union under Mikhail S. Gorbachev's leadership, and for Mr. Reagan, whose carefully scripted remarks aimed at rapprochement with Moscow contradict a career of denouncing the Kremlin.

Mr. Reagan's soothing words, eight months before leaving office, will be recorded for posterity, whether or not the president has changed in his heart of hearts.

His decades-long anti-Communist stride culminated in a speech to Protestant evangelicals in Orlando in March 1983, when he said that the Soviet Union was "the focus of evil in the modern world," and that the West must guard against the "aggressive impulses of an evil empire."

This week in Moscow, the president criticized the Soviet Union's human-rights record, as he should, and wasted few opportunities to laud America's democratic processes. But he also recanted the evil empire theme, lauded Soviet culture, hailed the economic and political reforms of Mr. Gorbachev and told Soviet students that they stood on the threshold of a fantastic new age.

Mr. Reagan's new approach is better for the United States and the world as well as for his place in history than his saber rattling of earlier years. He stands a good chance of leaving office as a realist who made the world a safer place through arms control measures and confidence-building rhetoric.

Mr. Reagan's most conservative supporters will not swallow the new line. Many of them feel that the president shouldn't try to help Mr. Gorbachev succeed because the Soviet Union would be a stronger adversary as a result. They discount the persuasive argument that a more prosperous and secure Soviet Union would be less likely to seek security and prosperity by going to war.

It's ironic that in the end, Mr. Reagan may disappoint his most devoted supporters, who tend to shrink from the idea of détente. But he'll make a lasting contribution if he can devalue the currency of the paralyzing, irrational kind of anti-communism that for too long dominated U.S. politics.

The Register-Guard

Eugene, OR, June 4, 1988

Just before the recent Moscow summit, The New York Times and CBS News commissioned a poll of Soviet citizens' views. Public opinion polling is not new in the Soviet Union, but this survey asked sensitive questions about the Soviet political system. Many of the responses were of interest, but the most illuminating findings relate to the poll itself.

The Soviets allowed questions on such touchy subjects as whether Soviets favor a one-party system (51 percent yes, 28 percent no) and whether multi-candidate elections should be conducted (77 percent yes, 4 percent no). People were asked their opinion of former Soviet leaders (Stalin, Trotsky and Brezhnev rated low, Bukharin and Khrushchev high).

But the pollsters were denied permission to ask people their opinion of current Soviet leaders, including Mikhail Gorbachev. That defines the limits of political debate.

The government was not the only source of resistance. Respondents often did not believe the pollsters' promises of anonymity. Some refused to participate, and others gave the answers they thought corresponded to official policy. Yet people's initial suspicions soon passed, and on the average they gave responses that departed from official policy one-third of the time.

Soviet leaders clearly have some distance to go before they permit uninhibited gathering and dissemination of information about public opinion. And citizens will need further assurance that they can speak with candor. But still, there's evidence of a new willingness to seek the truth from among the people. Such a willingness is one of the more convincing demonstrations to date of change in the Soviet Union.

The Kansas City Times

Kansas City, MO, June 3, 1988

There were handshakes all around and expressions of hope and good will, but Mikhail Gorbachev exhibited an unmistakable and no doubt calculated surliness in the final hours of the Moscow conference. He spoke of lost opportunities to advance arms reductions and said that "Mr. Reagan had missed an important chance to take a step forward."

Gorbachev must have been bridling under the president's insistence on talking about human rights and his meetings with dissidents, some of them only freshly out of the *gulag.* "I'm not filled with admiration for this part of the visit," the general secretary said.

Yet human rights is inextricable in the total equation of relations that includes arms control and reductions. It is not the mere existence of Soviet power that is the central issue, but the use to which that power is put. It is used to occupy Eastern Europe. It blots out freedom and national self-determination wherever it can reach. The Soviet-style police state that grinds down its own nonconformists is the pattern in Poland, Hungary, Czechoslovakia, Cuba, Nicaragua, Vietnam — wherever it is installed.

The model is Section 1 Article 70 of the Criminal Code of the Russian Republic which says in part:

Agitation or propaganda carried out with the purpose of subverting the Soviet regime..

the dissemination for the said purposes of slanderous inventions defamatory to the Soviet political and social system . . . are punishable by imprisonment for a period of from six months to seven years and with exile from two to five years.

Similarly, Article 190 outlaws:

. . . The systematic dissemination by word of mouth of deliberately false statements derogatory to the Soviet State and social system and also the preparation or dissemination of such statements in written, printed or any other form. . . .

That's about as plain as can be.

Yet Gorbachev's final emphasis on weapons reductions is a shrewd if hoary ploy. Soviet apologists in the West can always turn to the nuclear question whenever the nature of Soviet totalitarianism is acknowledged. Everything must be subordinate to "peace." Without "peace" there will be no humans to have human rights.

This assumes that the only alternative to nuclear war is to accept the Soviet position on all questions, to let Gorbachev, "the good guy," go unchallenged in all matters. Of course this is absurd. Some is naive stupidity. Some is deliberate and dishonorable service in the cause of despotism, the same warped mentality that excused Josef Stalin's 30 years of terror.

The Soviet Union, under Mikhail Gorbachev, is moving in a new direction. But the movement is only beginning. With all good will the United States and other democracies can hope it will proceed swiftly to real freedom. But to ignore the reality of the Soviet Union as it is would in no way aid the process. It could only slow or negate it entirely.

News-Tribune & Herald

Duluth, MN, June 3, 1988

Columnist Ellen Goodman doesn't feel much safer in the wake of the the Reagan-Gorbachev Moscow summit (her opinion is elsewhere on this page), do you?

How safe we feel from being blown up in a nuclear war varies with individual personalities. And while, by most accounts, there were no "major breakthroughs" in the Moscow meetings, those same accounts exude optimism that relations between the United States and Soviet Union are vastly improved.

Yes, the INF (Intermediate-range Nuclear Forces) treaty was delivered (it had already been been signed and sealed at the Washington summit). It's a start. Cutbacks in strategic nuclear weapons were not agreed upon. It could still happen.

But there is a feeling that there were developments that are broader than weapons reductions. The generally amicable meetings between President Reagan and Soviet leader Gorbachev, their warm public appearances on the world's stage and the willingness of the pair to talk frankly in all areas of mutual interest all bode well for future relations between the two countries.

It is truly astonishing to observe the progress — and we mean progress — of Reagan's thinking from the old "evil empire" days to a series of one-on-one summits with the evil emperor. But then this Soviet leader doesn't seem as "evil" as past ones. Gorbachev doesn't seem evil at all; he seems earnestly interested in a peaceful relationship with the United States.

While the world might not be appreciably safer in terms of nuclear throw-weight, it has to be progress when those responsible for doing the throwing are shaking hands.

HERALD·JOURNAL

SYRACUSE

Syracuse, NY, June 3, 1988

Superpower summitry is symbolism first and substance second. The just-concluded Moscow meeting between President Reagan and Mikhail Gorbachev was no exception.

When the tangible accomplishments of the past week are totaled up, they don't amount to much in the context of history. It was a media show. The most important real event of the summit was the exchange of ratified INF treaty documents. The rest was mostly feel-good stuff. The best the two leaders could do on a strategic arms reduction agreement was to express the common hope that it could be accomplished — sometime.

This is not to belittle what happened in Moscow this week. It may have been largely rhetoric, but it was extraordinary rhetoric indeed when measured against the old-fashioned Cold War saber-rattling of just a few years ago. The two leaders have added impetus to a trend toward better relations between the two old enemies.

The momentum established at the Moscow love-feast will not be checked easily. Neither government will want to be perceived as the spoilsport who ruined the progress that is earning broad approval among the citizens of both countries, as well as the rest of the world. Over the long haul, this could make for a more peaceful world. But there could be short-term benefits as well.

Among the likely beneficiaries of this momentum are Soviet citizens seeking to leave their country. After getting in his customary licks on human rights, Reagan made the amazing statement — to the chagrin of his conservative followers in this country — that the dissidents' inability to secure exit visas was due more to bureaucratic ineptitude than to state policy. Even giving the Soviets the benefit of every doubt, such a conclusion is nonsense.

But when we consider a possible upshot, there may have been a method to the madness. The American president has said for all the world to hear — including the Soviet Union — that the visa-seekers are not the victims of oppressive policy. In order to lend credibility to those kind words, the reasoning could be, it would be in the Kremlin's best interests to make things easier for people who want to emigrate. The last thing the Soviets want to do, in Reagan's opinion apparently, is make a liar out of him when he's praising them.

The most important thing that happened in Moscow this week was affirmation of a feeling the Cold War is beginning to thaw. It may have been mostly warm fuzzies, but it inspires a confidence that U.S.-Soviet relations will continue to improve.

"Silence must never again be permitted to fall between us," said President Reagan at the end of his visit.

Amen.

The Record

Hackensack, NJ, June 1, 1988

In presuming to lecture Mikhail Gorbachev on human rights, President Reagan has seriously miscalculated. Although he and the thousand of Western journalists may think otherwise, in Moscow the fourth Reagan-Gorbachev summit is viewed as little more than a warm-up act for the really big show due at the end of the month, the general conference of the Soviet Communist Party.

The assembly, the first of its kind since 1941, is shaping up as the final showdown between the forces of perestroika and glasnost on one hand, and the self-aggrandizing, go-slow Soviet bureaucracy on the other. Boris Yeltsin, the recently-deposed mayor of Moscow who accused Mr. Gorbachev of not moving fast enough, has called for the resignation of Yegor Ligachev, the party's most prominent neo-conservative; demonstrations have broken out in Leningrad over charges that neo-cons are rigging the voting for the conference; and mass protests in Soviet Armenia are again adding to the underlying tension.

Thus, while the summit is important to U.S.-Soviet relations, the Communist Party conference, which begins on June 28, is even more significant in that it could set the course for the Soviet Union for years to come.

With that in mind, Mr. Reagan's comments on human rights could not be more clumsy. Their inevitable effect is to weaken Mr. Gorbachev's position. If he pushes for more human rights, he puts himself in the position of submitting meekly to schoolboy lectures from an American president and only succeeds in making himself look weak. If he responds with defiance, he might wind up putting a chill back on U.S.-Soviet relations and undermining the very policies he espouses. Either way, he loses, while the xenophobic Soviet right, which is deeply suspicious of the West as a source of military competition, liberalization, and economic change, gains. It is a no-win proposition, for Mr. Gorbachev and the West. Mr. Reagan's message may well backfire.

Mr. Reagan's remarks are also inappropriate because they are out of date. Take the matter of Alexander Solzhenitsyn, whom he invoked during a tour of the restored Danilov Monastery and again in an address before prominent Soviet performers and artists. Mr. Reagan thinks of the exiled writer as a patriot and anti-Communist. But ever since his famous 1978 Harvard commencement address, in which he railed against decadent Western democracy, questions have arisen about Mr. Solzhenitsyn. Those who know the Soviet scene well, such as Alexander Yanov, the exiled Soviet political scientist who is the author of "The Russian New Right," point to anti-semitic references in his writings in arguing that Mr. Solzhenitsyn is a Russian nationalist, an apologist for czarism, and anything but a supporter of the pro-Western liberal policies espoused by Mr. Gorbachev.

The situation in the Soviet Union is complex and explosive, which is why slogans imported ready-made from the United States are inappropriate. They are all too likely to produce opposite results. Rather than barge ahead, Mr. Reagan should listen and learn before proffering advice.

Herald ⚓ News

Fall River, MA, June 1, 1988

The Senate finally approved the treaty between the United States and the Soviet Union that eliminates medium range nuclear missiles.

Approval came after the President was on his way to the Moscow summit meeting with Mikhail Gorbachev.

It was, however, in time for Howard Baker, the chief White House aide, to fly to Moscow to deliver it to the President. Baker had remained behind with this in mind after the Reagan party had taken off.

The Senate, and for that matter the country, had been in two minds about the treaty ever since President Reagan and Secretary Gorbachev reached agreement about it at their last summit session in Washington.

In the end, however, it was ratified less because the Senate's doubts were dispelled than because refusal to do so would have prejudiced the chances of further negotiations with the Soviet Union, and the senators, on the whole, preferred to give them a chance.

The President and Gorbachev are talking about further reductions in the superpowers' stockpiles of nuclear weapons. There is no likelihood they will arrive at another treaty during the current summit session, however, and the President has even mentioned the possibility of another, similar meeting before he leaves office in January.

Presumably another meeting would be scheduled only if a new treaty to reduce nuclear weapons still further were near completion.

In that case the President might wish to sign it before turning the reins and prerogatives of office over to his successor.

The fact is, however, that the Moscow summit meeting is not producing much that is strikingly new or decisive in terms of disarmament.

Its importance is more as a demonstration of good will by the President than as a major step forward in the ongoing negotiations between the United States and the Soviet Union.

As such, the demonstration may be worth much or nothing. The President is exceptionally good at conveying good will, probably because he genuinely feels it.

But whether any such display of American friendliness will have a lasting effect on relations between this country and Russia is dubious at best.

It may, however, give Milhail Gorbachev some support in his endeavor to bring about internal reforms in the Soviet Union, and this, it appears, is more likely to promote peaceful relations between the superpowers than the reverse.

As always, negotiations of any kind with the Soviet Union are difficult or uncertain, but the President and Congress are doing what they can to help them succeed.

Arkansas 🦌 Gazette.

Little Rock, AR, June 4, 1988

The Intermediate-range Nuclear Forces treaty that was the centerpiece of the Moscow summit is a powerful symbol for arms control efforts and for any reason it is welcome. However, it should be understood that the INF agreement still leaves the world with far too many nuclear weapons.

Consider some of the benefits. INF helps to ease tensions between the United States and the Soviet Union because it is the first ratified arms control treaty between them in 16 years. It removes Soviet fears of a fatal strike on their command and control facilities, so they would not feel it necessary to strike first. It sets precedent for "on-site inspections" in negotiating additional treaties. It requires the Soviet Union to destroy 857 deployed missiles capable of carrying 1,667 warheads while it requires the United States to destroy only 429 single-warhead missiles.

Essentially the treaty provides that all missiles with a range of 300 miles to 3,400 miles be destroyed within three years. This means the 1,286 deployed missiles will be joined on the dump by 1,417 training and testing missiles.

This much accomplished, where do the two stand?

Neither is a 98-pound weakling. None of the warheads will be destroyed, just the missiles themselves. In one accounting, these weapons represent only about 3 per cent of the nuclear arsenals anyway. The United States still will have about 4,300 short-range nuclear weapons of various types in Western Europe, and they will be complemented by French and British arsenals. Western sources have found it more difficult to estimate what will be left of the Soviet arsenal although it is known that about 1,000 short-range land-based missiles are deployed.

This may be a slightly safer world now that the INF treaty has gone into effect, and that is to the common good. But there is still plenty of bang left for anyone who thinks the United States and the Soviet Union have engaged in any significant measure of disarmament.

The Union Leader

*Manchester, NH,
June 5, 1988*

Aides are blaming either fatigue or a wish to be polite to his host for President Reagan's appalling remark that mere bureaucracy is responsible for the plight of Soviet dissidents and refuseniks.

Whatever the reason, we think the President's words and Soviet boss Gorbachev's response to them sum up forcefully what was wrong with this summit and what ails the fading Reagan administration.

The President told Moscow and the world last week that any problem Soviet Jews and other dissidents have in getting out of the Soviet slave state is probably one of bureaucratic red tape and certainly not because of Communist government policy.

"I'm not blaming you," Reagan told a Communist newsman who had asked about the President's earlier criticism of the Soviet Union's human rights violations.

"I'm blaming bureaucracy. We have the same type of thing happen in our country."

With that one incredible response, the President severely damaged what had been the only saving grace of this deplorable summit love-in with the Communists.

Until then, on the matter of human rights, Mr. Reagan had been forthright, candid, and eloquent in speaking out against Soviet repression of religion, of free speech, of free thought and movement.

But in return for his "bureaucracy apology" and his glowing remarks about Gorbachev's hard work on reform, what did Mr. Reagan get from his new friend?

Gorbachev figuratively spit in the President's face, chastising him at their joint appearance for failing to do more on East-West relations. Later, as the President's plane was leaving the USSR, the chief thug was telling so-called "peace activists" that he didn't need lectures by others on human rights and that he had no intention of changing his government's repressive policies.

President Reagan has convinced himself that the man who heads the evil empire has ended its treachery and is trying to be one of the good guys, and facts to the contrary will not sway him.

It was a sad week for the free world, indeed.

New U.S. Embassy in Moscow Found Riddled with 'Bugs'

The head of a U.S. State Department special panel June 8, 1987 called for an overhaul of the chancery building of the new U.S. embassy in Moscow in order to rid the facility of eavesdropping devices planted by the Soviets. The recommendation came from James R. Schlesinger, a former U.S. defense secretary and an ex-director of central intelligence. Schlesinger made his comments at a press conference in a wing of the chancery. He spoke at the conclusion of a 10-day investigation of the Moscow facility conducted with the aid of U.S. intelligence agencies.

The embassy complex, which was nearing completion, was being built by Soviet workers under U.S. supervision. Under an agreement with Moscow, the Soviets could not occupy their new embassy in Washington, D.C. until American personnel moved into the new Moscow embassy.

Schlesinger said the investigation revealed that the chancery was riddled with sophisticated Soviet listening devices. The devices were planted in precast concrete pillars and beams that had been molded away from the construction site. The bugs had eluded U.S. X-ray screening machines at the embassy site, but some had been discovered with the aid of a new U.S. detection device, about which Schlesinger declined to give details.

Schlesinger called the Soviet bugs an "ingenious" advance in eavesdropping technology. He criticized the "naivete" of U.S. officials who had permitted the concrete sections to be prefabricated away from the construction site. It was unclear how many of the bugs had been detected. However, Schlesinger said he was troubled by evidence that parts of the chancery that were intended to be secure areas were honeycombed with listening devices. He estimated that it could take over two years and "many tens of millions of dollars" to achieve a "significant restructuring" of the embassy with Soviet cooperation. He said that overhaul would probably require the addition of new secure areas to the existing chancery.

Without Soviet cooperation, Schlesinger estimated, it might by "decades" before American personnel could move into a secure Moscow facility. Schlesinger disclosed that he had spoken to some Soviet officials about compensating the U.S. for the costs of overhauling the new embassy. But, he said, those discussions "did not proceed very far."

A U.S. Senate Committee April 29 had recommended the demolition of the chancery building of the new embassy in Moscow. A Senate Select Committee on Intelligence voted, 15-0, that the chancery should be torn down. The recommendation was based on evidence gathered by the panel that the Soviets had been planting listening devices in the new facility as early as 1979.

The U.S. Senate July 1, 1987 agreed to a compromise with the House of Representatives on the issue of security at the new U.S. embassy in Moscow. The move cleared the way for approval of a delayed supplemental spending bill. The House compromise called for a moratorium on spending for construction of the new embassy until Nov. 1. It also prohibited Soviet personnel from moving into their new embassy in the U.S., located on Mount Alto in Washington, D.C., during the moratorium period.

President Reagan had decided to recommend that the new U.S. embassy in Moscow be razed because it was infested with electronic bugging devices, the *Washington Post* reported Oct. 26, 1988. The final decision would be made by incoming President George Bush.

The Honolulu Advertiser
*Honolulu, HI,
October 30, 1988*

Good luck to the Reagan administration in trying to claim damages for shoddy Soviet workmanship in the bug-riddled U.S. embassy in Moscow. Even with *glasnost*, the Russians are unlikely to admit the obvious.

And good luck to the next administration in trying to get Congress to vote upwards of $500 million to tear down the newly-built-but-bugged structure and replace it with a clean one.

The Moscow embassy has been compared to the pyramids in Egypt as a construction epic. But as a fiasco is is more akin to France's supposedly impregnable Maginot Line, which the Germans simply went around at the start of World War II.

The sick joke is the KGB was the prime contractor for our new Moscow embassy. Thanks to our incredible 1970s naivete, we let them sell us prefabricated building modules full of devices and didn't monitor construction strictly enough. The result is not only a monumental waste of money but embarrassment as well.

About the only leverage the United States seems to have is that Soviet diplomats are being barred from moving into their newly-built embassy compound in Washington until the new U.S. embassy is Moscow is finished.

But even then it is well to remember the "old Russian proverb" cited by President Reagan on his Moscow visit: negotiate but verify.

The Washington Times

Washington, DC, October 28, 1988

After several years of bureaucratic, congressional and diplomatic haggling, President Reagan has recommended that the United States tear down the flawed U.S. Embassy building in Moscow and build a new one. He is absolutely correct. Even though a new embassy may cost as much as $300 million and take five years to construct, the old one is so riddled with KGB eavesdropping gadgets as to be useless.

The controversial building, located on a swampy lowland site chosen by the Soviets and right next to the ambassador's residence, was built by Soviet workers with Soviet materials. A 1987 a study commissioned by the State Department showed, not surprisingly, that it was full of Soviet bugs. Former Secretary of Defense and CIA director James Schlesinger, who headed the study commission, noted that "Soviet security services have permeated our new chancery building in Moscow with a full array of intelligence devices — for which we do not yet understand either the technology or the underlying strategy."

Mr. Schlesinger recommended, among other things, that the top three floors of the chancery be rebuilt, that the 1972 agreement permitting the construction of a new Soviet embassy in Washington and a new American embassy in Moscow be adjusted so that American personnel carry out the new construction and that the Soviets be allowed to move into their new Washington home only after the reconstructed Moscow complex was ready for occupancy. Perhaps most important, he urged that the United States think realistically about embassy construction, particularly in communist countries, and develop a strategy to prevent or at least minimize hostile espionage activities in and around our embassies.

Mr. Reagan's decision to get rid of the new chancery building won't help morale among our embassy personnel in Moscow, many of whom are anxious to move into a new building, but it was the right move. He knows that our security and our relationships with the Soviets will be enhanced by looking Soviet espionage in the eye, scrapping the boondoggle of the past and building anew.

The Atlanta Journal
THE ATLANTA CONSTITUTION

Atlanta, GA, October 31, 1988

The new U.S. Embassy office building in Moscow is uninhabitable as a place to conduct confidential business. The fault for that lies mainly with a sneaky KGB but partly, too, with Nixon-era officials who were seduced by sweet visions of detente and allowed the Soviets to pull a fast one on them in deciding how the facility was to be constructed.

President Reagan wants to tear the new $22 million chancery down and start over, and who can blame him? It is so honeycombed with listening devices that there's probably no place within where an embassy staffer can sneeze without a KGB officer somewhere outside murmuring gesundheit.

The problem is that razing and rebuilding might delay up to five years moving U.S. personnel from their current dilapidated firetrap to modern quarters. Because of a reciprocal agreement we have with Moscow, that means a corresponding wait for Soviet envoys in Washington, themselves eager to move to an already finished facility.

Wouldn't it be better for the United States to propose an arrangement that would save both sides time and money? The new and presumably more practical crowd in the Kremlin just might be receptive.

We never cared much for the new chancery's location in the first place. Rather than tear it down, why not offer it as a public building for whatever use the Soviets choose for it — that is, in exchange for another, better site? All this would be in the interests of minimizing wrecking costs and expediting construction, with the shared objective of getting diplomats of both sides in more commodious (and in our case, safer) surroundings as quickly as possible.

Arkansas Gazette

Little Rock, AR, November 7, 1988

The United States has been left with no practical choice but to tear down its partly finished embassy in Moscow and then replace it with an entirely American-built structure that would be free of Soviet listening devices. Chalk up one for Soviet intelligence on this one, although one must assume that the American government can make it a costly triumph for the Soviets.

In making the announcement President Reagan said the several hundred million dollars required to do the job would have to be financed by taking the money away from something else. Reagan's days of commie-bashing clearly are over if he's not even willing to seek compensation from the Soviet government for rendering the embassy unusable by planting all those bugs. On the assumption that in foreign intelligence things are now always what they seem to be there could be some compensation that shapes the mess to our advantage. An equally bad mistake was made when the United States allowed the Soviets to build a new embassy compound in Washington at a location that gives it great advantage for electronic spying on our own seat of government.

It is to our advantage to delay Soviet occupation of the compound until new measures can be devised to thwart at least some of the Soviet listening facilities. Under previous arrangements the Soviets cannot move to the higher ground until the United States embassy in Moscow is completed.

PORTLAND EVENING EXPRESS

Portland, ME, October 29, 1988

It's a little late in the day, but President Reagan has made the right decision to knock down the U.S. Embassy building in Moscow and start from scratch.

There's never really been any other choice. After all, the new quarters will be housing our diplomatic corps in the Soviet Union for perhaps half a century.

As it is, the building is worse than useless. It is riddled with listening devices implanted by the Soviets in the raw materials used to construct the building.

At the time the eavesdropping apparatus was discovered last year, Sen. Patrick J. Leahy, D-Vt., observed tartly, "Our general contractor is the KGB."

Replacing the embassy will be expensive. Initial estimates last year were that the project would cost $160 million and take about 45 months to complete. Now the State Department figures it will cost more than $300 million and take five years.

Still, the costs must be swallowed. We simply must have an embassy which can be relied upon to be reasonably secure — particularly in the Soviet Union.

But the Soviets must not be let off the hook in this matter, considering the fact that they are the cause of the problem. At the very least, they should be kept out of their own new embassy building in Washington until the United States is established in new quarters in Moscow, securely built to our specifications.

Since the decision to rebuild comes so late in Reagan's term, it will really be left to the next administration to carry out the reconstruction project. But regardless of who makes the final decision, it is a decision which can only be regarded as inevitable.

Gorbachev Sees Reagan, Bush in New York City, Vowing Troop Cut

Soviet General Secretary Mikhail S. Gorbachev visited New York City Dec. 6-8, 1988 for brief talks with U.S. President Ronald Reagan and President-elect George Bush. It was Gorbachev's second appearance in the U.S. The last Soviet leader to visit New York City had been Nikita S. Khrushchev in 1960.

Gorbachev's meeting with Reagan, Dec. 7, was the fifth time that the leaders of the superpowers had held discussions, and the second time (following the Moscow summit) in 1988. The New York meeting was hastily arranged. As late as October, the Reagan administration had been rebuffing Soviet calls for one more summit before Reagan left office.

The White House had taken pains to avoid calling the New York City meeting a "summit," in the sense of bargaining with Gorbachev over important issues. Rather, the administration viewed the meeting as a symbolic "passing of the torch" to Bush from Reagan in the area of relations with the Soviet leader. The Reagan administration had let it be known in advance that the U.S. did not plan to make any substantive proposals when the leaders got together. At the same time, the Soviets had hinted that Gorbachev would make a major announcement or offer (labeled a "Christmas surprise" by the wary administration) when he reached the U.S.

Gorbachev upstaged the meeting with a historic address to the United Nations General Assembly Dec. 7. During the speech, he announced a plan for a large, unilateral reduction in Soviet conventional forces.

Upon arriving at New York City's John F. Kennedy International Airport, Gorbachev made a brief speech saying that he expected his visit to "promote greater dynamism in the [U.S.-Soviet] dialogue and an expansion of cooperation between our two countries." The Soviet leader was accompanied by his wife, Raisa; Aleksandr N. Yakovlev, the Communist Party secretary in charge of foreign policy; Foreign Minister Eduard A. Shevardnadze; and a large contingent of other Soviet officials.

The Soviet leader addressed the U.N. General Assembly in New York Dec. 7 following an hour-long private meeting with U.N. Secretary General Javier Perez de Cuellar and General Assembly President Dante Caputo. Gorbachev was the first Soviet leader to address the U.N. since Premier Nikita Khrushchev in 1960. The general secretary expressed a willingness to have the Soviet Union take a place in the forefront of a new era of international peace and cooperation. He told the U.N. delegates that, while Marxism and the Russian Revolution had helped to shape the 20th century, "Today we face a different road to the future." Gorbachev continued: "Today, further world progress is only possible through a consensus as we move forward to a new world order."

The highlight of the Gorbachev speech was a pledge to reduce the Soviet military forces by 500,000 troops (an estimated 20% of total Soviet troops) by 1991. The troop cutback was to be coupled with the removal of 10,000 Soviet tanks (six armored divisions), 8,500 artillery pieces and 800 combat aircraft attached to the Warsaw Pact and based in East Germany, Hungary and Czechoslovakia. According to an estimate by the North Atlantic Treaty Organization, the Soviets had over 600,000 troops and up to 30,000 tanks in Eastern Europe outside of Soviet territory. In concert with the reductions, he promised to shift to a defensive posture in the U.S.S.R's military doctrine.

General Secretary Gorbachev and his aides lunched with President Reagan, President-elect Bush and their chief aides Dec. 7, following Gorbachev's U.N. speech.

Later on Dec. 7, Mrs. Gorbachev joined her husband in a motorcade through lower and midtown Manhattan. Thousands of cheering New Yorkers lined the streets to get a glimpse of the couple. The response of New Yorkers to the general secretary was, on the whole, very friendly.

The Idaho STATESMAN
Boise, ID, December 8, 1988

Soviet leader Mikhail Gorbachev did it again, wowing 'em at the United Nations — and around the world — with his unilateral troop cuts and proposals for international cooperation.

When it comes to splashy headline making, Mr. Gorbachev is a master. But beneath the pizazz lie solid initiatives for making this a more peaceful world.

Merry Christmas from the Kremlin.

General Secretary Gorbachev's announced intention to withdraw tens of thousands of troops and tanks from Eastern Europe and Asia along with slashing the Soviet Army by 10 percent are big presents, indeed. It's tough to argue with unilateral military cuts. The United States and NATO nations long have argued that the 2-1 bulge in Soviet conventional forces in Europe threaten peace and necessitate a Western nuclear deterrent.

The cuts add weight to Mr. Gorbachev's call for a move toward a 50 percent cut in the superpowers' nuclear stockpile — a goal President Reagan supports. A goal that would make the world a bit less likely to self-destruct.

The general secretary also called for an end to the fighting in Afghanistan — the United States is supplying the Afghan rebels and the Soviets want to be done with their version of Vietnam.

Mr. Gorbachev reinforced his call for a "period of peace" by saying that, "The use or threat of force no longer can or must be an instrument of foreign policy." He even paraphrased poet John Donne to declare: "The bell of every regional conflict tolls for all of us."

And then he gave us a peak at his motivation: "...one-sided reliance on military power," said the head of the world's largest military, "ultimately weakens other components of national security."

In other words, Mr. Gorbachev needs to lessen world tension in order to divert resources from defense to his ailing domestic economy. And, ideally, such a shift wouldn't hurt us either.

The Soviet leader also proposed a range of initiatives including cooperation in space, an expanded role for the United Nations and the World Court, reducing Third World debt, assembling a team of international scientists to solve environmental disasters and even a peace corps to rebuild Afghanistan.

It was a far cry from the Khrushchev shoe-banging episode in 1960 — the last time a Soviet leader visited New York. And his speech went farther than ever to show, as President Kennedy said in a different context, that the torch has been passed to a new generation.

It will be up to America and the incoming Bush administration to meet this peace initiative, to decide if a militarily weaker, economically stronger Soviet Union is in our best interests.

Clearly, it has become the premier foreign policy question of our time.

The TENNESSEAN
Nashville, TN, December 8, 1988

MR. Mikhail Gorbachev's address to the United Nations made him sound like a dove and a small-D democrat running for the title of the world's No. 1 Nice Guy — and that is not to disparage his remarks.

It was evident the Soviet leader wanted to project the image of a man of peace, ready to put the Cold War and its tensions behind, ready to referee regional conflicts and ready, as he put it, to meet the new American administration half-way on mutual and world problems. He reiterated his desire toward a treaty that would reduce by 50% the strategic nuclear missiles of the superpowers and his hope for "a period of peace."

Mr. Gorbachev had something for everyone. He praised the United Nations for its role in world affairs, suggesting that role could be even greater in the future. He talked of environmental concerns shared by East and West. And he spoke hopefully about non-political groups such as scientists and churches and others having some input in the international dialogue. He talked of the Third World and its debt problems in terms of moratoriums and forgiveness, certainly aimed at touching off a glow among the representatives of underdeveloped and undeveloped countries.

And, he had a Christmas card, if not a present, for the West. The Soviet leader said tens of thousands of tanks and a half million troops would be withdrawn from Eastern Europe — and that other forces would be pulled out of Asia in a major drawdown of the Soviet military machine.

Specifically he said that by 1991, the Soviet Union would withdraw 50,000 men and 5,000 tanks from East Germany, Czechoslovakia and Hungary. Considering that it has more than 500,000 troops and tens of thousands of tanks in those countries, that is hardly a reduction that would set off cheers among NATO commanders.

However, it is a step — albeit a small one — that could give new momentum to the long-stalled talks on reducing Warsaw Pact and NATO forces in Central Europe. If the talks could follow Mr. Gorbachev's initiative, perhaps more substantial reductions in troops could be made in what would be the flash point of any conventional war.

Mr. Gorbachev's troop reductions are not altogether altruistic but are a pragmatic realization that the drain on the Soviet economy is considerable. If his restructuring of the economy is to work, some of that drain has to be eased.

The Soviet president was conciliatory, offering cooperation to the U.S. and its allies, and holding out the possibility that greater things could be in the offing in the future of a new relationship. On the whole it is rather remarkable how far the U.S. and the Soviet Union have come in their relationship since President Reagan came into office railing about the "evil empire." That there has been progress in relations is encouraging. That may be the real significance of the Gorbachev appearance at the U.N. and his cooperative tone toward it and the U.S. ∎

The Register-Guard
Eugene, OR,
December 9, 1988

Mikhail Gorbachev's remarkable speech to the United Nations Wednesday appears to represent a genuine turn toward peace. It has rightfully elicited positive response from the entire Western world, with approval and at least cautious hopefulness expressed by everyone from military experts to cab drivers.

The highlight of the speech was the announcement of a plan to unilaterally reduce Soviet military forces, including those stationed in Eastern Europe and the European portion of the Soviet Union, over the next two years.

Subtracting all of the tanks and men that Gorbachev listed will still leave the Warsaw Pact nations with conventional force superiority over NATO. Nonetheless, the reductions will be significant, especially if they include some of the amphibious and river-crossing units that the Soviet leader mentioned.

These changes will represent the first tangible evidence that Gorbachev is serious about his claim, voiced repeatedly during the past two years, that the Soviets want to place their European forces on a defensive rather than offensive footing.

The way for both sides to confirm that highly important shift in strategy will be to proceed with negotiations to reduce and balance all NATO and Warsaw Pact conventional forces.

Gorbachev has ample reason to want to put the brakes on what has been a long and steady buildup of non-nuclear forces. These represent the most expensive part of an excessive Soviet military budget. If he is to have any hope of modernizing the Soviet economy and meeting the burgeoning demand for consumer goods, Gorbachev must shift resources — both dollars and people — away from the military.

It is a risky business for this daring middle-aged man on a leadership trapeze. Not only is a military reduction opposed by powerful forces inside the Kremlin, it may well increase the restlessness of East European nations under Soviet domination. A strong military presence is an important element of Soviet control.

Gorbachev's policies to date point toward a reduced threat of war and an improved domestic economy. If an unraveling of the Soviet empire becomes an unintended byproduct, of course, the West will have no less reason to applaud.

Minneapolis Star and Tribune
Minneapolis, MN, December 8, 1988

Soviet leader Mikhail Gorbachev has shown again that he is the grand master of the grand gesture. Although his statement apparently was long expected by Western leaders, Gorbachev captured the world's attention Wednesday by announcing to the United Nations that the Soviet Union will reduce its military forces by half a million troops, along with thousands of tanks and other weapons those troops field. The attention is deserved. So is the applause the move will generate in the United States and Western Europe.

Gorbachev did not signal unilateral disarmament. Against the awesome bulk of Soviet power, the cuts clearly are at the margin. The Soviet Union still will have more than 5 million troops, far the largest force in the world, backed by an oversized nuclear arsenal. But focusing on what remains misses the point of what's being eliminated and where that might lead.

It's unusual for a superpower unilaterally to chop 10 percent out of its military. Even more impressive is that a sizable portion of the cut will come in tanks and troops stationed in Eastern Europe, despite the economic and political turmoil in that region caused by Gorbachev's liberalization policies in the Soviet Union.

Ever the politician, Gorbachev coated his military announcements with soothing rhetoric designed to appeal to his U.N. audience and to the Western public. He also sought to create a night-and-day contrast with the behavior of the last Soviet leader to visit the United Nations — the shoe-wielding Nikita Khrushchev. "The use of threat of force no longer can or must be an instrument of foreign policy," Gorbachev pronounced, and pledged to convert the Soviet Union to "an economy of disarmament."

Those words are noble but, unfortunately, unrealistic. It would be equally unrealistic, and unwise as well, for his listeners to focus on that rhetorical excess and miss the larger point. Gorbachev isn't just playing with words and numbers to fool the West; he made clear that he hopes to help steer the world away from confrontation and toward cooperation.

For the United States, the proof of his commitment will come at the bargaining table. But the unilateral grand gesture should encourage George Bush to enter bargaining with an expectation similar to Gorbachev's — that arms-reduction progress and a more harmonious superpower relationship will be achieved, to everyone's benefit.

The Oregonian

Portland, OR,
December 9, 1988

Unquestionably, Soviet President Mikhail Gorbachev scored an international public relations point Wednesday with his announcement of a significant reduction in his nation's military forces. It is a win-win situation for Gorbachev, at least outside of his own nation, earning him plaudits for doing no more than what common sense dictated in light of the Soviet Union's economic distress and continuing numerical military superiority.

U.S. Secretary of State George Shultz put Gorbachev's U.N. speech in a good perspective when he called it "a significant step in the right direction." The proper U.S. response to this unilateral reduction in force should be cautious welcome, but no rush to declare the Cold War over, a hot war now impossible, or NATO unnecessary.

Most important, there is no need to rush into a major equivalent reduction in U.S. or NATO forces, popular as that move might be, especially in Europe, where Gorbachev has managed to bleed away considerable popular support for strong anti-Soviet defenses. The cuts announced by Gorbachev, when fully carried out, would reduce the disparity between NATO and the Warsaw Pact nations, but would not eliminate it.

In addition to the military cuts, Gorbachev sounded an upbeat tone, denouncing military solutions to international tensions and saying good things about personal freedom in the Soviet Union. We'll wait and see how much is rhetorical ruffles and how much a real sea change in a Soviet system that still imposes change from the top down.

Gorbachev has launched an initiative that certainly is intriguing and far more helpful to the cause of world peace than would have been an opposite decision to build up his military. Combined with the intermediate nuclear forces treaty, his U.N. comments offer real hope that negotiations on other arms reductions — nuclear and conventional — will succeed.

He seems to want that, and he seems to be in control of his country. That gives real opportunities to President-elect George Bush to join in building a positive relationship. Bush cannot afford to let the Soviet leader hold, in world opinion, the high ground as peacemaker.

But U.S.-Soviet relations have warmed and cooled before, and much intensive work remains to be done to produce 'a lasting thaw for all peoples of the world.

Gorbachev gave a good, positive speech. History will discover whether it was an epoch-making one.

The Hartford Courant

Hartford, CT, December 8, 1988

Mikhail S. Gorbachev made history at the United Nations on Wednesday.

Rarely, if ever, does a major power unilaterally disband a substantial portion of its military force. Mr. Gorbachev announced there will be half a million fewer Soviet men and women in uniform. Thousands of tanks and big guns will be withdrawn from East European countries and from the Soviet Union's European and Asian borders.

This is just the beginning, he said, of a drive to build an "economy of disarmament." Plans for converting defense plants and shifting military specialists into civilian industry will be published and made available for international inspection, he promised.

Although Mr. Gorbachev's emphasis was on conventional weapons, he reasserted his readiness for a 50 percent cut in strategic nuclear arsenals, provided the United States agrees to do the same. He went beyond military issues by declaring his government's support for, in effect, forgiving foreign debts owed the Soviet Union by Third World countries.

"The use of the threat of force no longer can or must be an instrument of foreign policy," said Mr. Gorbachev. This is a breathtaking pronouncement. If he means what he says, the cause of world peace will advance dramatically — no, miraculously.

To many Americans, the Gorbachev initiative is surprising, and perhaps unbelievable. After all, the Soviets have built the world's biggest military machine, and generals dislike unilateral cutbacks in conventional arms. Indeed, major Soviet military officials are said to have resigned or retired in response to the policy change.

But is it really unbelievable that a militarized nation will someday come to its senses? A first-rate military power built on a third-rate economic base does not make a superpower. The Soviet Union is a Third World country in many respects, and will remain in that group so long as roughly one-fifth of its gross national product is devoted to the military.

Mr. Gorbachev did not take these steps because he wants to be remembered as the Mother Teresa or Albert Schweitzer of superpower diplomacy. Pacifism obviously is not what drove him to seriously begin addressing issues that no Soviet leader had addressed before. What probably drove him is his desire to bring his country into the 20th century while the world prepares to enter the 21st century.

Even after the cutbacks, the Soviet Union's military might will remain awesome. But it will no longer be as threatening as it has been historically. The emphasis, if Mr. Gorbachev is to be believed, will be on defensive capability.

Disarmament has a bad meaning in certain U.S. quarters. It connotes weakness and surrender. Our policy-makers grew up with ideas about bargaining chips and about never giving up anything unilaterally. Members of the Warsaw Pact and NATO have been negotiating without success for two decades on balanced and mutual withdrawal of conventional forces from central Europe.

Mr. Gorbachev is challenging these ideas. Who, other than Soviet hardliners, will denounce his decision to trim Soviet conventional forces by an estimated 10 percent? Certainly not President Reagan or President-elect George Bush.

U.S. officials naturally welcomed Mr. Gorbachev's initiatives. But they will have to do more after the new administration is sworn in. They will have to show that they, too, are capable of bold initiatives — of converting swords into plowshares.

The Pittsburgh PRESS

Pittsburgh, PA, December 11, 1988

With his address to the United Nations, Soviet President Mikhail Gorbachev has impressed much of the world with his new thinking about international relations.

One would have to be churlish to deny that his words were encouraging and forward-looking. Who could be against peace, disarmament, cooperation, helping poor nations, toning down ideology and rejecting force as an instrument of foreign policy?

One also would have to be naive to equate Gorbachev's soaring words with facts. He may well cut the Soviet Army by 500,000 men two years from now. Or he may be kicked out of power by disgruntled generals and reactionary politicians.

There is, however, one thing that Gorbachev could do right now to assure the West that his words are more than skillful propaganda and carry real meaning. That would be to tear down the Berlin Wall.

The ugly, hated wall, which Gorbachev's predecessor Nikita Khrushchev erected in 1961 to complete East Germany's transformation into a huge prison camp, divides Germans from their brothers and belies the normal Europe that the Kremlin leader says he favors.

In his U.N. speech, Gorbachev strongly praised the Universal Declaration of Human Rights which the United Nations adopted 40 years ago (with the Soviet Union abstaining in the voting).

Article 13, Section 2 of the declaration states clearly: "Everyone has the right to leave any country, including his own, and to return to his country."

The Berlin Wall and the East German regime's barbed-wire fences, watchtowers, mine fields, attack dogs and border guards ordered to shoot to kill are unspeakable violations of human rights in general and the U.N. declaration in particular.

The wall epitomizes the use of force and coercion that Gorbachev so eloquently abjured. A word to his friend, Comrade Erich Honecker, about razing the front gate to his prison would go far to convince the world that Gorbachev means what he says.

Omaha World-Herald
Omaha, NE, December 9, 1988

The Bush-Gorbachev era seems to be off to a smooth start. Soviet President Mikhail Gorbachev was both dynamic and conciliatory in the proposals he made during his United Nations speech and his meeting with President-elect Bush and President Reagan. Bush wisely avoided premature commitments but clearly left the door open for a productive relationship with his Soviet counterpart.

Hastily arranged summit meetings with Soviet leaders have not always worked to the best interests of the United States. President Kennedy rushed into a summit with Nikita Khrushchev early in the first year of his presidency and achieved little more than an irritating and fruitless quarrel with Khrushchev, who — according to later reports — received the impression that Kennedy was a lightweight who could be bullied.

Kennedy should have waited until he was more secure in his office and until an agenda for substantive talks had been mutually arranged.

Reagan's meeting with Gorbachev at Reykjavik, Iceland, was hastily arranged, too, and from all appearances, Reagan was not prepared for Gorbachev's sweeping proposals on nuclear disarmament. Gorbachev apparently gambled on catching Reagan off guard and winning concessions that would otherwise be difficult to achieve. Reagan resisted, and the brief meeting left both sides bitter for a time.

Neither Reagan nor Bush was in a position to make deals over lunch on Governor's Island. They kept the exchanges to pleasantries in which the president and the president-elect could favorably comment on the general sense of Gorbachev's initiatives while making customary assurances of the importance of having good relations.

Gorbachev has made it clear that he wants to continue his disarmament dialogue with the Bush administration. The first election of a sitting vice president in 140 years — and the appointment of James Baker as secretary of state — helps the United States establish a theme of continuity in this crucial period.

Bush was circumspect after the meeting. He described Gorbachev's plans to reduce Soviet conventional forces as a good decision but added that Warsaw Pact forces still would outnumber NATO's forces in Europe.

Bush and Gorbachev said they would meet again. How much better the situation is than was the case in Reagan's first term when the Soviet Union, paralyzed by its succession of dying leaders, seemed unable to deal with the West without paranoia and suspicion.

Reagan and Gorbachev went on to demonstrate the importance of a personal relationship between the leaders of the world's most powerful nations. It is good that Bush and Gorbachev have built the groundwork for a similar approach.

THE INDIANAPOLIS NEWS
Indianapolis, IN, December 9, 1988

Ronald Reagan says the Cold War is over. That's no small news.

Is this seeming change of heart merely the wishful sentimentality of an outgoing president eager to secure his place in history books as the leader who ushered in a new era of peace? Is Reagan ignoring the reality of U.S.-Soviet relations?

Or is there something to what the man is saying?

Reagan's Russian counterpart, Mikhail Gorbachev, is making all the right moves to validate Reagan's statement.

Gorbachev's announcement this week that the Soviet Union plans a massive withdrawal of troops and weaponry from Eastern Europe is a dramatic break from the past. If he follows his words with action, the world can't help but stand up and take note.

Reagan's recognition of Gorbachev's efforts to redirect his nation away from monolithic statism shouldn't be dismissed as cockeyed optimism. Ronald Reagan remains a dedicated anti-communist warrior. His hopefulness is based on a spreading realization among Soviets that democratic, capitalist nations have left the U.S.S.R. behind and that the Soviet Union will have to become more like the West if it is to progress.

Another factor in the U.S.-Soviet thaw is the realization by both sides that their oversized military machines are sucking away the lifeblood of their economies.

This is certainly true of the Soviet Union, but Americans have also watched in frustration as Japan, West Germany, South Korea and other up-and-coming nations have beaten the United States in economic competition.

The feeling that change is due has spread among Americans. Rep. Pat Schroeder, D-Colo., expressed a widely held sentiment when she said, "We have all the burdens of empire and none of the benefits."

Reagan and Gorbachev both appear to see the writing on the wall. All great civilizations decline in power, but far-sighted leaders can greatly extend the productive life of a society with intelligent planning.

None of this, of course, is cause to lay down arms and embrace the Soviet Union. It remains a profoundly paranoid and dangerous nation. The best policy for the United States will always be to remain at full defensive readiness, for only then can stability be assured.

Still, the current changes in the Soviet Union should not be dismissed as inconsequential. A window of opportunity has opened, and it will take a fully engaged U.S. leadership that is at once skeptical and optimistic to meet and win a more peaceful future.

Wisconsin State Journal
Madison, WI, December 9, 1988

As always, caution and optimism should be blended in careful amounts when dealing with the Soviet Union. Too much optimism begs 40 years of postwar history and undersells the fundamental differences between East and West. Too much caution risks missing an important chance to test Soviet leader Mikhail Gorbachev's intentions and to encourage his reformist instincts.

Nonetheless, the reaction to Gorbachev's announcement that he plans to unilaterally cut the 5.6-million man Soviet military by nearly 10 percent over two years must tilt toward the optimistic.

Mikhail Gorbachev

Those Soviet leaders allied with Gorbachev seem intent on testing a new military doctrine they call "reasonable sufficiency," and that we might call a stunning reversal. Since the end of World War II, Western defense strategy has been based on the undeniable fact that Soviet and Warsaw Pact troops are massed in Eastern Europe in numbers that can only be interpreted as offensive.

The new Soviet doctrine seems closer to the strategy used since its inception by NATO — deploying conventional forces sufficient to repel an attack, rather than in numbers necessary to mount one. In Europe today, conventional NATO forces are outnumbered 2.5 to 1 by the Warsaw Pact. So even if Gorbachev pulls back 50,000 troops from Hungary, Czechoslovakia and East Germany, the Soviet edge will remain significant. Still, any cutbacks are a move away from an unnerving past.

If only 50,000 Soviet troops are pulling out of Eastern Europe, where is Gorbachev cutting the other 450,000? Perhaps along its long border with China, for there have been long and apparently friendly chats over the communist back fence in recent months. This initiative may then have less to do with the apparent thaw in East-West relations than with a thaw in East-East relations.

Most likely, however, is that Gorbachev's initiative is based on cold, hard economic facts at home. He realizes his nation's sluggish economy can no longer afford to maintain a standing army of 5.6 million people. The Soviet Union cannot feed itself. The stores are largely empty. Most of its citizens live under Third World conditions. Ethnic and social unrest is growing.

Gorbachev's speech to the United Nations may have been a concession that the West has won the Cold War on the economic front. It cost the United States its largest peacetime military buildup in history and has helped to create a huge national debt, but the Cold War may be winding down thanks to that resolve.

Now is a time to applaud Gorbachev's move; tomorrow is a time to test his intentions. That is a blend of optimism and caution we can all accept.

Part III: Eastern Europe

Eastern Europe emerged from World War II in the Soviet sphere of influence: The countries had communism imposed on them and were under the control of regimes subservient to Soviet leader Joseph Stalin. While Yugoslavia and Albania eventually broke with Moscow, the other members of the Eastern bloc – Poland, Hungary, East Germany, Romania, Bulgaria and Czechoslovakia – were little more than than puppet states.

Stalin died in 1953, but a succession of Soviet leaders kept a tight rein on Eastern Europe. Nikita S. Khrushchev, who denounced Stalin as a dictator, sent Soviet tanks to crush the 1956 Hungarian uprising. Leonid I. Brezhnev, who toppled Khrushchev from power, presided over the 1968 invasion of Czechoslovakia and the destruction of the "Prague Spring" reform movement in that country. (The Kremlin justified the 1968 invasion with a policy that came to be known in the West as the Brezhnev Doctrine. It expressed a Soviet right to intervene anywhere to preserve a Marxist regime.)

There was no immediate loosening of Moscow's hold on the Eastern bloc when Mikhail Gorbachev became the Soviet leader. But he baffled the leaders of Eastern Europe – nearly all of them aging traditionalists – by undertaking economic and political reforms in the U.S.S.R. and making it plain that they were expected to follow the new Soviet model. Adding to their confusion, Gorbachev indicated to his allies that they were freer than ever before to pursue their own policies.

East German leader Erich Honecker wanted nothing to do with reforms. Nor did Romanian leader Nicolae Ceausescu, already a maverick within the Soviet bloc. Bulgaria's Todor Zhikov vocally supported reforms, but was slow to implement them. In Czechoslovakia, arch-conservative Gustav Husak was succeeded in 1987 by Milos Jakes, who then led a purge of pro-reform elements from his regime.

But there were startling developments in Poland and Hungary, where the regimes were struggling with crippled economies, heavy international debts and populations anxious to be free of Soviet domination. In Poland, the regime of Gen. Wojciech Jaruzelski came to terms with the dissident labor union Solidarity (restored to legal status in 1989) and agreed to hold free elections. Hungarian leader Janos Kadar and his cronies were replaced by Karoly Grosz and a coalition of pragmatists and reformists in 1988. Hungary launched into an ambitious program of liberalization, capped by a 1989 decision to allow the creation of the first multiparty political system in Eastern Europe.

In a December 1988 United Nations address, Gorbachev promised to remove some Soviet troops from Eastern Europe. And in March 1989, he pledged to Grosz that the Soviet Union would not interfere with the Hungarian liberalization, a comment viewed by some Western observers as a tacit refutation of the Brezhnev Doctrine. Nevertheless, it remains in question whether the Kremlin would allow noncommunists to take power anywhere in Eastern Europe.

East German Leader Honecker Visits West Germany

East German leader Erich Honecker Sept. 7-11, 1987 became the first East German head of state to visit West Germany. Honecker's visit included 12 hours of talks with West German Chancellor Helmut Kohl. The talks produced only modest results, but the symbolism of the trip was widely regarded as setting the stage for improved relations between the two Germanys. The 75-year-old East German leader, who in 1961 had overseen the construction of the Berlin Wall, arrived the chancellery in Bonn on the morning of Sept. 7 and held talks with Kohl later that day and the next before a joint communique was issued Sept. 8. The ceremonial aspects of Honecker's arrival refelcted a primary issue between the two nations: that East Germany had long sought its neighbors' recognition as a sovereign nation while West Germany was committed by its constitution to a reunification of the two nations.

The communique issued Sept. 8 outlined agreements on economic and cultural issues that had been widely expected. Werst German Chancellery Minister Wolfgang Schaeuble explained that despite the lack of major breakthroughs "the important thing is that we have the intention, step by step, to develop cooperation further." One step was acceptance by Kohl of an invitation to visit Honecker in West Germany.

An impromptu remark by Honecker Sept. 10 about the border between the two Germanys drew much attention in the German press. While visiting his birthplace in Neunkirchen, Honecker said that the current borders understandably "were not as they should be" because the Germanys were members of opposing military alliances (the Warsaw Pact and the North Atlantic Treaty Organization). But the East German leader went on to say that the border between the two nations might someday be like that between the two Germanys. Bonn officials called that message "positive" but warned against too hopeful an interpretation. East German officials cautioned against "reading between the lines."

THE ARIZONA REPUBLIC
Phoenix, AZ, September 9, 1987

THERE is considerably more flash than substance to the meeting between West German Chancellor Helmut Kohl and East German leader Erich Honecker.

While historic in the sense that it is the first-ever meeting between two heads of state in a nation that was divided after its defeat in World War II, it is not likely to be memorable for anything that comes of it.

When Rudyard Kipling wrote in *The Ballad of East and West* that "East is East, and West is West, and never the twain shall meet," he might well have been referring to the two German states.

The tone of the modern-day East-West ballad was set early, at a formal banquet Monday evening in Bonn, the capital of West Germany, when Honecker was met with a demand from Kohl that East German security forces stop shooting people who try to flee the communist nation.

Kohl also condemned the Berlin Wall, the construction of which was supervised by Honecker in 1961.

Even as Kohl was speaking, demonstrators outside the banquet hall were chanting: "Down with the wall," and, "Scrap the shoot-to-kill orders."

Their chants, along with Kohl's demands, fell on deaf ears. Honecker was as stonily silent as the wall he helped build.

The East German Communist Party chief was equally cold to West German calls for a reunification of Germany.

Honecker said, "Socialism and capitalism can't be any more united than fire and water."

At best, the two-day summit brought little more than pledges to work for a more relaxed relationship between the two German countries.

That does not, of course, include any relaxation of tensions caused by the wall and East Germany's tight borders.

Honecker did promise improvements and relief in travel between East and West Germany, and treaties were signed calling for the protection of the environment, safeguards against radiation and cooperation in science and technology.

But as expected, despite the symbolic shaking of hands and the agreement on taking small steps toward improving relations, there was no meeting of minds on the big issues.

Reunification remains a dream, and the wall has not been breached.

DESERET NEWS
Salt Lake City, UT
September 9/10, 1987

Relations between West Germany and its communist counterpart, the German Democratic Republic, inevitably follow the rise and fall of tensions between the two superpowers.

Thus the current visit of the GDR's Erich Honecker to West Germany comes at a lull in U.S.-Russian relations when Washington and Moscow appear to be on the verge of a treaty to dismantle medium-range nuclear weapons on both sides.

Honecker has planned to visit Bonn twice previously. Both trips were cancelled after East-West relations suddenly deteriorated — the last time over the U.S. missile buildup in Europe.

While some issues divide the two Germanys as sharply as the Berlin Wall, both are finding that cooperation is becoming essential in at least some areas. That's indicated by the signing of three bilateral agreements this week on cooperation in science, technology, and radiation control from nuclear power plants. The Chernobyl nuclear plant disaster in the Soviet Union has made the need for radiation control agreements painfully evident.

As for human contacts, the best that can be hoped for is a gradual relaxing of East German travel restrictions for those who want to visit the West. In that respect, much has been accomplished since the Basic Treaty of 1972 when the GDR first established official relations with the West. At first, only old-age pensioners in East Germany were allowed to travel to the west. This year, some 2.3 million East German visitors will travel to West Germany and other western countries — more than half of them below retirement age.

But it's too much to expect, despite West German Chancellor Helmut Kohl's plea this week, that East Germany dismantle the Berlin Wall and quit shooting at those trying to flee to the west. For one thing, Honecker doesn't want a drain of East German talent fleeing to the west. For another, Russia will not permit its client state to go too far in reciprocity with West Germany. As the Soviets found in Czechoslovakia and Poland, a little freedom granted to the people soon results in demands for more freedom.

Honecker was right: capitalism and socialism won't mix any more than fire and water. But that's because socialism cannot keep pace with capitalist achievements in human freedom as well as in economic progress. A true rapprochement of the two Germanys can be achieved only if both are free or both are enslaved — and the Free World must never tolerate the latter course.

Roanoke Times & World-News

Roanoke, VA, September 9, 1987

TO NO ONE'S surprise, the wonders of West German capitalism did not sway Erich Honnecker's determination to keep East Germany a separate nation.

The East German leader, the first to visit West Germany, was likewise unswayed by the appeal of West Germany Chancellor Helmut Kohl to tear down the infamous Berlin wall.

Like it or not, Germany will remain a divided nation for the foreseeable future. That is no historical oddity. For most of its history, Germany has been divided into kingdoms, principalities and duchies under the sway of one or the other of the great Teutonic powers: Austria and Prussia.

East Germany's borders, in fact, approximate those of pre-Bismarck Prussia, and the country could get away with calling itself Prussia if it were of a mind to. But Prussian military tradition does not square with East Germany's pretense at being the "good Germany," the one that rejected Nazism after World War II and chose to build socialism on a peaceful foundation.

Those peaceful pretensions are hard to sustain with a straight face. The border between East Germany and West Germany is called the Iron Curtain. The gunfire that sometimes crackles across the border comes from East German guns. The targets are not West Germans, but East Germans trying to escape to the freedom and affluence of the West.

East Germany, officially, does not yearn for union with West Germany. It would do it no good to so yearn. It is a captive state of the Soviet Union, whose nightmarish experience with German invaders in World War II has left it loath to entertain the prospect of a reunited Germany. Soviet soldiers outnumber German soldiers on East German soil, keeping it a subservient satellite.

West Germany, on the other hand, refuses to recognize two German nations. It considers all those residing within the boundaries of pre-World War II Germany to be German citizens. Its constitution's preamble calls for a unified Germany.

West Germany's one-Deutschland policy leads to some interesting situations. East Germany normally doesn't allow emigration to West Germany. That's why the wall's there. But once an East German has retired, he is free to migrate to the West. The reason? Since West Germany regards him as a West German citizen, he immediately becomes eligible for liberal retirement benefits. East Germany has reaped the benefits of his productive life; West Germany gets stuck with the retirement bill.

East Germany is dwarfed by West Germany in most respects. West Germany is more than twice as large and has about three and a half times the population. When the world thinks of Germany, it thinks of West Germany.

East Germany therefore is jealous of its identity and adamant about its sovereignty. It even bridles at being called East Germany: It's official name is the German Democratic Republic. In its propaganda, West Germany is a fascist state built upon the remnants of the Third Reich. The Berlin Wall is not a monument of shame but, to quote one East German official, "the most effective building project the German Democratic Republic has ever put up."

Honnecker called upon West Germany to give his nation full diplomatic recognition. Reunification, he said, won't work: "Socialism and capitalism can't any more be united than fire and water."

Kohl contends that reunification "corresponds to the wishes and the will and even the yearnings of people in Germany."

He's doubtless right. But it doesn't correspond to the wishes of the Politburo in Moscow. And that, in the real world, is what counts.

THE SACRAMENTO BEE

Sacramento, CA, September 12, 1987

Erich Honnecker added a characteristic touch of cynicism to his visit this week to West Germany, the first ever by an East German Communist Party leader and head of state: The man who supervised construction of the Berlin Wall in 1961 and issued the standing shoot-to-kill order that has cost the lives of 188 East Germans trying to flee to the West since then, suspended — "for the time being," according to West German sources — that cold-blooded edict on the eve of his visit.

If the irony of that was lost on Honnecker, surely the significance of his visit was not. For years he has harbored the desire to visit the Saarland, a region of West Germany where he was born and grew up and where his parents are buried. More important, as a dedicated Communist and an East German patriot, he wanted to be received in West Germany as the head of a sovereign state. Technically, Honnecker didn't quite achieve that: West Germany still does not recognize East German sovereignty, because of Bonn's commitment to the goal of a reunified Germany and the abandonment of that goal that formal recognition would seem to imply.

Even so, Honnecker's reception was cordial, and although he and West German Chancellor Helmut Kohl totally disagreed — and said so — about the future of Germany, they signed agreements for cooperation on technical and environmental matters. West Germany agreed to pay for improvements in road and rail connections between the two countries. Honnecker promised to relax restrictions on visits by East Germans to relatives in the West, though it's not clear whether the practice of shooting those who try to leave without permission will be resumed after Honnecker's return home.

Those are minor steps forward in a practical sense, but symbolically they underline the growing willingness of both Germanys to harmonize their relations as much as their ideological differences and strategic ties allow. Honnecker could do a great deal to promote that harmony, and show a little unwonted humanity, by issuing a permanent hold-your-fire order to his border guards.

The Des Moines Register

Des Moines, IA
September 11, 1987

The Ethics in Government Act, born of Watergate, is up for renewal (or expiration) this fall. The Wall Street Journal, in a two-column-long editorial, calls it the Hypocrisy in Government Act, and that's hardly a misnomer. But it doesn't mean that the act should be scrapped, as the Journal proposes.

There is a long list of ethical offenses charged against members of the executive branch that have been or are being investigated under the ethics law. There is an equally long list of ethical offenses charged against members of Congress that have been ignored or whitewashed by the congressional ethics committees.

In the first category, to give only several examples, are (1) charges of illegal lobbying by former White House aides Michael Deaver and Lyn Nofziger, and (2) accusations against Attorney General Edwin Meese III relative to his financial dealings and possibly improper use of political influence in a conflict-of-interest situation.

The second category includes (1) a situation in which House Speaker Jim Wright appears to have influenced legislation sought by a Texas developer with whom Wright had a business partnership, and (2) refusal of the House to let its Ethics Committee continue probing the dealings of Banking Committee Chairman Fernand St. Germain, who, among other things, allegedly underreported his assets by more than $1 million.

There are unfortunately too many other examples in both the executive and legislative branches.

However, there is nothing wrong with the Ethics in Government Act except that it doesn't go far enough. It can be enforced against members of the executive branch, while Congress lets its own ethics committees investigate its members gently.

Instead of being allowed to die because of its one-sidedness, the act should be renewed and strengthened so that Congress will come under as close scrutiny as the other branch.

That isn't likely to happen, but it surely is better to punish some miscreants than make all immune merely because Congress exempts itself from impartial scrutiny.

THE DAILY HERALD

Biloxi, MS, September 9, 1987

Contrary to Rudyard Kipling's refrain that "East is east and west is west and never the twain shall meet," a historic meeting of East and West is now taking place in Bonn, West Germany. East German leader Erich Honecker is spending four days on the other side of the Berlin Wall whose construction he supervised. Europe and the world await to see what may develop from the visit.

No head of the German Democratic Republic has set foot in the Federal Democratic Republic since the separate states came into being in 1949 at the conclusion of World War II. For all practical purposes, the division of Germany has created two countries, but West Germany refuses to admit that East Germany is a separate country. The preamble of its constitution calls for the reunification of the two.

At the initial banquet in Bonn, West German Chancellor Helmut Kohl condemned the Berlin Wall and began their meeting by insisting that Honecker lift the shoot-to-kill orders on the boundaries between the two Germanys. At least 188 East Germans have been killed while trying to cross to the West since the wall was built in 1961. Honecker has resisted the plea for unity, remarking that "Socialism and capitalism can't be any more united than fire and water."

Yet for all the irresistible force and immovable object posturing of these two leaders, the very fact of the visit fosters hope that this face-to-face communication will lead to improved relations between the two Germanys. Twice before in the past six years, Honecker has accepted invitations to visit West Germany, only to renege under pressure from the Soviet Union.

The current visit indicates that the Soviet Union is also interested in improving relations between the two Germanys. Perhaps the visit may prove to be the first crack in the Berlin Wall.

Calgary Herald

Calgary, Alta., September 9, 1987

After 38 years of division, the two Germanys remain worlds apart, despite the heralded visit of East German leader Erich Honecker to Bonn.

The working visit — the term West Germany used so that it would not be interpreted as official recognition of the state of East Germany — began sourly.

Chancellor Helmut Kohl rattled the banquet china by calling for the reunification of Germany and decrying the shooting of escapers along the Berlin Wall.

"Germans suffer under the division. They suffer because of a wall that literally stands in their way and repels them," he said. "They want to come together because they belong together."

But while Honecker, the 75-year-old Communist party chief, recently ordered the dismantling of 54,-000 self-firing guns along the barbed-wire cordon which was erected under his orders in 1961, he dispelled any hope that the wall would be torn down.

Departing from his prepared text, he said flatly: "Socialism and capitalism can never be reconciled, just like fire and water can never be reconciled."

While the leaders proclaimed mutual respect for each country's political character and alliances as the official portion of the visit ended Tuesday, it's clear that ideology will keep Germany divided.

Polls show that few Germans on either side of the border believe the country will be joined before the year 2000.

The main agreements reached on environmental and scientific research issues were relatively insignificant. However, Honecker did give way on an issue close to the hearts of all German families — in future, it should be easier for long-divided families like Honecker's own to cross the border for visits.

However, this concession pales in comparison to the unresolved, nagging issue of the Berlin Wall. In the final analysis, no major barriers came down with the Honecker visit.

Post-Tribune

Gary, IN, September 5, 1987

The Berlin Wall won't come tumbling down soon and the political differences between West German and East Germany aren't about to fade away. But there is a symbolic crack in the wall and all that divides them: Eric Honecker will step over the line into West Germany on Monday. No head of the East German government has done that since the separation in 1949.

That visit will be a giant step forward in the Bonn government's continuing attempts to improve ties with its communist neighbors.

Our opinions

The five-day visit comes six years after the invitation from West Germany. Honecker's decision reflects the general improvement in East-West relations.

The political atmosphere seems right. Bonn has renounced the Pershing missiles planted on its soil, and East Germany recently announced an amnesty that included political prisoners and abolition of the death penalty.

Reunification remains more a dream than a possibility, but a new relationship is possible. Ordinary citizens in West Germany seem to be more interested in that than in pursuing a goal that is blocked by political realities.

A West German brochure puts it clearly. It notes that Germans on both sides of the border drink about the same amount of beer per person, smoke about the same number of cigarettes and eat about the same quantity of pork chops.

And through the years, these Germans who live in different worlds have adjusted to their own circumstances, which is a commentary on human ingenuity and sensibility. Some West Germans brag about their political freedom and high standard of living, and say they would not want to give that up to reunite with their compatriots. Visitors to East German report that many people there say they are happy with cradle-to-grave security and a system that produces top athletes and industrial goods.

East Germany says it will allow about a million of its people to visit West Germany this year, and it figures about 3,000 won't come back.

The political necessities and realities prevent a crumbling of the communist hold on East Germany, but it is clear that the two states need each other. The buying and selling of goods is essential to both.

The Honecker visit should improve relations. Expecting it to accomplish some ideological miracle or to even touch on reunification is folly. Judging it on that standard would make the meeting a failure, when in reality it is a historic move.

The San Diego Union

San Diego, CA, September 7, 1987

East German Communist Party boss Erich Honecker today set foot on his native soil for the first time in 52 years. He is the first East German leader to visit West Germany since the postwar partition of the nation four decades ago.

It was no ordinary state occasion. Matter of fact, it wasn't a state occasion at all. Neither country officially recognizes the other. But the long-awaited trip is a highly symbolic act that will have profound political and economic repercussions far beyond the borders of the two Germanies.

Small wonder, then, that Mr. Honecker's homecoming plans have twice been scotched by Mikhail Gorbachev. In public, Moscow is relentless in its opposition to a unified Germany. The sheer volume of horror stories about what reunification would mean to world peace has kept an army of Soviet hacks gainfully employed for decades. The private line, however, is entirely different.

East Germany plays a vital role in Moscow's untiring efforts to strike increasingly lucrative commercial deals with West Germany. These economic ties are crucial to Mr. Gorbachev's embryonic campaign to refurbish his economy. Without West German technology and credits, the U.S.S.R. would continue to write new definitions of the term economic stagnation.

For political and historical reasons, the Kremlin would never permit a strong, unified Germany. It is a position Mr. Honecker enthusiastically shares. But Moscow plays on Bonn's dream of reunification by allowing its East German satellite to establish a variety of economic and social links with the West.

Mr. Honecker is expected to sign agreements on environmental matters, scientific research, and nuclear safety. Additionally, he will pay lip service to the "sister city" program, in which nine pairs of towns in the two Germanies have been linked culturally and economically. All this is window-dressing. The big item is cash.

East Germany receives about $1 billion annually in aid from Bonn. Without hefty West German credits and loans, even if they do come in the form of ransom Bonn pays for political prisoners, East Germany could not possibly maintain its image as the Soviet bloc's economic showcase.

The dilemma West Germany faces is one of proportion: How to continue encouraging and broadening links to the East without triggering the Kremlin's latent Germanophobia. Solving the problem depends almost entirely on the tired old man who has returned to see his homeland for perhaps the last time.

The Honolulu Advertiser

Honolulu, HI
September 10, 1987

The historic first visit since World War II by an East German leader to West Germany has yielded little of real value.

West German Chancellor Helmut Kohl and East Germany's Erich Honecker signed some cooperation agreements. But Honecker ignored Kohl's pleas to tear down the Berlin Wall. It's not even clear if temporary orders not to shoot would-be escapees will be made permanent.

And West Germany rejected Honecker's demand for diplomatic recognition, though raising the East German flag and playing its national anthem did constitute recognition of sorts.

Despite historical ties, the two Germanys are divided by starkly different political and economic systems. Though East Germany has the strongest economy in the Soviet bloc, its citizens' incomes are only half those of West Germany. With four times the people and twice the land, the West's GNP is nearly six times that of the East.

Still, the goal of reunification is written into the West's constitution and 80 percent of West Germans say they would welcome a reunited, neutral nation. But the percentage who see that as possible "within 10 years" dropped from 30 to 10 percent in the last decade.

The Soviet Union, which was invaded by a united Germany in both world wars, bitterly opposes reunification. And the idea sends shivers up the spines of people in the rest of Europe and many Americans.

If a reunited Germany were neutral, it would harm NATO more than the Warsaw Pact and undermine western security. Even some Germans see the 75 years of unity from Otto von Bismarck to Adolf Hitler as an aberration, not the desirable norm.

For East Germany the hope was that this visit would lead to more respect as a nation, not just a Soviet puppet. West Germans hoped the result might be greater respect for human rights and arms control cooperation from the East.

But what will certainly *not* result is renewed movement toward a reunited Germany.

Jazz Section
Leaders Sentenced

A judge in Prague, Czechoslovakia March 11, 1987 convicted five leaders of the Jazz Section dissident organization of participating in illegal business activities. The judge gave the men sentences considerably lighter than those sought by the state prosecutor. The trial had opened March 10 to international attention. The defendants, who faced charges of up to eight years in prison apiece, all pleaded not guilty. Czechoslovakia was the most stubborn Eastern Bloc nation to accede to Moscow's new agenda of political and social liberalization.

Judge Vladimir Striborik March 11 found that the men had violated the law by publishing unsanctioned newsletters and books and using the gains for personal profit. Before pronouncing sentence, Striborik took the unusual step of praising the Jazz Section. "We don't want to limit cultural activity in our country, we want to develop it better for a young generation," he said. "The work [the organization] did was commendable, but needs a legalized forum." The judge's statements and the sentencing were nearly drowned out by syncopated hand clapping by about 150 young supporters of the Jazz Section outside the courtroom.

Striborik sentenced Karel Srp, the Jazz Section's chairman, to 16 months in prison, but subtracted the six months Srp had served in prison. Vladimir Kouril, the group's deputy chairman, was handed a 10-month sentence, with six months' credit for time served in detention. The three other defendants were placed on probation.

The Record

Hackensack, NJ, March 23, 1987

What's the state of cultural freedom in Czechoslovakia? Confused. In Prague recently, a judge praised leaders of a 16-year-old society called the Jazz Section, a group that met to share American-style music and other unorthodox art forms. "We don't want in any way to limit the cultural movements in our country," said Judge Vladimir Stiborik. "As there is a young generation with new interests, we want to support their concerns." He called the group's leaders "experts in their professions" and said that "their cultural work was commendable." Then he sentenced the group's two top leaders to brief prison terms for maintaining their 5,000-member organization after the state ordered it disbanded in 1984. Three other Jazz Section members, also defendants at the trial, received suspended sentences.

The judge's kind words and lenient punishment were seen as a compromise between conservative elements of the nation's Communist hierarchy, who want to silence the Jazz Section, and those within the party who hope to take advantage of the mood of cultural openness that seems to be emanating from Moscow. This ambivalence produced an exercise in theater of the absurd.

While the judge was passing sentence on the jazz lovers, some 150 of their supporters were allowed to stand outside the courtroom and clap for 20 minutes. (One observer noted that the clapping, fittingly, was "syncopated.") Western journalists were invited in to watch the proceedings and to hear some bizarre dialogue. For instance, an Interior Ministry official, who was part of the "liquidating commitee" convened to oversee the disbanding of the Jazz Section, explained that the group's written accounting of its assets was insufficient. Why, then, had the official not written for more information? "We could not address letters to an organization that did not exist." Well, would he have met with the Jazz Section leaders? "If they consented to be liquidated, of course we could have met them."

All this polite gobbledygook cannot mask the fact that music and poetry are still fearsome powers in Czechoslovakia. As Mikhail Gorbachev prepares to bring his smiles and talk of freedom to Prague in a few weeks, his hosts can be forgiven if they wonder how seriously to take him. It was only 19 years ago that Soviet forces put an end to a Czechoslovak experiment in cultural liberty. Which way is the wind really blowing, and how hard will it blow tomorrow?

Czechoslovakia, unsure of the answers, seems to be trying to take one step forward, one step back, and maybe one to the side as well. It is a strange dance, to a jazz accompaniment.

The Philadelphia Inquirer

Philadelphia, PA, March 13, 1987

Czech leaders apparently have become so unnerved by the new *glasnost* (openness) in Moscow that they are ending dissident jazz musicians to jail. That seems the best explanation or the persecution of the leaders of he Jazz Section, five Czech musicians who promoted jazz and published articles on culture written by dissidents.

In a country still tightly ruled by he men who crushed the 1968 "Prague pring," where culture is under wraps and even the word *reform* has been truck by censors, the sight of Soviet eader Mikhail Gorbachev wooing Moscow's intelligentsia must be sending shivers up many Czech spines. That the Czech leaders would prosecute the one Czech dissident group with a substantial domestic following shows how deeply ill at ease they feel at the prospect of even limited reforms.

Thus, when the organizers of the Jazz Section — originally a popular, legally sanctioned group of jazz fans attached to the state-sponsored Musicians' Union — began to publish an uncensored cultural newsletter, the government panicked. When the Musicians' Union refused to shut the group down, the government abolished the union. When jazz fans complained, the government organized public jazz festivals to try to counter their ire. And when the Jazz Section kept on publishing, the government concocted charges of illegal profit-making in order to jail its leaders.

The relatively light jail terms handed down Wednesday for two of those leaders reflect the debate within the Czech leadership over how to deal with the issue of reform. The sentencing judge took pains to praise the defendants' contributions to Czech culture — but he didn't dare let them go free. The fact that the trial was held at all — only a few weeks before Mr. Gorbachev is to visit Prague — is illustrative of the reactions to the Soviet leader's reforms by Moscow's more conservative allies in Eastern Europe. Only Poland and Hungary have generally welcomed the reforms, and even the Hungarian leadership is said to be somewhat uneasy.

Perhaps the other East bloc leaders recall that Soviet leader Nikita Khrushchev's move to de-Stalinize Eastern Europe in the mid-1950s led to upheaval in Poland and revolution in Hungary. Czech rulers remember that a dose of cultural freedom in 1968 inspired demands to change the whole system. Mr. Gorbachev will have a tough sales job ahead in the Eastern bloc, and if he can't push the *glasnost* product, it could make him look bad at home.

The Register

Santa Ana, CA, March 13, 1987

At first glance, it's just a typical story of Communist over-reaching, converting music into a political issue because of the misguided desire to control every conceivable human activity to serve the interests of the party and the state. At second glance, you wonder whether it's so different from some of the regulations we accept here with barely a second thought.

The problem arose in Czechoslovakia, where five leaders of the Jazz Section of the Musician's Union fell into official disfavor for publishing unauthorized art and culture books and arranging concerts without state sanction. They were charged with unauthorized economic activity, punishable by a maximum prison term of two to eight years. The judge, after praising their intentions and the quality of their work, found them guilty and sentenced the leader to 16 months in jail, his deputy to 10 months, and three other defendants to probation of up to four years.

The judge said that the government didn't want to limit cultural development, indeed it wanted to encourage cultural development. He noted that the defendants were serious and competent artists. But, "their cultural work was commendable, but it required a legal form because social values must be regulated."

The statement sounds absurd to people who take culture seriously. A culture that truly expresses the complexity of a given society is more often one that is permitted to develop freely, without overt regulation, by a process akin to spontaneous order. Of course such a cultural garden may sometimes contain as many weeds as flowers, but the subtle interplay of innovation and judgment by people with various degrees of taste will regulate its development more effectively than any all-wise central authority.

But is it only Communists who believe that social values must be regulated, that certain types of economic activity ought to be unauthorized? Hardly.

Some American cities want to ban the unauthorized economic activity of garage sales. Some have used economic regulations to ban private concerts held in private homes. There's little you can do in this country without first getting a permit from government at some level. And, of course, dozens of groups advocate outright bans on certain modes of cultural expression such as punk rock.

Few Americans embrace a theory of total control of all aspects of life approaching the totalitarian theory that underpins Communist regimes. But plenty of Americans seem quite comfortable with regulations that people living under Communism would find familiar.

In Czechoslovakia the trial of the Jazz Section leaders attracted 150 to 200 supporters of the musicians who clapped in syncopated rhythms in the hallway outside and pronounced the sentence scandalous. So cultural freedom has friends in Czechoslovakia. Does it have so many in our country, or will it take more systematic repression to arouse more concern?

The News and Courier

Charleston, SC, March 13, 1987

"Kafkaesque" is the word that describes the conviction on Wednesday by a Prague court of five jazz enthusiasts. But even Franz Kafka's imagination might have boggled at the idea of a story about the state persecuting and then prosecuting the seven leaders of a musical organization called Jazz Section.

Of course, Kafka died in 1924 before totalitarian fact outdid the Czech author's fiction. Who would have imagined that Stalin would have sent the NKVD to liquidate all stamp collectors and speakers of Esperanto as enemies of the state? Who would have imagined that the Argentine military regime would go after psychologists and ban modern mathematics, on the grounds that both induced communism?

The arrest last Sept. 2 and subsequent trial of the leaders of Jazz Section has, nevertheless, aroused a furor around the world. Had there been no international outcry, the sentences handed out might have been much more severe. The charge, of illegally profiting from publishing books and illegally promoting modern music, carries a maximum sentence of eight years. The judge, who solemnly announced that promoting culture "requires a legal form because social values must be attained," sentenced the leader of the group, Karel Srp, to 16 months in prison, while Vladimir Kouril, the secretary, was given a 10-month term. Both of them have been in jail since Sept. 2. Three other members of Jazz Section were given suspended prison terms and were placed on probation. The remaining two of the seven leaders were excused for health reasons but will be tried later.

Jazz Section took its name from the founders' declaration that jazz is "a symbol of creativity, humanity and tolerance" and "a way to mutual understanding between nations." It sought to spread independent culture, through jazz and rock sessions, books and art exhibits, throughout Eastern Europe. That, of course, was why Big Brother stamped on Jazz Section — despite the campaign that has been waged by leading writers like Kurt Vonnegut, by jazz musicians and human rights organizations. Culture is one of the tools that a totalitarian society uses to repress the people, and to succeed it must be in the hands of the state.

The jazz trials are not over yet. Apart from the defendants who were too ill to attend court and will be hauled before the judge at a later date, a young man by the name of Petr Pospichal faces 10 years in jail. Mr. Pospichal is guilty of an even greater crime than the leaders of Jazz Section. As well as being a member of the outlawed group, Mr. Pospichal has been monitoring human rights violations in Czechoslovakia.

The message that is coming from Prague is that, despite the advent of Soviet General Secretary Mikhail Gorbachev and the example of his much touted "glasnost" policies and talk of liberalization, nothing much has changed in communist Czechoslovakia.

The Charlotte Observer

Charlotte, NC, March 19, 1987

"We don't want in any way to limit cultural movements in our country," the Czech judge said to the five activists for cultural freedom on trial in his Prague courtroom. But, he said, "social values must be regulated." After praising the quality and seriousness of the defendants' work, he found them guilty of unauthorized commercial activities and gave them sentences ranging from probation to 16 months.

The five were leaders of the Jazz Section, an independent cultural group that was banned last fall. Begun as an officially tolerated jazz club, the group had enlarged its scope to the point of publishing uncensored works by leading writers. Perhaps because the group was reportedly preparing to take its case to a meeting discussing Eastern European compliance with the pledges of freedom made in the Helsinki accords, the government cracked down.

At the trial, supporters of the group were allowed to gather outside the courtroom and three Western reporters were admitted. The sentences were relatively light. Some suspect all that reflects ambivalence in the central committee of the Czech Communist Party, where there is said to be sharp division over the openness and reform being touted in Russia by Soviet leader Mikhail Gorbachev. The Czechs, of course, have vivid memories of the dangers of too much reform, recalling how Soviet power crushed their own efforts at liberalization during the "Prague Spring" of 1968. Similar ambivalence is seen elsewhere in the Soviet sphere as small signs of liberalization alternate with familiar patterns of repression.

Mr. Gorbachev is to visit Czechoslovakia soon and will have ample opportunity to say whether he means for openness to extend to cultural and intellectual activity in the U.S.S.R.'s satellites in Eastern Europe. If, say, he publicly calls for reestablishment of the Jazz Section and pardon of its convicted leaders, the world will know he really is serious about opening up more than public relations in the Soviet bloc. If, however, by his silence on the subject he blesses such repressive acts as the crackdown on the Jazz Section, then the world will see more clearly the limits of his zeal for reform.

THE CHRISTIAN SCIENCE MONITOR
Boston, MA, March 13, 1987

AUTHORITARIANS, whether of the left or right, have always feared ideas – even new thoughts coming in the form of music or popular culture. Untraditional ideas, after all – like the nononsense blare of a trumpet or the sweet wail of a saxophone in the night – have a way of catching one's attention and forcing fresh perspectives on the familiar.

Thus, the conviction of five members of the so-called Jazz Section of the Musicians' Union in Prague is not unexpected. Granted, the actual sentences turned out to be lighter than they might have been. Two defendants were given brief jail sentences; three others were placed on probation. Still, the verdict has to be seen as curious indeed, coming as it does against the backdrop of increasing political and cultural liberalization in the Soviet Union under Mikhail Gorbachev, who, by the way, is shortly to visit Prague. And jazz itself, it might be noted, has won a substantial following in the USSR since its founding in 1917.

What crimes were committed by the Jazz Section? It continued to publish newsletters and books after the government's interior minister had ruled the group should disband. Over the years the Jazz Section has promoted jazz as well as various forms of nonauthorized cultural activities.

Czechoslovakia's ruling Communist Party leadership is attempting to walk a fine line, bowing to some of the liberalization under way in parts of the East bloc while seeking to ensure domestic order to prevent any recurrence of the Soviet invasion after the "Prague Spring" of 1968. But that aside, the reasoning of the court in the Jazz Section case cannot be cheering to libertarians – or those valuing art for the sake of art. Noting the professionalism of the five convicted defendants, the judge said that "their cultural work was commendable, but it required a legal form because social values must be regulated."

The Virginian-Pilot

Norfolk, VA, March 17, 1987

The chief defendant, a 50-year-old chairman of a cultural group, sports a beard and moustache and shoulder-length hair, and was seen to flash his supporters. a "V" sign from manacled hands. Those supporters — many similarly long-haired — filled the hallway outside the courtroom during the trial, clapping in rhythm, singing John Lennon's "Give peace a chance," and cheering the defendants. The government's call for heavy fines and long jail terms were frustrated by the district court judge, who handed down only light prison terms to two defendants and probation to three others.

Chicago, 1968? No: Prague, Czechoslovakia, 1987.

The five social activists were tried for illegal economic activity, consisting of collecting dues from members of the Jazz Section organization (originally part of the official musicians' union) after the group had been ordered dissolved by the Czech government, and selling uncensored newsletters and books on the arts.

This is standard operating procedure for a repressive society. But the fact that representatives of three Western news agencies were allowed to attend the trial suggests that it was intended to demonstrate the spread of Mikhail Gorbachev's liberalizing influence in Eastern Europe. What it suggested, though, was that there is some truth in the old saw that Eastern European countries are 100 percent Marxist: 50 percent Karl, 50 percent Groucho. Witness, for example, this unintentionally comic exchange:

Chief defendant Karol Srp asked the official of the Ministry of Culture who had been responsible for liquidating the Jazz Section why he had not responded to letters sent by members of the section. The official's bland reply: "We could not answer letters from an organization that does not exist."

A TV interview with Chicago's Mayor Daley would have fit right in.

Richmond Times-Dispatch

Richmond, VA, March 16, 1987

Until now the "economic crime" in jazz has been considered the pay, or lack of it. Czechoslovakia this past week formally added another: Five members of the Jazz Section of the Musician's Union have been sentenced to jail terms for refusing a government order to disband, for disseminating opinions as dissonant to Czech authorities as some jazz chords are to untutored ears, and for making money off them.

Jazz Section leaders deny breaking even, much less making a profit. But their publications, initially newsletters on the arts, reached a wider, more eager audience than the 3,000 members of a union sanctioned and provided a printing press by a since-regretful government. Just as jazz aficionados will find or form a club, underground writers will find a publisher: Czech dissidents denied publication in other official forums found space in Jazz Section books and newsletters, as did articles on experimental music, rock music and punk bands.

The issue here is not taste in music, or the merits of underground literature, or illegal commercial activity, though Czechs in government and out see Western music, mimeograph machines and profits as both symbols and tools of a free society. The issue is control, and that Prague has chosen to exert control now, and so openly, is bad news for East Europeans who had hoped their capitals would emulate the apparent cultural thaw in Moscow, where Nobel Prize-winning author Boris Pasternak's "Doctor Zhivago" has gotten the official nod, if 30 years late. To Westerners so happily welcoming Mikhail Gorbachev's Russia to the 1950s as a precursor to peace and freedom for Europe in the 1980s jail terms for the Czech Jazz Section are a sour note of warning.

The Washington Post

Washington, DC, March 15, 1987

IN CZECHOSLOVAKIA, which has made immense contributions to the Western cultural heritage, five citizens have been convicted for belonging to a jazz club—not a jazz club fronting as a spy shop or a political party, but a jazz club. Why have the communist authorities chosen in this way to make their country an international laughingstock? Because the people in the so-called Jazz Section were setting out to conduct a performance and create an enterprise responsive to the varied and educated tastes of Czech citizens. The party took this as a threat to socialism in Czechoslovakia.

Perhaps the party knows best. The kind of socialism that is enforced by the Soviet army—which is the kind Czechoslovakia and the rest of Eastern Europe have—may well be unable to accommodate an innocent but independent cultural organization. The party with its police is in a position to know how shallow its support is. Still, it shames the country to have a leadership so frightened and so disrespectful of Czech traditions. It is cruel to the individuals involved, who went out of their way to make their enterprise acceptable to the authorities and who are now in prison or on probation for their pains.

Czechoslovakia, of course, still lives under the shadow of its trauma of 1968, when an effort to build "socialism with a human face" was crushed by half a million Soviet troops. The Czech leadership then installed by Moscow remains in power. This has created an extraordinary set of tensions. The first set is familiar: where other empires established (and since lost) by the West Europeans were built on the subjugation of less technologically developed countries, the Soviet Union took in more developed countries, such as Czechoslovakia. Meanwhile, however, Mikhail Gorbachev has come to the Kremlin, giving Moscow at least for a while a government that is, in appearance anyway, less uptight about these things than the regime in Prague—this, even though Czechoslovakia is a more Western country. The situation is unnatural and cannot last.

The best that can be said for the Czech government is that it understands the curious position it is in. Hence its feeble effort to temper its repressions by serving up relatively light sentences and holding a somewhat open trial. But these are palliatives. The Czech leadership of 1968-87 is an anomaly. It is afraid of letting citizens listen to jazz.

San Francisco Chronicle

San Francisco, CA, March 12, 1987

THE TRIAL OF FIVE jazz enthusiasts in Czechoslovakia for unauthorized commercial activity has drawn international attention as an indicator of just how far Mr. Gorbachev's vaunted "glasnost" will be allowed to stray from its Soviet home. The result — speedy conviction — warns that exportation of a commodity like cultural freedom will be strictly rationed to certain East Bloc countries.

What had these downbeat desperadoes been up to? They had been putting out a publication called Jazz Section for about 5000 fans. But trouble came when Jazz Section extended its coverage from jazz themes to developments in art and literature around the world and became the mostly widely read uncensored source of cultural information in the country.

That, it turned out, made Jazz Section illegal by decree of the Interior Ministry. Down swooped the police, and the stage was set for a political trial. The fans turned out to cheer as manacled musicians and editors entered the dock.

THE SENTENCES imposed after a brief trial were prison terms of 10 and 16 months for two defendants, and suspended terms for the others. That's better than the eight years each might have received. But the fact they were in court at all was outrageous. One handcuffed defendant shouted "Long Live Jazz" as he was led way. That defiant cry is one of long reverberation.

The Seattle Times

Seattle, WA, March 12, 1987

MIKHAIL Gorbachev may have somewhat loosened the state's grip on free expression in the Soviet Union, but that measure of enlightenment has yet to reach one of the western outposts of the Soviet empire.

A trial in a Prague courtroom this week demonstrated why Czechoslovakia, under hardline party chief Gustav Husak, remains one of the more backward states in the Warsaw Pact bloc.

Five leaders of the banned Jazz Section, a group of Czech activists, were convicted of "economic crimes" for illegally publishing books and promoting modern music. The five were sentenced to prison terms of several months, some being released for having served sufficient time since their arrest in September.

A crowd of 150 people sang "Give Peace a Chance" outside the courtroom, and their rhythmic clapping could be heard inside. One

Gustav Husak

defendant shouted, "Long live jazz!" before being led away.

Jazz Section is an independent publishing and musical organization founded in 1971 as part of the musicians' union. It continued operating even after the state banned the union in 1984.

Judge Vladimir Stiborik said the state does not want to discourage culture, but that promoting culture "requires a legal form because social value must be attained." Social value as defined exclusively by the state, of course.

The San Diego Union

San Diego, CA, March 13, 1987

It is fitting that the trial of five leaders of the Czechoslovakian group called Jazz Section took place in Prague, the hometown of Franz Kafka, the author whose brilliant, comedic works focused on the ironic absurdities that he saw as a staple of everyday life.

Only in an absurd arena could the act of publishing tracts on culture be deemed a crime. And only in a Kafkaesque world could it be suggested, as it has been in this case, that the defendants were lucky to receive "light" sentences.

All five leaders of the Jazz Section, a group daring to espouse cultural freedom, were convicted, and two were sentenced to jail. Their crime was daring to publish newsletters and books after the Czechoslovakian Interior Ministry had ruled arbitrarily that the group should be disbanded. Arbitrary rulings by obscure but powerful tribunals were, in fact, crucial elements in Kafka's great work, *The Trial*, published in 1925, a year after the author's death.

As though to complete the irony, the judge praised the five men for their contributions to Czechoslovakian culture before convicting them and pronouncing sentence. Karel Srp was sentenced to 16 months, and Vladimir Kouril to 10 months. The six months each of them spent in pre-trial detention was subtracted from their sentences. The other three men, who also spent six months in jail awaiting trial, received suspended sentences. As for the Jazz Section, it remained sentenced to "liquidation" by the Interior Ministry.

Significantly, the Jazz Section started out as a group dedicated to jazz, a Western art form. The freewheeling aesthetics of the jazz milieu became the foundation, the currency of the group's objections to the cultural tyranny imposed upon their nation by its communist regime. The Jazz Section, which had more than 5,000 members, published pamphlets and books that ultimately reached out to discuss a wide spectrum of cultural trends, most of them emanating from the West. The publications gained a broad following. Then, in 1984, the government ordered the group to disband. The leaders sought a clarification, didn't get one, and kept on functioning.

Glasnost, Soviet leader Mikhail Gorbachev's stated policy of economic liberalization and more cultural openness, faces opposition even among his own Russian communist cadres. It is perhaps even less admired by the skittish communist regimes along the western edges of the Soviet empire. The very word "reform" is often struck by Czechoslovakian censors.

Thus the travesty of the Jazz Section proceedings. After the judge pronounced his sentences and the defendants were being led away, one of them shouted toward Western correspondents, "Write it down, what they did to us." Kafka already did.

Houston Chronicle

Houston, TX, March 16, 1987

Jazz is a type of music that glories in individual experimentation and expression. Not by accident, its origins lie in America.

Czechoslovakia has a communist government that suppresses individual expression. Also not by accident, five jazz enthusiasts on trial in Prague for "economic crimes" were convicted.

The five defendants were members of a club called the Jazz Section, which published uncensored — and therefore very popular — books and newsletters on jazz, literature and other cultural affairs. When its influence became too widespread, the government ordered the club to disband.

The prosecutor in the case said, "It is not a question of jazz, but of failing to respect the decisions of the authorities of Czechoslovakia."

He is only partly right. In Czechoslovakia and other Soviet bloc countries, of course, those who do not let the decisions of the authorities govern every aspect of their lives risk a prison sentence or worse.

However, jazz was more than a symbolic element in this case. Jazz is a music that allows its performers the freedom to compose and improvise as they see fit. Eastern Europeans who try to take such freedom outside the concert hall are indeed threats to a totalitarian government's authority.

Hungarian Leader Kadar
Ousted at Party Meeting

Janos Kadar was removed as the general secretary of Hungary's Socialist Worker's (Communist) Party May 22, 1988 at a national party conference in Budapest. He was replaced by Premier Karoly Grosz. Kadar, 75, had been in power since 1956. He was the second aged Eastern European leader to step down in five months. Czechoslovakia's Gustav Husak had resigned in December 1987. The change was made on the third and final day of Hungary's first national conference since 1957. Nearly 1,000 delegates – party officials, workers, students and intellectuals – attended the gathering.

Kadar was given the newly created post of party president. Western observers expected his duties to be largely ceremonial. In addition to Kadar's removal, sweeping personnel changes in the policy-making Politburo and the party Central Committee were announced at the gathering. With the changes, a new generation took control of the party.

The conference had been called to set a course for the party amid Hungary's stagnant economy and rising political dissent. For several months prior to the conference, rumors had circulated around Budapest that major leadership changes were imminent. The *New York Times*, citing an unidentified party source, May 21 reported that Kadar had reluctantly accepted a Politburo decision May 16 that he should relinquish power. Younger party officials, those in their 40s and 50s, had grown impatient with Kadar's policies, which they regarded as too stubborn to cope with Hungary's current problems. That attitude was prevalent among the younger conference delegates, some of whom were in their 20s.

Under Kadar's leadership, Hungary since the 1960s had evolved as the most market-oriented economy of any Soviet-bloc country. But the economy had begun to decline in the mid-1970s, and Kadar had resisted far-reaching remedies. At the end of 1987, Hungary had been one of the first Eastern European countries to have multi-candidate parliamentary elections, but Kadar had remained staunchly conservative on the matter of further political liberalization. Since becoming premier in June 1987, Grosz had gained a reputation not so much as a reformist, but as a pragmatist.

THE SACRAMENTO BEE
Sacramento, CA, May 28, 1988

Janos Kadar began his 31-year reign as Hungary's Communist Party chairman as Soviet tanks were brutally crushing the Hungarian freedom fighters in the streets of Budapest during the darkest days of the Cold War. He ended it last Sunday as Ronald Reagan and Mikhail Gorbachev prepared for the next round in the process aimed at stabilizing relations between the world's two great power blocs. During one man's political career, much has changed.

The 76-year-old Kadar was ousted by younger leaders for reverting to the conservatism that caused Moscow to install him in the first place. After presiding over the most progressive economic reforms in Eastern Europe during the 1960s, Kadar had become an obstacle to reform now promoted, ironically, by the Kremlin. Hungary's economy has stagnated in recent years. The standard of living, still high by East-bloc standards, has fallen; Hungarians are so overworked — many of them hold two or three jobs to make ends meet — that the country's alcoholism and suicide rates are well above others in the region.

Karoly Grosz, the new party chairman, is, like Gorbachev, relatively young (57), pragmatic and, with his team of radical reformers, apparently willing to initiate sweeping economic changes and allow a greater degree of political expression, even at the risk of creating popular pressure for the kind of freedoms that incurred Soviet wrath in 1956.

It's noteworthy that Hungary appears to be taking full advantage of the change in Moscow, while others in Eastern Europe — notably East Germany, Czechoslovakia and Romania — resist reform. In those countries, old-line Communists cling to power and to orthodoxy, hoping, no doubt, that Gorbachev and Grosz will fail and that they, the hard-liners, will see their brand of communism vindicated. It's of vital importance, in the Communist world and beyond, that those hopes not be realized.

The West has little direct role in this drama, but it can nudge it toward the desired end by supporting diplomatically, and in some cases with trade and credit policy, reforms that promote economic efficiency and political pluralism. That will require an uncommon degree of skill and flexibility from Washington in an era when the United States, deprived for too long of strong leadership and preoccupied with its own problems, has become too inattentive to a part of the world that is more complex and, as this week's dramatic change in Budapest demonstrates, less monolithic than often imagined.

The London Free Press
London, Ont., May 26, 1988

That Janos Kadar has been replaced as general secretary of Hungary's Communist party is not surprising. Age, too many years in power and a sour national mood took their toll.

However, the manner of his going was unusual. He's the first leader in the Soviet bloc to be retired, ostensibly undisgraced, with most of his cronies.

Kadar's replacement, Karoly Grosz, emerged from months of infighting in the upper ranks of the party over economic reform. As premier since last June, Grosz has imposed austerity measures in a bid to reduce foreign debt, deregulate prices and close down money-losing state industries.

Kadar's hopes that such policies would hurt his rival were unfulfilled. Grosz drew influential support despite their unpopularity.

At the three-day national party conference last weekend, the two main advocates of economic and political change — Rezso Nyers and Imre Pozsgay — were also elected to the Politburo while seven of Kadar's closest lieutenants were dropped.

Grosz fits the mould of his pragmatic Soviet counterpart, Mikhail Gorbachev. To overcome his country's economic stagnation, he resolutely advocates reliance on market principles in place of centralized state control.

Still, he is not seen as a liberal and his loyalty to Moscow is not in question.

The situation in Hungary remains volatile. Kadar resisted the drive to remove him and there is speculation the wily former leader may not accept his demotion to president as purely ceremonial. Should he try to exercise authority, he could be supported by many party officials who fear the new leadership wants to remove them.

WORCESTER TELEGRAM

Worcester, MA, May 26, 1988

Mikhail Gorbachev's battle to restructure Soviet society has been the focus of the coverage of "perestroika" in the Western press. But the most dramatic demonstration of restructuring in the Soviet bloc to date came last weekend in Hungary.

Janos Kadar, Hungary's Communist Party head for 32 years, was replaced by Prime Minister Karoly Grosz. Kadar, a former hard-line Stalinist and capo of the secret police, evolved into something of a reformer after being installed as head of the Hungarian Communist Party. Kadar retreated to a more traditional stance in recent years, and reportedly his removal was partly in response to widespread popular resentment. The power shift came at the end of an unusual three-day national party conference, the first in 31 years.

Kadar turns 76 today, so the party action was not unexpected and might have been as much a generational change as an ideological one. Alone, the move would have been of limited significance.

However, the shift of Kadar to the honorary position of party president was accompanied by a wave of ousters in the top ranks of Hungary's Communist Party. Prominent among the victims were representatives of the old guard, including two party secretaries who had been close to Kadar and seven members of the 13-member politboro.

The winds of "glasnost" also seem to have reached the centers of Hungarian political power. Party insiders reported an unexpected degree of openness in the speeches made by many of the 50 conference delegates who took the floor to voice local concerns. The frankness apparently went well beyond the usual pro forma socialist self-criticism.

There is always the danger of reading too much into the recent changes in the Soviet bloc. As the Hungarian Communist Party made a public show of its political housecleaning, the Soviet tanks withdrawing from Afghanistan provided a grim reminder of the Soviet tanks that rumbled through the streets of Budapest in 1956 and of Prague in the spring of 1968.

Still, taken together with the re-emergence of Solidarity as a political force in Poland and Gorbachev's continuing moves to replace hardliners with more progressive party leaders, the developments in Budapest hold out real hope for liberalization.

Lincoln Journal

Lincoln, NE, May 27, 1988

Reformers have carried the day in Hungary. That Soviet satellite nation's Communist Party pretty well cleaned house last weekend, retiring its leader of 32 years, Janos Kadar, replacing eight septuagenarians on its 13-member politburo with younger, more forward-looking individuals and committing itself to a rather heady dose of democracy in the coming years.

These changes would not have happened without the blessing of the people now calling the shots in the neighboring Soviet Union. Yet what happened in Budapest is no sure sign that Mikhail Gorbachev can achieve a comparable upheaval when the Soviet Union's first Communist Party general conference in 47 years convenes next month.

Gorbachev is making the conference a focal point of his efforts to restructure the economy and politics of his country. In speeches that have been widely circulated, he has called for the selection of enthusiastic supporters of reform as delegates to the conference.

However, early returns, as it were, cast some doubt on Gorbachev's ability to achieve the composition of the conference he wants. Regional party leaders have great influence over the choice of delegates. They are part of the entrenched party bureaucracy and have a great deal to lose if the political structure is shaken up. Several of the most outspoken advocates of perestroika apparently aren't winning the favor of these regional powers.

But Gorbachev has proved himself a shrewd leader. It is doubtful that he would allow plans for the unusual general conference to proceed if he were not confident of its outcome. The June 29 meeting should be historic — either a staunch endorsement of Gorbachev's initiatives or an abrupt rejection of them, perhaps marking the end of his dramatic interlude in the Kremlin and on the world stage.

It is in the interest of the West to see Gorbachev prevail. His movement has been in the direction of improved relations with the non-communist world and a reduction of the superpowers' insane arms buildup. Is there anything Washington and other Western capitals can do to strengthen the Soviet leader's hand?

The answer to that is easily found in President Reagan's imminent summit visit to Moscow. Its timing is surely dictated less by Mrs. Reagan's astrologer than by Gorbachev's domestic political needs.

As he hosts Reagan, Gorbachev will be sending a signal to his ruling comrades and the Soviet people that their nation, under his leadership, is firmly back in the community of nations, playing a major if not pre-eminent role in the pursuit of peace and on the brink of a bright new day. How could the Communist Party conference repudiate such a leader?

The Washington Post

Washington, DC, May 24, 1988

THE LAST LEADER of communist-ruled Hungary was put in power by Soviet tanks. Janos Kadar, a former chief (and victim) of the secret police, having embraced "our glorious revolution" of 1956, within days betrayed it, defected to the Soviets as they intervened and became Moscow's man in Budapest. The wonder is that in a few years he worked himself out from under this unimaginable burden, finding ways to ease the strains of a riven society and establishing Hungary as a Soviet-bloc model of better living, civility and incipient reform. This "wise man," as George Shultz has called him, became over the weekend the first bloc leader to leave power in honor, undone not by violence or intrigue but by age.

The new leader was put in power by a remarkably public process of deliberation within the Hungarian Communist Party. The Soviet Union still dictates Hungary's general retention of a Moscow-oriented socialist system, but it does not dictate all the specific choices Hungarians make within it. Karoly Grosz, 57, is an energetic party veteran, currently serving as prime minister, who has had full exposure to the country's awesome economic cares. He has been one of those pushing impatiently to take reform beyond the retiring Mr. Kadar's cautious but pace-setting experiment with "market socialism." By Hungarian communist standards, nonetheless, he remains a moderate or, in the Kadar style, a balancer. He proposes to "renew" one-party rule by carefully expanding certain democratic procedures. He is less ready—only a few ranking figures are—to encourage the nonparty professional associations and social organizations that constitute the fragile shoots of "political pluralism" in Hungary today.

The ascension of Mikhail Gorbachev in Moscow has given a certain amount of heart and cover to would-be reformers throughout the Kremlin's East European realm. Because socialism was settled only recently and involuntarily on the region by Soviet power, however, attempts to nudge forward intrinsically difficult reform measures carry with them the constant possibility of an antisocialist and anti-Soviet explosion. A live fear of this possibility hovers over the daily struggle in the trenches in Poland. In Hungary, Janos Kadar taught—after 1956—a lesson of calculated discretion that has kept the national peace but has so far denied the sort of national breakthrough that the new leadership desperately hopes to bring.

Los Angeles Times

Los Angeles, CA, May 26, 1988

Janos Kadar devoted a good number of his 32 years in power to making Hungary a laboratory for economic experimentation unique within the Soviet Bloc. His "market socialism," with its easing away from ideological rigidities, drew the interest of reformers in China and the nervous attention of other Eastern European hierarchs. Hungarians came to speak of themselves as socialists in the morning, capitalists in the afternoon. But Hungarians who have had the chance under Kadar's long tenure to taste something of the better life still are a long way from achieving the good life. An economy that once seemed robust has stagnated, foreign debt has soared, political restiveness has grown. The blame has increasingly fallen on the 76-year-old man at the top. This week, in a quiet political coup, Kadar was put out to pasture.

His successor as head of the Communist Party is Karoly Grosz, named prime minister by Kadar just a year ago. Observers describe Grosz as a hard-nosed reformer. Add to that an apparent affinity for candor. In an interview two days after his election Grosz acknowledged his government's failure so far to revitalize Hungary's economy, and warned that his planned reforms won't bring improvements overnight. Those new approaches amount to a considerable agenda for change. They include encouraging more foreign investment and joint ventures, relaxing restrictions on the ownership of foreign capital, expanding private initiatives and giving Hungarians a greater voice in their political and economic affairs.

Kadar came to power in the wake of the 1956 rebellion that explosively showed how deep Hungarian hatred for Soviet domination and Communist rule was. Grosz comes to power at a time when economic and social restructuring and maybe even a dose of political liberalization are official if still not final doctrine in the Soviet Union. Leaders in other Warsaw Pact countries—in East Germany and Czechoslovakia particularly—look on Mikhail S. Gorbachev's reformist instincts with fear and loathing. Grosz gives every sign not only of supporting Gorbachev's reforms but also of being ready to introduce more progressive flourishes of his own.

Buffalo Evening News

Buffalo, NY, May 26, 1988

IN A DRAMATIC sign of change behind the Iron Curtain, Janos Kadar, the Hungarian Communist chief who was installed in office by Soviet tanks in 1956, was ousted from his post this week along with his aging followers on the ruling Politburo.

The party conference that made the changes was notable not only for its reformist leanings but for the open debate concerning economic and political issues. Kadar was roundly criticized for the country's recent economic stagnation. Usually, such leadership changes are arranged at secret party meetings.

Hungary has been the most innovative of the Soviet satellites under Kadar, who allowed some use of free enterprise and made Hungary the most prosperous and least repressive member of the Soviet bloc. But reform movements have been curbed in recent years.

Now there may be more progress. The party issued a policy statement calling for fewer economic restraints and greater autonomy for labor unions. There was no drastic break with the past, however. The statement rejected the idea of independent political parties and urged greater Communist Party discipline.

Continuity was also suggested by the choice of Premier Karoly Grosz as the new party chief. Grosz is faithful to Moscow and is unlikely to favor liberal political ideas, but he is also a new generation communist in the pragmatic mold of Soviet leader Mikhail Gorbachev. He is expected to favor greater use of free enterprise principles in order to stimulate the economy.

Change is likely to be sought by two newcomers to the Politburo, one of whom is the father of the economic reforms of the 1960s and the other a liberal supporter of independent political parties.

During the rigid Brezhnev years in the Soviet world, Hungary was a maverick with its economic innovation, but now Gorbachev is pushing many similar reforms and allowing some freedom of discussion. There is no sign yet that Hungary will plunge ahead again at a greater pace of reform than Moscow.

Nevertheless, the changes in Hungary are symptomatic of the spirit in other parts of the Soviet bloc. The people of Poland continue to press for new freedoms, and in Czechoslovakia another long-time Communist Party chief, Gustav Husak, was "kicked upstairs" to the presidency last November.

The United States is rightly responding to these yearnings for change by its diplomatic contacts with officials of the Soviet bloc. Many of the satellite countries are looking to Western nations for economic help. Trade and other ties should be linked to advances in human rights and the cause of freedom generally.

The Christian Science Monitor

Boston, MA, May 24, 1988

HUNGARY's Karoly Grosz adds a fresh twist of plot to the slow drama of reform in Eastern Europe. Mr. Grosz comes to power with a long history as a tough party functionary and propagandist and with a newfound faith in reform.

He has the earmarks of a consummate politician, somewhat in the mold of Mikhail Gorbachev – and indications are that the Soviet leader was pleased with Grosz's victory at a conference of the Hungarian Communist Party over the weekend.

Grosz replaces Janos Kadar as party chief. Mr. Kadar had held the post since 1956, when the Soviets smashed an anticommunist revolution in Hungary. Though a reformer in his own right, Kadar had increasingly been perceived as a man of the past. And his earlier experiments with free-market techniques had not been enough to save the country from its current economic morass.

Over the past year as prime minister, Grosz has been responsible for imposing discipline on the Hungarian economy by slashing price subsidies, taxing incomes, and taking other measures hardly designed to build popularity. Some speculate that Kadar gave Grosz the job thinking that it might give the ambitious younger man enough rope to hang himself. Instead, Grosz pursued his tasks while waving the banner of economic restructuring and succeeded in winning to his side many of Hungary's most influential people.

Now in power, along with a number of reform-minded Politburo members, Grosz has to take up the extraordinarily complex task of balancing change with stability. The central question he faces – the same one faced by leaders in Poland, Bulgaria, and the Soviet Union itself – is how far to go with the political side of reform. Grosz has said such iconoclastic things as "We have to have opposite interests competing in order to find solutions."

But so far neither the new party chief nor his like-minded Politburo members take that to mean genuine political pluralism; rather, they mean pluralism within the structure of the Communist Party. Radical change, including a multiparty system and true representative government, is not yet on the horizon.

What may be on the horizon is ferment within the Hungarian party as competing factions battle for position. Kadar, relegated to the ceremonial post of party president, could still wield a residue of power. Doubtless Grosz will push hard for further economic change. Such innovations as widespread private ownership and a stock market may come. Hungary is already further down this road than its East-bloc neighbors. But its over-commitment to unproductive heavy industry and its huge foreign debt make quick progress difficult.

Whatever the pace of change under its new leader, Hungary's experience will be watched closely on both sides of what was once routinely referred to as the "Iron Curtain." That image has in itself been rusting away in recent years – a process that could be accelerated a bit by the peaceful rise to power of Hungary's new reformers.

The Morning News

Wilmington, DE, May 27, 1988

TO NO ONE'S surprise, Janos Kadar, who had headed Hungary's Communist Party since 1956, stepped aside earlier this week at the party's national conference.

The 76-year-old Mr. Kadar had served his country remarkably well. He had come to power in 1956 as Soviet tanks rolled through Budapest and all thoughts of freedom and economic recovery threatened to evaporate before the eyes of the Hungarian people. But remarkably, in spite of the continuing presence of some Soviet troops, Mr. Kadar managed to make Hungary the politically most relaxed member of the Soviet bloc and also the one with the highest standards of living. Mind you, this is not to imply that life in Hungary was anywhere as pleasant as life in neighboring, democratic Austria, but it was a lot better than life in neighboring communist Czechoslovakia, for instance.

In the last couple of years, however, Hungary had incurred sizable budget deficits and the remedial measures Mr. Kadar imposed were not well received. Somehow he had lost his touch of making policies palatable. At age 76, he had lost some of his energy.

And so the Hungarians last weekend engineered a rare maneuver — a peaceful, smooth change of government. Karoly Grosz, whom Mr. Kadar last year named as prime minister, succeeded to the party leadership. Mr. Kadar was given the honorary title of party president.

While the Kadar-Grosz move had been expected for some weeks, there were also some surprising changes made at the party conference. Several Politburo members who had been close to Mr. Kadar did not get reappointed. It seems as though a major shift in leadership has been accomplished in one big swoop rather than in the gradual steps that Mikhail Gorbachev has had to take in the Soviet Union.

Not enough is known yet about Mr. Grosz for predictions about how he will run the country. For the sake of the Hungarian people, it would be nice if he could do it with a light hand, but not so light that Moscow once again feels obligated to run interference.

The Sun

Vancouver, B.C., May 25, 1988

A bloodless, quiet coup of the middle-aged has shaken the political structure of Hungary, ousting Communist party leader Janos Kadar who had been the nation s leader for 32 years.

Of communism's many repugnant features, one of the most stultifying is the lack of mechanism for revitalization of the Eastern bloc leadership. Politicians who were once idealistic and innovative grow hidebound and infirm in office, and stay there because only occasionally do men like Karoly Grosz work their way up and create the opportunity to change things.

Mr. Grosz, who became general secretary of Hungary's Communist party, thus unseating Mr. Kadar, is no young hothead. At 57 he is a contemporary of Mikhail Gorbachev, and he obviously shares many of the reformist ideas that have driven the architect of *glasnost* and *perestroika*.

Hungary is in great need of restructuring. Although it became, by Eastern bloc standards, a fairly open society in the early 1980s, the country's economy has stagnated badly. It has the Eastern bloc's highest per capita debt (about $22 billion is owed to Western banks), a high inflation rate, and a severe trade deficit. Last year Mr. Kadar gave Mr. Grosz the job of prime minister, and with it responsibility for economic turnaround and the potential for earning unpopularity that such overhaul can bring.

Mr. Grosz, who is most consistently described as pragmatic, managed to draw on the power the prime ministership gave him in order to orchestrate the unseating of the old guard.

That can't help but cause nervousness in other Eastern bloc nations. Mr. Kadar had been in office since 1956. Todor Zhivkov, 76, has led Bulgaria since 1954. East German leader Erich Honecker is 75.

Who was in power in the West in 1956? Well, Dwight Eisenhower was president of the United States, Louis St. Laurent was prime minister of Canada, Rene Coty was president of France, Anthony Eden was prime minister of Britain.

Those names are now the stuff of history, while the Communist leaders of that day have stayed on, and on.

Will reformers in neighboring countries emulate Mr. Grosz? Political and economic conditions in numerous nations appear ripe for overhaul, which will make watching Mr. Grosz, and his success at a Hungarian-style *perestroika*, fascinating both inside the Soviet orbit and beyond.

Czechoslovaks Mark '68 Invasion Anniversary

Thousands of anti-Soviet demonstrators in Prague Aug. 21, 1988 marked the 20th anniversary of the Soviet-led invasion of Czechoslovakia. Warsaw Pact troops entered Czechoslovakia Aug. 20-21, 1968 to overthrow the "Prague Spring" reformist regime of Communist Party leader Alexander Dubcek. Dubcek was formally removed from power in 1969. There was no official observance of the anniversary in Czechoslovakia. The authorities, expecting trouble, had reinforced police units in Prague and other cities. Some dissident leaders had been ordered to stay away from the capital during the anniversary or face imprisonment, according to sources in Prague cited by the Western press.

Early Aug. 21, some 200 demonstrators in Prague's Wenceslas Square were dispersed by police when their leaders attempted to lay flowers at the foot of St. Wenceslas, a 10th-century Bohemian monarch and religious hero. Several Czechoslovaks had been slain by Soviet troops in Wenceslas Square during the 1968 invasion.

The protest was led by Eva Kanturkova and Tomas Hradilek, activists in the Czechoslovak human-rights organization Charter 77. Another group of demonstrators was prevented from laying a wreath at the building that housed the national radio station, another site of Czechoslovak casualties during the Soviet intervention.

Later the same day, an estimated 10,000 people gathered in Wenceslas Square, signed petitions calling for democratic reforms, and then staged an impromptu march toward Hradcany Castle, the government's headquarters. The marchers shouted, "Russians go home!" and "Dubcek! Dubcek!" Security forces used tear gas and batons to break up the demonstration before it could reach the castle. There were at least five arrests. Dubcek, still in official disgrace, was a resident of the city of Bratislava, where he remained during the Prague protests.

The demonstrations were some of the largest in Czechoslovakia since 1969. However, observers noted that cities other than Prague were quiet, and that even in the capital the vast majority of citizens seemed to be apathetic.

THE ARIZONA REPUBLIC
Phoenix, AZ, August 23, 1988

THE young people marching in the streets of Prague could not possibly remember the Soviet tanks rumbling through those same stately avenues. Many were mere babes and others were not yet born 20 years ago when Leonid Brezhnev sent the Red Army into Czechoslovakia to put down ruthlessly the brief flowering of freedom there.

But even the brutish, cynical and kowtowing Czech Communist Party, Moscow's lap dog since the heady days of the "Prague Spring," has failed to quench the Czech people's longing to free themselves of oppression.

As thousands marched in Prague last weekend to mark the anniversary of those bittersweet days, the crowds taunted the government with Alexander Dubcek's old slogan from those few hopeful months in 1968 — "Socialism with a human face."

The taunt was particularly barbed. Although Mr. Dubcek, the Czech president who led the revolt against Moscow, was deposed and expelled in disgrace from the Communist Party, his rallying cry is now the favored slogan of none other than the successor to his persecutors, Mikhail Gorbachev — an irony not lost on the Czechs.

On this 20th anniversary of the Czechs' heroic uprising, restive stirrings are evident all over the Eastern bloc. In Poland tens of thousands of workers struck coal mines, steel mills and industrial plants. Workers seized the Lenin Shipyard in Gdansk demanding that the government recognize the outlawed Solidarity labor union, which Moscow's lackeys in Warsaw have tried unsuccessfully to exterminate.

And in Moscow itself, about 100 protesters gathered in the fashionable Arbat to mark the anniversary of Prague's quixotic rebellion. Socialism's human face notwithstanding, Soviet authorities graphically demonstrated the limits of glasnost when the state militia showed up to kick and punch out unresisting protesters.

In Prague, meanwhile, the police turned out in force to round up dozens of demonstrators, and in Poland, the government sent troops to break up industrial strikes by workers who, a government spokesman said, had raised the "specter of anarchy" in the country.

Following Moscow's merciless crushing of the uprisings in Hungary in 1956, Czechoslovakia in 1968 and Poland's Solidarity movement in 1980, Eastern Europe resigned itself to life under the heel of the Soviet jackboot. Moscow's satellites, however, watch closely and listen intently to what is going on behind the Kremlin's crenelated walls.

With Mr. Gorbachev now championing many of the same reforms his predecessors had previously smashed in Eastern Europe, captive populations from the Baltic to the Danube seem certain to push for greater independence.

The Register
Santa Ana, CA, August 23, 1988

In the West we often take our freedoms for granted. But actions the past few days by brave people behind the Iron Curtain show us that this most essential element of human life is worth everything else combined — worth even sacrificing one's life.

In recent days massive protests against Communist tyranny have taken place in Poland, Czechoslovakia, and Moscow. The protests — in which people risked jail and death — prove that the yearning for freedom cannot be stopped, even by the most powerful and repressive empire that has ever existed.

In Gdansk, Poland, workers have struck the Lenin Shipyard, scene of the famous 1980 walkout by Solidarity, the free trade union. Since 1980, Solidarity has been repressed and outlawed, but on Monday Solidarity leader Lech Walesa somehow slipped into the shipyard and led the strike. Strikes and work stoppages have also hit the Stalowa Wola steel mill south of Warsaw, a railway repair yard in Wroclaw, the Hipolit Cegielski engineering works in Poznan, and the docks and the public transportation system of Szczecin. The Poles have one major demand: legalization of Solidarity. "We will end [the strike] only after we get Solidarity, and then we will make real reforms in this of the Lenin shipyard strike committee, just before police cracked down again.

In Prague, Czechoslovakia, a spontaneous march of 10,000 people commemorated the 20th anniversary of the 1968 Soviet invasion of their country. They shouted "Freedom!" and "Russians go home!" while waving Czech flags. The major protest was held in Wenceslas Square (named after Good King Wenceslaus, a Czech national hero, and subject of the favorite song). Police goons moved in, beating protesters and carrying some away. But before the crowd was dispersed, hundreds of Czechs signed a petition calling for democracy, human rights, free speech, and the withdrawal of the Red Army occupation force.

In Moscow, the very heart of the Soviet empire, hundreds of demonstrators marched to mark the 20th anniversary of the Soviet regime's invasion of Czechoslovakia. "Prague, Prague, Prague," the demonstrators shouted, showing solidarity with their fellow Soviet slaves a few hundred miles to the west. When Soviet troops charged in, beating the protesters and hauling some away, the protesters shouted "Fascists!" at the troops. The protest was called by the Democratic Union, an illegal political party demanding freedom in the Soviet Union.

While these simultaneous protests were occurring, four people swam to freedom from East Berlin to West Berlin — across a polluted river, as if to symbolize the grime of oppression they had left behind. One of the defectors is Maigda Adryan, and she is three months pregnant. She broke her foot during the escape, all to ensure that her unborn baby will breathe his first air in a land of freedom.

Where will these protests and heroic acts lead? No one knows. The Kremlin still possesses tremendous repressive power and can be expected to thwart any threats to its power. But a slab of concrete must first crack before it crumbles.

The Boston Globe

Boston, MA, August 20, 1988

Twenty years have passed since Soviet tanks rumbled across the Czechoslovakian border and on to Prague, where, after a few days of doomed resistance, they crushed a tragically premature attempt to restructure a communist society.

The state of affairs in Czechoslovakia today forces the question of whether the "perestroika" – the restructuring – sought by Mikhail Gorbachev may be as premature as the "pestuba" sought by Alexander Dubcek.

The Soviet forces invaded Czechoslovakia to "save socialism." That slogan was implied when the Polish government imposed martial law rather than allow the restructuring sought by Solidarity; it also could be employed to justify Gorbachev's perestroika.

The question Gorbachev should be asking 20 years after a midsummer winter fell on "the Prague Spring," is whether socialism has proved to be worth saving.

It was indeed a Gorbachevian restructuring that Dubcek was proposing. He was no disaffected worker from outside the system like Lech Walesa, but a longtime party official in a nation that, unlike Poland, has traditionally had close ties to Russia. The Economist reports that Dubcek's program – openness, market-based economics, direct election of government officials – is seen by many Czechs as a blueprint for Gorbachev's proposals.

The message of the Soviet tanks was that those modest reforms were too much to ask for in 1968. Now, Czechoslovakia's socialist economy is as stagnant as those of the Soviet-bloc neighbors whose troops joined in Leonid Brezhnev's save-socialism invasion.

The same shoddy goods are being produced (the Czech government concedes there is $3.5 billion worth of unwanted goods piled up in warehouses) with the same Mickey Mouse price structures and the same heavy-handed bureaucracy.

Socially and culturally, Czechoslovakia is just beginning to awaken. But it is many years behind Poland, where the Solidarity movement, even driven underground, has inspired a cultural flowering. According to The Economist, the first "more or less independent art exhibition in 20 years" is opening this month in Prague – an event that would be considered routine in Warsaw and Krakow.

Radio Free Europe reports that a lecture at Prague University on perestroika was frequently interrupted by students' laughter: "Finally, one of the students rose to compare the idea of 'restructuring' in Czechoslovakia to opening a new whorehouse with old whores."

That does not suggest a high degree of optimism over the situation in Czechoslovakia or for the save-socialism solutions being attempted in the Soviet Union. It may be that 1968 was too early for restructuring to be accepted – and that 1988 is too late.

Winnipeg Free Press

Winnipeg, Man., August 23, 1988

More than 10,000 people marched through the streets of Prague on Sunday, shouting for freedom, demanding that the Russians go home and chanting the name of Alexander Dubcek, the unlikely hero who 20 years ago tried to put a human face on communism in Eastern Europe.

It was 20 years ago that the armies of the Warsaw Pact invaded Czechoslovakia, bringing to an end the Prague Spring, the brief but exhilarating period of reform initiated by the government led by Mr. Dubcek. This week's was the biggest demonstration since August of 1969, a year after the invasion, when 100,000 people protested their loss of liberty and the purge from the party of Mr. Dubcek. He was taken to Moscow and broken, his reforms dismantled and his country seized by an unrelenting repression that is only now beginning slightly to ease.

Since then, Czechoslovakia has been the greyest part of the Soviet Union's iron empire, a land it seems, where "it is always winter and never spring." Today, when the Czechs look east to Moscow, it is with a sense of bitter irony, for what is happening there under Mikhail Gorbachev has some strong similarities to what they attempted in 1968 with such cruel consequences. Even today, as the ripples of Mr. Gorbachev's glasnost and perestroika spread through Eastern Europe, they are felt most faintly in Czechoslovakia. Indeed, the situation there raises some doubts about how sincere the warm and reassuring smile the Soviet leader flashes at the world really is.

A better life in Czechoslovakia seems unlikely under the present leadership without a new, more subtle Soviet intervention. There was a brief burst of hope late last year when Gustav Husak, who had originally supported Mr. Dubcek but turned against him after the invasion and, with the zeal of the convert, presided over the return of his country to socialist normality, was replaced. His successor, however, is Milos Jakes, who encouraged the invasion and who is perhaps under-

standably reluctant now to denounce his own policies of the last two decades.

There have been small gestures in the direction of glasnost — an amnesty for some prisoners, a little more freedom for artists, writers and journalists — and a nod towards perestroika — some new economic plans for which the leadership seems to have no real enthusiasm — but Czechoslovakia, where these policies might be said to have been invented, remains one of the most repressive and centrally controlled of all the Eastern European satellites.

Mr. Gorbachev himself has been strangely silent about the situation there. He has urged the government and the people to economic reform, but has said nothing about the events of 1968, despite the fact that he has acknowledged and condemned several Soviet sins and errors of the past and encouraged others to go even further.

This silence has raised the question of whether glasnost is in fact intended for the satellites as well as the Soviet Union. Some of them — Hungary and Poland — enjoy more freedom that the Soviet Union has ever had, although not necessarily with the Soviets' unrestrained approval; others, such as Czechoslovakia, have far less than Moscow now allows its own people. If Mr. Gorabachev wants Eastern Europe to follow his lead, he must deal with the Czechoslovak problem. The memory of 1968 will loom large in the mind of any party contemplating dramatic reform; certainly, it must preoccupy Poland's Gen. Wojciech Jaruzelski as he debates how far he can go to reach a compromise with Solidarity.

If he does not, then the failure to repudiate the crushing of the Prague Spring serves a useful purpose. There may be more nods and gestures, paint and powder applied to the harsh face of the old regime, but unless Czechoslovakia is permitted, or encouraged, to deal with its past, it will be some time before spring comes again.

Buffalo Evening News

Buffalo, NY, August 24, 1988

SINCE SOVIET tanks rolled in and quelled the hopes for freedom in Czechoslovakia 20 years ago this week, the people there have lived sullenly amid an atmosphere of repression. But in observing the tragic anniversary, 10,000 people demonstrated in Prague, displaying a new activism that showed that the spirit of freedom is still alive.

The demonstrations, in the same Wenceslas Square where defiant youths braved Soviet tanks 20 years ago, were the largest since the Soviet occupation began. The gathering was apparently spontaneous and composed largely of young people who had never lived in freedom.

Scores of demonstrators were detained, but there was no concerted effort to prevent the gathering from taking place. This possibly reflected a slight easing of the communist government's repressive policy.

The world was shocked in 1968 when Alexander Dubcek, the Communist Party leader who had proposed broad reforms, was dragged off to Moscow to face Leonid Brezhnev's bullies. He returned to Czechoslovakia sadder and wiser, and after a brief time he was eased out of the leadership and the party. The "Prague spring," the rebirth of hope and freedom he inspired, became a vanished dream.

It is deeply ironic that the Soviet Union under Mikhail Gorbachev is now experimenting with some of the same reforms sought by Dubcek two decades ago. The people of Czechoslovakia can now see in the Soviet press and television that the Soviet people are freer than they are. Gorbachev recently described his reforms with the same phrase made famous by Dubcek: "socialism with a human face."

The reversed situation is embarrassing for Moscow, since it still officially maintains the position that Soviet troops intervened in Czechoslovakia to "save socialism." Dubcek's reforms did, indeed, seem likely to go beyond Gorbachev's "glasnost" and "perestroika," but Dubcek considered himself a loyal communist until the troops rolled in.

Some Soviet commentators are acknowledging that Dubcek's reforms had much in common with the changes introduced by Gorbachev, but Moscow is doing nothing to undercut the repressive Czechoslovakian government that was installed by Soviet tanks. That might prove too destabilizing in the Soviet empire, or perhaps Gorbachev feels he has his hands full with his own domestic changes.

Gorbachev's reforms remain in doubt, since he is seeking to introduce some elements of freedom in a basically repressive system. But at least the Soviet leader is introducing his changes without having to worry, like Dubcek, about a menacing, repressive superpower looking over his shoulder.

Chicago Tribune

Chicago, IL, August 30, 1988

Mikhail Gorbachev has peddled *glasnost* and *perestroika* up, down and across the Soviet Union with the evangelical, never-take-no-for-an-answer fervor of Madison Avenue. But as he has waged his impatient campaign to speed up the process in his country, he has carefully refrained, at least publicly, from pushing his counterparts in Eastern Europe to embrace his new gospel of openness and restructuring.

But freedom is a tough genie to keep in a bottle. And the unfamiliar ripples of *glasnost* and *perestroika* flowing from the Soviet Union these days must bear a hint of freedom to the long-repressed and eager watchers in Eastern Europe. Clear signs of contagion are appearing not only in the Soviet Baltic republics of Lithuania, Estonia and Latvia, but also in ideologically rigid Czechoslovakia, relatively prosperous Hungary and always simmering Poland.

In most of the Eastern-bloc states outside the Soviet Union, the entrenched Communist leadership has been hesitant to climb on the *glasnost* wagon. And absent a clear message from Moscow, it's been hard for the citizenry to know what's real and what's not. Without guidelines, as Gorbachev is learning at home, there's a tendency to test limits.

One of those risky efforts, born of curiosity and some youthful derring-do, came in Czechoslovakia at a protest marking the 20th anniversary of the Soviet-led invasion that ended the Prague spring reform of 1968.

Most prominent dissidents left Prague on the anniversary at the suggestion of security forces. But human rights activists and foreign diplomats said 10,000 young demonstrators joined in an unplanned march after a group called the Independent Peace Initiative spent hours without interference getting signatures on a 10-point petition demanding withdrawal of Soviet troops, free elections and an end to censorship.

Although 77 people were detained as police finally broke up the march, some older hands exuded wonder at the spontaneous involvement of youths with no activist history, and at the restrained response. "It is important for people to see," one said, "that they demonstrated and practically nothing happened. It will encourage them to repeat it."

But as Prague sampled what some felt was a real taste of freedom, in Moscow police and soldiers were roughly breaking up a demonstration by members of the Democratic Union, an outlawed party, who also were trying to mark the anniversary.

If those mixed signals didn't complicate matters enough for the confused East Europeans, tens of thousands of demonstrators, with official permission, marched through the Baltic capitals Tuesday denouncing the 1939 Soviet-Nazi pact that led to annexation. Some even demanded independence from Moscow.

In Poland, meanwhile, strikers at many sites, apparently emboldened by *glasnost*, have been demanding higher pay, better working conditions and that Solidarity be made legal again. And in Hungary, miners have struck against bonus cuts and a new income tax.

Well, Mikhail, we could have told you. A little freedom, like a little learning, can be a dangerous thing. You sow a bit of *glasnost* and *perestroika*, you can't keep the secret from a lot of folks out there—even in Czechoslovakia, Poland and Hungary. They may figure what they've been missing. Then, as your old pal Ronald Reagan would probably be happy to explain, it's Katy bar the door. So, you'd better mean it.

THE COMMERCIAL APPEAL

Memphis, TN, August 24, 1988

THE latest test of Mikhail Gorbachev's glasnost was the 20th anniversary of the Soviet invasion of Czechoslovakia. Unfortunately, glasnost flunked.

Official Soviet publications, which under Gorbachev have become refreshingly candid about many other misdeeds of past Soviet leaders, had almost nothing to say about the 1968 invasion. The few articles that did appear essentially repeated the pre-Gorbachev line: The invasion was necessary to combat a "threat to socialism."

Even more disturbing was the response to a demonstration in a Moscow park denouncing the invasion. Hundreds of policemen and soldiers converged to silence the protesters, arresting dozens.

The bravest heroes of glasnost are not Soviet leaders, but the citizens who constantly risk persecution by testing the limits of the new policies. Someday Moscow may pass their tests — but it still has a long way to go.

THE INDIANAPOLIS NEWS

Indianapolis, IN, August 25, 1988

Riot squads breaking up protests in Prague, Czechoslovakia.

Soviet police using clubs and bayonets against demonstrators in Moscow at several sites.

Milling workers in Poland yelling "strike — strike" as shipyards and steel mills close across the land.

Turmoil in Romania and Hungary, where the entrenched satellite governments are either unable or unwilling to adapt to Mikhail Gorbachev's perestroika.

The list is long: social and economic disturbances both inside the Soviet Union and among its European and Asian allies.

When Gorbachev announced his plan to open up a society that had been closed since the Russian revolution, he must have foreseen tense moments of inconsistency, even in his own intentions.

Does perestroika apply in Poland, for example?

Hardly. He is back-pedaling in this harried land, where he went out of his way in a July visit to tag the unpopular puppet dictator, Gen. Wajciech Jaruzelski, as his dear friend. He urged the Poles to appreciate and follow their great leader.

The Poles are not swallowing this line.

Neither did other East Europeans like his directive that they adopt foreign aid programs for Vietnam, Cuba and Mongolia. He also dropped the bad news that he could not continue to provide more oil and raw materials for export to Eastern Europe.

Perestroika? Yes, but "selective" perestroika as far as the satellite countries are concerned. He planted the notion earlier that the 65,000 Soviet troops in Hungary would be withdrawn, but it is now unclear when, if ever, those troops will go home.

Soviet military and economic aid to Nicaragua has also increased during the past three months. Gorbachev has not responded to the Arias peace plan in the slightest degree.

Inside the Soviet Union? Again, growing selectivity.

Although a few citizens are debating freely and reading books previously banned or unavailable, the dreaded KGB lurks in its usual places. It also stays in club-wielding practice by breaking up assemblies of which it does not approve.

Public libraries in some Soviet cities have been ordered to remove from their shelves all political and economic literature published before Gorbachev came to power.

So much for enlightened and uninhibited research and scholarship.

Even the mutual inspection of military equipment and sites is subject to suspicion. American teams have noted — and protested — what is a transparent intention by the Soviets to produce mostly offensive weaponry.

So much for Gorbachev's new doctrine of "defensive sufficiency."

It is encouraging to see a few cracks in the Soviet wall. And the Reagan administration rightly credits a combination of American power and internal Soviet failures for the loosening of the bonds. But this is not a time for euphoria — or the neglect of military defense.

Gorbachev's selective perestroika gives a little freedom at home and takes some away in Hungary or Nicaragua.

There is doubt among Soviet-watchers that the Russian people want the kind of freedom Americans have taken for granted for 200 years. There is even greater doubt that Gorbachev understands or believes in this kind of freedom or that he had it in mind when he announced perestroika.

Therefore, the watchword is caution.

"YOU SAID RESTRUCTURE!"

The Oregonian
Portland, OR, August 24, 1988

1988 is turning out to be a remarkable year. Not only has it brought peace or hopes of peace in wars from Afghanistan and the Persian Gulf to Angola, but it also has seen stirrings of demand throughout Eastern Europe for relief from the grip of the Soviet Union.

In Prague, 10,000 demonstrators marched Sunday to protest the day 20 years ago when Soviet tanks overthrew a Czechoslovakian government that was showing too much independence from the Soviet brand of communism. In Moscow itself police cracked down on sympathizers who put on their own demonstration Sunday, chanting "Prague, Prague, Prague."

Meanwhile, shipyard workers in Poland are striking for, among other things, recognition of Solidarity, the union that the Soviet-backed Polish government has suppressed.

Earlier and again Tuesday there were demonstrations for greater autonomy in the Baltic states — Latvia, Lithuania and Estonia — which the Soviet Union swallowed at the outset of World War II.

It is safe to say that a majority of today's protesters were not even born 40 years and more ago when the Soviet Union under Josef Stalin built its belt of puppet buffer states in Eastern Europe. Out of those grabs for political and economic domination came the Cold War and the huge buildup of armaments in both East and West that followed.

The status of Eastern Europe remains one of the great unsettled issues between the United States and the Soviet Union. As president, George Bush or Michael Dukakis will have to deal with it, and as candidates they are sure to be asked about it. It is of burning concern to many of the ethnic groups in the United States with ties to the old countries.

Experience has shown that the United States and its allies have little power to roll back the Soviet tide. Since World War II the West has watched helplessly as uprisings have flared and been suppressed at various times in East Berlin, Hungary and Poland. In 1968, the Czechs did not even have a chance to resist.

But the cautious restructuring inside the Soviet Union itself under Mikhail Gorbachev is producing echoes throughout Eastern Europe. The Western democracies may sympathize, but the changes will have to come from the Eastern Europeans themselves. 1988 has seen numerous signs that the spirit of freedom there is rising.

The Morning News
Wilmington, DE, August 24, 1988

A REPRESSIVE government is a repressive government. That truism has been amply brought home in the last couple of days by events in Czechoslovakia, the Soviet Union and Poland.

In Prague last weekend, 10,000 demonstrators marched in a 20th anniversary commemoration of the Prague Spring — the brief period in 1968 when freedom was making a comeback in Czechoslovakia. An invasion by Soviet and East German troops put a brutal end to the Prague spring on Aug. 20, 1968.

This summer, Czech authorities at first permitted the demonstration to proceed, then stopped it from going near the university, and ended up detaining some of the most persistent demonstrators.

In Moscow, on the same day, there was a sympathy demonstration for the lost Prague Spring. Here too the police intervened, beating and kicking many and arresting about a hundred protesters.

In Poland, the Solidarity labor union movement is trying to rise again, and the Warsaw government is doing its best to contain this revival. Strikes have popped up all over the country, including at the famous Gdansk Shipyards, where Lech Walesa gained fame.

In response, the Warsaw government has imposed curfews, forcefully ousted strikers from their work places and arrested some strikers.

These governmental actions are hardly in the spirit of glasnost that Soviet leader Mikhail Gorbachev has proclaimed. Regimes based on repression find it hard to loosen control gradually and gracefully. Sadly, we are still a long way from seeing liberty shine in the Soviet bloc.

Poland Beset by Labor Protests; Worst Unrest Since '81-82

Paramilitary police May 5, 1988 staged a predawn raid on Poland's Lenin Steel Mill, forcing an end to a nine-day strike at the plant. The mill, located in Nowa Huta, near Krakow, was Poland's largest and most modern industrial facility. At least 15,000 of the plant's 32,000 workers participated in the strike. The assault by the police signaled a new, hard-line approach by the government to widespread labor protests that had begun in late-April. The unrest was the worst since the 1981-82 period, prior to and during the imposition of martial law.

The police set off stun (percussion) grenades as they stormed into the Lenin Steel Mill and confronted the workers who had been staging a sit-in there since the start of the strike. Thirty-eight strikers were arrested, including most of the ad hoc committee that had led the job action. According to unconfirmed reports that reached the West, about 40 steelworkers were injured in the raid. The U.S. government May 5 criticized the use of force to end the strike. Later on May 5, riot police sealed off the Lenin Shipyard, the site of another strike, in the Baltic port city of Gdansk. About 2,500 strikers were in the shipyard, among them Lech Walesa, the founder of the outlawed Solidarity union movement.

The labor protests were mainly directed against government's price increases. In increases implemented April 1, the cost of gas and electricity doubled and the cost of coal quadrupled. The first stoppage began April 25 in Bydgoszcz, an industrial city with a population of 370,000 people northwest of Warsaw. Hundreds of transportation workers walked off their jobs, demanding higher pay to offset the price hikes. The government gave the Bydgoszcz strikers a 63% pay increase less than 24 hours after the strike began.

Tens of thousands of Polish workers stayed off their jobs Aug. 15-26 in a renewal of the labor unrest that had paralyzed the nation in April and May. The government used force to break some of the strikes and was also relying on mediation by the Roman Catholic Church to restore a semblance of peace. Amid the turmoil, there were indications that the government might be prepared to talk directly with the opposition, including the banned Solidarity union. Gen. Czeslaw Kiszczak, Poland's interior minister, Aug. 26 publicly stated that he wanted Solidarity included in any such talks, a major reversal of government policy.

The unrest had been preceded by a clash between police and pro-Solidarity demonstrators in Gdansk Aug. 14. The demonstrators were marking the eighth anniversary of the protests that had led to the creation of Solidarity. About 300 workers at the Manifest Lipcowy (July Manifesto) coal mine, near Jastrzebie in the southwestern Silesia region, refused to report for work Aug. 15.

The job-action escalated Aug. 16 into a full-scale strike involving 3,000-4,000 miners. The miners demanded higher pay, better working conditions and legalization of Solidarity. Four other Silesian coal mines were struck Aug. 17-18, raising to about 9,000 the number of coal miners on strike. In nearly all the strikes, a principal demand was the legalization of Solidarity. The government flatly rejected the demand Aug. 19.

Lech Walesa Aug. 19 warned that workers at the Lenin Shipyard in Gdansk, where he was employed, would join the strikes unless the government granted legal status to the union.

The central committee Aug. 22 issued emergency regulations empowering local authorities to impose curfews in three regions beset by strikes. The regulations were the strongest steps taken to restore public order since the imposition of martial law in 1981. Riot police clashed with striking transport workers in Szczecin Aug. 22 and sealed off the striking Silesian coal mines and the Lenin Shipyard the same day. Momentum appeared to shift to the government Aug. 23, when the strikes began to wane.

The Miami Herald

Miami, FL, May 9, 1988

AT FIRST glance, the current labor unrest in Poland seems to be a rerun of the 1980 disturbances that gave birth to the independent Solidarity union. Indeed, judging from the Polish government's crackdown, there is a similarity. Yet important developments have taken place in the last few years that alter Poland's political scenario significantly.

First, there are strong signals of *glasnost* and *perestroika* coming from Moscow. These signals spell reform, not only inside the Soviet Union but spreading to its satellite neighbors as well. And reform is what the whole Polish situation is about.

Polish workers and Solidarity leaders support Mr. Gorbachev's new ways. Theoretically, the government of Gen. Wojciech Jaruzelski also supports the Soviet leader's reform programs. And yet the clash continues, and street action resembles the early 1980s, with crushing raids against workers and labor leaders.

The government conducted its raid with percussion grenades at the Nowa Huta plant shortly before labor-management talks were to begin at 8 a.m. It came one day after the powerful Roman Catholic Church in Poland was named mediator to defuse the labor crisis. Reportedly, the strikers were beaten to the point of requiring medical treatment. Such an action from the Polish government is surprising only because of the new openness permeating the political climate in Eastern Europe.

The Reagan Administration commendably has urged the Polish government to "begin a productive dialogue with all segments of Polish society, including Solidarity." The United States applied economic sanctions against Poland when the regime imposed martial law in 1981 in the aftermath of the Solidarity turmoil. In 1986, President Reagan properly lifted those sanctions in response to improvements in the Polish situation.

Rather than avoid the Poland issue for fear of jeopardizing the U.S.-Soviet summit scheduled for later this month, President Reagan should add it to the agenda. Considering that the Brezhnev Era is over, the new man in the Kremlin should be asked to review the matter from his more-positive perspective.

The Philadelphia Inquirer

Philadelphia, PA, May 6, 1988

The strikes by Polish workers must be giving Soviet leader Mikhail Gorbachev nightmares. They are a worst-case scenario of how attempts at economic reforms in a communist country can tear it apart if the government does not command the trust and loyalty of its population.

It's ironic that Poland's workers have returned to the barricades just when their government is imitating the Gorbachev regime in trying to shake up a failing, state-run economy by letting the market play a role. But, as Mr. Gorbachev knows well, such reforms cause pain before gain. Prices rise and inefficient state factories face closure, a shock in communist countries. And so far consumers — whether in Warsaw or Moscow — have yet to see the benefits.

There is little question that such reforms are needed. Neither Poland nor the Soviet Union can afford to continue paying workers for producing shoddy, subsidized goods that no one wants. But the last couple of years have shown that communist leaders can't get support for such reforms from their skeptical citizenry unless they provide more than promises of a rosy future. In Moscow the carrot has been a relaxation of restrictions on press and culture, in hopes that happy journalists and intellectuals will convince the public to join the reform team. But in volatile, alienated Poland, the price of worker consent comes higher.

Lech Walesa, standing among striking workers in the Gdansk shipyards where the banned Solidarity trade union was born, demanded Wednesday that the government again make the union legal. He appealed directly to Mr. Gorbachev, hinting that had this Soviet leader been around in 1980 Solidarity would never have been crushed. The Polish authorities, while talking of "reform and reconciliation," have so far responded only with strike-breaking riot police, who yesterday smashed the strike at the giant Lenin steel mill near Krakow and were threatening to do the same in Gdansk.

That Polish hunger for political reform — for a workers' voice independent of the authorities — is a direct challenge to Mr. Gorbachev. He, too, foresees greater political freedom as part of his larger plan for economic restructuring, but the Communist Party would retain its dominant role. In Poland, where the average worker is *anti*-communist, that kind of arrangement would never fly.

Whether or not the strikers win this round, they are sending Mr. Gorbachev an important message: Once the winds of change begin to blow, their direction can't be so neatly controlled. That message will provide Moscow conservatives with ammunition with which to press Mr. Gorbachev to slow Soviet reforms and to tighten his loose reins on the Eastern bloc. It might also force the Soviet leader to reconsider the necessary link between economic and political change.

ST. LOUIS POST-DISPATCH

St. Louis, MO, May 12, 1988

The communist government of Gen. Wojciech Jaruzelski should be under no illusions that the end to the nine-day strike at the Gdansk shipyard is a crushing blow to the Solidarity free trade union. Polish strikers vowed that their leaving the yard was only a "truce, not a defeat."

Within hours of the strike's end, the government placed before the parliament a new, draconian economic "reform" bill that includes authority for mass firings of workers and managers, a freeze in wages and prices, the forced merger or bankruptcy of state firms and a new tax law. However, the government did drop provisions banning all strikes and other kinds of work stoppages after the regime's official unions protested the ban.

That concession is not likely to bring labor peace, however, because the Polish economy is on the verge of collapsing. Real per capita income has dropped by more than 20 percent in the last 10 years. Nearly a third of the population lives in poverty, and more than 60 percent of Polish families have no savings to fall back on. Meanwhile, the government — facing huge international debts and dwindling reserves — raised prices on most Polish consumer goods and food between 40 and 200 percent earlier this year.

At best, Warsaw's new economic policies are a desperate attempt to buy time. Few think that these measures will work. Even the government's own labor union federation is cool to the economic reform package.

The best hope for Poland is the establishment of a new social contract among the communist government and the Catholic Church and Solidarity that would allow for a larger and freer mixed economy. The party may have the gun, but only the church and Solidarity have moral and political legitimacy in the eyes of the Polish people. Without the clear support of these two institutions, the government's efforts are are almost certainly doomed.

But there is a fourth party in this power equation — the Soviet Union. In the past, the Kremlin has been brutally swift to crush any threats to the Warsaw regime, and that danger remains.

Ironically, though, the Soviet Union could also provide the chance for reforms in Poland. Early in the strike, the founder of Solidarity, Lech Walesa, was careful to frame his call for major reforms in Poland in terms of Soviet leader Mikhail Gorbachev's plans for *perestroika* (economic restructuring).

For Mr. Gorbachev, a failure in Polish economic reforms would reflect badly on his own reform efforts, and that would help his Kremlin opponents. For these reasons Mr. Gorbachev might be willing to tolerate greater political roles for the Catholic Church and Solidarity.

Chicago Tribune

Chicago, IL, May 3, 1988

On May Day, which the Soviet bloc has designated as a time for celebrating Communism and the rise of the working class, the people of Poland made it resoundingly clear they felt no reason to do so. On the contrary, and in spades.

Antigovernment protests broke out in a dozen cities and were quickly broken up by truncheon-wielding police officers and plainclothes goons. That set the stage for a strike at the giant Lenin Shipyard in the northern port of Gdansk, where Solidarity was born. The echoes of history are unmistakable.

Lech Walesa, once thought to be a fading figure, is back. His followers responded when the Nobel Peace Prize-winning electrician cried: "Show me tomorrow what you can do. If you have an army, Gen. Lech Walesa is at your disposal."

What is the government going to do, deport him? That would ruin any chance it has of obtaining the infusion of Western economic aid it desperately needs.

Gen. Wojciech Jaruzelski's government may yet weather the storm of protest, but its carefully drawn plans for smooth economic reform have gone awry. Its best hope can be for only a Pyrrhic victory: damned if you do and damned if you don't.

Furious over higher prices despite government warnings for months that they were coming, thousands of workers went on strike last week in Nowa Huta, Bydgoszcz and Stalowa Wola. These are unfamiliar places, but the significance of their unrest reverberates all the way up to Mikhail Gorbachev's Kremlin office.

Poland has been an economic disaster for years, its natural capitalistic instincts drained by centralized Communist mismanagement. Worker anger produced government shakeups in 1956, 1976 and 1980. No one in Poland has forgotten that, not the workers and certainly not Gen. Jaruzelski, who has been casting about for years to develop an economic reform plan that would get the country back on its feet without a replay of the Solidarity turbulence of the early 1980s.

It's not working. Recent consumer price hikes of 42 percent (shoppers at the markets say they're higher) were accompanied by some selective pay increases, but that wasn't enough. Instead of striding forward under Communism's banner, Poles are walking away from the workplace.

Until now, protest has been directed at bread-and-butter issues. The crucial question is whether the current volatile mood will transform into another, wider call for political reform. That would give unreconstructed hardliners in the government the excuse they want to crack down hard.

It's not clear yet whether the Jaruzelski government can jawbone the workforce or at least provide the financial incentives to keep it on the job. By doling out new pay increases to some of the strikers, the government is playing a dangerous inflationary game. It was rampaging inflation that toppled a regime and created the conditions for Solidarity's emergence at the beginning of this decade.

With a crushing external debt approaching $40 billion and industrial technology a decade or more behind the West, Poland's leaders don't have a lot of room to operate. No matter how they try to wiggle out of it—a pay raise here, lowered prices there—they're stuck in a crack of their own devising.

None of this will be lost on Mikhail Gorbachev, who has praised Gen. Jaruzelski's problem-solving ability (you know, like imposing martial law to wreck the Solidarity movement). Poland's experiments with reform reflect the Soviet leader's own *perestroika* program of economic restructuring. If one doesn't work, why should the other? After all, it's the same system.

San Francisco Chronicle

San Francisco, CA, May 13, 1988

SOLIDARITY'S STRIKE at the Lenin shipyard lasted only nine days, and by the end only about 400 of the plant's labor force of 10,000 were on hand to protest the Polish government's economic policies. The authorities offered some concessions, but the strikers chose instead to walk out the gates with "our heads held high," proud that they would sign no agreement short of their full demands.

The strikers found themselves isolated. The reasons fellow shipyard workers at Gdansk gave for not joining the sit-in included complaints that the effort was too political in nature, too hastily planned and far too likely to end in violence and joblessness.

As it turned out, the strikers' heads were not bloodied because Polish officials chose a softer and more sensible course. Though police moved quickly to break up a strike at the Lenin Steelworks in Nowa Huta in southern Poland, protests elsewhere ended when the government retreated from its policy of economic austerity by raising wages instead.

AFTER WALESA LED the strikers out of the shipyard, he emphasized his commitment to continue his long campaign against oppression by telling an interviewer, "There is no freedom without Solidarity." At that point, Walesa's wife, Danuta, broke in with the bitter comment, "There is no Solidarity."

The failed effort at the shipyard in Gdansk is a sad episode in a long line of gallant but unsuccessful protests that have marked so much of Poland's history. What is not clear is how permanent the defeat will be.

ALBUQUERQUE JOURNAL

Albuquerque, NM, May 10, 1988

Soviet leader Mikhail Gorbachev speaks from the top of restructuring communist society to give a greater voice and a greater motivation to the common people. In Poland, the common people are demanding the same thing from the bottom.

Both events attest to the stagnation and atrophy of world communism as a force for the betterment of the workers of the world.

The Polish experience demonstrates again that freedom begets the demand for more freedom. Poland is already the Soviet bloc trend-setter on individual liberty. The Catholic Church is strong and respected.

Economic conditions are bad, but have been improving since the unrest of 1981. The price increases that triggered the labor unrest are a bitter but probably necessary pill if Polish leader Gen. Wojciech Jaruzelski's economic reforms are ever to succeed. And that is the crux of the problem: If the government gives in and raises wages, the economic reform is diluted; if it resists, further political unrest and economic instability is likely.

Strikers in the Lenin Shipyard in Gdansk have dwindled in number from as many as 5,000 to about 500. The hoped-for national outburst of support didn't come to pass.

The striking workers rejected a compromise offered by the government to end the stand-off. Ultimatum deadlines have come and gone. The shadow of the police solution already inflicted on steel mill strikers looms long over the shipyard.

Poland, whose labor union Solidarity is banned but clearly still influential, is putting to the test Gorbachev's policy of loosening the reins of authority. Strike leaders — and the Jaruzelski government — will need to tread lightly to avoid making the Polish unrest a victory for the reactionary hardliners.

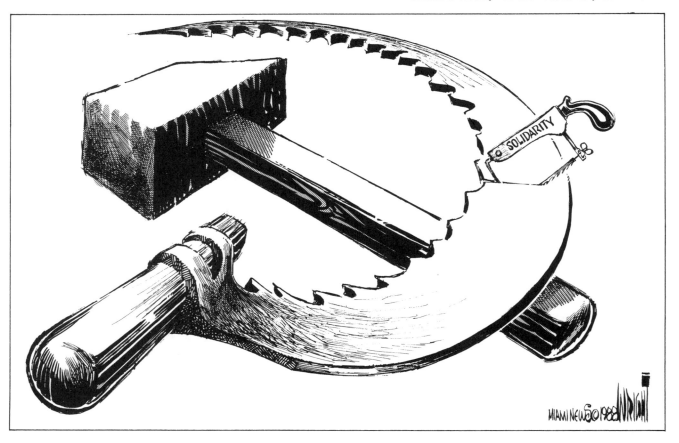

The TENNESSEAN
Nashville, TN, August 23, 1988

THE Communist government of Gen. Wojciech Jaruzelski in Poland is in crisis as a result of mounting labor unrest and worsening economic conditions.

Mr. Lech Walesa, head of the outlawed Solidarity trade union, has called his followers out on strike until the government enters into "serious" discussion of grievances.

But the government has not agreed to talks. It ordered troops to secure major industrial plants and ordered curfews in several provinces. Despite the military action, the government seems to be basing much of its response to the strike on an appeal to the public to recognize the seriousness of Poland's economic plight. It claims the strike is seriously damaging the country's chances of coming out of its economic crisis.

The government also says that losses of hard currency earnings needed to repay Poland's $37 billion foreign debt are totaling $222,000 a day, and that the strikes can only exacerbate this condition.

The government has even resorted to the highly unusual strategy of sending state-run television to interview workers who oppose the strike and claim it is bad for the economy. The television also reported on the refusal of striking workers to allow teams into the mines to prevent damage.

Government-endorsed labor unions had already denounced the strikes but were critical of the government for failing to revive the economy. With wages lagging far behind the 60% inflation rate, all Polish workers are in a pinch.

Mr. Walesa says a settlement must encompass economic, political and social factors and that he is ready to call off the strike when the government agrees to talks.

With world attention centered on political and economic changes taking place in the Soviet Union, there is intense interest in how the Polish government will handle its crisis.

There have been some reported cases of violence by the police in arresting or evicting workers. Also the government has begun to induct draft-age striking miners who chose to work in the mines in lieu of military service. But so far it seems to be trying to avoid the imposition of martial law which touched off major riots six or seven years ago.

It remains to be seen if Mr. Walesa will be able to extract major concessions from Mr. Jaruzelski. The Solidarity leader has had virtually unanimous support from workers in the past.

If the government will avoid the rough stuff and stick to the theme that the strikers are harming the economy and themselves, the enthusiasm for striking could begin to wane. But resort to military suppression could plunge the nation into deeper conflict. Either way, the struggle for political and economic justice in Poland seems certain to continue. ■

The Washington Post
Washington, DC, August 26, 1988

AGAIN POLAND seethes with a condition that is becoming increasingly common in the age of glasnost. The condition is nationalism, an expression both of national longing and of individual dignity. It is touching not just Poland and other parts of the Soviet Union's East European empire, but also the small subject nationality groups in the trans-Caucasus and the Baltic region, which earlier were absorbed into the Soviet Union itself. Glasnost is presented by Mikhail Gorbachev as essential to unlocking the initiative and energy needed for vital economic reform. But glasnost is also broadening the political space in which East Europeans and the subject nationalities voice demands that the authorities can neither satisfy nor suppress.

Poland is the pace setter. The Red Army liberated it from the Nazis in World War II but also imposed communism and Soviet control. Solidarity represents popular opposition to both of the latter. Actually, Solidarity is a responsible mass organization whose leaders have a realistic understanding of the constraints on the workers' and on Poland's freedom of action. The Polish regime, however, remains unwilling to take Solidarity as the patriotic and efficient partner it is prepared to be. Instead it uses its superior forces of compulsion to deny Solidarity its deserved role as spokesman for most of the Polish people. Given the chance, the Poles would probably choose, at this constrained moment in their history, a policy that was respectful enough of Soviet security interests not to risk reprisal and yet expressive of their own native political desires. This is the policy that would serve stability.

The agitation in the Baltics is different and perhaps harder to deal with, since, theoretically anyway, the satisfaction of local desires could lead to the territorial fragmentation of the Soviet Union. Recently the Soviet Baltic republics have been learning, from their own press no less, of the Nazi-Soviet Pact of 1939, which resulted in the Kremlin's swallowing of the then-independent nations of Estonia, Latvia and Lithuania. No country willingly participates in its own dismemberment. At the least, however, the Soviet Union is going to have to explore new forms of association with the parts of its country—as with the parts of its empire—that were involuntarily attached to it. Self-determination is a powerful political current, and no ruler can forever ignore it.

The Soviet Union needs a generation or more to come to terms with the consequences of its multiple past aggressions. Whether Mikhail Gorbachev can do it, and survive it, is a real question. Some well-meaning Americans would look for ways to ease his burden, or at least not to make it heavier. But the right American attitude is to be on the side of freedom. That does not mean egging others on: they need no egging anyway. It means being faithful and sympathetic to the victims in a responsible way. That is the work of a generation too.

AKRON BEACON JOURNAL
Akron, OH, August 24, 1988

LABOR UNREST has returned to Poland. In a week's time, strikes have spread to coal mines, factories, ports and transportation depots in several regions of the country.

The crackdown has begun as well. Riot police stormed a streetcar facility in Szczecin. Local authorities have been given the power to impose curfews in Szczecin, Katowice, Jastrzebie and Gdansk. Gen. Czeslaw Kiszczak, the interior minister, warned that, without strong measures, Poland would degenerate into "a land of lawlessness and anarchy."

This most recent unrest comes just four months after Poland was shaken by 15 days of labor turmoil. Then workers focused their demands on economic issues. Now the focus is political. Strikers are calling for the return of Solidarity, the independent labor union outlawed in 1981, which remains the most popular political movement in Poland today.

The Polish economy is ailing severely, burdened by a large foreign debt and a rigid bureaucracy. Standards of living have declined significantly. Poland's largest economic problem, however, is its lack of spirit and cooperation. Government officials can vow incessantly that there will be "no return to August 1980," when Solidarity was born; they can even crush the unrest with their overwhelming strength. But until the authorities agree to compromise with Solidarity, the economy has little chance for revival.

Solidarity's leaders understand the stakes. Their demands are fair, even in the context of Poland's one-party state. They are far more credible than Gen. Kiszczak's words to the nation this week. "To continue the dialogue," he told a national television audience, "we must put an end to illegal excesses, and in particular to illegal strikes, because an element of force and pressure has been introduced into our political and social life." Of course, there is no dialogue; and the destructive "element of force" is the brutality of the state.

The government has announced a special Aug. 31 session of parliament to review its economic policies. Still, no matter how promising a series of reforms may be, the setting is most important. Poland could use a substantial dose of *glasnost* and *perestroika*, openness and restructuring. Without a viable Solidarity, it faces a bleak future of continued stagnation and labor unrest.

Polish Regime, Opposition Reach Concilliation

The "round-table" talks in Poland between the regime and opposition concluded April 5, 1989 with accords on broad political and economic reform. The talks had lasted for two months. The political changes outlined in the accords placed Poland, along with Hungary, in the forefront of democratic reform in Eastern Europe. (See pp. 154-157.) The agreements were singed in a nationally televised ceremony at the government palace in Warsaw. Gen. Czeslaw Kiszczak, the interior minister, represented the regime. Lech Walesa, founder of the outlawed Solidarity trade union, represented the opposition. Walesa called the accords "the beginning of the road for democracy and a free Poland."

Popular reaction to the accords was reported to be muted. Caution was said to result in part because of the serious economic problems faced by the nation and also from a fear of investing too much hope in the new system.

The ceremony was delayed for three hours because of a walkout by Alfred Miodowicz, the party official in charge of labor relations. The dispute centered on a compromise provision in the accords calling for worker wages to be indexed to 80% of any rise in the cost of living. Miodowicz, backed by OPZZ – the federation of government-supervised unions – wanted wages indexed to 100% of inflation. Miodowicz returned for the ceremony, but vowed to continuing the fight for full indexing.

In other major provisions:

■ *Senate and Free Elections* – The signatories agreed to a restructuring of the current unicameral national legislature into a bicameral body. The existing Sejm (parliament) would be the lower house and have 460 seats. A new Senate would be the upper house and have 100 seats.

Senators would be chosen through free elections, set for June. The Senate would have the power to veto key legislation, thus having a check on the Sejm. The ruling United Workers (Communist) Party and its allies, the Democratic and Peasant parties, were guaranteed 65% representation in the Sejm. The remaining 35% of the seats would be filled by opposition figures and independents through free elections. The Communists and their allies, therefore, would not be guaranteed the two-thirds majority in the Sejm needed to override legislative vetoes.

■ *Strong President* – The head of state, currently a largely symbolic post, was to be elected by a joint session of the legislature for a six-year term and would have strong executive powers. He or she would have the authority to veto legislation, dissolve parliament and supervise foreign policy. Current Communist President Gen. Wojceich Jaruzelski was widely expected to be named the first president under the new system.

■ *Solidarity Legalization* – Solidarity, formally banned since 1982, was to be returned to legal status, perhaps by the end of April 1989. Two other outlawed organizations – the farmers' union Rural Solidarity and the Independent Students Association (NZS) – were also to be legalized. Mechanisms were established for the official recognition of other opposition groups.

■ *Opposition Media* – The pact provided for the creation of official opposition media outlets, including newspapers and broadcasting stations.

Poland April 5 announced agreement on a draft law that for the first time in the Soviet bloc would grant official recognition to the Roman Catholic Church. Recognition would be a step toward possible diplomatic relations between Warsaw and the Vatican. Polish church represenatives had participated in the round table talks, but the agreement was the product of separate negotiations with the regime.

The Courier-Journal & Times

Louisville, KY, April 17, 1989

WHEN the Solidarity movement came to Western attention nine years ago, it was seen as a gallant, quixotic — and characteristically Polish — challenge to overpowering opposition. The question was whether the Soviets would crush the upstarts sooner or later.

But unlike the Polish cavalrymen who charged Nazi tanks, the labor union survived and, to a degree, triumphed. Irony of ironies, Poland's Communist overlords finally conceded that sharing power with Solidarity is their best hope for reversing Poland's economic, political and social decline.

Thus, after months of rocky talks, government representatives joined Lech Walesa in agreeing to make Solidarity legal again and Poland the second East bloc nation to experiment with free elections.

Communists. retain control, but a third of parliament's lower house will be reserved for the opposition. A new upper house will be chosen in open elections. Other astounding reforms permit opposition news media and independent courts. The Soviets, far from objecting, seem willing to tolerate deviations from Marxist orthodoxy in Eastern Europe if the result is economic revival and political stability.

While America should take delight in encouraging these developments, euphoria is premature. Even a more representative government will not hold a magical solution to Poland's devastating problems, which include crippling foreign debt, insufficient food and Europe's worst pollution. Communist hardliners are ready to pounce if the new system falters. Solidarity's early idealism has given way to cynicism and division — hardly a good omen. And all bets are off if Mikhail Gorbachev, father of *perestroika*, falls by the wayside.

But momentum. is on the side of change. Polish visionaries may actually succeed, for once, in pointing the way to a new order.

DESERET NEWS
Salt Lake City, UT, April 5/6, 1989

Taking its cue from reforms in the Soviet Union, the Communist Party leaders in Poland have approved sweeping changes in the political system. Those changes allow for political diversity and an end to the communist monopoly in government.

This is most encouraging and is another example of the world tide that seems to be running strongly toward greater freedom, more democracy and even free market economics in nations formerly locked into Marxism.

The announcements in Poland this past week included only the political changes. Other socioeconomic reforms are promised for the Communist Party conference May 4-5.

Just how profound are the political changes in Poland? Consider:

• Laws allowing opposition parties in the lower house of parliament will be liberalized and a democratically elected senate will be created. The two will join to elect the nation's president.

• The Communist Party will lose its majority in parliament for the first time since Stalin installed communists in power in 1944.

• For the first time in postwar Poland, Communist Party candidates will face direct electoral competition from opposition candidates.

• Inner workings of the Communist Party will be opened and covered by the media. Closed party administrative departments will be replaced by commissions in which non-party members may participate as consultants.

• Solidarity and other unions and student associations, banned since martial law was imposed in 1981, will be legalized.

• Opposition parties will be guaranteed access to the mass media, including a daily newspaper, two weeklies, and at least one program on national television.

Of course, all of this does not mean that Poland will suddenly become a democracy. The lower house in parliament will be weighted so that the Communist Party holds about 65 percent of the 460 seats. But that will leave a sizeable opposition and the senate is expected to be controlled by opposition parties.

For years, Poland has been gripped by one economic or political crisis after another. Communist leaders have agreed that the only solution is more democracy and a freer economy. It's a lesson that more and more of the world seems to be learning.

FORT WORTH STAR-TELEGRAM
Fort Worth, TX, April 7, 1989

Today, the Polish parliament, the Sejm, is to turn into law the far-reaching political and economic agreements forged this week between the communist government and the Solidarity union.

As it has since 1946, the communist-dominated Sejm has been told what to do, and will do it. But what it does today is effectively to rewrite Poland's constitution and swerve radically away from the last 43 years of Polish history.

Poland, the first link in the chain of subservient communist-ruled Eastern European nations that were molded into a Soviet "outer empire" after World War II, becomes the first Soviet satellite state to weaken the communist grip on its political life.

Poland will have two houses in its next parliament. In the lower house, the communist party will be guaranteed 38 percent of the seats. Solidarity and its allies in opposition to the government will have 35 percent — a formidable opposition bloc. A new upper house, with veto power over lower house decisions, will be chosen in June in free and open elections.

No more rubber-stamp. No more strict party control over Polish government and Polish life without the voice of opposition being heard.

It is a history-making moment for Poland, for Eastern Europe (can other Soviet client states. Czechoslovakia for instance, be far behind? They have yearnings, too) and for the world.

The grumbling of decades led in 1980 to the challenge of communist rule in Poland by working people, illegally organized to protest economic conditions. After almost 10 years of arrests and broken promises, Solidarity has won. The Polish people have won, if not complete freedom and true independence, then at least a major victory.

The Soviet Union contributed to the change, setting a recent example of free expression and relatively democratic elections. In Poland, as in the Soviet Union, the driving force behind political change has been economic malaise. Poland is broke, its people saddled with rising inflation and its government badly in debt and needing help from the West.

But the Polish about-face is also further evidence that the world, as its approaches the last decade of the 20th century, is in a period of the most rapid change it has seen since the aftermath of World War II. Traditional 19th century colonialism came to an end, sometimes painfully, in the 1940s, 1950s and 1960s. Now the new Soviet colonialism, born of Stalinist xenophobia and cold war tensions, is under severe strain and itself may be coming apart at the seams.

It is an exciting era, one full of challenges for policymakers on both sides of the crumbling Iron Curtain. But nowhere on earth should it be more exciting, on this day, than in beleaguered Poland.

Chicago Tribune
Chicago, IL, April 7, 1989

Lech Walesa sounded an understandable note of caution as he signed accords with the Communist government providing for the restoration of Solidarity's legal status after seven years as an outlaw and for the first free elections in Poland since World War II. Accepting that, the wonder of the moment was that he was there to speak at all.

"Either we'll be able to build Poland as a nation in a peaceful way, independent, sovereign and safe, with equal alliances, or we'll sink in the chaos of demagogy, which could result in civil war, in which there will be no victors," warned the 45-year-old shipyard electrician who founded the union in 1980 and won a Nobel Peace Prize for his struggle on its behalf.

Think about it, coming from the difficult man from Gdansk, arrested, detained, shunned after Solidarity was banned in 1981, but never successfully silenced by the regime that's finally conceded it needs him.

"Independent, sovereign and safe, with equal alliances." And nobody shut him up, or even corrected him. "There's only one victor, the nation, our fatherland," said Gen. Czeslaw Kiszczak, the interior minister, who with Gen. Wojciech Jaruzelski, the nation's leader, imposed martial law in 1981 and ordered the arrest of Walesa and most of the union's other leaders.

Now, under the agreement expected to be approved by the parliament Friday, Solidarity and other independent unions and associations will be legal again. And in June, elections will be held for a new two-house parliament with 35 percent of the seats in the lower house allocated to the Solidarity-based opposition to the communists. An upper house also will be restored. It will be chosen in open elections with no guarantee of seats for the communists and it will have veto power over legislation passed in the lower house.

If this comes off as planned, the voting for the upper house will be the first democratic election in Eastern Europe since it fell under the sway of the Soviet Union more than 40 years ago. The two houses will choose a president of the republic.

In spite of Walesa's brave words—independent, sovereign and safe, with equal alliances—a slight shadow was cast by the first reaction from the ally he obviously had most in mind. The official Soviet news agency Tass reported only that the talks had ended and that Walesa had participated. Even Radio Moscow's English-language service, while noting the legalization of trade unions and establishment of the two-house parliament, didn't mention free elections.

Mikhail Gorbachev's *glasnost* and *perestroika* notwithstanding, someone appears to think the Soviet people aren't prepared yet to digest news of the pace of change elsewhere in the socialist bloc. It will be interesting—and certainly telling—to see how Moscow deals with Walesa's suggestion that he visit the Soviet Union to explain the Polish reforms.

"I'd like to go to that beautiful country and learn something about it," Walesa said, " . . . but I wouldn't like to disturb *perestroika* and reforms." Obviously, somebody fears he and Solidarity already have.

The Seattle Times

Seattle, WA, April 7, 1989

ONLY two months ago in Warsaw, Lech Walesa was publicly heckled by young Solidarity members who branded him a traitor for agreeing to negotiate with the Polish government on policial and economic reforms.

But now, after eight weeks of talks, Walesa has reached a remarkable agreement with the government that should give Poland the most open, democratic society in Eastern Europe.

Walesa called it "the beginning of the road for democracy and a free Poland." That may sound overly optimistic considering Poland's recent history, but Walesa could be right.

The commendable new accords, to be made law today by the Sejm (Polish parliament), will:

■ Restore the legal status of the trade union Solidarity, which was banned when martial law was imposed in 1981.

■ Provide for free parliamentary elections in June – Poland's first since 1946.

■ Give Solidarity delegates 35 percent of the 460-seat Sejm; the Communists, 38 percent and other parties the rest.

■ Restore Poland's 100-member upper house of parliament, which was disbanded just after World War II.

■ Give Solidarity its own daily national newspaper, regional weekly papers, and weekly airtime on government-controlled radio and television.

■ Make sweeping changes in Poland's economy, including a wage-indexing system to help workers fight high inflation.

The country's disastrous economic situation virtually forced the government to strike a bargain with Solidarity. But the agreement also reflects Soviet President Mikhail Gorbachev's new policy of looser controls over Eastern Europe.

Polish government leaders now openly describe communism as "obsolete." They talk of "borrowing from Western democracies" and seeking a "humanitarian, democratic socialism."

Poland still has horrendous problems to overcome – especially economic ones. The United States and Western Europe, through trade, investment and debt relief, should make every effort to encourage Poland's peaceful escape from the communist domination that has crippled the nation for more than 40 years.

The Philadelphia Inquirer

Philadelphia, PA, April 7, 1989

In the ongoing race to see which communist country can democratize fastest, Poland pulled ahead of Hungary and the Soviet Union on Wednesday.

The communist government of Poland and the leaders of the Solidarity trade union movement signed a historic agreement that would have seemed unthinkable only months ago, reinstating the banned union and setting the stage for the first free elections since World War II.

Solidarity has gone through bitter times since its heady triumphs in 1980 as the first and only free trade union movement in the communist world. With the union he founded crushed and banned by martial law in 1981, its leaders forced underground or put in jail, few would have predicted that Lech Walesa, his face a bit puffier, his mustache still drooping, would be joining a de facto alliance with the government this week.

What has happened over the last decade is that the government and the Communist Party found that they could not rule alone. Their credibility was gone. The workers wouldn't work, and Poland's economy had sunk below Third World status. With the changes in the Soviet Union, and Mikhail S. Gorbachev's blessing, Poland's communist leaders had to turn to the only institutions that commanded any respect — the illegal-but-still-active Solidarity and the church.

Now Mr. Walesa has signed on to an accord that calls for open elections in June for a lower chamber in which the communists and their allied front groups are guaranteed a 60 percent majority, and an upper chamber, or Senate, totally up for grabs. The opposition is expected to control the Senate, which will have a veto over key legislation.

This does not mark the end of Communist Party control in Poland — far from it — but it is the furthest any communist regime has moved towards giving political power to non-communist forces. The population at large remains skeptical, and the risks for Solidarity are high. Many of Solidarity's younger members believe that the leadership has sold out.

Becoming part of the system means that Solidarity officials will have to talk harsh economic realities to their membership, who, like any constituency, do not like hearing about more budget cuts and unemployment. The biggest threat to the process may come not from the government but from popular protests and strikes if the skeptical public is not convinced that tough economic reforms will bring results.

But for the first time, with Moscow's blessing, an East Bloc regime has recognized openly that the communist political system no longer works. A wholly new political formula is being tried. This historic shift deserves the strongest support from the United States. The White House should look hard for ways to help Poland improve its economic conditions in order to give these experiments with partial democracy a fair chance.

The Houston Post
Houston, TX, April 7, 1989

POLAND'S LONG-OUTLAWED Solidarity has won reinstatement as a legal trade union, along with sweeping reforms that include the communist nation's first free elections in 42 years. The next step must be to heal the economic ills that forced the Polish government to cut a deal with the union.

The accords signed this week by Solidarity leader Lech Walesa and Gen. Wojciech Jaruzelski's government, was a triumph for Walesa, the union and all freedom-loving Poles. But it is inconceivable that the Warsaw regime acted without a nudge and nod from the Soviet Union's reform-minded leader, Mikhail Gorbachev. It was the pre-Gorbachev Soviet leadership, after all, that pressured Jaruzelski to declare martial law and crush Solidarity in 1981.

The new reform package embodies many of Solidarity's goals when Walesa founded it in 1980 as the only independent trade union in the Soviet bloc. Poland's one-house parliament will become a two-house body, a 460-seat lower house and a 100-seat Senate.

Parliamentary elections will be held in June. Legislators will then choose a president. In this first vote, the Communist Party will be guaranteed 65 percent of the lower house seats, though later elections are to be more open. But the entire Senate will be freely elected and will have limited veto power over the lower house.

Besides the political changes, however, there are free-market economic reforms designed to cure Poland's ailing agriculture and industry. The United States should encourage the success of both.

BUFFALO EVENING NEWS
Buffalo, NY, April 6, 1989

THE SOLIDARITY labor union in Poland has achieved a remarkable breakthrough for itself and the nation, winning the Communist government's agreement to legalize the union and to hold free elections for the first time since World War II.

In return, Solidarity has pledged to assist the government in solving Poland's deep-seated economic problems, discouraging its members from striking during the difficult period of austerity that will be necessary to get the economy moving again.

The historic accord came after two months of talks and after hundreds of pages of agreements had been hammered out dealing with many details of economic and political reforms. A government official called the agreement a "social contract," and it has brought together in a compromise broad elements of Polish society.

Solidarity had only a brief legal existence before it was suspended with the imposition of martial law in 1981. Ever since then, leaders of both the Roman Catholic Church and Solidarity have appealed for a national dialogue and a national reconciliation.

The Communist government of Gen. Wojciech Jaruzelski for a long time scorned Solidarity as an insignificant, outlaw group, but finally it has realized it must enlist its help in marshaling the nation's resources in a program of economic recovery and political reform.

The negotiations over the past two months came after a series of crippling strikes, which Solidarity helped to end. The dialogue begun then has led to the new accord.

The legalization of Solidarity will come immediately, but free elections will be handled in phases. Elections will be held in June, but the government will be guaranteed 65 percent of the seats in the lower parliamentary house. Solidarity will enter the lower house as an opposition party — in itself a important concession — and later elections will be more democratic.

In addition, a newly created Senate will be freely elected, and it is expected to be controlled by the opposition. Both houses will elect the president, who is expected to be Jaruzelski. The compromise and the sharing of power implicit in the agreement means that the Communist Party's 45-year monopoly of power would be ended.

A significant part of the accord is what Solidarity calls a new "infrastructure of democracy" — independence for judges, the right to form associations and political clubs and a national newspaper in which Solidarity could express its views.

The pact also includes greater economic freedom. The country will work toward a more market-oriented economic system as a means of stimulating growth and reducing Poland's massive $38 billion foreign debt.

Solidarity leader Lech Walesa, who played a leading role in the negotiations, said the union did not achieve all of its goals, but that new gains could be made "when we are a legal union."

Walesa has already conducted a remarkable labor negotiation, apparently winning a large chunk of freedom for an entire country. Solidarity has always been a national movement as well as a labor union.

Many problems, both political and economic, lie ahead, and the gap between the military government set up by Jaruzelski over seven years ago and true democracy will be difficult to bridge.

Walesa rightly warned that the promised reforms could still end up as empty words, but he said the historic accord "can be the beginning of the road to democracy and a free Poland."

The Miami Herald
Miami, FL, April 8, 1989

HISTORY HAS shown time and again that winning at war, no matter how protracted, often is easier than winning at peace. The challenges facing the victors rarely end with the cessation of conflict. Rather, that's when they truly begin.

Such is the case with Solidarity, the Polish independent trade union. Its battle for recognition has just reached a fascinating climax with the signing of a historic accord with the government of Poland. The treaty restores Solidarity's legal status and opens the way for the establishment of a new and more-representative parliament.

In achieving this hard-won objective, Solidarity has proved that the Communist Party does not truly represent the workers, as official propaganda has always proclaimed. But in assuming its rightful place in Polish society, Solidarity now begins the daunting task of proving that *it* does.

Not an easy task at that. Poland faces runaway inflation, severe shortages, and lack of housing. The market-type economic reforms on which it must now embark require that, for the short run at least, the people be prepared to bear the trying austerity measures that are sure to follow. The ability to be more effective than the government in persuading the desperate and apathetic workers to endure prolonged sacrifices and lower standards of living toward this end will be the test of Solidarity's authority.

To become a legitimate political force in Poland requires Solidarity's leaders to demonstrate that they possess enough political vision and moral authority to succeed where the Communists failed. It also means that they will need as much assistance as they can get, both politically and economically. Washington can help by moving quickly to further ease trade restrictions imposed on Poland on the heels of the government's crackdown on Solidarity in 1982.

The ball is now in Solidarity's court to show that it is capable of co-governing the nation. And while its followers celebrate and bask in the glow of a democratic victory that is almost too sweet and overwhelming for words, they must also keep in mind the hardships that lie ahead.

Nice going, Solidarity, and good luck.

Part IV: Ethnic & Nationality Issues

Although foreigners commonly refer to Soviets as "Russians," it should be pointed out that ethnic Russians make up little more than one-half of the U.S.S.R.'s nearly 300 million people. Over 100 distinct ethnic groups live in the nation's 15 constituent republics. In addition to Russians, the largest groups include Ukrainians, Uzbeks, Byelorussians, Kazakhs, Tatars, Azerbaijanis, Armenians, Georgians, Moldavians, Tadzhiks and Lithuanians. Some cling to centuries-old languages, cultures and traditions. Moslem non- Russians, concentrated in the southern and west-central regions of the U.S.S.R. have the fastest rising birthrate in the country.

Under the Soviet constitution, all ethnic groups are equal. But ethnic Russians fill the highest ranks of the Communist Party and the central government. Russian is the official language of the Soviet Union. And Russian culture dominates all others.

Long-simmering inter-ethnic tensions and nationalist aspirations exploded when Mikhail Gorbachev, himself an ethnic Russian, took power. Ironically, the eruption appeared to be in part an unintended outgrowth of *perestroika* and "democratization." Many non-Russians took Gorbachev's liberalization to be sign that he would accept more autonomy among the diverse nationalities. In-stead, he has maintained a hard-line stance, warning that nationalist unrest perils his reforms.

In 1986, anti-Russian riots erupted in the Central Asian republic of Kazakhstan. The same year, the Chernobyl nuclear accident fed the resentment of Ukrainians and Byelorussians against the central government. In 1987, Tatars began a public clamor for a re-establishment of their ancestral homeland on the Black Sea.

In 1988, troops had to be sent into the southern Transcaucasus to quell
bloody clashes between Christian Armenians and Moslem Azerbaijanis over the political control of an Armenian enclave in the Azerbaijan republic. (The Kremlin placed the enclave, the Nagorno-Karabakh Autonomous Region, under the direct control of the central government in 1989.)

A strong upsurge of nationalism swept through the Baltic republics (Estonia, Latvia and Lithuania) 1987-89 led by independence-minded organizations that, in some cases, had the active support of party chiefs in that region. The latest hotspot was the Transcaucasus republic Georgia, where 20 nationalist demonstrators died in a clash with soldiers in the capital of Tblisi in April 1989.

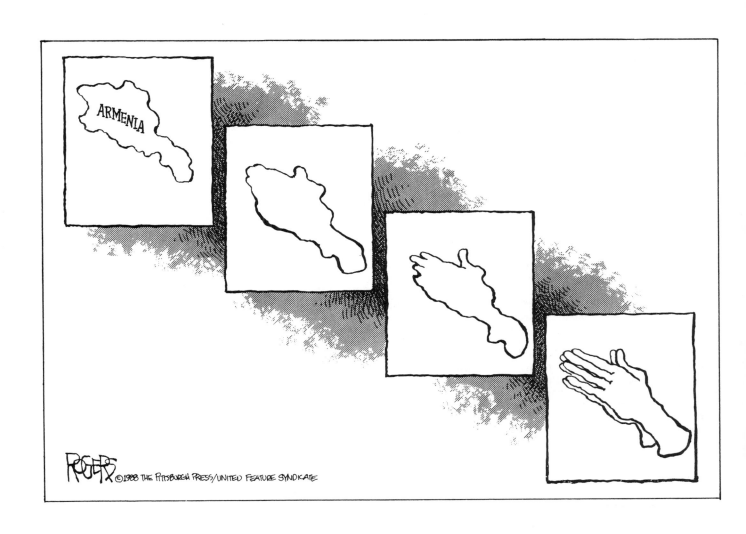

Riots in Kazakhstan Ensue as Soviet Leader is Ousted

Anti-Russian riots broke out in the central Asian city of Alma-Alta Dec. 17, 1986, one day after the removal of the head of the Communist Party (CP) of the republic of Kazakhstan. Alma-Alta was the capital of Kazakhstan. The Central Committee of the Kazakhstan CP dismissed Dinmukhamed Kunayev as the regional party first secretary Dec. 16. Tass, the Soviet news agency, said that Kunayev had asked to be relieved of the post in preparation for voluntary retirement. Kunayev, 74, an ethnic Kazakh, had been the regional party chief for nearly 25 years. He had once been a close associate of the late Soviet General Secretary Leonid Brezhnev, who had made him a full (voting) member of the Politburo in 1971. As of Dec. 22 Kunayev retained his seat on the Politburo.

Western analysts viewed Kunayev's dismissal as a further move by Soviet leader Mikhail S. Gorbachev to consolidate power by removing holdovers from the Brezhnev era. Kunayev's ouster had been preceded by a shakeup of the Kazakhstan CP involving corruption charges against some party officials.

Kunayev was replaced by Gennadi Kolbin, 59, an ethnic Russian who had been the head of the Ulyanovsky Province in central Russia. Kolbin was a member of the national Communist Party Central Committee. Ethnic Russians outnumbered ethnic Kazakhs in Kazakhstan. Nevertheless, it was unusual for a regional party to be headed by anyone other than a member of the region's native ethnic group. The riots were viewed in the West as a sign of growing tensions between the traditionally Moslem population in the southern U.S.S.R. and the northern Slavs. Slavs, particularly Russians, dominated the national leadership.

The Soviet press reported that "several hundred students...incited by nationalist elements" took to the streets of Alma-Alta on the night of Dec. 17 to protest Kolbin's appointment. "Hooligans, parasites and other antisocial persons made use of this situation and resorted to unlawful actions against the representatives of law and order," Tass reported Dec. 18. "They set fire to a food store, to private cars, and insulted townspeople."

The disorders continued through Dec. 19. The Soviet media did not mention casualties in the rioting, but a French diplomat, citing unidentified Soviet sources, claimed that there had been several deaths. Unconfirmed reports in the Western press, based on eyewitness accounts, later said that unidentified persons had distributed vodka, marijuana and nationalist leaflets to the rioters. Kolbin and Mikhail Solomentsev, a member of the Politburo, were dispatched to Alma-Alta following the riots and met with regional party officials Dec. 21.

𝕽𝖎𝖈𝖍𝖒𝖔𝖓𝖉 𝕿𝖎𝖒𝖊𝖘-𝕯𝖎𝖘𝖕𝖆𝖙𝖈𝖍

Richmond, VA, December 28, 1986

Alma Ata is a city in Soviet Kazakhstan. But it is far closer to Kabul, the capital of Afghanistan, than to the Soviet capital, Moscow. As of yesterday, Afghan rebels have spent seven years fighting Russian domination of their nation. Earlier this month, the same sort of national and ethnic pride that drives the Afghan resistance erupted within Soviet borders, though not for the first time. But for once, Moscow acknowledged the confrontation.

The Soviet Union has many non-Russian minorities. Within most Soviet republics, the minority is actually the majority. Kazakhstan is an exception: Its Kazakh population is, at the moment, outnumbered by ethnic Russians, a distinction the Kazakhs dislike and will probably rectify with their higher birth rate. Meantime, they prefer that at least the nominal leader of the state which bears their name be one of their own, however corrupt or inept he may be.

Until recently, he was — that is, longtime Communist Party boss in Kazakhstan Dinmukhamed Kunaev was Kazakh, and corrupt, and, from Moscow's point of view, inept. The other day, Mikhail Gorbachev, in his ongoing fight against corruption and for Russian hegemony, replaced Mr. Kunaev with a Russian, Gennadi Kolbin. Kazakhs in Alma Ata, where loathing of Russians is often shown in small but unmistakable ways, rioted. For two days — Russian patience was shorter than Beijing's and Russian rioters more violent — "hooligans" burned cars, looted stores, roamed streets.

Writing all the rioters off as hooligans won't wash. Kazakhstan has exhibited in microcosm a larger Soviet problem. Mr. Kunaev typifies the old order that Mr. Gorbachev must replace to get the Soviet Union moving. Mr. Kolbin, former top aide to Foreign Minister Edvard Shevardnadze, typifies the new technocrats on whom Mr. Gorbachev is counting to get his nation moving. Kazakhs typify the ethnic animosity that could undercut his moves throughout the Soviet Union.

So why publicize the rioting? Partly because doing so would boost Mr. Gorbachev's calculated reputation for *glasnost*, or openness; partly because news of such fervent protest would circulate anyway. Non-Russians have been warned that riots won't roust Russians. Mr. Gorbachev's own Russian constituency has been alerted to the attempt. He seems to have learned, from his predecessors' willful ignorance of it, that unacknowledged problems only worsen.

Alma Ata was not a real-life prelude to "Red Storm Rising." But the strains that run through Tom Clancy's new novel — ethnicity, religion and loyalties which transcend the fear of Russian rulers — are real enough.

Birmingham Post-Herald

Birmingham, AL, December 24, 1986

For the protesting students in mainland China, the cause is mainly ideological: a thirst for democracy and freedom of expression. For those in Soviet Central Asia, it seems nationalistic: tension between ethnic Russians and Turkic-speaking Moslems. Despite these differences, the recent street demonstrations in both countries underscore difficulties that old-fashioned Marxists will find harder than ever to meet.

Moscow provoked an anti-Russian backlash in the Asian province of Kazakhstan by dismissing its veteran Communist Party boss and replacing him with a follower of Mikhail Gorbachev. The Gorbachev regime evidently wanted to consolidate its position by ousting an aging — and allegedly corrupt — crony of the late Leonid Brezhnev. But in doing so it transferred the top job in Kazakhstan from a Kazakh to a Russian. Young protesters saw that change as symbolizing their region's domination by an alien culture.

The Soviet Union has a huge Moslem minority — some 44 million people, mostly concentrated in Kazakhstan and five other "republics" bordering Iran, Afghanistan and China. But nearly all its central government leaders are European Slavs, and its official creed is atheism. Clearly Moscow cannot take the Moslems' loyalty for granted, especially when it is butchering their co-religionists in Afghanistan. With the Moslem groups growing at least twice as fast as the country's European population, ethnic strains will almost certainly become even more acute.

China is far more ethnically cohesive than the Soviet empire — and more advanced in discarding Marxism's economic myths. But that very advance has created ideological contradictions: Peking has been trying to move toward capitalism but not toward democracy, and many of its citizens yearn for both.

Several Chinese cities have now seen massive student marches, featuring huge placards with slogans such as "Long Live Freedom" and "Give Us Democracy." The students are pressing four demands: restoration of their right to express their views through wall posters and open debates, an end to censorship of press reports on their activities, a guarantee against punishment for demonstrating and official recognition that their demonstrations are "just, patriotic and legal."

These students are members of China's future technical and managerial elite, beneficiaries of Peking's turn toward Western methods. They seem to be trying to teach their elders a lesson that some of us Westerners have forgotten: that economic and political freedom are inseparable.

The Salt Lake Tribune

Salt Lake City, UT, December 23, 1986

Soviet leader Mikhail Gorbachev's purge of yet another aging Brezhnev protege from the ruling Politburo nearly completes a consolidation of Kremlin power, the swiftness of which is unsurpassed in Soviet history.

The latest member of the old guard to be removed from the Kremlin's inner sanctum is Dinmukhamed Kunaev, the 74-year-old chairman of the Communist Party in the Kazakhstan Republic. His imminent departure leaves only one Brezhnev loyalist in a leadership role on the 12-man Politburo, Vladimir Shcherbitsky, 68, the Ukrainian party boss.

Shortly after taking power in March 1985, Gorbachev moved swiftly to consolidate his position. Almost immediately he appointed three of his close personal associates to the Politburo, and he sacked one of his principal rivals, Grigori Romanov, the former party boss of Leningrad. By year's end he had eliminated another pretender to the throne, Viktor Grishin, the former party baron of Moscow, and added two other of his own men to the ruling council, including Eduard Shevardnadze, the new foreign minister.

Gorbachev's purification of the party has gone much deeper than the ruling elite. By the end of his first year of rule, he had replaced about 20 percent of the party bureaucracy, some 20,000 positions.

The Soviet leader reportedly has wanted to remove Kunaev and Shcherbitsky from the beginning, but was cautious because of the strong local support they enjoyed in their republics. Gorbachev's fears apparently were justified. The Soviet news agency, Tass. took the unusual step thi past week of reporting riots in Alma Ata, the capital of Kazakhstan, presumably in response to Kunaev's ouster and his replacement by an ethnic Russian, Gennady Kolbin, a protege of Shevardnadze.

The appointment of Kolbin violates the tradition in which the top party post in republics outside the Russian Federation are reserved for representatives of the local nationality, who ordinarily are then assigned a Russian deputy.

In his assault on the Brezhnevites in the ruling elite and the party bureaucracy, Gorbachev is staying the course set by his mentor, the late Yuri Andropov. The Andropov-Gorbachev wing of the party represents a younger, better-educated generation of communist leaders predisposed toward pragmatism rather than old line dogma. They are dedicated more to leadership by merit than to Brezhnev-style cronyism.

Their foremost goal is to reform the plodding, centrally planned economic system established by Stalin and perpetuated by Brezhnev, and they are particularly concerned with rooting out the official corruption and system of egregious privilege that became so distasteful to the ordinary Soviet citizen during Brezhnev's rule. Kunaev was ousted after a campaign charging officials in Kazakhstan, a major grain-producing region, with corruption and inefficiency.

Part of the Andropov-Gorbachev strategy has been to admit that difficulties do exist in the Soviet Union. hence the reporting of the Alma Ata riots.

The political demise of Kunaev and the events surrounding it should be viewed in this context.

The Dispatch

Columbus, OH, December 19, 1986

Mikhail Gorbachev's campaign to clean up the Soviet bureaucracy took another step forward recently when a top official known for his tolerance of corruption was stripped of his provincial party leadership. This is likely to lead to his removal from the 12-member ruling Politburo.

Dinmukhamed Kunaev, 74, a Politburo member for 15 years, was relieved of his job as Communist Party secretary in the central Asian republic of Kazakhstan "in connection with his retirement."

His re-election earlier this year as Kazakhstan party chief came as a surprise since the vote was in the midst of Gorbachev's efforts to revitalize the economy and make the huge Soviet bureaucracy more efficient. While the factors leading to the re-election have never become clear, Kunaev's ouster had been expected for some time.

If the chain of events leads to his removal from the Politburo, he will be the fourth member of the elite group removed by Gorbachev, who has vowed to fight corruption and inefficiency in the bureaucracy.

It would also serve to strengthen his control on the all-powerful Politburo and help to position himself for a long tenure as the Soviet Union's top leader.

Gorbachev is moving carefully and effectively, biding his time until the moment for action is right. Western officials can learn much about Gorbachev's leadership style from watching the way this man conducts domestic business.

The Times-Picayune
The States-Item

New Orleans, LA, December 21, 1986

It is a common observation in the West that the Soviet Union is potentially unstable domestically because ethnic Russians are, in effect, colonial rulers of non-Russian provinces that could conceivably rebel. Such a view seemed confirmed recently by ethnic riots in Alma Ata, the capital of Kazakhstan, protesting the Kremlin's removal of the veteran Kazakh Communist Party chief and his replacement by a Russian from Siberia.

Several hundred students demonstrated, and serious riots followed. The disorders had to be put down by police and troops, and a member of the Politburo was sent down from Moscow put things back together with "warm, friendly meetings."

But this is not quite a textbook case of an empire beginning to come apart. In the first place, Kazakhstan, though it retains its Kazakh culture and usages, has a slight Russian majority. The Soviet system allows such provinces to follow their traditional culture, but also strives to progressively Russify and communize the population. Locals may head the provincial party and provide most of the party bureaucracy, but Moscow has its people there, too, and they are really in charge.

This policy, by all reports, has been generally successful. People in such provinces seem to have little difficulty maintaining a sort of cultural-political split personality. When disputes with Moscow arise, it is natural for protests to be couched in terms of ethnic rights regardless of the real content of the dispute.

In this case, the content seems to be not cultural repression but General Secretary Mikhail Gorbachev's program of rooting out entrenched corruption, incompetence and conservatism. The Kazakh party chief retired by Moscow had been in office for 22 years and at 72 was one of the last top officials remaining from the Brezhnev era. With him went two-thirds of the regional party central committee and many local party officials.

Mr. Gorbachev has cited Kazakhstan as ripe for exemplary action. Moscow's move, then, was clearly not against Kazakhs as Kazakhs — most of the party posts will doubtless be refilled with Kazakhs — but against party members needing discipline.

Presumably Moscow expects the population of Kazakhstan to approve and applaud a more effective and productive party management. Thus is solved the mystery of why the Tass domestic service reported the demonstration and riots to the Russian people — the first time it has been known to do so.

Some have speculated that Moscow feared word would get around, magnified in the retelling, and that it was better to report it even at the risk of encouraging thoughts of similar actions among other "nationalities." But the reporting might be explained more simply as Moscow advertising to the nation how swift and thorough it is moving to throw local rascals out and come to the aid of the people. Mr. Gorbachev, too, is known as a Great Communicator.

The Des Moines Register

Des Moines, IA, December 25, 1986

Two things might be noted about the ethnic riots in the Soviet republic of Kazakhstan.

• The first is short-range and encouraging: the fact that the Soviet public and the rest of the world have been learning about them from current news reports, and not in bits and pieces by word of mouth weeks later.

It's another example of Chairman Mikhail Gorbachev's new policy of *glasnost*, openness. By Western standards, the openness thus far is a mere crack, but by historic Soviet standards it's remarkable, and it looks hopeful.

• Long-range, and less hopeful, the riots in the Kazakh capital, Alma Ata, are a vivid reminder of the fragmented nature of the Soviet Union and of the fact that Russians will soon be — if they are not already — a minority in the Union of Socialist Soviet Republics.

The Russian republic is much the largest of the 15 in population (137 million) and area (6,593,391 square miles). It has about half of the total population of the USSR, but is by no means all Russian.

The Kazakh republic is second in area (1,064,032 square miles), but is largely desert and mountains, so its population is much smaller (14 million) than that of the second most populous republic, the Ukrainian (49 million).

Moscow's relations with the non-Russian republics have been varied and ambivalent. The trappings of independence are flaunted: soviets (parliaments), flags and even the right spelled out in the Soviet constitution to withdraw from the Soviet Union (but they know they'd better not try it).

Most important, the local languages and cultures are encouraged, with Russian the language for communication among the various ethnic groups — and for getting ahead in life.

The present trouble in Kazakhstan arose from the replacement of an ethnic Kazakh by an ethnic Russian as Communist Party leader. The big worry for Moscow, however, is not this kind of local political hassle.

It is the fact that the Kazakhs and the other Asian minorities are multiplying with families of five or 10 children while the Russians are subtracting with families of one or two children. Moreover, 50 million of the Asians are practicing Moslems.

If Ukrainians or the relatively few Estonians or Latvians had high birthrates, it would be less concern, for those peoples are "like us," while the Kazakhs and Uzbeks are Asians (the cities and villages down there remind one much more of China than of Russia). And Russians are no better than white Americans about really accepting dark-skinned peoples.

•

The future of so heterogenous a union is a deep concern for thoughtful Russian leaders and scholars. Maybe it can be made to work, but the Alma Ata riots are one — probably not the first such — reminder that at some point it may break down.

For Americans the question is whether a troubled, disintegrating Soviet Union would be an unpredictable, more dangerous foe than a calm and prosperous one. We think the latter kind of Soviet Union would make a better citizen of the world.

SATURDAY POST-COURIER

Charleston, SC, December 27, 1986

The riots in the Soviet Socialist Republic of Kazakhstan have been attributed to nationalism. Although the protests, including street demonstrations, which are rare enough in the USSR to make news, were centered on the removal of Dinmukhamed A. Kunayev and his replacement by a Slav, there is more to it than Kazakh pride.

Kazakhstan has been ruled by Russians before and has a sizable minority of resident Slavs. These factors suggest that the anger over Mr. Kunayev's ouster, on grounds of corruption, stems from Islamic reaction against renewed centralization of power under Mr. Gorbachev.

With the removal of Mr. Kunayev, the Asian people of the USSR have lost their sole representative on the Politburo. Their manifest discontent can only be satisfied if they see that their lot will improve as the result of Mr. Gorbachev's reforms.

THE SACRAMENTO BEE

Sacramento, CA, December 20, 1986

The murmurs coming from the Soviet Union are not the sound of ice cracking, however deeply one might wish for such an event. Still something is going on. On the day after Tass officially reports ethnic street riots against a new first secretary in the central Asian republic of Kazakhstan — highly unusual both for the event itself and for the disclosure by the Soviet press — the government releases Andrei Sakharov and his wife Yelena Bonner, the Soviet Union's best-known dissidents, from internal exile in Gorky.

One can only be grateful that physicist Sakharov, after some seven years in Gorky, will be allowed to return to Moscow and to resume his scientific work there. Coming not long after the release of dissidents Yuri Orlov and Alexander Shcharansky, next to Sakharov the best-known Soviet dissidents, that might signal at the very least an effort by Soviet leader Mikhail Gorbachev to reduce the ongoing international embarrassment that the Soviet Union suffers for its treatment of dissidents. Orlov, among others, believes that pressure from abroad, combined with the publicity attendant on the death two weeks ago of another long-persecuted dissident, Anatoly Marchenko, contributed to the decision.

But neither the decision to let Sakharov leave Gorky nor the disclosure of the riots in Alma-Ata by "hooligans, parasites and other anti-social persons," nor the recent moves to allow the occasional publication of other officially unwelcome news and unorthodox literature, nor the authorization of a little more private enterprise ought to be taken as evidence of any fundamental shift. So far, at least, what evidence there is points much more to a realization, certainly by Gorbachev, and presumably by others, that there are more effective — or least less clumsy — means of maintaining order and achieving social objectives. The Russians are not releasing all dissidents, and are not allowing all spouses of foreigners to emigrate at will, much less the thousands of others who have applied to do so.

Still there's at least a change in style. As Gorbachev has already shown in other instances, he understands the importance not only of the Soviet Union's image abroad but of the need to generate more economic efficiency and to rid himself of dead bureaucracy at home. That requires more open communication internally, fewer embarrassments abroad and thus presents an opportunity for the West: Just as seven years of pressure worked in the Sakharov case, it can work in others.

For 300 years, the Russians have swung back and forth between attempts to open themselves to the West, on the one hand, and rigid isolation, on the other. No doubt there were will be more swings in the future. Yet, for the moment, it's clear that they badly want Western technology and some semblance of Western economic progress and more influence in the world. The more they want those things, the more difficult it will be to exclude the ideas and processes that produce them.

Los Angeles Times

Los Angeles, CA, December 24, 1986

For months Soviet leader Mikhail S. Gorbachev has been complaining that bureaucratic defenders of the status quo were stubbornly resisting his efforts to modernize the creaky Soviet economy. However, last week's student riots in Alma-Ata—the capital of the Central Asian Soviet republic of Kazakhstan—were the first known instance of resistance taking a violent turn.

Gorbachev has used economic shortcomings in Kazakhstan as a horrible example of old-style Communist leadership. Two-thirds of the members of the regional Communist Party central committee have been purged, along with many local party officials.

A week ago the new regional central committee dutifully fired Dinmukhamed Kunaev, a 74-year-old Kazakh who had headed the republic's Communist Party organization for 22 years, and replaced him with Gennady Kolbin, an ethnic Russian from Siberia. Kunaev, a protege of the late Leonid I. Brezhnev, is also expected to lose his membership in the ruling Politburo.

This, on the face of it, was a risky business. The Soviet Union is in actuality a colonial empire in which non-Russian nationalities are dominated by Moscow. Kazakhstan is one of several Central Asian republics, most of them predominantly Muslim, that border on China, Afghanistan and Iran. The country's unwritten rule has previously been that the provincial governments are headed by the representatives of local ethnic groups, whose power has frequently been more apparent than real, with Moscow's man sitting in as No. 2.

By unseating Kunaev, the Kremlin offended the ethnic sensitivities of the Kazakhs. The day after Kunaev's downfall, rioting broke out among several hundred students who burned autos and a store, fought police and "insulted townspeople," according to an unprecedented Tass report that blamed the riots on "hooligans and parasites" who were "incited by nationalistic elements."

Order was restored by police and troops on the second day—but not before several people were killed, according to Soviet sources cited by the Washington Post. The Post also reported that the students were supplied with vodka and narcotics, apparently with the connivance of local officials who feared that Kunaev's removal endangered their own jobs and privileges.

The Kremlin sent in a Politburo member, Mikhail Solomentsev, to restore ideological order. According to reports circulating in Kazakhstan, dozens of local party officials have been arrested. Communist youth organizations are being castigated by the Kremlin for "poor moral and ideological teaching" and for failure to cope with "growing problems."

From where Gorbachev sits, all this has to be a disturbing demonstration of the fact that his anti-reform enemies in the bureaucracy are willing to go to any lengths—including the stoking of racial hatreds among the Soviet Union's dozens of nationalities—to oppose his efforts to bring the country out of the economic and social dark ages.

The Philadelphia Inquirer

Philadelphia, PA
December 28, 1986

The closest thing to an open rebellion against Mikhail S. Gorbachev's continuing shake-up of the Soviet power structure took place last week in Kazakhstan, a sparsely populated Central Asian "republic" that is roughly the size of Western Europe. Replacement of the longtime provincial Communist Party chief, an ethnic Kazakh, with a Russian from Siberia led to student riots in the Kazakh capital of Alma-Ata.

Details remain sparse, but there is evidence that local party officials, in defiance of the strict hierarchical control that is the heart of the Soviet system, encouraged the student rampage to show their displeasure with Moscow's attempt to exert its political authority. The rebellion showed that the "nationalities question" remains a potent source of conflict beneath the surface calm of Soviet rule.

Despite their absolute political dominance, ethnic Russians make up only half the population of the Soviet Union. The 90 or so other nationalities are so ethnically and geographically divided — and often so antagonistic toward each other — that it is inconceivable to imagine them rising in unison against the Russians. Passive resistance has proved a more effective weapon, and the Russians have kept the peace by adopting a low political profile in the non-Russian republics and allowing local languages and other cultural trappings to thrive.

Kremlin-watchers noted that when Mr. Gorbachev conducted a major purge of the party leadership during his first year in power, the only two Brezhnev loyalists to keep their seats on the Politburo were the chiefs of the two largest ethnic republics, the Ukraine and Kazakhstan. Now he has moved against the Kazakh leader, and the sharp reaction explains why he hesitated earlier.

In naming a Russian to head the Kazakh party organization, Mr. Gorbachev abandoned the customary practice of choosing the top man from the local population and then installing a Russian as his deputy. Apparently he could not find a Kazakh who was sufficiently competent and loyal, and thus brought in an outsider — the new man's last post was on the Volga — to bring the local party in line with Moscow's new emphasis on reform.

These are fascinating times in the Soviet Union. Soon after cracking down in Kazakhstan, Mr. Gorbachev telephoned human rights leader Andrei Sakharov to personally inform him that he was free to return to Moscow from seven years of internal exile, and free to continue a life that has included frequent protests against the Soviet system. It is as if Mr. Gorbachev wants to rally even the dissidents to his side in his effort to root out recalcitrant, Brezhnev-era party officials and bureaucrats who, far more than the Sakharovs, represent the real threat to his programs.

The San Diego Union

San Diego, CA, December 29, 1986

The violent student uprisings of several weeks ago in Alma-Ata, the capital of the Central Asian Soviet republic of Kazakhstan, is undoubtedly a sobering business for Mikhail Gorbachev and his colleagues in the Kremlin. For they are an ominous reminder of the Soviet Union's inability to suppress the resurgent nationalism among the nation's numerous ethnic groups that has haunted Soviet leaders since the Bolsheviks seized power in 1917.

The Kazakhstan outburst was prompted by Mr. Gorbachev's replacement of long-serving native party leader, Dinmukhamed Kunaev, with a non-Moslem Russian. By putting in his own man to deal with what he charged was rampant political corruption and economic inefficiency, Mr. Gorbachev seeks to strengthen his hold over the second largest of the U.S.S.R.'s 15 republics.

Mr. Gorbahev's controversial gambit is a dramatic departure from the longstanding Kremlin policy of tolerating the occasional incompetence of indigenous leaders in return for their political loyalty. Consequently, his determination to weaken local distinctions is almost certain to provoke additional protests as the Kremlin continues to push for political and economic integration throughout the Soviet Union.

Not without significance is that the European Russians, who constitute barely half of the Soviet Union's population of 280 million, are hanging on to a disproportionate position of political and cultural dominance. Russian dominance has long been a source of tension particularly among the Central Asian republics, where the Moslem majority resents the steady erosion of its heritage.

Apparently unconcerned with this simmering discontent, Mr. Gorbachev is insisting that all of the Soviet republics join his campaign against corruption and economic inefficiency on his self-serving terms. If a few nationalistic sensibilities are bruised in the process, then so be it.

Mr. Gorbachev drives wild horses in trying to improve the economy of the Central Asian republics and simultaneously reasserting Kremlin control over that volatile region of the U.S.S.R. Inherent tribalism and resistance to change are too much to be trampled underfoot even in a police state.

Soviets Report 31 Dead in Armenian Ethnic Clashes

The Soviet Union March 4, 1988 revealed that 31 people had died in ethnic clashes in Sumgait, a city in the Azerbaijan Republic. It was believed to be the most serious outbreak of nationalist violence in the U.S.S.R. since the anti-Russian riots in the central Asian city of Alma-Alta in December 1986. (See pp. 172-175.) The rioting was an outgrowth of tensions between the republic's majority population of Shiite Moslem Azerbaijanis and a minority made up of Christian ethnic Armenians. Armenians were demanding that Nagorno-Karabakh, an autonomous region in Azerbaijan, be politically reunified with the Armenian Republic, Azerbaijan's western neighbor in the Caucasus area.

Tass, the official Soviet news agency, March 4 reported that "immature people" had "committed violent actions and engaged in robberies" in Sumgait Feb. 28, resulting in 31 deaths. Sumgait was a Caspian Sea port city about 20 miles northwest of the Azerbaijan capital of Baku. According to various estimates, its population ranged from 150,000 to 200,000. The Sumgait disturbance had apparently been triggered by a disclosure Feb. 28 that two Azerbaijanis had been killed in strife with Armenians in Nagorno-Karabakh sometime during the Armenian nationalist protests earlier in the month. Tass had first reported the Sumgait violence Feb. 29, attributing the unrest to a "group of hooligans." The chief spokesman of the Soviet foreign ministry, Gennadi Gerasimov, March 1 confirmed that troops had been sent to the city and were enforcing a dusk-to-dawn curfew.

Soviet leader Mikhail S. Gorbachev and the Politburo met March 9 to discuss the troubling developments in the Caucasus region. Tass said that officials agreed to an Armenian request to establish a commission to study the possibility of reunifying the Armenian Republic with the Nagorno-Karabakh Autonomous Region.

In a related development, a crowd of Armenians estimated to be in the tens of thousands held a silent march through Yerevan, the capital of Soviet Armenia, March 8 to mourn the victims of Sumgait. The march symbolically climaxed with a ceremony at a monument to Armenians massacred by the Turks in 1915.

The Hartford Courant

Hartford, CT, March 13, 1988

Until recently, most of the attention paid by Westerners to repressed minorities in the Soviet Union has focused on the plight of Jews, who are unable to practice their religion freely and whose ability to emigrate is tightly restricted.

But unrest in Transcaucasia over the past two weeks, involving the deaths of scores of people during protests for greater cultural and political autonomy, has highlighted the grievances of all non-Russian ethnic and national groups that live under the Soviet system.

The aspirations of Armenian nationalists, and the desire of Armenians living in the Soviet republics of Armenia and Azerbaijan for freer expression of their culture, have been brought to the boiling point — probably because Soviet General Secretary Mikhail S. Gorbachev's policy of openness has made people bolder.

Other nationalist groups in the Soviet Union, including the Tatars, Ukrainians and Latvians, are also growing restive under Moscow's rule. They too have staged protests and demonstrations.

Glasnost, it seems, is a double-edged sword: It is tragic that Armenians' openly expressed desire for greater freedom should result in so many deaths, and it is remarkable that the deaths were officially made known by Soviet authorities.

The Soviet Union, spanning 11 separate time zones from the Baltic Sea to the Kamchatka Peninsula in Asia, is home to more than 100 ethnic groups. Many of them will presumably be emboldened by the Armenian protests to assert themselves more aggressively as time and glasnost go on.

Perhaps never again will the Kremlin's leaders be able to take minority groups' compliance with Moscow's agenda for granted.

Among other things, the protests show that Russians' dominance in Soviet political affairs is under assault. With the ethnic genie out of the bottle, and with hardliners watching his every step, Mr. Gorbachev will be hard pressed to find ways to deal with an expanding demand for human rights in his country. That must not prevent the West from insisting that he do so.

The Register

Santa Ana, CA, February 29, 1988

Has People Power come to the Soviet Union? On Friday 1 million Armenians gathered in Yerevan, capital of the Armenian "Republic" of the USSR. It was the largest anti-government demonstration ever inside the Soviet Union, and in the Soviet bloc has been equaled only by the Solidarity protests in Poland.

The Armenian protesters demanded that the territory of Nagorno-Karabakh, now part of the Azerbaijan Republic but whose population is predominantly Armenian, be re-attached to Armenia. Nagorno-Karabakh was traditionally part of Armenia until 1923, when the new Communist regime in Moscow, which had just conquered both Armenia and Azerbaijan, transferred the region to the latter.

Armenian culture and language go back to antiquity; around the year 300 Armenia became the first country to convert to Christianity. By all rights Armenia should be an independent country with its own laws and institutions. Instead, it is a slave "republic" of the Soviet Union. Moscow dictates policy and imposes the the Soviet Union's official atheism and "socialist realism," though Armenian Christianity and culture are somewhat tolerated.

Today Armenians cannot, alas, protest for independence. To do so would mean swift suppression by the Red Army. In the same way, Solidarity never demanded that Poland withdraw from the Warsaw Pact. But in both cases, mass demonstrations have provided the foundation for unity against the far larger structure of tyranny.

A larger question is how all this fits into Soviet dictator Mikhail Gorbachev's glasnost campaign. Glasnost is, in essence, a propaganda ploy to hoodwink Westerners into thinking that the Kremlin is making fundamental moves toward democracy and freedom. A coat of whitewash is slapped over the gulag prisons and psychiatric torture chambers. The Western media, always eager to be duped, believe.

But something else has also happened. Dissatisfied national groups have taken Gorbachev at his word and are demanding satisfaction for the injustices done them. The Baltic nations, invaded and annexed by Josef Stalin in 1940, have turned important dates in their nations' histories into annual demonstrations. For example, last Wednesday Estonians at a rally shouted "Independence to Estonia!" and "Get the Russians out!" And Crimean Tartars, deported by Stalin to Siberia, have demanded a return to their warmer homeland.

Are we seeing the breakup of the Soviet Empire? Might it jettison Communism for a kind of Russian nationalism far more tolerant? Or will a new wave of Stalinist purges, deportations, and mass murders begin?

No one knows. But the momentous protest of 1 million Armenians is another sign that Marxism-Leninism is a dying ideology.

THE SACRAMENTO BEE
Sacramento, CA, March 1, 1988

Hundreds of thousands of Soviet Armenians took to the streets last week in an unprecedentedly large display of popular displeasure with the Soviet government. The Armenian unrest is but one of many emanating from minority groups that together make up nearly half the population of the Soviet Union. If such discontent grows, it could imperil Soviet leader Mikhail Gorbachev's reformist program, which centers on greater openness about public issues.

Other groups that have raised their voices include the three Baltic peoples — Latvians, Lithuanians and Estonians — who demonstrated last summer on the anniversary of their countries' absorption into the Soviet Union in 1940. Last month, 14 Estonian nationalists demanded the formation of an independent political party; more recently, Soviet officials closed Estonia temporarily to foreign travelers to prevent them from witnessing demonstrations commemorating the day in 1918 when Estonians won a short-lived independence.

Last summer, Crimean Tatars staged a public demonstration in Red Square, demanding the right to return to their homeland on the Black Sea from which they were expelled in 1944; in December 1986, several thousand people rioted in Alma Ata, capital of Kazakhstan, to protest the appointment of a Russian to head the government of the region; and demonstrations by students in the Georgian republic in opposition to military maneuvers were reported to have taken place last week.

Each complaint arises more out of local circumstances than from any general opposition to the Soviet system or to communism. In Armenia, for example, the 200,000 who came into the streets demand the rejoining of Soviet Armenia with an area of neighboring Soviet Azerbaijan with a 75 percent Armenian majority but a local hierarchy that is predominantly Muslim. The area was split off in the 1920s by Stalin to placate Muslims in the region and as a means of diluting Armenian nationalism. Leaders of the protest movement have suspended their protests only because Gorbachev has promised to address their grievances.

No outsider can be sure to what extent such outbursts occurred in the pre-*glasnost* days, although those incidents known to Westerners were dealt with harshly. Nor is it certain how far this new clamor for autonomy and human rights will be tolerated by Moscow should it become more widespread or more violent; so far, only a few isolated deaths have occurred. And how far will the dozens of critical newspapers now popping up like spring flowers in Moscow be allowed to go before being reined in?

To Western democrats, all this popular ferment is exciting stuff. Yet such enthusiasm must be tempered with a concern that, in promoting greater openness, Gorbachev may have opened a Pandora's box that he — or his more conservative colleagues — will feel at some point powerless to control and thus may resort to a more familiar method of dealing with dissent: repression by force. That would be tragic.

THE SUN
Baltimore, MD, March 2, 1988

General Secretary Mikhail Gorbachev, in a prescient statement Feb. 18, described the Soviet nationalities problem as "a most fundamental, vital question of our society." Less than a week later, protest crowds of a size unprecedented in Soviet history took to the streets of Yerevan, the capital of the Soviet Armenian republic, for a demonstration that indeed raises fundamental questions.

Specifically at issue is whether Armenia (largely Christian) is to regain control of Nagorno-Karabakh, a district ceded to Azerbaijan (largely Muslim) by Josef Stalin in 1923. Of far greater consequence is whether the Soviet Union can keep its ethnic divisions from tearing it apart as Mr. Gorbachev pursues his ballyhooed reforms.

Although the United States, like the Soviet Union, is a heterogeneous nation, our polyglot population is scattered throughout most of the 50 states. We are a nation of immigrants. The Soviet Union, in contrast, is a patchwork of long-established societies sewed together by the Russian empire builders of the 19th and 20th centuries. Today, the 15 Soviet republics comprise scores of nationality groups with distinctive religions, languages, cultures — and a lingering resentment toward Russian hegemony.

Like the czars before them, the Kremlin's Communist rulers have always been interested in Russian aggrandizement, even though Moscow has permitted ethnic theater, art, language and architecture as a cultural safety valve. It has also instituted better medical care, leading to an explosive Asian birth rate foreshadowing a non-Russian Soviet majority. The Kremlin, however, has never relinquished Russian control on real power or tolerated any form of separatism.

Nonetheless, centrifugal tendencies are the stuff of Kremlin nightmares, as exemplified by dissident Andrei Amalrik's 1969 treatise, "Will the Soviet Union Survive until 1984?" Now, we suspect, Kremlin hardliners are asking, "Will the Soviet Union survive *glasnost* and *perestroika*?" Mr. Gorbachev, the progenitor of openness and economic restructuring reforms, must be asking, "Will I survive Yerevan?" Since he took office, there have been serious disturbances in Kazakhstan, Lithuania, Latvia and Estonia, and Crimean Tatars have tried to storm Red Square.

Strains in Soviet society increase. No sooner had Mr. Gorbachev promised the Armenians he would look into their grievances than Azerbaijanis started protesting violently. Unrest could spread.

The nationality problem is the greatest challenge yet to face Mr. Gorbachev. So it is no wonder that the Soviet leader seeks an exit from Afghanistan and detente with the United States as foreign policy initiatives while he tests the limits to which the Soviet state can tolerate his reforms. Whether Kremlin hardliners will tolerate Mr. Gorbachev is another "fundamental, vital question."

AKRON BEACON JOURNAL
Akron, OH, March 3, 1988

THE SIGHT is rare in the Soviet Union — huge crowds gathering in protest — but for two weeks that's what the men in the Kremlin have faced. No, the shouting has not been from Red Square. The protests have been in the southwestern Soviet republics of Azerbaijan and Armenia. But the issue is close to Soviet officials: maintaining order in their ethnically diverse and far-flung country.

The unrest is Armenian-inspired. The Armenian Republic would like to annex a region of the neighboring republic of Azerbaijan. The region is dominated by Armenians, who are largely Christians. The Azerbaijanis, on the other hand, are mostly Moslems. The Armenians of the region argue they've become the victims of the Moslem majority. It's not hard to imagine the tensions evoked. Keep Lebanon in mind.

There's little question Mikhail Gorbachev understands the stakes involved. Last month he told the Central Committee that the country's problems with ethnic diversity — there are more than 100 ethnic groups in the Soviet Union — posed the "most fundamental, vital issue of our society." Soviet leaders, for instance, worry about the influence of Iranian fundamentalists in Azerbaijan, which borders Iran.

In typically bureaucratic fashion — it happens over there, too — Gorbachev appointed a commission to study the problem. Unfortunately, for him, at the same time, Moscow rejected a request from Armenia to annex the region within Azerbaijan. Thus, the protests began. And already officials are backpedaling. Gorbachev pledged to listen to Armenian demands.

Not surprisingly, that hardly eased matters. Indeed, the Soviet leader faces a difficult challenge. The traditional Kremlin method of simply crushing the protesters would scarcely serve as good PR in the era of *glasnost*. And yet, actually redrawing boundaries in the face of great pressure could set a troubling precedent in a country unused to democratic rule and home to so many fiercely nationalistic ethnic groups.

Ah, the perils of *perestroika*. What are its boundaries?

Lincoln Journal

Lincoln, NE, March 2, 1988

Detailed information from the southern reaches of the Soviet Union, where pro-Armenian protests apparently have been going on for weeks, is scarce. But plainly one casualty is the spirit of *glasnost.*

Not since the nuclear disaster at Chernobyl have officials in Moscow been less open about events within their borders. This suggests the trouble in Soviet Armenia and Azerbaidzhan represents a serious challenge and Kremlin leaders are uncertain how to react.

The belated and terse Kremlin statements on the trouble are notably conciliatory, pointing to a priority effort to calm things down. Soviet leader Mikhail Gorbachev reportedly promised that the Communist Party Central Committee would review relations among the nationalities that make up the nation. Similiar pledges have been made to other restive ethnic groups, but reviews do not necessarily mean action.

More interesting was a Soviet Foreign Ministry spokesman's remarks this week that "mistakes were made" 65 years ago when the territory of Nagorno-Karabakh, mostly Armenian, was included in the Soviet Moslem republic of Azerbaidzhan.

Will these errors be corrected and Nagorno-Karabakh restored to Soviet Armenia, as the protestors want? One might gather from the Foreign Ministry's spokesman that yes, this will happen. But that's not easily done.

For one thing, Armenia and Nagorno Karabakh share no common boundary. Uniting them would seem to require a kind of "Armenian corridor," a creation unlikely to set well with other Azerbaidzhanians.

More importantly, yielding to the Armenians on so major a point surely would inspire demands by other national groups in the Soviet Union, leading to widespread unrest and agitation. And for many Armenians, union within the Soviet context would be only a first step. Demands for independence would inevitably follow.

What Moscow does will be interesting to watch. Again a basic problem facing the Soviet Union is underlined: how to govern a diverse population made up of more than 100 nationalities. It's not hard to believe Gorbachev truly wants out of Afghanistan. He has enough trouble at home.

The Atlanta Journal
THE ATLANTA CONSTITUTION

Altanta, GA, March 12, 1988

There's more than meets the eye in the recent mass demonstrations in one Soviet republic and what looked for all the world like murderous race riots in another.

The Kremlin may have barred the press from the scenes of the turmoil, but it has divulged uncommonly revealing bits of the story itself. Also, independent voices from Soviet Armenia have not been silenced.

This week they appealed to Party Secretary Mikhail Gorbachev to protect Armenian enclaves in the Moslem republic of Azerbaijan from Shiite fanatics' attacks during Iranian new year festivities, starting March 18. Judging from reports of Azeri ferocity during rampages in Sumgait, which took an official toll of 32 lives (and likely more than that), Armenian unease seems warranted.

But the antipathy between these two feuding peoples is only part of the story.

The Soviet press began an orchestrated expose of the Armenian problem early this year not out of concern for minority grievances, but because of the corruption reportedly rampant within the local government and the party structure. This was the same tack the Kremlin took last year before replacing a Kazakh party boss renowned for his venality with an ethnic Russian, a miscalculation that ignited serious (and staged) rioting in Alma-Ata, the Kazakh capital.

The Armenian bosses knew better than to challenge Moscow directly. Instead they reawoke resentment over a blunder dating back to Lenin's time when a largely Armenian region called Nagorno-Karabakh was ceded to Azerbaijan. Their appeal to nationalism sent thousands of demonstrators into the streets of Armenia's cities and, viewed cynically, the Armenian cause then won sympathy worldwide when the Azeris responded to the threatened loss of territory with a small-scale pogrom of Armenians.

The larger question here is Moscow's management of its empire. Its ability to dictate to the non-Russian republics has rested for years on a see-no-evil accommodation with crooked regional bosses. Their waste and thievery, though, is a colossal obstacle for Gorbachev's structural reforms, so vital for the Soviets' economic resuscitation. But rooting out corruption in the provinces risks being interpreted as declaring war on his country's myriad minorities.

And Gorbachev thought he had troubles with bureaucratic heel-draggers in Moscow.

THE ARIZONA REPUBLIC

Phoenix, AZ, March 2, 1988

LIKE the ancient mariner's albatross, the symbol of guilt in Samuel Taylor Coleridge's poem, the intractable "nationalities" problem hangs from the neck of the Soviet empire 70 years after the Bolshevik revolution.

The recent riots and mass demonstrations in Soviet Armenia, Azerbaijan and the autonomous region of Nagorno Karabakh — following on the 1986 Alma Ata riots and last year's demonstrations in the Baltic — are vivid evidence of how persistent non-Russian nationalism is in the Soviet Union.

The Soviet empire is a conglomeration of more than 100 ethnic groups uneasily united under the umbrella of the Communist Party and the Great Russian Muscovite state. Soviet spokesmen talk about their country as if it were a harmonious entity linked by the common bonds of patriotism and communism.

In fact, it never has cut the Gordian knot of recusant non-Slavic nationalism. Despite sometimes bloody "Russification" campaigns, non-Russian nationalism refuses to expire, especially in the Baltic and Moslem republics, in Georgia, Armenia, Ukraine and other ethnic regions.

By early 1918, just months after the Bolsheviks shot their way into power, the Czarist empire had disintegrated. Virtually every ethnic region of the old imperial state had declared independence and elected its own government. The Red Army fought a savage war to restore the Russian empire, despite pre-revolution promises of self-determination for the ethnic republics.

But the Bolshevik conquest of the 1920s failed to resolve the nationalities conundrum, for Lenin's approach was authentically Marxist, embracing two mutually contradictory principles: the self-determination of nations and a powerful, centralized state.

The nationalistic demonstrations in Armenia and Azerbaijan, the largest since the revolution, are thought to be partially a reaction to Mikhail Gorbachev's *glasnost* and *perestroika* campaigns, probing the limits of openness and economic restructuring.

It is on the issue of nationalism, however, that Gorbachev's power may be most vulnerable. Hard-liners may view his recent appeal for more latitude for ethnic diversity as the proximate cause of the disturbances. Gorbachev also is the first general secretary to have no working experience in the non-Slavic regions, a real liability.

For the perpetually public-order-obsessed Moscow, the Armenian-Azerbaijani rampages could not have occurred in a more unsettling place. Moscow long has feared that Shiite fundamentalism might spill over from Iran into the Moslem republics. With a Soviet military withdrawal from Afghanistan looking distinctly like a *mujahideen* victory, Kremlin concerns for the stability of its southern border are not wholly without cause.

The Record

Hackensack, NJ, March 3, 1988

For years, the West has depicted the Soviet Union as a prison house of nations, with everyone from Estonians to Uzbeks yearning to break free of Russian domination and go their separate ways. But the recent extraordinary demonstrations in Soviet Armenia indicate the situation is more complicated.

Last week, thousands of Armenians took to the streets to demand formal annexation of Nagorno-Karabakh in the neighboring Soviet republic of Azerbaijan. Armenians are Christian. They are culturally and scientifically advanced, prosperous, and historically oriented to Western Europe and European Russia. Azerbaijanis are predominately Shiite Moslem, speak a Turkic language, and are traditionally oriented to Turkey and Iran. Conflict between the two groups goes back centuries, with the Armenians a Christian outpost in a Moslem sea.

The coming of Soviet power imposed a rough measure of peace. But in 1923, under heavy pressure from Turkey, the young Soviet government detached Nagorno-Karabakh from Armenia and handed it over to Azerbaijan as an "autonomous region." Sixty-five years later, the move still rankles. The desire among the Armenians in Nagorno-Karabakh to be reunited with their countrymen to the west remains undiminished.

Hence last week's extraordinary demonstrations. Peaceful and disciplined, the protests nonetheless had something of the nature of a national revolt. The economy in Soviet Armenia came to a halt, radio and television employees revolted and demanded full news coverage of the protests, and the local police sided with the demonstrators. In Moscow, Foreign Ministry spokesman Gennady I. Gerasimov made the extraordinary admission (by Soviet standards) that Moscow may have made "some mistakes" in handing Nagorno-Karabakh over to Azerbaijan.

But then came the reaction in Azerbaijan. On Sunday, mass demonstrations broke out in the Caspian seaport of Sumgait. News reports are sketchy, but it appears that Armenians were attacked in the streets and that at least two people died. Apparently, Nagorno-Karabakh is hardly less explosive an issue in Azerbaijan than it is in Armenia.

What does it all mean? Simply that even as they seek to have the wrong of Nagorno-Karabakh corrected, Armenians are more dependent on Moscow than ever. They rely on Moscow to protect them from their larger neighbors (those in the Soviet Union as well as those outside) and to mediate disputes such as the one over Nagorno-Karabakh. The Armenians are not calling for a breakup of the Soviet Union, or for their own independence. Either course would mean a return to the dark days of massacres and pogroms and foreign domination. Soviet Armenians want a solution to the Nagorno-Karabakh issue, but as the organizers of last week's mass demonstrations were careful to stress, they want a solution within the Soviet framework.

The Boston Globe

Boston, MA, March 7, 1988

There is a specter haunting the Soviet Union, a specter of ethnic, religious and racial conflict among the more than 100 nationalities that make up the Soviet Union. It has begun to take human shape in the form of the thousands of protesters in the streets of Yerevan, the capital of Armenia.

The Russians who remain the dominant group in the USSR are actually only its largest minority. They keep control because they practice the divide-and-conquer techniques that were perfected over the centuries by the czars of the Romanov dynasty. The czars annexed the territories and populations of scores of nations, from Poland and Lithuania in the west to Georgia and Armenia in the South and Mongolia and parts of China along the borders of Siberia in the distant East.

The Romanovs tried to unify their heterogeneous domains by an aggressive policy of Russification. When the communists came to power, they professed that theirs was to be a union of autonomous republics in which the cultural heritage of each nationality would be acknowledged and respected.

The reality was quite different. Power remained concentrated in the central government in Moscow, although lip service was paid to cultural pluralism, and some tolerance was afforded to different nationalities.

During Joseph Stalin's terrifying reign, the autonomy of the Soviet republics proved a sham. Millions of Ukrainians were killed or starved into submission to Moscow. When certain populations excited his distrust, Stalin deported them all – men, women and children –to Siberia. He also reshuffled the boundaries of the republics to serve his political objectives, rather than the democratic wishes of the subject people.

One such gerrymander in 1923 caused the district of Nagorno-Karabakh to be transferred out of Armenia into neighboring Azerbaijan, although its population is 75 percent Armenian. Armenians are a Christian people with an old and rich culture. They feel no kinship with the Azerbaijanis, who are predominantly Moslem. Huge demonstrations in Armenia now demand the return of the district to Armenia.

At the same time, there are acute ethnic tensions within Azerbaijan. There are sizable Armenian minority communities in Baku, its capital, and in smaller cities. The Soviets have reported that "rampage and violence" have been caused by the usual unidentified "hooligans" and have resulted in several deaths and injuries.

This ethnic unrest causes grave concern in Moscow. Mikhail Gorbachev quieted the demonstrations in Armenia only by promising to review the issues. He has also called a special conference of the Communist Party to reconsider "the nationalities question."

The whole subject is pregnant with danger. Any concession made to the Armenians might be an awkward precedent for bigger claims by the Ukrainians or the Lithuanians or any one of a dozen other dissatisfied groups. Although Marxist theory asserts that economic motives are the controlling ones in human behavior, experience has shown the enormous power of racial and religious rivalries and hatreds.

Ultimately, Gorbachev and his colleagues could fall back upon military force to crush dissidence, as Stalin did in his day and the czars did in theirs. Ruthless repression has its own price. It would hardly further the modernization and restructuring of an already stagnant and resentful society.

MILWAUKEE SENTINEL

Milwaukee, WI, February 27, 1988

Although many Americans may be surprised to even learn that Armenia is part of the Soviet Union, it probably is not a total surprise to Soviet leader Mikhail S. Gorbachev that ethnic problems there could provide a major test of his program of perestroika, or restructuring.

The diversity of the Soviet population throughout the 15 republics that constitute the country, particularly those in Central Asia such as Armenia, is the stuff from which discontent and factional fighting are bred.

Gorbachev's unprecedented personal appeal for calm in the streets of the Armenian capital of Yerevan — backed by 1,500 paratroopers he ordered to the trouble spot — was his recognition that the five days of demonstrations there were a serious matter.

The sight of Armenian soldiers who fought in Afghanistan throwing their medals into the street and tearing up their Communist Party membership cards had to be unsettling to the Kremlin.

And those abroad who view the Soviet Union as a monolithic entity peopled by Ivans and Tatanyas may get a different perspective on the country before this issue is settled.

What is at issue are claims that the predominantly Armenian region of Nagorno-Karabakh be incorporated into Armenia. One banner carried by the demonstrators in Yerevan, it was reported, read "Karabakh is a test of perestroika."

Meantime, ethnic Russians in Armenia, many of whom were born in the republic as the descendants of resettled parents and grandparents, must be wondering whose side to cheer for and what this assertion of ethnic rights will mean to them.

Gorbachev has promised to devote one of the party's Central Committee plenary meetings to examining relations between the country's more than 100 ethnic groups.

Small wonder that the Soviets are ready to pull out of Afghanistan. They may have more serious problems within their own borders.

Armenian Earthquake Kills Thousands

A massive earthquake, registering 6.9 on the Richter scale and centered in the Soviet republic of Armenia, Dec. 7, 1988 devastated a large area of the southern Soviet Union near the Turkish border. Initial reports placed the death toll in the tens of thousands, with the possibility that thousands were still trapped in collapsed buildings awaiting rescue. An early estimate of the number of people left homeless was over 100,000.

Soviet leader Mikhail S. Gorbachev had been in New York City visiting with President Reagan and President-elect George Bush. Gorbachev and his entourage left the United States for the U.S.S.R. on the morning of Dec. 8, one day earlier than had been planned. (See pp. 140-143.) The decision to end the trip had been announced early Dec. 7 by Soviet Foreign Minister Eduard Shevardnadze. Before departing from Kennedy International Airport, the Soviet leader revealed that he had received telephone condolences from President Reagan and President-elect Bush.

The earthquake had left several cities and towns in ruins. Few multistory structures were left standing in Leninakan, a city of 290,000. The town of Spitak, close to the epicenter, was completely demolished, and 90% of the 20,000 people who had lived there were dead.

As of Dec. 15, the estimated death toll was 55,000. Some Soviet officials believed that as many as 100,000 had been killed. In the worst earthquake in recent history, at least 100,000 people had died in Tangshen, China in 1976.

Thousands of Armenians missing and presumed dead were under the rubble of collapsed buildings. Also, the estimated death toll did not take into account fatalities in remote regions affected by the quake. Soviet authorities estimated that at least 12,000 had been injured, and that 500,000 people had been left homeless. The earthquake prompted a massive outpouring of international aid to the U.S.S.R.

Gorbachev and his wife, Raisa, toured the disaster region, Dec. 10-11.

The Des Moines Register

Des Moines, IA, December 13, 1988

It is normal and right that the loss of life and property from a natural disaster enables rivals to put aside political differences for the sake of restoring order.

It is, therefore, instructive to learn that ethnic violence has flared in areas of the Soviet Union most devastated by an earthquake.

The disaster left hundreds of thousands dead and homeless.

It also spawned an extraordinary outpouring of humanitarian aid from the world community.

Even Turkey, considered by many the historical enemy of Armenia, sent a caravan of medical supplies, blood transfusions and food.

Amidst the rubble of the quake, however, Armenian nationalists armed with bricks and pipes clashed with Soviet troops and tanks.

Demonstrators complained that relief efforts were intentionally slow in regions where ethnic violence has flared since February. Others blamed Moscow for not predicting the quake.

Anger directed at Moscow is largely in response to Mikhail Gorbachev's handling of a long-standing feud between Christians in the republic of Armenia and Muslims in the republic of Azerbaijan.

Last July, the Soviet parliament rebuffed Armenia's demand for annexation of the Nagorno-Karabakh region, now part of Azerbaijan but heavily populated by Christian Armenians. Since then, violence has flared periodically between Armenians and Azerbaijanis.

That such a feud persists despite the most devastating earthquake in more than 1,000 years shows the intensity of ethnic hatreds within the Soviet Union, and the danger such conflicts pose to Gorbachev's leadership.

"This is the edge of the abyss," Gorbachev warned the protesters. "One more step and it's the abyss."

The Kansas City Times

Kansas City, MO, December 10, 1988

Imagine, if you can, hundreds and hundreds of Hyatt Hotel collapses, but imagine them as entire buildings crashing down, and imagine that the buildings are schools, offices, apartments and factories jammed with people.

That is the emerging picture in the Armenian Republic of the Soviet Union. The toll from the earthquake may never be really known, but it appears to be immense. The response from the United States and other countries should be large and immediate. Technical and medical help and personnel familiar with earthquake relief are important in the first aftermath. When needs are determined, material aid should be swift, constant and generous. The United States should play a leading part.

A terrible blow has fallen on some of the best and yet longest-suffering people on Earth. The Armenians have endured hardship from the earliest days of recorded history. Survival always has been terribly difficult. In ancient times they were buffeted by Assyrians and Persians. They were conquered by Alexander, the Romans, the Mongols, the Turks. From time to time a nation with boundaries has emerged. Almost always it has been swallowed up in the shifting boundaries of the region. Armenia probably was the first Christian state.

Modern history has seen the worst of times. In the early part of this century the Ottoman sultan set about a systematic plan of extermination. At the end of World War I there was briefly an independent Armenian republic. In 1920 it was occupied by the Red Army and a year later a Russo-Turkish treaty established lines.

All this has happened to a cultivated, civilized people famous for their friendliness and hospitality. No visitor to an Armenian community is a stranger. In the Soviet Union, Armenians stand out as a stylish, sophisticated segment of the population who have made a large contribution to culture and the economy. They have been steadfast in maintaining their identity despite both subtle and overt campaigns of Russification. The earthquake came in the midst of new struggles in neighboring Soviet Azerbaijan where an Armenian minority is under siege.

For the Armenian people the blows of fate never seem to end.

THE CHRISTIAN SCIENCE MONITOR

Boston, MA, December 13, 1988

MIKHAIL GORBACHEV and his Soviet Union find themselves in an unusual position: They are the objects of worldwide humanitarian concern and of a flow of aid to that country unprecedented since World War II.

The Soviets are getting a glimpse of the deeper benefits from being more responsible players on the global scene. Beyond trade agreements and progress in arms lies the world's readiness to help shoulder the load when hardship strikes, as it did last week when an earthquake devastated cities in Soviet Armenia.

The grim statistics – as many as 60,000 dead, at least half a million without homes as winter sets in – are enough to bring out the humanitarian in even the most hardened critics of the Soviet Union.

One of the biggest challenges those numbers bring is the need to resist cynicism, disillusionment, and political manipulation, which appear to be surfacing among some inhabitants of the stricken region.

Ethnic tensions in the region erupted into violence prior to the quake, and Moscow was unwilling to accept Armenia's call for a transfer of territory, inhabited largely by Armenians, from neighboring Soviet Azerbaijan to Armenia. This has led some residents to suspect that Moscow is intentionally slowing aid as a stick to get militants back in line. That reasoning does a gross injustice to those who are supplying the assistance and conducting rescue efforts. It also does disservice to the 85 Soviet relief workers who have died in plane crashes trying to bring supplies to the region.

Beyond the immediate search-and-rescue efforts looms the larger task of reconstruction.

Recovering from the accident at a nuclear power plant in Chernobyl in 1986 cost the Soviets an estimated $12.8 billion. Recovering from the Armenian quake will easily eclipse that figure. This demands of shortage-weary Soviets, already criticizing Gorbachev's economic reforms for not showing tangible gains, an extra measure of patience.

It also demands of Soviet officials a level of ethical behavior equal to the billions of rubles that will be funneled into Armenia.

Dipping into the till, which seems too often to be a job requirement among some Soviet officials, would only fuel suspicion and mistrust among an already disaffected Armenian population.

The heartwarming global response to the Armenian tragedy should serve the historically insecure Soviet Union notice that the world is worthy of more trust than Moscow has traditionally been willing to give it.

The Soviet Union's humble willingness to accept the aid that is offered may hint at that growing trust.

The Hartford Courant

Hartford, CT, December 9, 1988

If there is a silver lining in the disastrous earthquake that struck Soviet Armenia, it lies in the promise that it holds for a bond between the peoples of the United States and the Soviet Union.

That promise was in part realized Thursday as Mikhail S. Gorbachev, his visit to New York cut short by the earthquake, flew home to lead reconstruction efforts with a pledge of American aid from President Reagan.

"If there is any way we can be of assistance, either bilaterally or through the international community, please let me know," Mr. Reagan told the Soviet leader.

The administration should quickly follow up on the president's offer, perhaps by suggesting direct government-to-government assistance or offering logistical help or funds, if appropriate, to private agencies mounting disaster-relief efforts.

The American Red Cross and the U.S. Armenian community have already started. The Red Cross sent an "immediate gift" of $50,000, and Richard F. Shubert, president of the organization, said that donations can be sent to local chapters or to the American Red Cross, International Disaster Relief, P.O. Box 37243, Washington, D.C. 20013, and marked "Soviet-Armenian Earthquake."

Archbishop Torkom Manoogian, primate of the Eastern Diocese of the Armenian Church in America, said, "we are asking all people of good will and compassion . . . to assist financially."

A tremendous amount of aid will be needed if reports of the damage are accurate. A disaster on the scale of the one that struck Wednesday would tax the resources of any country. Several towns were obliterated and an estimated 75 percent of Soviet Armenia's second-largest city, Leninakan, was destroyed. Perhaps as many as 80,000 people were killed by the earthquake and hundreds of thousands are injured. A greater number are homeless. The grave situation is further aggravated by the presence of 100,000 refugees who fled to Armenia from the neighboring Soviet republic of Azerbaijan, where the existence of the Armenian minority is endangered by ethnic strife.

Mr. Gorbachev's pledge at the United Nations of a unilateral reduction in Soviet troop strength and the dismantling of some defense plants continued the work of building a bridge of peace between two peoples highly suspicious of each other. Coincidentally, the Soviet leader's dramatic offer came on the same day as the earthquake that leveled so much of Soviet Armenia. The American people and their leaders can nail down another plank or two on that bridge by responding generously to the suffering of the disaster victims.

THE DAILY OKLAHOMAN

Oklahoma City, OK, December 13, 1988

NOT since World War II has there been such an outpouring of support from the world community toward the Soviet Union.

Sympathy for the victims of the disastrous Armenian earthquake has been translated into a massive international relief effort.

The United States, whose adversarial relationship with Moscow has lessened with Mikhail Gorbachev in power, is in the forefront of the humanitarian efforts.

There is hardly anything remarkable about the response of Americans and other citizens of the free world to this tragedy. In countries which place a high value on the welfare of individuals, helping a neighbor in need is a natural endeavor.

What is different about the current situation in Armenia is the fact that the Soviets are not only willing to accept outside assistance but are even asking for it. In times past, the Kremlin's policy was one of unswerving self-reliance.

For years, disasters behind the Iron Curtain were covered up by Soviet officials. Now the doors are open to planes carrying rescue workers, medical personnel and emergency supplies. The scope of the destruction, as well as blame for its causes, is being fully reported and analyzed.

Gorbachev has had a knack for turning misfortune to his advantage. It is ironic that nature's violence struck an area where ethnic strife has been a mounting problem for the Soviet leader. By personally involving himself in responding to the local crisis, it's possible he can ease the unrest.

On the other hand, the presence of Westerners lending assistance may give the Armenians just enough of a taste of freedom to make them even more antagonistic toward the Soviet central government.

DAILY NEWS

New York, NY, December 10, 1988

IT WILL BE DAYS, PERHAPS WEEKS, before the final death toll in Wednesday's earthquake is known. The conservative estimate is 50,000. It could be 100,000. It could be higher.

On the Richter scale, the quake measured 6.9. On the scale of human suffering and misery and horror, it was immeasurable.

In the city of Leninakan, near the epicenter, the hands of a clock stand at 11:41, marking the exact minute when disaster began—and the world stopped. It was 11:41 a.m., an hour when the factories were filled with workers. The factories are now rubble. An hour when the schools were filled with children. The schools are now rubble.

At least one city, Spitak, was obliterated. It simply no longer exists. In some cities and towns and villages, an entire generation of children simply no longer exists.

Churches throughout this country will hold requiem services in memory of the dead. Prayer is all that can be done for them. But then, there are the living. Hundreds of thousands of people, hurt and homeless and hungry. In desperate need of food and clothing and blankets and shelter and medical supplies.

The Armenian community in the United States is, of course, in the vanguard of the relief effort. But it's an effort anyone with any sense of humanity should join.

Contact the local Armenian churches to make a donation or to find out how you otherwise can help. Or call the American Red Cross, which has established a toll-free number for its Armenia aid: 1-800-453-9000. Or contact other charitable organizations.

Relief planes from around the world are flying to the disaster area. The response has been extraordinary. Immense. It must continue on that level. For the suffering is immense. And the suffering continues.

The Sun Reporter

San Francisco, CA, December 14, 1988

At the last count, over forty-eight nations, including the United States, have responded positively by sending aid to the victims of the earthquake in Armenia, the first instance since World War II that the USSR has accepted U.S. aid; in fact, no person's or country's aid has been refused. The horror which these people have endured has been quoted by the authorities as "indescribable."

Some of the Soviet residents, and millions of Armenians at home and abroad, have leveled severe criticism at the central government of the Soviet Union as incompetent and doing far too little and too late to cope with the disaster. This criticism, we feel, is unfounded.

Many villages were wiped out, and no structure over four stories tall remained standing. This condition approximates that of a holocaust, in that the living envy the dead.

We feel that the presence of international teams from the West and the East, which include the United Nations disaster teams, the British brigades that dealt with the bombing of Britain during the war, and the surgical teams from the U.S., Great Britain and France, will add immeasurably to the feeling that the world cares.

Added to the misery is the fact that the weather is getting colder, and several planes containing soldiers on missions of mercy were wrecked on landing, with all aboard killed. The Armenian people have long known suffering, and the response of the average U.S. citizen, as well as the Armenians American, has been encouraging.

Many more dollars are needed to be raised so as to adequately supply the enormous needs created by this emergency.

The response of the international community has been excellent to two of the crises which have recently arisen on the world scene: the drought and starvation in East Africa in '86, '87 and '88, and now this great catastrophe in the Soviet Union.

In this season of giving, we urge Blacks to share equally with these two dire needs. Their gifts should be divided between Airlift for Africa and the Armenian Relief Society. It is not the amount one gives which is as important as the fact that one gives. In this regard, the window's mite is as precious as the rich man's millions.

For aid to the victims in Armenia, the address a contribution is: Armenian Relief Society, 51 Commonwealth Ave., San Francisco, CA 94118.

For aid to the starving people of the Sudan, the address is: Airlift for Africa, Third Baptist Church, 1399 McAllister St., San Francisco, CA 94115.

The Record

Hackensack, NJ, December 9, 1988

Less than 48 hours after he arrived in Manhattan, Mikhail Gorbachev was boarding an Aeroflot jet for an emergency dash to earthquake-devastated Soviet Armenia. Behind him lay a vintage Gorbachev handshaking excursion on Broadway, and a pledge to the United Nations to unilaterally cut his country's armed forces. Ahead lay a region where the death toll is in the thousands and entire cities were destroyed. For drama alone, history will remember the time Mr. Gorbachev played the Big Apple. With luck and effort, history may also record that his speech marked an important change in superpower tensions that have shaped the world for 40 years.

In the address to the United Nations, Mr. Gorbachev said he would cut his country's armed forces by 500,000 men, pull tanks and troops back from eastern Europe and the Chinese border, and shift from a military doctrine based primarily on offense to one based on defense. If the move is carried out, President Reagan said, it would be "important, significant." Britain's Margaret Thatcher, Western Europe's most experienced head of state and generally a skeptic on Soviet intentions, said she warmly welcomed the pledge. His announcement raises important new possibilities and questions:

Is Mr. Gorbachev's proposal for real? Yes, with reservations. The cutback is unilateral, and requires no negotiations. Hard-line conservatives in the Soviet Union oppose the cuts, and the chief of the Soviet General Staff quickly resigned. But it's inconceivable that Mr. Gorbachev would announce such a move without enough support in his own government to carry it out. A test of his sincerity will be whether he removes new tanks from Eastern Europe, or obsolete models ready for scrapping. Pulling back support personnel rather than combat-ready frontline troops would be another way to undercut his pledge. But analysts remain impressed by details such as a promise to move out of Eastern Europe units that can quickly build new bridges if old ones are destroyed. Without such units, an offensive attack is almost impossible.

Why is Mr. Gorbachev taking such a step? Because it benefits the Soviet Union, and because it's forced on him by a crumbling economy. Although there may be other, more idealistic reasons, Mr. Gorbachev sounded like he meant it when he assured his U.N. audience that he's a realist, not a romantic. Soviet citizens are demanding better food, consumer goods, housing, and health care. The inefficient Soviet economy can't deliver without easing up on military spending that's been rising for years. And Mr. Gorbachev is keeping more than enough military strength to defend his country, protect its Communist government, put down ethnic insurgencies, and keep his rebelious East European empire in line. But he's still scoring a propaganda coup in Western Europe, where he hopes to build new business ties that will bring in cash and technology.

What should the United States do in response? In the short run, little but study and make plans. Mr. Gorbachev has caught the United States in a transition between two presidents. In the long run, the United States should respond with imaginative arms reduction plans, possibly including a unilateral gesture of its own. More important, President-elect Bush must develop an overall strategy for regaining the initiative from Mr. Gorbachev and reaching goals of our own devising. With his energy and talent for bold, appealing, surprise gestures, Mr. Gorbachev has the United States locked into a mode of reacting.

Why is Mr. Gorbachev's proposal significant? Under the best of conditions, it could signal that the Soviet Union is ready to stop its military buildup, to cooperate with the United States, and to focus on its domestic economy. Such a policy could make it easier for the United States to cut its own military spending, thereby easing its own budget deficit. And America could devote more resources to strengthening its own economy and competing with Japan and other economic powers.

Can Mr. Gorbachev last long enough to implement his new policies? This may be the most important question of all, and it's the hardest to answer. His policies of change have angered conservative Soviet critics, without delivering enough tangible benefits to guarantee him popularity with everyday citizens. This week's U.N. announcement will turn a significant portion of the military against him. Unless he can produce some form of payoff soon, he could well be ousted. If that happens, Mr. Gorbachev's 48 hours in New York will probably be remembered chiefly for a raising of hopes that were never fulfilled.

The Pittsburgh
PRESS

Pittsburgh, PA, December 11, 1988

The forces of nature know no ideological or political boundaries; nor does the human heart.

So it was fitting and unsurprising that when a devastating earthquake struck Soviet Armenia, nations around the world responded with an outpouring of sympathy and offers of help.

Strikingly, the Soviet Union's new policy of openness has made it easier for outsiders to help. It's another indication of change being brought about in that country by Soviet President Mikhail Gorbachev.

In the past, Moscow has gone to great lengths to conceal accidents and natural disasters from outsiders and even from its own people. But the government-controlled Soviet press is giving full coverage to the catastrophe in Armenia, and Gorbachev explained his hurried departure from New York as necessary to go home to deal with an earthquake that "was extremely severe and had extremely grave consequences."

President Reagan telephoned the Soviet leader before he left and conveyed to him "the deep sympathy of the American people and our anxiousness to provide any humanitarian assistance we possibly can." Government sources said medical and other supplies at U.S. military bases abroad would be made available to the stricken area.

The Armenian Assembly of America immediately set up a relief effort, and donations of goods and money began pouring in. The Armenian American Club of Pittsburgh also quickly established a relief fund for the victims. The Red Cross in America and elsewhere geared up its far-flung facilities to help.

The damage is vast, and so is the help now arriving in Armenia.

The Philadelphia Inquirer

Philadelphia, PA, December 14, 1988

The Armenian earthquake, a tragedy of almost unfathomable proportions, is providing the world a vivid lesson in the gross deficiencies of the Soviet system. As such, the disaster stands as evidence both of the crying need for fundamental reforms and of the enormous obstacles facing Mikhail S. Gorbachev's reform program.

That this lesson is taking place at all is tribute to Mr. Gorbachev's major domestic success, the greater openness of the Soviet news media. In 1948, when an earthquake killed 110,000 people in the remote Soviet city of Ashkhabad, the Soviet press published not one word. Just two years ago, when a nuclear reactor exploded at Chernobyl, the Soviets stonewalled for a week while the world cried out for information.

This time the cameras and reporters have been let in. And the information being sent back to the Soviet people and the world beyond has been brutal. The press has revealed not only Armenian suffering, but terrible inefficiencies that have contributed to the scope of the disaster. It has shown a rescue effort undermined by primitive roads and railroad systems, inadequate medical supplies and havoc at the airports. It has questioned shoddy construction techniques that led to the collapse of new apartment blocks built without any thought to seismic conditions.

Tom Brokaw of NBC-TV watched rescue helicopters sit idle on the ground while Armenians dug frantically with plates in the rubble because they didn't even have shovels. And Soviet Prime Minister Nikolai Ryzhkov told reporters that in one village a bureaucrat refused to give out a shipment of bread because the official whose signature was needed had been killed.

The news hasn't been all bad. The televised scenes of suffering have bound Soviets together in humanitarian concern. Relief supplies have poured in from all over the country. And Moscow's unprecedented decision to accept — and publicize — a massive influx of foreign aid (including American and Israeli shipments) goes far toward ending the Soviet Union's self-imposed isolation. Mr. Gorbachev's willingness to let the world, and his own people, see the Soviet Union's shame and pain is a necessary catharsis. To his own people, it underlines the message that the Soviet Union must change or stagnate at the economic level of a Third World nation. To the outside world it says the Soviet leader wants his country to become part of the global village.

Baltic Unrest Increases as Protests Sweep Region

Large public protests in the Baltic region Aug. 23, 1987 were the latest sign of a resurgence of nationalism in the Soviet Union. A month earlier, Crimean Tatars had created a furor by calling for autonomy in a series of protests in Moscow. The U.S.S.R. had over 100 separate nationalities and ethnic groups, but the Communist Party and central government hierarchies were dominated by Russians.

On Aug. 23, thousands of people marched through the streets of the capital cities of Latvia, Lithuania and Estonia calling for a restoration of independence. The protests had been coordinated by human-rights groups in the region. The date marked the 48th anniversary of a 1939 pact between Soviet leader Joseph Stalin and Nazi German leader Adolf Hitler. The accord had paved the way for the Soviet Union to annex the three Baltic republics in 1940.

The exact number of people taking part in the demonstrations was unclear. The Western press, citing unconfirmed figures from emigre sources, estimated that there were over 2,000 demonstrators in the Latvian capital of Riga, about 2,000 in the Estonian capital of Tallinn, and over 500 in the Lithuanian capital of Vilnus. It was also unclear what actions were taken by the authorities against the protests. Emigre sources in the West claimed that at least eight persons were arrested in Riga, and that police broke into the apartments of some organizers in the city.

The state-controlled Soviet media gave limited coverage to the Baltic protests. Tass, the official national news agency, Aug. 23 mentioned an expression of "national feelings among Estonians" and characterized the Lithuanian demonstration as a "hate rally" conducted by a "paltry group of aggressive extremists."

The Peoples Front of Estonia, a nationalist political organization, had been accorded official recognition by the Estonian Republic of the U.S.S.R., it was reported June 20. The front was believed to be the first large-scale non-Communist political group to be recognized by a Soviet republic and, by extension, the Kremlin itself. The People's Front had roots in a January call by some Estonians nationalists for the creation of an independent party. The organization was reported to have grown to 40,000 members since May. The group's stated policy was to allow Communists to join but to bar them from holding leadership positions.

A Peoples Front rally in the Estonian capital, Tallinn, June 17 had attracted 100,000 people, including high-ranking party officials of the republic. The group supported Gorbachev's reforms, but was also dedicated to increased political and economic independence from Moscow. The group's nationalist orientation was evident in the fact that it had adopted as its banner the blue, black and white flag of pre-Soviet Estonia. The flag had been banned since 1940, when the U.S.S.R. had annexed the Baltic republic.

Tatyana I. Zaslavskaya, a sociologist and Gorbachev adviser, May 23 had suggested that the creation of popular fronts throughout the nation would be beneficial as democratic counterbalances to the Communist Party. But she said she did not envision the fronts acting as opposition political parties. Some Western analysts saw a policy of recognizing unofficial political groups as having an additional benefit for Moscow – the creation of approved outlets for venting nationalist feelings.

Unions representing writers and cultural figures in Latvia had called on the Kremlin to grant the republic the status of a "sovereign state" within the U.S.S.R., it was reported in the West June 21, 1988. The call, in the form of a proclamation published in Latvian newspapers, was perhaps the boldest nationalist appeal ever made by state-supervised organizations. The proclamation urged that Latvia be allowed to control its own press, have greater power over military and secret-police activities.

Nationalist and ethnic ferment swept through Soviet republics July 25 through Nov. 10, 1988. Mass movements and protests (some of them violent) were particularly evident in the Baltic and Transcaucasus regions. The unrest tested the limits of the Kremlin's tolerance in an era when Gorbachev was pushing *glasnost* (openness) and "democratization." Moscow's responses ranged from a military crackdown in the Transcaucasus area to tacit approval of grassroots nationalist movements in the Baltic region encompassing Estonia, Latvia and Lithuania.

THE KANSAS CITY STAR

Kansas City, MO, June 26, 1988

The People's Front of Estonia, which the Soviet Union has permitted to take shape in the Baltic republic, is one more fascinating departure in the Gorbachev experiment. It's hard to believe. Why would the party allow this in one of the most nationalistic regions of the country?

Bill Keller of *The New York Times* suggests that the Estonian group may be a model for future pro-Gorbachev fronts designed to shake the party out of its lethargy. It may also take the heat out of implacable nationalistic stirrings elsewhere, as in this period of violent confrontation between Armenians and Azerbaijanis.

Keller says that most of the leaders of the Estonian organization are members of the Communist Party, and all are devoted to Gorbachevism. A reporter for *Sovtskaya Estoniya* told Keller that "the party does not control the movement. The movement supports the party and the party supports the movement."

That's fine for now, but the nationalism of the Baltic states, Lithuania, Latvia and Estonia, that rose in the late 19th century is not something that can be turned on and off. They were proudly independent from 1918 until 1940 when Hitler and Stalin decided their fate in a secret protocol of the 1939 pact that partitioned Poland and began World War II. There was a brief period of protectorate status under the Russians followed by the the German invasion of the Soviet Union. In 1944, when the tide had turned, Stalin incorporated them totally. Since then there has been considerable migration of Russians and Ukrainians to the area.

So now a People's Front in Estonia and perhaps other People's Fronts elsewhere may serve the purpose of perestroika and provide alternatives to a party apparatus that has paralyzed the economy.

But what comes after Gorbachev? These spirits released are not easily contained. In the best Hegelian dialectic, the leapfrogging syntheses lead in many directions. Who can say where the Estonians will go? Unlike the Armenians and Aberzaijanis, whose nationalism is directed against each other, Baltic nationalism is directed against Mother Russia.

The Oregonian

Portland, OR, June 28, 1988

No more striking examples have surfaced of the new openness to dissent in the Soviet Union than the recent nationalist demonstrations in Latvia and Estonia.

For most of the past three centuries the Baltic states — Latvia, Estonia and neighboring Lithuania — have been part of the Russian empire. But for a little more than 20 years between the two World Wars they were independent countries, until in 1941 Stalin sent his army to occupy and absorb them again.

The United States and other Western countries never have recognized their re-annexation to the Soviet Union. They have maintained governments in exile, and Baltic-Americans have kept the memory of their independence alive.

As recently as last year police in Riga, the capital of Latvia, broke up nationalist demonstrations there and arrested some of the leaders. Now, suddenly, things are different.

According to Latvian-American reports and articles in Soviet Latvian newspapers, tens of thousands of Latvians marched in Riga's streets recently and listened to speeches at a rally. From Estonia have come reports of the formation of a political group outside the Communist Party with 40,000 members and a platform that combines support for Mikhail Gorbachev's reforms with calls for greater political and economic independence for Estonia. In both countries the campaigners asked for increased use of their own languages instead of Russian and greater control over their own affairs.

Their demands differed in some symbolic details. The Estonians said they wanted to be included in a European time zone. The Latvians asked for a Latvian team in the Olympic Games and a seat for Latvia in the United Nations. While extremely unlikely to succeed, there is precedent for that request: The Soviet republics of Byelorussia, which borders on Lithuania, and the Ukraine hold U.N. seats due to the horsetrading by which the organization came into being in 1945.

So far none of the demands from inside the Baltic states has included independence. If the Soviet Union continues on its current path toward reorganization and more open political debate, though, it will have increasingly to deal with the desires and longings of the many non-Russian peoples like the Balts who have found themselves folded within the boundaries of the Soviet empire.

BUFFALO EVENING NEWS

Buffalo, NY, August 26, 1988

LAST YEAR, nationalist groups in the three occupied Baltic republics held demonstrations and were harshly suppressed by the Soviet government. This year, unprecedented mass demonstrations were held legally under government permits. That is a measure of the progress of the new Soviet policy of "glasnost," or openness.

The observances were to mark a day of mourning in the three republics of Estonia, Latvia and Lithuania, the 49th anniversary of the signing of the Nazi-Soviet treaty, by which the three independent republics were soon annexed into the Soviet system.

The demonstrations were of surprising scope. In Vilnius, the Lithuanian capital, 200,000 people — a third of the population — turned out to hear appeals for independence.

Soviet leader Mikhail Gorbachev has allowed the three republics greater control of their economic affairs and greater recognition of their language and cultural heritage. He may be particularly interested in the region because it has been more successful than the rest of the country in implementing his economic reforms, which allow greater individual initiative.

The new freedom to condemn the 1939 treaty with Nazi Germany also advances the new Gorbachev policy of denouncing Stalin, who annexed the republics. The official Tass news agency, while noting the nationalistic aspects of the demonstrations, portrayed them as honoring the victims of Stalin. Thousands were deported from the Baltic republics and died in labor camps.

There have been increasingly frank revelations about Stalin in the Soviet press since Gorbachev's speech last fall in which he said Stalin's crimes had been "enormous and unforgivable" but did not go into detail. Recently, a documentary film on Soviet national television gave the details.

It equated Stalin with Hitler and said he was a deranged dictator who had sent countless people to their deaths. It noted the execution of military officers before World War II and said this had left the nation unprepared for the Nazi onslaught in 1941. A Western diplomat who saw the film said he was "blown out of my chair."

We are becoming accustomed to surprises from the Soviet Union since Gorbachev took over, but we can be sure that the freedom allowed the Baltic demonstrators does not mean that Moscow is even considering granting them outright independence. The official line now is that their ties to the Soviet Union are so close that independence would result in economic disaster for them.

Nevertheless, the changes in Moscow are coming very fast since Gorbachev took over only three years ago. There could be more surprises ahead.

THE PLAIN DEALER

Cleveland, OH, August 27, 1988

The Soviets took a big gamble earlier this week in permitting citizens of three Baltic countries to mass in the streets in belated protest of the Stalin-Hitler pact of 1939 that paved the way for Soviet annexation of Lithuania, Latvia and Estonia. Of course the Baltic peoples, at home and as exiles, have long lamented their countries' loss of freedom. Never before, however, has Moscow sanctioned such demonstrations. Quite the opposite.

Moscow defended its policy against demonstrations by restating the official Soviet view that the three countries voluntarily joined the Soviet Union. As for the pact with Nazi Germany, the Soviets contend it was a delaying action to allow the Kremlin to prepare for an inevitable invasion. They deny the existence of a secret protocol, published by the West after World War II, which ceded the Baltic countries to the Soviet Union. Yet now, and for the first time in a Soviet publication, they have allowed excerpts to be published in Estonia.

So why take a risk on being able to contain the obviously powerful nationalistic emotions of Lithuanians, Latvians and Estonians? Obviously *glasnost*, introduced by Soviet leader Mikhail S. Gorbachev and still having its limits tested, has created a more moderate climate for political expression, perhaps deceptively so. The futile campaign of Armenians to resolve a territorial dispute earlier this year demonstrated that the Soviets will not allow nationalistic aspirations to tear the fabric of the Soviet Union itself.

But Gorbachev and his colleagues evidently learned a lesson from Armenia, where protests turned militant and troops had to be called in. In the Baltic republics, the Soviets undoubtedly reasoned that by providing an authorized outlet for protest, even if it meant denunciation of the Soviets by name, they could keep the situation under control. They even encouraged local communists to join in, blaming Stalin for what happened in 1939.

Nobody can be sure the new tactics will work in the long term. Liberalization of discussion, should *glasnost* survive, might divide the Baltic peoples into those who advocate restoration of independence and those who believe that a more realistic goal would be to allow the three republics greater autonomy. Still, having legitimized denunciation of the origins of the Soviet connection, Moscow may have encouraged a force that will be difficult to contain.

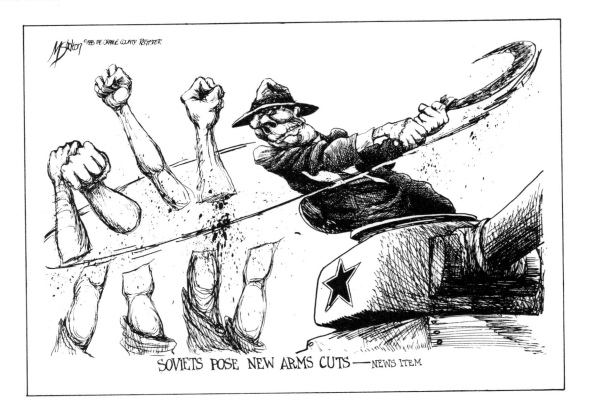

SOVIETS POSE NEW ARMS CUTS——NEWS ITEM

Pittsburgh Post-Gazette
Pittsburgh, PA, July 5, 1988

One good thing that emerged from the carnage of World War I was independence for Latvia, Lithuania and Estonia. The three Baltic nations maintained that status until 1940, when Josef Stalin's infamous pact with Adolf Hitler allowed their annexation by the Soviet Union.

Now, in what may prove a historic irony, the small, unwilling "Soviet republics" are leading an effort to bring more political and economic independence, home rule and pluralism to all the lands ruled by Moscow.

In Estonia, with only 1.5 million people but the highest per capita income in the Soviet Union, the Communist Party has permitted the formation of a political group that could evolve into a rival party in all but name.

The Peoples Front of Estonia has signed up 40,000 members in less than two months. A recent rally attracted more than 100,000 in Tallinn, the capital. Party authorities see the front as a weapon against opponents of Mikhail Gorbachev's reforms, but it expresses nationalistic goals that must worry the Kremlin.

For example, the front flies the formerly banned flag of independent Estonia. It wants Estonian to replace Russian as the republic's official language. It demands an end to Moscow's control over industry, agriculture, prices and taxes in all 15 republics.

Similar fronts have been formed in Lithuania and in the cities of Moscow, Leningrad, Kiev and Yaroslavl. If they spread and grow and are not suppressed, Russia could get a two-party system without admitting it.

It is too soon to say the Soviet Union is changing from a one-party dictatorship. But Gorbachev has granted a bit of freedom, and human nature is to strive for more.

The Wichita
Eagle-Beacon
Wichita, KS, October 25, 1988

WITH Lithuania's yellow, green and red-striped flag of independence rippling in the Baltic breeze, the people of that Soviet-occupied republic celebrated a new taste of freedom over the weekend. An estimated 20,000 Lithuanians sang the songs of their nationhood and gave thanks to God on Sunday in the first Mass at the historic Vilnius Cathedral since the Soviets closed it down 30 years ago. Elsewhere in the capital of Vilnius, delegates of the Lithuanian Restructuring Movement condemned almost every aspect of Soviet rule in what one observer called a "national catharsis."

Throughout the Baltic republics, ferment is in the air, and changes are being made in the three countries' political and social lives that would have astounded even the most ardent nationalists just weeks ago. Lithuania, Latvia and Estonia aren't free yet, by any means. But they are freer than they have been at any time since the notorious Molotov-Ribbentrop Pact of Aug. 23, 1939, that supposedly sealed their fates forever.

It was a secret protocol to that mutual non-aggression pact between Hitler's Germany and Stalin's Soviet Union that delivered the three Baltic nations into the Soviet "sphere of in-fluence." Stalin invaded the republics the following year, and within days, Soviet-style "elections" were staged to legitimize Soviet rule. The results were predictable. In Lithuania, for example, 99.2 percent of the "votes" went to the communist ticket.

The Soviets didn't fool anyone with their duplicity; to this day, the United States and the other Western democracies continue to recognize the independence of the three Baltic states. And every year, the peoples of the Baltic republics have continued to celebrate their independence days, risking beatings or imprisonment.

The first breath of perestroika, wafting over the Baltic boundaries from the east, changed all that. In August, authorities gave permission for one of the greatest outpourings of Baltic discontent ever, on this year's anniversary of the Molotov-Ribbentrop Pact. Soon the legislatures of the three states were drafting bills making Lithuanian, Latvian and Estonian the official languages, rather than the hated Russian. The flags of the three nations flew freely again, and authorities did nothing to prevent it.

Where it all will stop, nobody knows — but again the free nations of the world dare to dream of freedom for the Baltic states as well.

WORCESTER TELEGRAM

Worcester, MA, November 8, 1988

Nationalist movements in Lithuania, Latvia and Estonia, the Baltic republics annexed by the Soviet Union during World War II, must now tread the tightrope between the quest for independence and the risk of sharp repression.

Through changes thought impossible only a year ago, Moscow has demonstrated remarkable tolerance in the Baltic region. New national movements with all the trappings of alternate political parties have sprung up overnight; they have publicly recited lists of grievances against the Soviet Union and its Russian majority. They have stirred feelings of national pride and the resentments of centuries.

It is not clear how far Mikhail Gorbachev will allow ethnic and political minorities to go in opening Soviet society. Veiled calls for independence defy decades of Soviet orthodoxy. Yet cracking down on millions of people would destroy credibility in his reform movement.

Lithuanian speakers at the inaugural congress of the Movement for the Support of Perestroika were careful to point out that Lenin, still the patron saint of Soviet-style Marxism, approved independence for Lithuania but that Stalin, the arch-villain of the moment, was responsible for its annexation. This whole line of reasoning attempts to thread a way through the minefields of dissent.

Lithuania's first prelate in 300 years, Cardinal Vincentas Sladkevicius, has intimated that the Roman Catholic Church might be a natural ally for the newly formed nationalist movement. Such a public role for the church defies years of Soviet policy, but the model for it exists in Poland.

It is difficult to imagine the Soviet Union releasing one of its constituent republics from central rule. But then only months ago, it was just as difficult to imagine the emergence of nationalist movements in the Baltics, where such actions would have brought harsh criminal sentences in the past.

The fear of sudden repression when some undefined ideological line has been crossed hovers over the independence movements constantly. The euphoria of the new nationalist expressions can be a heady wine; intoxication now could prove fatal.

The fate of Lithuania and its sister nations in the Baltic are of deep concern to many in Worcester and Central Massachusetts. We join them in their anxiety, hopes and prayers for the eventual freedom of their ancestral homes — a freedom that until only recently seemed an impossible dream.

ST. LOUIS POST-DISPATCH

St. Louis, MO, November 21, 1988

It was a remarkable scene. The Estonian Supreme Soviet, in the name of protecting local autonomy, approved a measure saying that it had a right to veto laws passed down from Moscow. The communist parliament then voted a "declaration of sovereignty" for the small Baltic republic within the borders of the Soviet Union. It was not an outright declaration of independence, but it was an unprecedented official statement asserting Estonian nationalism.

Even more remarkably, the tanks of the Red Army did not immediately roll on Estonia's capital of Tallinn. Rather, General Secretary Mikhail Gorbachev, through the Presidium in Moscow, declared the Estonian action "unconstitutional" and the local leaders were invited to the Kremlin to talk the matter over. Later, the Council of Ministers in Moscow made a vague promise about sharing more economic powers with the republics, and Mr. Gorbachev characterized the Estonian action as "purely emotional."

This low-key approach helped to defuse the situation. Also, the refusal on Friday of the Supreme Soviet in neighboring Lithuania to take a similar hard-line position on local sovereignty weakened the Estonian move.

There is a double irony here. First, the Estonian communist leaders pressed their nationalistic demands in the name of Mr. Gorbachev's own democratization reforms. But they also acted to block at least part of Mr. Gorbachev's proposed changes in the Soviet Constitution, changes that are set to be approved by the Supreme Soviet in Moscow on Nov. 29. Besides bestowing more political powers on the general secretary and the Soviet president, the changes would eliminate the decades-old provision in the Soviet Constitution that allows individual Soviet republics to secede.

Under Josef Stalin or Leonid Brezhnev, this provision — like the amendment granting religious freedom — meant nothing. But under the liberalizing reforms of Mr. Gorbachev, it might. Hence, Estonia's attempts at asserting its legal rights.

Mr. Gorbachev appears to have handled the Estonian situation fairly well and could have set a precedent on how Moscow deals with new nationalistic outbursts in other Soviet republics, which are increasingly taking the form of parliamentary action by the local Communist Party.

In the other two Baltic republics, Lithuania and Latvia, such nationalistic feelings are becoming increasingly strong. Moreover, this cry for greater local autonomy has already been heard in Armenia and some of the Soviet Moslem areas; it is only a matter of time before it arises in the Ukraine, the Soviet Union's breadbasket and home of 50 million people.

Mr. Gorbachev must rein in these nationalistic emotions while avoiding damage to his political and economic reforms. That will not be easy. Moreover, his hard-line opponents will seize on these nationalistic outbreaks as a sign that "anti-party elements" are running amok. Mr. Gorbachev is learning that interjecting a little democracy into to an old-time dictatorship can have explosive side effects.

THE ARIZONA REPUBLIC

Phoenix, AZ, November 18, 1988

THE trouble with giving freedom-starved people a little taste of liberty is that, like Oliver Twist, they always hunger for more. Mikhail Gorbachev is discovering this insatiable appetite, which now threatens to devour his much-heralded plans for an economic restructuring of the Soviet Union.

The problem for Mr. Gorbachev and his *perestroika* campaign to invigorate the workers' paradise is that some of the workers are taking him at his word. What Mr. Gorbachev himself refers to as Russia's "second revolution" is now being borne out — too literally for many in the Kremlin — in the Baltic states.

Although the three Baltic republics — Estonia, Latvia and Lithuania — comprise but a small snippet of the vast Soviet empire, their role has become increasingly important in Mr. Gorbachev's perilous attempt to relax the state's powerful grip on the country's moribund economy.

They were the first republics to set up so-called popular fronts, envisioned and authorized by the Gorbachev reformers as a way to lessen the Communist Party's heavy drag on farms and factories. Estonia has been officially selected by the Kremlin as the first republic to use "cost accounting" procedures in economic planning and industrial operations.

But along with their enthusiastic support for *perestroika*, the Baltic republics are also pushing, even more enthusiastically, independent notions of their own. This summer mass demonstrations in all three republics were held to denounce the 1939 Hitler-Stalin pact, whereby the Soviets and the Nazis dismembered Eastern Europe. These protests were followed by rallies calling for more religious, cultural and political freedoms.

Now Estonia's Supreme Soviet, which has no real power except that it appears to have the support of the majority of the people, has passed overwhelmingly a "declaration of sovereignty" that proclaims independence from Moscow except in defense and foreign affairs. Although a declaration from a powerless republic presents no real threat to Moscow's authority, it does represent the most serious test to date of Mr. Gorbachev's commitment to economic reform.

Since the entire concept of *perestroika* is based on what Mr. Gorbachev calls the "democratization" of the Soviet economy, independent thinking and action are necessary to effect change. But giving ordinary people a say in how their lives are to be conducted also has consequences that directly threaten the authority and ideological legitimacy of the Marxist-Leninist system.

If the Baltic upstarts in Tallinn, Vilnius and Riga are tolerated, other republics surely will want to follow their example. If that should occur, Mr. Gorbachev's second revolution could undo Russia's first.

Part V: Human & Religious Rights

In June 1988, the Russian Orthodox Church marked the 1,000th anniversary of the introduction of Christianity in medieval Russia. The celebration, attended by religious dignitaries from around the world, had the whole-hearted support of the Soviet authorities. The millennial observance indicated that a new era of church-state relations had arrived in the U.S.S.R.

Religions have had a difficult time in the U.S.S.R. since the 1917 Bolshevik Revolution because the Communist Party has traditionally viewed religion as incompatible with Marxism. Worship was discouraged and religious activists jailed. An estimated 63,000 Russian Orthodox churches had been closed since the revolution. Joseph Stalin outlawed the Ukrainian Uniate Church in 1946. And Jews, the target of vicious persecutions in czarist Russian, encountered periods of blatant anti-Semitism following the revolution, particularly during the Stalin era.

Religion is now emerging from the shadows in the U.S.S.R. In April 1988, the general secretary met with Patriarch Pimen, the head of the Russian Orthodox Church, and said that the party had made "mistakes" in its relations with the church. In May 1988, the government announced that the Russian Orthodox Church had been granted permission to build a cathedral in Moscow, the first new church in the capital in more than 30 years. In October 1988, the newly appointed Roman Catholic primate of Lithuania conducted the first mass in the republic's capital in 40 years.

More recently, Soviet Jews were permitted to open their first rabbinical school in 60 years.

Religious freedom is just one aspect of the broader issue of human rights. Although the Soviet constitution guarantees fundamental liberties, the Kremlin's use of repression to control the populace is well documented. Western leaders repeatedly raised the rights in their meetings with Gorbachev, and the pressure has achieved results. Even the most vociferous critics of the Soviet system now concede that there has been substantial progress since he came to power.

In one of his first gestures of good faith, the general secretary in 1986 freed from internal exile two of the country's most famous dissidents—Nobel Prize-winning physicist Andrei D. Sakharov and his wife, Dr. Elena G. Bonner. Imprisoned Jewish activist Anatoly B. Shcharansky was set free in an East-West prisoner exchange the same year. In 1987, the government pardoned 140 jailed dissidents, the largest single release since the 1950s. Many more dissident were freed in the 1988-89 period, and there were encouraging gains in the emigration of Soviet Jews, including such prominent "refuseniks" as Iosif Z. Begun, Naum Meiman and Aleksandr Lerner.

After considerable wrangling, the U.S. in January 1989 dropped its objection to a Soviet proposal that Moscow host an international human-rights conference in 1991. The idea of holding such a conference in the Soviet Union would have been virtually unthinkable before the Gorbachev era.

Jackson Confronts Gorbachev; Maneuver Draws Criticism

The Rev. Jesse L. Jackson, a U.S. civil rights leader and presidential aspirant, had an impromptu discussion with Soviet leader Mikhail S. Gorbachev in Geneva Nov. 19, 1985. (See pp. 94-97.) Jackson had come to Geneva as the head of a contingent of U.S. peace activists. They brought petitions, signed by more than one million Americans, urging the U.S. and Soviet Union to halt nuclear weapons tests.

The encounter between Jackson and Gorbachev took place in the crowded lobby of the Soviet mission when the Soviet leader returned from his first meeting with U.S. President Ronald Reagan. The two men stood close together and talked for about 45 minutes. Gorbachev smiled throughout the confrontation and politely responded to Jackson through an interpreter.

Jackson raised the peace issue, but soon focused on the subject of Soviet Jewry. Jackson told Gorbachev that there was "great anxiety among the American people about the plight of Soviet Jews." Gorbachev responded: "We would like to say that Jews are part of the Soviet people. They contribute a lot to the development of our country. They are very talented people." He added: "Therefore the so-called problem of Jews in Soviet Union does not exist."

Following the discussion, Jackson told reporters that Gorbachev's response on the Jewish issue was "not adequate. He recognized no problem."

Reagan aides were reported to have privately denounced Jackson's intervention as a blatantly political move, noting that Jackson had come under fire from American Jews during his 1984 presidential campaign.

The Dispatch

Columbus, OH, November 21, 1985

The Rev. Jesse Jackson's performance at Geneva will do nothing to advance world peace and human rights. Indeed, it will impede progress in these areas and compromise the position of his country in the vital talks between President Reagan and Soviet leader Mikhail Gorbachev.

Jackson has every right to say what he wants and to be exploited by any foreign government he wishes. But there is no justification for him to trample on the hopes of people everywhere for a safer world, to stomp on the dreams of Jews in the Soviet Union, freedom-loving people in Poland, Afghanistan and elsewhere.

Anyone who watched the tapes of the 40-minute meeting between Jackson and Gorbachev Tuesday could see that the Soviet leader knew that Jackson was a pawn to be used to serve the Kremlin's own ends. Gorbachev could use the film of the encounter as propaganda in Third World countries around the world as "proof" that the American people are divided on foreign policy and that the government does not enjoy the support of its citizens. They won't get the message from Soviet manipulators that dissent is what makes America strong.

But there is a time for dissent and there is a time to put forth a unified front — to rally behind the president as this nation's representative in foreign affairs. The summit is one such time for unity, but Jackson saw only an opportunity for self-aggrandizement.

The consequence of Jackson's performance is contempt from his countrymen and from all of those around the world looking to Reagan to confront Gorbachev with evidence of Soviet aggression and human rights abuses.

But Jackson gave Gorbachev the opportunity — before all the world — to be patronizing on one of the most sensitive issues at the summit: the plight of Soviet Jews.

In response to Jackson's request that he discuss that issue, Gorbachev said, "Jews are a part of the Soviet people. They are fine people. They contribute a lot to disarmament. They are very talented people, and they are very valued in the Soviet Union.

"The problem — the so-called problem — in the Soviet Union does not exist. Perhaps this problem only exists with those who would like to mar the relations with us, who cast their doubts and aspersions."

A superpower summit is not a three-ring circus. It is serious business — a meeting of the two most powerful men on Earth trying to find ways to reduce the threat of nuclear war and to live together in peace. Good things can come from a summit, but they will come from the meeting of the minds of the men who lead their countries and from the forged understanding between governments.

The News and Courier

Charleston, SC, November 22, 1985

The leaders of the world's two superpowers, Ronald Reagan and Mikhail Gorbachev, met for their first personal confrontation this week in Geneva. With the one exception — an official welcoming ceremony hosted by the president of Switzerland — the two men neither met publicly nor talked with anybody not working for the media or in their personal entourage. That was as it should be since all Americans stood behind their leader knowing one voice would speak for all.

That was true until the Rev. Jesse Jackson entered the scene and was granted a 45-minute meeting with Gorbachev during a break in the summit talks. Accompanied by a delegation of peace activists, Jackson delivered a petition with supposedly more than one million signatures calling for an end to the arms race. The civil rights leader also raised questions about the Soviet Union's human rights record. He had the gall to defend his third-man mission to the two-man summit meeting on the grounds that he had a "right to be here, as well as a moral imperative."

Well, thanks to the news blackout on Tuesday agreed to by both powers, the international media had a break from interviewing each other and had a field day with the Jackson encounter, quoting his impressions that Gorbachev "did not flinch," "responded in kind" and displayed a "kind of openness that was impressive," — all very generous descriptions of the man who heads up one of the most repressive governments in the history of the world.

Why did the Soviet Secretary General — an acknowledged practitioner of media manipulation — spare so much time of his already tight schedule on an open meeting with Jackson, with the media present? One need only have seen the play given to the encounter by Soviet television for its home audience comsumption. Every minute was milked to give the impression to Soviet citizens that black and other minority Americans somehow felt they had to send their own representative to the summit because they failed to trust the nation's elected leader to accurately describe their positions on issues.

Of course, that's not true and Jesse Jackson was the first to say he was not "challenging the president." But that's the perception received in countries where the state controls the media and such perceptions are quite often passed on as truths. Jackson didn't accomplish anything positive for the causes he espoused as far as the Soviets are concerned. It's difficult to estimate the damage to America's reputation he contributed by thrusting himself on the scene.

The Providence Journal

Providence, RI, November 21, 1985

The tangible results of the summit in Geneva (however they are defined) remain to be measured. President Reagan and Mikhail Gorbachev may have been anticipating only meager results when they posted a news blackout on substantive information about the talks until after they are over.

But the news blackout had no deterrent effect on the Rev. Jesse Jackson, who surprised almost everyone by materializing in Geneva on Tuesday morning. Mr. Jackson's 45-minute chat with Mr. Gorbachev, conducted in a crowded lobby of the Soviet mission, turned out to be relatively benign, merely contributing to an impression that the Soviet leader was beating Mr. Reagan in the realm of public relations. Mr. Jackson even insisted that his presence should

not be construed as anything but support for the President.

Well and good. But it could have been worse. The Reagan summit staff had denied Mr. Jackson's request for a meeting with the President. If Mr. Jackson had not responded to this as responsibly as in fact he did, the apparent superpower thaw could have been upset. If Mr. Reagan's staff had been confronted by a media barrage over the matter, things could have been even worse.

Yet while Mr. Jackson behaved responsibly in the spotlight, his decision to put himself in this spotlight at this time was the height of irresponsibility. He talked about significant issues, presenting a petition of Americans in support of a nuclear freeze, and urging Mr. Gorbachev to

ease up on Soviet Jewry. But it was unecessary — and, for an outsider, quite inappropriate — to raise those issues under those delicate conditions. It was not worth the risk of tripping the two most powerful men in the world as they danced their delicate *pas de deux*.

Whether Mr. Jackson's meeting with the Soviet leader was a public relations coup for Mr. Gorbachev is debatable. It could not but reflect poorly upon the Soviet system that the U.S. system can produce a respected black candidate for the American presidency who vigorously disputes most policies of the current President. If there were a Soviet version of Mr. Jackson, he would be clinking chains in Siberia, or under house arrest in, say, Gorki.

THE DENVER POST

Denver, CO,
November 21, 1985

THE REV. Jesse Jackson's ego has taken him on another excursion, this time to the Geneva summit where he served as a useful propaganda prop for Soviet Premier Mikhail Gorbachev.

Jackson insinuated himself as the spokesman for a legitimate cause — nuclear disarmament — into a setting in which Gorbachev could be portrayed as embracing that goal while President Reagan stood opposed. Predictably, Soviet television played the scene as the black U.S. religious figure and unsuccessful candidate for the 1984 Democratic presidential nomination in solidarity with Gorbachev against the warlike intransigence of the U.S. president.

Jackson's relentless pursuit of the spotlight in this critical moment of U.S.-Soviet relations damaged both his country and the cause of peace. It encouraged the perception — fed by the Soviets — that Jackson speaks for the American people in their honest desires for peace and Reagan does not.

As if to reinforce that perception, Jackson told reporters, after presenting Gorbachev with petitions containing more than 1 million U.S. signatures on behalf of a nuclear test ban, that the Soviet leader "made it clear that his business is disarmament."

Jackson should remember that he was not elected to speak for America or to serve as the U.S. interpreter of Soviet intentions. Ronald Reagan was elected president, and only he can represent us at Geneva. Nothing, not even Jackson's gigantic ego, should diminish or confuse Reagan's responsibility — for either the Soviet or the American peoples.

THE RICHMOND NEWS LEADER

Richmond, VA, November 20, 1985

The Summit has brought the world's press to Geneva, and the press attracts activists of all stripes.

One such: Jesse Jackson, seemingly ever on the road to Damascus.

Jackson was lucky. Yesterday he enjoyed a 45-minute chat with Boss Gorbachev.

Afterwards Jackson said:

"On the question of Soviet Jews, his answer was not adequate to us. He recognized no problem."

Did the intrusively ubiquitous Jackson seriously expect anything else — other than attention from the press?

Top Jewish Dissidents Given Exit Visas

Moscow Dec. 30, 1985 denied reports that it was negotiating an agreement with Israel for the increased emigration of Soviet Jews. Edgar Bronfman, head of the World Jewish Congress, claimed to have held secret discussions with Soviet officials during trips to Moscow in September and December, and with Polish officials in Warsaw in December. Israeli officials Dec. 23 had stated that Bronfman was acting as an intermediary between Jerusalem and Moscow on behalf of a proposal to airlift Soviet Jews to Israel via Poland. However, the officials indicated that there had been no progress in the talks.

The Soviet government Dec. 21, 1987 informed Aleksandr Lerner, a leading "refusnik" (persons, mainly Jews, who had been denied permission to emigrate), that he could leave the country. Lerner, a 74-year-old cyberneticist, had been attempting to emigrate for 17 years. Lerner was one of several famous refuseniks/dissidents granted exit visas during the year. Western analysts attributed the liberalized emigration policy to a Kremlin attempt to improve its human-rights image and rid itself of persons regarded as troublemakers. As of Dec. 21, Moscow had provided no firm count on Jewish emigration in 1987, but Western observers believed the figure would top 8,000, a substantial increase over previous years.

Naum Meiman, a Jewish mathematician, had received permission to emigrate to Israel, it was reported Jan. 23, 1988. Meiman, 76, had been seeking to emigrate for 12 years. He had repeatedly been denied an exit visa on the ground that he held state secrets. Two other Jewish dissidents, Iosif Z. Begun and Aleksandr Lerner, left the U.S.S.R. for Israel in 1987. Begun and six family members left Jan. 18. Lerner and three family members left Jan. 24.

THE RICHMOND NEWS LEADER
Richmond, VA,
May 14, 1985

A student relying on Soviet sources for information about World War II would read about the liberation of the concentration camps. He would *not* read that the victims of the Holocaust were Jews.

The Soviet newspaper *Izvestia* recently ran a front-page story about the camps. It never mentioned the Jews. The reason is simple. The USSR is anti-Semitic, and telling the truth about the Holocaust might arouse sympathy for Jews.

Dimitri Simes of the Carnegie Endowment for International Peace — a group hardly known as a Red-baiting outfit — writes in *The Christian Science Monitor*:

"Nor does the Politburo ever talk about the Soviets' own anti-Semitic campaign shortly after the war. Thousands upon thousands of Jews were arrested on fabricated charges of Zionist activity, spying for the United States, and plotting against Joseph Stalin. Many more were fired from their jobs, denied college admission, and harassed.

"Stalin was planning his own 'final solution' for the Jews. Anti-Semitic mobs encouraged by the authorities were supposed to proceed with pogroms. Several leading Jewish personalities were already asked to sign a petition to Stalin 'apologizing' for Zionist crimes but still begging him to protect Jews from the 'anger of the people.' Stalin intended to oblige. All Jews would be expelled to concentration camps and exiled in harsh areas to the east of the Urals."

Stalin's death intervened. But although the Communists have not exterminated the USSR's Jews, government-sanctioned anti-Jewish persecution persists. As Simes observes, a Catch-22 confronts Soviet Jews. The USSR forbids assimilation. It also forbids the observance of Jewish customs. Jews are denied entry to the political elite. They also are generally prevented from emigrating to Israel. Some Jews do emigrate, of course — but not nearly so many as would like to leave.

The USSR tried to score propaganda points off President Reagan's ill-chosen visit to a German military cemetery. "The other day the same *Izvestia* that fails to acknowledge the Holocaust went so far as to use the occasion of the Bitburg controversy to compare Ronald Reagan to Adolf Hitler," writes Simes. "The concept of shame seems to be alien to the Soviet propaganda writers." Shame is indeed alien to the Soviets. But anti-Semitism is not.

The Wichita
Eagle-Beacon
Wichita, KS, September 16, 1985

SOVIET leader Mikhail Gorbachev — Mr. Congeniality to some — is continuing the hard line against Soviet Jews begun by his predecessor, Yuri Andropov. The High Holy Days of the Jewish religion, beginning today with Rosh Hashanah, is a good time to remember that behind the new leader's smiles, the harassment and oppression continue. President Reagan should insist on improvements in Soviet human rights — especially the treatment of Soviet Jews — when he meets Mr. Gorbachev in Geneva.

U.S. Jewish groups monitoring the situation say the oppression, if anything, has worsened under Mr. Gorbachev's regime. Of the Jews currently in Soviet jails for practicing their faith, 30 percent were arrested this year. Jewish emigration has all but come to a halt in recent years. In 1984, more than 350,000 Jews requested emigration papers — only 896 were allowed to leave the country. So far this year, 702 people of Jewish faith have been permitted to leave. These figures represent a trickle compared to the 50,000 Jews the Soviets allowed to leave in 1979.

Jews aren't the only religious group being persecuted. Vladimir Khailo, an evangelical Baptist in the Ukraine, has been interred in psychiatric hospitals since 1980 for his faith and his efforts to emigrate with his family. He is not alone.

Not only does the oppression of religious groups violate the Helsinki human rights accords — which the Soviet Union signed — it violates the 1975 Jackson-Vanik amendment, which prohibits export credits to nations that refuse to let citizens emigrate. Mr. Reagan should make clear to Mr. Gorbachev that the harsh treatment of Jews and other political and religious dissidents simply won't be tolerated.

The fundamental importance of human rights mustn't be lost in the debate over arms control and the "big issues." Indeed, the Soviets' credibility as a negotiating partner is related directly to their adherence to past human rights accords. In Geneva, the U.S. message should be clear: Soviet Jews won't be forgotten.

The News American

Baltimore, MD, July 7, 1985

Not all of the news from the Soviet Union last week was welcome. The prospect of a working summit conference between President Reagan and Soviet party leader Mikhail Gorbachev is overdue and is a sign that the leaders of the strongest nations on earth are at last coming to their senses. But reports also reached the West of yet another round in the persecution of Soviet Jews. If ever there was a factor that truly distinguishes the United States and the Soviet Union it is the matter of religious freedom. It is something we protect and cherish, and in the Soviet Union religious freedom does not exist.

Leonid Volvovsky is 43, a computer scientist, married with one child. Eleven years ago, Volvovsky had the temerity to ask Soviet officials if he might leave the country. He was refused. Seven years ago, he was exiled to Gorky, the city shrouded in a cloak of secrecy. On June 25, he was arrested and jailed, and police ransacked the homes of students in his Hebrew classes.

Though the specific charges against Volvovsky haven't been revealed, it's known that he worships a God in a nation that allows only the worship of the state. He teaches Hebrew in a nation where teachers of Hebrew are harassed and jailed. And he encourages others to practice their faith in a nation where religion and faith are barely tolerated.

Volvovsky was the third Soviet Jewish activist to be arrested in the month of June and the sixth since the start of the year. It is a dismal trend, reflecting a paranoic and zealous Soviet repression that has forcibly detained some 250,000 people seeking to leave the country, separating parents, children, siblings and spouses — including at least a dozen Americans married to Soviets.

We have been honoring the declaration of this nation's independence these past few days and celebrating the freedoms we cherish. The celebration of freedom is a time to share hope and to remember those like Volvovsky who have only the dream of freedom.

There is a small way to remember people like Volvovsky and to bring pressure on the Soviet authorities who persist in their misguided oppression. It is called Operation Hope. *The News American,* with the help of the Baltimore Jewish Council, has been publishing lists of prisoners and their mailing addresses, and does so again today on the Letters/Opinion page. Sadly, it is an incomplete list that keeps growing — in all parts of the world.

We are encouraging Baltimoreans to write to these religious prisoners. They are people who are being punished for practicing their religious beliefs, not merely for opposing the governments in their home nations.

Volvosky is of primary concern this week. His address is Krylova 14-115, Gorky, RSFSR, USSR. But there are many more. In the name of the freedom we celebrate, join Operation Hope. Pick up a pen or pencil or sit down at the typewriter or computer keyboard and share your thoughts. It is a small way of extending a lifeline where there is no hope and of offering a ray of light in a land of darkness.

DAYTON DAILY NEWS

Dayton, OH, June 6, 1985

Gilbert Martin, respected biographer of Winston Churchill, spent some time in Russia among Jews in 1983 and now has written a book about that experience (*The Jews of Hope).* He reports that things are bad and getting worse.

At the heart of the problem is the desire of many Jews to get out of the Soviet Union. The government has cracked down. In 1979, 50,000 Jews were allowed to leave, whereas in 1984 only 1,000 were, though countless thousands still want to.

Why won't the Russians let them go? Apparently because the state doesn't want other minority groups getting any ideas, which they were starting to as Jewish immigration soared in the 1970s. Christian groups, Moslems and others also want greater freedom to worship and are suffering at Soviet hands.

People with good jobs who express a desire to leave lose their jobs immediately and have to take menial ones, while their applications pend for years at a time. You can't get out until the authorities check with all your relatives; if one relative wants you to stay, you stay. And if a relative gives permission for you to go, that relative is in trouble with the state.

It's not just the would-be emigrants who are coming under government harassment. It's Jews in general. More and more, anti-Semitic lies are appearing in the Soviet press. One popular "journalist" is writing that the Holocaust was a Zionist plot designed to result in the creation of the state of Israel.

The Soviet Union does not appear to be a society that is mellowing or evolving.

Newsday

Long Island, NY, April 8, 1985

For those disposed to read tea leaves, there's a hint from Moscow of possible improvement in the Soviet human rights situation: Dozens of Soviet Jews — including many who have been awaiting permission to emigrate for years — have been notified by the authorities to reapply for visas to leave the country. That usually means the applicants are going to get their exit permits.

At the same time, Israeli radio reported that about 1,000 Soviet Jews would be allowed to emigrate soon. Only 896 were permitted to leave the Soviet Union during all of 1984. By comparison, 51,000 were given exit visas in 1979, when relations between Washington and Moscow were cordial.

It's still too early to hail the easing of Soviet emigration restrictions. But conditions appear encouraging.

For one thing, the Soviets have tended to permit more Jews to emigrate whenever the Kremlin wanted to improve relations with the United States. Right now, Moscow may well be trying to smooth the road to a summit meeting between President Ronald Reagan and Soviet leader Mikhail Gorbachev.

Furthermore, rising emigration has reflected Moscow's desire for increased trade with this country.

During a recent meeting in Moscow, an American official was told by the head of the Soviet State Bank that 50,000 Soviet Jews could be given exit visas if U.S.-Soviet trade relations improved. For its part, Washington has repeatedly made it clear that any easing of U.S. trade restrictions would depend at least to some extent on looser Soviet constraints on emigration.

Jewish emigration has been a fairly reliable gauge of the general level of repression in the Soviet Union. So some readers of Soviet tea leaves might be tempted to rush to the conclusion, based on the recent emigration reports, that the new Kremlin leadership is likely to adopt a less repressive style than its predecessors.

That's premature, of course. But who knows? Maybe British Prime Minister Margaret Thatcher was right when she said that Gorbachev was someone she could do business with.

⒪maha Ⓦorld-Ⓗerald

Omaha, NE,
August 22, 1988

When the Soviet Union opens its long-hidden files on the Nazi concentration camps, it will add an immeasurable amount of knowledge and perspective to the historical accounts of that terrible era. Those who study Hitler's persecution of the Jews and other ethnic groups appear to have glasnost to thank for this new information.

Experts at the U.S. Holocaust Memorial Council estimate that 30 to 40 percent of all the material about the Holocaust is in the Soviet Union, including Nazi documents, photographs and other records captured by Soviet troops at the end of World War II in Eastern Europe. Until now the material has been restricted, and most of it has never been seen by scholars or Nazi-hunting investigators. The Soviets have provided specific documents on request but have never before thrown open their files to outsiders.

It was a Nazi identity card provided by the Soviets from their extensive files that proved a key piece of evidence in convicting John Demjanjuk, a former Cleveland autoworker, of war crimes perpetrated when he was a concentration camp guard. He was sentenced to death by an Israeli court in April.

The Holocaust Council, which arranged the agreement with the Soviets, will be allowed to copy what could be several million documents for its planned U.S. Holocaust Memorial Museum, expected to open in 1991. The materials are scattered among dozens of archives in the Soviet Union. The council also hopes to borrow original documents to display in its museum.

The Soviet collection is a repository of horror, one that is likely to be sorted through and pored over by scholars, investigators and experts for many years to come. This gift of glasnost is a welcome one.

THE ARIZONA REPUBLIC

Phoenix, AZ, April 13, 1988

I T doesn't take a chemist to know that you can catch more flies with sugar than vinegar. Shrewd diplomats know it probably better than anybody.

Take Soviet General Secretary Mikhail Gorbachev, for example, who's sharp as a tack in the ways of diplomacy.

As even a casual student of the Soviet Union knows, Moscow never has been particularly fond of Israel or the Jewish people. Jews in Russia have had a rather rough time of it, and it's been only in recent years that they've been allowed to leave the country in any numbers.

The situation got so bad that Soviet Jews became known as "refuseniks" because of Moscow's hard-line policy of refusing them permission to emigrate.

Along with that, the Soviets have been a principal supporter of the Palestine Liberation Organization, which dislikes Israel to the point of denying its existence.

So what do we hear coming from within the walls of the Kremlin? Not what one might expect, given the historical backdrop.

According to a report in the Communist Party newspaper *Pravda,* Gorbachev has urged Palestinian leader Yasser Arafat to recognize Israel's right to exist as an important step in achieving peace in the Middle East.

"The Palestinians are a people with a difficult fate," Gorbachev told Arafat during a meeting in Moscow. "But they receive broad international support, and this is the guarantee for resolving the main question for the Palestinians — self-determination."

Some diplomats view Gorbachev's remarks as signaling a further evolution in the Soviet Union's position on the Mideast, showing greater flexibility toward Israel and a desire to steer Palestinian leaders away from armed struggle and toward a negotiated settlement.

There's no denying that since Gorbachev came to power Moscow has indeed softened its stance toward Jerusalem. Informal meetings between the two countries even suggest a move toward restoring the diplomatic ties that were broken after the 1967 Six-Day War.

Moreover, Gorbachev has been talking like an uncle to Syrian President Hafez Assad, telling the leader of the Soviet client state that it was "abnormal" for Syria not to have relations with Israel. Heretofore, the Kremlin fomented Syrian aggression against Israel.

Gorbachev's sugar-coated comments clearly were not intended for Arafat's consumption only. For one thing, Arafat already favors a negotiated settlement; for another, he heads only one faction of the PLO.

It's the radical groups that Gorbachev needs to convince, and they're very much addicted to vinegar. A lot depends on the influence Arafat can muster, and the sincerity of what has been called Gorbachev's "new political thinking."

Phoenix, AZ, May 20, 1988

D ON'T by fooled by Mikhail Gorbachev's official title as general secretary of the Communist Party. The Soviet leader actually is a highly gifted artist who is in the process of painting a Rubens-esque portrait of Mother Russia.

Gorbachev wants the world to view Moscow through rose-colored *glasnost.* How else to explain the rapid rise in the emigration of Jews from the Soviet Union in recent days?

Until last year, the number of Jews permitted to leave the country was severely limited. After peaking at a high of 51,320 in 1979, emigrations declined sharply and steadily, hitting a low of fewer than 1,000 in 1986.

Then came Gorbachev's introduction of changes intended to foster a climate of openness. The total of emigrants grew to 8,011 in 1987, with indications that the number would continue climbing.

Last month more than 1,000 Jews received permission to leave Russia. April emigration, which the New York-based National Conference on Soviet Jewery said numbered 1,086, was the highest monthly total since May 1981 when 1,141 departed. If the current trend continues, May 1988 could top that. What goes on here?

It's no mystery. The why and wherefore really is fairly simple. Later this month President Reagan will be meeting with Gorbachev in Moscow on a wide-ranging agenda of arms control, regional conflicts, bilateral relations and human rights.

The Soviets are anxious to be seen in a favorable light, hence the extra effort to make moves designed to counter longstanding criticism from the West.

The Soviets' withdrawal from Afghanistan is seen as another example of the Kremlin's bid to ease tensions with the United States and other Western countries. Along with concluding that he had little choice but to cut his losses, a clever Gorbachev timed the withdrawal to begin just two weeks before Reagan was scheduled to land in Moscow.

Western sources estimate that more than 400,000 of the Soviet Union's 1.8 million Jews want to emigrate. The Kremlin discounts that figure, saying the figure is closer to 15,000.

Quibbling over numbers is academic. Whether 15,000 or 400,000, the point is there are a great many Soviet Jews who would love to be gone from Russia. The sooner the Soviets accomodate them, the more believable the image that Gorbachev is trying to portray will become.

The Atlanta Journal
THE ATLANTA CONSTITUTION
Atlanta, GA, June 2, 1988

It is a new era. On that, we have the testimony of no less than Ronald Reagan and Mikhail Gorbachev.

The "evil empire" to which he had often alluded early in his presidency was, as Reagan pointed out Tuesday (in, of all places, Red Square), of "another time, another era."

Indeed, the Soviet general secretary declared Wednesday that "the era of nuclear disarmament has begun."

The first chapter of their new age closed, then, with the signing of the intermediate-range nuclear forces (INF) treaty, the only U.S.-Soviet arms-control accord thus far to reduce weapons on both sides.

The next installment, the one concerning strategic missiles and their nuclear warheads, is a far more difficult one to compose, with fiendishly complex questions of force structure and verification yet to be resolved. Reagan handled the question of a strategic weapons reduction neatly at the summit's close, holding out the hope it might be completed during his remaining months in office but refusing to be locked into a deadline, often an artificial device producing more last-minute stresses or disappointments than genuine results.

In terms of concrete results, it is true that this fourth Reagan-Gorbachev summit, in the main, put finishing touches on important work begun during the two leaders' third meeting. But that limited assessment fails to take into account deep currents of emotion that were tapped in the visiting American president, in the Soviet citizens who saw and heard him and among viewers around the world who were electronic witnesses to this interchange.

Reagan was at his very best while lecturing intellectuals and students at Moscow State University on the virtues (and the utility) of personal liberties and economic freedom. His warmth and sincerity touched many of those who were predisposed to be suspicious of him. (His unfortunate aside concerning American Indians shouldn't detract from the moving impression he made.)

If anything, the president was a trifle too generous in crediting Gorbachev for the progress made in reaching the INF accord. The world and Western Europe in particular mustn't overlook the fact that the treaty is as much a product of his administration's resolve, and Jimmy Carter's preceding it, to undo a lopsided Soviet missile advantage.

But he's right that this is indeed "another era." Just this week brought news of a record number of Soviet Jews permitted to emigrate (a blossoming May development that could wither in June, of course) and also of a new Soviet income tax being reduced, simply because Soviet lawmakers, usually a docile lot, said no, it was too high.

Processes are under way in the Soviet Union that have a momentum that is difficult to resist. The visit of President Reagan and his party, for all the little irritations that arose during the week, gave his newfound friend in the Kremlin a helpful push.

The Pittsburgh PRESS
Pittsburgh, PA, September 22, 1988

Forced to choose between offending the government of Israel and upholding a key principle of U.S. foreign policy, Secretary of State George Shultz made the right decision. Mr. Shultz told a Senate committee that the Reagan administration opposes efforts to make Soviet Jewish emigres settle in Israel against their will.

"We feel that there is a fundamental principle involved in the human rights field, namely the principle of freedom of choice," Mr. Shultz said. "A person who is allowed to emigrate from the Soviet Union should have a freedom of choice as to where to go."

The Gorbachev regime has allowed nearly 18,000 Soviet Jews to leave since the beginning of 1987 — still only a small fraction of those who got out in 1979, the peak year for such emigration.

The great majority of these recent emigrants have chosen to make the United States their permanent home, even though they could become full-fledged citizens of Israel merely by entering that country.

Israeli officials are understandably concerned, for their nation faces a long-term demographic crisis: It is surrounded by hostile Arab lands with higher birth rates. Israel wants to increase its Jewish population by enticing as many of Moscow's refugees as possible.

Enticement, of course, is perfectly acceptable; coercion is not. The Israeli Cabinet stepped over that line several months ago when it decided that most Jews leaving the Soviet Union should travel via Romania rather than Austria.

The significance of this change is that once in Austria, a free country, Soviet emigrants can pick any other free country they like as their next destination. In Romania they would have no choice but to do what that country and Israel require: fly on to Israel.

Fortunately, this new arrangement has still not taken effect — partly because Dutch officials dislike it. The Dutch embassy in Moscow has represented Israeli interests there ever since the Soviets broke diplomatic relations with Israel in 1967.

Refugees should be free to settle in any country that will welcome them. Israel should follow its Dutch and American friends in reaffirming that principle, not eroding it.

THE TENNESSEAN
Nashville, TN, May 24, 1988

THE most gratifying news to welcome President Reagan on his upcoming trip to Moscow is the news of a healthy increase in emigration of Soviet Jews.

In April, more than 1,000 Jews received official permission to emigrate from the Soviet Union, and 1,088 actually left the nation. Those numbers have not been so high since 1981.

There is no way to guess how many of the 1.8 million Soviet Jews want to emigrate since Soviets refuse to release the actual figure. They scoff at the Western estimate of 400,000, saying that the number is closer to 15,000.

The success of Soviet Jewish emigration seems to be in direct proportion to the friendliness of the relationship between that nation and this one. In 1979, more than 51,000 Soviet Jews were allowed to emigrate, but the number fell to about 20,000 in 1980, and 10,000 in 1981. Only about 1,000 were allowed to emigrate each year from 1982-1986.

Last year, the United States put the plight of Soviet Jewry high on its pre-summit agenda and the numbers started to come up with a total of 8,000 Soviet Jews emigrating in 1987.

Just prior to last year's Washington summit, the Soviet Union released some of its most prominent Jews, including Ms. Ida Nudel and Mr. Vladimir Slepak. The freedom of these and other refuseniks was cause for great celebration — but there was still concern that the Soviets were releasing well-known dissidents to quieten the clamor in this nation for more lenient emigration laws and more religous freedom for Soviet Jews.

Although the news of increased emigration of Soviet Jews is good, it should not be met in the United States with satisfaction, but with resolve. Many Soviet Jews want to emigrate. Many others want exit visas in order to temporarily leave the nation. And many Soviet Jews have no relatives in other nations, which under current Soviet regulation, makes emigration virtually impossible.

Thousands of individuals in this nation and others have taken up the cause of Soviet Jewry. Still, the Soviet Union responds most directly and most immediately when the issue is raised by the White House. At the Moscow summit, President Reagan should strike a blow for freedom by complimenting the Soviets on the increased numbers, but also telling them that the success of Jewish emigration will be gauged not in the names of the emigrates but in their numbers. ∎

THE PLAIN DEALER

Cleveland, OH, January 23, 1988

Josef Begun's arrival in Israel this week, following his 17-year-old quest to leave the Soviet Union, raises two questions regarding the effectiveness of the Reagan-Gorbachev summit and its impact on human rights. Did the summit improve the chances for refuseniks to leave? To what extent?

The Jewish activist's release from Soviet prison last February was part of a celebrated pre-summit plan by the Kremlin to improve Soviet relations with the West and let the world witness its changing approach to human rights. Demonstrations in the United States and by Begun's family and friends in the Soviet Union had kept an international focus on the the plight of the refuseniks. While Begun was still awaiting clearance to emigrate to Israel, the United States pledged to keep human rights at the head of the agenda in September talks between Secretary of State George P. Shultz and Soviet Foreign Minister Eduard A. Shevardnadze. Reagan also pledged the same in his talks with Gorbachev. But upon the conclusion of the December summit, only one line about human rights was written in the joint statement of Reagan and

Gorbachev. The sentence said the matter had been discussed thoroughly and candidly.

Reagan repeatedly has said that U.S. pressure and discussions on the issue had increased the numbers of exit visas. Relatively speaking, the Soviet emigration policy has improved. In 1986 only 914 Jews were allowed to leave. In 1987, 5,000 were given permission to emigrate. But that is less than half of the 11,000 the Soviet Union had promised to free last year, Jewish leaders say. In reality, Soviet emigration policy has been much more lenient, even when U.S. and Soviet leaders were on far more hostile terms. Between 1971 and 1981, 280,000 Jews were permitted to leave, an average of 28,000 each year.

The number of Soviet Jews still wishing to emigrate is about 400,000, according to former refuseniks. It is doubtful that the Summit talks will help free those activists any sooner than the Soviets have scheduled. Nonetheless, the fact that human rights have advanced to high-level discussions is a sign of hope. The Soviets' changing approach is just that—changing. What should remain constant are the efforts by Western nations to keep the pressure on the Kremlin.

San Francisco Chronicle

San Francisco, CA, July 27, 1988

THE OPENING of a small Israeli consulate in Moscow tomorrow marks a preliminary but significant advance toward a full resumption of diplomatic relations that can mean important benefits for both Israel and the USSR.

Six Israeli officials in Moscow have been issued only two-month visas, but it is expected that the documents will be extended repeatedly as has been the case for a similar group of Soviet diplomats who have been stationed in Israel for the past year. Out of concern for possible Arab resentment, the Soviet mission has operated quietly while evaluating Soviet property left behind when the two countries broke off ties during the 1967 Mideast war.

A consulate in Moscow will provide Israel with an opportunity to negotiate an expanded emigration of Russian Jews while sending notice to the world that Israel is achieving an international stature on a par with more venerable nations.

CONVERSELY, closer relations with Israel would fulfill an aim of Soviet leader Mikhail Gorbachev and bring the Soviet Union nearer to participation in any international peace conference on the Middle East. The establishment of a permanent Israeli presence in Moscow is a diplomatic initiative that can clearly serve the interests of both countries.

The Evening Gazette

Worcester, MA, November 3, 1988

A plan to force Jewish emigrants from the Soviet Union to settle in Israel has foundered for the time being, much to the relief of some American Jews and United States officials. Impediments to the plan were set up by the Netherlands, whose embassy in Moscow processes visas for Israel.

This is a thorny issue that begs for a solution soon.

Israel wanted the 2,000 Jews now leaving the Soviet Union each month to depart through Romania directly to Israel. Israel grants the visas guaranteeing the emigrants residence, upon which, in turn, the Soviet Union gives exit permits. Once the emigrants reach the West, however, they have been choosing where they want to go, and many opt for the United States.

If the emigrants go to Israel, under the Law of the Return they become Israeli citizens upon arrival. That changes their status as far as the United States is concerned: There is a quota for Israeli citizens with a wait of several years to emigrate to the United States. For Soviet Jews fleeing oppression, there is no quota in most Western countries.

The United States stands by the Helsinki Accords on freedom of choice for emigrants. Eleven American Jewish organizations had tentatively supported the Israeli proposal to require Soviet emigrants with Israeli papers to go to the Israel — but only if the Soviets would allow the American embassy to give visas to Jews also.

That option is still being negotiated, but the Soviets have been reluctant to grant exit visas to the United States for anybody. Their official justification for issuing permits to Soviet Jews is that those emigrants are going to the Jewish homeland.

The Netherlands government has handled Israel's diplomatic business since the 1967 Mideast war when Israeli-Soviet relations ceased. The Hague apparently agrees with the United States on freedom of choice and has refused to do the consular work to force the Soviet Jews to Israel.

It is understandable that Israel fears the dispersion of potential citizens and wants the Soviet Jews to settle in the homeland. But the hard line that the emigrants must go to Israel — or stay in the Soviet Union — is difficult for Americans to accept.

Perhaps when both the Israeli and U.S. elections are over, the two governments could review the problem and find a compromise.

Birmingham Post-Herald

Birmingham, AL, July 29, 1988

Mikhail Gorbachev's steps toward open political debate would be more impressive if his spokesmen would stop telling impudent lies about issues such as human rights. For example, Soviet Foreign Minister Eduard Shevardnadze told Israeli Premier Yitzhak Shamir at their recent meeting in New York that Moscow places no obstacles in the path of Soviet Jews who wish to leave the country.

The only "constraint," said Shevardnadze, is on Jews who possess "military secrets" and whose emigration would therefore threaten Soviet security.

If this were true, the proportion of Soviet Jews with access to classified information would be the highest of all ethnic groups in the Soviet Union. Hundreds of thousands of Jews wish to emigrate, but Gorbachev has been letting them go at a rate of only about 10,000 a year — roughly one-fifth the rate allowed by Leonid Brezhnev in the late 1970s.

The Hartford Courant

Hartford, CT, January 23, 1988

Scarcely more than a month after Soviet General Secretary Mikhail S. Gorbachev told NBC anchorman Tom Brokaw that outside agitators were responsible for protests on behalf of Jewish refuseniks, Mr. Gorbachev's government has let Josef Begun go.

Mr. Begun, a tireless champion of open emigration, had struggled 17 years to be allowed to go to Israel. As he left Moscow, he pledged to continue to fight. "We will not forget those we are leaving behind," he said. "That's the most important thing — not to forget."

What to make of Mr. Begun's liberation, coming so soon after Mr. Gorbachev's outrageous pre-summit denial that Soviet Jews suffer?

Clearly, the refusenik question continues to haunt the Kremlin — an irritant, from Moscow's point of view, that won't go away. Mr. Gorbachev and his colleagues understand that winning agreements and improved relations with the West will be more difficult so long as they detain Soviet Jews wishing to emigrate.

Moscow deals with the problem by denying that it exists, all the while acting on it. As a result, the pace of Jewish emigration from the Soviet Union picked up noticeably in the past year.

A blessing though that is, it is no miracle: Western pressure has had its effect. Honor Mr. Begun's courage; applaud the agitators.

The Atlanta Journal
AND
THE ATLANTA CONSTITUTION

Atlanta, GA, March 4, 1988

It won't be clear for some weeks whether the U.S. concessions that Secretary of State George Shultz made in Moscow during his recent visit will produce a breakthrough in negotiations to reduce strategic missiles by 50 percent. But Shultz apparently did carry the day with an ancillary concern — Soviet emigration policy, particularly Jewish emigration.

Foreign Minister Eduard Shevardnadze continues to insist that emigration is an internal matter not subject to negotiations, but he indicated some provisions of the policy are under review, and both U.S. and Soviet officials agree that "misunderstandings" have been cleared up at least for the rest of this year.

U.S officials have been appropriately worried about a new Soviet law that took effect last year and under some interpretations could further restrict the already reduced numbers of Jews and others who have been permitted in recent years to resettle outside the country.

Last year, when the Soviets were trying to get in good odor for a summit between President Reagan General Secretary Mikhail Gorbachev, the Kremlin allowed 8,000 Jews to leave, eight times the previous year's total but still sharply down from the 51,000 high-water mark in 1979.

Kremlin policy counts far more than Soviet law, and with indications from Gorbachev and Shevardnadze that flexibility is the current order, perhaps improvement even beyond last year's total is possible. That would be in the Soviets' own interests on two counts. Soviet performance on emigration, religious freedom and other human rights is one key to the quality of the superpower relationship. And if Moscow wants to become a more important player in Middle East affairs, as it clearly does, increased emigration and religious freedom are necessary to make its activities in the region even remotely acceptable to Israel.

Emigration would allow the Kremlin to unburden itself of manifestly discontened citizens and into the bargain improve its standing internationally. Continued coyness on the point will be doubly self-defeatng.

The Philadelphia Inquirer

Philadelphia, PA, June 20, 1988

During the Moscow summit, a crew of Soviet painters showed up at the apartment building of Jewish refuseniks Tanya and Yuri Zieman to spruce the place up. The crowds soon followed, breaking into the entryway and frightening the poor Ziemans.

It seems that the Reagans had been considering visiting the Ziemans after the couple's 12-year-old daughter appealed to the President for help in leaving the country, something her parents had been trying to do for 11 years. As it turned out, the Reagans never came. A Soviet deputy foreign minister had warned that if the Reagans made the call the Ziemans would never get out.

It appears now that the President's understandable caution did the Ziemans no good. On Wednesday Tanya Zieman learned that her latest appeal has been turned down and that the family cannot reapply until 1992.

What purpose does such stubbornness serve when Mikhail Gorbachev is trying to project a new image of Kremlin civility?

Yuri Zieman, a former computer specialist who has worked as a plumber since applying to emigrate in the late 1970s, was never engaged in top-secret work, and even if he had some inside knowledge it would be outdated by now. Seriously ill with a blood disease Soviet doctors have been unable to treat, he recently contracted hepatitis in a Soviet hospital and nearly died.

Holding hostages like the Ziemans, along with hundreds of other Jewish families, only reinforces the notion that justice is selective in the Soviet Union. The officials who sent the painters to the Ziemans' door would do a far greater service to their country if they sent an exit permit instead.

Soviets Free Shcharansky; Israel Welcomes Dissident

Soviet Jewish dissident Anatoly B. Shcharansky was freed Feb. 11, 1986 in an East-West exchange that involved a total of nine persons either accused or convicted of espionage. The exchange took place on the Gilenicke Bridge between East Germany and West Berlin. Shcharansky, 38, had been convicted in the U.S.S.R. in 1978 of spying for the West. His supporters maintained that he had been targeted by the Kremlin because of his outspoken criticism of Moscow's policies with regard to Jews. His release came after eight years of imprisonment and forced labor. Shcharansky's plight had mobilized Jewish activists and human-rights advocates throughout the world.

Shcharansky was the first of nine prisoners set free. As hundreds of journalists watched, he crossed the bridge – which connects Potsdam and West Berlin – and was warmly greeted by West German authorities and Richard R. Burt, the U.S. ambassador to West Germany. Witnesses described Shcharansky as "fit," "ebullient," and "exhilarated."

In addition to Shcharansky, the Eastern bloc released three others. They were Wolf-Georg Frohn, an East German sentenced as a U.S. spy to life imprisonment in 1981; Dietrich Nistroy, an East German sentenced as a West German spy to life imprisonment in 1985; and Jaroslav Javorsky, a Czechoslovakian-born West German arrested in Czechoslovakia. The West freed five persons. They were: Karl and Hana Koecher, a Czechoslovakian-born couple accused by the U.S. in 1984 of spying for their native country; Yevgeny Zemlykov, a Soviet jailed in West Germany, and Detlef Scharfenoth, an accused East German spy arrested in West Germany in 1985.

Shcharansky flew to Jerusalem Feb. 11, where he was met by his wife, Avital, Israeli Prime Minister Shimon Peres and a crowd of onlookers, some of whom had been friends and fellow dissidents in the Soviet Union. Avital, an Israeli resident, had campaigned tirelessly around the world to obtain her husband's freedom. They had been apart for 12 years. Saying it was the "happiest day" in his life, Shcharansky told the audience that he would not forget those left in the [labor] camps, in the prisons, who are still in exile or who still continue their struggle for their right to emigrate, for their human rights."

THE SAGINAW NEWS
Saginaw, MI, February 13, 1985

Anatoly Shcharansky is free in Israel, with the Soviet Union's permission — and that is the operative word in this episode.

Shcharansky came to symbolize the plight of many thousands of Soviets, by no means all Jewish, who wish to emigrate. In his persecution for that desire, he also symbolizes what is so deeply wrong, even repulsive, about the system the Soviets tout as a global model, with some success among some people who should know better.

His liberty is welcome, both for its own sake, and for the personal testimony he can submit to the world court, if it is willing to listen and to judge. That's why his release is worth the contorted, sham "spy-exchange" rigmarole the United States and West Germany had to go through to win it.

The case is simply this: In the Soviet Union, wishing to leave risks prison and repression. Public questioning of Kremlin policies can bring a death sentence.

Shcharansky was a member of the Moscow Helsinki Monitoring Group, a tiny clutch of 20 people organized to check Soviet compliance with the human-rights section of those misbegotten accords. He was convicted as a spy. His depar-

ture makes six who have been allowed to emigrate. Two were forced out. Ten are in prison or internal exile. The two others are old and sick.

The record is as dismal with members of similar groups. At least 17 members of the Ukrainian Helsinki committee are in prison; three other activists have died in labor camps recently.

It is such an ordinary thing, going from one country to another. Nor is it necessary to be a "dissident." People cross borders for any number of innocent reasons — marriage, family, opportunity, study. And it is such a simple freedom, the right to speak, to petition. Yet the Kremlin of Gorbachev, like that of his predecessors, cannot tolerate either.

By itself, that should be all anyone needs to know about the roots of the differences between powers who may be equivalent in their military capacities, but assuredly not in their moral claims.

After Shcharansky's release, President Reagan promised to press the Soviets for human rights reforms. Press on, we say. Nothing seems to irritate Moscow more. Nothing draws the lines of the essential conflict — one of conscience — so clearly.

The Times-Picayune
The States-Item
New Orleans, LA, February 13, 1986

The Soviet Union's release of Anatoly Shcharansky was a typical charade that should fool no one. Mr. Shcharansky's release was camouflaged as a spy swap, preserving for the Soviets their fiction that he was an agent of the U.S. Central Intelligence Agency. But the Soviets clearly expect the world to look through that transparent fiction to see the release as a gesture of good will that shows the Soviets are honorable people with whom the world can confidently deal on such matters as arms control and trade.

But the release does not reflect a change in Soviet policy or indicate high principles. It was a purely tactical political move for the Kremlin's own purposes. The Soviets have let other highly publicized dissidents leave, and it has a large supply left in captivity for future use — notably its ace in the hole, Andrei Sakharov.

Soviet leader Mikhail Gorbachev asks understanding in Mr. Sakharov's case: He was in the top circle of Soviet nuclear weapons development and still knows national secrets. But the time may come when some Soviet interest will override protecting old secrets, and Mr. Sakharov, too, may be freed.

Mr. Shcharansky's sins would not be sins most other places in the world. A Jew, he wanted to emigrate to Israel; a citizen, he worked in an organization that monitored Soviet compliance with the Helsinki treaty, which guarantees certain human rights. Both acts in the Soviet Union are considered virtual treason.

Yet Mr. Shcharansky persisted, and for 12 years bravely bore the consequences. In 1974, he was separated from his wife of one day by official insistence that if she did not leave the country at once, her exit visa would be revoked. In 1977, he was charged with spying and spent nine years in prisons and labor camps.

The Shcharanskys are now united in Jerusalem, which Mrs. Shcharansky made her home and her base for a campaign to keep Mr. Shcharansky's case before the court of world opinion. Mr. Shcharansky vows to resume his struggle for those still captive in their own country.

Among these are a brother and a 77-year-old mother. The founder of the Moscow Helsinki Watch group Mr. Shcharansky belonged to is still exiled in Siberia after seven years in a labor camp. Of 20 people who were active in the group, six have been allowed to emigrate, two expelled and 10 sentenced to prison or internal exile. At least 17 members of the Ukrainian Helsinki committee are still in jail. Four have died in labor camps, one by suicide.

The world should not forget these people and the ordinary, non-activist Soviet Jews who would simply like to leave. While Soviet interests are the chief determiner of whether they free their own citizens, those interests can be shaped to some extent by worldwide opinion. Keeping the heat on maintains an incentive to the Kremlin and keeps open the escape route to freedom.

Herald ✦ News
Fall River, MA, February 13, 1986

The release of Anatoly Shcharansky, the Russian dissident, was arranged as part of an east-west prisoner exchange, and like so many similar exchanges took place on a bridge between East and West Berlin.

As expected, Shcharansky was no sooner handed over to United States authorities than he took off by plane for Israel.

Presumably, the full story of his years of imprisonment in Soviet labor camps will be told later.

The exchange is considered the most important of its kind since 1962 when Francis Gary Powers, the U-2 pilot, was swapped for Colonel Rudolf Abel, the Soviet spy.

Shcharkansky was sentenced to 13 years in prison in 1977 on a charge of spying for the United States. He has consistently denied the charge, and no evidence supporting it has ever been produced.

On the other hand Shcharansky had been one of the leaders of the Human Rights movement in Russia and in various efforts to win Jews who wished to emigrate to Israel the right to do so.

In relation to the Human Rights movement, he had been involved with Andrei Sakharov, the Nobel prixe-winning physicist, who now lives in detention in Gorki by government order.

Shcharansky was a computer programmer by profession. It was the Human Rights movement that brought him together with Sakharov, and presumably it was his activities in relation to that movement which led to his arrest and imprisonment.

There is no reason to think he was a spy for this country or any other.

All the same he has been in prisons or labor camps since 1977, and all through that time his family, friends and associates in the Human Rights Movement have clamored for his release.

Why has that release come now?

It may be that it is part of Mikhail Gorbachev's campaign to improve relations with the west.

If so, it can only be welcomed.

Yet the Soviet Union refused to release him except in an exchange for known Soviet spies in American custody. In spite of State Department disclaimers, the fact of the exchange will be used by Russia as substantiation of its original charges against the dissident leader.

Washington's view is "So be it. His release was worth it."

And this will be the view of Americans as a whole.

But it is worth stressing the exchange factor here in the United States lest the whole episode be misconstrued as evidence of simple humanitarianism on the part of Mikhail Gorbachev.

Whatever else it was, it certainly was not that.

Yet whatever its motive, Shcharansky's release has happened, and is worth celebrating for its own sake.

ST. LOUIS POST-DISPATCH
St. Louis, MO, February 12, 1986

It made sense from the Kremlin's viewpoint to be rid of Anatoly Shcharansky, who was sentenced in 1978 to 13 years in prison for being a spy for the U.S. Central Intelligence Agency, as smoothly as possible. That was done when Mr. Shcharansky, a Jewish Russian dissident, was released this week with three West German spies.

This never was a simple East-West spy case. Though Mr. Shcharansky was put away in the gulag, his cause grew larger than life. He came to symbolize the plight of Soviet Jews (and by extension, other minorities) who, acting under the promises of the Helsinki accord on human rights, sought to exercise their right to emigrate.

While the spy swap that immediately followed Mr. Shcharansky's release was standard Cold War chess, what about the issues Mr. Shcharansky came to represent so movingly? By freeing one jailed Jewish dissident whose name has become a cachet in human rights circles of the left and the right, the Soviets released a pressure valve and won short-lived praise. But what about well-documented cases of official anti-Semitism, in which the Soviet state has sought to disrupt, if not destroy, Jewish cultural and religious life? If this is the way non-Russian cultures are treated, then the large Moslem minority in the south of the Soviet Union must be taking note.

There are approximately 2.5 million Jews in the Soviet Union, with 100,000 to 350,000 who wish to emigrate, presumably to Israel. While Mr. Shcharansky is now a free man, emigration of Soviet Jews has dropped from its peak of 51,320 in 1979 (before the Soviet invasion of Afghanistan and when the U.S. Senate's ratification of SALT II was sought) to 1,140 last year. The issue Mr. Shcharansky represented — basic human rights — is not resolved with his freedom.

The Cincinnati Post
TIMES ✦ STAR
Cincinatti, OH, February 12, 1986

After unjustifiably jailing him for nearly nine years, the Soviet Union has released Anatoly Shcharansky, hoping to achieve two things: win praise from naive foreigners for an act of compassion, and convince its own citizens that dissidents are traitors.

Those two goals explain why it leaked word of his release long in advance and insisted on a package deal, trading Shcharansky and three imprisoned Western spies for five Soviet-bloc agents convicted in the West.

The KGB, of course, knows Shcharansky never spied for the West. It brutalized him for something it considers equally offensive: campaigning for human rights.

Shcharansky applied for permission to emigrate to Israel in 1973. When his application was denied, he protested and was fired from his job as a computer programmer. He soon became a leader of the Jewish emigration movement and of the Helsinki Watch group formed to monitor Moscow's compliance—and non-compliance—with its human-rights pledges.

In 1977, Shcharansky became the first major dissident since Stalin's time to be accused of espionage. The authorities kept him in jail for more than a year before bringing him to trial; they then tried him behind closed doors, denying him access to anyone but the KGB. After convicting him on trumped-up charges, they sentenced him to 13 years of imprisonment.

Shcharansky's jailers tried hard to break his spirit. They repeatedly placed him in solitary confinement, confiscated his mail and canceled visits from his family. He suffered eye and heart ailments, and once undertook a 110-day hunger strike. He maintained his innocence even though that resulted in far harsher treatment.

Thanks to Shcharansky's wife, Avital, Moscow never succeeded in sweeping him under the rug. Though forced to emigrate without him just one day after their wedding, she proved as indomitable as he—lobbying American and West European officials, haunting public appearances of Soviet officials in the West and constantly prodding the media.

How much credit do the Soviets deserve for freeing a man who should never have been arrested to begin with? None.

The Miami Herald

Miami, FL,
February 12, 1986

THERE WERE no toasts or trumpet flourishes, no public pronouncements of goodwill. In the gelid stillness of a subzero Berlin morning, the transaction took on the prosaic quality of a real-estate closing. A few formalities, handshakes all around, and Anatoly B. Shcharansky was off to a new land, a new life, a new freedom.

Imprisoned since 1978 on trumped-up charges of espionage, Mr. Shcharansky had become the most prominent symbol of the *refusenik* movement. To the Soviet leadership, he was a constant embarrassment, a reminder of the limits to even the most totalitarian regime's ability to silence its critics. The greater the punishment inflicted on Mr. Shcharansky, the louder his indictment of the Soviet system echoed in the West.

Mr. Shcharansky's release thus may represent nothing more than the Soviet leadership's latest, subtlest attempt to bump its detractors out of the international spotlight. Soviet officials appear to have concluded that their former prisoner will be a smaller liability in the West than in a Soviet labor camp, where he served as a living monument to religious oppression.

Americans err if they view Mr. Shcharansky's liberation as a simple triumph of good over evil. It was that, of course — but only coincidentally. Fundamentally it was a pragmatic, calculated Soviet response to an assessment of their self-interest. Yet it's precisely this sort of cost-benefit analysis that is most likely to impel Soviet leaders in the direction of real emigration reform.

It would be naive to conclude that Mr. Shcharansky's release signals fundamental changes in Soviet leaders' attitude toward the *refuseniks*. For the sad fact is that Jewish emigration from the USSR has dwindled to a trickle in recent years. So while the release of high-profile prisoners such as Mr. Shcharansky is cause for joy, there is no evidence that it portends relief for thousands of lesser-known *refuseniks* who yearn just as fervently for deliverance.

But a Soviet leadership shrewd enough to perceive the extent of Mr. Shcharansky's influence may yet come to understand that *every* prisoner of conscience poses a similar liability. By raising their voices on behalf of those who remain behind, Westerners may help Mikhail Gorbachev conclude that a humanitarian emigration policy is the most cost-effective way to excise this continuing Soviet embarrassment.

The Salt Lake Tribune

Salt Lake City, UT, February 12, 1986

The manner in which the Soviet Union released Russian dissident Anatoly Shcharansky is as significant as the fact that he was actually released. It is less the "good will" gesture than it might first appear.

By most accounts, Kremlin decision-makers set Mr. Shcharansky free in an attempt to eliminate his imprisonment as a constant irritant complicating various Soviet Union diplomatic initiatives. But the compromise method used was, well, compromising.

The prisoner exchange on the Glienicke Bridge, connecting East and West Germany, was of mostly convicted espionage agents, Mr. Shcharansky included. While the United States and his defenders have always denied Mr. Shcharansky had anything to do with espionage, he was tried and convicted eight years ago of working for the Central Intelligence Agency. His custodians may have decided freeing him removed an irritant, but that's not fully possible since they refused to simultaneously admit the trumped-up charges.

A mathematician and computer expert, Anatoly Shcharansky was one of several Russian Jews who, in the 1970s, actively focused attention on human and civil rights violations occurring in the Soviet Union, especially a crack-down on Jews filing for emigration to Israel. The government response was to jail some of the more prominent "refuseniks," usually accusing them, not of political opposition, but of treasonous acts such as spying.

One of these victims, Mr. Shchar-

ansky never stopped denying the phony charges against him, nor did Western world spokesmen who made him and others similarly held in Soviet detention a cause for their complaints against the Kremlin leadership. In fact, during their summit conference last year, President Reagan reportedly suggested to Communist Party chief Mikhail Gorbachev that Mr. Shcharansky be released as a sign of "good will."

Now, that very release has been arranged, with substantial help from West Germany, which held three of the five communist spies given up for the exchange. Considerably more "good will" would have been achieved had the Russians not stuck to their fiction that Mr. Shcharansky was a CIA stooge.

Moreover, if this is but an isolated incident, little diplomatic capital has been earned. If, on the other hand, it actually signals revised Soviet Union policy on Russian Jews leaving for Israel, it could make a difference in Soviet-Israeli relationships, with ripple effects on U.S.-Soviet relations, U.S.-Israeli relations, Soviet-Arab world relations, ad infinitum.

As important would be a Kremlin realization that fraudulently imprisoning detractors as prominent as an Anatoly Shcharansky generates more bad press than such suppression is worth. This is not very likely. Still, for the commutation of Anatoly Shcharansky's sentence to have utmost value in the easing of East-West tension, it will have to be representative of a definite trend, rather than merely a single case of calculated second thoughts.

THE INDIANAPOLIS STAR
*Indianapolis, IN,
February 13, 1986*

Anatoly Shcharansky is free. Eastern Europe is not.

That is the first thing which must be said to keep the "spy swap," the detente fever and the "peace" campaigns in perspective. More Soviet "refuseniks" may get out. Millions will remain prisoners.

The day that Shcharansky gained his release from the imprisonment that is the cost of speaking freely in the USSR, Lech Walesa went to court for speaking freely.

The Polish prosecutor halted a slander action against Walesa, though Walesa refused to retract his estimate of lower voter turnout than was announced in October by authorities. Walesa said he meant to slander no one, and the prosecutor allowed that complaining officials "might" be satisfied they had an apology for the voicing of an opinion that "humiliated" them.

Walesa smiles, and he knows he is dealing with an evil empire. Under his jacket he wears a sweater with the legend, "God and Motherland." The day before his court appearance he declared in an interview, "Only force linked with all kinds of threats keeps the anger of the people under control."

The West can rejoice that dissident Shcharansky is free while recognizing the swap as the diversion that it is, to the Kremlin.

Shcharansky is expendable, but the chains for the millions of others are not. Yet those chains will fall some day.

The San Diego Union
San Diego, CA, February 12, 1986

Clearly, the release of Soviet dissident Anatoly Shcharansky yesterday is cause for rejoicing among his family and friends. It culminates a protracted struggle by Mr. Shcharansky's wife to secure his freedom so he can join her in Israel.

Nevertheless, the circumstances surrounding the Shcharansky case underscore the lengths to which the Kremlin will go to crush domestic dissent and then seek rewards for a brief respite in its brutish behavior.

Nine years ago, Mr. Shcharansky was arrested by KGB agents, convicted of high treason, and sentenced to three years in prison and 10 years in a labor camp. The formal charge was that he was a spy for the CIA. In fact, his so-called crimes consisted of advocating Jewish emigration from the Soviet Union and condemning the Kremlin's human-rights violations.

In making an example of this Jewish activist with a passion for human rights, the Kremlin sent a powerful message to other dissidents who dared to question the Soviet State.

During his imprisonment, Mr. Shcharansky was subjected to countless brutalities including beatings, forced feedings, and the injection of powerful drugs designed to break his body and spirit. Still he refused to submit to his captors and soon became a worldwide symbol of the "Refuseniks" — Soviet Jews denied permission to emigrate.

Mr. Shcharansky's plight proved a continual source of embarrassment to the Soviet Union. When Soviet boss Mikhail Gorbachev visited Paris recently, he was urged by French President Francois Mitterrand to release the ailing Jewish activist. A similar request was made by President Reagan last November when he met with the Soviet leader at Geneva.

Mindful of improving his image and his bargaining power at the forthcoming summit meeting, Mr. Gorbachev consented earlier this month to the release.

Even so, the Soviet Union sought to extract several concessions from the United States. Mr. Shcharansky's release coincided with an exchange of convicted spies, an arrangement demanded by the Soviets to lend credence to their absurd contention that he is an American agent. The Kremlin, moreover, demanded $2 million for his freedom.

To its credit, the Reagan administration refused to pay the ransom and further insisted that Mr. Shcharansky be released ahead of the other prisoners so as to distance him from the spy swap.

Lest anyone mistake the Shcharansky release as a sign of liberalization in the U.S.S.R., it should be noted that thousands of Soviet dissidents are still imprisoned and thousands of Soviet Jews are not permitted to emigrate. That Anatoly Shcharansky was allowed to leave, merely confirms the Soviets' cynical campaign to defuse the human-rights issue.

His release should in no way diminish U.S. pressure on the Soviet Union for an improvement in human rights and a corresponding increase in the overall levels of Jewish emigration. To do anything less would surely mock Mr. Shcharansky's valiant struggle for freedom.

The State
Columbia, SC, February 15, 1986

THE FREEING of political dissident Anatoly Shcharansky by the Soviet Union in a trade of intelligence agents Tuesday set off jubilant celebrations in Israel and was cheered by liberty-loving people around the world. For a dozen years his ordeal has been international news.

The 38-year-old Soviet Jew, a mathematician and computer analyst, led a group who sought to monitor Moscow's compliance with the human rights agreements of the 1975 Helsinki Accords. He was sentenced in 1978 to 13 years at hard labor, charged with being an agent of the Central Intelligence Agency — a charge he and the United States have resolutely denied.

The West handed over spies that could still be valuable to Soviet intelligence for this human rights advocate — clear evidence of the value we put on freedom. Among communist spies we exchanged were Karl F. Koecher, 52, and his wife, Hana, 42. He is the first communist agent caught after working inside the CIA. A Czech, he probably still has information about U.S. intelligence that will be helpful to the KGB.

In the years since his imprisonment, the group of dissidents has been broken up. One of its most prominent figures, Andrei Sakharov, a physicist who developed the hydrogen bomb for the Soviet Union, is still interned in the closed city of Gorki. He was awarded a Nobel Peace Prize for his stand against Soviet repression of civil and human rights.

Of the dissidents, Shcharansky has been an inspiration with a display of remarkable courage in the face of his oppressors. He would pretend not to hear his guard's orders, or deliberately do the opposite of their directions.

Even at the last moments at the Gliennicke Bridge, when he was told by a Soviet KGB official to walk straight across the bridge to the Western side where freedom waited, Shcharansky deliberately walked a zig-zag path to show his contempt.

Within the day he was reunited with his wife, whom he had not seen since the day after their wedding 12 years ago, and was flown to Israel to a hero's welcome. Although his personal ordeal has ended, Shcharansky promptly renewed his campaign for free emigration of Jews from the Soviet Union by calling for the release of his 77-year-old mother and a brother.

Shcharansky's compelling story must be put in a much larger context. While we may rejoice for him and his family, 300,000 others are refused the right to leave the Soviet Union. Not the least among them is Sakharov, whose fate appeared sealed last week in a French newspaper interview with Soviet leader Mikhail Gorbachev.

Gorbachev has declined to discuss Sakharov publicly before, but in the interview with *L'Humanite*, republished in Moscow, he flatly said Sakharov "still has knowledge of secrets of special importance to the state and for this reason cannot go abroad." Diplomatic authorities say that by speaking directly of this case, Gorbachev leaves little hope Sakharov's status will be changed.

Human rights interests around the world must continue to focus attention on Andrei Sakharov as they did on Shcharansky, for such international interest provides a cloak of protection and the warmth of hope.

Sakharov Freed From Exile; Physicist Immediately Speaks Out

The Soviet Union Dec. 19, 1986 announced that dissident Andrei Sakharov and his wife, Dr. Yelena Bonner, had been released from their eternal exile in the city of Gorky. The internal exile of Sakharov had become a worldwide symbol of human-rights abuses in the Soviet Union. The announcement also said that Sakharov, a renowned physicist, would be permitted to resume his work at the Soviet Academy of Sciences.

Sakharov revealed that Soviet leader Mikhail S. Gorbachev had personally informed him of the pardon in a telephone call Dec. 16. Sakharov vowed to continue his human-rights activities.

The Sakharovs returned to their native Moscow Dec. 23 and were greeted by 200 friends, supporters and journalists. The physicist resumed his outspoken ways, denouncing the treatment of Soviet dissidents and calling for an end to the war in Afghanistan. Later on Dec. 23, Sakharov attended a seminar at the Physics Institute in Moscow and was warmly greeted by his fellow scientists.

THE TENNESSEAN
Nashville, TN, December 22, 1986

IT is doubtful that the leaders in the Kremlin could be imbued with the spirit of Christmas, but there are at least some rays of cheer for the Soviet Union's most prominent dissidents.

Mr. Andrei Sakharov is being allowed to return to Moscow after nearly seven years of internal exile in the closed city of Gorky and his wife, Ms. Yelena Bonner, has been pardoned, according to a government official.

Deputy Foreign Minister V. F. Petrovsky said Mr. Sakharov had asked permission to return to the Soviet capital and said that had been granted. He also indicated that the Nobel Peace laureate could resume his scientific research as a member of the Academy of Sciences.

Mr. Sakharov, 65, once the leading physicist in the Soviet Union, won the 1975 Nobel Peace Prize for his work in behalf of human rights. He was arrested after criticizing the 1979 Soviet invasion of Afghanistan and was exiled to Gorky in 1980.

Mrs. Bonner was sent to Gorky in 1983 after being charged with slander against the Soviet state. Mr. Sakharov went on several hunger strikes seeking permission for her to visit the United States and Italy for medical treatment. She was later permitted to leave the country for medical help and spent six months in the West undergoing eye and heart operations.

In a related case, the wife of another Soviet dissident, Mr. Naum Meiman, is reportedly being allowed to leave the country for experimental cancer treatment. Mrs. Meiman suffers from an inoperable tumor on her neck. Despite years of appeals from prominent scientists and political figures in the West she had been denied permission to seek the specialized radiation treatment she believes is her only hope of survival.

Mr. Meiman is one of the few early members of the Moscow Helsinki group, organized 10 years ago to monitor Soviet compliance with human rights accords, who has not been imprisoned, subjected to internal exile or forced to emigrate. He has been trying to emigrate since 1975, but has been refused because of his work many years ago on classified mathematical formulas. In Soviet eyes he is a security risk because of what he knows. But Mr. Meiman said the foreign ministry is reconsidering his case. That may be a hopeful sign that he could join his wife in the U.S. at a later date.

It is extremely unlikely that Mr. Sakharov will be permitted to leave. Soviet leader Mikhail Gorbachev told a French interviewer recently that Mr. Sakharov — who helped his country develop the atom bomb — could not leave the Soviet Union because he knows state secrets.

Nevertheless it is good news that he is now to leave exile for a more normal life in Moscow. Whether there are stipulations to this, such as talking to foreigners or engaging in criticism of the government, is not known.

It is obvious that pressure from the West has had some influence on Soviet authorities. Mr. Sakharov and his wife have been a major focus of Western criticism of Soviet human rights abuses. Mr. Yuri Orlov, a dissenter freed by the Soviet Union, has said the criticism may have reached a peak with the death in prison of dissident Mr. Anatoly Marchenko earlier this month.

In any case the West should learn from this that persistent and continuing pressure on the Soviet Union about human rights abuses can and often does pay off. ∎

The Boston Herald
Boston, MA, December 30, 1986

WHILE we bow to none in our admiration for dissident Andrei Sakharov, his pronouncements on strategic defense must be viewed skeptically.

The physicist, recently released from internal exile, has expressed pessimism concerning the Reagan administration's space-based anti-missile program. Though he conceded it was possible to develop such a system, Sakharov also stated that a powerful adversary could harness high technology to counter its effects.

As the father of the Soviet hydrogen bomb, Sakharov's views certainly carry weight. But is this really his candid opinion, or did Moscow have a hand in "shaping" his perspective?

Assuming the statement does indeed reflect Sakharov's sentiments, his conclusions are disputable. Granted, the dissident is a renowned scientist. However, for seven years he was isolated in Gorki, unable to conduct scientific research.

Given this hiatus, it's quite likely that Sakharov is unaware of the latest developments in his field, which make an effective strategic defense system far more feasible than a decade ago.

A group of eminent Soviet scientists is equally certain that Star Wars could be quite effective. In June, 30 emigre scientists from the Soviet Union released a letter urging our nation to proceed posthaste with the development of SDI. The letter's signatories, including physicists and engineers, all are currently employed by universities, corporations or research institutes in the U.S.

The scientists stated they were convinced both that the space shield was practical and that the Kremlin was busy at work on its own Star Wars program, and expending considerably more in the effort than is America.

On a concept as revolutionary as a space shield, even experts may disagree. When it comes to something as vital as our security, we should err on the side of caution, by following the course these emigre scientists believe the U.S.S.R. is taking.

THE ATLANTA CONSTITUTION
Atlanta, GA, December 22, 1986

The decision of Soviet authorities to release the physicist and human-rights advocate Andrei Sakharov from internal exile and to pardon his wife, Yelena Bonner, is welcome, of course, but the move should not be mistaken as indicating any general change of Soviet heart or policy.

Unless followed by more substantial changes, the clemency for Sakharov and Bonner will be just another sop to Western criticism of the Soviet Union's mistreatment of its political dissidents, criticism that had intensified after the recent death in prison of 48-year-old Anatoly Marchenko.

Sakharov is 65, Bonner 63. Both are in fragile health. At least in part, the Kremlin's action was motivated by its desire not to have another famous dissident die in abusive circumstances. Although never tried for any crime, or even charged with one, Sakharov in 1980 was sentenced to exile in Gorky, a city closed to foreigners, after criticizing the Soviet invasion of Afghanistan. Bonner was sent to Gorky after being convicted of anti-Soviet slander in mid-1984. She had been protesting her husband's exile.

The decision to allow Sakharov and Bonner to return to Moscow and the physicist to resume his academic life is one of several well-publicized concessions by the Kremlin this year. Anatoly Shcharansky was allowed to emigrate to Israel. Yuri Orlov was permitted to leave the Soviet Union after eight years in prison and internal exile. The Kremlin also has shown some increased willingness to let Soviets with relatives in the West join their families and to permit citizens suffering serious illnesses to leave the country for treatment.

But those moves are a gloss on a general picture that is not bright at all. At the peak of emigration in the 1970s, the Soviets permitted 52,000 citizens, most of them Jews, to leave. Last year, the number did not quite reach 1,000, and it appears slightly fewer will be allowed out this year.

In addition, the government is planning to adopt an emigration law that, although billed as setting up ways to regularize the emigration process, bears prohibitions that could have the effect of increasing the statutory and operational authority for restraining rather than facilitating emigrations.

The release of Sakharov and Bonner from internal exile suggests the Soviet system is aware, and somewhat painfully, of the concern in other countries about its human-rights abuses. So far, General Secretary Gorbachev has responded with clemencies chosen to give the Soviet Union maximum public-relations payoff, without any broad easing toward dissenters and would-be emigrants. The governments that welcome this latest such gesture should let him know at the same time that they expect far more.

The Times-Picayune
The States-Item
New Orleans, LA, December 26, 1986

Soviet dissidents Andrei Sakharov and his wife, Yelena Bonner, have now been permitted to return to Moscow from internal exile and constant harassment in the closed city of Gorky. Only in a national prison like the Soviet Union would orders to Moscow constitute a lesser sentence. But such it is, and admirers of the two staunch political moralists rejoice with them in the easing of their travail.

How permanent and how eased that will be remains the decision of the leadership in the Kremlin. General Secretary Mikhail Gorbachev has received the expressed appreciation of Dr. Sakharov himself and some Russian dissident emigres for his leniency.

But it remains a political fact that in the Soviet Union clemency for internationally celebrated figures like the Sakharovs tends to spring from foreign pressure and to serve national, not humanitarian, purposes. The Sakharovs are still under Kremlin control; if they again step over the line only the Kremlin knows where it has drawn, they can be sent back to Gorky — or worse.

Several notable Soviet dissidents have recently been allowed to leave the Soviet Union — Mrs. Bonner herself for medical treatment in the West. The pattern suggests that Mr. Gorbachev is trying to brush up his country's record on human rights to further Soviet diplomatic initiatives in other areas.
Soviet diplomatic intiatives in other areas.

Writes Peter Reddaway, director of the Kennan Institute for Advanced Russian Studies, in The Washington Post: "The physicist Orlov, the mathematician Shcharansky, the computer programmer Grivnina, and now the Kiev poet Ratushinskaya have, one by one, been released and allowed to leave the country. In these and other cases, the main goal has been to create a better Soviet image abroad."

This puts the outside world, anxious for the fates of those known to be imprisoned for exercising what in most other places would be basic civil and political rights, in a difficult position. Attacks on the Soviet leaders and system could be dismissed by charges of slander or interference in internal affairs. Pleas, cajolings — even praise when some detainee is cynically turned loose — only prove to the Kremlin the value of its hostages.

Yet there is no alternative but to continue the pressure and make the Soviets hurt from the consequences of their behavior. The Soviets are not the only ones with carrots and sticks, and Mr. Gorbachev himself has given the widest opening with his policy of "openness" to publicity, comment and criticism.

The Charlotte Observer
Charlotte, NC, December 26, 1986

There should be joy and satisfaction, but no illusions, about the Soviet Union's decision to release one of its most distinguished citizens from seven years of exile in the closed city of Gorki.

Nuclear physicist Andrei Sakharov, winner of the 1975 Nobel Peace Prize for his leadership in the Soviet human rights movement, becomes the fourth major dissident to be spared further cruelty by the Soviets in the past few months. Yuri Orlov and Anatoly Shcharansky were both permitted to emigrate. And Mr. Sakharov's wife, Yelena Bonner, was pardoned by the Soviet regime and will be allowed to join her husband in Moscow, where Mr. Sakharov has said he would prefer to live.

None of this means there has been any fundamental improvement in the Soviet system. That nation remains steadfast in its denial of human rights, and there appears scant hope that it will change. Indeed, the December death of another prominent dissident, Anatoly Marchenko, in a Soviet prison is a reminder of the continuing barbarism of Soviet repression.

But the Sakharov case, in combination with the others, is a reminder of the effectiveness of international pressure — the possibility of influencing the outcome in specific human rights cases, and even of achieving incremental improvements in the overall picture.

As columnist Jeane Kirkpatrick noted on Sunday's Viewpoint page, victims of the repressions by governments, left and right, are virtually unanimous in the view that international attention makes a difference. As a matter of U.S. policy, linkage is important. Governments around the world must be made to understand that their human rights policies are of grave concern to the United States and can affect negotiations on other issues of mutual interest.

To its credit, the Reagan administration continues to drive home that point to the Soviet Union. But Mr. Reagan has been less consistent than his predecessor in defending human rights in his dealings with *all* nations — regardless of the ideologies by which they rationalize their cruelty.

THE DENVER POST

Denver, CO, December 30, 1986

DISSIDENT Soviet physicist Andrei Sakharov has been making the most of his new-found freedom, continuing to press the Kremlin to clean up its act on human rights. But his popularity with some ardent Soviet-bashers may fade because of his renewed criticism of the "star wars" plan.

Sakharov told reporters last week that space defense systems will be technically possible "in the distant future." But he added "it will always be impossible from the military-strategic point of view, since any strong opponent with a sufficiently high level of technology can always overcome the technical achievements of the other side — and he won't even have to invest as much" as the other side.

On this issue, at least, official Soviet opinion seems to be coming around to Sakharov's views. The Soviets once seemed to genuinely fear that star wars could disarm them and leave them open to a U.S. first-strike. But earlier this month a blue-ribbon comittee of Soviet scientists reported that star wars could be overwhelmed with a varied attack that would cost "only a fraction" of the cost of building such a system.

Most U.S. scientists similarly agree agree with Sakharov that the Reagan administration's vision of covering America with a leak-proof umbrella against nuclear attack is utterly unworkable — unless it is closely tied to arms control efforts.

Without the limits on nuclear weapons imposed by such treaties as SALT II — which the Reagan administration unilaterally scrapped last month — it is easy to overwhelm any defense by sheer brute force of numbers. Similarly, if President Reagan and Secretary Gorbachev had made true progress toward the "nuclear-free world" they envisioned in their Iceland summit, a modified star wars system could have ensured against efforts by either superpower to cheat — or against attack by such unstable third parties such as Libya's Moammar Khadafy.

Sakharov, who has long sought true bilateral arms control, has picked a timely forum to warn the world that there is no magical technological fix to the nuclear nightmare. Until the Reagan administration devotes as much attention to serious diplomacy aimed at curbing the arms race as it has to technological efforts to escalate it, the world will move no closer to Sakharov's dream.

The Washington Times

Washington, DC, December 29, 1986

In an astonishing remark, Mikhail Gorbachev told the French Communist daily *L'Humanite* earlier this year that "there are no political prisoners in the Soviet Union." How he accounted for Andrei Sakharov's seven-year exile in Gorki was unclear, and now the very government that sent the Sakharovs into exile is proving to be the chief beneficiary of their release.

For all the wrong reasons, of course. Despite the worldwide approbation that has been heaped on the Kremlin, springing Dr. Sakharov says less about the state of human rights in the U.S.S.R. than it does about the intense pressure applied to Mr. Gorbachev from foreign and domestic sources. And while Dr. Sakharov continues to urge the release of political prisoners (whose number he puts in the thousands) and rapid withdrawal from Afghanistan, in other respects he has been co-opted by Mr. Gorbachev. Dr. Sakharov expresses "great respect" for Mr. Gorbachev, pronounces President Reagan's Strategic Defense Initiative a military and strategic impossibility, and credits Mr. Gorbachev with pressing for those internal reforms advocated by dissidents in the 1960s and '70s. "I very much welcome these moves in favor of greater openness," he says.

What Mr. Gorbachev accomplished by "freeing" the Sakharovs was to enlist them in a public-relations game in which the strategic stakes for the Soviet Union are inordinately high. There are others players, too. Just last October, Moscow inexplicably released the celebrated young poet Irina Ratushinskaya from prison and subsequently permitted her to travel to the West for medical care with her husband. Two weeks ago U.S. presidential hopeful Gary Hart was given a spirited welcome to Moscow and spent several hours closeted with Mr. Gorbachev in what were described as a "constructive frank" exchange. As Mr. Hart left the Soviet Union, a Soviet cancer patient was loaded aboard his aircraft to receive health care in the West.

All this is a PR windfall for Mr. Gorbachev, whose policy of *glasnost*, or openness, continues to win plaudits worldwide and even from Dr. Sakharov. But public-relations gimmickry cannot mask the horrendous problems Moscow faces. Mr. Gorbachev's heralded shakeup of the fossilized Soviet bureaucracy has not produced the hoped-for economic rejuvenation; many economists, some of them Soviet, suggest that the economy is even worse off than it was when Mr. Gorbachev assumed power three years ago. Moreover, the recent rioting in the central Asian republic of Kazakhstan, which many Westerners (missing the point) viewed as yet another example of *glasnost*, testify to the severe nationalistic and ethnic crises that continue to bedevil the Kremlin.

Just recently, *Pravda* printed a series of scapegoating articles critical of the late party boss Leonid Brezhnev, laying the blame for such problems squarely at his grave. Again, naive Westerners rushed to applaud *glasnost*. Had they read the articles carefully, they would have seen that the only achievement for which Mr. Brezhnev was praised was his "policy of detente." For Mr. Gorbachev nothing would be more welcome than a comfortable seat on the detente express, with its cheap Western grain, abundant foreign credits, and access to the bottomless well of U.S. technology.

Moscow has learned over the years that the road to detente is smoothed by public-relations spectaculars, deceptive blandishments that foolishly hopeful Westerners are unable to resist. The release of Dr. Sakharov, as welcome as it is on humanitarian grounds, must be viewed in this realistic light.

The Dallas Morning News

Dallas, TX, December 20, 1986

The abuse of human rights can have myriad sordid faces. The Soviet Union may rank No. 1 in showing them all. Its treatment of dissidents like Andrei Sakharov is one such glaring example. A Nobel Peace laureate and renowned physicist, Sakharov finally has had his internal exile lifted, but only now that his health has been nearly destroyed under the conditions of his seven-year detention.

The Soviets do not deserve accolades for allowing this man to return to Moscow. Their actions are but a further reminder of their penchant for manipulating the lives of dissidents to suit the whimsies of their propaganda apparatus.

Perhaps far more damaging to the viability of the Soviet state is the abuse of human rights of the ethnic minorities which constitute 50 percent of the U.S.S.R. Rioting erupted this week in the Soviet Central Asian Republic of Kazakhstan over a Kremlin decision to replace a longtime leader of that Moslem state with an ethnic Russian. The Soviet Union, it should be remembered, is not a federal state. It is a colonial empire of 15 republics, dominated by ethnic Russians. The entity is held together by the intimidation and military might of the Russian-controlled Kremlin.

The U.S.S.R. also is a country whose national identity is shaped by the ethnic Russians, a privileged class within the so-called classless Soviet society. Its sense of manifest destiny has been the use of military conquest to broaden its boundaries in ever-widening concentric circles, absorbing Central Asia and dominating Eastern Europe. The resources of the state bolstered by the exploitation of its internal colonies have been channeled into building and sustaining an awesome military machine to the neglect of economic development.

But the system engenders hostility on the part of the non-Russian republics, which are neither adequately represented in the Kremlin nor culturally assimilated even to the extent of speaking Russian. Many of the Asian republics are dominated by Moslems who eschew the atheism of the state. It was this reality that forced the Soviet army to remove its Central Asian troops from Afghanistan because of the greater loyalty they began showing to the Moslem Afghans.

The Soviet Union's greatest vulnerability is not to foreign attack, but to the disintegration of its colonial empire. The United States in its advocacy of human rights should begin to reflect that reality, expressing as much moral indignation to the oppression of Soviet ethnic minorities who number in the millions, as it now does to the abuse of the rights of individual Russian dissidents.

AKRON BEACON JOURNAL
Akron, OH, December 22, 1986

THE BEST news out of the Soviet Union in a while came last week, with the announcement that Andrei Sakharov's internal exile was to end, and that the dissident's wife, Yelena Bonner, was being pardoned on her conviction of slandering the state.

After six years in the closed city of Gorky — two years for Mrs. Bonner — it all

Mr. Sakharov

seemed so simple. Mr. Sakharov asked permission to return to Moscow, and the request was granted. Even international human rights groups such as Amnesty International, which had been working for Mr. Sakharov's release, were surprised by the announcement.

Mr. Sakharov has been considered a criminal by the Kremlin for his "anti-Soviet behavior." As late as a few weeks ago, at a news conference for International Human Rights Day, there was no indication of any change in Soviet attitudes concerning the Sakharovs.

In addition, the Soviet official making the announcement, said that "academician Sakharov can actively join the scientific life of the Academy of Sciences."

Mr. Sakharov, of course, is a distinguished scientist. The 65-year-old physicist helped develop the Soviet hydrogen bomb, yet he was awarded the Nobel Peace Prize in 1975 for his human rights work.

In 1979, he got into trouble for criticizing the Soviet invasion of Afghanistan, and was exiled to Gorky the following year.

As usual, it is hard to know what to make of this move by the Soviets. It might be a public relations ploy, on the order of the Nicaraguans release of American gun-runner Eugene Hasenfus.

But seeing the move simply as propaganda misses the point. For whatever reason, the action is a good move, one that the United States and human rights groups have been lobbying for.

There is also the possibility that the international pressure has worked. Perhaps the Soviets were tired of the situation in which Mr. Sakharov was seen as a symbol of the Soviet abuse of human rights.

In any case, the release from Gorky is a positive sign. The Reagan administration should recognize it as such, encourage similar action in the future, and use the change in attitude to try to rebuild communication between the two superpowers.

The Philadelphia Inquirer
Philadelphia, PA, December 21, 1986

Name a Soviet dissident who is now in prison or banished to internal exile. Not easy, is it? The name Yosef Begun does not have the resonance of names like Andrei Sakharov, Yelena Bonner, Anatoly Shcharansky and Yuri Orlov, all of whom would have been at the top of anyone's list a year ago. The Soviet Union may not be making fundamental changes in its human rights policy, but it is certainly taking serious steps to clean up its image.

The announcement Friday that Mr. Sakharov is being allowed to return to his Moscow home with Ms. Bonner, his wife, is the Gorbachev regime's most dramatic move on the human-rights front to date. In one simple step, the Soviet leader stole from his ideological adversaries a club with which they have been persistently beating him and his predecessors since the day Mr. Sakharov was snatched off the street and summarily banished to Gorky nearly seven years ago.

No longer will Mr. Gorbachev have to listen to pleas for Mr. Sakharov's release from virtually every Western politician who comes through his office. No longer will he get nasty questions about the Sakharovs at his news conferences abroad.

The Sakharovs still may prove troublesome now that they are returning to a place where foreign correspondents can reach them, but nothing they can say or do could match the damage created by their continuing confinement in Gorky.

The Sakharovs' release represents a victory for the Reagan administration and for countless political leaders, scientific organizations and human rights activists who campaigned steadily on their behalf. When it comes to influencing Soviet human rights policy, noisiness has its place.

It goes without saying that this welcome event should not still criticism of Soviet human rights abuses nor discourage campaigning for lesser-known prisoners of conscience like Mr. Begun. But those stressing the need to press on should not dismiss the importance of this particular gesture too lightly.

The Kremlin has been saying in a number of ways recently that it remains anxious to do business with the Reagan administration, despite the breakdown of the Reykjavik summit and the distraction of the Iran-contra arms scandal. Soviet spokesmen are promoting ways to compromise on the sticky question of "Star Wars" research and thus clear the way for a major nuclear arms agreement before the end of Mr. Reagan's term. The Sakharovs' release should be viewed as a possible sign that the Kremlin is in the mood for accommodation.

The Register-Guard
Eugene, OR, December 23, 1986

George Orwell once wrote that there could be a thousand Gandhis in the Soviet Union, and no one would ever know it. His point was that a voice of dissent cannot be heard in a closed society. Andrei Sakharov's release from internal exile is heartening proof that the silence is not absolute.

The physicist and Nobel Peace Prize laureate is the most prominent victim of Soviet repression of religious and political opposition. By freeing Sakharov to return to Moscow, the Soviet Union has offered the most convincing sign to date of movement toward living up to its obligations to respect basic human rights.

One robin, of course, does not make a spring. Amnesty International, the worldwide human rights organization, knows of 600 prisoners of conscience in the Soviet Union, and it suspects there are many more. Jewish emigration has slowed to a trickle. The freedom to travel, speak and publish is closely circumscribed. The Soviet Union clearly has far to go before it can be considered in compliance with the Helsinki human rights accords of 1975.

Yet Soviet leader Mikhail Gorbachev's decision to allow Sakharov and his wife, Yelena Bonner, to leave the closed city of Gorky was enormously significant. Sakharov's credibility as a critic of the Soviet system is unsurpassed. His words carry weight everywhere they are heard, whether the topic is nuclear armaments, Afghanistan or human rights.

The Soviet Union could not silence Sakharov, because when he could not speak, an international chorus spoke on his behalf. Sakharov's exile handicapped the Soviets' efforts to negotiate trade and arms control agreements. And despite his isolation, news of his thoughts and reports of his medical condition seeped out of Gorky.

Sakharov's release may be a sign that a genuine thaw is occurring in the Soviet Union. That possibility is reinforced by such scattered events as the emigration of dissidents Anatoly Shcharansky and Yuri Orlov and by recent criticism of former Soviet leader Leonid Brezhnev in the Soviet press.

A more limited interpretation is that Gorbachev decided that keeping Sakharov in exile was not worth the political price. Even that, however, would be encouraging. It would prove that international pressure on behalf of an individual prisoner inside the Soviet Union can have an effect. It would show that a Soviet leader is capable of concluding that the benefits of repression are outweighed by the costs.

Sakharov has said he will test the limits of his new freedom by speaking openly on political and human-rights subjects. By doing so he will discover whether there has been any real change in the atmosphere of Soviet society. But he has already proved Orwell wrong in one vital respect: A courageous voice can be heard, even in the Soviet Union.

Soviet Dissidents Freed;
Moscow Claims 140 Pardoned

The Soviet foreign ministry Feb. 10, 1987 announced that 140 dissidents had been released from prisons and labor camps through legislative pardons. The announced figure was believed to be the largest release of political prisoners in the U.S.S.R. since 1956, when the regime of Nikita Khrushchev had set free thousands of persons imprisoned under the regime of Joseph Stalin. Western observers viewed the pardons as a move by Moscow to defuse international criticism of the Soviet human-rights record.

Gennadi Gerasimov, the chief spokesman of the foreign ministry, disclosed the releases at a press conference in Moscow. He said that, in addition to the 140 set free, the government was considering the release of 140 other prisoners. Gerasimov explained that the pardons had come from decrees, enacted Feb. 2 and Feb. 9, by the Presidium of the Supreme Soviet, the nation's nominal parliament. Western analysts differed on their estimates of the number of persons imprisoned in the Soviet Union for political acts. The estimates ranged from 750 to 3,000.

Those pardoned had been convicted under Article 70 of the national criminal code, which prohibited "anti-Soviet agitation and propaganda." Those receiving pardons apparently had to sign statements pledging to refrain from such activities in the future. The releases were given little coverage in the state-controlled Soviet media. Some prisoners had apparently been set free in late January, before the first legislative decree. The news of the earliest releases had reached the Western press via the Soviet dissident community. Gerasimov declined to supply the names of the 140 pardoned prisoners. Western journalists learned that they included Sergei Grigoryants, a former literary critic; Yuri Shikhanovich, a mathematician and former editor of the clandestine human rights journal the *Chronicle of Current Events*, and Roald Zelichenok, an activist on the Jewish emigration issue.

Richmond Times-Dispatch

Richmond, VA, February 13, 1987

Whether for sure or for show, time alone will tell. For now, the release from labor camps, prisons and internal exile of more than a hundred political prisoners is welcome as a break in, perhaps an end to, their anguish and that of their families. Mikhail Gorbachev must know that their release is also a test of his intentions to make the Soviet Union a freer, and more productive, place and his ability to see them through.

According to the best estimates of international human rights organizations, these 140 men and women now free are only a tenth of Soviets imprisoned for such crimes as disseminating opinions and information, monitoring human rights abuses, maintaining Western contacts, preaching and practicing their religious faith. According to the best estimates of international Jewish organizations, the 500 Soviet Jews who are now to be permitted to emigrate are a sixtieth of those who would like to.

The praise for these moves, coming as they do on the heels of a visit by a high-level American delegation, and on the eve of a Soviet-sponsored conference on nuclear disarmament, must be muted by the Kremlin's past record of very cynically manipulating Western concern for the civil and human rights of Soviets. Doors opened suddenly to dissidents and would-be emigrants have closed just as fast. "Pardons" granted can be revoked. The pardoned can be held under pain of reimprisonment to their promises to recant and forswear the activities for which they were imprisoned. They have to wonder when and how they are going to overstep a mark they won't see until they've crossed it.

If the Soviet Communist Party, its leadership, its bureaucrats have more to gain than the West from a Soviet Union which can abide freedom of thought, assembly, expression, religion, movement, they also have more to fear. The Western press and publics have been made well aware of Mr. Gorbachev's policy of *glasnost*. American critics of the Soviet system are invited to the Kremlin for three hours of frank give-and-take with the general secretary; they come away impressed, if wary. Soviet officials give American correspondents access hitherto unheard of. But those Soviet dissidents just released from prison are not invited to the Kremlin for a frank discussion of differences. Soviet print media have given only the tersest attention to this latest release, and television none.

"What can we do," said a Soviet youth this week in reply to Phil Donahue's exasperation with a placid teen-age audience in Moscow, "if everything is all right? Do you want us to create problems?" Problem-creators is how many Soviets see the dissidents in their midst. Mikhail Gorbachev, for all his overtures to the West, seems content to keep it that way.

The Honolulu Advertiser

Honolulu, HI, February 11, 1987

Word of the release from prison of 140 Soviet dissidents, and the possible freeing of an equal number more, is welcome indeed. As always with reports of Soviet openness, however, the caveat "as far as it goes" must be added.

Those now being released had been convicted of "anti-Soviet activity." They are said to be mostly scientists and clericals.

In order to gain release, they had to apply and to promise not to engage again in illegal acts, most of which would be considered normal political activity in the West. Those who would not promise have no chance of release.

So clearly, this is neither a general amnesty nor a major relaxation of Soviet repression. It has also been announced that laws governing anti-Soviet activity will be reviewed, but how far that will go remains to be seen.

Also, there will apparently be no relaxation of strict rules that prevent emigration of those wishing to leave the Soviet Union, including many Jews and other religious and ethnic minorities. This is one of the Soviets' most severe violations of basic human rights.

Ever since Soviet leader Mikhail Gorbachev allowed the release of the dissident physicist Andrei Sakharov before Christmas, it has been clear that an effort was being made to improve the Soviet Union's image before the world.

Still, it must be remembered that hundreds more are imprisoned for criticizing the state, and the KGB remains the scourge of those who try to inform the West about such abuses.

And while Gorbachev seems to be making limited progress on his reforms, there is always the chance the entrenched party hierarchy and government bureaucracy will turn on him if he goes too far too fast. It has happened to other Soviet leaders, including Nikita Khrushchev.

So, welcome as the current moves are, they only amount to a small modification of one of the world's most repressive systems. That is why the new release policy is to be applauded, but "only as far as it goes."

THE CHRONICLE-HERALD

Halifax, N.S., February 2, 1987

IF THE UNDER-RULERS in the Kremlin continue to accept the policies of Mikhail Gorbachev, as for the moment it seems they do, how far will he go?

Chairman Gorbachev, seen in the West almost from the start of his selection as a new face for an old foe, also appears to be trying some of the new thought — at least it's new in Moscow — he complains has been universally missing for the past half century.

He has introduced to his personal and political styles ideas and methods that are radically different for the sombre Soviets, although most are so old that they exist for Western leaders as an exhibition of the "common touch" of the politician.

Mr. Gorbachev has travelled widely, for a Russian, and has an endless streak of inquisitiveness. He has a ready smile, an eye-appealing spouse with her own list of questions, and both dress more stylishly than perhaps any Soviet envoys since the days of the Czar.

The Communist Party chief gets out of his Kremlin office on a regular basis, glad-hands factory workers, debates openly with shoppers, mutters incessantly about slow delivery of consumer goods, angrily chastizes sloppy management and berates Russians for their love affair with alcohol.

In the last several months, he has appeared determined to change the face of Russia — in minor but meaningful ways.

Last fall, he showed up in Iceland and dropped on President Reagan an arms proposal for which his U.S. counterpart may have been unprepared, may even have misunderstood. Clearly, Mr. Gorbachev expected some help from the United States in dealing with the potential political damage back in Moscow. He didn't get even that, perhaps because Mr. Reagan's America hasn't yet decided whether to help, even peripherally, or just watch.

There's the promise of a pull-back from Afghanistan, as yet unfulfilled, so we don't know if that's a typical Russian ploy or an unexpected policy development. Just before Christmas, long-suffering scientist and dissident Andrei Sakharov was allowed to leave Gorky and return to Moscow, where, his banishment ended, the physicist promptly engaged in an open round of interviews that described his life in exile.

It was Dr. Sakharov who wondered whether his release was a propaganda trick or part of a genuine change. He seemed as puzzled by his new state of bliss as outsiders seem to be of the new Soviet rationale.

A recent decision to stop jamming the Russian-language broadcasts of the British Broadcasting Corporation had not been expected and in London it's an abrupt change that has the Thatcher administration waiting and watching.

Now we're told that Mr. Gorbachev wants competition at election time, has urged workers to choose their managers, and has instituted basic planning for some forms of limited individual enterprise.

Pravda has been filled with reader complaints that only a year ago might well have consigned the writer to some distant Gulag.

It's all Mr. Gorbachev's doing, and it seems clear that he has support, and a lot, because he's been able to dump old Brezhnev hands and to develop a smaller politburo of his own appointees. Whatever debate, if there is one, may be raging within the Soviet inner circle, Mr. Gorbachev's basic contentions seem to have the sway.

But, if not enough of them are serious about Gorbachev's reforms, how long can he survive? Less than 20 years ago, the wonderful "Prague Spring" brought the Czechoslovak people a new life; within a few months, the cold winter of orthodoxy blew harshly in from Moscow, and it was back to the drudgery of socialist reality.

Post-Tribune

Gary, IN, February 13, 1987

The Soviet Union has released 140 dissenters and is on the verge of freeing at least that many more. That won't leave the jails empty of political prisoners, because there is a generous supply. And it does not mean that the totalitarian system has undergone a radical conversion. But this is the largest release of its kind in decades, and that is significant.

At least some of those pardoned have promised not to violate the ban on "anti-Soviet agitation and propaganda," used mostly in cases of religious or political dissent. If that means people are being freed in exchange for their silence, it is a neat trade for the government.

Our opinions

Some were freed without such a promise, and the move appears to be, as a Soviet spokesman said, "in line with Mikhail Gorbachev's policy on more democratization of Soviet life."

It is not necessary to see Gorbachev as a great humanitarian, but it is smart to see him as astute enough to know that the Soviet policy on human rights is a barrier to his credibility in the free world. And he is realistic about his credibility at home. Gorbachev will be limited, though, in his "democratization" moves, because the old guard leaders view it as a threat.

There was a previous surge of democratization under Nikita Khrushchev, who turned loose an estimated million people as he denounced the regime of Josef Stalin. And on the 50th and 60th anniversaries of the 1917 revolution, some amnesties were granted.

The current releases come in a different atmosphere. Gorbachev apparently has been listening to the outside denunciations of the Soviet human rights policies. Soviet and American leaders will never define liberty and security the same way, because they begin from very different perspectives. So expecting a drastic Soviet turnaround is like believing in fairy tales.

The significance in the release of dissidents is that it has occurred under the spotlight of world attention. It is real. Whatever political meaning people want to read into it cannot detract from the positive aspect of these decisions.

The Dallas Morning News

Dallas, TX, February 10, 1987

The release from prison of 42 Soviet dissidents is certainly cause for celebration.

And the reason for their being freed at this time is also worth some speculation. It's not inconceivable that the Soviet Union is loosening its harsh penalties for political dissidence. But then again, it's not too likely. The present moves may just be Mikhail Gorbachev's way of sprucing up his image in an attempt to influence Western public opinion on behalf of new proposals Moscow will be presenting at ongoing arms control negotiations.

Whatever Gorbachev's motives in this instance, it's time to admit that the West's human rights policy toward the Soviet Union always has been flawed. For why, really, should the abuse of the human rights of a handful of Russian dissidents be viewed as a more serious offense than the abuse of the rights of 36 million Poles, 15 million Czechoslovaks, 10 million Hungarians, 23 million Yugoslavians and 8 million Baltics all held in the Soviet system against their will?

The categories of prisoners not freed in this new move at amnesty also is worth noting. Among the political prisoners still remaining in jail are Ukrainian and other nationalists in addition to religious leaders.

Now may just be the appropriate moment to fuse the two essential elements of the Soviet human rights equation. They are, on one hand, the continued imprisonment of from 1,000 to 3,000 political dissidents and, on the other, the circumstances of virtual house arrest under which Eastern Europe is bound to the Soviet empire.

Christian Millenium Celebrated as Soviets Widen Religious Rights

The Russian Orthodox Church June 5-12, 1988 celebrated the 1,000th anniversary of the introduction of Christianity into Medieval Russia. The church had over 40 million followers, most – but not all – living in the Soviet Union. The celebration had the full support of the Kremlin, which appeared anxious to shed its reputation of hostility.

Christianity had gained a foothold in the region when a pagan prince, Vladimir I of Kievan Rus (an Eastern Slavic state centered at what was to become the Soviet Ukraine city of Kiev), converted to the religion in the year 988. Christianity subsequently flourished to a point where there had been an estimated 70,000 churches in the Russian Empire before the 1917 Bolshevik Revolution. Soviet religious dissidents contended that Communist Party persecutions had reduced the number of functioning churches to about 7,000 in 1988.

The festivities formally opened with a Russian Orthodox mass at Moscow's Epiphany Cathedral June 5. The service was attended by theologians and officials of Christian denominations from around the world. Among the dignitaries in attendance were Johannes Cardinal Willebrands, the head of the Vatican's Secretariat for Christian Unity, and the Most Rev. Robert Runcie, the archbishop of Canterbury. The celebrations, which also took place in Kiev, Leningrad and other Soviet cities, featured press receptions, academic forums and conferences on religion. The festivities climaxed June 12 (All Saints Day) with an open-air mass at Moscow's 13th-century Danilov Monastery. The service was conducted by Patriarch Sergei Pimen, primate of the Russian Orthodox Church. An estimated 10,000 people attended.

In related developments:

■ Soviet leader Mikhail S. Gorbachev met with Agostino Cardinal Casaroli, the Vatican secretary of state, at the Kremlin June 13. Casaroli carried a letter to Gorbachev from Pope John Paul II. The content of the letter was not made public, but a Vatican source quoted by the Western press said that John Paul expressed the hope that the changes underway in the Soviet Union would include more religious freedom.

General Secretary Gorbachev and Casaroli held an hour-long private discussion. A Soviet press account of the talks stated that the general secretary assured the cardinal that there now existed "a basis for a dialogue" between Moscow and the Vatican. However, Gorbachev was said to have warned his visitor that Soviet religious freedom was an "internal affair" not subject to outside "interference." The cardinal later described the discussion as "friendly." He added: "We can raise questions about the life of [Soviet] Catholics, which was difficult before because there were no direct contacts."

■ General Secretary Gorbachev conferred with Patriarch Pimen and other top officials of the Russian Orthodox Church April 29 at the Kremlin. Soviet television showed Gorbachev receiving the visitors. The general secretary was reported to have admitted to the churchmen that the party had made "mistakes" with regard to the church. Soviet believers, he said, should have "the full right to express their conviction with dignity."

THE INDIANAPOLIS STAR
Indianapolis, IN, January 25, 1988

The vicious Soviet campaign against religion goes on.

But one student of the subject thinks the Soviets are stumbling along in their strenuous efforts to stamp out religious faith.

William Fletcher, professor of Soviet and East European Studies at the University of Kansas, doesn't minimize the barbarity of the Soviet government when it does go after religious believers.

"More and more, the state's anti-religious campaign consists of a fair number of isolated acts of barbarity, while generally atheism becomes less and less noticeable across the vast country," he writes in Policy Review magazine.

For example, he notes the proliferation of house churches, which are even highlighted occasionally in government publications, with disapproval of course. But apparently the government can't stop them all and has eased some of its past strenuous attempts to stamp out all indigenous religious meetings.

It's nice to know that the Soviet machine is losing a bit of its grip.

But his comments don't mean that the U.S. should soften attempts to promote freedom behind the Iron Curtain. One of the problems with new Reagan-Gorbachev "detente" is that the well-meaning pleas for peace and dialogue will tend to overshadow the crying need for U.S. influence on behalf of persecuted Jews, Christians, Moslems and other religious believers in the Soviet Union.

The New York Times
New York, NY, June 11, 1988

An extraordinary gathering of world religious leaders assembled in atheist Moscow this week to celebrate a true millennium — the 1,000th anniversary of the Russian Orthodox Church. Participants included Cardinal O'Connor of New York, the Archbishop of Canterbury, the Vatican's Secretary of State and the Rev. Billy Graham.

Mikhail Gorbachev himself met with Orthodox Church leaders in preparation for the event, and returned several monasteries to the church's control. Meantime, the Soviet press has rung with open debate on religious issues. And all this occurs in a state that calls religion a superstition unworthy of the modern scientific age.

But the millennium also serves as a reminder of how much has *not* changed between the Soviet state and religious believers: the continuing repression of millions of Catholics, Jews, Protestants and Moslems whose religions are less favored.

True, there are some hopeful gestures even here. For 42 years Moscow has suppressed the Ukrainian Catholic Church. But on the eve of the millennial celebration, a Russian Orthodox official agreed to begin talks on the status of the Ukrainian church. Soviet officials have agreed in principle to open a rabbinical school. There have also been promises that the 1929 law restricting religion will be revised. And Russian Orthodox leaders this week approved statutes aimed at reclaiming some religious functions from the state.

Yet strict state control remains the rule. No one can worship except in officially registered congregations. The state owns the buildings, oversees clergy and remains the sole publisher of Bibles and other religious literature, constantly in short supply. Religious instruction for children is prohibited. Two hundred Soviet citizens remain imprisoned for their religious beliefs, though down from more than 400 in 1985. Countless others suffer education and professional discrimination.

Many Communist leaders fear that genuine independence even for the Russian Orthodox Church would threaten party supremacy. Other churches, their traditions foreign, their allegiances directed to places other than Moscow, seem even more menacing. And in the Baltic states and Poland, the Catholic Church is inevitably associated with struggles for greater independence from Soviet control.

Yet the time now seems propitious for positive change. As Russians begin to look honestly at their history, the Russian Orthodox Church commands fresh attention for the rich role it has played in that history. More generally, Mr. Gorbachev is plainly eager to improve his country's human rights image abroad. And organized religions tend to stress community involvement, family life and hard work, values Mr. Gorbachev would like to see applied toward his reforms.

This week's assembly of religious notables, in a monastery restored by the world's proudest atheist state, is specifically designed to look back at a thousand years in the life of one church. By calling attention also to less-favored faiths, this celebration can serve the future, too.

"OH, ЯATS! IF HE'S GOING TO GIVE US MORE SERMONS ...!!"

St. Louis Review

St. Louis, MO, June 10, 1988

World opinion, western pressure, and enlightened self-interest have apparently impelled the leadership in the USSR toward greater openness and recognition of the need for restructuring its society. The underlying truth is that the Communist system has failed. Unless party obstructionism, the entrenched bureaucracy, the military and the specter of unemployment combine to derail a much-needed reform, the USSR may be evolving toward something like European socialism.

One manifestation of change-in-the-making is the first stirrings of religious liberty. Make no mistake there is no religious liberty in the USSR at the present. Religion and religious leaders have been persecuted throughout the Communist epoch. Yet,

if openness means anything, it must mean liberty of conscience. Some tentative moves in the direction of greater freedom for members of the Russian Orthodox Church have been made in recent weeks.

It is tragic that leaders of the Orthodox Church have manifested their opposition to an extension of religious liberty to Ukrainian Catholics. The Ukrainian Catholic Church which is in union with Rome is thought to number some 4 million members in the Soviet Union. In 1946, Dictator Josef Stalin compelled the official dissolution of the Ukrainian Catholic Church. Nevertheless, its members have continued to meet and worship together. They have petitioned the Soviet government for official recognition of their existence

and their right to gather for worship. Metropolitan M. Filaret, head of the Russian Orthodox Church in Kiev, would like to compel the Ukrainian Catholics to become amalgamated into the Russian Orthodox Church. It is for this reason that Ukrainian Catholics have repeatedly petitioned the Holy See to be established as an independent partriarchate to preclude any such forced absorption.

Representatives of the Russian Orthodox Church and the Vatican will be meeting in Finland to hold discussions on the status of Ukrainian Catholics. It is unlikely that there will be any substantial agreement at this time, but it is important that the churches meet to discuss this vital issue.

Newsday

Long Island, NY, August 30, 1988

Maybe it's because the Soviet leadership understands that Marxism-Leninism has lost its mass appeal and people are seeking other values as an alternative. But in the era of Mikhail Gorbachev's glasnost and perestroika, religion is gradually becoming more acceptable in the Soviet Union. Increasingly it's seen as a matter of personal conscience rather than a form of political or social deviance.

Churches are gradually reopening. More than 200 religious prisoners were released this year. At the special Communist Party conference in June, Gorbachev called for full

acceptance of religious believers in Soviet society. But there's a long way to go before anything like western-style freedom of religion becomes a fact of Soviet life.

A quasi-official Soviet human rights commission recently called for release of all religious prisoners jailed under two articles of the code restricting religious activities. The appeal received wide publicity. But only about 15 of 130 religious prisoners known in the West would be affected. The rest were convicted of other offenses. Nor did the commission demand repeal of the law,

which sharply curtails religious education and requires groups to have official approval before they hold worship services.

That has to change and more. Even if they stay within the existing law, Soviet citizens who practice their religion face harassment and discrimination. Higher education and job advancement are still denied many, particularly if they're outside the Russian Orthodox church. Yet, as in so much else, there seems to be a new dispensation with more leniency than could have been imagined just a few years ago. The trend should be encouraged.

The Pittsburgh PRESS

Pittsburgh, PA, May 13, 1988

Just weeks before President Reagan's scheduled trip to Moscow, Mikhail Gorbachev pledged greater toleration of religion in a televised meeting with leaders of the Russian Orthodox Church. Whether this dramatic gesture will lead to genuine change remains to be seen.

So far, Gorbachev's reforms have mainly affected prominent secular intellectuals, not ordinary churchgoers who want to practice their faith without persecution. But now he says that "Believers are Soviet people ... Perestroika and democratization concern them, too — in full measure."

Those are noble words, but supporters of human rights are entitled to be skeptical.

For many months Soviet officials have been talking about possible changes in the law on religious associations — which explicitly denies freedoms taken for granted in the West — but have remained coy about what those changes might be.

Gorbachev's promise that the new law "will reflect the interests of religious organizations" adds nothing specific.

Anyone who thinks the Soviet leader has become an advocate of religious pluralism should note his statement that "The attitude to the church should be determined by the interests of strengthening the unity of all working people, of the entire nation."

If the church is acceptable only as an engine of national unity, persecution will not end but will merely take on more subtle forms. Reinforcing this fear is the fact that Gorbachev met only with Orthodox leaders — not with the Catholic, Protestant, Moslem or Jewish minorities.

As Ukrainian Catholics know, it is all too easy for Moscow to make the Orthodox Church an agent of oppression, not just a victim.

The richest irony in Gorbachev's speech was his boast that Moscow is "restoring in full measure the Leninist principles of attitude to religion."

It was Lenin, of course, who launched the Bolshevik regime's bloody war against religion — calling it "the opium of the people" and jailing or killing thousands of church leaders.

Most of the restrictions ordered or inspired by Lenin, such as the law against teaching religion to children, are still in force. Moscow must clearly repeal them — in both letter and spirit — to earn the image that Gorbachev now claims.

WORCESTER TELEGRAM

Worcester, MA, March 29, 1988

Orthodox Christianity is about to celebrate its millenium in the most ungodly place of all — the Soviet Union. The celebration of 1,000 years of the Russian Orthodox Church is even being recognized by the officially atheist government.

As with the rehabilitation of some church buildings, the Kremlin sees the millenium as a tourist attraction rather than an anniversary of faith. Unlike the Roman Catholic Church that has retained its influence in Poland and elsewhere in the communist bloc through struggle and peril, the Russian Orthodox Church has been severely co-opted since the 1917 revolution. Even now, church activities are legally confined to parish property and monitored closely, although some clandestine services are held.

The Russian Orthodox church and Patriarch Pimen have been promised they can return to the 700-year-old Danilov Monastery in Moscow once the property is rehabilitated. The Soviet government says it will spend $45 million to restore the monastery that has been used as an umbrella factory, a refrigerator plant and a juvenile detention center.

Mikhail Gorbachev may have something to do with this religious glasnost. Rumor has it that the general secretary was secretly baptized as a child and that his mother still attends church. For the first time in decades, Soviet parents may now have their children baptized without registering with the police.

Just how Soviet Christians will be allowed to celebrate 1,000 years of faith remains to be seen. Prince Vladimir, founder of the Russian church, is remembered for deciding that he and his countrymen would be baptized in the Dnieper River. The blessing of any river for baptism was re-enacted for hundreds of years as Russians prepared for Easter. Since 1929, the rite has been forbidden.

For the 50 million Soviet citizens who claim to be Christians, even small changes are welcome. But the real celebration of Russian Orthodoxy will come only if all churches are allowed to open and function without government interference.

The Wichita Eagle-Beacon

Wichita, KS, June 18, 1988

VLADIMIR the saint accepted Christianity in 988 and commenced the conversion of the regions of Russia. It was the beginning of the Russian Orthodox Church. In 1988 the Russian Orthodox Church, while celebrating its 1,000-year anniversary, is at a new beginning as a result of General Secretary Gorbachev's new policy of openness.

The event celebrates the Russian Church as a newly confirmed force in Soviet society. The Russian Church officially has been acknowledged as having a place in Russian history and culture. The regions of Russia, Byelorussia and the Ukraine, once principalities of Kievan Russia and now republics in the Soviet Union, date their birth as nations to the Russian Orthodox Church and their acceptance of Christianity 1,000 years ago. Mr. Gorbachev in the past 18 months has permitted the Russian Church a greater degree of fulfillment of its members spiritual needs.

The Russian Church is beginning to test the dimensions of these new freedoms. The church says the most significant activity that will be reinstated is the right to "perform charitable works and the right for priests to administer their churches." Religious education also is to be expanded. Mr. Gorbachev is giving back to the Russian Church what once had been decisively taken from it with force.

On Sept. 4, 1943, Stalin received the Russian Orthodox Church leaders in the Kremlin. The Russian Church, while supporting the Soviet government strongly in the nation's fight against Nazism, hailed Stalin as the appointed leader of the nation. The Russian Church collected 150 million rubles and many valuables to help support the war effort.

A victory in that war required the enlistment of all segments of Soviet society. Stalin in return softened his anti-religious propaganda. Stalin also disposed of the League of Militant Atheists. On Sept. 7, he restored the patriarch of the Russian Orthodox Church and allowed the election of a synod. He also permitted children to receive religious instruction.

Stalin attempted to reconcile the Russian Church to the Soviet state. By 1946, the Ukrainian Catholic Church officially united with the Russian Orthodox Church, but unofficially, the Ukrainian Church was forced underground. Today, it has 4 to 5 million members. Meanwhile, the Russian Church was obscured by the Kremlin.

The Russian Church must repent for its submission to Stalin, says church leader Father Gleb Yakunin. Many believers were killed under Stalin's rule. Issues remain to be resolved within the church structure. But under Mr. Gorbachev, there are new opportunities for all believers. The Russian Church first must decide how far it wants to go before it can know how far it will be allowed to go under Mr. Gorbachev's banner.

The ⚘ State

Columbia, SC, May 15, 1988

PRESIDENT Reagan is catching a good deal of flak in Congress and in some church circles over his decision to visit a Russian Orthodox monastery near Moscow during the upcoming summit meeting with Soviet leader Mikhail Gorbachev.

"We have a situation where the Soviets hope to showcase what they hope the world will believe is religious tolerance and religious freedom, when we know that the exact opposite has been the case for 70 years," said Rep. Christopher Smith, R-N.J.

Mikhail Gorbachev

The head of the Ukrainian Catholic Church, which is outlawed in the Soviet Union, asked the President to cancel the visit. Mr. Reagan refused, saying he was simply trying to promote religious freedom in the Soviet Union.

Indeed, this rather minor event comes at a time when something significant may be happening in official Soviet attitudes toward religion, which Karl Marx branded as "the opium of the people" as early as 1844. In 1929, slightly more than a decade after the Bolshevik Revolution, the Soviet government imposed a series of highly restrictive laws on the practice of religion and, in effect, substituted Marxism as the state religion. It was scientific, they said, and religion was superstition. Soviet rulers were to be the dispensers of the ultimate truth, and the party would direct the moral life of society.

Religious intolerance, particularly against Jews, was present in the days of the Czars, but the persecution of all religion intensified under "Old Joe" Stalin. Although the Russian Orthodox Church is tolerated by the state, believers are banned from Communist Party membership, which limits their choice of careers, and religious practices are mostly underground.

Still, the government figures that 40 million of the USSR's 280 million people are religious. Unofficial estimates put the total at twice that, the majority of them Russian Orthodox.

In an event thought to be unprecedented, Mr. Gorbachev met with the Russian Orthodox hierarchy in the Kremlin on April 29, reportedly to discuss plans for the 1,000th anniversary of Christianity in Russia, which falls shortly after the summit.

The Soviet leader used the occasion, which received heavy play on Soviet television, to say some fairly remarkable things. "Believers are Soviet people, workers, patriots, and they have the full right to express their conviction with dignity. *Perestroika* (his policy of restructuring the system) and democratization concern them too — in full measure and without any restrictions."

He called for an official policy toward religion that assures the right of the church to "carry out its activity without outside interference" and said "a new law on freedom of conscience, now being drafted, will reflect the interests of religious organizations as well." The new attitude, he added, was important for strengthening national unity during a period of change.

It seems clear that Mr. Gorbachev, who is engaged in a struggle with opponents of change within the party, is seeking to enlist believers in religion in his program of social and economic revitalization. He is trying to avoid the fate suffered by Nikita Khrushchev, an earlier reformer, in the 1960s, and he needs all the support he can get.

But he is playing with fire. Nationalism and fundamentalism are hard to control once loosed, and both are stirring in the vast Soviet empire. Furthermore, tolerance of religion, even more than his ideas of political and economic reform within the system, goes to the heart of Soviet orthodoxy and may be seen by the old Bolsheviks as his most serious provocation to date.

We are not sure how serious Mr. Gorbachev is about this. After all, Stalin, seeking national unity, relaxed religious persecution during World War II and returned to it thereafter. But we see no reason for Mr. Reagan not to encourage this change while it seems to have a chance.

Pittsburgh Post-Gazette

Pittsburgh, PA, June 7, 1988

Even before the spectacle of the Reagan-Gorbachev summit, observers of the Soviet Union watched with fascination as one taboo after another was broken — how permanently, it is unclear — in the ferment of glasnost. Now comes a policy shift with theological as well as political implications.

In the midst of the celebration of the millenium of Christianity in what is now the Soviet Union, a Russian Orthodox bishop has announced that his church will hold discussions with the Vatican on the status of the Ukrainian Catholic Church, a denomination that supposedly was absorbed by the Russian Orthodox Church after World War II but which survives in the U.S.S.R. as an underground movement with millions of adherents.

The overture from Metropolitan Filaret of Kiev was less than gracious. The prelate warned Catholics not to be "aggressive" in seeking to restore their church, which the Orthodox regard as an artificial creation of Ukraine's 16th-century Polish overseers. That grudging tone strengthens the impression that the Orthodox gesture resulted less from ecumenical stirrings than from Mikhail Gorbachev's policy of glasnost. Criticism of the plight of Ukrainian Catholics has made it hard for Mr. Gorbachev to boast about religious tolerance in his society.

Ukrainian Catholics, who are numerous in the United States, share a Byzantine liturgy and other traditions with the Russian Orthodox Church. But, since the 16th century, they have regarded the pope in Rome rather than the Orthodox patriarch in Moscow as their ultimate pastor. That affiliation cost them dearly in the late 1940s, when, as part of a general repression of religion, Soviet authorities forced the merger of the Catholic and Orthodox churches and imprisoned Catholic clergymen — including the church's chief archbishop, who was released in 1963 to the custody of Pope John XXIII.

The "merger" of the two churches long has been denounced by the United States as repression pure and simple, and even a prominent Orthodox writer concedes that, while some of the Ukrainian Catholics might have desired to unite with Orthodoxy, "many others who wished to continue subject to the pope ... have suffered seriously for their religious convictions."

The possibility that Stalin's successor is agitating for Catholic freedom is only one of the ironies in this development. The other is that, as part of the ecumenical movement, Catholics and Orthodox Christians have surmounted many of the antagonisms of the past. Still, that doesn't alter the fact that many Ukrainians have chosen, at the risk of persecution, to identify themselves as Catholics. A society that respects religious liberty will not thwart a citizen's choice of creed or church. If Mr. Gorbachev is extending his blessing to that precept, he is truly a revolutionary.

Index